Genealogical Encyclopedia
of the
COLONIAL AMERICAS

Genealogical Encyclopedia
of the

COLONIAL AMERICAS

A Complete Digest of the Records of
All the Countries of the Western Hemisphere

Christina K. Schaefer

Published by Genealogical Publishing Co., Inc.
1001 N. Calvert St., Baltimore, Md. 21202
Second printing, 2000
Library of Congress Catalogue Card Number 98-72263
International Standard Book Number 0-8063-1576-8
Made in the United States of America

Contents

Part Three: The Caribbean

Part Four: The Thirteen Colonies, Maine, and Vermont

Part Five: Other U.S. States with settlements prior to the Revolution

Part Six: Canada

List of Maps

Preface

Genealogical Encyclopedia of the Colonial Americas: A Complete Digest of the Records of All the Countries of the Western Hemisphere has been written out of my frustration at the lack of an existing single-source reference for Colonial America. During my experience in helping researchers determine *where* to look, I have often found them overwhelmed by this confusing period of history. The competing colonial powers came and went, sometimes with such frequency that it took years for record keeping to transition over to a new government. Often, by that time, someone else was in charge, and the process began all over again.

In my writing, my approach has been to write "where-to" books rather than "how-to" books. Researchers are bombarded with information on the how or the why of genealogy, but often have trouble knowing where to begin their research. The immense body of records of the colonial period in the Western Hemisphere presents perhaps the greatest challenge of all, and thus I have attempted in this book, as I have in others, to show the researcher where to find the most important genealogical records of the period and how to access them. Equally important, I have defined the various classes of records in each country, identified as many of them as is practicable in a book of this size, provided historical background and brief sketches of the records themselves, added a description of the principal holdings of the major repositories of each country, and have interwoven selected reading lists. The reader will appreciate that the subject matter is vast, covering the colonial records of all the Americas, from Latin America to the Caribbean, from the original Thirteen Colonies to Canada and New France, and while I have tried to be comprehensive— knowing that such an aim is ultimately futile— I have nevertheless put together a book that I believe will help to guide all researchers, beginners and professionals alike, to the most direct and reliable route to the colonial records of the Western Hemisphere.

Scope

The scope of this book covers the period of colonial history from the beginning of European colonization in the Western Hemisphere up to the time of the American Revolution. The time line has been extended to provide more complete information in the following instances:

> U.S. states other than the Thirteen Colonies with records that begin prior to the Revolutionary War, until such time as they became part of the U.S. (possession, territory, state)

> Latin American countries, which did not declare their independence from Spain and Portugal until 1808 and later

➤ Caribbean countries and dependencies to about 1810
➤ The subject of slavery up to the abolition of the slave trade, and including dates of emancipation

Wherever possible, the areas covered have been identified by their colonial names rather than present-day political or governmental designations. Calendar dates are given according to the Gregorian Calendar in North America from 1752, when Great Britain stopped using the Julian Calendar. As Spain adopted the Gregorian Calendar in 1582, the Latin American colonies discontinued using the Julian Calendar almost 150 years earlier.

Every attempt has been made to provide up-to-date information on the extent and location of original records. For that reason, all the published compilations of the colonial time period have not been included, except where original records have been lost, destroyed, or are not readily available.

European Records
The best sources of information regarding an immigrant ancestor are usually in the country to which he immigrated. There can be, however, many records in the country of origin, such as church records, emigration and trade company records, indenture agreements, military records, missionary society records, probate records and wills, provincial land grants, public records involving colonial administration, tax records, etc. The last section of this book provides information as to the whereabouts of colonial records which are still in Denmark, England, France, Germany, The Netherlands, Portugal, Scotland, Spain, Sweden, and Switzerland, and at the Library of Congress in Washington, DC.

Citations Used
For purposes of identification, all seven-digit numbers following a record, given in parenthesis with the word "film" or "fiche," are call numbers for material in the Family History Library Catalog (FHLC), used by the Family History Library (FHL) in Salt Lake City, Utah, and Family History Centers worldwide. The letters "ff" indicate that the number is a first folio and that there are other reels or fiche in the series (e.g. film 1679949 ff.).

Sometimes given alone or with a film or fiche number are other letters and numbers. Numbers such as these have been provided for:
➤ The National Archives of the United States
➤ The National Archives of Canada
➤ The Public Record Office of the United Kingdom (PRO)
➤ The Scottish Record Office, Edinburgh

Online Information
Most major archives, libraries, societies, and other record repositories have Web sites that can be accessed via the Internet. One site with links to most of the organizations cited in this book is *Repositories of Primary Sources*, available online at <www.uidaho.edu/special-collections/other>. Links include facilities in all U.S. states, Puerto Rico, and most federal archives and libraries; all Canadian provinces and most European national facilities: Denmark, France, Germany, The Netherlands, Portugal, Spain, Sweden, Switzerland, and the United Kingdom; as well as Argentina, the Bahamas, Bolivia, Brazil, Chile, Colombia, the Dominican Republic, Jamaica, Mexico, and Venezuela. These locations are current as of March 1998.

Acknowledgments
Numerous individuals have made it possible for me to complete this book. Some of the individuals who gave extra time and attention to this project are:
- Stella Colwell, Family Records Centre, Public Record Office, London
- Russell Gasero, Archivist, Archives of the Reformed Church in America, Rutgers University, New Brunswick, New Jersey
- Victoria Robinson, friend and colleague, Annandale, Virginia Family History Center
- Stephen Bahrendt, Professor, Harvard University
- Laurie A. Rofini, Archivist, Chester County Archives and Records Service, West Chester, Pennsylvania
- Elizabeth C. Bouvier, Head of Archives, Supreme Judicial Court Archives, Boston
- Judy Johnson, Genealogist, Connecticut Historical Society, Hartford
- Gail Saunders, Public Records Office, Nassau, Bahamas
- John Stayer, Pennsylvania State Archives, Harrisburg
- Peter Carr, Editor, *Caribbean Genealogical and Historical Journal*

Organizations that provided me with support are:
- The Geography and Map Reading Room, and the Manuscript Division, at the Library of Congress, Washington, DC
- Allen County Public Library, Fort Wayne, Indiana
- American Antiquarian Society, Worcester, Massachusetts
- Archives of Ontario, Toronto
- The Center for American History, University of Texas, Austin
- Fortress of Louisbourg National Historic Park, Archives Library, Louisbourg, Nova Scotia
- Georgia Department of Archives and History, Atlanta
- Historical Society of Delaware, Wilmington
- Huntington Library, San Marino, California

➤ Indian and Colonial Research Center, Old Mystic, Connecticut
➤ Institute of Early American History and Culture, College of William and Mary, Williamsburg, Virginia
➤ Library of Michigan, Lansing
➤ Louisiana Historical Center, Louisiana State Museum, New Orleans
➤ Maine State Archives, Augusta
➤ Maryland State Archives, Hall of Records, Annapolis
➤ Massachusetts Historical Society, Boston
➤ Memorial University, Saint John's, Newfoundland
➤ Mississippi Department of Archives and History, Jackson
➤ Newberry Library, Chicago
➤ New England Historic Genealogical Society, Boston
➤ New Hampshire Historical Society, Concord
➤ New Jersey State Archives, Trenton
➤ New Mexico Records Center and Archives, Santa Fe
➤ New York Genealogical and Biographical Society, New York
➤ New York State Archives, Albany
➤ State Historical Society of Wisconsin, Madison
➤ Virginia State Library and Archives, Richmond
➤ North Carolina State Archives, Raleigh
➤ Ohio Historical Society, Columbus
➤ Provincial Archives of New Brunswick, University of New Brunswick, Fredericton
➤ Public Archives of Nova Scotia, Halifax
➤ Rhode Island State Historical Society, Providence
➤ South Carolina Department of Archives and History, Columbia
➤ University of Missouri Western Historical Manuscript Collection, Columbia
➤ Vermont Public Records Division, Montpelier
➤ P.K. Younge Library of Florida History, University of Florida, Gainesville

Most importantly, I owe my thanks to Eileen Perkins and Mike Tepper at Genealogical Publishing Company, and to my family. My mother, Lareine Richardson, a teacher and historian, corrupted me at an early age with an obsession for colonial history, and when she became the recipient of the Schoolmen's Medal from the Freedoms Foundation of Valley Forge, I learned how many others have a desire to preserve and record America's heritage. My son, Eric, whom we call History Boy, and my daughter, Alice, who helped to illustrate the cover of my last book, have always been supportive and have never complained when I disappear under a pile of research. My husband, Doug, is always there, telling me that I can do anything that I decide will make a difference. They make all things possible.

Genealogical Encyclopedia
of the
COLONIAL AMERICAS

Part One

Beyond the line,
a chronology

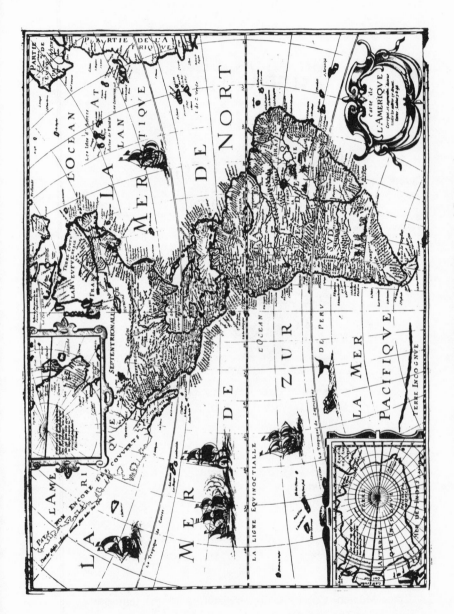

1 The Western hemisphere, 1634 (Library of Congress)

Chronology of Colonial American History

1492 Columbus lands at San Salvador (Bahamas), known as Guanahani by Lucayan Arawak Indians.

1493 Columbus' second expedition brings settlers to Hispaniola (present-day Dominican Republic and Haiti). Columbus discovers present-day Saint Croix and names it Santa Cruz.

1496 Spain begins construction of the city of Santo Domingo on Hispaniola.

1500 Portuguese land in Brazil.

1502 Spain first transports African slaves to its Caribbean colonies. It rebuilds the city of Santo Domingo which had been destroyed by a hurricane. More settlers arrive at Santo Domingo.

1507 Sugarcane is first cultivated on Hispaniola.

1508 Spain founds a settlement at San Juan Bautista, Puerto Rico and forces the inhabitants into slavery. The first sugar mill is built on Hispaniola.

1509 Spain establishes a colony for raising cattle on Jamaica. The colony of Tierra Firme (Panama) is established.

1510 Darién, Panama is founded by Spain.

1511 Spanish conquerors found Baracoa, Cuba and bring their African slaves. The first *audiencia* (high court) and *cabildo* (city council) in the West Indies are established at Santo Domingo. A Roman Catholic bishop is appointed to Santo Domingo.

1513 Spain lays claim to Florida.

1514 The city of Santiago de Cuba (Cuba) is founded.

1515 Charles V, King of Spain and Emperor of Germany, also becomes Count of Holland and ruler of the southern Netherlands (until 1555). Sugarcane is first cultivated in Puerto Rico.

1516 Bananas are brought to Hispaniola from the Canary Islands.

1518 Smallpox strikes the West Indies.

1519 Havana, Cuba is founded.

1520 Venezuela is first colonized. Spain conquers the Aztecs in Mexico, also called Nueva España. Sugarcane is first cultivated in Mexico. Wheat is brought from Spain to Mexico.

1521 African slaves are transported to Hispaniola to work in gold mines that had been taken from the Amerindians. The first smallpox epidemic strikes Mexico. Courts of the Holy Office of the Inquisition are instituted in The Netherlands.

1524 Franciscan missionaries arrive at Tenochtitlán (Mexico). The first sugar mill in Puerto Rico is built. The King of Spain creates the office

3

of the Royal Governor and Supreme Council of the West Indies to hold authority over all Spanish colonies.

1525 German financiers build a silver factory on Hispaniola. German miners immigrate to work in Venezuela.

1526 A permanent Portuguese settlement is founded at Pernambuco, Brazil and begins sugar production. Franciscans open the College of Santiago Tlatelolco (near Mexico City).

1527 Smallpox strikes Peru.

1528 Roman Catholic bishop is appointed to Mexico.

1529 Spain institutes the first *audiencia* (high court) in Mexico at Nuevo Galicia (near present-day Mexico City). Germans establish a settlement at Maracaibo, Venezuela.

1530 Silver is discovered in Mexico.

1531 Spain begins colonizing New Mexico and Arizona. Measles epidemics strike Mexico and Peru.

1532 Spanish troops conquer the Incas in Peru. The first *fazendas* (sugar plantations) are established in Brazil.

1533 La Fortaleza is built at San Juan, Puerto Rico. Cartagena and Santa Marta (Colombia) are established. Sugarcane is cultivated in Peru.

1535 Ciudad de los Reyes (Lima, Peru) and Asunción (Paraguay) are founded.

1537 A Papal Bull, *Sublimis Deus,* declares that American Indians are "truly men," with rights to own property and become Christian, but the Indian slave trade continues unabated. The first printing press in the New World is brought to Mexico.

1538 Portugal transports the first shipment of African slaves to Brazil.

1540 Santiago, Chile, and Quito, Ecuador are founded by Spain.

1541 An earthquake devastates Guatemala City.

1545 Silver is discovered in Bolivia.

1547 Portugal institutes Tribunals of Inquisition.

1549 Jesuit missionaries arrive at Bahia, Brazil, and the colonial capital is established there.

1550 On the North American continent, the Iroquois Confederation, or the Five Nations, is formed by the Mohawk, Oneida, Onondaga, Cayuga, and Seneca tribes (date approximate).

1551 Augustinian missionaries arrive in Mexico. Dominicans open the University of San Marco at Lima, Peru. The University of Mexico is established in Mexico City.

1552 The discovery of gold in Chile brings more than 1,000 colonists from Spain.

1553 French forces attack settlements along the coast of Hispaniola and Puerto Rico.

1554 French forces sack and burn Santiago de Cuba.

1555 French forces sack and burn Havana. Spain intro-duces tobacco into North America. French colonists settle near the site of Rio de Janeiro, Brazil.
1556 The plague strikes Europe.
1559 War between France and Spain ends.
1560 French colonists are expelled from Brazil. French settlers build a fort at Port Royal, off the coast of Florida (destroyed by Spain in 1565).
1562 English corsairs begin trading in the West Indies.
1564 French Huguenots settle Fort Caroline on the Saint Johns River in Florida (destroyed in 1565). The Papal Bull, *Benedictus et Pater,* requires recording of parish records.
1565 Spain founds a presidio at Saint Augustine, Florida, most of the colonists and soldiers coming from Cuba. A Catholic parish is established there. Rio de Janeiro, Brazil is founded by Portugal.

Gregorian vs. the Julian Calendar

The Julian Calendar — instituted in 46 B.C. by Julius Caesar — was ten days behind the solar year by 1582. That year Pope Gregory introduced the Gregorian Calendar, which was adopted in the Catholic countries in Europe and some of the Protestant ones. To distinguish between the Old Style (O.S.) and the New Style (N.S.), dates are written as (i.e.) 14/24 July, or with the initials O.S. and N.S. The dates of adoption of the new calendar are:

➢ Spain and France, 1582
➢ Germany (Catholic), 1582–5
➢ Mexico, 1583
➢ Peru, 1584
➢ Scotland, 1600
➢ Germany (Protestant), 1600s
➢ Denmark, The Netherlands, Norway, 1700
➢ England, 1752
➢ Sweden, 1753

1566 Jesuit missionaries settle in Florida.
1568 Jesuit missionaries settle in Peru. The island of Barbados is named by a Portuguese explorer, but no settlement is made.
1570 A Court of the Holy Office of the Inquisition is instituted at Lima, Peru.
1571 A Court of the Holy Office of the Inquisition is instituted at Mexico City. The last of the Inca rulers is executed near Cuzco, Mexico.
1572 The Powhatan Confederation is formed by tribes in the Chesapeake Bay area. Jesuits abandon their Florida missions.
1573 Franciscans take over the Jesuit missions in Florida.
1576 Smallpox epidemics strike all of Central America.
1578 England claims the California coast.
1579 The northern provinces of The Netherlands break away from Spain.
1584 Roanoke Colony is founded in Virginia.

1585 English forces sack Cartagena, Colombia. Yellow fever strikes the West Indies.

1586 Saint Augustine, Florida is attacked and burned by the English.

1588 The Roanoke Colony disappears. England defeats the Spanish Armada.

1590 Gold is discovered in Brazil.

1593 The Dutch found a permanent settlement at Guiana.

1595 The king of Spain approves the colonization of the Kingdom of New Mexico.

1596 Spain unsuccessfully attempts to colonize California.

1598 San Juan, New Mexico is founded by Spain. In France, the Edict of Nantes grants religious toleration to French Huguenots (Protestants). The trail known as Camino Real links Santa Fe, New Mexico and Mexico City.

1601 The plague returns to Europe.

1604 The French establish forts at Port Royal, Acadia (Nova Scotia), and Île Saint Croix (New Brunswick).

1605 Jesuits from Spain establish the first missions in Paraguay.

1607 The Virginia Company of London arrives at Cape Henry, Virginia, and Jamestown is founded by Captain John Smith. The French abandon the settlement at Port Royal.

1608 The first permanent French settlement is founded at Quebec.

1609 Holland lays claim to New Netherland (New York region). French settlers reoccupy Port Royal. Bermuda, known as the Somers Islands, is colonized by shipwrecked settlers bound for Virginia. Portugal institutes a *relaçao* (high court of appeals) in Salvador, Brazil. Santa Fe is established as the capital of New Mexico. The Netherlands gain independence from Spain. Brownists (English Calvinists) arrive in The Netherlands (the same group that founds the Plymouth Colony in Massachusetts in 1620).

1610 A Court of the Holy Office of the Inquisition is instituted at Cartagena, Colombia. Spain founds a mission at Santa Fe, New Mexico. French colonists establish a permanent settlement at Île Saint Jean (Prince Edward Island).

1611 A Presbyterian congregation is established in Virginia.

1612 Tobacco growing is introduced into Jamestown. Saint George, Bermuda is founded.

1613 The Compagnie de Canada is given exclusive trading rights in the Gulf of Saint Lawrence. Port Royal, Acadia is destroyed by the English. The French establish a colony at Cayenne (Guyane).

1614 The Dutch found Fort Nassau (Albany, New York).

1615 The Bermuda Company is established.

1616 The first African slaves are brought to Bermuda. A plague devastates

the American Indian population along the coast of New England.
1617 English convicts are first transported to the New World.
1618 The struggling Jamestown (Virginia) colony receives new laws, the introduction of wheat cultivation, supplies, new settlers, and a contingent of women.
1619 Virginia receives the first shipment of Africans, probably slaves, transported by the Dutch. The House of Burgesses is established in Virginia as the first governing body in the colonies. Virginia endorses the Church of England as the official church of the colony.
1620 Massachusetts' first permanent settlement is established by the Plymouth Company — Protestant Pilgrim dissenters from England — at New Plymouth.
1621 The Pilgrims and the Wampanoag Indians sign a peace treaty. The Dutch West India Company is chartered. The Scots lay claim to Acadia and call it Nova Scotia. A blast furnace is built at Falling Creek, Virginia (destroyed a year later by American Indians).
1622 A large number of Jamestown, Virginia settlers are massacred by American Indians. The Gorges Colony is founded in Maine.
1623 Piscataqua (Rye), New Hampshire is settled by Plymouth Colony merchants. Dover, Portsmouth, and Natascot (Hull), New Hampshire are settled. Wessaguscus (Weymouth), Massachusetts is settled by a group from the Gorges Colony (Maine).
1624 The Virginia Company is dissolved and Virginia becomes a Royal colony. The colony of New Netherland is founded by the Dutch West India Company, with settlements at Fort Orange (Albany, also site of a Fort Nassau) and Fort Nassau (a second Fort Nassau, near present-day Woodbridge, New Jersey). The first settlers are Walloon immigrants from Amsterdam and Leiden. The Dutch capture the Portuguese colony at Bahia (San Salvador), Brazil. English settlers from Guiana arrive at Saint Christopher (name shortened to Saint Kitts) in the Leeward Islands.
1625 New Amsterdam is founded by the Dutch on Manhattan Island. The English settle Barbados. Jesuits establish a mission in Quebec. The Portuguese recapture San Salvador, Brazil. Both the English and the Dutch — with a group of French Huguenots from Saint Kitts — establish settlements at Saint Croix, and the English build a sugar mill.
1626 Manhattan Island, the site of New Amsterdam, is purchased from the Manhattan Indians by the Dutch West India Company. The first African slaves are transported to New Amsterdam. Salem, Massachusetts is settled by Dorchester colonists from Cape Ann.
1627 Scots colonists settle at Port Royal, Acadia (Nova Scotia). French colonists from Normandy and Brittany settle at Saint Kitts. English colonists and a few captured African slaves settle at Barbados.

1628 English colonists from Saint Kitts establish settlements on the islands of Nevis and Barbados. The Dutch fleet captures the Spanish treasure fleet off the coast of Cuba, signaling the decline of Spain's preeminence in the New World. Dover Point, New Hampshire is settled by colonists from New Plymouth. Pemaquid and Pejepscot, Maine are settled. The *Compagnie des Cents Associes* is founded to encourage permanent settlement in New France. The first Reformed Dutch congregation is organized in New Amsterdam.

1629 Augusta, Maine is settled. Patroonship, the manorial land system, is introduced in the New Netherland Colony. The English settle Barbuda. English buccaneers organize a company on Providence Island, off the coast of Nicaragua. The Spanish fleet attacks the settlement at Saint Kitts. The Dutch West India Company grants large estates in New Netherland along the Hudson, Connecticut, and Delaware rivers.

1630 Boston is founded by the first settlers of the Massachusetts Bay Company, at the beginning of the "Great Migration." The Dutch establish a settlement at Pavonia, New Jersey (Jersey City). The Providence Island Company establishes a Puritan colony on Santa Catalina, off the coast of Nicaragua. Refugees from Saint Kitts and runaway sailors establish a buccaneer stronghold on the island of Tortuga, and it becomes a haven for Dutch, English, French, Portuguese, and Spanish privateers. The Dutch occupy Pernambuco, Brazil.

1631 Portsmouth, New Hampshire is founded by settlers who name the area "the Strawberry Banke." The Dutch establish a settlement on the Delaware Bay, called Zwaanendael (Lewes). A fire destroys part of Boston. Tobacco growing is introduced into Maryland. The Dutch capture the island of Saint Martin from Spain.

1632 Maryland is chartered as a proprietary colony. The Scots give up the settlement at Port Royal, and control of Acadia reverts to France. English colonists from Saint Kitts settle at Montserrat and Antigua. Irish Catholic servants and planters are recruited to settle on Montserrat. English pirates raid Bristol, Maine.

1633 Smallpox strikes Massachusetts, and fatalities are especially high among the American Indians. The Collegé de Québec is established by Jesuits. The first permanent settlement at Portland, Maine is established. Dutch settlers build a fort at Hartford, Connecticut. The English take the island of Saint Martin from the Dutch.

1634 Maryland's first colonists establish the city of Saint Mary's, on the western shore of the Chesapeake Bay. The Dutch take possession of Curaçao from Spain and also occupy the islands of Aruba and Bonaire. Bubonic plague strikes French settlements in Canada.

1635 Connecticut's first towns of Hartford, Wethersfield, and Windsor are settled by Puritans from Massachusetts. Puritans build a fort at the mouth of the Connecticut River, at Saybrook. The Dutch conquer northern Brazil. French settle Basse-Terre on Guadeloupe and plant another colony on Martinique. Spain conquers Tortuga. A hurricane causes destruction at Plymouth Colony.

1636 The Pequot War begins in New England. Harvard College is founded at Cambridge, Massachusetts. The Providence (Rhode Island) Colony is settled by Puritan dissenters from Salem, Massachusetts. Barbados' governor and council declare Indians and blacks to be slaves for life. Fort La Tour (Saint John's, New Brunswick) is founded by the French. Plymouth Colony passes a pension act.

1637 The Pequot War ends. Barbados becomes the first English colony to cultivate sugar.

1638 The Swedish West India Company establishes the colony of New Sweden at Fort Christina (Wilmington) in the Delaware Valley, and a Lutheran congregation is established there. Pocasset (Portsmouth, Rhode Island) is founded by Puritan dissenters from Massachusetts. New Haven Colony is founded in Connecticut by Puritans from England. Exeter and Hampton, New Hampshire are settled.

1639 Puritans from England establish settlements at Guilford and Milford, Connecticut. The Fundamental Orders for Connecticut are drafted. Newport (Rhode Island) is founded by Puritan dissenters. The first Baptist Church in America is organized in Providence (Rhode Island).

1640 The first English settlement in New York is planted at Southampton by colonists from Massachusetts. Springfield, Massachusetts is settled.

1641 The city of York, Maine is chartered by the English Crown. New Hampshire Colony becomes part of Massachusetts. The Massachusetts Body of Liberties limits the powers of the magistrates (members of the Puritan clergy). Montreal, Quebec is founded on the Saint Lawrence River. Spain conquers the island of Providence. The Dutch recapture Saint Martin from Spain.

1642 Civil War breaks out in England. The Dutch on Saint Croix name their settlement *Nieuw Zeeland*. Sugar refining begins in Barbados.

1643 Swedes establish settlements in the Delaware Valley area of Pennsylvania. The United Colonies of New England are formed by the colonies of Connecticut, Massachusetts Bay, New Haven, and Plymouth for purposes of defense. Warwick (Rhode Island) is founded by Puritan dissenters. The settlements of Portsmouth, Providence, and Newport unite under the Providence Plantations in Narragansett Bay in New England. The name of the colony is then changed to Rhode Island. Settlers in Barbados — mostly white males — begin to migrate to other colonies. The Dutch try to sell Portuguese prisoners from Brazil at Barbados, but the prisoners are freed by the Barbadian governor. Kieft's War is waged between the Dutch and the Indians in the Hudson River Valley area.

1644 Virginia establishes a treaty with the Powhatan Indians. Rhode Island and the Providence Plantations receive a charter. Dutch refugees flee from Brazil to Curaçao and then are transported to New Amsterdam.

1645 An English settlement is established in the Bahamas, and a salt-making station is established on the island of Eleuthra. On Saint Croix, the Dutch governor kills the English governor; the English settlers shoot the Dutch governor. The Dutch settlers migrate to Saint Eustatius and Saint Martin. The French Huguenots on Saint Croix migrate to Guadeloupe.

1646 Puritan settlers from Bermuda begin to migrate to the Bahamas and attempt to establish a settlement at Eleuthra. Breuckelen (Brooklyn) becomes the first town to be chartered in New Amsterdam.

1647 Rhode Island adopts a civil code, separating church and state, and Warwick unites with the Rhode Island Colony. In Massachusetts, Catholic priests are forbidden to enter any Puritan settlements. Yellow fever in the West Indies and Mexico kills thousands. The first sugar plantation on Guadeloupe is begun. A major outbreak of influenza strikes all of New England, Saint Kitts, and Barbados.

1648 The Netherlands are officially recognized as a nation in Europe. More colonists from Bermuda migrate to Eleuthra, Bahamas, and the colony receives a charter. The Society of Friends (Quakers) is founded in England. The first execution for witchcraft takes place at Charleston, Massachusetts. The first orphans' court held in English North America is convened in Virginia. Smallpox strikes Massachusetts.

1649 Charles I of England is beheaded, and Oliver Cromwell establishes the Commonwealth. The Toleration Act in Maryland guarantees religious freedom to Protestants and Catholics. Royalist refugees from England migrate to Virginia.

1650 The Puritan Parliament passes the first Navigation Act, which bans foreign ships from trading with English colonies. Almshouses are established at Beverswyck (near Albany), New Netherland. Colonists from Martinique settle Grenada. English colonists migrate from Barbados to Suriname. English colonists establish a settlement on the island of Anguilla. Spain attacks Saint Croix, and English settlers are killed or flee to Bermuda, after which France claims the island. The Treaty of Hartford establishes the border between the Dutch (New York) and the English (Connecticut).

1651 Scots Highlanders and prisoners from the Battle of Dunbar are transported to Massachusetts and Virginia. Witchcraft trials begin in Bermuda (through 1696). French Knights of Malta and other colonists settle at Saint Croix.

1652 Maine settlements are incorporated into the Massachusetts Bay Colony. Scots Highlanders and prisoners from the Battle of Worcester are transported to Bermuda and Jamaica. In Rhode Island, Warwick and Providence enact legislation that Englishmen may keep black slaves for life servitude.

1653 The Anglo-Dutch War begins. A wall (site of the future Wall Street) is built in New Amsterdam to keep out invaders from New England.

1654 In Maryland, the Toleration Act is repealed, and Protestants seize control of the colony from the proprietors. Over the next thirty years, 10,000 emigrants depart from Bristol as indentured servants, mostly from the counties of Somerset, Gloucestershire, and Wiltshire in England and Monmouthshire in Wales. More than half book passage to Virginia, settling in Henrico, James City, Charles City, Isle of Wight, Gloucester, Surry, and Prince George's counties. Portugal retakes Dutch-held Brazil, and the Treaty of Taborda expels the Dutch and Jewish colonists from that country. The first Jewish settlers arrive in New Amsterdam as refugees from Brazil's Dutch colony. The Dutch who are ejected from Brazil migrate to many of the West Indian islands. The English capture Port Royal, Acadia from France.

1655 Scots Highlanders and prisoners of war in Plymouth Castle are transported to Barbados. New Sweden is conquered by New Netherland. The Peach War is waged between the Manhattan Indians and the settlers at New Amsterdam. The first Quakers arrive at Barbados. England recruits men from Saint Kitts, Nevis, Montserrat, and Barbados to fight against Spain. They are defeated at Hispaniola but capture Jamaica. Colonists from Saint Kitts and Barbados migrate to Jamaica. Barbadian soldiers settle at Jamaica and Port Royal (Jamaica) becomes a base for buccaneers. Buccaneers invade the city of Grenada and sack Costa Rica.

1656 Quakers arrive at Massachusetts, are imprisoned, and then deported, eventually settling in Rhode Island. They are forbidden to settle in Massachusetts. Scots Highlanders and prisoners are transported to Antigua.

1657 The Scots Charitable Society is established at Boston. Spain organizes Mission San Luis at the site of Tallahassee, Florida. Colonists from Barbados and Nevis migrate to Jamaica. Virginia organizes a postal system. Quakers arrive at New Amsterdam, and after imprisonment, go to Rhode Island.

1658 Typhoid strikes New Amsterdam.

1659 The Reformed Dutch Church of Esopus (Kingston, New York) is founded.

1660 The English monarchy is restored, and Charles II becomes King. Bergen, New Jersey is founded by Dutch colonists. Parliament reenacts the Navigation Act on colonial trade. Virginia writes slavery into statute law, although it has been practiced for years. Connecticut law requires all men to live with their wives.

1661 English colonists settle on the island of Barbuda. Jamaica acquires a civil government.

1662 Connecticut receives a Royal charter and becomes a corporate colony. Virginia law declares that a child born of a black mother is a slave, even if the father is white.

1663 A large tract of land in the area of Georgia and the Carolinas is granted to eight proprietors. The Province of Carolina is established. France sends a Royal governor to Canada, and Quebec becomes a Royal colony. The French government sends the *filles du roi* (774 marriageable women) to Canada. A Royal charter is granted to the United Colony of Rhode Island and the Providence Plantations, creating a corporate colony. The Staple Act requires that goods shipped to the colonies must transit through English ports. The last major plague epidemic strikes Europe.

1664 The Anglo-Dutch War ends. New Amsterdam is conquered by the English. The Kill van Kull Patent is granted in New Jersey. New York, New Jersey, and Delaware become proprietary colonies. A German Lutheran church is founded at New York City. Maryland law declares that all blacks in Maryland are bound to life servitude. The Compagnie des Indies Occidentales (French West Indies Company) is created and assumes control of New France. Barbadians settle at Cape Fear in Carolina. The Classis of Amsterdam (Reformed Dutch Church) declares that slave owners are responsible for "instructing their Negroes in the Christian Religion."

1665 The New Haven Colony is absorbed into Connecticut. The Monmouth Patent is granted in New Jersey. A Jesuit mission is established at Chequamegon Bay (Minnesota). Puritan settlers migrate from Massachusetts and establish the Clarendon Colony in Albemarle Province (near Wilmington, North Carolina). The Concessions and Agreements of Albemarle Province are written.

1666 Newark, New Jersey is founded by Puritans from Connecticut. The Presbyterian Church is established in New Jersey. The French build

Fort Isle la Motte in Vermont. The French invade the Iroquois Confederation. French forces capture the English colonies of Saint Kitts, Antigua, Anguilla, and Barbuda. English settlers from Saint Kitts flee to Jamaica, New England, Virginia, and nearby Nevis and Montserrat. Colonists from Bermuda settle the island of New Providence, Bahamas. Smallpox strikes Boston.

1667 Scots colonists emigrate from Leith to Virginia. Montserrat is taken by the French. The English colony on Saint Kitts is restored. Dutch forces take Suriname from England. The Barbadians at Cape Fear abandon their settlement and migrate to Virginia, New England, the Albemarle settlement, or return to Barbados. Smallpox strikes Virginia. Virginia law states that baptism as a Christian does not alter the bondage of a slave.

1668 Sault Sainte Marie, Michigan is founded by the French. Charles Fort is established by the English on the Rupert River (site of Rupert's Land) in Canada. English buccaneers attack Saint Augustine and capture the city of Panama (originally named Porto Bello).

1669 Scots Covenanters are deported to Virginia. The Fundamental Constitution of Carolina is written, granting freemen absolute authority over black slaves. Jesuits establish a mission at Green Bay, Wisconsin. English buccaneers sack the city of Maracaibo, Venezuela.

1670 English colonists settle at Albemarle Point, Albermarle Colony (North Carolina). The Governor and Company of Merchant Adventurers establish Rupert's Land on Hudson Bay. Control of Acadia reverts from England to France. Slaves in Massachusetts become legally inheritable. The Treaty of Madrid establishes the boundaries of the English and Spanish settlements in North America and yields Spanish West Indian territories that are occupied by the English. English loggers migrate from Jamaica and found (English) Honduras. Charlestown, Nevis becomes the principal slave market of the Leeward Islands. The Lord Proprietors of the Carolinas take over New Providence, Bahamas.

1671 A group of Dutch settlers migrate from New York to South Carolina. Virginia begins the naturalization of white non-English settlers. Saint Kitts, Antigua, Montserrat, Anguilla, and Barbuda are restored to the English. A Seventh-Day Baptist Church is founded at Newport, Rhode Island.

1672 The Royal African Company controls most of the English slave trade. Port Nelson is established by the Hudson's Bay Company. The Dutch island of Tortola is taken by the English. Danish forces take Saint Thomas in the Virgin Islands. The first Quaker meeting house in New

Jersey is built at Shrewsbury.

1673 The Dutch recapture New York. Parliament passes the Plantation Act, imposing duties on goods shipped from one colony to another. The first post road is designated from New York to Boston. The first mail in North America is dispatched from New York to Boston. Biloxi, Mississippi is settled by the French.

1674 The English retake New York. Dutch inhabitants are recognized as English subjects. New France reverts to the French Crown. England cedes Suriname to the Dutch in exchange for New York.

1675 King Philip's War begins. Quakers suffering from religious persecution immigrate to Pennsylvania and West Jersey. A hurricane levels Barbados. The Lords of Trade is established as a committee of the Privy Council in England to centralize enforcement of the Trade Acts. A fire in Boston destroys part of the city.

1676 Bacon's Rebellion begins in Virginia. King Philip's War ends. New Jersey is divided into the provinces of East Jersey and West Jersey. The Covenant Alliance is made between the Iroquois Confederation and the English colonies. An influenza outbreak strikes Quebec.

1677 The Powhatan Confederation of Virginia tribes sign a peace treaty with the English settlers. Massachusetts purchases the Gorges land rights to Maine. Quakers settle at Burlington, New Jersey. Smallpox strikes the Carolina colony and Boston.

1679 New Hampshire is converted into a separate Royal colony by the Lords of Trade. A smallpox epidemic strikes New York and New England. Another fire destroys part of Boston.

1680 Charles Town (name changed to Charleston upon its incorporation in 1783), South Carolina is founded by settlers from England and Barbados. A small group of Huguenots settle at Charles Town. Scottish Quakers begin to emigrate to New Jersey. Both Jersey provinces become part of the United Colonies of New England. Pueblo Indians drive the Spanish colonists from Santa Fé, New Mexico to Mision Guadeloupe in the district of El Paso, Texas. Hurricanes cause massive destruction in Jamaica and the Leeward Islands.

1681 Philadelphia, Pennsylvania is founded. Two counties are established in the province of West Jersey. East Jersey is sold to Quaker proprietors. Virginia becomes the first North American colony to draft a slave code.

1682 A representative assembly is established in Pennsylvania. The Duke of York deeds the three counties of Delaware to Pennsylvania. Pennsylvania issues a law guaranteeing religious liberty. The Mississippi Valley area is claimed by France and is named the

Louisiana Territory. Three counties are established in Carolina. Fort Saint Louis is built on the Illinois River.

1683 New York creates a legislative assembly and issues the Charter of Liberties. The twelve original counties in New York are formed. Four counties are established in the Province of East Jersey. Scots colonists settle at Perth Amboy in East Jersey. German Mennonites begin settling in the area of Germantown, Pennsylvania. Scots colonists begin settling in Carolina. The Jamaica Act requires that all buccaneers are to be prosecuted as pirates. Pennsylvania holds its first witchcraft trial.

1684 The United Colonies of New England are dissolved. Large numbers of Quakers begin to emigrate from Bristol, England. The Treaty of Albany allies the Iroquois and the English. New York becomes a Royal colony. Mision El Paso is organized in Texas. Spanish forces sack English settlements in the Bahamas and the colonists flee to Jamaica and Massachusetts. The Bermuda Company's charter is forfeited to the Crown. Massachusetts' original charter is withdrawn by Charles II.

1685 Charles II dies, and his Catholic brother, James, Duke of York, accedes to the throne. The Edict of Nantes, which granted religious toleration, is revoked, beginning the French Huguenot emigration to America. Huguenots settle at New Rochelle, New York, Virginia, Massachusetts, Rhode Island and South Carolina. Scots Covenanters and prisoners are deported to Jamaica. Louis XIV's *Code Noir* (Black Code) declares that a freed slave (either by his master or by purchasing his freedom) becomes a full citizen of France. He may also own slaves.

1686 The Dominion of New England is formed by the Crown and includes New Jersey, New York, and Pennsylvania. French traders from Louisiana establish the Arkansas Post. French Huguenots begin to be transported to Martinique. Scots Covenanters are deported to Virginia. A diphtheria epidemic strikes Virginia.

1687 Mision Pimería Alta is organized in Arizona. The first Anglican services are held in Boston. James II suspends the Test Act, allowing Catholics to serve in the English army and hold public office. A measles epidemic strikes Quebec. A malaria epidemic strikes Virginia.

1688 The French begin to establish a chain of forts in the Minnesota area. Abenaki Indians capture Pemaquid, Maine. A measles epidemic strikes New England and Virginia. The Germantown Protest becomes the first organized action taken by Quakers toward the abolition of slavery.

1689 James II is ousted and his Protestant daughter, Mary, and her Dutch husband, William of Orange, are crowned. King William's War begins. The Dominion of New England is dissolved. During Leisler's Rebellion, New Yorkers temporarily overthrow the Royal governor. Spain organizes Mision Apalachicola in western Georgia. Saint Kitts and Anguilla are taken by the French. An epidemic on Nevis kills over half the men on the island. Diphtheria strikes Connecticut and Virginia. Smallpox strikes New England and Quebec.

1690 New Hampshire and Massachusetts are reunited. English forces capture Port Royal, Acadia. French Canadians and American Indians raid Falmouth, Maine, Salmon Falls, New Hampshire, and Schenectady, New York. Spain begins colonizing Texas.

1691 Albemarle Province is renamed North Carolina and has its own legislature. Massachusetts Colony is granted a new charter by the king, and the Plymouth Colony is annexed to Massachusetts. Maine is incorporated as part of Massachusetts. The union of New Hampshire and Massachusetts is dissolved and Massachusetts becomes a separate Royal colony. Maryland becomes a Royal colony. Interracial marriage is banned by law in Virginia.

1692 Witchcraft trials are conducted at Salem, Massachusetts. The Church of England is recognized in Maryland. Port Royal, Jamaica is devastated by an earthquake, destroying the stronghold of the buccaneers. York, Maine is raided by French Canadians and Indians.

1693 William and Mary College is founded at Williamsburg, Virginia. Santa Fe, New Mexico is reoccupied by Spanish colonists. Postal service begins between New York and Philadelphia. Spanish Florida offers freedom to any African slave willing to embrace Catholicism. Yellow fever strikes Barbados and is carried to Boston.

1694 The English resettle the Bahamas.

1695 Santa Cruz, New Mexico is founded. Nassau, Bahamas (originally named Charles Town) is founded. French colonists on Saint Croix abandon their settlement and migrate to Santo Domingo.

1696 Control of New Mexico reverts to Spain. The English and Iroquois Indians attack Quebec. Smallpox strikes Jamestown, Virginia.

1697 King William's War ends. A Vice-Admiralty court is created at Nassau. French forces take over the western end of Hispaniola and name it Saint Dominigue. France and Spain divide Hispaniola. Smallpox strikes Charles Town, South Carolina.

1698 The Spanish found Pensacola, Florida. Scots colonists attempt to colonize Darien, on the Isthmus of Panama. Bernalillo, New Mexico is settled.

1699 French priests found a mission at Cahokia, Illinois. The French establish Fort Maurepas on Biloxi Bay, Mississippi. Scots colonists arrive in Jamaica, and the settlers at Darien migrate to Jamaica. Yellow fever strikes Barbados and is carried to Charles Town and

Philadelphia.[1] All freed slaves in Virginia are required to leave the colony.

1700 Over the next thirty years, the French establish the Waubash-Maumee trade route in Indiana.

1701 Queen Anne's War begins. Yale College is founded at New Haven, Connecticut. Fort Ponchartrian is founded by the French at the site of Detroit, Michigan. The Society for the Propagation of the Gospel in Foreign Parts founds a slave school in New York City.

1702 The two Jersey provinces are united as a Royal colony and establish an assembly. French settlers found the city of Mobile, Alabama. Smallpox and yellow fever strike New York City. English settlers from the Carolinas burn Saint Augustine, Florida.

1703 Delaware withdraws from the Pennsylvania Colony. Jesuits found a mission at Kaskaskia, Illinois. Nassau, Bahamas is sacked by French and Spanish from Cuba.

1704 The first colonial newspaper is published in Boston, the *Boston-News Letter* (1704–76). Deerfield, Massachusetts is destroyed by French-Canadians and Indians. English forces attack Port Royal, Acadia.

1705 Virginia enacts legislation declaring black, mulatto, and Indian slaves to be real estate and slaves for life. The Anglican Church is established in North Carolina. Pennsylvania establishes separate courts for Negroes.

1706 Albuquerque, New Mexico is founded. The first Presbytery of the Presbyterian church in North America is founded at Philadelphia. The first Anglican Church is established in Connecticut. To curb the runaway slave problem, the Privy Council of Saint Thomas orders all trees to be cut down that are big enough to carve into canoes. Yellow fever strikes Charles Town.

1707 England and Scotland are united as Great Britain. The first association of Baptist churches in North America is organized in Pennsylvania.

1708 Congregationalism becomes the official church of Connecticut. Palatine refugees from London found Quassaic Creek (Newburgh), New York. Haverhill, Massachusetts is destroyed by American Indians. The Saybrook Platform is adopted by Congregational churches in Connecticut.

1709 Slaveholding is legalized in New France. Swiss immigrants settle in New Bern, North Carolina. The first mining charter in British North America is granted by the Connecticut General Assembly for a copper mine at Simsbury.

1710 About 13,000 German Palatines emigrate to Britain. Port Royal,

---

[1]Known as "Barbados distemper" in Philadelphia.

Acadia is captured by troops from New England. The British rename Port Royal Annapolis Royal. Acadia becomes the British province of Nova Scotia. German and Swiss Protestants settle in the Carolinas.

1711 A fire in Boston destroys three hundred homes. France cedes Newfoundland to Britain.

1712 South Carolina drafts a slave code. Slaves are executed after an uprising in New York City. Smallpox strikes all of South Carolina.

1713 Queen Anne's War ends. British forces gain control of Acadia, Hudson Bay, and Newfoundland by the Treaty of Utrecht. England is granted an *asiento* (license) to import 4,800 slaves to Spanish North America on a yearly basis for the next thirty years. Saint Kitts and Anguilla are returned to the British by the Treaty of Utrecht. France retains Cape Breton Island. North and South Carolina are officially divided.

1714 Natchitoches, Louisiana is established by the French as a military and trading post. Tea is imported into the colonies. Germans and German Swiss colonists settle in the Germanna Colony in the Valley of Virginia.

1715 Maryland reverts to a proprietary colony. Jacobite prisoners from the 1715 rebellion in Scotland are exiled to the Americas. The Yamassee War is waged between the Yamassee Indians and South Carolina settlers. North Carolina establishes separate slave courts for criminal trials.

1716 Maine is called York County of Massachusetts. Fort Rosalie (Natchez), Mississippi is settled by the French. Smallpox strikes New York and New Jersey.

1717 The French West Indies Company is granted rights to settle in Louisiana. The first migration of Ulster Scots to Pennsylvania begins. Mision San Antonio is organized. France founds Fort Toulouse on the Alabama River.

1718 Ulster Scots begin to emigrate to New England and settle at Wiscasset, Maine, Worcester, Massachusetts, and Londonderry, New Hampshire. Smallpox strikes New York City. The French establish the Province of Louisiana. New Orleans is founded by settlers from Canada and France. The Yamassee War ends in South Carolina. A smallpox epidemic strikes Peru and lasts for two years. The Bahamas become a British Crown colony. The presidio of San Antonio, Texas is founded by Spain.

1719 The newspapers *American Weekly Mercury* (Philadelphia) and *Boston Gazette* are established. South Carolina declares itself a Royal colony. Dunkards begin settling in the area of Germantown, Pennsylvania. Pensacola, Florida is captured by French from Mobile, Alabama. The French rebuild Fort Niagara (New York).

1720 Spanish forces attempt to occupy Texas. France founds Louisbourg on Cape Breton Island. French Canadians begin settling in the Illinois area.

1721 A smallpox epidemic strikes the West Indies and is carried to Boston. A regular postal service commences between New England and London.

1722 Spain retakes Pensacola from the French. Dummer's War is waged between the Abenaki Indians and Massachusetts. The Iroquois Confederation and Virginia establish a treaty.

1724 Vermont's first British settlement is founded at Fort Dummer (Brattleboro). Diphtheria strikes South Carolina.

1725 The *New York Gazette* is licensed as a newspaper. Dummer's War ends in Massachusetts. The second migration of Ulster Scots begins to emigrate to Pennsylvania. The Colored Baptist Church is established at Williamsburg, Virginia. Russians explore the northwest coast of North America.

1729 The *Pennsylvania Gazette* newspaper is established. North and South Carolina officially become separate Royal colonies. Baltimore, Maryland is founded. Settlers begin to migrate south on the Great Wagon Road that stretches from Philadelphia to Georgia. A measles epidemic strikes New York City. The Natchez Rebellion begins in Louisiana.

1730 A synagogue is built at New York City. The first major slave rebellion occurs in Jamaica.

1731 The boundary between Connecticut and New York is settled. The French build Fort Saint Frédéric on Lake Champlain (Crown Point, New York). Spanish colonists from the Canary Islands are sent to San Antonio, Texas. Yellow fever strikes Bermuda. Smallpox strikes New York City, Boston, and Philadelphia.

1732 Georgia is chartered by the British Crown. Moravian missionaries settle at Saint Croix. French colonists settle at Vincennes (Indiana). Yellow fever epidemics strike Charles Town and New York City.

1733 Savannah, Georgia is settled. Parliament passes the Molasses Act to collect levies on imports from the French West Indies. The Danish West India Company buys Saint Croix from the French Crown. Danish law imposes penalties of torture, amputation, and death on runaway slaves.

1734 Immigrants from Salzburg, Germany settle in Georgia. Schwenk-felders begin settling in the area of Germantown, Pennsylvania. Scots colonists begin to migrate from Leith and Inverness to Georgia. Ulster Scots emigrate directly to North Carolina and settle in New Hanover County. Yellow fever strikes the Bahamas.

1735 The *New York Weekly Journal* begins publication. Saint Genevieve, Missouri is established by French lead miners. German Moravians emigrate to Georgia and establish a church at Savannah. The Great Awakening is begun by Jonathan Edwards in Massachusetts. Diphtheria strikes New England and Saint Kitts.

1736 Ulster Scots begin to settle in the Valley of Virginia. A stagecoach service begins between Boston and Newport, Rhode Island.

1737 The Delaware Indians sell the Lehigh Valley to Pennsylvania. Richmond, Virginia is founded. Smallpox strikes Rhode Island and Martha's Vineyard, Massachusetts. Yellow fever strikes Virginia.

1738 Over the next four years Scottish Highlanders from Islay settle in New York. Smallpox strikes Charles Town and New York City.

1739 Scottish Highlanders begin emigrating to Cape Fear Valley in North Carolina. The governor of Jamaica negotiates a truce with armed slaves. Yellow fever strikes Charles Town. White planters in Saint Paul's Parish, South Carolina are attacked by Angolan slaves during the Stono Rebellion. Conflicts begin between the British settlers in South Carolina and Georgia and the Spanish settlers in Florida. British forces begin raiding Spanish colonies in the West Indies. Diphtheria strikes Connecticut. Measles strikes New England, New York, and New Jersey.

1740 A fire in Charles Town destroys over three hundred buildings. A famine in Ireland precipitates the third migration of Ulster Scots to Pennsylvania, who also settle in Virginia and the Carolinas. Parliament passes a law granting British citizenship to foreigners living in any colony, providing they are Protestants and take the oath of allegiance. Parliament forbids Catholics in British colonies from becoming naturalized citizens. The War of Jenkins' Ear begins between British settlers in South Carolina and Georgia and settlers in Spanish Florida. Yellow fever is carried from the Bahamas to Philadelphia and New Jersey.

1741 A Moravian settlement is established in the area of Germantown, Pennsylvania. Three thousand Americans are enlisted by Britain to attack Cartagena, Colombia. More than half of them die of disease. The Society for the Propagation of the Gospel in Foreign Parts founds a slave school in Charles Town. Smallpox strikes New Hampshire.

1742 Spanish troops trying to unseat the British settlers in Georgia are defeated at the Battle of Bloody Marsh. Yellow fever is carried from the West Indies to Connecticut and New York City.

1744 The French capture the British settlement at Canso, Nova Scotia. King George's War begins between British and French colonists. By

the Treaty of Lancaster the Iroquois cede most of western Maryland
and Pennsylvania to the British. Diphtheria strikes Massachusetts, New
Hampshire, and New York.

1745 British and colonial troops capture the French Fort Louisbourg on
Cape Breton Island. The second group of Scottish Jacobite prisoners,
from the 1745 rebellion, is exiled to the colonies. Canadians capture
Fort Massachusetts (on the Hoosick River) and take prisoners to
Canada.

1746 Yellow fever strikes Albany, New York. Diphtheria strikes
Philadelphia.

1747 Princeton College is founded at Elizabeth, New Jersey. Rhode Island
gains the towns of Bristol, Tiverton, Little Compton, and Warren from
Massachusetts. The capitol building burns at Williamsburg, Virginia.
The border between Massachusetts and New Hampshire is settled. The
Ohio Company of Virginia is formed to expand Virginia's settlements
to the west. Measles strikes South Carolina, Pennsylvania, Massachusetts, Connecticut, New York, and the Ohio Valley.

1748 King George's War ends. The Lutheran Synod of America is officially
organized in Pennsylvania. The British found Halifax, Nova Scotia.

1749 The Ohio Company of Virginia is granted a charter to land already
claimed by the French and the Iroquois Confederacy. A severe drought
builds in New England. French establish a mission at Ogdensburg, New
York.

1750 The ban on slavery in Georgia, existing from the founding of the
colony, is lifted and slaves begin to arrive. Yellow fever epidemics
strike Philadelphia and Charles Town.

1751 The first hospital in America opens at Philadelphia. Portugal creates
a second *relaçao* (high court) at Rio de Janeiro, Brazil. Missionaries
from Santo Domingo introduce sugarcane into Louisiana. The first
Scottish immigrants are recruited by the Hudson's Bay Company to
settle in Canada. Diphtheria strikes South Carolina.

1752 A hurricane destroys the settlement at Santa Rosa Island, Florida and
the colonists resettle at Pensacola. Georgia becomes a Royal colony.
The French begin to build a series of forts across Ohio and Pennsylvania.

1753 Large numbers of colonists migrate from Antigua to South Carolina.
German Moravians settle Betharabia in the Wachovia Tract, North
Carolina.

1754 The French and Indian Wars begin. The French build Fort Duquesne
(Pittsburgh). They capture the British expedition at Fort Necessity. The
fourth major migration of Ulster Scots brings colonists who settle in

areas from Pennsylvania to North Carolina. Moravians settle at Antigua.

1755 French Acadians are expelled from their homes by the British and are deported to the Carolinas, Connecticut, Georgia, Maryland, Massachusetts, New York, Pennsylvania, and Virginia. Fort Duquesne is the site of the first major battle of the French and Indian War. A war council is held with five colonial governors to design a strategy to remove the French from the Ohio Valley. Quakers decide to expel any of their membership who are importing slaves. The Danish slave law of 1755 states that slaves who have Christian marriages may stay together as nuclear families; baptism, however, does not bring freedom or change their status as chattel property. The French build Fort Carrillon (New York). Saint Croix becomes a Crown colony of Denmark. A major smallpox epidemic strikes Canada and spreads to New York.

1756 Great Britain officially declares war against the French and the Indians. France captures Fort Oswego, New York. The Cherokee Uprising begins in North and South Carolina. Acadians who had been deported to Virginia are shipped to England. Stagecoach service begins between Philadelphia and New York. The *New Hampshire Gazette* is established.

1758 The French colony of Île Sainte Jean (Saint John's Island) is captured by the British, and Acadians who fled there in 1755 are shipped back to France. Quakers recommend that all their members should free their slaves. British forces capture Louisbourg (Cape Breton Island) and Fort Frontenac (Lake Ontario). The French burn Fort Duquesne. The British rebuild it and name it Fort Pitt. The first American Indian reservation in New Jersey is established.

1759 Quebec is captured by British and colonial forces. British forces capture the French island of Guadeloupe. British forces capture the French Fort Carrillon (renamed Ticonderoga) and Fort Frederic (renamed Crown Point).

1760 Two more counties are added to Maine, and the area becomes known as the Province of Maine of the Massachusetts Bay Colony. A fire in Boston destroys over four hundred buildings. New France surrenders to the British. Smallpox strikes Charles Town and New England.

1761 The Cherokee Uprising in the Carolinas is defeated. British forces capture the French island of Dominica. Smallpox strikes Bermuda.

1762 British forces capture Havana, Cuba and the French islands of Martinique, Saint Lucia, Grenada, and Saint Vincent. France cedes the Louisiana Territory to Spain. A major yellow fever epidemic strikes Philadelphia and Havana, Cuba.

1763 The French and Indian Wars end. France cedes Canada and all claims east of the Mississippi River to Great Britain and the West Indian islands of Saint Vincent, Dominica, and Tobago. England returns Havana, Cuba to Spain. Spain cedes Florida to England. France retains the islands on the Gulf of the Saint Lawrence River and the West Indian islands of Martinique, Guadeloupe, and Saint Lucia. Acadians who had been shipped from Virginia to Britain are now sent to France and eventually emigrate to Louisiana in 1785. Other Acadians who had been transported to the North American colonies begin to migrate to Louisiana. The Sugar Act is adopted by Parliament. The Creek Indians cede 2.4 million acres of land to Georgia. The Argyle Patent allocates land in Washington County, New York to Scottish settlers. Southwest Pennsylvania is settled along the Forbes Road that extends to Ohio. Great Britain issues a proclamation ordering no white settlements to be made west of the Appalachian Mountains. The British Crown establishes East and West Florida. A famine in Europe leaves 30,000 people dead in Sicily.

1764 New Hampshire's and Vermont's boundaries are established along the Connecticut River. Saint Louis, Missouri is founded by French fur traders. Six hundred frontier settlers march on Philadelphia and demand protection from the Indians. British Parliament adopts the Currency Act. Diphtheria strikes Philadelphia.

1765 The Stamp Act and the Quartering Act are adopted by Parliament. An angry mob in Newport, Rhode Island destroys a British warship. Sons and Daughters of Liberty are organized in the thirteen colonies.

1766 The Stamp Act is repealed. The Declaratory Act and the Townshend Acts are adopted by Parliament. Sons of Liberty in Wilmington, North Carolina prevent stamps and stamped paper from landing at port.

1767 The Mason-Dixon Line survey establishes the border between Pennsylvania and Maryland. The Philadelphia Company establishes a settlement in Nova Scotia. Spain expels Jesuits from all of its territories. The New York Assembly is suspended for failure to comply with the Quartering Act of 1765.

1768 The Massachusetts Assembly is dissolved. The Methodist Church is established in New York City. Colonists from Italy and Greece settle at New Smyrna, Florida.

1769 Rhode Islanders burn a crown revenue ship at Newport. The Townshend Acts are repealed, except for the tax on tea. The Virginia Assembly is dissolved by the British governor. The boundary between New York and New Jersey is settled. The first permanent Spanish settlement in California is founded at San Diego Bay. Some Virginia and North Carolina settlers migrate to the Watauga Valley in

Tennessee. Six judicial districts are established in South Carolina. Saint John's Island, later renamed Prince Edward Island, is parceled off in a land lottery to British Protestants. Diphtheria strikes New York.

1770 Five Americans are killed by British troops at the Boston Massacre. The Green Mountain Boys are formed in Vermont to protect local residents' land claims. The last major migration of Ulster Scots begins. Spain founds the presidio of Monterrey at San Francisco Bay. A famine in Europe leaves 150,000 people dead in Saxony and 80,000 people dead in Bohemia. Quakers in Philadelphia found a slave school.

1771 British troops engage farmers in North Carolina. Moravians found missions in Labrador. The Separate Baptist Church Association is formed in Orange County, Virginia. The "Great Fresh" flood on the James and Rappahannock rivers destroys a major portion of Virginia's tobacco crop. Diphtheria strikes South Carolina.

1772 Slavery is abolished in Great Britain. A hurricane devastates a large part of Saint Croix. Scarlet fever strikes New Haven, Connecticut.

1773 The Tea Act is adopted by Parliament. The Boston Tea party protests the tea tax by throwing tea chests into the harbor. The British blockade Boston Harbor. Falmouth, Maine is raided by the British. The boundary between New York and Massachusetts is settled. Scottish Highlanders settle in the Mohawk Valley in New York. Large numbers of English and Scottish colonists settle in Georgia. Some Ulster Scots migrate to Newport, Rhode Island.

1774 The First Continental Congress convenes in Philadelphia. The Coercive (also called Intolerable) Acts and the Quebec Act are adopted by Parliament. Settlers from Virginia traverse the Wilderness Road and settle at Harrodsburg, Kentucky. Shaker colonists settle at New Lebanon, New York. Lord Dunmore calls upon Shenandoah Valley settlers to fight Indians at Point Pleasant in the Ohio Valley. A cargo of British tea is burned in Greenwich, New Jersey as a tax protest. The tea brig *Peggy Stewart* is burned at Annapolis, Maryland. A group of women in Edenton, North Carolina burn tea as a protest. Virginia counties begin to form independent militia companies.

1775 Battles are fought at Lexington, Concord, and Bunker Hill in Massachusetts. Portland, Maine is razed by the British. The Second Continental Congress convenes at Philadelphia. In Rhode Island the Providence Tea Party protests the tea tax by burning tea in the market square. Lord Dunmore seizes the powder from the public magazine in Williamsburg, Virginia, occupies Norfolk, and offers to free any black slaves who will fight to subdue the colonists. Fort Ticonderoga is captured by the Green Mountain Boys, and Vermont declares its independence from New York and New Hampshire. New Hampshire becomes the first colony to expel its Royal governor. North Carolina issues the Mecklenburg Declaration of Independence. The Transylvania Company purchases about half the land in Kentucky. Boonesboro, Kentucky is founded. King Charles III of Spain grants permission to all Spaniards to settle wherever they choose in Spanish America.

Suggested Reading

Bannon, John Francis. *History of the Americas.* 2 Vols. 2nd ed. (New York: McGraw-Hill, 1963).

Carruth, Gordon. *The Encyclopedia of America Facts and Dates.* 8th ed. (New York: Harper and Row, 1978).

Cooke, Jacob Ernest. *Encyclopedia of North American Colonies.* 3 Vols. (New York: Charles Scribner's Sons, 1993).

Cordasco, Francesco. *Dictionary of American Immigration History* (Metuchen, NJ: Scarecrow Press, 1990).

Duffy, John. *Epidemics in Colonial America* (Baton Rouge: Louisiana State University Press, 1953).

Dupuy, R.E. and T.N. Dupuy. *Encyclopedia of Military History* (London: Jane's Publishing Co., 1986).

Urdang, Laurence. *The Timetables of American History* (New York: Simon and Schuster, 1981).

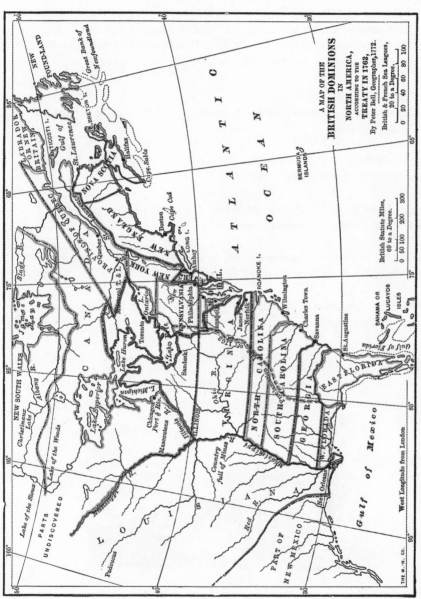

2 North America in 1763 (Edward Channing, *A Short History of the United States*. New York: Macmillan & Co., 1911)

Dates of the First European Colonial Governors in America

CA = Central America   SA = South America
NA = North America   WI = West Indies

Year	European Dominion	Colony
1496	Spain	Santo Domingo (Dominican Republic), WI
1504	Portugal	Brazil, SA
1508	Spain	Puerto Rico, WI
1509	Spain	Jamaica, WI
1511	Spain	Cuba, WI
1514	Spain	Tierra Firme (Panama), CA
1521	Spain	Nueva España (Mexico), NA
1522	Spain	Nicaragua, CA
1524	Spain	Guatemala, CA
1525	Spain	Santa Marta (Colombia), SA
1526	Spain	Honduras, CA
1527	Spain	Venezuela, SA
1532	Spain	Trinidad, WI
1535	Spain	Peru, SA
1536	Spain	Río de la Plata (Argentina), SA
1540	Spain	Chile, SA
1556	Spain	Quito (Ecuador), SA
1567	Spain	Florida, NA

1568	Spain	Costa Rica, CA
1599	Spain	Nuevo México (New Mexico), NA
1604	France	Acadia (later Nova Scotia, New Brunswick), NA
1607	England	Virginia, NA
1609	England	Bermuda, WI
1611	England	Newfoundland, NA
1612	France	New France (Québec), NA
1618	Spain	Paraguay, SA
1620	England	New Plymouth (Massachusetts), NA
1623	England	Anguilla, WI
1623	England	Saint Christopher (Saint Kitts), WI
1624	Netherlands	New Netherland (New York, New Jersey), NA
1628	England	Barbados, WI
1628	France	Saint Croix, WI
1628	France	La Désirade, WI
1628	France	Marie-Galante, WI
1628	England	Nevis, WI
1629	England	Massachusetts Bay Company (parts of Massachusetts, Maine, and New Hampshire), NA
1630	England	Providence Island, WI
1632	England	Montserrat, WI
1634	Netherlands	Curaçao, WI

1634	England	Maryland, NA
1635	France	Guadeloupe, WI
1635	England	Antigua, WI
1635	France	Martinique, WI
1636	Netherlands	Sint Maarten, WI
1636	Netherlands	Saint Eustatius, WI
1638	France	Saint Martin, WI
1638	Sweden	New Sweden (New Jersey, Delaware), NA
1638	England	Rhode Island, NA
1639	England	Connecticut, NA
1641	France	Saint-Domingue (Haiti), WI
1649	France	Grenada, WI
1664	France	French Guiana (Guyane), SA
1664	England	North Carolina, NA
1665	Netherlands	Suriname, SA
1670	England	Rupert's Land (Hudson's Bay Company), NA
1670	England	South Carolina, NA
1671	England	Bahama Islands, WI
1671	England	Virgin Islands, WI
1672	Denmark	Saint John, WI
1672	Denmark	Saint Thomas, WI
1680	England	New Hampshire, NA
1681	England	Pennsylvania, NA

1699	France	Louisiana, NA
1712	Great Britain	Nova Scotia, NA
1714	France	Île Royale (Cape Breton), NA
1716	Spain	Texas (briefly from 1691–3), NA
1720	France	Île Saint-Jean (Prince Edward Island), NA
1733	Great Britain	Georgia, NA
1763	France	Saint Lucia, WI
1763	Great Britain	Saint Vincent, WI
1763	France	Saint-Pierre-et-Miquelon, NA
1764	Great Britain	Tobago, WI
1764	Great Britain	Quebec, NA
1766	Great Britain	Falkland Islands, SA
1767	Spain	California, NA
1768	Great Britain	Dominica, WI
1770	Great Britain	Prince Edward Island, NA
1784	Sweden	Saint-Barthélemy, WI
1784	Great Britain	Cape Breton, NA
1784	Great Britain	New Brunswick, NA
1786	Great Britain	British Honduras (Belize), CA
1791	Great Britain	Upper Canada (Ontario), NA
1803	Great Britain	British Guiana (Guyana), SA

Part Two

Latin America

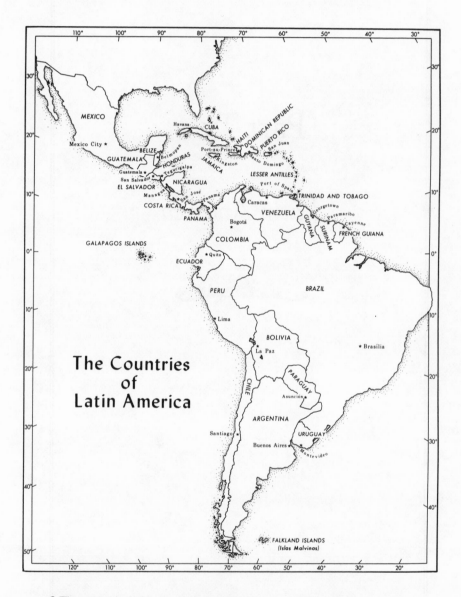

3 The countries of Latin America (Cathryn L. Lombardi, et al., *Latin American History: A Teaching Atlas*. Madison: University of Wisconsin Press, 1983)

Colonial Records of Latin America

In 1493 Pope Alexander VI created a line of demarcation — known as the Tordesillas Line — west of the Azores and the Cape Verde Islands, establishing Spain's right to claim territory to the west. The following year the line was moved father west, which allowed Portugal to begin colonizing Brazil. Over the course of the next two centuries, Spain colonized territory that became the present-day countries of Argentina, Bolivia, Chile, Colombia, Costa Rica, Cuba, the Dominican Republic, Ecuador, El Salvador, Guatemala, Honduras, Mexico, Nicaragua, Panama, Paraguay, Peru, Puerto Rico, Uruguay, and Venezuela. Between 1810 and 1830 the Latin American colonies of Spain and Portugal became independent.

Parish, Diocesan, and Other Ecclesiastical Records

With the first Spanish and Portuguese conquerors to America came priests. Caught up in the religious zeal of the sixteenth-century Inquisition, the first missionaries baptized tens of thousands of Amerindians.

Registros parroquiales y eclesiásticos diversos (parish registers, diocesan, and other ecclesiastical records) are the major source for vital records. Record keeping was obligatory after the Council of Trent in 1563. In Peru the First Council of Lima (1551–2) established rules for record keeping, and some of the earliest registers date from 1538.

The basic ecclesiastical divisions are the *arquidiócesis* (archdiocese), *dióceses* or *obispado* (diocese), and *parroquia* (parish). By 1600 five archdioceses existed in Spanish America. They were: Santo Domingo, Lima, Mexico, Santa Fé de Bogotá, and Charcas. Parish records are usually kept at the original parish. If a parish is disestablished, the records are transferred to a bishop's or archbishop's archive. Diocesan

SEE ALSO
Caribbean
Portugal
Spain

33

archives also hold administrative records, church court records, marriage information, notarial, and other records.[2] Some of the types of records are:

> *bautismos* (baptisms).
> *matrimoniales* (marriages).
> *defunctos* (deaths).
> *entierros* (burials).
> *confirmaciónes* (confirmations).
> *testamentos* (wills).
> *divorcios y nulidades* (divorces and annulments).
> *de universidades y academias* (university records).
> *Inquicision: limpieza de sangre* (purity of blood): proof of pure Christian ancestry; includes names, residences, parentage, and pedigrees. For more information on records of the Inquisition, see the chapter on sources of colonial records in Spain.

Missionaries
From Columbus' second voyage in 1493, missionaries were a presence in the colonizing of the New World. The Dominicans were the first to arrive, followed by the Franciscans, Augustinians, and Jesuits. The Incas and Aztecs readily accepted the idea that one supreme being was responsible for creating the world. The organization of the Christian church was also familiar to them, as they also had an order of priesthood, baptism with water, confession and repentance, plural marriage, and the symbol of the cross.[3]

Census Records

Padrones (civil census records) and *matrículas* (ecclesiastical censuses, sometimes also called *padrones* and *visitas*) or *róis* (in Portuguese) were taken to formulate tax lists or elevate the status of a chapelry to a parish. They usually contain information on complete family units. The most common terms and neighborhood geographical divisions are the *anexo* (sub-parish), and *parroquia* (parish), *manzana* (block), and *solares* (plot).

Notarial Records

Notariales (notarial records) are the instruments drawn up to record a variety of

---

[2] For a chronological listing of the creation of dioceses in Latin America, see Lyman D. Platt, *Investigaciones Genealógicas en Latinoamerica* (Salt Lake City: Instituto Genealógico e Histórico Latinoamericano, 1989), 20–3.

[3] Huber Herring, *A History of Latin America from the Beginnings to the Present.* 2ⁿᵈ ed. (New York: Alfred A. Knopf, 1989), 171.

transactions:

➣ *testamentos* (recordings of wills).

➣ *testamento cerrado* (will written in secret and sealed before a notary).

➣ *intestados* (estate records).

➣ *tutelas* (guardianships).

➣ *prohijaciones* (adoptions).

➣ *limpiezas de sangre* (cleanliness of blood).

➣ *tierras y propiedades* (land transactions).

➣ *aprendizages* (apprenticeships).

➣ *cartas de dote* (dowry information).

➣ *conciertos y contratos* (contracts).

➣ *poderes* (powers of attorney).

➣ *hipotecas* (mortgages).

Governmental and Municipal Records

De Gobernación, de las provincias, y municipales (governmental and municipal records) are at various municipal archives throughout Latin American countries. Examples of such are:

➣ *de impuestos, contibuyentes, y alcabalas* (tax records).

➣ *exoneraciones* (names, residences, and places of birth of Indians who were exempted from paying tributes because of noble descent — *caciques).*

➣ *de los tribunales y cortes* (court records), including *actuaciones civlies y criminales* (civil and criminal cases) and *juzgados sobre biens de difuntos* (administrations of estates).

➣ *pensiones* (pensions).

➣ *del ayuntamiento* (town records).

➣ *del hospitales* (hospital records) including lists of patients, residences, and places of birth, etc.).

➣ *de los Indigenas* (Indian records).

➣ *inmigración* (records of European origins and immigration).

➣ *degremios* (guild and association records).

Viceroyalties

The *virreinato* (viceroyalty) system of government was transplanted from Spain and Portugal to the New World. The viceroy (vice-king) was the highest ranking colonial official, reporting directly to the Crown. He served as governor and often as captain general and president of the *audiencia.* The dates of establishment of the viceroyalties are:

➣ Santo Domingo, 1509–26

➣ Nueva España (Mexico), 1534–1821

➣ Peru, 1543–1821

➤ Brazil, 1549–1822
➤ Nueva Granada (Colombia, Ecuador, Panama, and Venezuela), 1717–23
    and 1739–1891
➤ Río de la Plata (Argentina, Bolivia, Paraguay, and Uruguay), 1776–1810

Captaincy Generals
Capitanía general (captaincy general) was the next administrative division under
a viceroyalty. The captain general, a military officer appointed by the Crown,
governed the province. Some of the most important captaincies were: Buenos
Aires, Cuba, Chile, Guatemala, El Salvador, Nueva España, Nueva Granada,
Peru, Puerto Rico, Santo Domingo, Venezuela, Yucatán, and Florida and
Louisiana.

Audiencias
Courts known as *audiencias* were instituted to supervise the local courts and to
administer Spanish and Portuguese law. These courts paralleled the admin-
istrative divisions of the captaincy generals. A group of judges appointed by the
Crown held both civil and criminal jurisdiction, and served as a court of appeals
within the territory. The dates of the institution of the *audiencias* are:
➤ Santo Domingo (Hispaniola), 1511
➤ Nueva España (Mexico), 1527
➤ Tierra Firme (Panama), 1536
➤ Lima (Peru), 1542
➤ Guatemala, 1543 and 1570
➤ Guadalajara, Nueva Galicia (Mexico), 1548
➤ Bogotá (Colombia), 1549
➤ Charcas (Boliva), 1559
➤ Quito (Ecuador), 1563
➤ Santiago (Chile), 1609
➤ Buenos Aires (Argentina), 1661
➤ Caracas (Venezuela), 1786
➤ Cuzco (Peru), 1787

Cabildos
The basic unit of government was the *cabildo* (city council). The first cabildos
were appointed by the Crown; after 1523 most were elected by landholders,
although many offices were still sold by the Crown. An important contribution
of this system was the practice of holding a *cabildo abierto* (open town meeting).

Land Records
De tierras y propiedades (land records) are found in notarial, ecclesiastical, and
municipal records. Types of land records are:

➤ *encomiendas* (original colonial grants which involved the assignments of Indians as laborers).[4]

➤ *capellanías* (land donated to the Catholic church by individuals and from estates).

➤ *títulas de propriedad* (land titles) found in notarial records, including mortgages, disputed wills, and probates involving land.

➤ *vínculos and mayorazgos* (family hereditary properties).

➤ *casas* (sale of houses).

➤ *donaciónes* (donations of property prior to donor's death).

The basic unit of land measurement was the *tercia,* based on the Castillian yard, about four hand-breadths in length. A *cordel* was equal to fifty *tercias.* In terms of distance, a league equaled 5,000 Castillian yards. A Portuguese *alquier* equaled between 24.2 and 48.4 square meters.

Names for specific plots and uses of land were *huerta* or *suerte* (garden plot, about 552 x 276 yards), *venta* (50 x 50 yards), *molino* (same size as a *venta*), and *caballería* (1,104 x 552 yards).

Political Land Divisions
Terms most frequently used to designate political geographical divisions were:

➤ *Departamento, provincia, estado, intendencia* (state and provincial divisions).

➤ *Municipio, ayuntamiento, barrio, canton* (municipal divisions).

These divisions generally paralleled the ecclesiastical divisions. Terms varied from country to country.[5]

Military Records

Militares y milicias (military records) are found in most national archives in Central and South America and archival repositories in Spain (see the chapter on sources of colonial records in Spain). Terms most frequently used to describe military records are:

➤ *hojas de servicio* (service sheets of those enlisted — often includes ancestry).

---

[4]An *econmienda* owner was required to erect a church on his estate for the baptism of the Amerindians and infants within a week of their birth. In Cuba and Hispaniola, the names of the Amerindians in the original grants of *ecomienda* in 1514 were recorded in the church visitations.

[5]For a chart describing these divisions, see George R. Ryskamp, *Finding Your Hispanic Roots* (Baltimore: Genealogical Publishing Co., 1997), 117.

➣ *comisiones* (comissions of officers).
➣ *listas de revistas* (troop lists).
➣ *marinas* (naval records).
➣ *expedientes personales* (officer service records, including marriage information and pension records).
➣ *capellanías* (military parish records).
➣ *cofrídia y confraternidades* (entry into military orders).
➣ *filciaciones* (military registers of soldiers' enlistments).
➣ *meritos y servicios* (merits and services; information on noble lineage).

Suggested Reading

Carlo, Agustín Millares. *Los Archivos Municipales de Latinoamérica: Libros de Actas y Colecciones Documentales* (n.p., n.d., film 0897926). A listing of the collections of the municipal archives in Latin America.

Catalog of the Latin American Library of the Tulane University Library, New Orleans. 9 Vols. Supps. (Boston: G.K. Hall, 1970–8).

Catalog of the Latin American Collection of the University of Florida Libraries, Gainesville, Florida. 13 Vols. Supp. (Boston: G.K. Hall, 1973, 1979). The concentration includes a large map collection, most Latin American and Caribbean newspapers (on microfilm), census materials, books, manuscripts, and rare books.

Diffie, Bailey W. *Latin American Civilization: The Colonial Period*. 2nd ed. (New York: n.p., 1967).

Driver, Steven L. and Rafael Espejo-Saavedra. *Spanish-English Dictionary of Human and Physical Geography* (Westport, CT: Greenwood Press, 1993).

Feldman, Lawrence. *Anglo-Americans in Spanish Archives: Lists of Anglo-American Settlers in the Spanish Colonies of America; A Finding Aid* (Baltimore: Genealogical Publishing Co., 1991). Abstracted original census documents, 1781–97, from major Spanish archives, about individuals and families who settled in the French territories of Louisiana and the Floridas after they came under Spanish rule in 1766. The areas correspond to the present-day states of Delaware, Florida, Alabama, Mississippi, Louisiana, and Missouri and to Belize, formerly British Honduras.

Gropp, Arthur Eric. *Guide to Libraries and Archives in Central America and the West Indies, Panama, Bermuda, and British Guiana* (New Orleans: Middle

American Research Institute, Tulane University, 1941). This includes Central America, Bermuda, the West Indies, Guyana, and Panama.

Grow, Michael. *Scholar's Guide to Washington, DC: Latin American and Caribbean Studies.* 2nd ed. (Washington, DC: Woodrow Wilson Center Press, 1992).

Hill, Roscoe R. *Los Archivos Nacionales de la América Latina* (Havana: Archivo Nacional de Cuba, 1948). The national archives of Latin America, including a history and description of the collection, and a listing of the publications of each archive.

Indice biográfico de España, Portugal e Ibero-América (New York: K.G. Saur, 1990). Biographical works in Spain, Portugal, and Latin America, indexed.

Lombardi, Cathryn L. and John V. Lombardi. *Latin American History: A Teaching Atlas* (Madison: University of Wisconsin Press, 1983).

Platt, Lyman D. *Hispanic Surnames and Family History* (Baltimore: Genealogical Publishing Co., 1996).

Platt, Lyman D. *Census Records Latin America and the United States* (Baltimore: Genealogical Publishing Co., 1998). Covers Argentina, Arizona, Bolivia, California, Chile, Colombia, Costa Rica, Cuba, the Dominican Republic, Ecuador, Florida, Guatemala, Louisiana, Mexico, New Mexico, Nicaragua, Panama, Peru, Puerto Rico, El Salvador, Texas, Uruguay, and Venezuela.

Querexeta, Jaime. *Diccionario omnástico y heráldico basco* (Bilbao: La Gran Enciclopedia Basca, 1970–5). Dictionary of Basque surnames and heraldry.

Ryskamp, George S. *Finding Your Hispanic Roots* (Baltimore: Genealogical Publishing Co., 1997).

Sweet, David G. and Gary B. Nash. *Struggle and Survival in Colonial America* (Berkeley: University of California Press, 1981).

Ulibarri, George S. and John P. Harrison. *Guide to Materials on Latin America in the National Archives of the United States* (Washington, DC: The National Archives, 1974).

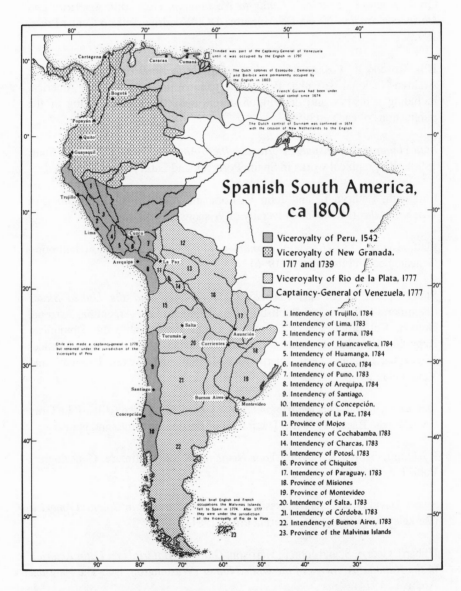

Trinidad was part of the Captaincy General of Venezuela until it was occupied by the English in 1797

Cartagena

Caracas Cumaná

The Dutch colonies of Essequibo, Demerara and Berbice were permanently occupied by the English in 1803

Bogotá

French Guiana had been under royal control since 1674

Popayán

Quito

The Dutch control of Surinam was confirmed in 1674 with the cession of New Netherlands to the English

Guayaquil

Spanish South America, ca 1800

Trujillo

Lima Cuzco

Arequipa La Paz

▦ Viceroyalty of Peru, 1542

▦ Viceroyalty of New Granada, 1717 and 1739

▦ Viceroyalty of Rio de la Plata, 1777

▦ Captaincy-General of Venezuela, 1777

Salta

Tucumán Asunción

Corrientes

Chile was made a captaincy-general in 1778, but remained under the jurisdiction of the Viceroyalty of Peru

Santiago

Buenos Aires

Montevideo

Concepción

1. Intendency of Trujillo, 1784
2. Intendency of Lima, 1783
3. Intendency of Tarma, 1784
4. Intendency of Huancavelica, 1784
5. Intendency of Huamanga, 1784
6. Intendency of Cuzco, 1784
7. Intendency of Puno, 1783
8. Intendency of Arequipa, 1784
9. Intendency of Santiago,
10. Intendency of Concepción,
11. Intendency of La Paz, 1784
12. Province of Mojos
13. Intendency of Cochabamba, 1783
14. Intendency of Charcas, 1783
15. Intendency of Potosí, 1783
16. Province of Chiquitos
17. Intendency of Paraguay, 1783
18. Province of Misiones
19. Province of Montevideo
20. Intendency of Salta, 1783
21. Intendency of Córdoba, 1783
22. Intendency of Buenos Aires, 1783
23. Province of the Malvinas Islands

After brief English and French occupations the Malvinas Islands fell to Spain in 1774. After 1777 they were under the jurisdiction of the Viceroyalty of Rio de la Plata

4 Spanish South America, 1800 (Cathryn L. Lombardi, et al., *Latin American History: A Teaching Atlas*. Madison: University of Wisconsin Press, 1983)

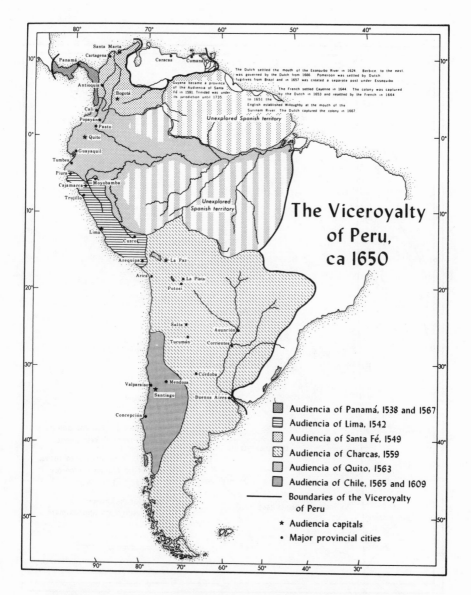

The Viceroyalty
of Peru,
ca 1650

The Dutch settled the mouth of the Essequibo River in 1624. Berbice, to the east, was governed by the Dutch from 1666. Pomeroon was settled by Dutch fugitives from Brazil and in 1657 was created a separate post under Essequibo

The French settled Cayenne in 1644. The colony was captured by the Dutch in 1653 and resettled by the French in 1664

In 1651 the English established Willoughby at the mouth of the Surinam River. The Dutch captured the colony in 1667

Unexplored Spanish territory

Unexplored
Spanish territory

Audiencia of Panamá, 1538 and 1567
Audiencia of Lima, 1542
Audiencia of Santa Fé, 1549
Audiencia of Charcas, 1559
Audiencia of Quito, 1563
Audiencia of Chile, 1565 and 1609
Boundaries of the Viceroyalty of Peru
★ Audiencia capitals
• Major provincial cities

5 Viceroyalty of Peru, 1650 (Cathryn L. Lombardi, et al., *Latin American History: A Teaching Atlas*. Madison: University of Wisconsin Press, 1983)

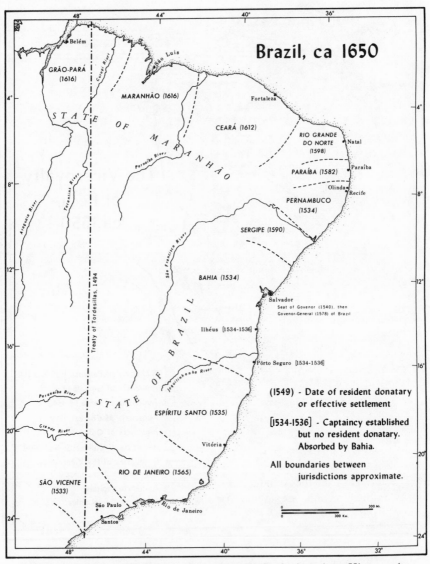

Brazil, ca 1650

GRÃO-PARÁ (1616)

MARANHÃO (1616)

Belém

São Luis

STATE OF MARANHÃO

CEARÁ (1612)

Fortaleza

RIO GRANDE DO NORTE (1598)

Natal

PARAÍBA (1582)

Paraíba

Olinda

Recife

PERNAMBUCO (1534)

SERGIPE (1590)

BAHIA (1534)

Salvador
Seat of Govenor (1540), then
Govenor-General (1578) of Brazil

Ilhéus [1534-1536]

Pôrto Seguro [1534-1536]

Treaty of Tordesillas, 1494

STATE OF BRAZIL

ESPÍRITU SANTO (1535)

Vitória

RIO DE JANEIRO (1565)

SÃO VICENTE (1533)

São Paulo

Santos

Rio de Janeiro

(1549) - Date of resident donatary
or effective settlement

[1534-1536] - Captaincy established
but no resident donatary.
Absorbed by Bahia.

All boundaries between
jurisdictions approximate.

0   300 Mi.
0   300 Km.

6 Brazil, 1650 (Cathryn L. Lombardi, et al., *Latin American History: A Teaching Atlas.* Madison: University of Wisconsin Press, 1983)

Argentina

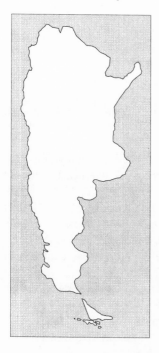

The first permanent settlement in Argentina was at Asunción (now Paraguay) in 1541. Argentina was part of the Viceroyalty of Peru until 1776. At that time the Viceroyalty of Río de la Plata was created and included Argentina, Bolivia, Paraguay, and Uruguay. Argentina declared independence from Spain in 1810. The earliest cities founded were Santiago del Estero (1553), San Juan and Mendoza (1562), Tumucán (1565), Córdoba and Santa Fé (1573), Buenos Aires (1580), Salta (1582), Corrientes and Paraná (1588), La Ríoja (1591), and San Luis (1596).

Parish, Diocesan, and Other Ecclesiastical Records

Parroquiales (parish registers) date from 1610 and include baptisms, marriages, deaths and burials, and other records. Examples of parish records are:

Arquidiócesis de Córdoba, Iglesia Católica.
- Documentos eclesiásticos, 1557–1937 (film 0720490 ff.). Registers of miscellaneous ecclesiastical documents from the Archdiocese of Córdoba, including *capellanías*, 1643–1884, *juicios eclesiásticos*, 1692–1905, *juicios criminales*, 1699–1871, and documents from the Archivo General de Indias in Seville referring to the Obispado and Cathedral at Córdoba, 1566–1783.
- Documentos eclesiásticos tocante a matrimonio: 1664–1914 (film 0756643 ff.). Registers of marriage petitions, divorces, annulments, separations, and decisions of ecclesiastical courts in cases involving proposed or already contracted marriages from the Archdiocese of Córdoba.

SEE ALSO
Chile
Latin America
Peru
Spain

The original records are at the Arquidiócesis de Córdoba in Córdoba.

Records of the Inquisition from the sixteenth to nineteenth centuries are at the Archivo Histórico Nacional in Madrid, Spain, the Archivo Nacional in Lima, Peru, and the Archivo Nacional in Santiago, Chile.

For more information on records of the Inquisition, see the chapter on sources of colonial records in Spain.

Census Records

Padrones (civil census records) date from 1622 and *matrículas* and *padrones* (ecclesiastical censuses) from 1610. Examples of such records are:

Contaduría General de Retasas, La Plata.
* Padrones, 1780–1807 (film 1840704 ff.). Censuses of the Indian populations who lived in some of the old tax districts of the Viceroyalty of La Plata.
* Padrones, 1780 (film 1840709 ff.). Census and tax lists of emigrants from countries ruled by Great Britain to the territories governed by the old Viceroyalty of La Plata.
* Padrones, 1657–1801 (film 1840693 ff.). Censuses of the Indian populations who lived in the old tax districts of Misiones Province, Viceroyalty of La Plata. These districts are now part of Misiones Province, Argentina. Old Misiones Province included the present-day countries of Paraguay and Uruguay.
* Padrones, 1667–1772 (film 1840690 ff.). Censuses of the population who lived in the old tax districts of Buenos Aires Province, Viceroyalty of Peru. These districts are now part of the city or province of Buenos Aires.

The original records are in the *Interior* collection of the Archivo General de la Nación in Buenos Aires.

Frías, Susana R. *Censos y Padrones Existentes en el Archivo General de la Nación, 1776–1852* (Buenos Aires: Centro para Investigaciones Históricas en la Argentina, 1974, film 1614821). This is a guide to censuses available at the National Archive in Buenos Aires for the years 1776–1852.

Notarial Records

Notariales (notarial records) date from 1571. Examples of notarial records are:
* Archivo General de la Nación. Indice alfabético y cronológico de sucesiones, 1600–1920 (film 1614822). Alphabetical and chronological index of probate and inheritance records.
* Escribanía, Trinidad, Perú. Protocolos, 1584–1756 (film 1700187 ff.). Notarial record books from Trinidad (also known as La Trinidad and La Santíssima Trinidad), a city in the Buenos Aires district of Río de la Plata Province, Viceroyalty of Peru.

The original records are at the Archivo General de la Nación in Buenos Aires.

Governmental and Municipal Records

De Gobernación, de las provincias, y municipales (governmental and municipal records) dating from 1554 are at various municipal archives throughout Argentina. Examples of such records are:

Córdoba del Tucumán. Documentos civiles, 1571–1784 (film 0756638). The original manuscripts are at the Archivo del Arzobispado in Córdoba.

Archivo General de la Nación.

- Catálogo de nombres y materias: fichero general, 1544–1880 (film 1614816 ff.). Personal name and subject index to court and government records housed in the Argentine National Archives. The majority of the references pertain to the Viceroyalty of Río de la Plata, and the countries of Argentina, Bolivia, Paraguay, and Uruguay.
- Catálogo, Sala IX, División Colonia, Sección Gobierno: Indice por materia, 1584–1861 (film 1614821). Subject index to the Colonial Division of documents in Room IX of the Argentine National Archives.

The original records are at the Archivo General de la Nación in Buenos Aires.

Military Records

Militares (military records) dating from the eighteenth century at the Archivo General de la Nación in Buenos Aires. For other records, see the chapter on sources of colonial records in Spain.

Land Records

De tierras y propiedades (land records) dating from 1571 are found in notarial, ecclesiastical, and municipal records at the Archivo General de la Nación in Buenos Aires.

Suggested Reading

Bibliografía Argentina: Catálogo de Materiales Argentinos en las Bibliotecas. 7 Vols. (Boston: G.K. Hall, 1980). Argentine bibliography: a union catalog of Argentine holdings in the libraries of the University of Buenos Aires.

Bruno, Cayetano. *Historia de la Iglesia en la Argentina* (Buenos Aires: Editorial Don Bosco, 1966). History of the Catholic Church in Argentina.

Calvo, Carlos. *Novilaiario del Antiguo Virreynato del Río de la Plata* (1936. Reprint. Austin, TX: Golightly-Payne-Coon Co., 1958, film 0283551). Genealogy of viceroys of old La Plata (Argentina, Uruguay, Paraguay, and Bolivia).

Fernández de Burzaco y Barrios, Hugo. *Aportes Biogenealógicos para un Padrón de Habitantes del Río de la Plata* (Buenos Aires: Myrta Chena de Fernández Burazco, 1986). Biogenealogical contributions for a listing of residents of the Viceroyalty of Río de la Plata (Argentina, Bolivia, Paraguay, and Uruguay).

Gammalsson, Hialmar Edmundo. *Los Pobladores de Buenos Aires y Su Descendencia* (Buenos Aires: Municipalidad de la Ciudad de Buenos Aires, n.d.). The first settlers of Buenos Aires and their descendants.

García Quintanilla, Julio. *Historia de la Iglesia en La Plata* (Sucre, Bolivia: Talleres Gráficos Don Bosco, 1964). A story of the church in La Plata. The diocese of Charcas or La Plata, founded in 1553, includes parts of what are today Argentina, Bolivia, Chile, Paraguay, and Peru.

Konetze, Richard. *La Emigración Española al Río de la Plata Durante el Siglo XVI* (Madrid: Instituto Gonzalo Fernández de Oviedo, Consejo Superior de Investigaciones Científicas, 1952). Spanish emigration to Río de la Plata in the sixteenth century.

Muzzio, Julio A. Diccionario *Histórico y Biográfico de la Repùblica Argentina.* 2 Vols. (Buenos Aires: Librería La Facultad de Juan Roldán, 1920, film 0824202). Historical and biographical dictionary of Argentina.

Santillán, Diego A. de. *Gran Enciplopedia Argentina: Todo lo Argentino Ordenado Alfabéticamente; Geografía e Historia, Topo Nomías, Biografías, Ciencias, Artes, Letras, Derecho, Economía, Indus Tria y Comercio Instituciones, Flora y Fauna, Folklore, Lexico Regional.* 9 Vols. (Buenos Aires: Ediar, 1956). Great Argentine encyclopedia of geographical, historical, toponomical, biographical information, etc.

Serrano Redonnet, Jorge Alberto. *La Sociedad de Buenos Aires en Sus Derechos a Mayorazgos y a Otras Fundaciones Españolas* (Buenos Aires: Academia Americana de Genealogía, 1992). Family estates among the socially prominent citizens of the city of Buenos Aires in the seventeenth century.

Bolivia

Bolivia was colonized by Spain in 1536. It was part of the Viceroyalty of Peru until 1776. At that time the Viceroyalty of Río de la Plata was created and included Argentina, Bolivia, Paraguay, and Uruguay. Bolivia declared independence from Spain in 1825. The earliest cities founded were Charcas (1539) and Potosí (1545).

Parish, Diocesan, and Other Ecclesiastical Records

Parroquiales (parish registers) date from 1558 and include baptisms, marriages, deaths and burials, and other records. The Diocese of la Plata was established in 1552. Records can be found in Bolivia, Argentina, Chile, and Peru.

Records of the Inquisition from the sixteenth to nineteenth centuries are at the Archivo Histórico Nacional in Madrid, Spain, the Archivo Nacional in Lima, Peru, and the Archivo Nacional in Santiago, Chile. For more information on records of the Inquisition, see the chapter on sources of colonial records in Spain.

Census Records

Padrones (civil census records) and *matrículas* and *padrones* (ecclesiastical censuses) from 1558. Examples of such records are:

Alto Perú Contaduría General de Retasas. Padrones, 1645–1780 (film 1840691 ff.). Census lists of the Indian population who lived in old tax districts of Alto Perú, a province of the Viceroyalty of Peru which is now known as the Republic of Bolivia. The original records are at the Sala IX del Archivo General de la Nación en Buenos Aires, Argentina.

SEE ALSO
Argentina
Latin America
Paraguay
Peru
Spain

Archivo General de la Nación, Argentina, Contaduría General de Retasas. Padrones y revisitas de indios: 1607–1807 (film 1700449 ff.). Censuses of the Indian population who lived in many of the old tax districts of La Plata Province, viceroyalties of Peru and La Plata. Most of these districts are now part of *cantones* (provinces) in the departments of Oruro, Cochabamba, Chuquisaca, and Potosí, Bolivia. The original records are at the Archivo General de la Nación in Buenos Aires, Argentina.

Notarial Records

Notariales (notarial records) date from 1540. They can be found at the Escrituras Pública in La Plata and the Libros de Acuerde del Cabidode in Potosí.

Governmental and Municipal Records

De Gobernación, de las provincias, y municipales (governmental and municipal records) dating from 1548 are at various municipal archives throughout Bolivia and Argentina.

Military Records

Militares (military records) dating from the 1558 are at the Archivo de Indias in Seville, Spain, the Biblioteca de las Universidad Mayor de San Andreas, and other archives in Argentina and Peru. For more information, see the chapter on sources of colonial records in Spain.

Wilde Cavero, M. Fernando. *Historia Militar de Bolivia* (La Paz: n.p., 1963, film 0873666). Military history of Bolivia.

Land Records

De tierras y propiedades (land records) dating from 1548 are found in notarial, ecclesiastical, and municipal records at the Archivo General in Lima, Peru.

Repartimiento de Tierras por el Inca Huayna Capac: Testimonio de un Documento de 1556. 2nd ed. (Cochabamba, Bolivia: Universidad Mayor de San Simón. Departamemto de Arqueología, 1977). Distribution of land by the Inca Huayna Capac in a document from 1556.

Suggested Reading

Arze Quiroga, Eduardo. *Historia de Bolivia: Fases del Progreso Hispano Americano, Origenes de la Sociedad Boliviana en el Siglo XVI* (La Paz: Los Amigos del Libro, 1969, film 0897094). History of Bolivia: origins of Bolivian society in the sixteenth century.

Bakewell, Judith R. *Research Guide to Andean History: Bolivia, Chile, Ecuador, and Peru* (Durham, NC: Duke University Press, 1981).

Martarelli, Angélico. *El Colegio Franciscano de Potosí y Sus Misiones: Noticias Históricas.* 2nd ed. (La Paz: Tallares Gráficos Marinoni, n.d.). The Franciscan academy of Potosí and its missions, with historical notes.

Moreno, Gabriel René. *Catálogo del Archivo de Mojos y Chiquitos.* 2nd ed. (1888. Reprint. La Paz: Librería Juventud, 1973). A collection of manuscripts dealing with the Jesuit Missions in Upper Peru (colonial Bolivia), made by Moreno and presented by him to the Bolivian Government.

Nino, Bernardino de. *Misiones Franciscanas del Colegio de Propaganda Fide de Potosí* (La Paz: Tallares Gráficos Marinoni, 1918). Franciscan missions of the Academy of Propaganda Fide of Potosí. This is a continuation of the historical work of Angélico Martarelli.

Urquidi, Arturo. *Las Comunidades Indígenas en Bolivia* (Cochabamba, Bolivia: Los Amigos del Libro, 1970, film 0897294). A sociological study of native Bolivians.

South American Indians.

Chile

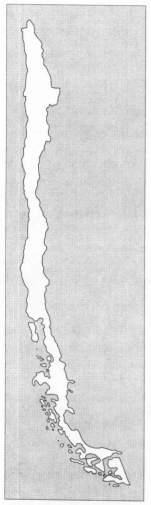

Chile was first settled by Spain in 1536. The city of Santiago was founded in 1541, Concepción in 1550, and Valdivia in 1552. A captaincy general was established in 1561. From 1561 to 1810 it was part of the Viceroyalty of Peru. An *audiencia* was created at Santiago in 1609. Chile declared independence from Spain in 1810.

Parish, Diocesan, and Other Ecclesiastical Records

Parroquiales (parish registers) date from 1550 and include baptisms, marriages, deaths and burials, and other records.

Díaz Vial, Raúl. *Situación de los Libros Parroquiales* (n.p.: Revista de Estudios Historicos, 1960). List of parishes in Chile and some in Argentina, with registry years.

Mansilla Vidal, Luis. *Las Misiones Franciscanas de la Araucania* (Angol, Chile: El Misionero Franciscano, 1904. Reprint. Washington, DC: Library of Congress, 1977, film 1155436). Franciscan missions of Araucania.

Arzobispado de Santiago. *Guía Parroquial y Guía Eclesiástica de Chile* (Santiago: Librería San Pablo, 1969). Parochial and ecclesiastical guide to Chile.

Arzobispado de Santiago. *Catálogo Biográfico Eclesiástico Chileno* (Santiago: Provedora del Culto, 1963, film 0873924). Parish registers of ecclesiastical documents.

Records of the Inquisition from 1550 to 1820 are at the Archivo Histórico Nacional in Madrid, Spain and the Archivo Nacional in Santiago. For more

SEE ALSO
Argentina
Guatemala
Latin America
Peru
Spain

information on records of the Inquisition, see the chapter on sources of colonial records in Spain.

Census Records

Padrones (civil census records) date from 1579 and *matrículas* and *padrones* (ecclesiastical censuses) from 1641. They can be found at the Archivo Nacional in Santiago and the Achivo General de Indias in Seville, Spain. Examples of such records are:

Iglesia Católica, Obispado de Santiago. Padrones, 1777–8 (Syracuse, NY: Syracuse University, n.d., film 1162403 ff.). Church census records from the Bishopric of Santiago. The original records are at the Archivo General de Indias in Seville.
Archivo Nacional de Chile. Padrones, 1777–1816 (film 1410432 ff.). Census information for various localities in Chile. The original records are at the Archivo Nacional in Santiago.

Notarial Records

Notariales (notarial records) date from 1550 and are at the Archivo Nacional in Santiago.

Governmental and Municipal Records

De Gobernación, de las provincias, y municipales (governmental and municipal records) dating from 1550 are at various municipal archives throughout Chile. Examples of such records are:

Real Audiencia. Documentos jurídicos, 1609–1828 (film 1410451 ff.). Judicial records from colonial Chile.
Registro Civil. Bienes de difuntos, 1568–1769 (film 1410433 ff.). Information about the dead.
The original records of the above are at the Archivo Nacional in Santiago.

Catálogo del Archivo de la Real Audiencia de Santiago. 2 Vols. (Santiago: Litografía y Encuadernación Barcelona, 1898–1903, film 1162488). Catalog of the archive of the Real Audiencia of Santiago, 1609–1811 and 1814–17.

Military Records

Militares (military records) dating from 1550 are at the Archivo Nacional in Santiago and various archives in Chile, Argentina, and Peru. For earlier records, see the chapter on sources of colonial records in Spain.

Land Records

De tierras y propiedades (land records) dating from 1550 are found in notarial, ecclesiastical, and municipal records at the Archivo Nacional in Santiago and the Archivo General de la Nación in Lima, Peru.

Suggested Reading

Bakewell, Judith R. *Research Guide to Andean History: Bolivia, Chile, Ecuador, and Peru* (Durham, NC: Duke University Press, 1981).

Galdames, Luis. *A History of Chile* (Chapel Hill: University of North Carolina Press, 1941).

Muñoz, Juan Guillermo. *Pobladores de Chile, 1565–1580* (Temuco, Chile: Universidad de La Frontera, 1989). Colonizers of Chile.

Silva, Osvaldo. *Atlas de Historia de Chile* (Santiago: Editorial Universitaria, 1984).

Thayer Ojeda, Tomás. *Formación de la Sociedad Chilena y Censo de la Población de Chile en los Años de 1540 a 1565: Con Datos Estadísticos, Biográficos, Etnicos y Demográficos* (1939–41. Reprint. Santiago: Centro de Historia Familiar de Santiago, 1988, film 1224503 ff.). Formation of the Chilean society and census of the population of Chile in the years 1540–65, with statistical, biographical, ethnic, and demographic data. These volumes contain biographies.

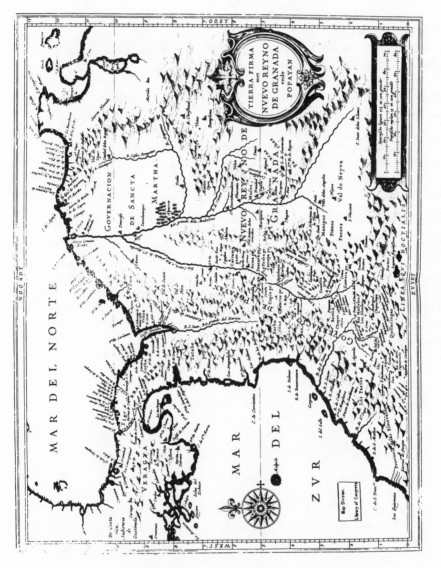

7 Colombia, 1625 (Library of Congress)

Colombia

Colombia was first settled when the city of Santa Marta was founded in 1525. The Audiencia de Santa Fé de Bogotá was established in 1550. It became part of the Viceroyalty of Peru in 1559, and the Viceroyalty of Nuevo Grenada in 1718. The viceroyalty was suspended in 1723 and reestablished in 1739. Colombia declared independence from Spain in 1810 and was part of the Republic of Greater Colombia, consisting of Ecuador, Panama, Colombia, and Venezuela, until 1830. The first cities founded in Colombia were Cartagena and Santa Fé de Bogotá in 1538.

Parish, Diocesan, and Other Ecclesiastical Records

Parroquiales (parish registers) date from 1540 and include baptisms, marriages, deaths and burials, and other records. Examples of parish records are:

Iglesia Católica, Arquidiócesis de Nueva Pamplona. Registros parroquiales, 1580–1944 (film 1511673 ff.). Marriage documents, including licenses, dispensations, and ecclesiastical court judgments issued by the bishop as well as church censuses, records of property given to the church, and other administrative church records of the Archdiocese of Nueva Pamplona, Colombia. The original records are at the Archivo Arzobispal de la Arquidiócesis de Nueva Pamplona in Pamplona.

Records of the Inquisition from the eighteenth and nineteenth centuries are at the Archivo Histórico Nacional in Madrid, Spain. For more information on records of the Inquisition, see the chapter on sources of colonial records in Spain.

Consejo de Inquisición, Cartagena.
* Procesos de fé, 1612–1799 (Madrid: Centro Nacional de Microfilm, 1977, film 1224001 ff.). Professions of faith of persons tried by the Holy Office of the Inquisition of Cartagena.
* Pleitos civiles relativos a Cartagena de Indias, 1634–1864 (Madrid: Centro Nacional de Microfilm, 1982, film 1418266 ff.). Civil

SEE ALSO
Latin America
Peru
Spain
Venezuela

lawsuits relative to the Tribunal de Cartagena de Indias during the Inquisition. The original records are at the Archivo Histórico Nacional in Madrid.

Census Records

Padrones (civil census records) date from 1777 and *matrículas* and *padrones* (ecclesiastical censuses) from 1586. See the above section on parish records for ecclesiastical censuses. An example of a civil census record is:

Censo del 1777–84 de Nueva Granada (Syracuse, NY: Syracuse University, n.d., film 1162416 ff.). The original records are at the Archivo Nacional de Historia in Bogotá.

Notarial Records

Notariales (notarial records) date from 1540 and can be found at the Archivo Nacional de Historia in Bogotá and the Archivo Historico in Popayán. Examples of notarial records are:

Bogotá, Cundinamarca. Notaría Segunda. Protocolos, 1570–1895 (film 1511754 ff.). Notarial records of Bogotá, including information from various municipalities in the departament of Cundinamarca. The original records are at the Archivo Nacional in Bogotá.

Governmental and Municipal Records

De gobernación, de las provincias, y municipales (governmental and municipal records) dating from 1537 are at various municipal archives throughout Colombia.

Historical documents in the Colonia collection of the Archivo Central del Cauca deal with all aspects of colonial life in the old *Gobernación* of Popayán, an administrative unit of the Viceroyalty of Nuevo Granada, or Santa Fé. Popayán in the colonial era included more than half of present-day Colombia, namely the departments of Antioquia, Caldas, Valle, Cauca, Nariño, and Huila; the intendencies of Chocó and Amazonas; and the commissariats of Putumayo and Caquetá. The documents include public records, court records, and notarial records.

Military Records

Militares (military records) dating from 1631 are at the Archivo Nacional de Historia in Bogotá. For other records, see the chapter on sources of colonial records in Spain.

Land Records

De tierras y propiedades (land records) dating from 1575 are found in notarial, ecclesiastical, and municipal records at the Archivo Nacional de Historia in Bogotá and the Archivo Historico in Popayán.

Suggested Reading

Acevedo Latorre, Eduardo. *Atlas de Mapas Antiguos de Colombia, Siglos XVI a XIX* (Bogotá: Litografía Arco, film 0873924). Atlas of old Colombian maps, sixteenth to nineteenth centuries.

Arboleda Llorente, José María. *Archivo Central del Cauca, Fondo Colonia, 1537-1800* (Bogotá: Ministerio de Educación, Departamento de Extensión Cultural y Bellas Artes, n.d., film 1698860 ff.). Manuscripts in the Instituto de Investigaciones Históricas, la Universidad del Cauca, in Popayán.

Arboleda Llorente, José María. *El Indio en la Colonia: Estudio Basado Especialmente en Documentos del Archivo Central del Cauca* (Bogotá: Ministerio de Educación, Departamento de Extensión Cultural y Bellas Artes, 1948). The treatment of Indians in the Spanish colony of Nueva Granada, mostly based upon documents in the Archivo Central del Cauca.

Diaz, Manuel A. *Catálogo de Genealogías, 1565-1810* (Bogotá: Archivo Nacional de Colombia, 1981, film 1389100). Catalog of genealogies housed at the Archivo Nacional de Colombia in Bogotá.

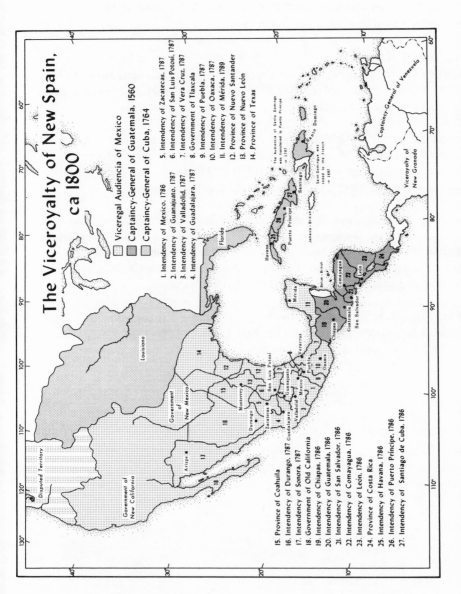

8 Viceroyalty of New Spain, 1800 (Cathryn L. Lombardi, et al., *Latin American History: A Teaching Atlas.* Madison: University of Wisconsin Press, 1983)

Costa Rica

Costa Rica was first explored in 1502, but no permanent settlement was made for some time. During the colonial period Costa Rica was a province in the Captaincy General of Guatemala under the Viceroyalty of Nueva España. Costa Rica declared independence from Spain in 1821.

Parish, Diocesan, and Other Ecclesiastical Records

Parroquiales (parish registers) date from 1594 and include baptisms, marriages, deaths and burials, and other records. Many of these are indexed in *Indización de Documentos del Archivo de la Curia Metropolitana: Fondos Antiguos* (film 1909905 ff.), an index to historical ecclesiastical records of Costa Rica held in the archives of the Archdiocese of San José. Examples of parish records are:

Iglesia Católica. Arquidiócesis de San José.
* Fondos antiguos, 1519–1965: Documentación encuadernada (film 1909906 ff.). Parish registers of various church records and different marriage issues from several localities in the Archdiocese of San José. This includes records from other localities, including Nicoya, Alajuela, and Cartago.
* Fondos antiguos, 1608–1906: Documentación suelta (film 1910934 ff.). Parish registers of various church records and some marriage issues from several localities in the Archdiocese of San José. This includes records from other localities such as Heredia, Esparza, and Cartago.

The original records of the above are at the Archivo Metropolitano de la Arquidiócesis de San José.

Census Records

Few *padrones* (civil census records) exist before 1844. *Matrículas* and *padrones* (ecclesiastical censuses) were taken from the late sixteenth century. An example of a census record is:

Virreino de Nueva España. Padrones, 1776–8 (film 0741739). Census to establish the status of the dispensations granted by the Commissioner General of the Crusades to persons appropriating property of unverified ownership. The original records are at the Archivo General de Centroamérica in Guatemala City.

SEE ALSO
Guatemala
Latin America
Spain

Notarial Records

Notariales (notarial records) date from 1569. They can be found in the Archivo Nacional in San José and the Archivo de Centroamérica in Guatemala City.

Governmental and Municipal Records

See Guatemala. There are excellent secondary published sources at the Library of the Universidad de Costa Rica (University of Costa Rica) in San Pedro de Montes de Oca, and the Biblioteca Nacional in San José. The University also has an exchange program with the University of Kansas Libraries, where a sizeable collection of materials on Costa Rica (and adjacent countries) has been developing since 1958.

Military Records

Militares (military records) dating from the 1549 are at the Archivo Nacional in San José. For other records, see the chapter on sources of colonial records in Spain.

Land Records

See Guatemala.

Suggested Reading

Blanco Segura, Ricardo. *Historia Eclesiástica de Costa Rica, del Descubrimiento a la Erección de la Diócesis* (San Jose: Editorial Costa Rica, 1967, film 1149535). History of the church in Costa Rica, from discovery to the founding of the diocese, 1502–1850.

El Archivo Nacional: *Su Creación, Legislación y Organismos Internacionales* (San Jose: The Archive, 1975).

Estrada Molina, Ligia María. *La Investigación Histórica y los Archivos Nacionales* (San Jose: n.p., 1964).

Jones, C.L. *Costa Rica and the Civilization in the Caribbean* (Madison: University of Wisconsin Press, 1935).

Ecuador

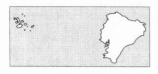

Ecuador was colonized when the Incan civilization fell to Spanish conquerors in 1532. It was part of the Viceroyalty of Perú from 1543 until 1734 under the name *Obispado de Quito* (Diocese of Quito). Quito was established as an *audiencia* in 1563. From 1740 until 1809 it was part of the Viceroyalty of Nuevo Grenada. The viceroyalty was suspended in 1723 and reestablished in 1739. Ecuador declared independence from Spain in 1809. After the war for independence it was part of Greater Colombia, consisting of Ecuador, Panama, Colombia, and Venezuela. Ecuador became a sovereign country in 1830.

Parish, Diocesan, and Other Ecclesiastical Records

Parroquiales (parish registers) date from 1534 and include baptisms, marriages, deaths and burials, and other records. These also contain *padrones*, 1772–93. They can be found in parochial and diocesan archives throughout Ecuador and Peru.

Records of the Inquisition from 1569 are at the Archivo Histórico Nacional in Madrid, Spain, the Archivo Nacional in Lima, Peru, and the Archivo Nacional in Santiago, Chile. For more information on records of the Inquisition, see the chapter on sources of colonial records in Spain.

Census Records

Padrones (civil census records) date from 1737 and can be found at the Archivo Nacional de Historia in Bogotá, Colombia and the Archivo Nacional de Historia in Quito. An example of a census record is:

Departamento de Empadronamientos. Padrones, 1737–1864 (film 1398293 ff.). Population census for Cotopaxi Province, Ecuador. The original records are at the Archivo Nacional de Historia in Quito.

SEE ALSO
Colombia
Latin America
Peru
Spain

Notarial Records

Notariales (notarial records) date from 1550 and can be found in various judicial archives in Ecuador. Examples of notarial records are:

Quito, Pichincha, Ecuador.
- Notaría Tercera. Protocolos, 1600–1801 (film 1667290 ff.).
- Notaría Cuarta. Protocolos, 1586–1805 (film 1667778 ff.).
- Notaría Quinta. Protocolos, 1599–1813 (film 1698889 ff.).
- Notaría Sexta. Protocolos, 1581–1807 (film 1699094 ff.).

Notarial records, including inheritance decisions, land and property disputes, and criminal records from Pichincha. The original records are at the Archivo Nacional de Historia in Quito.

Governmental and Municipal Records

De Gobernación, de las provincias, y municipales (governmental and municipal records) dating from 1534 are at various municipal archives throughout Ecuador and the Archivo Nacional de Historia in Quito. Documents dealing with the territory governed by a native chieftain, land decisions, genealogy of the chieftains, lists of subjects, etc., are known as *cacicazgos*. They include land and property settlements, tribute matters, criminal cases, and censuses, many of which were presented to the Protector General de Indígenas.

Examples of *cacicazgos* and probate records are:
- Pichincha Registro Civil. Cacicazgos, 1606–1809 (film 1521105 ff.).
- Tungurahua Registro Civil. Cacicazgos, 1582–1812 (film 1521106 ff.).
- Real Audiencia de Quito. Indígenas, 1579–1845 (film 1520289).
- Registro Civil. Registros civiles, 1588–1915 (film 1511900 ff.). Probate records from all parts of Ecuador.

The original records are at the Archivo Nacional de Historia in Quito.

Military Records

Militares (military records) dating from the sixteenth century are at the Archivo Nacional de Historia in Quito and the Archivo Historico de Guayas and Archivo Histórico Biblioteca Municipal in Guayaquil. For other records, see the chapter on sources of colonial records in Spain.

Noboa Icaza, Luis. *Hojas Coloniales de Servicios Militares: Guayaquil* (Guayaquil: Imprint de la Benemérita Sociedad Filatrópica de Guayas, 1960). Colonial pages of military service, Guayaquil.

Land Records

De tierras y propiedades (land records) dating from the sixteenth century are found in notarial, ecclesiastical, and municipal records in the Archivo Municipal de Quito, the Archivo Nacional de Historia in Bogotá, Colombia, and other local archives.

Suggested Reading

Freile-Granizo, Juan. *Breve Guía de Fuentes Genealógicas en Dos Archivos Ecuatorianos* (Guayaquil: Archivo Historico del Guayas, 1972). Brief guide to genealogical sources in two Ecuadorian archives.

Freile-Granizo, Juan. *Guia del Archivo Nacional de Historia* (Guayaquil: Archivo Historico del Guayas, 1973).

Jurado Noboa, Fernando. *La Migración InterNacional a Quito Entre 1534 y 1934.* 6 Vols. (Quito: Sociedad Amigos de la Genealogía, 1989). Biographical sketches and genealogical data on Spanish immigrants.

Moreno Egas, Jorge. *Algunos Viajeros de España a la Real Audiencia de Quito Entre 1636 y 1649* (Quito, 1977, film 1410954). Some of the passengers who came from Spain to the Real Audiencia de Quito between 1636–49.

Savoia, P. Rafael. *El Negro en la Historia: Aportes Para el Conocimiento de las Raíces en América Latina* (Cayambe, Ecuador: Tallares Abya-yala, 1990). The Negro in Latin America, especially in Ecuador.

Suárez Baquerizo, Raul. *Real Audiencia de Quito: Colonizadores* (Quito: Tirso de Molina, 1951). Colonizers of the Real Audiencia of Quito, Ecuador, together with officials and nobility associated with the government of Quito.

El Salvador

E l Salvador was conquered by Spain in 1524. During the colonial period it was part of the Viceroyalty of Nueva España in the Captaincy of Guatemala. In 1548 the area known as Cuzcztlán was divided into the four separate dominions of Soconusco, Honduras, Nicaragua, and Costa Rica. In 1574 El Salvador became part of the Province of Gracias a Dios, in Honduras. El Salvador declared independence from Spain in 1821.

Parish, Diocesan, and Other Ecclesiastical Records

Parroquiales (parish registers) date from 1631 and include baptisms, marriages, deaths and burials, and other records. They can be found at the Archivo General de Centroamérica in Guatemala City and the Archivo del Palacio Arzobispal in San Salvador. An example of a parish record is:

Iglesia Católica, Palacio Arzobispal, San Salvador. Registros parroquiales, 1741–1947 (film 1159992 ff.). Marriage information and confirmations from several parishes in the Diocese of San Salvador. The original records are at the Archivo del Palacio Arzobispal in San Salvador.

Records of the Inquisition from the sixteenth century are at the Archivo General de la Nación in Mexico City. For more information on records of the Inquisition, see the chapter on sources of colonial records in Spain.

Census Records

Padrones or *matrículas* (ecclesiastical censuses) date from 1746. An example of such records are:

Dirección General de Estadística, Guatemala. Padrones, 1746–1821 (film 0746867 ff.). Census records of El Salvador. The original records are at the Archivo General de Centroamérica in Guatemala City.

Notarial Records

Notariales (notarial records) date from 1543 and can be found at the Archivo General de Centroamérica in Guatemala City, and the Archivo de la Corte Suprema de Justicia in San Salvador.

SEE ALSO
Guatemala
Latin America
Spain

65

Governmental and Municipal Records

De Gobernación, de las provincias, y municipales (governmental and municipal records) dating from 1571 are at the Archivo General de Centroamérica in Guatemala City. Examples of such records are:

Juzgado General de Bienes de Difuntos. Testamentos, 1610–1781 (film 0741885 ff.). Probate records from El Salvador and Nicaragua, when those countries were part of the Captaincy General of Guatemala in the Viceroyalty of New Spain.

Military Records

Militares (military records) dating from the seventeenth century are at the Archivo General de Centroamérica in Guatemala City. For other records, see the chapter on sources of colonial records in Spain.

Land Records

See Guatemala.

Suggested Reading

Barberena, Santiago Ignacio. *Historia de El Salvador* (San Salvador: Imprenta Nacional, 1914–17, film 0824306). History of El Salvador; the ancient era and the period of conquest.

Documentos Historicos para El Salvador (Tegucigalpa: Unidad Móvil de la UNESCO, 1959, film 0802893 ff.). Various historical documents on El Salvador. Some deal with the titles to public lands.

Ministério de Obras Públicas. *Guía Para Investigadores de El Salvador* (Ciudad Delgado, El Salvador: Instituto Panamericano de Geografía e Historia, 1977). Guide book for research on El Salvador, including maps and bibliography.

Jiménez, Tomas Fidias. *Toponimia Arcaica de El Salvador: Significado de los Nombres Geográficos Indígenas* (San Salvador: El Salvador, 1936). Glossary of indigenous geographical terms of El Salvador.

Guatemala

Guatemala was the center of Mayan civilization until A.D. 800. It was conquered by Spain in 1524, and became part of the Viceroyalty of Nueva España in 1534. The Captaincy of Guatemala was established in 1542. The capital was moved from Santiago to Ciudad Vieja in 1527, to Antigua in 1593, and to Guatemala City in 1773. Guatemala declared independence from Spain in 1821.

Parish, Diocesan, and Other Ecclesiastical Records

Parroquiales (parish registers) date from 1527 and include baptisms, marriages, deaths and burials, and other records. They can be found in local church and other ecclesiastical archives and the Archivo General de Centroamérica in Guatemala City. Examples of parish records are:

Registros parroquiales, 1694–1915 (film 0746803 ff.). Baptism and marriage records from Central America, chiefly baptisms performed in Guatemala City. The original records are at the Archivo General de Centroamérica in Guatemala City.

Records of the Inquisition from 1556 to 1820 are at the Archivo General de la Nación in Mexico City. There is also information contained in civil records on *limpieza de sangre* (purity of blood) under records titled *Informaciones Personales* in the Archivo General de Centroamérica in Guatemala City. These are described below in governmental and municipal records. For more information on records of the Inquisition, see the chapter on sources of colonial records in Spain.

Inquisición, Procesos del Santo Oficio de México, 1522–1820 (film 0034797 ff.). Trial proceedings and genealogies of persons indicted by the Inquisition, including persons residing in Guatemala, Mexico, other parts of Central America, and the Philippines.

Chinchilla Aguilar, Ernesto. *La Inquisición en Guatemala* (Guatemala: Edition del Ministerio de Educación Pública, 1953, film 0908390).

SEE ALSO
Mexico
Latin America
Spain

67

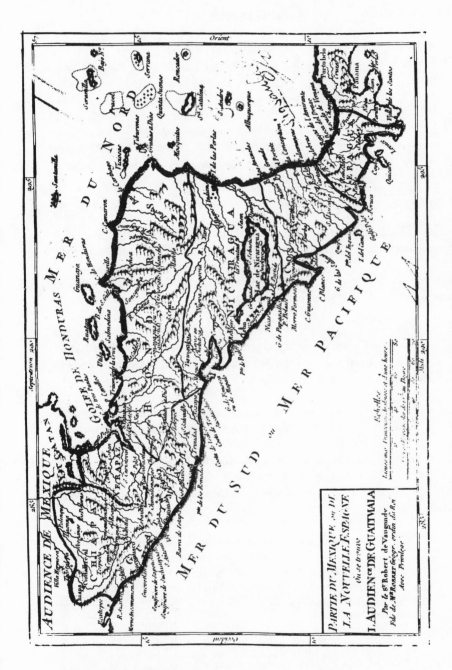

9 The Audiencia of Guatemala (Library of Congress)

Census Records

Padrones (civil census records) date from 1662 and *matrículas* or *padrones* (ecclesiastical censuses) from 1740. Examples of such records are:

Dirección General de Estadística, Guatemala. Padrones, 1662–1778 (film 0745817 ff.), 1698–1836 (film 0746825 ff.). Census records and *tributos* (tax records).

Real Tribunal y Audiencia de la Contaduría Mayor de Cuentas. Padrones, Capitanía General El Salvador, 1731–1820 (film 0741887 ff.). Census and tax lists from the Captaincy General of El Salvador, Audiencia of Guatemala, of New Spain.

Padrones de Guatemala: Epoca pre-independencia (film 0748131 ff.). Census records from various localities in pre-independence Guatemala. The earliest are 1635.

The original records of the above are at the Archivo General de Centroamérica in Guatemala City.

Notarial Records

Notariales (notarial records) date from 1543, and most are found at the Archivo General de Protocolos in the Archivo General de Centroamérica. A 123-volume index is available at the Archive in Guatemala City. Examples of notarial records are:

Archivo General de Centroamérica

The Archivo General de Centroamérica in Guatemala City is the repository for colonial, ecclesiastical, notarial, municipal, provincial, and university records not only for Guatemala but also Costa Rica, El Salvador, Honduras, Nicaragua, Yucatan and Chiapas, Mexico, and even some records for Peru and Chile. These records date from the time of conquest until 1824, when the United Provinces of Central America were formed, and later for Guatemala.

There is a card index for many records dating from 1536 to 1830. It includes dates of records, abstracts, and surnames. Places of origin — including in Europe — are included. Many records have also been filmed, including an index to the ancient archives of the government from 1560–1833 (film 0744844 ff.).

Virreinato de Nueva España. Audiencia de Guatemala.

- Protocolos, 1543–1722 (film 0744404 ff.). Notarial records of Guatemala, Honduras, and Nicaragua.
- Protocolos: testamentos, dotaciones de matrimonios, traslados de propiedad, contratos, ajustes, etc., 1508–1898 (film 0717517 ff.). Notarial records. This includes Guatemala, Honduras, Nicaragua, El Salvador, and Costa Rica.

- Protocolos y providencias, 1579–1842 (film 0747154 ff.). Civil documents and notarial records from Guatemala City.

The original records of the above are at the Archivo General de Centroamérica in Guatemala City.

Governmental and Municipal Records

De Gobernación, de las provincias, y municipales (governmental and municipal records) dating from 1543 are at various municipal archives throughout Guatemala and at the Archivo General de Centroamérica in Guatemala City. Examples of such records are:

Virreino de Nueva España.
- Registros civiles, 1639–78 (film 0741740). Royal letters or decrees and patents. Includes civil registration in Guatemala, Chiapas, Mexico, Honduras, El Salvador, Costa Rica, and Nicaragua.
- Documentos jurídicos, 1602–1730 (film 0741876 ff.). Court records of assignments, petitions, approvals, titles and judgments with the provisions, names of individuals, and geographical location of each case. The localities and countries of Guatemala, Chiapas, Mexico, Honduras, Nicaragua, Costa Rica, and Panama are included.
- Registros civiles, 1571–1824 (film 0745107 ff.). Central American marriage records, mainly from Guatemala City but also including El Salvador and Nicaragua.
- Bienes de difuntos, 1638–1713 (film 0744961). Probate records from Guatemala, Honduras, Costa Rica, and Nicaragua when they were provinces of the Captaincy General of Guatemala.
- Registros civiles: pasaportes, 1579–1824 (film 0745421 ff.). Passports. There are also later records that have been filmed in this series.
- Divorcios y causas matrimoniales, 1603–1824 (film 0745075). Marriage and divorce records from Guatemala. Later records in this series have also been filmed.

The original records of the above are at the Archivo General de Centroamérica in Guatemala City.

Informacion personal includes petitions, proclamations, complaints, criminal judgments, pension applications, powers of attorney, letters of reference, appointments, granting of titles, *limpieza de sangre* (purity of blood), and other kinds of official personal documents.

Virreinato de Nueva España, Audiencia de Guatemala.
Capitania General de Guatemala.

- Información personal, 1540–1836 (film 0745422 ff.), and 1668–1755 (film 0744763). Public records for Guatemala.
- Información personal, 1541–1805 (film 0745813 ff.), and 1624–1819 (film 0744398 ff.). Public records for Guatemala and Nicaragua.
- Información personal, 1574–1624 (film 0744761). Public records for San Salvador (1574), Mexico (1584 and 1600), Peru (1624 and 1702–45), and Chile (dates unknown).
- Información personal, Provincia de Chiapas, 1551–1789 (film 0744580 ff.). Public records for Chiapas, formerly a province in the Audiencia of Guatemala but now a state of the Republic of Mexico.

Capitanía General El Salvador.

- Información personal, 1587–1809 (film 0741894 ff.). Public records for El Salvador and Guatemala.

Military Records
Militares (military records) dating from the seventeenth and eighteenth centuries are at the Archivo General de Centroamérica in Guatemala City. For other records, see the chapter on sources of colonial records in Spain.

Land Records
De tierras y propiedades (land records) dating from 1568 are found in notarial, ecclesiastical, and municipal records at the Archivo General de Centroamérica in Guatemala City. Examples are:

Capitania General, Real Audiencia.

- Tierras y propiedades, 1570–1820 (film 0744759 ff.). Land and property records of Guatemala and Honduras.
- Tierras y propiedades, 1518–1902 (film 0746979 ff.). Land records of various localities, most pertaining to Guatemala City.
- Tierras y propiedades, 1579–1820 (film 0744588 ff.). Land and property records for Guatemala, El Salvador, Nicaragua, and Chiapas, Mexico. Later records in this series have also been filmed.

Murga, Gustavo Palma. *Indice General del Archivo del Extinguido Juzgado Privativo de Tierras: Depositado en la Escribanía de Cámara del Supremo Gobierno de la República de Guatemala; Segunde Parte, que Comprende el Indice Alfabético General* (Mexico, DF: Centro de Investigaciones y Estudios Superiores en Antropología Social, 1991). Index to colonial Guatemalan land records, from the sixteenth to nineteenth centuries, arranged by locality, found in the Archivo General de Centroamérica in Guatemala City.

Suggested Reading

Guía de la Iglesia en Guatemala (Guatemala City: Santa Isabel, 1967, film 0873807). Roman Catholic Church directory for Guatemala.

Fuentes y Guzmán, Francisco Antonio de. *Libro Viejo de la Fundación de Guatemala: Año de 1524* (16–. Reprint. Guatemala: Sociedad de Geografía e Historia, 1932, film 1410699). An old book on the founding of Guatemala, 1524.

O'Ryan, Juan Enrique. *Bibliografía Guatemalteca de los Siglos XVII y XVIII.* 2nd ed. (Guatemala City: Editorial del Ministerio de Educación Pública José de Pineda Ibarra, 1960). Guatemalan bibliography of the seventeenth and eighteenth centuries.

Otazu y Llana, Alfonso de. *Hacendistas Navarros en Indias* (Bilbao: Gráficas Ellacuria, 1970). Genealogies of families from the Navarra region of Spain who settled in Spanish America.

Ordóñez Jonama, Ramiro. *Biblioteca Genealógica Guatemalteca: Notas, Comentarios, Adiciones* (Nueva Guatemala de la Asunción: Academia Guatemalteca de Estudios Genealógicos, Heráldicos e Historicos, 1991). Annotated bibliography of published works dealing with Guatemalan genealogy, heraldry, and nobility.

Remesal, Antonio de. *Historia General de las Indias Occidentales y Particular de la Gobernación de Chiapas y Guatemala.* 2 Vols. (Madrid: Ediciones Atlas, 1964). General history of Spanish America, with emphasis on the government in Chiapas, Mexico and Guatemala.

Honduras

Honduras was conquered by Spain in 1523. During the colonial period it was part of the Viceroyalty of Nueva España in the Captaincy of Guatemala. In 1548 the area known as Cuzcztlán was divided into the four separate dominions of Soconusco, Honduras, Nicaragua, and Costa Rica. In 1574 Honduras was part of the Province of Gracias a Dios, along with El Salvador. Honduras declared independence from Spain in 1821.

Parish, Diocesan, and Other Ecclesiastical Records

Parroquiales (parish registers) date from 1702 and include baptisms, marriages, deaths and burials, and other records and can be found in local parishes and diocesan archives, notably the Archive of the Cathedral of Tegucigalpa. Types of records available on microfilm are:

Colección de registros parroquiales de Honduras. Registros parroquiales, 1633–1937 (film 1507758 ff.), 1694–1916 (film 1645345 ff.). Parish registrations from various localities of deaths and baptisms, with some marriages. The original records are at the Archivo Eclesiástico del Museo Colonial de Comauagua in Comayagua.

Records of the Inquisition from 1556 to 1820 are at the Archivo General de la Nación in Mexico City. For more information on records of the Inquisition, see the chapter on sources of colonial records in Spain.

Census Records

Padrones (civil census records) and *matrículas* and *padrones* (ecclesiastical censuses) from 1587. Examples of such records are:

El Adelanto, Jutiapa, Registro Civil. Padrones, 1587–1722 (film 0744403 ff.). Census records.
Dirección General de Estadística, Guatemala. Padrones de Comayagua, Honduras, 1741–1806 (film 0744866). Census of Comayagua, Honduras.
The original records of the above are at the Archivo General de Centroamérica in Guatemala City.

Notarial Records

See Guatemala.

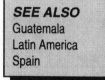

SEE ALSO
Guatemala
Latin America
Spain

Governmental and Municipal Records

De Gobernación, de las provincias, y municipales (governmental and municipal records) dating from 1551 are at the Archivo Nacional and the Archivo del Consejo del Distrito Central in Tegucigalpa, various municipal archives throughout Honduras, and the Archivo General de Centroamérica in Guatemala City. Examples of such are:

Documentos y expedientes de la época colonial, 1745–7 (Tegucigalpa: Unidad Móvil de la UNESCO, 1958, film 0802917). Colonial court records. The original records are at the Archivo Nacional de Honduras in Tegucigalpa. There are also court records deposited at the Archivo del Juzgado de Tegucigalpa.

Juzgado General de Bienes de Difuntos. Testamentos, 1633–1819 (film 0741751 ff.). Probate records from Honduras, when that country was part of the Captaincy General of Guatemala, Viceroyalty of New Spain. The original records are at the Archivo General de Centroamérica in Guatemala City.

Several excellent research libraries in Tegucigalpa are also open to the public:
➢ The Biblioteca Nacional
➢ The library at the Archivo Nacional
➢ The library at the Banco Central
➢ The Universidad Nacional Autónoma de Honduras
➢ The Instituto Hondureño de Antropologíae

Military Records

See Guatemala.

Land Records

De tierras y propiedades (land records) dating from the sixteenth century are found in notarial, ecclesiastical, and municipal records at the Archivo General de Centroamérica in Guatemala City.

Vallejo, Antonio R. *Indice Alfabético y Cronológico de los Títulos de Amparo y de Mas Documentos Relativos a los Terrenos de la República de Honduras* (1884. Tegucigalpa: Unidad Móvil de la UNESCO, 1958, film 0802918). Index of titles, writings, etc., relative to the lands of Honduras.

Suggested Reading

Carías, Marcos. *La Iglesia Católica en Honduras* (Tegucigalpa: Guaymuras, 1991). The evolution of the Roman Catholic Church in Honduras since 1492.

Chamberlain, Robert Stoner. *The Conquest and Colonization of Honduras, 1502–1550* (Washington, DC: Carnegie Institute, 1948. Reprint. New York: Octagon Books, 1966, film 0896861).

Graiño, Antonio. *Documentos referentes a los Indios Llamados Xicaques en la America Central* (Madrid: Librería General de Victoriano Suárez, 1907. Reprint. Tegucigalpa: Unidad Móvil de la UNESCO, 1958, film 0802918). Documents relating to the Xicaque (Zicaque) Indians of Central America.

Sevillano Colom, Francisco. *Misión de la UNESCO en Honduras: Lista de Materiales Microfilmados* (Tegucigalpa: n.p., 1958). List of materials microfilmed by UNESCO in Honduras.

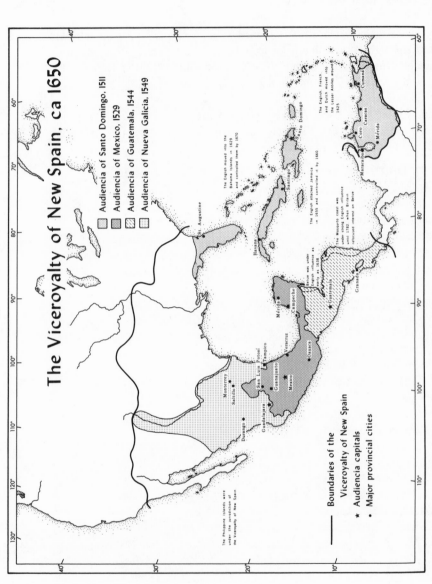

10 Viceroyalty of New Spain, 1650 (Cathryn L. Lombardi, et al., *Latin American History: A Teaching Atlas*. Madison: University of Wisconsin Press, 1983)

Mexico

 **M**exico was permanently settled after the Spanish conquest of the Aztec civilization in 1520. Ciudad de México was founded in 1521 and is the oldest capital city in continental America. The first *audiencia* was created in 1527. The Kingdom of Nueva Galicia was created in 1548. Mexico was part of the viceroyalty of Nueva España until it declared independence from Spain in 1810 and became a republic in 1824.

Parish, Diocesan, and Other Ecclesiastical Records

Parroquiales (parish registers) date from 1524 and include baptisms, marriages, deaths and burials, and other records. Parish records can be found in national and ecclesiastical archives. Examples of ecclesiastical records are:

Iglesia Católica, Arquidiocesis de México. Documentos eclesiásticos, 1527–1957 (film 0645811 ff.). Documents of an administrative, judicial, financial, and pastoral nature dealing with the work of the Roman Catholic Archdiocese of Mexico.

Iglesia Católica, Sagrario Metropolitano, Ciudad de México.

* Registros parroquiales, 1536–1953 (film 0035132 ff.). Parish registers of baptisms, confirmations, marriages, marriage petitions, and deaths from the Cathedral Church (La Asunción) of the Archdiocese of Mexico.

* Documentos eclesiásticos, 1527–1966 (film 0645727 ff.). Administrative records from the Holy Cathedral Church, La Asunción, of the Archidiocese of Mexico.

The original records are at the Archivo del Cabildo Metropolitano in the Arquidiocesis de México in Mexico City.

Secretaría General, Distrito Federal, Real Hacienda. Catalogo del Ramo Misiones, 1622–1825 (film 1521015 ff.). Financial accountings, foundings, synods, and tribunals dealing with the missions of Chihuahua and Sonora. The original records are at the Archivo General de la Nación in Mexico City.

> **SEE ALSO**
> Arizona
> California
> Guatemala
> Latin America
> New Mexico
> Spain
> Texas

Iglesia Católica, Diócesis de Campeche. Registros parroquiales, 1638–1895 (film 0764527ff.).

Miscellaneous records of baptisms, confirmations, marriages, and deaths from many parishes in the Diocese of Campeche, Mexico which comprised localities in the states of Campeche and Yucatán. The original records are at the local diocesan archive.

Iglesia Católica, Arquidiocesis de Morelia.

* Documentos eclesiásticos, 1579–1937 (film 0783246 ff.). Church documents of assessments, aspirants to religious orders, description of merits, declarations of faith, general accounts, civil and royal decrees, funds, statistics, probate juries, ecclesiastical seals, resolutions, and miscellaneous documents. The miscellaneous documents include wills, judgments, marriage banns, baptismal certifications, edicts, petitions, memberships lists, and other unspecified documents. The original records are at the archdiocesan archive in Morelia.

* Registros parroquiales, 1555–1875 (film 0764165 ff.). Parish and church records of marriage information and miscellaneous documents which include wills, judgments, marriage banns, baptismal certificates, ecclesiastical documents, edicts, petitions, dispensations, church membership lists, royal licenses, and other unspecified documents. The original records are at the archdiocesan archive in Michoacán.

Iglesia Católica, Díocesis de Chiapas. Registros parroquiales, 1599–1933 (film 0733716 ff.). Parish registers of baptisms, marriage petitions, marriages, deaths, wills, and other ecclesiastical documents. These records cover parts of Chiapas, México and Guatemala. The original records are at the Archivo Diocesano de San Cristóbal de la Casas.

Robinson, David J. *Research Inventory of the Mexican Collection of Colonial Parish Registers* (Salt Lake City: University of Utah Press, 1980).

Records of the Inquisition from 1519 to 1820 are at the Archivo General de la Nación in Mexico City, the Archivo Historical Nacional in Madrid, Spain, and the Library of Congress in Washington, DC. For more information on records of the Inquisition, see the chapter on sources of colonial records in Spain.

Procesos del Santo Oficio de México, 1522–1820 (film 0034797 ff.). Trial proceedings and genealogies of persons indicted by the Inquisition in Guatemala, Mexico, and the Philippines. The original records are at the Archivo General de la Nación in Mexico City.

Indice del Ramo de Inquisicion (n.p., 1978, film 1149544). List of people charged with crimes under the Inquisition.

Census Records

Padrones (civil census records) date from 1689 and *matrículas* and *padrones* (ecclesiastical censuses) from the early sixteenth century and can be found at the Archivo General de la Nación in Mexico City. An example of a civil census is: Dirección General de Estadística, México. Padrones, 1752–1865 (film 1224506 f.).

Notarial Records

Notariales (notarial records) date from 1524 and can be found at notarial archives throughout Mexico and the Archvio del Notarías de México in Mexico City. Examples of notarial records are:

Millares Carlo, Agustín and José Ignacio Mantecón. *Indice y Extractos de los Protocolos del Archivo de Notarías de México.* 2 Vols. (Mexico: El Colegio de México, 1945). Index and extracts of notarial records of the Archive of Notaries, Mexico City, 1524–53.

Records Outside of Mexico

Original parish registers, notarial records, court records, and other documents have been deposited at many locations outside of Mexico. Some of the many repositories are:

➤ The Library of Congress, Washington, DC
➤ The Newberry Library in Chicago, Illinois
➤ Middle American Research Institute, Tulane University, New Orleans, Louisiana
➤ Spanish American Collection, University of Texas, Austin
➤ The New Mexico Historical Society, Santa Fe, New Mexico
➤ The Bancroft Library, University of California, Berkeley
➤ William Clements Library, Ann Arbor, Michigan

Puebla de Zaragoza, Notaría. Protocolos, 1697–1798 (film 0650720 ff.). Records from the Fifth Notarial Office of Puebla de Zaragoza, Puebla. The original records are at the Archivo General de Notarías in Puebla.

García López, Ricardo. *Guía de Protocolos de Instrumentos Públicos del Siglo XVIII* (San Luis Potosí: Editorial Universitaria Potosina, 1988). Guide to the protocols of the sixteenth century found in the department of public documents in San Luis Potosí.

Governmental and Municipal Records

De Gobernación, de las provincias, y municipales (governmental and municipal records) dating from 1519 are at various municipal archives throughout Mexico. Examples of some records at the Archivo General de la Nación in Mexico City are:

• Ramo Civil: 1533–1857 (film 1563786 ff.). Civil court cases of all kinds originated by judicial bodies in the various states of the Republic of Mexico.

- Contaduría General de Temporalidades. Capellanías y testamentos, 1667–1860 (film 1563780 ff.). Wills of Mexico City.
- Virreinato de Nueva España, Comandancia General de las Provincias Internas. Documentos civiles, 1626–1886: asignaciónes, sueldos y empleados, asuntos financieros, asuntos de gobierno, aceptación de soldados, acusados, contadurías, correspondencia, descripciones geográficas y económicas, gastos militares, homicidios, intendencias, inventarios, minutas, real haciendas, regresos a España, revistas de tropas, temporalidades, tesorerías (film 1520588 ff.). Documents comprising the *Provincias Internas* collection in the National Archive of Mexico, including Nueva Vizcaya, Sonora (including Arizona), Sinaloa, Nuevo México (New Mexico), Texas, and the Californias.
- Archivo General de la Nación. *Indice del Ramo de Reales Cedulas* (Mexico: The Archive, 1967). Index of royal dispatches in the National Archive of Mexico.

Audiencia de Nueva Galicia, Guadalajara. Libros de gobierno, 1670–1752 (film 0269815 ff.). Public records from the *Audiencia* or Kingdom of Nueva Galicia, the present-day states of Colima, Jalisco, and Zacatecas, Mexico. The original records are at the Archivo de Instrumentos Públicos in Guadalajara.

Juzgado General de Bienes de Difuntos, Guatemala. Bienes de difuntos, 1554–1821 (film 0744567 ff.), 1557–1821 (film 0746581 ff.). Probate records from the state of Chiapas, Mexico when the area was a part of the Captaincy General of Guatemala. The original records are at the Archivo General de Centroamérica in Guatemala City.

Jiménez y Vizcarra, M. Claudio. *Indice del Archivo del Juzgado General de Bienes de Difuntos de la Nueva Galicia, Siglos XVI y XVII* (Mexico: Instituto Nacional de Antropología e Historia, 1978). Index in the archive of the General Court of Property of the Deceased in Mexico during the sixteenth and seventeenth centuries.

Millares Carlo, Agustin and J.R. Mantecón. *El Colegio de México* (Mexico: n.p., 1945). Indexes to the Archive of Notaries, 1524–53.

Military Records

Militares (military records) dating from 1524 are at the Archivo Historico Militar Mexicano, the Archivo Historico de Hacienda, and the Archivo General de la Nación in Mexico City. The main categories of military records are: Spanish troops assigned to permanent or temporary duty; provincial militia comprised of units within a province; and urban militia formed in specific cities. For other records, see the chapter on sources of colonial records in Spain.

Alístamiento del reximiento de milicias: filiaciones del reximiento de milicias de esta Nbiña Ciudad de Puebla (film 0228256 ff.). Militia regimental enlistments, military genealogies, 1760–9, petitions before the cabildo, 1776. The original records are at the Archivo del Ayuntamiento in Pueblo.

Land Records

De tierras y propiedades (land records) dating from 1524 are found in notarial, ecclesiastical, and municipal records at the Archivo General de la Nación in Mexico City, and various local archives. There are some records of *casas* (house sales) for the eighteenth century at the Archivo General del Centroamérica in Guatemala City.

Records at the Archivo General de la Nación in Mexico City include:
* Juz gado General de Naturales, México. Ramo de Tierras (film 1563720 ff. and 1857028 ff.). *Ramo de Tierras* is collection of legal documents from 1523 to 1822, representing complaints arising from the expropriation of native lands and properties by the Spanish government.
* Departamento Agrario, México. Vínculos, 1700–1800 (film 0034613 ff.). Bonds and miscellaneous information on heirs and index, 1560–1825.

Robinson, David J. *Catálogo del Archivo del Registro Público de la Propiedad de Guadalajara: Libros de Hipotecas, 1566–1820* (Guadalajara: Unidad Editorial del Gobierno de Jalisco, 1986). Catalog and indexes of the mortgage records of the Archive of the Public Register of Property of Gualalajara.

Suggested Reading

Archivo General de la Nación. *Guía General de los Fondos que Contiene el Archivo General de la Nación* (Mexico: The Archive, 1981). General guide to the resources of the Archivo General de la Nación.

Barnes, Thomas C. *Northern New Spain: A Research Guide* (Tucson: University of Arizona Press, 1981). Northern New Spain includes parts of California, Nevada, Utah, Colorado, Kansas, Oklahoma, and Texas, and all of Arizona and New Mexico. In Mexico it includes parts of Aguascalientes, Jalisco, Nayarit, San Luis Potosi, and Zacatecas, and all of Coahuila, Chihuahua, Durango, Nuevo Leon, Sinaloa, Sonora, Tamaulipas, and Baja California Norte and Sur.

Beers, Henry Putney. *Spanish and Mexican Records of the American Southwest* (Tucson: University of Arizona Press, 1979). This includes Arizona, California, New Mexico, and Texas.

Buglio, Rudecinda Lo. *The Archives of Northwestern Mexico* (Salt Lake City: Corporation of the President, 1980, fiche 6085818).

Carrera Stampa, Manuel. *Misiones Mexicanas en Archivos Europeos* (Mexico, DF: Instituto Panamericano de Geografía y Historia, 1949). Documentary sources relative to the history of Mexico; information stored in European archives.

Chamberlain, Robert Stoner. *The Conquest and Colonization of Yucatán* (New York: Octagon Books, 1966).

Chevalier, François. *Land and Society in Colonial Mexico* (Berkeley: University of California Press, 1963).

Diccionario Universal de Historia y de Geografía. 6 Vols. (Mexico: Tipografía de Rafael, 1853, film 0599332 ff.). Historical and geographical dictionary of the Americas, especially Mexico.

Fancourt, Charles Saint John. *The History of Yucatan, from Its Discovery to the Close of the Seventeenth Century* (London: John Murray, 1854, film 1162474).

García Cubas, Antonio. *Diccionario Geográfico, Historico y Biográfico de los Estados Unidos Mexicanos.* 5 Vols. (Mexico: Antigua Murguia, Oficina Tipográfica de la Secretaría de Fomento, 1888–91. Reprint. Washington, DC: Library of Congress, 1966, film 1102587 ff.). Geographical, historical, and biographical dictionary of Mexico.

González Navarro, Moisés. *Repartimientos de Indios en Nueva Galicia* (Mexico: Museo Nacional de Historia, 1977). Distribution of Indians to Spaniards in Nueva Galicia.

Hanke, Lewis. *Guía de las Fuentes en el Archivo General de Indias Para el Estudio de la Administración Virreinal Espanola en México y en el Perú: 1535–1700.* 3 Vols. (Madrid: Atlas, 1976). Guide to the sources in the Archivo General de Indias in Seville for studying the administration of the Spanish viceroyalties in Peru and Mexico, 1535–1700.

Icaza, Francisco A. de. *Diccionario Autobiográfico de Conquistadores y Pobladores de Nueva España*. 2 Vols. (Madrid: El Adelantado de Segovia, 1923, film 0873574). Biographical dictionary of the conquistadors and founders of Mexico.

Icazbalceta, Joaquín García. *Bibliografía Mexicana del Siglo XVI: Catálogo Razonado de Libros Impresos en México de 1539 a 1600* (Mexico, DF: Fondo de Cultura Economica, 1954). Mexican bibliography of the sixteenth century, 1539–1600.

Indice de Documentos de Nueva España: Existentes en el Archivo de Indias de Sevilla. 4 Vols. (Mexico, DF: Secretaría de Relaciones Exteriores, 1925–31). Index to the documents concerning New Spain in the Archive of the Indias in Seville.

Relaciones Geográficas del Siglo XVI: Tlaxcala (Mexico: Universidad Nacional Autónoma de México, 1984). Geographical reports of the sixteenth century: Tlaxcala, Mexico. Includes information on history, religion, society, etc.

Rodríguez de Lebrija, Esperanza. *Guía Documental del Archivo Historico de Hacienda*. 3 Vols. (Mexico, DF: Archivo General de la Nación, 1985). A guide to documents in the Historical Archive of Finance in Mexico City.

Simpson, Lesley Byrd. *The Encomienda in New Spain: The Beginnings of Spanish Mexico* (Berkeley: University of California, 1950).

Thompson, John Eric Sidney. *The Rise and Fall of Maya Civilization* (Norman: University of Oklahoma Press, 1954).

Temple Mound in Mexico.

Nicaragua

Nicaragua was first settled in the 1520s. The city of Córdoba was founded in 1524. During the colonial period Nicaragua was part of the province Gracias a Dios in the Captaincy General of Guatemala under the Viceroyalty of Nueva España. In 1548 the area known as Cuzcztlán was divided into the four separate dominions of Soconusco, Honduras, Nicaragua, and Costa Rica. Nicaragua was under the jurisdiction of the Audiencia de Panamá from 1538 and became a part of the Audiencia de Guatemala in 1570. From 1740 to 1786 Britain claimed the area of the Mosquito Coast as a protectorate, after which it was ceded back to Spain. Nicaragua declared independence from Spain in 1821.

Parish, Diocesan, and Other Ecclesiastical Records

Parroquiales (parish registers) date from 1801 and include baptisms, marriages, deaths and burials, and other records. They can be found in local archives. Many records were destroyed by a fire at the National Archives. The majority of the existing records are at the parish archives in Merced, San Miguel, and Santa Ana.

Records of the Inquisition from 1556 to 1820 are at the Archivo General de la Nación in Mexico City. For more information on records of the Inquisition, see the chapter on sources of colonial records in Spain.

Census Records

Padrones (civil census records) and *matrículas* and *padrones* (ecclesiastical censuses) from 1676. An example of such records are:

Padrones de Guatemala: varios pueblos de Nicaragua: 1708–54 (film 0763385 ff.). Census records from localities in old Nicaragua Province including Santísima, Trinidad, Telpaneca, and La Laguna. The original records are at the Archivo General de Centroamérica in Guatemala City.

Notarial Records

See Guatemala.

SEE ALSO
Guatemala
Latin America
Spain

85

Governmental and Municipal Records

De Gobernación, de las provincias, y municipales (governmental and municipal records) dating from 1536 are at the Archivo General de Centroamérica in Guatemala City. Examples of such are:

Capitanía General de Guatemala, Virreino de Nueva España, Real Audiencia.
• Registros civiles, 1754 (film 0745814). Civil marriage registration.
• Juzgado General de Matrimonios. Disputas de matrimonios, 1638–1810 (film 0745073 ff.). Marriage disputes.
• Pensiones, 1659–1792 (film 0745814). Pension records.

Military Records
See Guatemala.

Land Records
See Guatemala.

Suggested Reading

Guerrero, Julián N. and Lola Soraino de Guerrero. *Diccionario Nicaraguense Geográfico e Historico* (Managua, Nicaragua: Editiorial Somarriba, 1985).

Molina Argüello, Carlos. *Misiones Nicaraguenses en Archivos Europeos* (Mexico: Instituto Panamericano de Geografía e Historia, 1957). Documentary sources for a study of Nicaraguan history, collected from European archives.

Panama

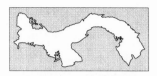

Panama was first established as the colony of Tierra Firme in 1509. The city of Darién was founded in 1511 and Panama City in 1519. The area was part of the Audiencia de Santo Domingo until 1535. It was given its own *audiencia* in 1538, but later came under that of Guatemala in 1543. The Audiencia de Panamá was reestablished in 1563. It did not become a province until 1821, under the Republic of Greater Colombia.

Parish, Diocesan, and Other Ecclesiastical Records

Parroquiales (parish registers) date from 1707 and include baptisms, marriages, deaths and burials, and other records. The Diocese of Panama was established in 1513. Examples of parish records are:

Iglesia Católica, Santo Domingo de Guzmán, Parita. Registros parroquiales, 1727–1973 (film 1089172 ff.). Parish registers of baptisms, marriages, marriage information and deaths. The original records are in the local parish archive.

Iglesia Católica, La Merced, Ciudad de Panamá. Registros parroquiales, 1742–1972 (film 0760713 ff.). Parish registers of baptisms, confirmations, marriages, and deaths. The original records are in the local parish archive.

Census Records

Padrones (civil census records) date from 1740 and are at the Archivo Nacional de Historia in Bogatá, Colombia and the Archivo General de Indias in Seville, Spain.

Notarial Records

Notariales (notarial records) dating from 1776 are at the Archivo Nacional, Edificio del Registro Civil, in Panama City. Earlier records can be found at the Archivo General de Centroamérica in Guatemala City.

Governmental and Municipal Records

See Guatemala and Colombia.

Military Records

See Colombia.

SEE ALSO
Colombia
Guatemala
Latin America
Spain

Land Records

De tierras y propiedades (land records) dating from 1776 are found in notarial, ecclesiastical, and municipal records in local notarial archives. For earlier records, see Guatemala and Colombia.

Suggested Reading

Carles, Rubén Darío. *220 Años del Período Colonial en Panamá* (Panama: n.p., 1969, film 1162495). Two hundred and twenty years of the colonial period in Panama, 1519–1739.

Gropp, Arthur Eric. *Guide to Libraries and Archives in Central America and the West Indies, Panama, Bermuda, and British Guiana* (New Orleans: Middle American Research Institute, Tulane University, 1941).

Jaen Suarez, Omar. *La Pobalción del Istmo de Panamá del Siglo XVI al Siglo XX* (Panama: n.p., 1978). The population of the Isthmus of Panama from the sixteenth to the twentieth centuries.

Paraguay

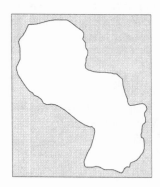

The first settlement in Paraguay was at Asuncion in 1537. Paraguay became a province in 1617 and was part of the Viceroyalty of Peru until 1776. At that time the Viceroyalty of Río de la Plata was created and included Argentina, Bolivia, Paraguay, and Uruguay. Paraguay declared independence from Spain in 1811.

Parish, Diocesan, and Other Ecclesiastical Records

Parroquiales (parish registers) date from 1763 and include baptisms, marriages, deaths and burials, and other records. Most parish records can be found in the local parish archives.

Records of the Inquisition from the eighteenth and nineteenth centuries are at the Archivo Histórico Nacional in Madrid, Spain, the Archivo Nacional in Lima, Peru, and the Archivo Nacional in Santiago, Chile. For more information on records of the Inquisition, see the chapter on sources of colonial records in Spain.

Census Records

Padrones (civil census records) date from 1537 and *matrículas* and *padrones* (ecclesiastical censuses) from 1763. They can be found at the Archivo General de la Nación in Buenos Aires, Argentina and the Bibilioteca y Archivo Nacionales in Asunción.

Notarial Records

Notariales (notarial records) date from 1537. They can be found at the Archivo de los Tribunales in Tacuarí, Asunción and the Archivo Nacional in Asunción. The Archivo Nacional has cataloged wills from 1537 in *Cátalogo de Testamentos y Codicilios,* by José Doroteo Bareiro (Asuncion: The Archive, 1971).

Governmental and Municipal Records

De Gobernación, de las provincias, y municipales (governmental and municipal records) dating from 1537 are at various municipal archives throughout Paraguay and Argentina.

SEE ALSO
Argentina
Brazil
Latin America
Spain

Military Records

Militares (military records) dating from the sixteenth century are at the Archivo General de la Nación in Buenos Aires, Argentina and the Archivo Militar in Asunción. For other records, see the section on sources of colonial records in Spain.

Land Records

De tierras y propiedades (land records) dating from 1537 are found in notarial, ecclesiastical, and municipal records at the Archivo Nacional in Asunción. These records are cataloged in *Cátalogo de Títulos de Propiedades,* which contains names and transactions from 1541 to 1870.

Suggested Reading

Pastells, Pablo. *Historia de la Compañía de Jesús en la Provincia de Paraguay: Según los Documentos Originales del Archivo General de Indias.* 8 Vols. (Madrid: Librería General de Victoriano Suárez, 1912–49). History of the Jesuits in the province of Paraguay (Argentina, Paraguay, Uruguay, Peru, Bolivia, and Brazil) according to documents in the Archivo General de Indias, in Seville, Spain.

Poz Cano, Raul del. *Paraguay-Bolivia, La Real Cedula de 1743 a la Luz de la Geografía de la Epoca* (Asuncion: Imprenta Nacional Asunción, 1935).

Whigham, Thomas and Jerry W. Cooney. *A Guide to Collections on Paraguay in the United States* (Westport CT: Greenwood Press, 1995).

Peru

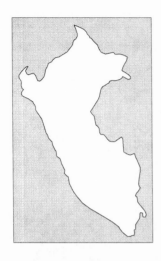

Peru was colonized when the Incan civilization fell to Spanish conquerors in 1532. Ciudad de los Reyes (Lima) was founded in 1534. An *audienca* was created in 1542, and the Viceroyalty of Peru was estab lished in 1543. It included the *audiencias* at Santa Fe de Bogotá (Colombia), Quito (Ecuador), Panama, Buenos Aires (Argentina), Santiago (Chile), and Caracas (Venezuela) until 1740 and 1776. Peru declared independence from Spain in 1821.

Parish, Diocesan, and Other Ecclesiastical Records

Parroquiales (parish registers) date from 1538 and include baptisms, marriages, deaths and burials, and other records. Examples of parish records are:

Iglesia Católica, Arquidiócesis de Trujillo. Documentos eclesiásticos, 1772–1831 (film 1083258). Parish registers of ecclesiastical documents from the Archidiocese of Trujillo, Colombia. These contain *padrones*. The records cover most of northern Peru and parts of Ecuador. The original records are in the Archivo Nacional de Historia in Bogotá, Colombia.

Iglesia Católica.

- Arquidiócesis de Lima. Registros parroquiales, 1600–1944 (film 1933516 ff.). Marriage petitions from la Ciudad de los Reyes (Lima).
- San Marcelo, Lima. Registros parroquiales, 1570–1921 (film 1110678 ff.). Baptisms, marriages, deaths, confirmations.
- San Sebastián, Lima. Registros parroquiales, 1561–1954 (film 1110232 ff.). Baptisms, marriages, deaths, confirmations.
- Santiago Apóstol, Lima. Registros parroquiales, 1573–1921 (film 1149551 ff.). Baptisms, marriages, and deaths.
- El Sagrario, Lima. Registros parroquiales, 1556–1901 (film 1110200 ff.). Registers of baptisms, confirmations, marriages, and deaths.

The original records of the above are at the Archivo Arzobispal in Lima.

Iglesia Católica, Diócesis de Chachapoyas.

- Registros parroquiales, 1678–1956 (film 1389081 ff.). Baptisms, confirmations, marriage

SEE ALSO
Colombia
Guatemala
Latin America
Mexico
Spain

petitions and marriages, deaths, church census, and other records.

• Documentos eclesiásticos, 1605–1908 (film 1523326 ff.). Miscellaneous ecclesiastical records, including *visitas, informaciones matrimoniales, expedientes,* and *capellanías* from the Diocese of Chachapoyas. The original records are in the diocesan archive.

Iglesia Católica, San Carlos, Amazonas. Registros parroquiales, 1613–1955 (film 1389135 ff.). Baptisms, marriage petitions, marriages, and deaths. The original records are at the parish archive in San Carlos.

Iglesia Católica, Obispado de Cuzco. Documentos eclesiásticos: Sumario demográfico de las parroquias, 1689 (Syracuse, NY: Syracuse University, n.d., film 1162402). Church census records for parishes in the Roman Catholic Bishopric of Cuzco, Peru. The original records are at the Archivo General de Indias in Seville.

Iglesia Católica, Lima.

• Documentos eclesiásticos, 1599–1795 (Lima: Paul Ganster, 1972, film 1104841). Ecclesiastical documents of the Catholic Church.

• Documentos eclesiásticos, 1634–1818 (Lima: Paul Ganster, 1970-2, film 1100841 ff.). Ecclesiastical and public documents.

The original records are at the Biblioteca Nacional in Lima.

Iglesia Católica, Arzobispado de Lima. Concilios provinciales y sínodos diocesanos del ilustrisimo y reverendisimo Señor Santo Toribio Alfonso Mogrovejo, segundo Arzobispo de Lima (Lima: Unidad Móvil de la UNESCO, 1960, film 0802892). The provincial councils and diocesan synods conducted during the tenure of Toribio Alfonso Mogrovejo as the second Archbishop of Lima, 1579–1606. During that period, the Archbishopric included places in the present-day countries of Ecuador and Colombia. It includes historical data regarding the Roman Catholic Church in Peru from its foundation up to 1606. The original records are at the Archivo Arzobispal in Lima.

Records of the Inquisition from 1550 to 1820 are at the Archivo Histórico Nacional in Madrid, Spain, the Archivo Nacional in Lima, and the Archivo Nacional in Santiago, Chile. For more information on records of the Inquisition, see the chapter on sources of colonial records in Spain.

Consejo de Inquisición, Lima.

• Procesos de fé, 1564–1804 (Madrid: Centro Nacional de Microfilm, 1977, film 1224016 ff.). Professions of faith of persons tried by the Holy Office of the Inquisition of Lima.

• Pleitos civiles relativos a Lima (Madrid: Centro Nacional de Microfilm, 1982, film 1418251 ff.). Civil suits relative to the Tribunal de Lima during the Inquisition, 1636-9.

The original records are at the Archivo Histórico Nacional in Madrid.

Lohmann Villena, Guillermo. *Informaciones Genealógicas de Perúanas Seguidas Ante el Santo Oficio* (Lima: n.p., 1957, film 0873987). Genealogical information of Perúvians appearing before the Holy Office of the Inquisition.

Medina, José Toribio. *Historia del Tribunal de la Inquisición de Lima, 1569-1820.* 2 Vols. (Santiago: Fondo Histórico Bibliográfico J.T. Medina, 1956, film 0896618). History of the Inquisition of Lima, 1569-1820.

Census Records

Padrones (civil census records) from 1606 and *matrículas* and *padrones* (ecclesiastical censuses) from 1535 and can be found at the Archivo General de la Nación in Lima, and the archives of the archbishoprics in Lima and Trujillo. For ecclesiatical censuses, see the section for parish records.

Notarial Records

Notariales (notarial records) date from 1533 and can be found in various national and local archives. Examples of notarial records are:

Escribanía. Protocolos, 1538-48: Pedro de Castañeda y Pedro de Salinas (Lima: Unidad Móvil de la UNESCO, 1961, film 0802881 ff.). Notarial records of Pedro de Castañeda and Pedro Salinas, 1537-48. The original records are at the Archivo Nacional in Lima.

Trujillo, Notaría. Expedientes, 1550-1893 (Trujillo, Peru: Archivo Notarial de García Flores, 1979-1982, film 1100813 ff.). Notarial record books from Trujillo. The original records are at the Archivo Notarial de García Flores in Trujillo.

Archivo General de la Nación. *Indice de Notarios de Lima y Callao: Cuyos Protocolos Se Hallan en el Archivo Nacional de Perú, Siglos XVI, XVII, XVIII, XIX, XX* (Lima: Imprenta Gil, 1928, fiche 6030595). Index of notary publics of Lima and Callao from the sixteenth to twentieth centuries whose records are found in the National Archive of Peru in Lima.

Governmental and Municipal Records

De Gobernación, de las provincias, y municipales (governmental and municipal records) dating from 1528 are at various municipal archives throughout Peru. An example of such is:

Cabildo de Lima. Cédulas y provisiones 1529-1739 (Lima: Filmado Unidad de Microfilm de la UNESCO, 1961, film 0590428 ff.). Decrees and writs. The original records are at the Archivo Histórico in Lima.

Military Records

Militares (military records) dating from 1550 are at the Archivo Histórico Militar, the Archivo General de la Nación, and the Biblioteca Nacional — all in Lima. For other records, see the chapter on sources of colonial records in Spain.

Land Records

De tierras y propiedades (land records) dating from 1528 are found in notarial, ecclesiastical, and municipal records at the Archivo General de la Nación in Madrid, and the Biblioteca Nacional and the Archivo Nacional in Lima. For *capellanias*, see the above section on parish records.

Suggested Reading

Arona, Juan de. La *Inmigración en el Perú* (Lima: Biblioteca Pública de la Cámara de Diputados, 1971). Immigration to Peru, with bibliography.

Bakewell, Judith R. *Research Guide to Andean History: Bolivia, Chile, Ecuador, and Peru* (Durham, NC: Duke University Press, 1981).

Bromley, Juan. *La Fundación de la Ciudad de los Reyes* (Lima: n.p., 1935). The founding of the City of the Kings (Lima), including a list of the first Spaniards in Peru to 1534.

Clemente, Stella R. *The Harkness Collection in the Library of Congress: Calendar of Spanish Manuscripts Concerning Peru, 1531-1651* (Washington, DC: USGPO, 1932).

Collapiña, Supno. *Relación de la Descendencia, Gobierno y Conquista de los Incas* (1892. Reprint. Lima: Ediciones de la Biblioteca Universitaria, 1974). An account of the descent, government, and conquest of the Incas as recorded in 1542 by the last *quipucamayos*, who were the native historians of the Inca empire.

Crespo, R. Alberto. *El Corregimiento de La Paz, 1548-1600* (La Paz: n.p., 1972). The ministry of justice over Bolivia and Peru, 1548-1600.

Cúneo-Vidal, Rómulo. *Historia de la Guerra de los Ultimos Incas Perúanos Contra el Poder Español: 1535-1572* (Barcelona: Maucci, 1925, film 0873987). History of the last wars of the Incas against the Spaniards in Peru.

García de Proodian, Lucía. *Los Judíos en América: Sus Actividades en los Virreinatos de Nueva Castilla y Nueva Granada, Siglo XVII* (Madrid: Universidad de Madrid, Seminario de Estudios Americanistas, 1966, film

0908099). The Jews in South America; their activities under the viceroys of New Castile and New Granada in the seventeenth century.

García Quintanilla, Julio. *Historia de la Iglesia en La Plata* (Sucre, Bolivia: Talleres Gráficos Don Bosco, 1964). A story of the church in La Plata. The diocese of Charcas or La Plata, founded in 1553, includes parts of what is today Argentina, Bolivia, Chile, Paraguay, and Peru.

Hanke, Lewis. *Guía de las Fuentes en el Archivo General de Indias Para el Estudio de la Administración Virreinal Española en México y en el Perú: 1535-1700.* 3 Vols. (Madrid: Atlas, 1976). Guide to the sources in the Archivo General de Indias in Seville for studying the administration of the Spanish viceroyalties in Peru and Mexico, 1535-1700.

Lockhart, James. *Spanish Peru, 1532-1560: A Colonial Society* (Madison: University of Wisconsin Press, 1968, film 0873987).

Martín, Luis. *Daughters of the Conquistadores: Women of the Viceroyalty of Peru* (Albuquerque: University of New Mexico Press, 1983).

Mateos, F. *Historia General de la Compañía de Jesús en la Provincia del Perú: Crónica Anónima de 1600 Que Trata del Establecimiento y Misiones de la Compañía de Jesús en los Países de Habla Española en la América Meridiana.* 2 Vols. (Madrid: Instituto Gonzalo Fernández de Oviedo, 1944). History of the Jesuits in Peru.

Morales, Adolfo de. *Revista del Insitututo Perúano de Investigaciones Genealógias* Vols. 6-8 (Lima, n.d.). Catalog of passengers arriving at Peru from 1560 to 1594.

Rivera Serna, Raúl. *Libro del Cabildo de la Ciudad de San Juan de la Frontera de Huamanga, 1539-1547* (Lima: Ediciones de la Casa de la Cultura del Perú, 1966, film 0908251). Documents pertaining to the founding of the city of Ayacucho, 1539-47.

Rodríguez, Jesús Jordán. *Pueblos y Parroquias de el Perú* (Lima: Imprenta Pasaje Piura, 1950, film 1162495). Towns and parishes of Peru.

Vargas Ugarte, Rubén. *Historia de la Iglesia en el Perú* (Lima: Imprenta Santa María, 1953). History of the Catholic Church in Peru, 1511-1900.

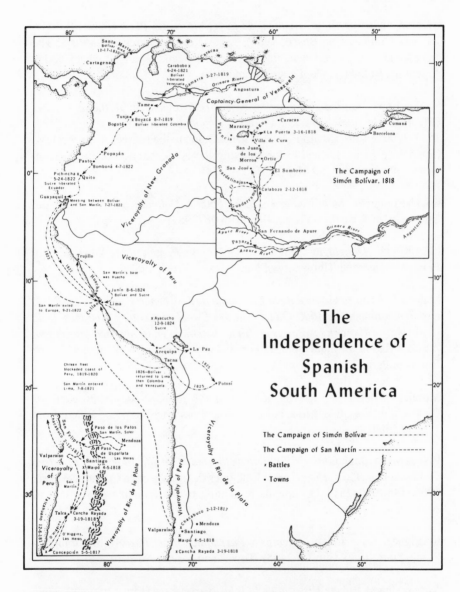

11 Independence of Spanish South America (Cathryn L. Lombardi, et al., *Latin American History: A Teaching Atlas*. Madison: University of Wisconsin Press, 1983)

Uruguay

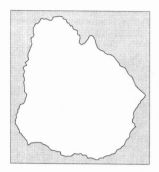

Portuguese colonists settled Montivideo in 1749. Uruguay was part of the Viceroyalty of Peru until 1776, when the separate Viceroyalty of Río de la Plata was established, and included Argentina, Bolivia, Paraguay, and Uruguay. Uruguay declared independence from Spain in 1828.

Parish, Diocesan, and Other Ecclesiastical Records

Parroquiales (parish registers) date from the seventeenth century and include baptisms, marriages, deaths and burials, and other records. An example of a parish record is:

Iglesia Católica. Santísimo Sacramento, Colonia. Registros parroquiales, 1766–1958 (film 0625361 ff.). Parish registers of baptisms, confirmations, marriage petitions, marriages, and deaths from Colonia. The original records are in the parish archive.

Records of the Inquisition from the eighteenth and nineteenth centuries are at the Archivo Histórico Nacional in Madrid, the Archivo Nacional in Lima, Peru, and the Archivo Nacional in Santiago, Chile. For more information on records of the Inquisition, see the chapter on sources of colonial records in Spain.

Census Records

Padrones (civil census records) date from 1726 and *matrículas* and *padrones* (ecclesiastical censuses) from the early seventeenth century. They can be found at the Archivo General de la Nación in Montevideo.

Notarial Records

Notarilaes (notarial records) can be found at the Archivo General de la Nación in Montevideo and at other archives in Uruguay and Argentina.

Governmental and Municipal Records

De Gobernación, de las provincias, y municipales (governmental and municipal records) dating from the seventeeth century are at the Suprema Corte de Justicia and the Archivo General de la Nación in Montevideo and various municipal archives throughout Uruguay.

SEE ALSO
Argentina
Brazil
Latin America
Paraguay
Spain

Apolant, Juan Alejandro. *Padrones Olvidados de Montevideo del Siglo XVIII.* 3 Vols. (Montevideo: Imprint Letras, 1966, fiche 6030580 ff.). Eighteenth century tax lists of Montevideo.

Military Records

Militares (military records) dating from the eighteenth century at the Archivo del Ministerio de Defensa Nacional, Archivo General del la Nación, in Montevideo. For other records, see the chapter on sources of colonial records in Spain.

Land Records

See Argentina.

Suggested Reading

Apolant, Juan Alejandro. *Génesis de la Familia Uruguay: Los Habitantes de Montevideo en Sus Primeros Cuarente Años, Filiaciones, Ascendencias, Entronques, Descendencias.* 4 Vols. 2nd ed. (Montevideo: Imprenta Insituto Histórico y Geográfico de Uruguay, 1966).

Archivo General de la Nación. *Inventario de los Fondos Documentales del Archivo General de la Nación* (Montevideo: n.p., 1965, film 0897479). Inventory of documents in the National Archive of Uruguay.

Azarola Gil, Luis Enrique. *Apellidos de la Patria Vieja* (Buenos Aires: Librería y Editorial la Facultad, 1942, film 0897479). Origins of Uruguayan surnames.

Ferréss, Carlos. *Epoca Colonial: La Compañía de Jesús en Montevideo* (Barcelona: Luis Gili, 1919). The Jesuits in Montevideo.

Hartmann, Américo. *500 Años de Historias de Familia.* 3 Vols. (Montevideo: Centro de Estudiantes de Ingeniería, Oficina de Publicaciones, 1994). Families of the Rio Plata Region and Uruguay, from the fifteenth century to the present time, with some history of Montevideo.

Museo Histórico Nacional, Uruguay. *Catálogo Descriptivo, VII: Colección de Manuscritos* (Montevideo: A. Monteverde, 1953, film 0896736). Descriptive catalog of manuscripts in the National Historical Museum of Uruguay.

Musso, Luis Alberto. *Archivos del Uruguay* (Montevideo: n.p., 1974). Archives of Uruguay.

Ponce de León, Luis R. *La Ciudad Vieja de Montevideo: Trazado Inicial y Evolución en Su Primer Cuarto de Siglo* (Montevideo: Impresora Rex, 1968, film 0908055). The ancient city of Montevideo: the first quarter century.

CITY OF CARACCAS.

Venezuela

Although Venezuela was explored by Christopher Colombus in 1498, no permanent settlement was made until 1520 at Cumaná. German colonists founded Maracaibo in 1529. Caracas was founded by Spanish settlers in 1566. Venezuela was made part of the Viceroyalty of Nueva España in 1534 and Nueva Granada in 1717. The viceroyalty was suspended in 1723 and reestablished in 1739. In the interim Venezuela was an independent captaincy. Caracas was established as the capital of a captaincy general in 1777, and as an *audiencia* in 1786. Venezuela declared independence from Spain in 1821 and became part of Greater Colombia, which consisted of Ecuador, Panama, Colombia, and Venezuela. It became an independent republic in 1830.

Parish, Diocesan, and Other Ecclesiastical Records

Parroquiales (parish registers) date from 1550 and include baptisms, marriages, deaths and burials, and other records. Examples of parish records are:
Iglesia Católica.

* Inmaculada Concepción, San Carlos. Registros parroquiales, 1677–1939 (film 1995985 ff.). Registers of baptisms, confirmations, marriages, and deaths from Inmaculada Concepción Parish, San Carlos, gathered into books that reflect social classes.
* San Juan, San Carlos. Registros parroquiales, 1729–1916 (film 1996062 ff.). Registers of baptisms, marriages, and deaths from San Juan Parish and San José Parish, San Carlos.

The original records of the above are at the Archivo Diocesano de San Carlos.
Iglesia Católica, San José, Carayaca. Registros parroquiales, 1692–1931 (film 1995980 ff.). Parish registers of baptisms, confirmations, marriages, and deaths from Carayaca. The original records are at the Archivo Diocesano de La Guaira.

Iglesia Católica, El Sagrario, San Cristóbal. Registros parroquiales, 1601–1960 (film 1873407 ff.). Registers of baptisms, confirmations, marriage petitions, marriages, and deaths from the Parish of El Sagrario in San Cristóbal. The original records are at the Archivo Diocesano de San Cristóbal.

SEE ALSO
Colombia
Latin America
Spain

101

Iglesia Católica, Nuestra Señora de la Paz, Trujillo. Registros parroquiales, 1607–1940 (film 1934342 ff.). Parish registers of baptisms, marriage petitions, marriages, and deaths from Trujillo, gathered into books that reflect social classes. The original records are at the Archivo Diocesano de Trujillo.

Iglesia Católica, Nuestra Señora del Rosario, Humocaro, Bajo Lara. Registros parroquiales, 1648–1977 (film 1855938 ff.). Parish registers of baptisms, confirmations, marriages, and deaths from Humocaro Bajo, Lara. The original records are at the Archivo de la Arquidiócesis de Barquisimeto.

El Libro Parroquial Mas Antiguo de Caracas (Caracas: Ediciones del Concejo Municipal del Distrito Federal, 1968, film 1162491). The oldest parish book of Caracas. Baptisms and marriages, 1579–1615.

Iturriza Guillén, Carlos. *Matrimonios y Velaciones de Españoles y Criollos Blancos Celebrados en la Catedral de Caracas Desde 1615 Hasta 1831: Extractos de los Primeros Once Libros Parroquiales* (Caracas: Instituto Venezolano de Genealogía, 1974, film 1224509). Marriages and marriage vigils of Spaniards and white Creoles celebrated in the cathedral of Caracas between 1615–1831.

Nagel, Kurt von Jess. *Registro Civil de la Catedral de Maracaibo, 1723–1775* (Maracaibo: Concejo Municipal del Distrito Maracaibo, 1980, film 1162479). Baptismal records kept in the Cathedral of Maracaibo, 1723–75.

Records of the Inquisition from 1609 are at the Archivo General de la Nación in Caracas and the Archivo Histórico Nacional in Madrid. For more information on records of the Inquisition, see the chapter on sources of colonial records in Spain.

Census Records

Padrones (civil census records) date from 1617 and *matrículas* and *padrones* (ecclesiastical censuses) from 1600. They can be found in the Archivo Nacional de Historia in Bogotá, Colombia and the Arquivo Arquidiocesano de Caracas in Caracas. An example of such records are:

Iglesia Católica, Obispado de Caracas. Padrones, 1756–98 (Syracuse, NY: Syracuse University, film 1162408 ff.). Church census records from Roman Catholic parishes in Venezuela.

Notarial Records

Notariales (notarial records) date from 1590 and can be found at various judicial offices in Venezuela and Colombia.

Governmental and Municipal Records
De Gobernación, de las provincias, y municipales (governmental and municipal records) dating from 1550 are at various municipal archives throughout Venezuela, the Archivo General de la Nación in Caracas, and the Archivo Nacional de Historia in Bogotá, Colombia.

Military Records
Militares (military records) dating from 1762 are at the Archivo General de la Nación in Caracas. For other records, see the chapter on sources of colonial records in Spain.

Austria, José de. *Bosquejo de la Historia Militar de Venezuela* (Caracas: Academia Nacional de la Historia, 1960). A sketch of Venezuelan military history.

Land Records
De tierras y propiedades (land records) dating from 1575 are found in notarial, ecclesiastical, and municipal records at the Archivo Nacional de Historia in Bogotá, Colombia and the Archivo Arquidiocesano de Caracas.

Suggested Reading
Academia Nacional de la Historia. *Actas del Cabildo Eclesiástico de Caracas: Compendio Cronológico* (Caracas: La Academia, 1963). Chronological listing of the acts of the Ecclesiastical Council of Caracas, 1580–1808.

Aguado, Pedro. *Historia de Venezuela.* 2 Vols. (Madrid: Imprenta y Editorial Maestre, 1951). History of Venezuela.

Arciniegas, German. *Germans in the Conquest of America* (New York: Macmillan & Co., 1943).

Briceño Perozo, Mario. *El Archivo de la Academia Nacional de la Historia* (Caracas: Biblioteca Venezolana de Historia, 1966). The archive of the Venezuelan National Academy of History.

Fundación Polar. *Diccionario de Historia de Venezuela* (Caracas: The Foundation, 1988). Dictionary of Venezuelan history.

Gabaldón Marquez, Joaquin. *Misiones Venezolanas en los Archivos Europeos* (Mexico: Instituto Panamericano de Geografía y Historia, 1954). Documentary sources for a study of Venezuelan history, collected from European archives.

Gómez Canedo, Lino. *Los Archivos Historicos de Venezuela* (Zulia, Venezuela: Universidad del Zulia, 1966). The Historical Archives of Venezuela.

Groot, José Manuel. *Historia Eclesiástica y Civil de Nueva Granada: Tomo II.* 2nd ed. (Bogotá: Ministerio de Educación Nacional, edición de la revista Bolivar, 1956, film 1090239). Ecclesiastical and civil history of Nueva Granada.

Herrera de Weishaar, M. L. *Guía del Archivo General de la Nación* (Caracas: Archivo General de la Nación, 1984). A guide to the General National Archive of Venezuela.

Iturriza Guillén, Carlos. *Algunas Familias Caraqueñas.* 2 Vols. (Caracas: Escuela Técnica Industrial Salesiana, 1967). Genealogy of some families of Caracas.

Jiménez Graziani, Morella A. *La Esclavitud Indígena en Venezuela* (Caracas: Academia Nacional de la Historia, 1986). Slavery of the native races in Venezuela during the sixteenth century.

Lombardi, John V. *People and Places in Colonial Venezuela* (Bloomington: Indiana University Press, 1976).

Morón, Guillermo. *Historia de la Provincia de Venezuela* (Caracas: Consejo Municipal del Distrito Federal, 1977). History of the province of Venezuela.

Nagel, Kurt, von Jess. *Archivo Arquidiocesano de Maracaibo* (Maracaibo: Concejo Municipal del Distrito Maracaibo, 1980). Inventory of the holdings of the archive of the Archdiocese of Maracaibo.

Brazil

Brazil was discovered by Portugal in 1500. The first settlements were at Salvador da Bahia and São Vicente in 1532, and Olinda in 1537. Brazil was originally established as thirteen *captinias*. A viceroyalty was created in 1549. Sugar was brought to São Vicente in 1552. Between 1555 and 1567 a group of French Catholics and Huguenots settled in the area of Rio de Janeiro. The French were expelled in 1567, but did not completely leave the area until 1615. Foreigners as individuals were treated very liberally, as long as they were Roman Catholic. English, Flemish, French, Florentine, Genoan, German, and Spanish Europeans were present among the first colonizers.

From 1580 to 1640 Portugal was united with Spain under one crown. The first *relação* (high court) was established at Bahia in 1609. From 1624 to 1654 the Dutch seized and controlled the northeastern part of Brazil. The capital of Brazil was moved from Bahia to Rio de Janeiro in 1763. When French troops captured Lisbon, Portugal in 1807, the Prince of Portugal and his entire court moved to Brazil and ruled there in exile until 1821. Uruguay was annexed as a province three years before Brazil declared independence from Portugal in 1822.

Parish, Diocesan, and Other Ecclesiastical Records

The bishopric of Brazil was created at Bahia in 1551, before which time it belonged to the Diocese of Funchal in the Azores. An archbishopric was created at Bahia in 1676. Records are kept at parish and diocesan archives. *Reistors paroquias* (parish registers) contain baptisms, marriages (of freemen and slaves), deaths and burials, rolls of families, proceedings of matrimonial cases, etc. Many marriages were *de juras* (common-law) and have no church record. Examples of parish records are:

Igreja Católica, Arquidiocese de São Paulo.

- Documentos eclesiásticos, 1667–1933 (film 1251612 ff.). Church records from the Catholic Archdioceses of São Paulo, Curitiba, and Botucatu.
- Autos de habilitação de genere et moribus, 1644–1920 (film 1153284). Collections of documents in support of candidates for appointment to the holy orders of the Catholic priesthood.

SEE ALSO
The Guianas
Latin America
The Netherlands
Neth. Antilles
Portugal
Spain

105

• Nossa Senhora da Assunção, Centro, São Paulo. Registros paroquiais, 1784–1802 (film 1251617). Ról de famílias, 1784, 1800, and 1802. Church census of the city of São Paulo.
The original records of the above are at the Arquivo da Cúria Metropolitana in São Paulo.

Igreja Católica.
• Nossa Senhora Mãe dos Homens, Madre de Deus do Boqueirão. Registros paroquiais, 1661–1927 (film 1285093 ff.). Parish registers of baptisms, marriages, and deaths from Madre de Deus do Boqueirão, Bahia.
• São Sebastião do Passé. Registros paroquiais, 1712–1921 (film 1284815 ff.). Registers of baptisms, marriages, and deaths from the parishes of São Sebastião do Passé, Catu, and Candeias, Bahia.
• Santo Amaro, Catu. Registros paroquiais, 1612–1931 (film 1285031 ff.). Registers of baptisms, marriages, and deaths from the parishes of Catu and Itaparica, Bahia.
• Nossa Senhora do Monte, Conde. Registros paroquiais, 1661–1908 (film 1284917 ff.). Parish registers of baptisms, marriages, and deaths from Conde, formerly known as Itapicurú da Praia, Bahia.
• Nossa Senhora da Conceição da Praia. Registros paroquiais, 1598–1910 (film 1251847 ff.). Registers of baptisms, marriages, and deaths from Conceição da Praia Parish in the city of Salvador, Bahia.
The original records of the above are at the Arquivo Arquidiocesano de Salvador, Bahia.

Vasconcellos, Vasco Smith de. *História da Província Eclesiástica de São Paulo* (São Paulo: Saraiva, 1957, film 1102976). History of the ecclesiastical province of São Paulo.

Dutch Reformed Church, Pernambuco. Registros paroquiais, 1633–53 (film 0113070). Baptism records of the Dutch Reformed Church in Pernambuco, Brazil. The original records are at the Gemeente Archief in Amsterdam.

Wasch, C.J. *Doopregister der Hollanders in Brasilie, 1633–1654*('s-Gravenhage: Genealogisch en Heraldisch Archief, 1889, film 0375563). Transcription of the Dutch church records.

Patterson, Frances. *Index to Doopregister der Hollanders in Brazilie* (n.p., 1964, film 0599501). Index to *Doopregister der Hollanders in Brasilie, 1633– 1654*, by C. J. Wasch.

Records of the Inquisition in Brazil are not as extensive as those in the Spanish colonies. The process was conducted as three visitations, 1591–5, 1681, and 1763–9. The original records are at the Arquivo Nacional da Torre do Tombo in Lisbon. The records of Dutch who were condemned by the *Counseil des Troubles* (Council of Troubles) are at the Bibliotheque Royal in Brussels, Belgium. For more information on records of the Inquisition, see the section on sources of colonial records in Spain.

Inquisição de Lisboa, 1591–1737 (Lisbon: Laboratórios Fototécnicos, 1975, film 0784501.) Documents of trials of New Christians (*Marranos*), persons taken prisoner in Brazil, accused of being Jewish, and sent to Portugal to face the Inquisition. The original records are at the Arquivo Nacional da Torre do Tombo in Lisbon and copies at the archives of Hebrew College in Cincinnati, Ohio.

The Bandeirantes

Bandeirantes were persons that belonged to armed bands known as *bandieras*, which existed around São Paulo in the sixteenth to eighteenth centuries. They were adventurers seeking the gold, silver, and diamonds that were fabled to exist in the wilderness of Brazil's interior. The *bandierantes* became pioneers, being among the first to open that part of the country for settlement. One of the first settlements was at Villa Nova do Principe in 1714.

Carvalho Franco, Francisco de Assis. *Dicionário de Bandeirantes e Sertanistas do Brasil: Séculos XVI, XVII, XVIII* (São Paulo: Editora da Universidade de São Paulo, 1989). Biographical dictionary of explorers and colonizers of Brazilian wilderness areas, most from the State of São Paulo.

Prado, Eduardo. *Primereia Visitação do Santo Ofício as Partes do Brasil, pelo licenciado Heitor Furtado de Menonça — Confissões da Baía — 1591-1592* (Sao Paolo: Paulo Prado, 1922). First visitation of the Holy Office to the Regions of Brazil, by the Licentiate Heitor Furtado de Mendonca — confessions of Bahia.

Verheyden, A.L. *Les Conseil des Troubles, Liste de Condamnés* (Brussels: Palaisdes Académies, 1961). Records of Dutch who were condemned by the *Counseil des Troubles* (Council of Troubles).

Census Records

Róls (civil census records) date from the sixteenth century and were usually a church census. For an example, see church records.

Notarial Records

A *notarius* (notary) performed functions similar to the notaries in the Spanish colonies. One of the most important documents for genealogical research is the *testimentum* (will), *conta de testamento* (will inventory), and *titulo de herdeiros* (title of heirs). The Brazilian sociologist, Gilberto Freyre, in *The Masters and the Slaves,* examined a collection of wills of the sixteenth and seventeenth centuries and identified the European origins of some of the first settlers. He determined that about one quarter of the colonists in São Vicente came from southern Portugal (Alentejo, Portuguese Estremadura, and the Algraves) and another quarter from Lusitania in the north.[6]

Inventários e Testamentos (Sao Paulo: Departamento do Arquivo do Estado de São Paulo, 1966, film 0962230). Extracts from the inventories and wills in the historical archive of the State of São Paulo. For a list of other public archives, see government records, following.

Governmental and Municipal Records

Relações (high courts) were established at Bahia in 1609 and Rio de Janeiro in 1752 and were the court of last resort for most colonial matters. The *Junta de Fazenda* (Board of Review) handled tax and treasury administration. Some of the duties collected were *entradas* (duties on merchandise, slaves, and cattle) and *dízimos* (taxes on agricultural products).

Local government was conducted by the *senado da câmara* (municipal council), and was comparable to the *cabildos* in the Spanish colonies, except that the *senado* functioned more independently. Town courts were the court of first instance in most proceedings.

Actas da Câmara da Villa de São Paulo (São Paulo: Typographia Piratininga, 1915, film 1162490). Transcribed records of the town council of São Paulo, 1653–78. The Registro General (General Registers) series has also been published (Vols. I–XXIII).

---

[6] Gilberto Freyre, *Masters and the Slaves* (New York: Alfred Knopf, 1963, originally published as *Casa-Grande e Senzala*, 1946), 221–2.

Arquivo do Estado, São Paulo. *Diagnóstico da Situação dos Arquivos do Governo do Estado de São Paulo: Órgãos da Administração Direta Sediadas na Capital* (São Paulo: The Archive, 1987). Summary description of the archival system for São Paulo, with the extent of document holdings.

Records of the Dutch administration can be found in archives in The Netherlands and Brazil. Some of the records at the Royal Archives of The Hague have been published in *Revista do Instituto Arqueológico Histórico e Geográfico de Pernambuco*. No. 33 (Recife, 1887). Some Dutch records are kept at the Archaeological Institute of Recife.

West-Indische Compagnie, Nederland, Kamer van Middelburg. Notulenboeken: 1623–74 (film 0488127). Records of the Dutch West India Company, Middleburg Chamber, including minutes, financial reports, correspondence, business transactions, settlements of wills, death notices, and other documents. The original records are at the Algemeen Rijksarchief in 's-Gravenhage, The Netherlands.

Research libraries in Brazil include:
➢ Biblioteca Nacional (National Library) in Rio de Janeiro
➢ State Library of Pernambuco (manuscripts on English colonists)
➢ Library of the Brazilian Historical Institute
➢ Archaeological Institutes of Pernambuco and Recife
➢ Institute of History in São Paulo
➢ Nina Rodrigues Museum in Bahia

Military Records

Militares (military records) dating from the sixteenth century are at the state archives in Brazil. Most military functions were conducted on a local level, carried out by the local militia, and commanded by a *capitão-mor* (colonel).

Bento, Cláudio Moreira. *Estrangeiros e Descendentes na História Militar do Rio Grande do Sul, 1635 a 1870* (Porto Alegre, Brazil: Gráfica Editora A Nação, 1976). Foreigners and their descendants in the military history of Rio Grande do Sul, Brazil, 1635–1870.

Land Records

Semarias (original land grants), dating from 1534, formed the sugar plantations and cattle ranches. The large estates were called *latifundias*. A land tax— a *fôro*—

was a type of quit rent paid on the *sesmarias*. In order to acquire a land grant in colonial Brazil it was necessary to be a Roman Catholic or to be willing to convert to Catholicism. These records can be found in federal, state, and municipal public archives, some of which are:

➤ Arquivo Público, Minas Geraes
➤ Arquivo do Distrito Federal, Brasília
➤ Arquivo do Distrito Federal, Rio de Janeiro
➤ Arquivo Público. Rio Grande do Sul, Porto Alegre
➤ Arquivo Público, São Paulo
➤ Arquivo Público, Pernambuco
➤ Arquivo Público, Bahia
➤ Arquivo Público, Mineiro, Belo-Horizonte

The National Archives has abstracted and published many of the early plantation records, such as Bezerra, Alcides. "Synopsis das Sismarias Registradas nos Livros Existentes no Archivo da Thesouraria de Fazenda da Bahia." *Publicacões deo Arquivo Nacional* XXVII (synopsis of the Acts of Allotment registered in the books existent in the Exchequer of the Plantation of Bahia).

Suggested Reading

Alden, David. *The Colonial Roots of Modern Brazil* (Berkeley: University of California Press, 1973).

Arquivo Nacional. *Catálogo dos Arquivos Brasileiros* (Rio de Janeiro: The Archive, 1977, film 1218975). Inventory of Brazilian archives; facsimiles of catalog cards, each card listing the name of an archive, its address, founding date, and brief description of its document collections.

Arquivo Nacional. *Guia Brasileiro de Fontes para a História da África, Daescravidão Negrae do Negro na Sociedade Atual: Fontes Arquivistas.* 2 Vols. (Rio de Janeiro: The Archive, 1988). A directory of Brazilian archival resources for a study of Africa, black slavery in Brazil, and the place of blacks in contemporary society.

Arquivo Público Estadual de Pernambuco. *Documentos do Arquivo: Presidentes de Províncias* (Recife: Secretária do Interior e Justiça, Arquivo Público Estadual, 1937). Documents housed in the Arquivo Público Estadual de Pernambuco which deal with the provincial presidents of northeastern Brazil, as well as Santa Catarina.

Bacellar, Carlos de Almeida Prado. *Família, Herança e Poder em São Paulo, 1765–1855* (São Paulo: Universidade de São Paulo, CEDHAL, 1991). Social-demographic study of the establishment, growth, and development during the colonial period of wealthy families in western São Paulo.

Barreto, Carlos Xavier Paes. *Os Primitivos Colonizadores Nordestinos e Seus Descendentes* (Rio de Janeiro: MELSO, 1960, fiche 6030568). The first colonizers of the Brazilian northeast and their descendants.

Bloom, Herbert I. *A Study of Brazilian Jewish History 1623–1654, Based Chiefly Upon the Findings of the Late Samuel Oppenheim* (n.p.: American Jewish Historical Society, 1934, film 1162475).

Boxer, C.R. *The Dutch in Brazil, 1624–1654* (Oxford: Oxford University Press, 1957).

Brotero, Frederico de Barros. *Tribunal de Relação e Tribunal de Justiça de São Paulo: Sob o Ponto de Vista Genealógica: Aditamentos a Silva Leme* (São Paulo: n.p., 1944). Genealogy of magistrates and ministers of the Tribunal de Relação and the Tribunal de Justiça in São Paulo.

Burns, E. Bradford. *A History of Brazil.* 3rd ed. (New York: Columbia University Press, 1993).

Córdova-Bello, Eleazar. *Compañías Holandesas de Navegación: Agentes de la Colonización Neerlandesa* (Seville: Escuela de Estudios Hispano Americanos, 1965). The Dutch navigation companies as agents for Dutch colonization in Brazil, Curaçao, and Guyana during the seventeenth to nineteenth centuries.

Metcalf, Alida Christine. *Families of Planters, Peasants, and Slaves: Strategies for Survival in Santana de Paraíba, Brazil, 1720–1820* (Austin: University of Texas at Austin, 1983).

Monbeig, Pierre. *Pionniers et Planteurs de São Paulo* (Paris: Librairie Armand Colin, 1952). Immigration to and colonization of São Paulo.

Moonen, Francisco José. *Holandeses no Brasil: Verbetes do Novo Dicionário Holandês de Biografias* (Recife, Brazil: Universidade Federal de Pernambuco, 1968, film 0962230 ff.). Biographical sketches of Dutch in Brazil. A Portuguese translation by Moonen of applicable entries found in the ten volume work, *New Dutch Biographical Dictionary*, published in Leiden during the period 1911–37.

Prado, Caio. *The Colonial Background of Modern Brazil* (Berkeley: University of California Press, 1967).

Salvador, José Gonçalves. *Os Cristãos-Novos: Povoamento e Conquista do Solo Brasileiro* (São Paulo: Edição da Universidade de São Paulo, 1976). The New-Christians; the colonizing and conquest of Brazilian soil; Jewish migration to Brazil during the period, 1530–1680.

Silva Leme, Luéz Gonzaga da. *Genealogia Paulistana*. 9 Vols. (São Paulo: Duprat, 1903–5, film 0823694 ff.). Genealogy of families from São Paulo.

Tyler, Samuel Lyman. *Indians of Brazil, with Reference to Paraguay and Uruguay* (Salt Lake City: University of Utah, 1976).

Wätjen, Hermann. *Das Holländische Kolonialreich in Brasilien: Ein Kapitel aus der Kolonialgeschichte des 17. Jahrhunderts* (The Hague: Martinus Nijhoff, 1921). The Dutch colonial kingdom in Brazil: a capital during the colonial history of the seventeenth century.

The Guianas

Originally known as the Spanish Main, the present-day countries of Suriname, Guyana, and the overseas Department of French Guiana were discovered by Christopher Columbus in 1498. He named the area Guiana. Guyana — formerly British Guiana — was settled by the Dutch and the English. Suriname was first settled by the English but became a Dutch colony in the seventeenth century. French Guiana — also known as Cayenne — was a French colony which also had some English settlements.

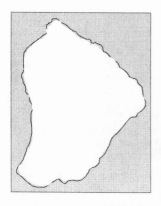

Guyane (French Guiana)

The Spanish attempted to settle this area in 1568 but were driven out by the Indians. In 1602 the King of France gave permission to create a Guiana colony. The first permanent settlement was made at Cayenne by the French North Company, but it failed after one year.

More French colonists from La Rochelle returned in 1664. Between 1651 and 1667, five hundred English and French slave plantations were established in the area of Suriname and French Guiana. Slavery was abolished in 1793 but was reintroduced nine years later. In the interim, France established a penal colony, the famous prison known as Devil's Island. Guiana remained under French control, except for the period from 1809 to 1817, when it was seized by Portugal.

Most of the colonial records for French Guyana are at the French National Archives, Section Outre-Mer, Paris, and the Library of the Université des Antilles et de la Guyane in Schoelcher, Martinique.

Eglise catholique.
* Mission des Îlets-du-Salut. Registre de sépultures, 1764–5 (film 1092737). Burial register for the Catholic mission on Îles-du-Salut.
* Saint-Sauveur, Cayenne. Registres paroissiaux, 1677–1830 (film 1092730 ff.). Parish registers of baptisms, marriages, and burials for Cayenne.

SEE ALSO
Brazil
Caribbean
France
French Antilles
Great Britain
The Netherlands
Neth. Antilles

- Notre-Dame, Kourou. Registres paroissiaux, 1717–97 (film 1092745). Parish registers of baptisms, marriages, and burials for Kourou.
Juge auditeur au Tribunal d'Instance. Tables alphabétiques, 1685–1830 (film 1092731 ff.). Alphabetical index to parish registers and early civil registration for French Guiana.
Île-du-Diable, Guyane: Poste Militaire, Commandant. Etat des personnes qui font décédés, 1766 (film 1092737). List of persons who died at the military post on Devil's Island.
The original records are at the French National Archives, Section Outre-Mer, Paris.

Guyana (British Guiana)

Guyana was first settled by the Dutch in 1581, who founded Georgetown in 1596. Dutch and English settlers founded Kijk-over-al in 1616. In 1621 the Dutch West India Company gained control of the colony. Great Britain seized the settlements at Berbice, Essequibo, and Demerara in 1781. The Dutch continued to immigrate to the area and founded the settlement of New Amsterdam in 1792. The entire colony came under British control in 1814.

Most of the colonial records for Guyana at the Algemeen Rijksarchief in 's-Gravenhage, The Netherlands, the Public Record Office (PRO) in Kew, Surrey, England and the National Library of Guyana in Georgetown, Guyana.[7]

The following church records have been filmed:
Eglise Wallonne Réformée, Demerara. Kerkelijke registers, 1758–1811 (film 0106810). Walloon Reformed Church registers of the colonies of Demerara and Essequibo. The original records are at the Algemeen Rijksarchief in 's-Gravenhage.

Many records remain in European archives. Berbice land grants, 1735–55, mortgages, 1737–63, tax returns, 1765–94, and court records, 1764–93, are in the Colonial Office records in the PRO in Kew, Surrey, England. Military

---

[7] The Public Record Office in London, hereinafter referred to as the PRO.

records, including muster lists, of British troops who served in the West Indies can also be found in this series. Some Dutch muster lists for 1796 are also at the PRO. There are also miscellaneous records dating from 1681.

Suriname (Dutch Guiana)

Suriname was claimed by Spain but not colonized. The first settlement was by the English in 1651. Jewish refugees from Brazil resettled in Suriname in 1654. It became a proprietorship under the English Crown in 1662, and in 1665 Paramaribo became the provincial capital. The Netherlands acquired Suriname from England in exchange for New Amsterdam (New York) in 1677. Moravian Brethren missionaries established a mission in 1735, and a Catholic mission was founded in 1787. The city government of Amsterdam, The Netherlands became two-thirds owner of Suriname in 1770. Suriname was under British control most of the time between 1791 and 1816.

The majority of the colonial records for Suriname are at the Algemeen Rijksarchief in 's-Gravenhage, The Netherlands and the Library of Anton de Kom Universiteit van Suriname in Paramaribo, Suriname.

The following church records of Suriname have been filmed:
Lutherse Kerk kerkelijke registers, 1787–1828 (film 0038836 ff.). Lutheran Church parish registers, baptisms, and marriage announcements.
Nederlands Hervormde Kerk kerkelijke registers, 1687–1828 (film 0038835 ff.). Dutch Reformed parish registers.
Rooms Katholieke Kerk kerkelijke registers, 1742–1830 (film 0038837 ff.). Roman Catholic Church parish registers, baptisms, and marriage intentions.
The original records of the above are at the Algemeen Rijksarchief in 's-Gravenhage, The Netherlands.

Some records of the Jewish community have been filmed:
* Hoogduits Joodse Gemeente. Geboorten, overlijden, 1773–1838 (film 0038837). Register of births and deaths in the German Jewish community in Suriname.
* Portugees Joodse Gemeente. Geboorten, overlijden, 1742–1828 (film 0038835 ff.). Register of births and deaths in the Portuguese Jewish community in Suriname.

The original records of the above are at the Algemeen Rijksarchief in 's-Gravenhage, The Netherlands.

An 1811 census of free and slave populations is at the PRO in Kew, Surrey, England. Also at the PRO are military records of the British occupation, 1799–1816, state papers, 1667–1832, and a passenger manifest of English subjects and slaves transported from Suriname to Jamaica, 1675.

Suggested Reading

Dalton, Henry G. *The History of British Guiana*. 2 Vols. (London: Longmans, 1855).

Gropp, Arthur Eric. *Guide to Libraries and Archives in Central America and the West Indies, Panama, Bermuda, and British Guiana* (New Orleans: Middle American Research Institute, Tulane University, 1941).

Meilink-Roelofsz, M.A.P. *Een Archiefreis in West-Indie: De Caribbean Archives Conference in Jamaica* ('s-Gravenhage: n.p., 1966). A description of the Caribbean Archives Conference in Jamaica. The public archives in The Netherlands Antilles and Suriname, and private archives of Dutch documents in the Antilles and Suriname.

Price, Richard and Sally Price. *Steadman's Surinam: Life in an Eighteenth-Century Slave Society* (Baltimore: Johns Hopkins University Press, 1992).

Storm van's Gravesande, Laurens. *The Rise of British Guiana* (Nedeln, Liechtenstein: Kraus Reprint Co., 1967, film 1224751). Extracts from the despatches written by Laurens Storm van's Gravesande to the directors of the Zeeland Chamber of the West India Company, 1738–72.

Swan, Michael. *British Guiana, the Land of Six Peoples* (London: HMSO, 1957).

Waddell, D.A.G. *The West Indies and the Guianas* (Englewood Cliffs, NJ: Prentice-Hall, 1967). 　Guiana.

Anaconda.

Belize/British Honduras

Belize — formerly British Honduras — was claimed as part of the Viceroyalty of Nueva España in 1543. English loggers from Jamaica founded a settlement on the Belize River in 1670. British Honduras was a colony of Great Britain until it gained independence in 1964.

Records for British Honduras can be found at the PRO in Kew, Surrey, England. These records include:

- War Office Papers (WO 55), list of persons who have received grants of land in George Town, no dates given.
- War Office Papers (WO 17), monthly returns of regiments stationed in British Honduras.
- Colonial Office Papers, 1744–1951 (CO 123), original correspondence, government gazettes, etc. For more information on the content of these records, see Great Britain.

The Society for the Propagation of the Gospel in Foreign Parts (SPG) in London holds journals of the Central American mission records (from 1701), Mosquito Shore papers (1769–85), and British Honduras papers (1812–47). There are additional SPG records in the Honduran Archives of the Royal Commonwealth Society Library, also in London.

Records of Spanish settlements can be found in the Archivo General de Indias in Seville, and are abstracted in Feldman, Lawrence H. *Anglo-Americans in Spanish Archives: Lists of Anglo-American Settlers in the Spanish Colonies of America, A Finding Aid* (Baltimore: Genealogical Publishing Co., 1991).

The National Archives of Belize in Belmopan date from the late eighteenth century, including British records, 1776–89, and are indexed. Saint John's College in Belize City is the home for the Belize Institute of Social Research and Action and has also become the depository for Jesuit records of Belize.

> **SEE ALSO**
> Great Britain
> Latin America
> Mexico
> Spain

Also in Belize City is the Central Library in the Bliss Institute, which contains published materials for historical research.[8]

---

[8] Kenneth J. Grieb, *Research Guide*, 119–20.

Suggested Reading

Belize (Oxford: Clio Press, 1980).

Bibliography of Books on Belize in the National Collection (Belize City: Central Library of Belize, 1977).

Bolland, O. Nigel. *The Formation of a Colonial Society: Belize, From Conquest to Crown Colony* (Baltimore: Johns Hopkins University Press, 1977).

Burdon, John Alder. *The Archives of British Honduras.* 3 Vols. (London: Sifton Praed and Co., Ltd., 1931).

Caiger, Stephen Langrish. *British Honduras, Past and Present* (London: George Allen and Unwin, 1951).

Calderón Quijano, José Antonio. *Belice, 1663–1821: Historia de los Establecimientos Britanicos del Rio Valis Hasta la Independencia de Hispanoamerica* (Seville: n.p., 1944).

Castellanos, Francisco Xavier. *La Intendencia de Yucatán y Belice* (Mexico: n.p., 1962).

Gregg, A.R. *British Honduras* (London: HMSO, 1968).

Winzerling, E.O. *The Beginning of British Honduras, 1506–1765* (New York: North River Press, 1946).

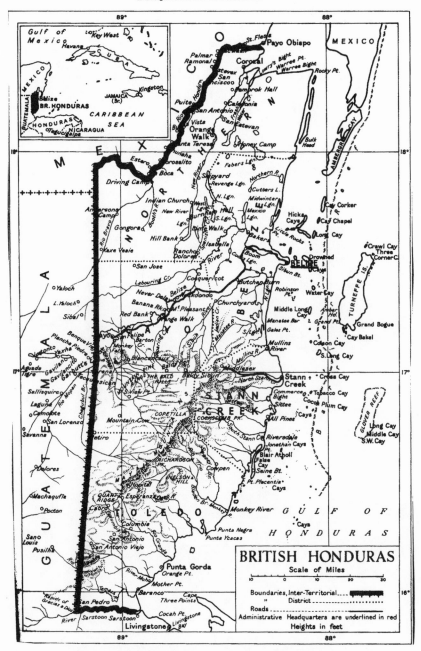

12 British Honduras (Colonial Office, 1948)

The Falkland Islands

Six hundred and forty kilometers off the southern coast of Argentina are a group of 600 islands known as the Falklands, which include the South Sandwich Islands and South Georgia. Originally claimed by Spain, the Dutch called them the Sebald Islands in 1600. The English renamed them the Falklands in 1690, in honor of the English Viscount Falkland.

The islands were first settled by the French from Saint-Malo at Port Louis, East Falkland, in 1764. They named the islands Las Malvinas, from the French *Les Malouines,* the nomenclature for sailors and seal hunters from Saint-Malo. The islands were returned to Spain for monetary compensation in 1770. Also in 1764, the British founded a colony at Port Egmont, on West Falkland, which they abandoned in 1774. Spain installed a governor at Saint Louis and renamed it Puerto del la Soledad. It was administered from Buenos Aires, Argentina from 1776 to 1806, and 1820 to 1833. After 1833 a British governor was appointed and the British resettled the islands. Since that time the islands have remained in British possession, although they continue to be disputed between Great Britain and Argentina.

Records for the Falklands are at the Public Record Office in Stanley, East Falkland, the Archivo General de la Nación in Buenos Aires, Argentina, and the PRO in Kew, Surrey, England. There are also military records for Spanish troops at the Archivo General de Simancas in Valladolid, Spain, under the viceroyalties of Río de la Plata from 1776 and Buenos Aires after 1787.

War Office, Great Britain. *Pension Returns, Falkland Islands [WO 22/248-9, 251]* (London: National Library of Australia, n.d., film 1483394). Pension returns for British troops, nineteenth century. The original records are at the PRO in Kew, Surrey, England.

Suggested Reading
Goebel, J. *The Struggle for the Falkland Islands* (New Haven: Yale University Press, 1982).

Muñoz Azpiri, José Luis. *Historia Completa de Las Malvinas* (Buenos Aires: Oriente, 1966).

SEE ALSO
Argentina
Great Britain
Spain

Part Three

The Caribbean

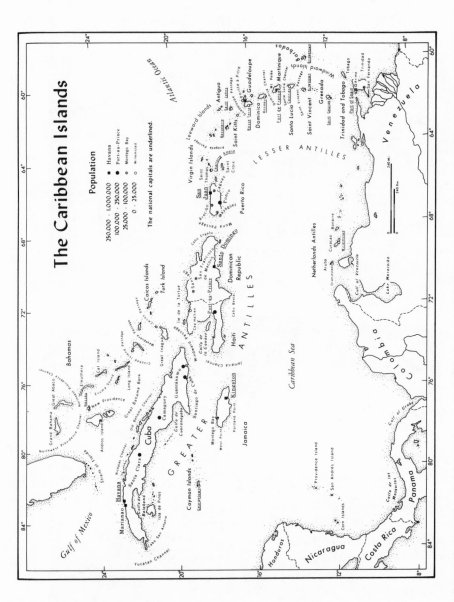

13 The Caribbean Islands (Cathryn L. Lombardi, et al., *Latin American History: A Teaching Atlas*. Madison: University of Wisconsin Press, 1983)

Colonial Records of the Caribbean

The islands of the Caribbean occupy a unique place in colonial history. Because they play a role in the settlement of North, South, and Central America, they provide a great resource to examine the European nations that competed for domination of the New World. The colonies were occupied first by Spain, and to a lesser extent Portugal, in the sixteenth century. Permanent settlements by England, Denmark, France, Germany, and The Netherlands were not successful until the seventeenth century.

The islands and the adjacent coastal and peninsular areas of mainland Central, North, and South America were contested throughout the seventeenth and eighteenth centuries. The mix of societies — both politically and culturally — created hybrid worlds that evolved into countries in a way that their European conquerors and colonizers could not have anticipated or imagined.

Of all the Americas — with the exception of Brazil — the colonizers of the Caribbean islands were the most responsible for building on the bones of the decimated native populations and the enslaved Africans, captured and sold to replace the dying indigenous people of the region. In the case of the Arawak Indians, they were completely eradicated by western disease and overexertion in the mines of Santo Domingo. The warlike Caribs managed to retain control of the windward islands into the eighteenth century, until the colonists eventually overran and subdued them.

Because of the mix of western cultures, the court systems, churches, and land distribution differ from island to island. As an individual island passed from the control of one European power to another, some elements of the language and culture of the previous conqueror would remain.

During most of the sixteenth century, Spain was the only nation with settlements in the West Indies, with the exception of Portugal's slave trade. After the conquest of Mexico (1519) and Peru (1531-3), many people left the islands for the mainland. The islands became ports of call for vessels traveling to and from the mainland. After 1528 King Charles V of Spain began to allow foreigners to enter the islands. This encouraged the settlement of some German, Italian, and Portuguese farmers and artisans.

SEE ALSO
Denmark
France
Great Britain
The Guianas
Latin America
The Netherlands
Spain

When the "Great Migration" from England began in the seventeenth century, along with freedom of worship, the European economic climate was a major factor in motivating emigration to the New World. The devaluation of money from the influx of gold and silver from Spanish possessions in New World, the loss of the European market for English cloth due to the religious wars, the increased cost of living and difficulty in earning a living, and the hardship to obtain land either by rent or purchase — all of these circumstances preceded the period of emigration.

In 1640 the English settlements in the West Indies were more prosperous than those in New England and Virginia. Most settlers in the English West Indian colonies were "small settlers" who rented or leased plantations from the Lord Proprietor of the island (who held the land for the King), or indentured servants, receiving a small parcel of land after three to five years of bound servitude. Island colonies were founded as tobacco plantations and were also important for crops such as dye-stuffs, ginger, cacao, and citrus.

Geographic Division

The Greater Antilles
Cuba
Hispaniola: Dominican Republic and Haiti
Jamaica
Puerto Rico

The Lesser Antilles
Windward Islands
Aruba
Barbados
Bonaire
Curaçao
Dominica
Grenada
Martinique
Saint Lucia
Saba

Saint Vincent and the Grenadines
Trinidad and Tobago
Leeward Islands
Anguilla
Antigua and Barbuda
British Virgin Islands: Caymans, Tortola, Turks and Caicos
Guadeloupe: Guadeloupe, Marie-Galante, Saint Martin, Saint-Barthélemy, La Désirade
Montserrat
Saint Eustatius
Saint Kitts and Nevis
U.S. Virgin Islands: Saint Thomas, Saint Croix, Saint John

The Bahamas and Bermuda

The islands of the Caribbean can be divided into three areas: Greater Antilles, Lesser Antilles, and the Bahamas (Lucayos). Within the Lesser Antilles are the two groups of islands known as the Windwards and the Leewards. Only two islands remain divided between two countries: Hispaniola by Haiti and the Dominican Republic, and Saint Martin by France and The Netherlands. Bermuda actually lies within the Atlantic Ocean, not the Caribbean Sea.

The Dutch, French, and Spanish tradition called the islands leeward and windward, according to the direction of the northeast trade winds from the South American mainland. The Windward Islands were considered all the islands between Puerto Rico and Trinidad. The British split the islands by the strength of the trade winds, dividing the islands from Dominica southward as windward, and those to the north as leeward. The use of the terms windward and leeward here are in the context of the British colonial tradition and do not reflect nineteenth- and twentieth-century governments.

Frequent Change of Hands

Because of the many European wars, the islands were continually being, captured, ceded, occupied, evacuated, and resettled by the Spanish, Dutch, English, French, and to a lesser extent the Danes and Swedes. Most of the islands were originally inhabited by the Arawak and Carib Indians; with little exception most Amerindians did not survive European settlement. The following list gives a rough idea of who controlled what from the time of western settlement to the end of the eighteenth century.

Anguilla. England, 1650, France, 1666, England, 1671, France, 1689, Great Britain, 1713.

Antigua. England, 1631, France, 1666, England, 1671, Moravian settlement added in 1754.

Aruba. The Netherlands, 1634.

Bahamas. England, 1645, Spain, 1684, England, 1694, pirates from Spain and France, 1703, Great Britain, 1708.

Barbados. England, 1627.

Barbuda. England, 1629, France, 1666, England, 1671.

Bermuda. England, 1612.

Bonaire. The Netherlands, 1634.

Cuba. Spain, 1511.

Curaçao. The Netherlands, 1634.

Dominica. England and France, 1627, neutral, 1748, Great Britain, 1756, France, 1778, Great Britain, 1783.

Dominican Republic. see Hispaniola.

Grenada. England, 1609, France, 1650, Great Britain, 1762, France, 1779, Great Britain, 1783.

Guadeloupe. France, 1635, Great Britain, 1759, France, 1763.

Haiti. see Hispaniola.

Hispaniola (Dominican Republic/Haiti). Spain, 1493, France takes over western end of island, 1697.

Jamaica. Spain, 1509, England, 1655.

Martinique. France, 1635, Great Britain, 1762, France, 1763.

Montserrat. England and Ireland, 1632, France, 1666, England, 1671.

Nevis. England, 1628.

Providence Island. England, 1630, Spain, 1641.

Puerto Rico. Spain, 1508.

Saba. The Netherlands, 1634.

Saint Bartholomew. France, 1648, Sweden, 1784, France, 1878.

Saint Kitts (Saint Christopher). England, 1623, France with England, 1625, France, 1666, England, 1667, France, 1689, Great Britain, 1713.

Saint Croix. England, The Netherlands, and France, 1625, England, 1645, France, 1650, Denmark 1733.

Saint-Domingue. see Hispaniola.

128 *The Caribbean*

Saint Eustatius. The Netherlands, 1600.
Saint John. Denmark, 1672.
Saint Lucia. France, 1639, England, 1663, France, 1667, Great Britain and France, 1713, France, 1723, neutral, 1748, Great Britain, 1756, France, 1763, Great Britain, 1778, France, 1783.
Saint Martin. France and The Netherlands, 1648.
Saint Thomas. Denmark, 1672.
Saint Vincent. England, 1627, neutral, 1660, Carib Indians, 1672, Great Britain, 1722, neutral, 1748, Great Britain and

France, 1756, Great Britain, 1763, France, 1779, Great Britain, 1783.
Tobago. England, The Netherlands, and France, 1632, neutral, 1748, Great Britain, 1763, France, 1781, Great Britain, 1793.
Tortola. The Netherlands, 1666, England, 1672.
Tortuga. Buccaneers from England, France, The Netherlands, Portugal, and Spain, 1630, Spain, 1635.
Trinidad. Spain, 1509, French settlement added in 1777, Great Britain, 1797.

Suggested Reading

Augier, F.R. and S.C. Gordon. *Sources of West Indian History* (London: Longman Caribbean, 1980).

Carr, Peter. *Caribbean Historical and Genealogical Bibliography* (San Luis Obispo, CA: TCI Resources, 1996).

Carter, E.H., G.W. Digby, and R.N. Murray. *History of the West Indian Peoples.* Book III: *From Earliest Times to the Seventeenth Century* (Sunbury-on-Thames, England: Thomas Nelson and Sons, Ltd., 1959).

Chittwood, Oliver Perry. *A History of Colonial America* (New York: Harper and Brothers, 1931).

Coke, Thomas. *A History of the West Indies, Containing the Natural, Civil and Ecclesiastical History of Each Island: With an Account of the Missions Instituted in Those Islands, from the Commencement of Their Civilization, but More Especially of the Missions Which Have Been Established in That Archipelago by the Society Late in Connexion with the Reverend John Wesley.* 3 Vols. (Liverpool: Nutter, Fisher, and Dixon, 1808–11, film 1224517).

Durham, Harrier F. *Caribbean Quakers* (Hollywood, FL: Dukane Press, 1972).

Fortune, Stephen A. *Merchants and Jews: The Struggle for British West Indian Commerce, 1650–1750* (Gainesville: University of Florida Press, 1984).

Grannum, Guy. *Tracing Your West Indian Ancestors: Sources in the Public Record Office* (London: PRO Publications, 1995).

Grieb, Kenneth J. *Research Guide to Central America and the Caribbean* (Madison: University of Wisconsin Press, 1985).

Lowenthal, David. *West Indian Societies* (London: Oxford University Press, 1972).

Lucas, C.P. *Historical Geography of the British Colonies*. Vol. 2. *The West Indies* (Oxford: Clarendon Press, 1890).

Nauman, Ann K. *A Handbook of Latin American and Caribbean National Archives* (Detroit: Blaine Ethridge Books, 1983).

Newton, Arthur P. *The European Nations in the West Indies, 1493-1688* (London: A. and C. Black, 1933).

Oliver, Vere Langford. *Caribbeana*. 6 Vols. (London: Mitchell Hughes and Clarke, 1910-19, film 0038848 ff.). Contains a 1677-8 census for Saint Kitts and Nevis, 1716 and 1717 censuses for Anguilla, 1677-8 census for Montserrat. Also included are lists of wills proved in the Prerogative Court of Canterbury, 1628-1818, including abstracts for Saint Kitts, Nevis, Jamaica, and Barbados. All British subjects dying abroad who held land in England or Wales — including military personnel — would have wills proved in the Prerogative Court of Canterbury.

Taeuber, Irene Barnes. *General Censuses and Vital Statistics in the Americas: an Annotated Bibliography of the Historical Censuses and Current Vital Statistics of the Twenty-One American Republics, the American Sections of the British Commonwealth of Nations, the American Colonies of Denmark, France, and The Netherlands, and the American Territories and Possessions of the United States* (Washington, DC: USGPO, 1943).

Walne, Peter. *A Guide to Manuscript Sources for Sources for the History of Latin America and the Caribbean in the British Isles* (London: Oxford University Press, 1973).

Waugh, Alec. *A Family of Islands: A History of the West Indies* (Garden City, NY: Doubleday and Co., 1964).

Williams, Eric. *From Columbus to Castro: The History of the Caribbean*. 2nd ed. (New York: Vintage Books, 1995).

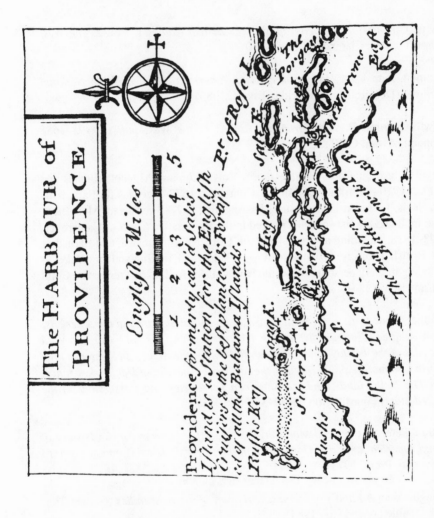

14 Map of the harbor of Providence (Department of Archives, Ministry of Education and Culture, Nassau, Bahamas)

The Bahama Islands

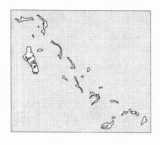 The Bahamas is an archipelago of almost 700 islands, only seventeen of which are inhabited. Christopher Columbus made his first landfall in the New World at the island of San Salvador in 1492. Spain did not attempt to colonize the Bahamas; they were used primarily as a source of labor. Colonists from Bermuda migrated to Eleuthra, Bahamas in 1648. More settlers from Bermuda arrived at the island of New Providence in 1666. In 1670 the Lord Proprietors of the Carolinas took over New Providence. The English settlements were sacked by Spanish forces in 1684, and most of the settlers fled to Jamaica and Massachusetts. The English resettled the Bahamas in 1694. Charles Town, Bahamas — renamed Nassau — was founded in 1695. In 1703 the islands were attacked again by French and Spanish from Cuba. After a period to rebuild, the Bahamas became a Crown colony in 1718.

The earliest surviving parish registers are from the parish of Christ Church. The parish was formed in 1670, but records only exist from 1744. The original records though 1803 are at the Public Record Office, Bahamian Archives, in Nassau.

Other manuscripts at the Public Record Office in Nassau include:
- Register of freed slaves, eighteenth and nineteenth centuries.
- Slave trials and manumissions, 1740–1834. The first slave manumissions appear in records as early as 1733.
- Records of supreme, general, chancery, vice-admiralty, bankruptcy, common pleas, and divorce courts from 1788.
- Land documents and index from 1792.
- Will index, 1700–1944 (film 0223469 ff.).
- Civil registration from 1799.
- Land grants from New Providence and the Out Islands from 1785.
- Mortgages, bonds, bills of sale, deeds of gift, powers of attorney, etc., 1764–1882 (Nassau: Dakota Southern Microfilm, Inc., 1955–6, film 0223445 ff.).

SEE ALSO
Bermuda
Caribbean
Cuba
Florida
Great Britain
Spain

The first census of the Bahamas — dated 1671 — names the freemen listed in A. T. Bethell's *Early Settlers of the Bahamas and Colonists of North America* (1937. Reprint. Baltimore: Clearfield Co., 1992). The information was taken from a registry book in the Bahamian Archives in Nassau; the original document appears lost.

Wood, David E. *A Guide to Selected Sources for the History of the Seminole Settlements at Red Bays, Andros, 1817–1980* (Nassau: Department of Archives, 1980). Contains records of baptisms, marriages, and other information of Seminole Indians living on Andros Island who came originally from the state of Florida.

The following records can be found at the PRO in Kew, Surrey, England:
- Colonial Office Papers (CO 23/25) includes censuses from 1731 and 1734, tax list for 1734, 1784 list of Loyalists households arriving in the Bahamas.
- High Court of Admiralty records, 1742–3, including the Acts of the Assembly of New Providence (HCA 30).
- Vice-Admiralty Court records, 1673–1859 (HCA 49).
- War Office Papers: 1660–1868, military returns, muster and pay lists for the West Indian regiments, correspondence regarding West Florida.
- Board of Treasury Commissioners: records for Loyalist claims dating from 1777–1841 (T 797), 1780–1835 (T 50), 1776–1831 (AO 12), 1780–1835 (AO 13), 1795–1846 (AO 14).
- Privy Council Office plantation books, 1678–1806 (PR 5).
- Home Office denizations and naturalizations, 1789–1871 (HO 1).[9]

The University of Florida in Gainesville has filmed, in the *Caribbean Serials Titles,* the earliest newspaper, *Bahamas Gazette,* published from 1784 to 1857. This contains many advertisements for runaway slaves. The films are available at the University, the Public Records Office in Nassau, the Library of Congress in Washington, DC, and other libraries. The Public Library in Nassau has both printed and microfilm copies.

Some records of the first settlers from Bermuda at Eleuthra can be found at the Bermuda Library in Hamilton. These records date from the 1650s.

The South Carolina Historical Society has a manuscript collection of Commissioners of Trade and Plantations, 1719–40.

---

[9] For a complete list see D. Gail Saunders, *Guide to Records of the Bahamas* (Nassau: Government Printing Office, 1983), 72–80.

The archives in Spain also hold material relating to the Bahamas. One of the more important collections is at the Archivo General de Indias in Seville, and is included in the *Papers of Cuba* regarding the seizure and surrender of the Bahamas in the 1780s, the seizure of the islands in 1703, and slave returns relating to Cuba and Louisiana (1799–1811).

Suggested Reading

Craton, Michael. *A History of the Bahamas* (Waterloo, Ontario: San Salvador Press, 1986).

Ingram, Kenneth E. *Manuscripts Relating to Commonwealth Caribbean Countries in the United States and Canadian Repositories* (Barbados: Caribbean Universities Press, 1975).

Johnson, Charlene Kozy. "Index of Land Grants in the Bahama Islands." *Caribbean Historical and Genealogical Journal* II 1(January 1994): 7–8. Abstract from Old Series Record Books, 1778–1850 (film 0223445 ff.), at the Public Record Office in Nassau, containing names of Georgia Loyalists.

Public Records Office, Nassau. *Supplement to the Guide to the Records of the Commonwealth of the Bahamas* (Nassau: Government Printing Office, 1980).

Saunders, D. Gail. *Slavery in the Bahamas, 1648–1748* (Nassau: The Nassau Guardian, 1985).

Saunders, D. Gail and E.A. Carson. *Guide to the Records of the Bahamas* (Nassau: Government Printing Office, 1973).

15 Barbados, 1640 (Ligon's History, 1657)

Barbados

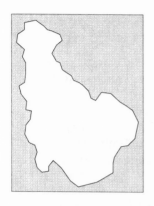

Barbados was colonized by English settlers in 1627. In 1649 many Royalists who escaped from England took refuge there. During the seventeenth and eighteenth centuries, Barbados was divided into eleven parishes.

Anglican parish registers exist from 1637 (with gaps), Methodist, Catholic, and Jewish records from 1660, and Moravian records from 1769. The following parish registers have been filmed:

Anglican Church. Saint Michael's parochial registers, 1637–1850 (1157951 ff.). Parish register transcripts of baptisms, marriages, burials, and indexes.

* Barbados parochial registers, 1660–1887 (film 1159602 ff.). Parish register transcripts of baptisms, marriages, burials, etc. for Wesleyan, Catholic, Moravian, Jewish, and congregations other than Anglican through 1886.

The original records are at the Department of Archives, Black Rock, Barbados.

Sanders, Joanne McRee. *Barbados Records, Baptisms, 1643–1800* (Baltimore: Genealogical Publishing Co., 1984).
Sanders, Joanne McRee. *Barbados Marriages, 1643–1800*. 2 Vols. (Baltimore: Genealogical Publishing Co., 1984).
The above are compilations of copies of parish registers in the Department of Archives, Black Rock.

The Department of Archives also holds Minutes of Assembly, 1650–present, land tax and militia rolls, deeds, 1640–1901, wills, 1647–1884, inventories, newspapers from 1784, and other records.

The Barbados Museum and Historical Society in Saint Michael has some plantation accounts and a large collection of published secondary sources.

The following parish registers are at the PRO in Kew, Surrey, England and begin with the dates indicated: Christ Church (1637), Saint George (1715), Saint John (1657), Saint Andrew (1825), Saint Joseph (1717), and Saint Peter (1779).

SEE ALSO
Bermuda
Caribbean
Great Britain

The Scottish Record Office in Edinburgh holds materials relating to Barbados in its manuscripts collections. An example of this would be the Seaforth Papers (GD46), which includes Admiralty Court papers, affairs of the Commercial Society of Barbados, and Attorney General letters containing capital crimes information (murders of Negroes, etc.).

Sanders, Joanne McRee. *Barbados Records, Wills and Administrations.* 3 Vols. (Marceline, MO: Walsworth Publishing, 1979–81). Covers the years 1639–1725.

Records of Jonathan Atkins, Governor, Barbados.
• The dispatches of Governor, Sir Jonathan Atkins, relating to the population of the island of Barbados, A.D. 1679–80 (film 1162149). Includes names of the landowners, with the number of acres, of white servants, and of Negroes, and the nominal rolls of the regiments of the horse and foot soldiers belonging to the island. Includes christenings and burials, 1678–9, and a list of tickets granted to people leaving the island in 1679. The original records are at the Department of Archives, Black Rock, Barbados.
• Census of Barbados, 1679 (film 1519514 ff.). List of landowners with quantity of land owned and servants; baptisms and burials, 1678–9; number of Negro slaves imported and sold, 1678–9; list of planters owning more than 200 acres, calendar of licenses to leave the island, 1678–9, with names of passengers, ships and ships' captains; nominal rolls of individual companies of the military force of Barbados; lists of masters of plantations, householders, tenants, etc., within the military companies; account of artillery; lists of judges and members of the King's Council and assembly. The original records are at the PRO in Kew, Surrey, England.

Hotten, John C. *Original Lists of Persons of Quality, and Others Who Went from Great Britain to the American Plantations, 1600–1700: Census Returns, Parish Registers, and Militia Rolls from the Barbados Census of 1679/80* (1880. Reprint. Baltimore: Genealogical Publishing Co., 1978, film 0784190). This does not include the parishes of Saint John, Saint Lucy, Saint Joseph, Saint Philip, and Saint Thomas, equal to about half of the population in the 1679/80 census. The censuses for 1678–80 and 1715 are at the PRO in Kew, Surrey, England.

Brandow, James C. *Omitted Chapters from Hotten's Original Lists of Persons of Quality, and Others Who Went from Great Britain to the American Plantations, 1600–1700: Census Returns, Parish Registers, and Militia Rolls from the Barbados Census of 1679/80* (Baltimore: Genealogical Publishing Co., 1982).

Kent, David, L. *Barbados and America* (Arlington, VA: C.M. Kent, 1980). A transcription of documents in the PRO in Kew, Surrey, England, including baptisms and burials, 1678-9, and census returns for 1680 and 1715.

Coldham, Peter Wilson. *The Complete Book of Emigrants, 1607-1660 . . .* (Baltimore: Genealogical Publishing Co., 1987). Contains listings of emigrants from Barbados to Virginia.

Suggested Reading

Alleyne, Warren and Henry Fraser. *The Barbados-Carolina Connection* (London: Macmillan Caribbean, 1988).

Brandow, James C. *Genealogies of Barbados Families* (Baltimore: Clearfield Co., 1997).

Chandler, M. *A Guide to Sources in Barbados* (Oxford: Basil Blackwell, 1965).

Genealogical Sources in Barbados (Salt Lake City: n.p., 1989, film 1224510).

Memoirs of the First Settlement of the Island of Barbados, and Other Carribbee Islands: with the Succession of the Governors and Commanders in Chief of Barbados to the Year 1742, Extracted from Ancient Records, Papers and Accounts Taken from Mr. William Arnold, Mr. Samuel Bulkly, and Mr. John Sumners, Some of the First Settlers . . . (London: Printed for E. Owen, 1743, film 0990299).

Pares, Richard. "Barbados History from the Records of the Prize Courts." *Journal of the Barbados Museum and Historical Society* XXXII (1966-7): 3-15.

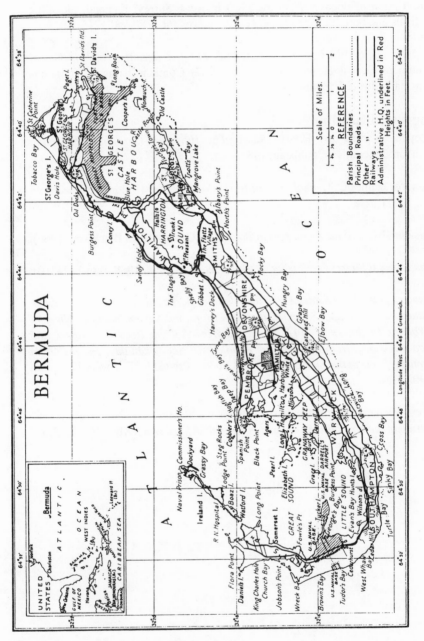

16 Bermuda (Colonial Office, 1948)

Bermuda

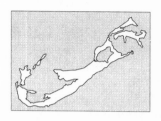

The Bermudas are sometimes called the Somers' Islands after Sir George Somers, whose ship *Sea Venture* was wrecked off these islands en route to Virginia in 1609 with a company of colonists. Saint George, Bermuda was founded in 1612, and the Bermuda Company was established in 1615. In 1646 Bermudians attempted to establish a colony on the Bahamian Island of Eleuthra. Trials for witchcraft began in Bermuda in 1651 and continued through 1696. In 1684 the Bermuda Company's charter was forfeited to the Crown and it became a Crown colony the next year.

Th oldest parish registers are of Port Royal, now called Southampton Parish (beginning in 1619). The dates of beginnings of other parish registers are Pembroke Parish (1645), Devonshire Parish (1668), and Saint George's (1710). These records are at the office of the Colonial Secretary in Hamilton. Baptisms and burials (dating from 1826) from the naval base at Ireland Island are in the Admiralty Records at the PRO in Kew, Surrey, England. A number of Irish convicts were transported to Ireland Island in the early nineteenth century.

Existing court records are:
- Chancery Court records, 1728–1841 (film 1909498).
- Court of Assizes records, 1694–1897 (film 1909478 ff). The Court of King's Bench, Court of Assize, Oyer and Terminer, General Goal Delivery, and Court of Common Pleas are included. The earlier records of the Court of Assizes from 1616–81 are not filmed. The records from 1647–71 include most of the witchcraft trials.
- Court of Quarter Sessions. Court records, 1790–1915 (film 1909499). There are also sessions, 1615–84, that have not been filmed. Volume IV contains information on Scots Highlanders and prisoners taken at the battle of Worcester and held in bondage in Bermuda.
- Probate Registry. Wills, inventories, and administrations, 1640–1954 (film 1667772 ff.). The original records are at the Bermuda Archives, Hamilton.

Colonial Secretary. Public records, 1612–1937 (film

SEE ALSO
Bahamas
Caribbean
Great Britain
Neth. Antilles
New France
Virginia

1857078 ff.). These records include
grants, deeds, bonds, bills, manumissions and bills of sale of slaves,
certificates of freedom, certificates
of naturalization, commissions,
deeds of gift, free passes of slaves,
powers of attorney, returns of
numbers of slaves and free black
people, shipping registers, and
oaths. The shipping registers, 1655–
71, and arrival lists to 1685 refer
mostly to passengers carried between Bermuda, Barbados, Eleuthra, Jamaica, and the settlement in
the Carolinas.

Some original records have been
lost, but the information has been
preserved in other sources. A
survey of the inhabitants by Governor Richard Norwood, taken in 1663 was lost,
but a copy was found in the British Museum in London in 1843.

English Tribes in Bermuda
In 1618 the Bermuda Company divi-
ded the islands into eight tribes, a
Biblical allusion to the Tribes of
Israel. The names of the tribes were:
➤ Bedfords Tribe (Hamiltons)
➤ Smiths Tribe
➤ Cavendish Tribe (Devonshire)
➤ Pembrookes Tribe
➤ Pagits Tribe
➤ Mansils Tribe (Warwicks)
➤ Southampton Tribe
➤ Sands Tribe
Each tribe was divided into fifty parts
called shares. These shares were
divided by lots cast in England.

The records of Richard Moore's government are gone, but their content was
recorded in Captain John Smith's, *The generall historie of Virginia, New
England and the Summer Isles: together with the true travels, adventures and
observations, and a sea grammar*. 2 Vols. (1627. Reprint. New York:
Macmillian & Co., 1907, film 1697615). The earliest council records of the
Bermuda Company can be found in *The Journal of John Winthrop, 1630–1649*
(1825. Reprint. Cambridge: Harvard University Press, 1996).

The Colonial Office Papers, 1574–1660, include information on transported
prisoners and proceedings against Quakers in Bermuda. These records were
published in an early account by Sampson Bond, *A Public Tryal of the Quakers
in Bermuda upon the First Day of May, 1678* (Boston, 1682).

Suggested Reading
Lefroy, John Henry. *Memorials of the Discovery and Early Settlement of the
Bermudas or Somers Islands, 1515–1685*. 2 Vols. (1877. Reprint. Toronto:
University of Toronto Press, 1981, film 1162479).

Rowe, Helen. *A Guide to the Records of Bermuda* (Hamilton: The Bermuda
Archives, 1980).

Hollis Hallett, A.C. *Early Bermuda Records, 1619–1826: A Guide to the Parish and Clergy Registers with Some Assessment Lists and Petitions* (Pembroke, Bermuda: Juniper Hill Press, 1991). Transcribed baptism, marriage, and burial entries from the earliest parish and clergy records in Bermuda.

Hollis Hallett, A.C. *Early Bermuda Wills, 1629–1835: Summarized and Indexed, a Genealogical Reference Book* (Pembroke, Bermuda: Juniper Hill Press, 1993).

Mercer, Julia E. *Bermuda Settlers of the Seventeenth Century: Genealogical Notes from Bermuda* (Baltimore: Genealogical Publishing Co., 1982).

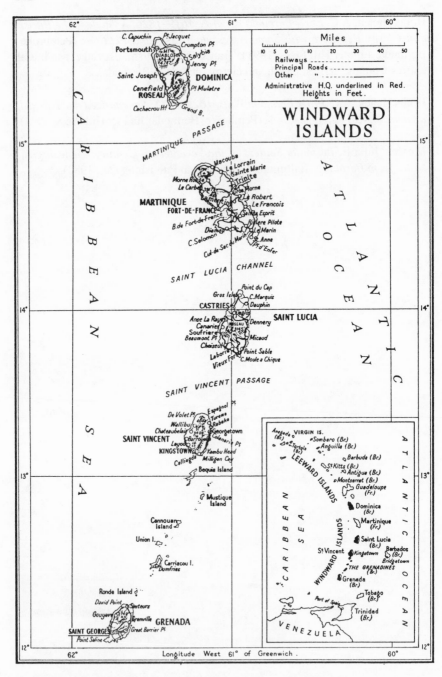

17 British Windward and Leeward Islands (Colonial Office, 1948)

The British Leeward Islands

Antigua and Barbuda

Antigua was colonized by English settlers from Saint Kitts in 1632. It came under the control of France in 1666 and was returned to England in 1671. Barbuda was colonized by the English in 1629. It was later sold to the Codrington family who held it as private property from 1685 until the late nineteenth century. Records for Antigua and Barbuda are at the National Archives in Saint John's and the PRO in Kew, Surrey, England.

Court of Common Pleas, Antigua.
* Court records, 1676–1907 (film 1855671 ff.). Record of enrollment books, which include deeds, wills and other estate documents, account books, mortgages, powers of attorney, documents subscribed before notaries, and other legal documents filed with the court.
* Acts, 1742–50 (film 1873639).

The original records are at the Antigua and Barbuda National Archives, Saint John's.

Colonial Office, Great Britain. Correspondence from Antigua and the Leeward Islands with the Board of Trade, 1727–30, 1734–5, 1744–7 (London: PRO, 1995, film 1818355 ff./ CO 1). The records include parish records, cargo and passenger lists, court records, taxation lists, and military records. The parish registers for Antigua include:
* Saint Peter. Baptisms and burials, 1726–7
* Saint Paul. Baptisms and burials, 1733–4, 1742–5
* Saint Mary. Baptisms and burials, 1733–4, 1742–5
* Saint John. Baptisms and burials, 1739–45
* Saint George. Baptisms and burials, 1739–45

The original records are at the PRO in Kew, Surrey, England.

> **SEE ALSO**
> Caribbean
> France
> French Antilles
> Great Britain

Saint Kitts and Nevis

Saint Kitts (Saint Christopher) was settled by England in 1623 and Nevis in 1628. French settlers from Normandy and Brittany arrived at Saint Kitts in 1625. From that time until 1727, the two countries competed for control of the islands. Records for Saint Kitts and Nevis are in the French

National Archives, Section Outre-Mer, Paris, the PRO in Kew, Surrey, England, and the Saint Kitts Archives in Basseterre.

Rossignol, Bernadette. *Recensement de l'Île de Saint-Christophe, Anné 1671: Liste des Personnes Figurant Dans le Terrier* (Paris: CGHIA, 1987). 1671 census of Saint Christopher (Saint Kitts).

The following Anglican Church parish registers (film 1818355 ff.) are at the PRO in Kew, Surrey, England:
Nevis:
- Saint Paul. Baptisms and burials, 1726-7
- Saint John. Baptisms and burials, 1733-4
- Saint Thomas. Baptisms and burials, 1733-4
- Saint George. Baptisms and burials, 1733-4
- Saint James. Baptisms and burials, 1740-5
Saint Christopher:
- Christ Church, Nichola Town. Baptisms and burials, 1721-30, 1733-40
- Saint John, Cabesatère. Baptisms and burials, 1721-30
- Saint Mary, Cayon. Baptisms and burials, 1721-30, 1733-45, marriages, 1738-45
- Saint George, Basseterre. Baptisms and burials, 1733-4, 1743-5
- Saint Ann, Sandy Point. Baptisms and burials, 1733-4

Anglican Church, Saint George (Saint George Basseterre). Church records, 1747-1968 (film 1699145 ff.).The original records are at the Registrar's Office in Basseterre.
Eglise Catholique. Les tables alphabétiques pour les paroisses de Saint-Pierre de Cayonne, La Cabesatère, et Sainte-Anne à l'Ouest sur l'Île de Saint-Christophe, 1682-1777 (film 0772740). Parish registers indexes for Saint Christopher churches. The original records are at the French National Archives, Section Outre-Mer, Paris.

Oliver, Vere Langford. *The Registers of Saint Thomas, Middle Island, Saint Kitts* (London: Mitchell, Hughes, and Clarke, 1915, film 1162487). Baptisms, 1729-1824, marriages, 1729-1832, burials, 1729-1802.

The Saint Kitts Archives in Basseterre holds the following and other records of genealogical value:
- Deeds, 1805-34
- Manumissions, 1780-1826
- Slave registers, 1818-35
A list of owners of French land in Basseterre and Cabesatère, 1721, is at the

PRO in Kew, Surrey, England. An account of losses of English subjects sustained in the French invasion, 1706, is also at the PRO.

Montserrat

Montserrat was first settled by English colonists from Saint Kitts and Irish colonists recruited directly from Ireland in 1632. A group of Irish Catholics who attempted to settle in Virginia in 1634 were also received at Montserrat.

The following Anglican Church parish registers (film 1818355 ff.) are at the PRO in Kew, Surrey, England:

- Saint Anthony. Baptisms, burials, and marriages, 1721–9
- Saint George. Baptisms, burials, and marriages, 1721–9
- Saint Patrick. Baptisms, burials, and marriages, 1721–9
- Various parishes, baptisms and burials, 1739–45

The Courthouse in Plymouth, Montserrat holds some early records, including deeds.

Anguilla

Anguilla was first colonized by the English in 1650. The island was seized by France from 1666 to 1671 and 1689 to 1713. Some of the early records for Anguilla are kept at the archive of the Registry Office in Basseterre, Saint Kitts.

Anglican Church, Saint Mary's Parish. Parish registers, 1826–1974 (film 1667894 ff.). The original records are at the parish archive.

Suggested Reading

Baker, E.C. *A Guide to Records in the Leeward Islands* (Oxford: Basil Blackwell, 1965).

Oliver, Vere Langford. *Caribbeana*. 6 Vols. (London: Mitchell, Hughes, and Clarke, 1910–19, film 0038848 ff.). Contains a 1677–8 census for Saint Kitts and Nevis, 1716 and 1717 censuses for Anguilla, and a 1677–8 census for Montserrat. Also included are lists of wills proved in the Prerogative Court of Canterbury, 1628–1818, including abstracts for Saint Kitts, Nevis, Jamaica, and Barbados.

Oliver, Vere Langford. *The History of the Island of Antigua: One of the Leeward Caribbees in the West Indies, from the First Settlement in 1635 to the Present Time.* 3 Vols. (London: Mitchell, Hughes, and Clarke, 1894–9, film 1149539). This contains a census of Antigua, 1678, wills, land records, parish registers, etc.

SCENE IN THE WEST INDIES.

The British Windward Islands

Most of the Windward Islands remained inhabited by the Carib Indians until the eighteenth century. Saint Lucia and Saint Vincent were declared neutral in 1660 by treaty with the Caribs, and all the Windwards were declared neutral in 1748. During the rest of the century and into the next, control of the islands passed among the French, British, and Caribs.

Dominica

First colonized in 1627, the island of Dominica was declared neutral in 1748. Continuing French settlement provoked a British attack in 1756. The island did not come under complete British control until 1805. It was originally classified as a Leeward Island.

Supreme Court Registry.
Land records: deeds and indentures, 1765–1927 (film 1699413 ff.).
Wills, 1790–1938 (film 1699767 ff.).
The original records are at the Supreme Court Registry, Roseau, Dominica.

The Carnegie Free Library in Roseau holds deed books from 1765, Assembly Minute Books from 1787, Vice-Admiralty Court records from 1792, and other records. Slave registers exist from 1817–1934.

The Colonial Office Papers at the PRO in Kew, Surrey, England contain a 1766 list of lands given by concession to French inhabitants. There is also a list of quit rent rolls, 1790–1803.

Grenada

Grenada's first English colony in 1609 was unsuccessful. The first permanent settlement of Grenada was by French from Martinique in 1650. The island remained under French control until the British captured it in 1762. After changing hands to France again in 1779, it came under British control in 1783.

SEE ALSO
Acadia
Caribbean
France
French Antilles
Great Britain
Nova Scotia

Supreme Court. Registers of records, 1764–1931 (film 1563217 ff.). Registers of land and property transactions before the Court of Common Pleas and the Supreme Court of Grenada. British records cover the period 1764–1931; French records cover 1766–1904; there are also records in Spanish. The documents include mortgages, indentures, conveyances, sales and manumissions of slaves, wills, and other kinds of public records. The original records are at the Supreme Court of Grenada in Saint George.

The Colonial Office Papers at the PRO in Kew, Surrey, England contain land sales for Saint George, 1762–4, a 1772 list of landholders, and a 1763 slave tax list.

Saint Lucia

Unsuccessful settlements of Saint Lucia were attempted by the English and French before 1650. Declared neutral in 1660, the island became a dependency of Martinique in 1667. From 1713 until 1748 Saint Lucia was disputed by the British and French and was again declared neutral. It passed back and forth between the two European countries until it came under British control in 1803.

Greffe du Tribunal Civil, Sainte-Lucie. Tables alphabétiques des paroisses, 1775–89 (film 1093928). Alphabetical indexes to parish registers for Saint Lucia during French administration. The original records are at the French National Archives, Section Outre-Mer, Paris.

The Saint Lucia Archaeological and Historical Society has an archive which holds most of the early records that are available locally.

The Colonial Office Papers at the PRO in Kew, Surrey, England contain an 1811 census for Saint Lucia and a slave register, various years, arranged by family and surname of the mother.

Saint Vincent and the Grenadines

From 1627 to 1783 the British and French competed over control of Saint Vincent. It became a British colony in 1783.

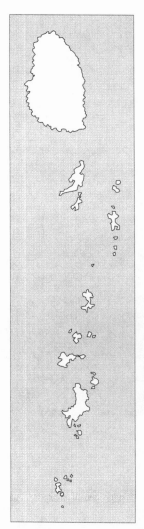

Ross, Richard A. and Lillian J. Ross. *Parish Records of Saint George Parish, Church of England, Saint Vincent, West Indies.* 4 Vols. (n.p., n.d., film 1162485). Extracts of parish registers of Saint George parish, Saint Vincent, 1765-1870.

The National Library in Kingstown holds most of the materials of archival and historical interest that are located in Saint Vincent itself. There are other materials in private collections.

The Colonial Office Papers at the PRO in Kew, Surrey, England contain a 1768-7 register of land and plantation grants, and claims by French inhabitants, 1766. There are also miscellaneous records, 1668-1873.

Suggested Reading

Atwood, T. *History of the Island of Dominica* (London: n.p., 1791).

Baker, E. C. *A Guide to Records in the Windward Islands* (Oxford: Basil Blackwell, 1968, fiche 6030570).

Brizan, George. *Grenada, Island of Conflict: From Amerindians to People's Revolution, 1498-1979* (London: Zed Books, Ltd., 1984).

Jesse, C. *Outlines of Saint Lucia's History* (Saint Lucia: Saint Lucia Archaeological and Historical Society, 1964).

Shepard, C. *Historical Account of the Island of Saint Vincent* (London: n.p., 1831).

CITY OF HAVANA, AND MORO CASTLE.

Cuba

 Cuba was named Juana by Christopher Columbus in 1492. Its name was changed to Fernandina in 1515, but has been known as Cuba since that time. The first cities founded were Baracoa (1512), Bayamo (1513), Santiago de Cuba (1514), and Havana (1519). It became a Captaincy General in 1607. The *Audiencia* of Santo Domingo was transferred to Cuba in 1800. Two years later, French and Spanish families from Louisiana began to migrate to Cuba.

Parroquiales (parish registers) date from 1514 and include baptisms, marriages, deaths and burials, and other records. The *Obispado de Cuba* (Bishopric of Cuba) was created in 1520 and sat at Santo Domingo (Hispaniola). They can be found in archdiocesan, diocesan, and parish archives throughout Cuba. Some parish registers have been filmed and are available at the Saint Augustine Historical Society in Saint Augustine, Florida.

Teste, Ismael. *Historia Eclesiastica de Cuba.* 5 Vols. (n.p., n.d.). History of all the parishes in Cuba.

Stibi, Ferdinand. *El Libro de Barajas de Catedral de Habana* (Madrid: Hidalguía, 1974, film 0973150). Alphabetical index of the first parish register for the cathedral of Havana contains marriages, 1588–1622, and baptisms, 1590–1600.

Santa Cruz y Mallen, Francisco Xavier de. *Registros Parroquiales, 1619–1874: Extractos de Registros de la Catedral de La Habana* (n.p., n.d., film 1162426). Extracts of parish registers from the Cathedral of Havana.

Records of the Inquisition from the sixteenth century are at the Universidad de La Habana in Havana and the Archivo Histórico Nacional in Madrid. For more information on records of the Inquisition, see the section on sources of colonial records in Spain.

Padrones (civil census records) date from 1774 and *matrículas* and *padrones* (ecclesiastical censuses) from the sixteenth century. The earliest civil census

SEE ALSO
Caribbean
Great Britain
Hispaniola
Latin America
Louisiana

records have been lost. Ecclesiastical censuses are found with the parish registers in church archives.

Notariales (notarial records) date from 1578 and can be found at the Archivo de Protocolos in the Archivo Nacional de Cuba in Havana, the municipal archives in Santa Clara, Santiago de Cuba, and Trinidad.

Rojas, Maria Teresa de. *Indice y Extractos del Archivos de Protocolos de la Habana* (Havana: Imprenta Ucar, Garcia y Cia). Notarial records from 1578–91.

De Gobernación, de las provincias, y municipales (governmental and municipal records) dating from 1536 are at the Archivo Nacional de Cuba in Havana and various municipal archives throughout Cuba. As of 1997, it is still illegal for a U.S. citizen to enter Cuba directly from the United States. Those seeking entry from other locations must first obtain authorization from the Cuban Academy of Sciences to use the Archivo Nacional.

There are also records for Cuba in the Foreign Office State Papers at the PRO in Kew, Surrey, England. For more information, see the section on colonial records in Great Britain.

Court records have been published in a series called *Gaceta de La Habana* (Madrid: n.p., n.d.). The volumes are available at:
> The Library of Congress, Washington, DC
> The University of Miami, Miami, Florida
> Yale University, New Haven, Connecticut
> The Boston Public Library, Boston, Massachusetts
> The Biblioteca Nacional de Cuba, Havana

Leuchsenring, Emilio Roig de. *Actas Capitulares del Ayuntamiento de la Habana.* Vol. 1 (Havana: Colección de documentos para la Historia de Cuba). Agreements and decisions made by the colonial government officials of Havana, 1550–65.

Malagón Barceló, Javier. *El Distrito de la Audiencia de Santo Domingo en los Siglos XV a XIX.* 2nd ed. (Santiago de los Caballeros, DR: Universidad Católica Madre y Maestra, 1977, fiche 6030607). The district of the *Audiencia* de Santo Domingo from the fifteenth to the nineteenth centuries, including a catalog of documents dealing with the period 1708–1800 that are housed in the Archivo Nacional de Cuba in Havana.

De tierras y propiedades (land records) dating from 1516 are found in notarial, ecclesiastical, and municipal records throughout Cuba. The *merced* system, by which land is granted but not owned, was used until 1729. In 1819 personal ownership of land was granted to lands previously given by *merced.* Grants were recorded in the municpal records and also by a notary. *Realengos* (royal grants) from 1682 can be found at the Archivo Nacional de Cuba in Havana.

Ruiz Cadalso, A. and A. Segura Cabrera. *Merecedes y Centros de Haciendas Circulares Cubanas* (Havana: n.p., 1916).

The Biblioteca National de Cuba in Havana includes among its holdings the Cuba Collection, which dates from the early sixteenth century.

In the Archivo General de Indias in Seville are a series of manuscripts entitled *Papeles de Cuba* (Papers of Cuba*),* which contain administrative and judicial manuscripts. Copies of these papers are at the North Carolina Department of Archives and Records in Raleigh and the Library of Congress in Washington, DC. Another series, *Papeles de Santo Domingo,* is the record of the exchange of Spanish and British prisoners at Havana, 1791, by three British truce ships. The lists of the prisoners are included.

Suggested Reading

Aimes, Hubert. *A History of Slavery in Cuba* (New York: G. Putnam and Sons, 1907).

Archivo Nacional de Cuba. *Catálogo de los Fondos de Las Floridas* (Havana: The Archive, 1944).

Archivo Nacional de Cuba. Indices y catálogos, 1532–1865 (film 1410927). Indexes and catalogs in the Archivo General de la Nación in Santo Domingo, Dominican Republic.

Bermúdez Plata, Cristóbal. *Catálogo de Documentos de la Sección Novena del Archivo General de Indias* (Seville: Escuela de Estudios Hispano Americanos, 1949). Catalog of the section of the Archivo General de Indias in Seville, Spain, containing records for Santo Domingo, Cuba, Puerto Rico, Louisiana, Florida, and Mexico.

"A Bibliography of Miscellaneous Sources for Cuban Research." *Caribbean Historical and Genealogical Journal* I (April 1993): 20–3.

Carbonell, Nestor and Emeterio S. Santovenia. *El Ayunmiento de La Habana, Noviembre 16, 1519–Noviembre 16, 1919* (Havana: Imprenta Seoane y Frenandez, 1919).

Carr, Peter E. *Guide to Cuban Genealogical Research: Records and Sources* (San Bernardino, CA: The Cuban Index, 1991).

Pérz, Luis A. *A Guide to Cuban Collections in the United States* (Westport, CT: Greenwood Press, 1991).

Pérez, Luis Marino. *Guide to the Materials for American History in Cuban Archives* (Washington, DC: Carnegie Institute, 1907. Reprint. New York: Kraus Reprint Corporation, 1967).

Platt, Lyman D. *Cuba General Research Guide* (Salt Lake City: Institute of Genealogy and History for Latin America, 1991).

Santa Cruz y Mallen, Francisco Xavier de. *Historia de Familias Cubanas* (Havana: Edition Hercules, 1940, fiche 6030546). History of Cuban families.

Santovenia y Echaide, Emeterio Santiago. *Fundadores de la Nación Cubana* (Miami, FL: Junta Educacional Patriótica Cubana, 1967). Founders of the Cuban nation.

Suchlicki, Jaime. *Historical Dictionary of Cuba* (Metuchen, NJ: Scarecrow Press, 1988).

Wright, Irene Aloha. *The Early History of Cuba, 1492–1586* (New York: Macmillan & Co., 1916, film 1224515). This also contains information on the Bahamas.

The French Antilles

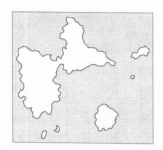

The islands of Martinique and Guadeloupe and dependencies comprise the group known as the French Antilles. The island of Saint Martin lies north of the British leewards among the Dutch Antilles and is shared by France and The Netherlands.

Guadeloupe

The islands that make up Guadeloupe and dependencies are Guadeloupe, Marie-Galante, Saint-Martin, Saint-Barthélemy, and La Désirade. Guadeloupe was first settled by the French in 1635. Saint Martin (Sint Maarten) was divided between the French and the Dutch in 1648 and remains so to the present day. Saint-Barthélemy was settled by the French in 1648 but was given to Sweden in 1784, which possessed it until 1887.

The Archives of Guadeloupe hold only records from 1912, with some microfilm copies of earlier records. All original records prior to this date are at the French National Archives, Section Outre-Mer, Paris. The exceptions are the records of the Swedish administration of Saint-Barthélemy, 1784–1878, and notarial records from 1759, which are at the Archives of Guadeloupe in Basse-Terre. There is also a reference library with published secondary sources.

Sources of information for both Guadeloupe and Martinique can be found at the Université de Antilles et de la Guyane, Point-Pitie, Guadeloupe. The Foreign Office Records, 1577 to 1780, at the PRO in Kew, Surrey, England contain state papers for Guadeloupe. For more information see the chapter on Great Britain.

Eglise Catholique, Notre-Dame, Saint-Barthélemy. Registres paroissiaux, 1682–1777 (film 0772740). Parish registers of baptisms, marriages, and burials for Saint-Barthélemy. Includes parish register indexes for Saint Christopher churches. The original records are at the French National Archives, Section Outre- Mer, Paris.

SEE ALSO
Acadia
British Windwards
Caribbean
France
Great Britain
The Guianas
Neth. Antilles
Nova Scotia

Martinique

The island of Martinique was first settled by French from Saint Kitts in 1635. The last of the native Carib Indians were driven out in 1660. Except for British occupation between 1794 and 1802 and 1809 and 1814, the island has remained under French control.

The following are examples of Catholic parish registers that have been filmed:

- Saint-Jean-Baptiste, Basse-Pointe. Registres paroissiaux, 1662–1830 (film 0771101 ff.). Parish registers of baptisms, marriages, and deaths for Basse-Pointe.
- Notre-Dame, Case-Pilote. Registres paroissiaux, 1675–1830 (film 0761453 ff.). Parish registers of baptisms, marriages, burials for Case-Pilote.
- Saint-Joseph, Le Prêcheur. Registres paroissiaux, 1665–1830 (film 0789111 ff.). Parish registers of baptisms, marriages, and burials for Le Prêcheur.

The original records are at the French National Archives, Section Outre-Mer, Paris.

The Société d'Histoire de la Martinique in Fort de France have identified more than 5,000 European immigrants from the seventeenth and eighteenth centuries. For more information see Hugh T. Law. *Tracing Your Ancestors from the U.S. to France* (Salt Lake City: Genealogical Society of Utah, 1969, fiche 6039359).

The Colonial Office Papers and the War Office Papers at the PRO in Kew, Surrey, England contain records of the British troops occupying Martinique, 1762-3.

Suggested Reading

Blanchard, Linn R. *Martinique: A Selected List of References* (Washington, DC: Library of Congress, 1942).

Bottin des Communes: Hameaux-Ecarts-Lieux-Dits, France Métropolitaine et Outre-Mer (Paris: Didot-Bottin, 1988). Gazetteer for France and the overseas departments of Guyane, Guadeloupe, Saint-Pierre-et-Miquelon, and Martinique.

Conseil Souverain de la Martinique, 1712–1791 (Fort-de-France, Martinique: The Archives, 1985). Analytical inventory of the Archives of Martinique.

Goddet-Langlois, Jean. *La Vie en Guadeloupe au XVIIe Siècle: Suivi du Dictionnaires des Familles Guadeloupénnes de 1635 à 1700* (Fort-de-France,

Martinique: Editions Exbrayat, 1991). Life in Guadeloupe in the seventeenth century, followed by a dictionary of families from 1635 to 1700.

Lore, Françoise. *Les Engagements à Nantes vers les Îles d'Amerique de 1690 à 1734* (Nantes: Impr. Contemporaine, 1987). Listing of indentured immigrants from France to the French West Indies, including Guadeloupe and Martinique.

Martinique Archives Départementales. *Guide des Archives de la Martinique* (Fort-de-France, Martinique: The Archives, 1978). Guide to the Archives of Martinique.

Petit-Jean Roget, Jacques and Eugéne Bruneau-Latouche. *Personnes et Famillies a la Martinique au XVIIe Siecle* (Fort-de-France, Martinique: Société d'Histoire de la Martinique, 1983).

Rennard, Joseph. *Historie Religieuse des Antilles Françaises des Origines à 1914, d'Après de Documents in Edits* (Paris: Société de l'Histore des Françaises, 1954). Religious history of the French Antilles to 1914, including Guadeloupe, Martinique, Dominica, Grenada, Saint Vincent, and Saint Lucia.

Robert, Walter Adolphe. *The French in the West Indies* (New York: Cooper Square Publishers, Inc., 1971).

18 Santo Domingo in 1673

Hispaniola: The Dominican Republic and Haiti

 The island of Hispaniola (La Isla Española) was discovered on Columbus' first voyage in 1492 and was the home of the first European colony in America. The first settlement was planted at Navidad in 1492 but did not survive. During the second voyage the settlement of Isabella was established. Santo Domingo was founded as the capital in 1498 and was the first permanent town in the New World. A viceroyalty was established in 1509 and an *audiencia* in 1511. In 1644 French colonists founded Port-de-Paix on the western end of the island. The island was divided between Spain and France in 1697. From 1795 to 1806 and 1822 to 1844, the French seized control of the entire island. The Republic of Haiti was established in 1822 and the Dominican Republic in 1844.

Santo Domingo / The Dominican Republic

The Archivo del Arzobispado de Santo Domingo (Archives of Santo Domingo) includes parish registers beginning in 1590, Libros de Capellanias, 1732–1815, records of bishops, a card file of clerics from 1494, and various correspondence, letters, and manuscripts.

Iglesia Católica, Santa María de la Encarnación. Registros parroquiales, 1590–1933 (film 0636797 ff.). Registers of baptisms, marriages, and deaths from the Cathedral Church of Santa María de la Encarnación, Santo Domingo. The original records are at the Cathedral in Santo Domingo. Many records before this time were destroyed.

Most of the earliest records of Santo Domingo were destroyed in 1586 by the English, led by Sir Francis Drake. In 1975 the records of the district of the *Real Audiencia* of Santo Domingo were transferred to Cuba, where they remain. Some are published in Malagón Barceló, Javier. *El Distrito de la Audiencia de Santo Domingo en los Siglos XV a XIX*. 2nd ed. (Santiago de los Caballeros, DR: Universidad Católica Madre y Maestra, 1977, fiche 6030607). This includes the district of the *Audiencia* of Santo Domingo from the fifteenth to the nineteenth centuries, including a catalog of documents dealing with the period 1708–1800.

SEE ALSO
Acadia
Caribbean
Cuba
France
Latin America
Nova Scotia
Spain

Some of the existing colonial records at the Archivo General de la Nación in Santo Domingo are:

- Notarial records. An example of records available on microfilm is the *protocolos* of Bayaguana, 1728–1900 (Santo Domingo: Unidad Móvil, 1959, film 0802921 ff.). Some notarial archives still remain in the original towns.
- The municipal archives of Bayaguana, Higuey, El Seybo, and Monte Plaza, dating from the early seventeenth century.
- Records of the Spanish dominion, 1492–1795, 1809–1821.
- Records of the French dominion, 1795–1809.
- Microfilm and photocopies of the Lugo and Coiscou collections and other manuscripts from the Archivo General de Indias in Seville and the Archivo Histórco Nacional in Madrid.

Rodríguez Demorizi, Emilio. *Los Domínicos y las Encomiendas de Indios de la Isla Española* (Santo Domingo: Editora del Caribe, 1971). The encomiendas of Hispaniola, including a census from 1514.

Rodríguez Demorizi, Emilio. *Familias Hispanoamericanas* (Ciudad Trujillo, DR: Editora Montalvo, 1959). Genealogy of Spanish American families in the Dominican Republic.

Bermúdez Plata, Cristóbal. *Catálogo de Documentos de la Sección Novena del Archivo General de Indias* (Seville: Escuela de Estudios Hispano Americanos, 1949). Catalog of the section of the Archivo General de Indias in Seville, containing records for Santo Domingo, Cuba, Puerto Rico, Louisiana, Florida, and Mexico.

Saint-Domingue / Haiti

The Amerindian name, Haiti, which the western portion of Hispaniola came to be called, was given by the black slaves, who learned it from the Arawak Indians. Most of the colonial records for Haiti are at the French National Archives, Section Outre-Mer, Paris. All of the records below are from the French Archives.

The following are examples of Catholic parish registers that have been filmed:

- Saint-Pierre. Registres paroissiaux, 1712–98 (film 1094169 ff.). Parish registers of baptisms, marriages, and burials for Arcahaie, Haiti.
- Saint-Joseph de Fort-Dauphin. Registres paroissiaux, 1705–96 (film 1094189 ff.). Parish registers of baptisms, marriages, and burials for Fort-Dauphin, now called Fort-Liberté, Haiti.

- Notre-Dame-de-la-Rosaire. Registres paroissiaux, 1693–1798 (film 1094161 ff.). Parish registers of baptisms, marriages, and burials for Croix-des-Bouquets, Haiti.

Greffes des Tribunaux Civils, Saint-Domingue. Tables alphabétiques des registres paroissiaux (film 1094159 ff.). Alphabetical indexes to parish registers of Haiti from 1698.

Notariat, Saint-Domingue. Minutes notariales, 1704–1803 (film 1095741 ff.). Notarial records: wills, marriage contracts, and land and property transactions for Saint-Domingue.

Greffe du Conseil Supérieur, Saint-Dominique. Réfugiés de Saint-Domingue, actes en registrés dans les consulats, 1750–1826 (film 0960760 ff.). Correspondence between the French consulates and the Council at Haiti regarding emigrants. The earliest records pertain to Charleston, South Carolina from 1750, and Norfolk, Virginia from 1752.

Greffe de l'Intendance, Saint-Domingue. Registres des libertés et affranchisements, 1776–7 (film 1093928 ff.). Slave emancipation records for Haiti, including the areas of Port-au-Prince, Cap-Français, Jérémie, Petite-Goave, and Léogane.

Greffe du Tribunal, Cap-Français. Délibérations, 1766–9 (film 1097687). Court records for Cap-Français, Saint-Domingue, now called Cap-Haitien, Haiti.

Greffe du Tribunal, Port-au-Prince. Délibérations, 1733–9 (film 1098201 ff.). Court records for Port-au-Prince, Saint-Domingue.

The Library of the Brothers of Christian Teaching in Port-au-Prince has published secondary sources and manuscript collections relating to Haitian history.

Suggested Reading

Brasseaux, Carl A. and Glenn R. Conrad. *The Road to Louisiana: The Saint-Domingue Refugees, 1792–1809* (Lafayette: University of Southwest Louisiana, 1992).

De Ville, Winston. *Saint-Domingue Census Records and Military Lists, 1688–1720* (Ville Platte, LA: The Author, 1988).

History of the Island of Santo Domingo: From Its First Discovery by Columbus to the Present Period (1821. Reprint. Westport, CT: Negro Universities Press, 1971, film 1102986).

Moya Pons, Frank. *Historia Colonial de Santo Domingo.* 2nd ed. (Barcelona: Universidad Católica Madre y Maestra, 1976).

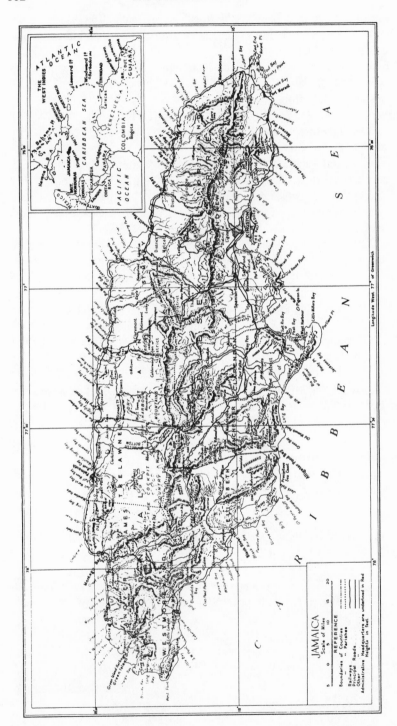

19 Jamaica (Colonial Office, 1948)

Jamaica

Jamaica was first established by Spain in 1509 as a colony for raising cattle. It remained under Spanish control until 1655, when it was seized by England. A number of English small planters arrived in 1662. In 1664, 600 English refugees fled from Montserrat to Jamaica, and in 1679 another 1200 arrived from Suriname. An earthquake in 1692 destroyed the stronghold of the buccaneers, who were operating from Port Royal.

List of Parish Registers Inventoried in Jamaican Archives (Jamaica: Jamaica Archives, 1971, film 0719936). Some of these records include slave baptisms and marriages. These parishes are Church of England, Church of Scotland/ Presbyterian, or an independent church.

Church of England, Diocese of Jamaica, Registrar. Parish register transcripts, 1664–1880 (film 1291761 ff.). Parishes included are Saint Andrew, Saint Ann, Saint Catherine, Clarendon, Saint David, Saint Dorothy, Saint Elizabeth, Saint George, Hanover, Saint James, Saint John, Kingston, Manchester, Saint Mary, Metcalfe, Portland, Port Royal, Saint Thomas in the East, Saint Thomas in the Vale, Trelawny, Vere, and Westmoreland. The original records are at the Registrar General's Department, Spanish Town, Jamaica.

In the Colonial Office Papers at the PRO in Kew, Surrey, England are censuses for Jamaica for 1680 (also muster rolls) and 1754 (CO 1), a list of landholders taken from the quit rent books, 1754, and slave returns, 1821–5 (T 71), lists of refugees from Suriname, 1679 (CO 1/35), and other records (see Great Britain).

The earliest records in the Jamaica Archives in Spanish Town date from 1674. Some of the documents include the following:

- estate journals, 1674–1881
- letters of administration
- poll tax lists
- plantation books and accounts, 1740–1927
- marriage registrations
- land patents, 1662–1704, index, 1661–1826

SEE ALSO
Barbados
Bermuda
Caribbean
Great Britain
Spain
Virginia

- court records, miscellaneous, 1680–1882
- manumission registers, 1740–1838
- slave registers, 1817–32

The Institute of Jamaica at Kingston has similar holdings, as well as minutes of the Slave Court, Saint Ann's Bay, 1787–1814.[10]

Giuseppi, Montague Spencer. *Naturalization of Foreign Protestants in the American and West Indian Colonies* (1921. Reprint. Baltimore: Genealogical Publishing Co., 1964, film 0847760). The naturalizations include Jamaica from 1740 to the end of the 1700s, taken from the returns sent from the colonies to the Lords Commissioners for Trade and Plantations at the PRO in Kew, Surrey, England.

Santa Marta, Colombia. Notaría Primera. Registros notariales, 1788–1930 (film 1563510 ff.). Registers from the First Notarial District of Santa Marta, capital city of the Department of Magdalena, Colombia. The records include documents notarized in Kingston, Jamaica. The original records are at the First Notarial District of Santa Marta, Colombia.

Suggested Reading

Bridges, George Wilson. *The Annals of Jamaica*. 2 Vols. (1828. Reprint. Westport, CT: Negro Universities Press, 1970, fiche 6030605).

Delany, Francis X. *A History of the Catholic Church in Jamaica, BWI, 1494 to 1929* (New York: Jesuit Mission Press, 1930).

Delatre, R. *A Guide to Jamaican Reference Materials in the West India Reference Library* (Kingston: n.p., 1965).

Ingram, K.E. *Sources of Jamaican History, 1655–1838: A Bibliographic Survey with Particular Reference to Manuscript Sources* (London: Inter Documentation Co., 1976).

Jamaica Record Office. *Real Estate Transactions Before the 1692 Earthquake, City of Port Royal, Jamaica* (Washington, DC: National Geographic Society, 1960).

---

[10] "Archival and Library Manuscript Collections on Various Caribbean Islands." *Caribbean Historical and Genealogical Journal* II 1 (January 1994): 14–15.

Karras, Alan L. *Sojourners in the Sun: Scottish Migrants in Jamaica and the Chesapeake, 1740–1800* (Ithaca, NY: Cornell University Press, 1992).

Livingston, Noël B. *Sketch Pedigrees of Some of the Early Settlers in Jamaica* (Kingston: Educational Supply, 1909, film 0277707). Compiled from the records of the Court of Chancery of the island, with a list of the inhabitants in 1670.

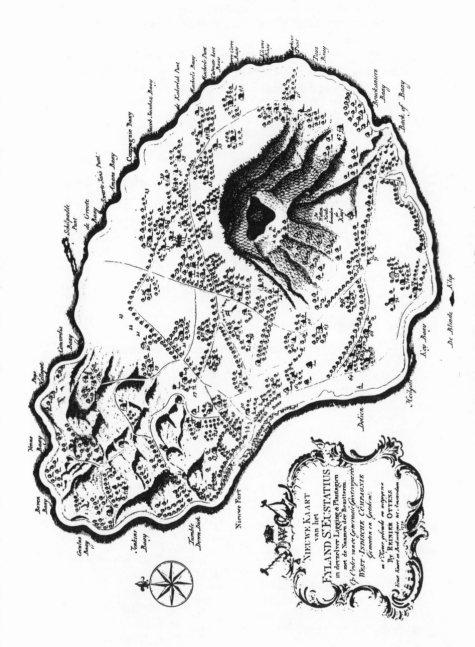

20 Saint Eustatius, 1775 (Library of Congress)

The Netherlands Antilles

The Netherlands Antilles formerly included Suriname (Dutch Guiana) and comprised the islands of Saint Eustatius, Saba, and Saint Martin / Sint Maarten — known as the Dutch Windwards — and Aruba, Bonaire, and Curaçao, located in the British Leewards. Aruba, Bonaire, Curacao, and Saba were first settled by the Dutch in 1634. Saint Eustatius was first colonized in 1600 by the Dutch. Saint Martin was colonized by both the Dutch and the French in 1648, and the island remains divided between the two countries.

The following parish registers have been filmed:

- Nederlands Hervormde Kerk, Curaçao. Kerkelijke registers, 1714–1822 (film 0038851 ff.). Reformed Dutch Church Registers: baptisms, marriages, and burials.
- Nederlands Hervormde Kerk, Sint Eustatius. Kerkelijke registers, 1709–91 (film 0038855). Reformed Dutch Church registers: baptisms and marriages of Saint Eustatius, Saint Martin, and Saba.

A Salute to the American Revolution

On 16 November 1776, Fort Orange, Saint Eustatius fired a salute to the brig or war *Andrew Doria* which was flying the United States flag. Saint Eustatius thus earned a unique place in American history as the first foreign power to acknowledge the sovereignty of the new nation.

- Lutherse Kerk, Curaçao. Kerkelijke registers, 1757–1831 (film 0038853 ff.). Lutheran parish registers: baptisms and burials.
- Rooms Katholieke Kerk, Curaçao Kerkelijke registers, 1768–1831(film 0038853 ff.). Roman Catholic parish registers: baptisms and burials.

The original records of the above are at the Algemeen Rijksarchief in 's-Gravenhage, The Netherlands.

Church of England, Parish Church of Saint Eustatius. Parish register transcripts, 1773–8 (fiche 6030542). The pastor who kept the record served in Bermuda, transferred to Saint Eustatius in 1773, and returned to Bermuda in 1778. This also includes Saint George, Bermuda marriages, 1772 and 1778–9, and burials, 1755–8, 1772. The original records are at the Bermuda Archives, Hamilton, Bermuda.

SEE ALSO
Brazil
Caribbean
France
French Antilles
Great Britain
The Guianas
The Netherlands
New York

167

The Colonial Office Papers at the PRO in Kew, Surrey, England contain miscellaneous records for Curaçao, Saint Eustatius, and Suriname, 1560–1780.

Portugees Joodse Gemeente, Curaçao. Joodse dokumenten, 1722–1831 (film 0038854). Portuguese Jewish births and burials. The original records are at the Algemeen Rijksarchief in 's-Gravenhage, The Netherlands. Original records at the American Jewish Archives, Cincinnati, Ohio are:

• Jewish marriages performed in Amsterdam, Curaçao, or Saint Eustatius of couples (one or both) born in New York, 1717–96 (film 1013426).

• Saint Eustatius Jewish Cemetery. Cemetery inscriptions, 1700–1825 (film 1012749).

Historical and other records are available at the Historisch Archief (Central Historical Archive) of The Netherlands Antilles, at Willemstad, Curaçao, including some records from Bonaire, Saint Martin, Saba, and Saint Eustatius. It has been reported that there may be some deeds and plantation records dating from the colonial period at the Department of Real Estate Management in Willemstadt.[11] The Bibliotheque National in Aruba also has a collection of published secondary sources on The Netherlands Antilles.

Suggested Reading

Attema, Y. *Saint Eustatius: A Short History of the Island and Its Monuments* (Zutphen: De Walburg, 1977).

Bijlsma, R. *Inventaris van Het Oud Archief Curaçao, Bonaire en Aruba Tot 1828* ('s-Gravenhage: Algemeen Rijksarchief Eerste Afdeling, 1989). Inventory of the old archives of Curaçao, Bonaire, and Aruba until 1828.

Córdova-Bello, Eleazar. *Companías Holandesas de Navegación: Agentes de la Colonización Neerlandesa* (Seville: Escuela de Estudios Hispano-Americanos, 1964). The Dutch navigation companies as agents for Dutch colonization in Brazil, Curaçao, and Guyana from the seventeenth to nineteenth centuries.

Gehring, Charles A. and J.A. Schiltkamp. *[New Netherland Documents] Curacao Papers, 1640–1665* (Interlaken, NY: Heart of the Lakes Publishing, 1987).

---

[11] Kenneth J. Grieb, *Research Guide to Central America and the Caribbean* (Madison: University of Wisconsin Press, 1985), 319.

Goslinga, Cornelius. *A Short History of The Netherlands Antilles and Surinam* (The Hague: n.p., 1979).

Goslinga, Cornelius. *The Dutch in the Caribbean and in the Guianas, 1680–1791* (Assen, The Netherlands; Dover, NH: Van Gorcum, 1985).

Goslinga, Cornelius. *The Dutch in the Caribbean and on the Wild Coast, 1580–1680* (Gainesville: University of Florida Press, 1971).

Hartog, John. *The Courthouses of Saint Maarten* (Aruba: DeWitt, 1974).

Hartog, John. *Curaçao from Colonial Dependence to Autonomy* (Aruba: DeWitt, 1968).

Hoff, Henry B. "Early Swedes on Saint Eustatius." *Swedish American Genealogist* 3 (1983):136.

Hoogendijk, E. *Inventaris van de Archieven van Curaçao en de Oderhorige Eilanden Bonaire en Aruba na 1828: Toegangsnummer 1.05.12.02* (The Hague: Algemeen Rijksarchief, 1995). Inventory of documents pertaining to the Dutch Antilles islands of Bonaire and Curaçao and the former colony of Aruba from 1828–75, found in the General Imperial Archive of The Hague, The Netherlands.

Krafft, A.J.C. *Historie en Oude Families van de Nederlandse Antillen: het Antilliannse Patriciaat: met een Historische Inleiding, Zestig Uitgewerkte Genealogieën, Genealogische Aantekenigen, Fragmenten van Genealogieën, Ongepubliceerde Documenten en een Overzicht van Bronnen Zowel Gedrukte als in Handschrift* ('s-Gravenhage: Martinus Nijhoff, 1951, film 0283583). History of prominent families from The Netherlands Antilles.

Meilink-Roelofsz, Marie Antoinette Petronella. *Een Archiefreis in West-Indie: De Caribbean Archives Conference in Jamaica, De Toestand van de Openbare Archieven in de Nederlandse Antillen en Suriname* ('s-Gravenhage: n.p., 1966). The public and private archives in The Netherlands Antilles and Suriname.

Palm, J. Ph. de. *Encyclopedia van de Nederlandse Antillen* (Zutphen: Walburg Pers, 1985). Encyclopedia of The Netherlands Antilles.

"Portuguese Jewish in Curaçao [1722–1741]." *Caribbean Historical and Genealogical Journal* II 1 (January 1994): 20.

Puerto Rico

In 1493 Columbus originally named the island San Juan Bautista and established the settlement of Caparra (renamed Ciudad de Puerto Rico) in 1508, forcing the native inhabitants into slavery. A bishop was installed in Puerto Rico in 1511. The first sugarcane was cultivated in 1515, and importation of African slaves began in 1518. Puerto Rico was made part of the Viceroyalty of Santo Domingo in 1509 and of Nueva España in 1534. It remained a colony of Spain until the end of the nineteenth century, when it was ceded to the United States.

Parroquiales (parish registers) date from 1550 and include baptisms, marriages, deaths and burials, and other records. They can be found at the Archivo General de Puerto Rico in San Juan, the Archivo Arzobispal de San Juan, and various parish and diocesan archives. Examples of parish records are:

Picó, Fernando. *Extractos de Registros Parroquiales, Siglos XVIII–XIX* (Puerto Rico: The Author, film 1563199 ff.). Extracts of parish registers from the municipalities of Utuado and Arecibo.

Iglesia Católica, Dulce Nombre de Jesús, Caguas. Registros parroquiales, 1730–1968 (film 1389035 ff.). Parish registers of baptisms, confirmations, marriages, and deaths from Dulce Nombre de Jesús Parish in Caguas. The original records are at the Archivo de la Diócesis in Caguas.

Iglesia Católica, San Blas, Coamo. Registros parroquiales, 1700–1922 (film 0820747 ff.). Parish registers of baptisms, confirmations, marriages, and deaths from Coamo. The original records are at the Archivo de la Parroquia de San Blas in Coamo.

Iglesia Católica, Santésimo Rosario, Yauco. Registros parroquiales, 1751–1962 (film 0538771 ff.). Parish registers of baptisms, confirmations, marriages, and deaths from Yauco. The original records are at the Archivo del la Diócesis in Ponce.

Directorio Arquidiocesano, San Juan: Sección II; Parroquias, Capillas, Personal Encargado. 2nd ed. (San Juan: The Archdiocese, 1980, film 1162471). Directory of the Roman Catholic Archdiocese of San Juan, Puerto Rico.

SEE ALSO
Caribbean
Great Britain
Latin America
Spain

Genealogical Society of the Church of Jesus Christ of Latter-day Saints. *Registros Parroquiales de Puerto Rico* (Puerto Rico: The Society, 1973, film 0924733). Parish registers of Puerto Rico; a table of eighteenth- to twentieth-century Catholic Church records, arranged by diocese, town, and parish.

Notariales (notarial records) date from 1751 and can be found at the Archivo General de Protocolo in San Juan and the Archivo de Protocolos Notariales in Guayama. The records at the Archivo General have been inventoried in Departamento de Justicia, Puerto Rico. *Protocolos Notariales: Archivo General de Puerto Rico* (San Juan: The Department, 1968), comprised of collections for the municipalities of San Juan (1751-1911), Bayamón (1738-1906), Humacao (1772-1915), Aguadilla (1790-1905), Mayagüez 1855-1923), and Arecibo (1800-1908).

De Gobernación, de las provincias, y municipales (governmental and municipal records) dating from 1730 are at the Archivo General de Puerto Rico in San Juan, various municipal archives throughout Puerto Rico, and the National Archives in Washington, DC (Record Group 186, T1120 ff.). The records at the National Archives date from 1767 and are for the communities of Aguada, Guaynbo, Toa Alta, and Toa Baja. Municipal archives have been transferred to the Archivo General de Puerto Rico, except for Ponce, Mayaguez, San Germán, Caguas, and Vega Baja.

The University of Puerto Rico is the depository for the Puerto Rico Collection, which contains books, microfilm, newspapers, and manuscripts. The Center for Historical Research at the University has been active in copying records on Puerto Rico in foreign archives (Spain, Great Britain, France, etc.), with emphasis on the fifteenth to eighteenth centuries.

Records regarding British citizens are in the Foreign Office State Papers, 1577-1780, at the PRO in Kew, Surrey, England. For more information, see the section on colonial records in Great Britain.

Militares (military records) dating from the 1550 are at the Archivo General de Puerto Rico in San Juan. For other records, see the chapter on sources of colonial records in Spain.

Ortega Benayas, María Angeles. *Inventario de la Serie Oficios de Guerra de Puerto Rico* (Madrid: Ministerio de Cultura, 1980). Inventory of the series *Oficios de Guerra* of Puerto Rico in the Archivo General de Indias in Seville.

De tierras y propiedades (land records) dating from 1761 are found in notarial, ecclesiastical, and municipal records at the Archivo General de Puerto Rico in San Juan and at local archives.

Suggested Reading

Báez, Vicente. *La Gran Enciclopedia de Puerto Rico: Historia* (Madrid: C. Corredera, 1976).

"Cabildo Records of Puerto Rico." *Caribbean Historical and Genealogical Journal* I 2 (April 1993): 18–19.

Campo Lacasa, Cristina. *Historia de la Iglesia en Puerto Rico, 1511–1802* (San Juan: Instituto de Cultura Puertorriqueña, 1977). History of the Catholic Church in Puerto Rico, 1511–1802.

"Canary Islands Families to Puerto Rico in 1692." *Caribbean Historical and Genealogical Journal* II 2 (April 1994): 23.

Codinach, Guadalupe Jiménez. *The Hispanic World, 1492–1898: A Guide to Photoreproduced Manuscripts from Spain in the Collections of the United States, Guam and Puerto Rico* (Washington, DC: Library of Congress, 1994).

Cuesta Mendoza, Antonio. *Historia Eclesiástica del Puerto Rico Colonial [1508–1700]* (Cuidad Trujillo, DR: Imprenta Arte y Cine, 1948).

Fernandez, Ronald, Serafin Mendez Mendez, and Gail Cuto. *Puerto Rico Past and Present: An Encyclopedia* (Westport CT: Greenwood Press, 1997).

Real Díaz, Joaquín. *Catálogo de las Cartas y Peticiones de Cabildo de San Juan Bautista de Puerto Rico en el Archivo General de Indias, Siglos XVI–XVIII* (San Juan: Municipio de San Juan e Instituto de Cultura Puertorriqueña, 1968). Chronological index to records in the Archivo des Indias in Seville, 1527–1800.

Ribes Tovar, Federico. *Historia Cronológica de Puerto Rico* (Panama: Editorial Tres Américas, 1973). Chronological history of Puerto Rico.

Rodríguez León, Mario A. *Los Registros Parroquiales y la Microhistoria Demográfia en Puerto Rico* (San Juan: Centro de Estudios Avanzados de Puerto Rico y el Caribe, 1990).

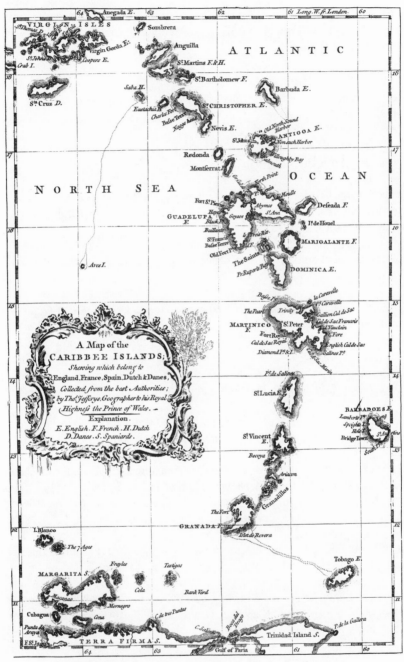

21 The Caribbean Islands (*Gentleman's Magazine*, 1756)

Trinidad and Tobago

Trinidad's first government was appointed by Spain from 1532 to 1534 and again in 1569. The first permanent settlement was at San José de Oruña (Saint Joseph) in 1592. Capuchin missionaries from Spain established a mission in 1687, but it was abolished in 1713. A smallpox epidemic in 1741 killed many of the inhabitants. Trinidad remained sparsely settled by the Spanish until 1770. French immigrants from Saint Lucia arrived in 1777. In 1797 the British seized control of the island. The *cabildo* form of government was replaced by the Port of Spain City Council in 1843, and Spanish law remained in effect until 1845.

Tobago was settled by English from Barbados in 1626, and in 1632 a small Dutch and English settlement known as Niewe Walcheren was formed. Spain and Carib Indians sacked and burned both settlements. Tobago was resettled by the Dutch and French in 1646, although the Dutch drove out the French colonists in 1662. Tobago was declared neutral in 1748 and ceded to Great Britain in 1763, but it passed back and forth from Britain to France until 1802, when it became a British possession as part of the Windward Islands. Tobago was removed from the windwards and joined with Trinidad in 1889.

Most of the colonial records in Trinidad are at the Registrar General, Red House, Port of Spain, and the Port of Spain Town Hall. Libraries with published records and newspapers include the West Indian

The Latvian Connection

In 1641 King Charles I of England gave as a present to his godson, James, Duke of Courland and ruler of Latvia, a land grant on the island of Tobago. Some 600 of the Duke's subjects, known as Courlanders, traveled to Tobago and established a colony on the north coast. They remained on Tobago until they were driven out by the Dutch in 1658. The Duke assigned his title to the Company of London Merchants in 1681. A bay still bears the name Courland and a monument in memory of the Duke.

SEE ALSO
Barbados
Caribbean
France
Great Britain
Latin America
Spain

175

Reference Collection at the Trinidad Public Library, Port of Spain and the public library in Scarborough, Tobago. The library in Scarborough is also the depository for records on Tobago prior to joining with Trinidad, including Assembly Minutes, 1794–1874, slave registers, 1820–22, and other manuscripts.

The Colonial Office Papers at the PRO in Kew, Surrey, England contain censuses for 1751 and 1770 and plantation grants, 1765–7, for Tobago. The records for Trinidad include an 1814 abstract of all land grants made by the Spanish government, lists of persons allowed to remain in Trinidad, 1814–15, and slave registers, various years, by family under the surname of the mother.

For information on military records, see the chapter on colonial records in Spain.

Suggested Reading

Bonde, P.G.L. *L'Île de Trinidad Sous le Government Español.* 2 Vols. (Paris: n.p., 1882).

Bryans, Robin. *Trinidad and Tobago: Isles of the Immortelles* (London: Faber and Faber, 1967).

Carmichael, Gertrude. *The History of the West Indian Islands of Trinidad and Tobago, 1498–1900* (London: Alvin Redman, 1966).

English Protestant Church of Tobago, Register of Baptisms, Marriages and Deaths from 1781 to 1817 (Trinidad: n.p., 1936).

Mount, G.S. and J.E. Mount. "Historical Resources in Trinidad." Conference of Latin American Historians, Washington, DC, December, 1976.

Ottley, Carlton Robert. *The Story of Port of Spain from the Earliest Times to the Present Day* (Diego Martin, Trinidad: Crusoe Publications, 1977).

Williams, Eric. *History of the People of Trinidad and Tobago* (Trinidad: PNM Printing, 1962).

The Virgin Islands
The Cayman Islands and Turks and Caicos

In 1493 Columbus discovered Saint Croix and named it Santa Cruz. By the time the island was settled in the early 1600s, all the Indians were gone, most of them carried off to work in the Spanish gold mines of Santo Domingo. In 1625 both the English and Dutch— with a group of French Huguenots from Saint Kitts — established settlements at Saint Croix.

The Dutch on Saint Croix named their settlement *Nieuw Zeeland* in 1642. The Dutch Governor of the island killed the English Governor in 1645. The Dutch Governor was then shot by the English settlers. The Dutch settlers migrated to Saint Eustatius and Saint Martin, and the French Huguenots migrated to Guadeloupe. The island was attacked by Spain in 1650. Those English settlers who were not killed fled to Bermuda. The abandoned island was claimed by France, and French Knights of Malta and other colonists settled at Saint Croix in 1651. French colonists abandoned their settlement in 1695 and migrated to Saint-Domingue (Santo Domingo).

Danish settlers colonized Saint Thomas in 1672. The Danes acquired Saint Croix from the French in 1733. A group of Moravian missionaries settled there in 1732. The islands, including Saint John, became the Danish West Indies in 1754. They were sold to the United States in 1917 and became the U.S. Virgin Islands.

The British Virgin Islands were first settled by English settlers from Anguilla. They arrived at Tortola, the largest of the islands, in 1666.

Germans in the Caribbean

The German state of Brandenburg-Prussia tried to get in on the action in the West Indies in 1689. After unsuccessful attempts to capture Spanish shipping in 1680, they attempted to buy Saint Vincent or Saint Croix from France. Under the Brandenburg Company, they bought a plantation from Denmark on Saint Thomas in 1685, which they held until 1734, when it became a Danish Crown colony. They also owned the tiny Virgin Island of Saint Peter from 1698 until 1734.

SEE ALSO
Caribbean
Denmark
France
Great Britain
The Netherlands

177

The Danish Islands

Records for the Danish West Indies can be found at local archives, the PRO in Kew, Surrey, England (Foreign Office State Papers, 1577–1780), The Netherlands National Archives, the National Archives in Washington, DC, and the French National Archives, Section Outre-Mer, Paris.

Reformed Dutch Church, Saint Thomas. Church records, 1744–1825 (Charlotte Amalie, VI: Saint Thomas Public Library, 1967, film 1520664). Register of members. The original records are at the Reformed Dutch Church in Saint Thomas.

Eglise Catholique, Sainte-Rose, Léogane, Haïti. Registres paroissiaux, 1666–1794 (film 1094163 ff.). Parish registers of baptisms, marriages, and burials for Léogane, Haiti, and the Virgin Islands. The original records are at the French National Archives, Section Outre-Mer, Paris.

Frederick Evangelical Lutheran Church, Saint Thomas. Church records, 1739–1974 (Charlotte Amalie, VI: Saint Thomas Public Library, 1974, film 1520639 ff.). Ministerial and administrative records of the Frederick Evangelical Lutheran Church, established in 1739. The original records are at the Frederick Evangelical Lutheran Church in Saint Thomas.

A list of Danish subjects going to Saint Thomas in 1796 is in the Foreign Office papers at the PRO in Kew, Surrey, England. The Foreign Office Series, State Papers, 1577–1780, also contains records for Saint Thomas and Saint Croix. For more information, see the section on colonial sources in Great Britain.

Governor of Danish West Indies. Records relating to the Danish West Indies: 1672–1860 (Washington, DC: National Archives, 1971, film 0847533 ff./ T952). Contains sentences, transfers of property, resolutions, wills, minutes, land registers, contracts, sales and transfers of sugar to New York from the Danish West Indies. The original records are at the National Archives, Washington, DC.

The British Islands

Sources of information for the British Virgin Islands are available at the National Library in Roadtown, Tortola, the Library of the College of the Virgin Islands in Charlotte Amalia, Saint Thomas, and the Saint Thomas Public Library, also in Charlotte Amalia.

Records and history for the Cayman Islands can be found at the Cayman Islands National Archive in George Town, The Cayman Islands National Museum, and the PRO in Kew, Surrey, England. A fire in 1972 destroyed the previous administration building, but some records may still be in alternate locations.

Records of the Turks and Caicos are located in Waterloo, Grand Turk at the Government Archives (mostly uncataloged), the Governor's Office, and the Judicial Department. Anglican parish records dating from 1799 are kept at the parish of Saint Thomas, Grand Turk. [12]

A 1717 census for Tortola is in the Colonial Office papers, 1711–1872, at the PRO in Kew, Surrey, England. The Turks and Caicos Islands records at the PRO are in the same series and date from 1799–1882.

Wesleyan Methodist Church, Tortola Circuit. Church records, 1815–1933 (film 1699188 ff.). The Tortola Circuit of the Wesleyan Methodist Church comprises Virgin Gorda, Anegada, East End, Road Town, West End, and Jost Van Dyke. The original records are at the Methodist Church archive, Road Town, Tortola.

Suggested Reading

Dooklan, Isaac. *A History of the British Virgin Islands* (Jamaica: Caribbean Universities Press, 1975).

Gutierrez de Arce, M. *La Colonización Danes en las Islas Virgenes, Estudio Histórico-Jurídico* (Seville: Escuela de Estudios Hispano Americanos, 1945). Danish colonization of the Virgin Islands.

Lawaetz, Eva. *Free Colored in Saint Croix, 1744–1816* (Saint Croix: n.p., 1979).

Lewisohn, Florence. *The Romantic History of Saint Croix: From the Time of Columbus until Today* (Christiansted, Saint Croix: Saint Croix Landmarks Society, 1964).

Lewisohn, Florence. *Tales of Tortola and the British Virgin Islands: Recounting Nearly Five Centuries of Lore, Legend and History of Las Virgines, Including Much Incidental Information on Virgin Gorda, Anegada, Jost Van Dyke, Fallen Jerusalem and Many Other Islands; Much Ado from the Time of Columbus to the Queen's Visit; Diverse Information on Pyrates, Personages, Shipwrecks,*

---

[12] Kenneth J. Grieb, *Research Guide*, 373.

Wars, Hurricanes and Buried Treasure; Tales of Plantation Life, Making Sugar and Rum, Insurrections, Emancipation and the Colony's Decline and Rise (n.p.: Alroy, 1966).

"List of Saint Thomas Colonists, 1678." *Caribbean Genealogical and Historical Journal* IV 4 (October 1996): 27.

Westergaard, W. *The Danish West Indies Under Company Rule, 1671–1754* (New York: Macmillan & Co., 1957).

Williams, Nigel. *The History of the Cayman Islands* (George Town, Grand Cayman: Government of the Cayman Islands, 1970).

Part Four

The Thirteen Colonies, Maine, and Vermont

22 Virginia, 1624 (Library of Congress)

The Thirteen Colonies: An Overview

Colony	Earliest Church Records	Earliest Land Records	Earliest Court Records
Connecticut	1636	1635	1636
Delaware	1646	1640	1642
Georgia	1733	1732	1751
Maryland	1640	1633	1635
Massachusetts	1620	1620	1620
New Hampshire	1634	1623	1629
New Jersey	1662	1629	1664
New York	1639	1630	1624
North Carolina	1677	1663	1663
Rhode Island	1636	1636	1638
Pennsylvania	1683	1683	1683
South Carolina	1694	1671	1671
Virginia	1646	1619	1608

Major English Colonies before 1640

1607	Jamestown Colony	1634	Connecticut Colony
1620	Plymouth Bay Colony	1634	Chesapeake Bay
1622	Piscataqua Plantation	1636	Providence Colony
1626	Massachusetts Bay Colony	1638	New Haven Colony

Major Non-English Colonies before 1640

1605	New France
1613	New Netherland
1638	New Sweden

New Netherland (1613-64)

New Netherland was colonized by the Dutch, many of whom were Walloons (French Protestant refugees) who had escaped persecution in Belgium and taken up residence in Holland. New Amsterdam (New York City area) was a trading post by 1612, owned by the Dutch East India Company. The Company also established a post at Fort Nassau in 1614, and received a charter for the colony of New Netherland in 1621. Fort Orange (Albany) was established in 1624. The Dutch conquered the colony of New Sweden in 1655, but were in turn conquered by the English fleet in 1664. From 1673 to 1674, they briefly retook the area.

New Sweden (1638-55)

The chancellor of Sweden chartered the New Sweden Company in 1637. The colony encompassed an area from Trenton, New Jersey to the mouth of the Delaware River and included parts of New Jersey, Delaware, and Pennsylvania. New Sweden was conquered by the Dutch in 1655.

New France (1605-1763)

See Canada: New France (Part Six).

British North America

Colonists came to the New World for both religious and economic reasons. The English economy was suffering from rapid inflation (influx of Spanish gold and silver from America into European markets) and not generating enough work. Unneeded and unwanted labor could come to America where a large labor supply was needed. The first permanent English settlement was at Jamestown, Virginia in 1607.

Settlers in the southern colonies had no difficulty recreating English laws and society. Those in a position to influence law and politics came for financial reasons and missed the life they left behind. They were granted large tracts of land and worked them using exploited labor, both slave and indentured. Between 1615 and 1775 about 50,000 convicts whose sentences had been commuted to specific periods of service in the colonies were transported, most to Maryland and Virginia.

The New England colonies were founded by religious dissenters from the Anglican Church. New England colonists wanted to create a society shaped to their faith, and developed laws on property and civil behavior that agreed with their religious ideology. Corporate charters gave them more leeway to develop their own systems — theocracies — than a royal or proprietary colony. Of the middle colonies, Pennsylvania, similar to New England, was also founded by religious dissenters. By 1640 most settlers were emigrating from the eastern counties of England and also some from the southern counties, mostly from the yeoman or artisan class. Scots, Irish, and Welsh made up less than two percent of the population.

Colonial Government under Great Britain

There were three basic charters by which a colony's administrative and other governmental functions were structured: a corporation, a proprietorship, and a Crown grant, in this order having increased control by the King and his Privy Council. A corporate colony had a governor elected, directly or indirectly, by qualified voters of the colony (white male landowners, usually members of the dominant church). A proprietary colony had a governor appointed by the proprietors (the entrepreneur or entrepreneurs purchasing the grant as a profit-making business venture), with approval of the King. A Royal colony was under direct control of the Crown, the governor being appointed by the King and Privy Council. The chart on the following page shows the distribution of these three types of charters throughout the thirteen colonies and their years of activity.

By 1702 eight of the private colonies had been royalized: Virginia, New Hampshire, Massachusetts, East and West Jersey, Barbados, Bermuda, and the Leeward Islands. Three other private grants came under the Crown by the mid-eighteenth century: the Bahamas, Carolinas, and Georgia. Maryland and Pennsylvania were returned to their original proprietors after periods of royal governorship. By the late seventeenth century, the greatest significance of the proprietaries was the revenue that was collected from land ownership.

Georgia, from 1732 to 1752, was neither royal, corporate, nor proprietary, but a trusteeship. Massachusetts had no charter from 1684 to 1691. New York City had a Royal Governor until 1783. The Northern Neck Proprietary existed within the Royal colony of Virginia.

Town Government

Regional diversity was reflected in the systems of law developed to meet the needs and values of the settlements. Geographic isolation played an important role in the sway and influence of differing European traditions. There were distinct differences in colonial town government:

➢ Boston and Newport: town meeting form of government
➢ New York and Philadelphia: governments modeled after the medieval English borough or town, ruled by a chartered corporation with a mayor, aldermen, and councilmen
➢ Charleston: never received a town charter during the colonial period. The South Carolina Governor and Council, followed by the Commons House, governed the town directly.

Colony	Corporate	Proprietary	Royal
Connecticut	1662–1775	—	—
Delaware	—	1664–1704	1704–76
Georgia	—	—	1752–76, 1779–82
Maryland	—	1632–91 1751–76	1691–1751
Massachusetts	—	1630–84	1691–1774
New Hampshire	—	1622–79	1679–1775
New Jersey	—	1664–1702	1702–76
New York	—	1664–84	1684–1775
North Carolina	—	1691–1729	1729–75
Pennsylvania	—	1682–92 1694–1776	1692–4
Rhode Island	1663–1775	—	—
South Carolina	—	1669–1721	1721–75
Virginia	1609–24	— 1649–1776	1624–1775

Headrights and Quit Rents

The great need for manpower on the plantations inaugurated the headright system. This system granted a defined tract of land to organized groups of Englishmen who agreed to settle servants on the land at their own expense. By paying the cost of bringing people to the colonies, a man could extend his own property. This devolved into the practice of indenturing. Indentured servants would bond themselves to serve for a period of time (typically four to seven years) after which they could buy their own land and bring others from England. The practice varied from colony to colony, and was mostly practiced in the plantation culture of the southern and West Indian colonies. In Jamaica, land was granted to any person who paid his own way to the colony, or paid the way of another person. Headrights belonged to the head of an immigrating family. Headrights were issued in Virginia from 1618 to 1738. The Carolinas were patterned after Virginia. When there was not enough response from Englishmen, headrights were extended to Irish and Scottish settlers. Quakers and settlers from Barbados were also invited. In New York the term *headright* indicated a share in a purchase of proprietary land.

An important item of discussion that particulary involved the proprietary colonies was the payment of quit rents. By and large land in New England was held freehold; but proprietary land was subject to a revenue paid on an annual basis to the proprietary landlords (often absentee in England). These rents were not always easy to collect. The following are some examples of how the practice functioned (or failed to do so):

- The Masonian proprietary in New Hampshire had received no quit rents at all when Robert Mason surrendered his patent in 1664.
- In Virginia quit rents were charged on proprietary estates, some owned by absentee landlords in England.
- In New York from 1681–8 many land grants were made, and numerous manors were created to increase the number of quit rents owed to the Duke of York for his proprietary.
- In Delaware planters refused to pay quit rents to the Penn Proprietary (Pennsylvania), claiming the rents should go to the Duke of York. The heirs of Penn were trying to collect quit rents as late as 1814. Some quit rents were collected in Kent County, 1681–1713, and Sussex County, 1702–13.

Discussion of land grants in New Jersey is quite complex. Freeholders paid quit rents to the proprietors and reserved one seventh of the lands in a town for the proprietors' use. Difficulties arose when conflicting land jurisdictions developed. Many patents were issued by Governor Nichols in the areas of Staten Island, Navesink (Elizabethtown and Monmouth grants), and Raritan during the Duke of York Proprietary; these freeholders were allowed their own general assembly, courts of trial, and seven years' tax exemption.[13] These grants took place before New Jersey was separated from New York. Additional proprietary grants were issued to Berkeley and Carteret, colonial proprietors who also took part in drafting the constitution of the Carolina colony.

Freeholders were required to take oaths of fidelity from 1665 to 1668, swearing allegiance to the King and faithfulness to the proprietors.[14] In 1670 many colonists in the Monmouth and Elizabethtown grants refused to pay quit rents on land issued under Nichols' grants. Payment would acknowledge the new

---

[13] *New Jersey Archives* I: 14–19, 43–6.

[14] *New Jersey Archives* I: 48–51.

proprietors and require the colonists to take out a new proprietary patent. Litigation regarding Elizabethtown lasted until the Revolution. Newark settlers offered to pay quit rent in wheat, not sterling, in 1666. In 1672 the Duke of York denied the validity of Nichols' grants and voided the titles; this was done in an attempt to require everyone to hold a proprietary patent and pay a quit rent in order to be a freeholder; however, this did not resolve the situation.

After the brief Dutch re-conquest of New Netherland (1673–4), the land grants to Berkeley and Carteret were leased and released again, except that Berkeley sold his proprietary rights to John Fenwick in 1674. The rights were transferred twice again, finally to three Quaker proprietors. Carteret issued a Quintpartite Deed (five party) in 1676 (confirmed in 1680) between himself and four Quaker proprietors, including William Penn, for the region known as West Jersey.

Upon the death of Carteret in 1680, his plantations were sold (release of sale issued 1683) to twelve proprietors, comprised primarily of English Quakers and Scots, Roman Catholics, Presbyterians, and Covenanters. This was the beginning of East Jersey. No uniform system of land purchase was adopted; grants were not always surveyed. Between 1683 and 1800 quit rents were infrequently collected in East Jersey. Freeholders rebelled when collection attempts were made. Those from New England especially felt that they held clear title to their land and were not subject to proprietors. In 1677 a regular system of land grants and quit rents was established in West Jersey, although the recording of deeds was irregular until after 1694. During the Dominion of New England from 1688 to 1692 the council of East Jersey did not function.

In 1692 part of West Jersey was sold to Anglican merchants from London; this became known as the West Jersey Society. They sold land shares and collected small quit rents. They also sold some lands in East Jersey in Middlesex and Somerset counties. Shares were often sold in fractions (i.e. 1/8, 1/24, etc.), making original ownership difficult to trace.

In 1702 the proprietary governments of East and West Jersey surrendered their rights to the Crown, and New Jersey became a single Royal colony. The proprietors retained their ownership and rights to the land, also the right to collect quit rents.[15] Thus, becoming a Crown colony did not end the land controversy.

The granting of land in the Carolina colony also bears close examination. As early as 1663 the Carolina proprietors were collecting quit rents from Virginia

---

[15] *New Jersey Archives* II: 517.

colonists along the northern shore of Albemarle Sound, who arrived in the area in 1653. In 1665 the Concessions and Agreements of Albemarle Province were written, and colonists from Barbados founded Charles Town on Cape Fear. The Fundamental Constitution, written in 1669, stated that only landholders could participate in government. It also established a feudal system of ownership for the large agricultural plantations whereby land was distributed two-fifths to hereditary royalty and three-fifths to manorial lords and common freeholders, and the proprietors collected quit rents.

➢ *Seignoires*: held by proprietors, allowed 12,000 acres in each county; (created 1678–90)

➢ *Baronies*: held by landgraves, each held four baronies totaling 48,000 acres (twenty-six created in 1671)

➢ *Caciques*: 24,000 acres each (first thirteen created in 1677)

➢ *Manors*: held by lords of the manors (mostly Huguenots in Craven County), comprised of 3–12,000 acres

➢ *Freeholders*: held a minimum of fifty acres

In 1691 the Province of Albemarle became North Carolina. South Carolina proclaimed a revolutionary government in 1719, no longer recognized the authority of the proprietors, and became a Royal colony. In 1729 the Carolina charter was officially surrendered and the Lords Proprietors of the Carolinas were abolished. North Carolina also became a Royal colony at this time.

Colonial Wars

Pequot War (1636–7): Massachusetts Bay Colony, Narragansett, and Mohican Indians allied to fight the Pequot Indians after the massacre in Wethersfield, Connecticut in 1637. This was the first major Indian war in New England

Dutch War (1653–64): There were three Anglo-Dutch wars in Europe that affected the colonies in that New Amsterdam was surrendered to the English 1664.

King Philip's War (1675–6): The two Massachusetts colonies, Connecticut, and Rhode Island, and the Mohegan Indians of the Mohawk Nation allied against Chief Philip (Nipmuck) and the coalition of Narragansett, Nipmuck, and Wampanoag tribes. At this time there were about 90 colonial settlements, 52 were attacked and twelve destroyed. The losses totaled more than 600 colonists and over 3,000 Indians.

Second Hundred Years' War (1689–1763): Actually four separate conflicts, this war began when William and Mary ascended the English throne and joined with Holland, Spain and Austria, Sweden, and a group of German states in the War of the League of Ausburg. The first hundred years' war was between England and France, 1337 to 1453. The four wars as they were known in the New and Old worlds are:

➤ King William's War (War of the League of Ausburg), 1689–97
➤ Queen Anne's War (War of the Spanish Succession), 1701–13
➤ King George's War (War of the Austrian Succession), 1744–8
➤ French and Indian War (after two years, conflict spread to Europe and was known as the Seven Years' War), 1754–63

After the Treaty of Paris in 1763, France ceded Canada and all French claims to all lands east of the Mississippi River to Great Britain; France also surrendered several West Indian islands to Great Britain. France retained two islands in the Gulf of the Saint Lawrence River. Spain ceded Florida to Great Britain, and Great Britain returned Martinique and Guadeloupe to France.

Seeds of the Revolution

As a result of the French and Indian War the British colonies had matured politically and developed a spirit of self-confidence. No longer united with Great Britain against a common enemy, many colonists began to chafe at the controls imposed upon them from abroad. The Crown barred settlement west of the Appalachian Mountains, supposedly to bring peace to the frontier, but actually in an attempt to confine the Americans to the coastal area, facilitating control. The colonists believed that a series of Parliamentary acts was a conspiracy designed to strip them of their basic political rights. They are briefly as follows:

Sugar Act (1763): Tax on sugar imported from the non-British West Indies.

Stamp Act (1765): Stamps attached to all types of legal documents, business papers, licenses, pamphlets, newspapers, almanacs, printed sermons, playing cards, and dice; paid for in hard cash in admiralty courts (granted no jury trials); to raise revenue to support the British Army in America (repealed in 1766).

Quartering Act (1765): Required colonists to find quarters for British soldiers in inns or barns and supply them with bedding, cooking utensils, condiments, and liquor.

Declaratory Act (1766): Affirmed Parliament's power to "bind the colonies and people of America . . . in all cases whatsoever."

Townshend Acts (1766): Levied customs duties (external taxes) on lead, paint, paper, glass, silk, and tea imported from England into the colonies; used to support British troops in America; all duties repealed in 1769 except tax on tea (repealed on the same day as the Boston Massacre).

Tea Act (1773): British East India tea could be exported to the colonies without paying customs duties; local merchants with large supplies of tea faced financial ruin against the British monopoly.

Coercive, or Intolerable Acts (1774):
➤ Boston Port Bill: closed the port of Boston to all trade except food and fuel
➤ Administration of Justice Act: regarding riot suppression
➤ Massachusetts Government Act: increased powers of governor and stripped them from the legislature
➤ Quartering Act: revised to provide quarters for troops at scenes of disturbances

Quebec Act (1774): Extended the boundaries of Quebec south to the Ohio River and westward to the Mississippi; Catholics given full religious rights; French civil law in effect.

Colonial Newspapers

Although the first printing press was brought from England to Massachusetts in 1639, it was decades before any regular newspaper was in circulation. Newspapers from London supplied some information, but local dissemination of news was primarily through letter. Manuscript newsletters known as broadsides were published when something that was considered momentous had taken place. A regular newspaper was attempted in Boston in 1690, but it was suppressed by the government after a single number. The first permanent newspaper was also started in Boston in 1704. The last of the colonies to acquire a printing press was Georgia, in 1762.

The earliest papers had news reprinted from London papers. As time progressed, local leaders made use of the press to present current views, and letters received were also published. Gradually they contained more contemporary information, such as advertisements, port arrivals (including name of ship and port of origin), tax lists, sales of slaves or runaways, reports of outbreaks of disease, real estate sold or leased, missing heirs, settlements of estates, stolen livestock, and eventually obituaries and marriages. Perhaps one of the greatest assets of examining period newspapers is that it provides a firsthand account of the tenor of daily life at a given time.

The Early American Newspapers Project, sponsored by the American Antiquarian Society, is an attempt to collect all newspapers printed between 1690 and

1820 and to put them on microfilm. They are listed in Brigham, Clarence. *History and Bibliography of American Newspapers, 1690-1820* (Worcester, MA: American Antiquarian Society, 1947, addendum published in 1961). A companion volume is Lathem, Edward C. *Chronological Tables of American Newspapers, 1690-1820* (Worcester, MA: American Antiquarian Society, 1972).

States with newspapers printed before 1800

Connecticut	1755	New Jersey	1765
Delaware	1762	New York	1725
(District of Columbia	1789)	North Carolina	1751
Florida	1783	Ohio	1793
Georgia	1763	Pennsylvania	1719
Kentucky	1787	Rhode Island	1732
Louisiana	1794	South Carolina	1732
Maine	1785	Tennessee	1791
Maryland	1727	Vermont	1781
Massachusetts	1704	Virginia	1736
New Hampshire	1756		

Mott, Frank Luther. *American Journalism: A History, 1690-1960* (New York: Macmillan & Co., 1962).

The New England Colonies

An extra explanation is required for searching in the New England colonies. Record keeping was primarily on a local level, with the town meeting as the basic unit of government. The importance of counties varied, and in Connecticut and Vermont an additional jurisdictional unit called a probate district was created. In addition, the earliest records can usually be found in the general assembly or court of the colony.

Town records in New England are generally comprised of:
➢ proprietors' records (the first grants of land)
➢ town meetings
➢ vital records (frequently recorded with land and town records)
➢ family records (vital records listed in family groups)
➢ livestock records (earmarks)
➢ society and parish records (except for Rhode Island)

The six colonies differ in level of administration, as follows:

Colony	Land records	Probate records	Vital records
Connecticut	town	district	town
Maine	county	county	town
Massachusetts	county	county	town
New Hampshire	county	county	town
Rhode Island	town	town	town
Vermont	town	district	town

The inventories of the towns discussed in this section include some or all of the records listed below under each colony:

Connecticut
tax receipts
highways
earmarks and strays
indentures
vital records
family records
land records
proprietors' records
earmarks
town meetings
society records

lists of electors and freemen
trainband (militia) rolls and musters
selectmen's records
school district records
grand (tax) and rate lists
boundary disputes
Indian deeds
lists of inhabitants
court records
tax abatements
poor relief

Maine
vital records
family records
town meetings
warnings out of town
marriage intentions
strays
taxes
tax notices
earmarks
parish and selectmen meetings
lists of jurors
boundary lines
roads
land grants

treasurer's accounts
plan of church pews
pew deeds
elections
indentures
soldiers and sailors
bills of sale
proprietors' deeds
mortgages
sale of property
adoptions
school district records
newcomers to town

Massachusetts

vital records
marriage intentions
town proceedings
publishments
warrants
earmarks
pew deeds
lists of men enrolled in the militia
earmarks for livestock
votes
land grants
strays
proprietors' (commoners') records
list of commoners/proprietors
town rates (tax records)
tax abatements
selectmen's records
accounts
perambulations of town lines
fence divisions

town boundaries
church records
warnings out of town
notifications of landlords harboring strangers
pews and pew-spots conveyed
tithingmen's records
fines: transgressions of the Sabbath
appointments
licences
apprenticeships
Indian records, manumissions
constables' returns
out-of-town marriages
deeds
school rate books
letters
overseers of the poor records
assessment records: school districts
inhabitants in school districts

New Hampshire

inventories and tax lists
town meetings
vital records
proprietors' records
society or parish records
church records
earmarks and strays
warnings out of town

surveyors' records
selectmen's records
provincial records
land records and grants
licenses
elections
school records
family records

Rhode Island

vital records
family records
lists of voters
marriage intentions
town council records
probate records
town meeting records
divorces
inquests
financial records
records of highways
orders for repair of highways
school district records

records of the poor
record of votes
bond [deed] books
administration bonds
miscellaneous bonds
town estate valuations
public indentures
land evidence documents
lists of freemen's names
town rates
laying out and letting of lands
exchange of lands
giving of lands

buying and selling of lands
records of people moving in or out of town
indentures
manumissions
wills and inventories

earmarks
certificates of residence
warrants for removal out of town
orders for guardianship
licenses

Vermont

town business
town meetings
road surveys
grants and land surveys
licenses
proprietors' records
vital records
minutes of meetings
election results
lists of officers and freemen
school district reports
road surveys

family records
warnings out of town
earmarks
religious opinions
school districts
Baptist church membership certificates
other religious certificates
cemetery records
freemen's meetings
adoptions
hawyard and hog reeve appointments
freemen's oaths

Church Records

With the exception of Rhode Island, the early Puritan church supervised not only the religious affairs of the community but the secular ones as well. Church membership was required to own land and vote in town meetings for many years. After 1657 the Half-Way Covenant (partial membership) was instituted in some areas, allowing the next generation of colonists to exercise their franchise and be baptized without owning the covenant. Marriage was not considered a sacrament but a civil contract, and marriages were not recorded in church records before the 1690s. Marriage intentions (similar to banns) were required in Massachusetts and in some areas settled by Massachusetts. These were recorded in the town records. Christenings are not found in Puritan churches, but can be found in Anglican records. Below are some of the categories found in church and society records:

infant and adult baptisms
marriages
admissions to the church
society meeting minutes
burials and deaths
bills of mortality
admissions to communion
confessions of faith
professions of faith
owners of the covenant
those renewing the covenant

persons recommended to other churches
transfers of memberships
certificates of dissent or withdrawal
removals
church charters
pew deeds, rents, subscriptions
seating plans
registers of pastors
lists of deacons
church committee records
warnings of meetings

meetings of inhabitants
historical sketches
rate or tax lists
freemen's lists
records of indigents from other communities

poor lists
disciplinary proceedings
excommunications
incorporation of new societies

Suggested Reading

General

Andrews, Charles M. *Our Earliest Colonial Settlements: Their Diversities of Origin and Later Characteristics.* 4 Vols. (1933. Reprint. Ithaca: Cornell University Press, 1987).

Channing, Edward. *Town and County Government in the English Colonies of North America* (1884. Reprint. New York: Johnson Reprint, 1973).

Greene, Jack P. and J.R. Pole. *Colonial British America* (Baltimore: Johns Hopkins University Press, 1984).

Hoffer, Peter Charles. *Law and People in Colonial America* (Baltimore: Johns Hopkins University Press, 1992).

Middle Colonies

Boyer, Carl. *Ship Passenger Lists, Pennsylvania and Delaware, 1641–1825* (Newhall, CA: The Author, 1980, fiche 6048670).

Butler, Jon. *Power, Authority, and the Origins of American Denominational Order: The English Churches in the Delaware Valley, 1680–1730* (Philadelphia: The American Philosophical Society, 1978).

Clay, Jehu Curtis. *Annals of the Swedes on the Delaware: From Their First Settlement in 1636, to the Present Time.* 2nd ed. (Philadelphia: H. Hooker and Co., 1858, film 1321096).

Eckert, Jack. *Guide to the Records of Philadelphia Yearly Meeting* (Philadelphia: Haverford College, Swarthmore College, 1989). Covers eastern Pennsylvania, western New Jersey, Delaware, and the eastern shore of Maryland.

Forbush, Bliss. *A History of Baltimore Yearly Meeting of Friends: Three Hundred Years of Quakerism in Maryland, Virginia, the District of Columbia, and Central Pennsylvania* (Sandy Spring, MD: Baltimore Yearly Meeting of Friends, 1972, fiche 6049733).

Holland Society of New York. *Inventory and Digest of Early Church Records in the Library of the Holland Society of New York* (New York: Holland Society of New York, 1912, film 1421917). Manuscript copies of seventeenth or early eighteenth-century baptisms, marriages, burials, lists of ministers, deacons and elders, member and pew holders for churches located in the New Netherland territory. Includes index of churches arranged by county.

Immigrants to the New World, 1600s-1800s (Broderbund, 1997). CD-ROM with images from four titles published by Genealogical Publishing Company:
➢ *New World Immigrants.* 2 Vols.
➢ *Emigrants to Pennsylvania, 1641-1819*
➢ *Immigrants to the Middle Colonies*
➢ *Passengers to America*

Lists of Officers of the Colonies on the Delaware and the Province of Pennsylvania, 1614-1776 (Baltimore: Genealogical Publishing Co., 1992, film 0823996). Republication of the *Pennsylvania Archives*, Second Series, 9: 621-818.

Parker, J. Carlyle. *Pennsylvania and Middle Atlantic States Genealogical Manuscripts: A User's Guide to the Manuscript Collections of the Genealogical Society of Pennsylvania, as Indexed in its Manuscripts Materials Index Microfilmed by the Genealogical Department, Salt Lake City* (Turlock, CA: Marietta Publishing, 1986).

Tepper, Michael. *Immigrants to the Middle Colonies: A Consolidation of Ship Passenger Lists and Associated Data from The New York Genealogical and Biographical Record* (Baltimore: Genealogical Publishing Co., 1978).

Vedder. H.C. *A History of the Baptists in the Middle States* (Philadelphia: American Baptist Publications Society, 1989).

Ward, Christopher. *The Dutch and Swedes on the Delaware, 1609-64* (Philadelphia: University of Pennsylvania, 1930, fiche 6101604).

Weslager, C.A. *The English on the Delaware, 1610-1682* (New Brunswick: Rutgers University Press, 1967).

New England Colonies
Banks, Charles Edward. *Topographical Dictionary of 2,885 English Emigrants to New England, 1620-1650* (1937. Reprint. Baltimore: Genealogical Publishing Co., 1981).

Clark, Charles E. *The Eastern Frontier: The Settlement of Northern New England, 1610–1763* (1970. Reprint. Hanover, NH: University Press of New England, 1983).

Cook, Edward M. *The Fathers of the Towns: Leadership and Community Structure in Eighteenth-Century New England* (Baltimore: Johns Hopkins University Press, 1976).

Crandall, Ralph. *Genealogical Research in New England* (Baltimore: Genealogical Publishing Co., 1984).

Demos, John Putnam. *Entertaining Satan: Witchcraft and the Culture of Early New England* (New York: Oxford University Press, 1982).

Martin, John Frederick. *Profits in the Wilderness: Entrepreneurship and the Founding of New England Towns in the Seventeenth Century* (Chapel Hill: University of North Carolina Press, 1991).

English Origins of New England Families: From The New England Historical and Genealogical Register, First Series. 3 Vols. (Baltimore: Genealogical Publishing Co., 1984, fiche 6047919 ff.).

English Origins of New England Families: From The New England Historical and Genealogical Register. Second Series. 3 Vols. (Baltimore: Genealogical Publishing Co., 1985, fiche 6047922 ff.).

Savage, James. *A Genealogical Dictionary of the First Settlers of New England.* 4 Vols. (1860. Reprint. Baltimore: Genealogical Publishing Co., 1981, fiche 6019972).

Torrey, Clarence Almon. *New England Marriages Prior to 1700* (Baltimore: Genealogical Publishing Co., 1985, film 1320548). See also:
➤ Torrey, Clarence Almon. Manuscript collection of New England marriages prior to 1700 (Andover, MA: Northeast Document Conservation Center, 1983, film 0929494 ff.).
➤ Sanborn, Melinde Lutz. *Supplement to Torrey's New England Marriages Prior to 1700* (Baltimore: Genealogical Publishing Co., 1991). A second supplement was published in 1995.
➤ Williams, Alicia. *Torrey Bibliography: Key to Reference Abbreviations in the Original Manuscript, New England Marriages Prior to 1700 by Clarence Almon Torrey* (Boston: New England Historic Genealogical Society, 1995).

Southern Colonies

Boyer, Carl. *Ship Passenger Lists, the South 1538–1825* (Newhall, CA: The Author, 1979, fiche 6050019).

Crane, Verner W. *The Southern Frontier, 1670–1732* (Ann Arbor: University of Michigan Press, 1956, fiche 6125073).

Doyle, John A. *The English in America: Virginia, Maryland, and the Carolinas* (1882. Reprint. Bowie, MD: Heritage Books, 1990).

Hardy, Stella Pickett. *Colonial Families of the Southern States of America: A History and Genealogy of Colonial Families Who Settled in the Colonies Prior to the Revolution* (New York: Tobias A. Wright, 1911, film 1033932).

Hill, Samuel S. *Encyclopedia of Religion in the South* (Macon, GA: Mercer, 1984).

Johnston, Mary. *Pioneers of the Old South: A Chronicle of English Colonial Beginnings* (New Haven: Yale University Press, 1920).

A History of the South. 10 Vols. (Baton Rouge: Louisiana State University Press, 1985).

Karraker, Cyrus H. *The Seventeenth-Century Sheriff: A Comparative Study of the Sheriff in England and the Chesapeake Colonies, 1607–1689* (Chapel Hill: University of North Carolina Press, 1930).

Peden, Henry C. *Marylanders to Carolina: Migration of Marylanders to North Carolina Prior to 1800* (Westminster, MD: Family Line Publications, 1994).

Robinson, W. Stitt. *The Southern Colonial Frontier, 1607–1763* (Albuquerque: University of New Mexico Press, 1979).

Smith, Abbot E. *Colonists in Bondage: White Servitude and Convict Labor in America, 1607–1776* (Chapel Hill: University of North Carolina Press, 1947).

Smith, John. *The generall historie of Virginia, New England and the Summer Isles: together with the true travels, adventures and observations, and a sea grammar.* 2 Vols. (New York: Macmillian & Co., 1907, film 1697615).

Wilson, Charles Reagan and William Ferris. *Encyclopedia of Southern Culture* (Chapel Hill: University of North Carolina Press, 1989).

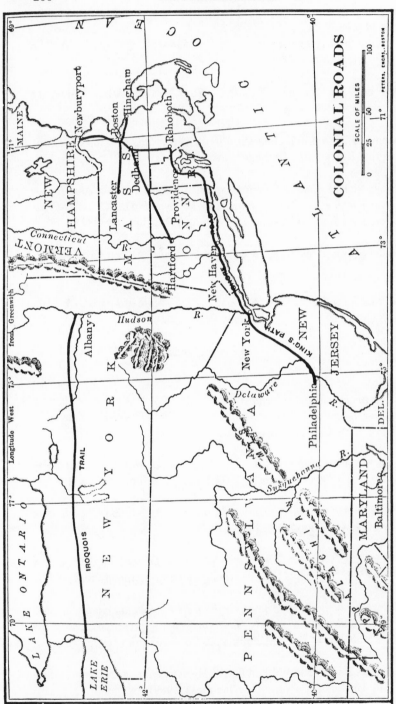

23 Colonial roads in the northeast (Katherine Coman, *The Industrial History of the United States*. New York: Macmillan & Co., 1910)

Connecticut

The first European settlement in Connecticut was a trading post established at Hartford (Suckiaug) by Dutch from New Netherland in 1633. Settlers from Watertown, Massachusetts migrated to Wethersfield (Pyquag) in 1634. About the same time, a group from Plymouth settled at Windsor (Mattaneaug), and were joined by more colonists from Dorchester in 1635. Also in 1635, more Puritans from Newtown, Cambridge, England emigrated to Hartford, and a military fort was built at Saybrook by a group from London. In 1637, after fighting against the Pequot Indians, the towns formed a government independent of Massachusetts.

Quinnipiac (New Haven) was founded in 1638, and the New Haven Colony came to include several towns along the shoreline, including Guilford (Menunketuck, 1639), Milford (Wepawaug, 1639), Southold, Long Island (1640), Stamford (Rippowam, 1641), and Branford (Totoket, 1644). New London (Nameaug) was founded independently in 1646. In 1662 an English Royal charter established Connecticut as a separate colony from Massachusetts, and within the next three years the New Haven Colony was absorbed into Connecticut. The towns on Long Island became part of New York. Four counties were created in 1666, and each was given a judicial unit presided over by a county court comprised of twelve jurymen. By 1740 most of Connecticut had been organized into incorporated towns.

Statewide Records and Resources

The colonial court records are the only source of records that encompass the entire colony. The most important are:

- **General Court (1636–1818):** Highest state court in the colonial era; held civil and criminal jurisdiction; came to be known as the General Assembly. The records have been transcribed in *The Public Records of the Colony of Connecticut* (see below for a description of the volumes).
- **Particular Court (1638–1666):** All types of cases, including appeals from town courts. These records are included in *The Public Records* and

SEE ALSO
Acadia
Great Britain
Massachusetts
New York
Pennsylvania
Vermont

201

abstracted in *Collections of the Connecticut Historical Society*. Vol. 22. *Records of the Particular Court of Connecticut, 1639–1663* (Hartford: Connecticut Historical Society, 1928, film 0897077). See probate districts for more information.

- **Court of Assistants and Superior Court (1669–1715, 1715–)**: Court of Assistants handled major civil and criminal cases. It was called the Court of Assistants, Superior Court, from 1687–1715, and was replaced by the county superior courts in 1715.
- **County Courts or Quarter Courts (1666–1855)**: Handled civil, criminal, chancery, and divorce proceedings. See individual counties.
- **Town courts (1630s–)**: Justice of the Peace courts handled cases without a town court. Most existing town records of the colonial era have been filmed.

The Public Records of the Colony of Connecticut, 1636–1776, Transcribed and Published in Accordance with a Resolution of the General Assembly. 15 Vols. (Hartford: Case, Lockwood, and Brainard Co., 1850–90, fiche 6051120). This important series contains the following records:

Vol. 1 General and Particular courts, 1636–49; General Court, 1650–65; wills and inventories, 1640–9; code of laws, General Court, 1650

Vol. 2 Charter of Connecticut; General Court, 1665–77; journal and correspondence of the Council, 1675–7

Vol. 3 Records of the colony of Connecticut, 1678–89; extracts from the records of the United Colonies of New England, 1652–84

Vol. 4 Colony records, 1689-1706; Council journal, 1696–8

Vol. 5 Colony records, 1706–16; Council Journal, 1710–17

Vol. 6 Colony records, 1717–25; Council Journal, 1717–26

Vol. 7 Colony records, 1726–35; Council

Journal, 1726–7/8

Vol. 8 Colony records, 1735–43

Vol. 9 Colony records, 1744–50

Vol. 10 Colony records, 1751–7

Vol. 11 Colony records, 1757–62

Vol. 12 Colony records, 1762–7

Vol. 13 Colony records, 1768–72 Council journal, 1770–2

Vol.14 Colony records, 1772–5; Susquehannah case (1774): respecting the boundaries of this colony and the Proprietaries of Pennsylvania; Norwich, 1774; inhabitants in the colony, 1774; Hartford, 1774; New London, 1775

Vol. 15 Colony records, 1775–6; journal of the Council of Safety, 1775–6; some council proceedings, 1663–1710

Until the New Haven Colony joined the Connecticut Colony, the records of that administration were kept separately. They have been transcribed in accordance with a resolution of the General Assembly of Connecticut in:

- Hoadly, Charles J. *Records of the Colony and Plantation of New Haven, from 1638 to 1649* (Hartford: Case, Tiffany, and Co., 1857, film 0944116).
- Hoadly, Charles J. *Records of the Colony or Jurisdiction of New Haven*,

from May 1653, to the Union: Together with the New Haven Code of 1656 (Hartford: Case, Lockwood, and Brainard Co., 1858, film 0944116). Series of original manuscripts known as the Connecticut Archives, ca. 1629–1820, are indexed in volumes and slip indexes at the State Library in Hartford.[16] Those that have been filmed are so indicated. Some — but not all — of the Connecticut Archives are:

- Civil officers' records 1669–1756 (series 1), with index (film 0003619 ff.). Series 2, 1673–1820, has not been filmed.
- Colleges and schools, 1657–1789 (series 1), 1718–1820 (series 2).
- Colonial boundaries, 1662–1827 (series 1), 1664–1820 (series 2).
- Court papers, 1649–1709. See *Public Records*.
- Crimes and misdemeanors, 1662–1789 (series 1), 1671–1820 (series 2).
- Estates of deceased persons, 1640–1820; estates of incompetent persons, 1711–1820; estates of minors, 1715–1820.
- Papers concerning transactions between Connecticut and the Indians, 1647–1789 (series 1) (film 0003624). Series 2, 1666–1820, has not been filmed.
- Land lotteries and divorces, 1755–89 (series 1), with index (film 0003617 ff.). Series 2, 1718–1820, has not been filmed.
- Militia records selected papers, 1678–1820 (series 1–3) (film 0003599 ff.). Includes tables of contents, calendar of the legislation on militia for the period covered, digest of the subject matter, and index to the three series. Many of these records have been published: *Roll and Journal of Connecticut Service in Queen Anne's War, 1710–1711 (*New Haven: Tuttle, Morehouse, and Taylor Press, 1916, fiche 6019415); *Collections of the Connecticut Historical Society.* Vol. 7. *Rolls of Connecticut Men in the French and Indian War, 1755–1762.* 2 Vols. (1928. Reprint. Bowie, MD: Heritage Books, 1993, film 0897070).
- Selected papers of colonial wars, 1675–1775 (series 1) (film 0003590 ff.). Covers the following conflicts: King Philip's War, 1675–6; King William's War, 1689–97; Queen Anne's War, 1702–12; Eastern Indian War, 1722–5; War with Spain, 1740–2; King George's War, 1744–8; French and Indian War, 1755–63; and also colonial agents in England, 1751–74. Series 2, 1689–1806, has not been filmed.[17]
- Towns and lands, 1629–1789 (series 1), 1649–1820 (series 2). Town charters, patents, deeds, proprietors' records, grants, etc.

---

[16] For more information, see Robert Claus, *Guide to Archives in the Connnecticut State Library.* 3rd ed. (Hartford: The Library, 1981).

[17] For earlier records, one published source is James Shepard, *Connecticut Soldiers in the Pequot War of 1637* (Meriden, CT: Journal Publishing Co., 1913, film 0438342).

- Trade and maritime affairs, 1668–1789 (series 1), 1685–1820 (series 2).
- Travel, highways, ferries, bridges, taverns, 1700–38 (series 1), 1737–1820 (series 2).
- Susquehannah Settlers, 1755–96 (series 1), 1771–97 (series 2).
- Colonial land records, 1640–1846: including patents, deeds and surveys of land (film 0003656 ff.). Land grants were issued by the Connecticut General Court to proprietors of the individual towns. The record of land distribution by proprietors can be found in town records.
- Revolutionary War papers, 1756–1856 (series 1–3), begin with records prior to the Revolution (film 0003530 ff.). Series 1 and 3 are indexed on microfilm; series 2 is indexed by a card file available only at the State Library in Hartford.

Examples of other records at the State Library in Hartford are:
- Indian deeds to Aquidneck (Rhode Island), 1638, Massapeage (Connecticut), 1658, Marlborough, Massachusetts, 1604, and Springfield, Massachusetts, 1636 (film 0002085).
- Miscellaneous French and Indian War records (film 0003626 ff.). Journals, orderly books, diaries, receipts for wages, orders, Pequot Indian papers, muster rolls, receipts of arms, pay orders, company accounts, etc.
- Robert C. Winthrop manuscript collection, 1631–1794 (film 0003644). Includes jurisdiction and land titles, 1631–1716, Indian, military and foreign affairs, 1651–1712; council, churches, shipping, etc., 1650–1784, and index.
- Samuel Wyllys papers: depositions on cases of witchcraft, assault, theft, drunkenness, and other crimes, tried in Connecticut, 1663–1728, supplement, 1662–93 (film 0003645). The supplement is copied from the Rhode Island State Archives in Providence, Rhode Island.

The Charles R. Hale Collection (film 0003076 ff.) of vital records copied from cemetery inscriptions (1640s–1934) and newspaper notices is indexed and also at the State Library in Hartford. The earliest newspapers abstracted are:

Connecticut Gazette (1755–1812)
Connecticut Journal (1767–1835)
Hartford Courant (1764–1865)
New London Gazette (1765–1836)

New London Summary, or Weekly Advertiser (1758–63)
Norwich Packet (1773–1812)

Records of Connecticut's attempted colonization in Pennsylvania can be found in the Connecticut Archives series and the Pennsylvania Archives, Second Series. Vol. 18: Egle, William Henry. *Documents Relating to the Connecticut Settlement in the Wyoming Valley* (Harrisburg, PA: E.K. Meyers, State Printer, 1890, film 0824000). This includes minutes of the Susquehanna Company claiming lands in Wyoming, 1753–1801, examination of the Connecticut claim to lands in Pennsylvania, 1774, miscellaneous papers relating to the Wyoming controversy, 1769–1808, and other records.

The Collections of the Connecticut Historical Society. 31 Vols. (Hartford: The Society, 1860–1967, film 0897070 ff.) are a series of published records, many of the colonial period, including governors and court records.

Probate Districts

From 1636 to 1649, all probates were handled by the Particular Court and General Court; the records of the two courts were kept together until 1649. The Particular Court continued to function until 1666 when it was succeeded by four county courts. These were the forerunners of the probate districts, established in 1698. The county and probate courts were coterminous until 1719.[18]

Probate districts comprised several towns and often crossed county boundaries. There is a statewide index (0166000 ff.) and selected probate packets of the districts (film 1015126 ff.). The index and packets do not contain references to all the files or surnames in the files. The complete records (within given years) for each district are also filmed and listed below. These are only the districts created before 1775.

Colchester District. Probate records, 1741–1922 (film 0003904 ff.). Contains the records of East Haddam District, 1741–1832, and Colchester District, 1832–1922. The original records are at the Town Hall in Colchester.

Danbury District. Probate records, 1744–1916 (film 0004024 ff.). The original records are at the Town Hall in Danbury.

Fairfield District. Probate records, 1648–1916 (film 0004287 ff.). The original records are at the Town Hall in Fairfield and the State Library in Hartford.

Farmington District. Probate records, 1769–1926 (film 0004207 ff.). The original records are at the Town Hall in Farmington.

Guilford District. Probate records, 1720–1920 (film 0004353 ff.). The original records are at the Town Hall in Guilford.

---

[18]For a list of probate districts by town and where records are included, see Charles W. Manwaring, *A Digest of the Early Connecticut Probate Records.* 3 Vols. 1(1904–6. Reprint. Baltimore: Genealogical Publishing Co., 1995, film 0873816): xvii–xxx.

Hartford District. Probate records, 1649–1917 (film 0004572 ff.), general index (film 0166067 ff.). The first six volumes also contain records of the county courts in Hartford County, sometimes called quarter courts, court of magistrates, particular courts, special courts, etc. The original records are at the Court of Probate in Hartford and the State Library in Hartford.

Litchfield District. Probate records, 1743–1917 (film 0004732 ff.). The original records are at the Town Hall in Litchfield.

Middletown District. Probate records, 1752–1917 (film 0004832 ff.). The original records are at the Town Hall in Middletown.

New Haven District. Probate records, 1647–1916 (film 0005293 ff.). The original records are at the Court of Probate in New Haven.

New London District. Probate records, 1675–1916 (film 1311924 ff.). The original records are at the Town Hall in New London.

Norwich District. Probate records, 1748–1917 (film 0005054 ff.), records of court proceedings, 1748–1852 (film 1310866 ff.). The original records are at the Town Hall in Norwich.

Plainfield District. Probate records, 1747–1918 (film 0005442 ff.). The original records are at the Town Hall in Plainfield.

Pomfret District. Probate records, 1754–1919 (film 0005414 ff.). The original records are at the Town Hall in Pomfret.

Sharon District. Probate records, 1757–1922 (film 0005681 ff.). The original records are at the Town Hall in Sharon.

Simsbury District. Probate records, 1769–1917 (film 0005641 ff.). The original records are at the Town Hall in Simsbury.

Stafford District. Probate records, 1759–1931 (film 0005742 ff.). The original records are at the Town Hall in Stafford.

Stamford District. Probate records, 1728–1916 (film 0005562 ff.).The original records are at the Town Hall in Stamford.

Stonington District. Probate records, 1767–1933 (film 0005605 ff.). The original records are at the Town Hall in Stonington.

Windham District. Probate records, 1719–1918 (film 0005930 ff.), probate records, special, 1734–1917 (film 0005925 ff.). The original records are at the Town Hall in Willimantic.

Woodbury District. Probate records, 1719–1916 (film 0006171 ff.). The original records are at the Town Hall in Woodbury.

Manwaring, Charles William. *A Digest of the Early Connecticut Probate Records.* 3 Vols. (Hartford: R.S. Peck, and Co., 1904–6, film 0873816 ff.). Covers Hartford District records, 1635–1750 (see footnote 18).

Godard, George Seymour. *Godard's Digests, Analytical and Chronological, of Connecticut Probate Papers* (n.p., n.d., film 1636684 ff.). Inventories of probate papers on file at the State Library in Hartford. Arranged first by probate district, and within each district by name of person.

County Records and Resources
Very few county court records have been filmed. County courts were established in 1666 and abolished in 1855. Superior courts held sessions in each county, and records begin 1711–15. Most records of the county and superior courts created before 1900 are at the State Library in Hartford. All records of land transactions are recorded in town records. The following are the only county court records that have been filmed to date:

Fairfield County (1666)
Fairfield County Superior Court. Divorce papers, 1720–99 (film 1673219 ff.).

Hartford County (1666)
Hartford County Superior Court. Divorce papers, 1725–1849 (film 1637917 ff.).

Litchfield County (1751)
Litchfield County Superior Court. Divorce papers, 1752–1922 (film 1664674 ff.).

New Haven County (1666)
New Haven County Superior Court. Divorce papers, 1712–1899 (film 1672069 ff.).

New London County (1666)
New London County Court. Records of trials, 1661–1700 (film 0005138).
New London County Superior Court. Divorce papers, 1719–1875 (film 1638067 ff.).

Windham County (1726)
Windham County Superior Court. Divorce papers, 1726–1907 (film 1638582 ff.).

Knox, Grace Louise and Barbara B. Ferris. *Connecticut Divorces: Superior Court Records for the Counties of New London, Tolland, and Windham, 1719–1910* (Bowie, MD: Heritage Books, 1987).

Town and Church Records and Resources

The Congregational Church was the state church until 1818, and the first vestiges of a town was the forming of a church, known as a society. Male members of the church were the only individuals who could vote at town meetings. The first Episcopal Church was not organized until 1722. Proprietors' records in Connecticut are the recordings of the earliest land grants. Vital records are recorded in the same volumes, mixed in with the deeds.

The early volumes of land records usually contain births, marriages, and deaths, often arranged by families. In some instances, towns have transcribed the early entries into separate volumes and included them with later vital records. There is a general index for almost every series of town land records, and volumes are also indexed individually. Some of the indexes also apply to vital records and proprietors' records. Between 1848 and 1854 vital records began to be kept by the Registrar of Vital Statistics in each town. Records entered previously were kept by the Town Clerk.

It is important to remember that land, town, and vital records are usually found together and that the title of the record will not exclude other information. Unless otherwise stated, all of the filmed town records are kept at the town hall under which they are listed. Many churches or ecclesiastical societies were established decades before a town was incorporated. Unless otherwise indicated, all filmed church records are at the State Library in Hartford, including original records, photocopies, and transcripts.

Indexes to town and church records at the State Library in Hartford are:
- Barbour Collection of Connecticut town vital records prior to 1850 (film 0002887 ff.). Abstracts from original town records organized by town; general surname index. This collection should not be considered definitive.
- Index cards to vital records of Connecticut churches at the State Library in Hartford (film 0002806 ff.).
- Bowman Collection: Index cards to Connecticut vital records in

Massachusetts, about 1800–1900 (film 0002884 ff.). Abstracts of death notices from Massachusetts newspapers and vital records in alphabetical order.

Ashford
Originally called New Scituate; incorporated as Ashford in 1714.
Church of Christ. Records, 1718–1834 (film 1007920).
Baptist Church of Christ at West Ashford. Records, 1765–1863 (film 0003692). Before 1755 known as the First Baptist Church of Christ in South Brimfield, Massachusetts.

Proprietors' records, 1705–70 (film 0003676).
Vital records, 1675–1849 (film 1376249).
Land records, 1715–1902 (film 0003677 ff.).

Barkhamsted
Land records, 1732–1913 (film 0003762 ff.).
Vital records, 1742–1912 (film 1451545).

Berlin
Congregational Church, Kensington. Records, 1709–1889 (film 0003744). Established in 1711 as Great Swamp or Second Society in Farmington.
Worthington Ecclesiastical Society. Records, 1772–1928 (film 0003746).

Bethlehem
Congregational Church. Records, 1738–1850 (film 0003803).

Vital records, 1761–1857 (film 1522005).

Bolton
Bolton Church. Records, 1725–1812 (film 1007926).
Congregational Church. Records, 1725–1922 (film 003720).

Land records, 1720–1911 (film 0003719 ff.).
Town and vital records, 1704–1855 (film 1376044).

Bozrahville
Congregational Church. Records, 1737–1890 (film 0003727). Includes records of New Concord Society in Norwich, 1737–1845.

Vital records, 1755–1861 (film 1312386).

Branford
First Congregational Church. Records, 1687–1899 (film 0003712). Organized as early as 1647 by settlers from Long Island; new church organized in 1688.

Land records, 1645–1906, vital records, 1645–1710 (film 0003697 ff.).

Bristol
First Congregational Church. Records, 1742–1897 (film 1008324).

Formerly called New Cambridge Society.

Brookfield
First Society. Records, 1755–1830 (film 1008325). Formerly called Newbury Society.
Saint Paul's Church, Episcopal. Records, 1707–1930 (film 0003842 ff.).

Vital records, 1764–1853 (film 1435600).

Brooklyn
First Congregational Church. Records, 1734–1926 (film 1008325).
First Trinitarian Church. Records, 1734–1897 (film 0003810).
Trinity Episcopal Church. Records, 1771–1866 (film 0003813).

Vital and town records, 1750–1917 (film 1378050 ff.).

Canaan
First Ecclesiastical Society. Records, 1741–1852 (film 0003948).
Second Church of Christ at East Canaan. Records, 1767–1942 (film 0003946).
Church of Christ. Records, 1752–1817 (film 0003947). In April 1762 the church removed to Stillwater, New York.
South and East Canaan church records, 1769–1870 (film 0234581). The location of the original records is unknown.

Land records, 1737–1935, early vital records, and proprietors' records (film 0003935 ff.). The original records are at the Town Hall in Falls Village.

Town and vital records, 1744–1898 (film 1503196).

Canterbury
Congregational Church. Records, 1711–1821 (film 0003983).
Separate Church. Records, 1748–99 (film 1008326).
Westminster Ecclesiastical Society. Records, 1770–1900 (film 1008327).

Land records, 1703–1914 (film 0003969 ff.).
Vital records, 1696–1907 (film 1378163 ff.).

Cheshire
Congregational Church. Records, 1724–1917 (film 0003998 ff.). Established in 1723 as the West Society in Wallingford.

Town records, 1765–1884 (film 1412759).

Colchester
Church formed in 1703; part set off as New Salem Society in 1725; Westchester Society established in 1728 as Colchester Southwest or Third Society (sometimes called Pine Swamp Society); part set off as Marlborough Society in 1747.

Westchester Ecclesiastical Society. Records, 1728–1835 (film 0003913).
First Congregational Church. Records, 1702–1937 (film 0003910).
First Society of Colchester. Records, 1729–1876 (film 1008331).
Second Church of Christ. Records, 1729–1876 (film 1008331).
Second Congregational Church. Records, 1729–1811 (film 0003911).

Land records, 1703–1909, early vital records (film 0003902 ff.).
Proprietors' records, 1713–1805 (film 0003888).
Vital records, 1712–1932 (film 1312155 ff.).

Colebrook
Land records, 1771–1912 (film 0003931 ff.).
Town and vital records, 1744–1835 (film 1503206).

Columbia
Congregational Church. Records, 1722–1917 (film 0003871 ff.). Also known as Northwest or Crank Society in Lebanon.

Town records, 1768–1868, marriages, 1768–1854 (film 0003870).

Cornwall
First Congregational Church. Records, 1755–1892 (film 0003966).

Land records, 1740–1908 (film 0003958 ff.).
Proprietors' records, 1730–1887 (film 0003957).
Vital records, 1732–1933 (film 1516243).

Coventry
First Congregational Church at South Coventry. Records, 1740–1936 (film 0003863).

First Ecclesiastical Society. Records, 1772–1819 (film 1008333).
Second Congregational Church at North Coventry. Records, 1740–1910 (film 0003862). Includes

extracts from town records, 1735– 40.

Land records, 1714–1905 (film 0003858 ff.).
Town and vital records, 1692–1853 (film 1376123 ff.).

Town records, 1692–1840 (film 0003861). The original records are at the State Library in Hartford.

Danbury
First Congregational Church. Records, 1754–1930 (film 0004035).

Vital records, 1711–1841 (film 1435525).

Darien
First Congregational Church. Records, 1739–1938 (film 1008338). Includes records of the Middlesex Ecclesiastical Society.

Town records, 1765–1873, vital records, 1765–1841(film 1434227).

Derby (see also Litchfield)
Saint James' Church, Episcopal. Records, 1740–1929 (film 1008339 ff.).

Land records, 1667–1907, early vital records (film 0004056 ff.).
Durham
Settled in 1698; called Coginchaug until 1704. All ecclesiastical affairs were voted upon in town meeting until 1804.
Congregational Church. Records, 1756–1938 (film 0004054).

Land records, 1698–1923 (film 0004044 ff.).

East Haddam
First Congregational Church and Ecclesiastical Society. Records, 1702–1927 (film 0004112). Established in 1702; Hadlyme Society in East Haddam and Lyme established in 1742.
Hadlyme Ecclesiastical Society and Congregational Church. Records, 1742–1932 (film 0004700 ff.).
Second Congregational Church and Ecclesiastical Society. Records, 1733–1931 (film 0004115).

Land records, 1704–1912, town and vital records, 1687–1761 (film 0004110 ff.).
Vital records abstracted from land records, 1687–1915 (film 1480163).

East Hampton
Chatham had its name changed to East Hampton in 1915.
Congregational Church. Records, 1748–1930 (film 0004193). Haddam Neck Society in Chatham and Haddam established in 1739 as Middle Haddam Society; part of Middletown including this Society was incorporated in 1767 as Chatham.
Haddam Neck Congregational Church. Records, 1740–1944 (film 0004194).

Land records, 1767–1912 (film 0003887 ff.).

Vital records, 1731–1909 (film 1480162 ff.).

East Hartford
First Congregational Church and Ecclesiastical Society. Records, 1699–1912 (film 0004130).

Vital records, 1739–1907 (film 1312792 ff.).

East Haven
First Congregational Church. Records, 1755–1905 (film 0004084). Organized in 1711 as the Old Stone Church. Early records destroyed by fire.

East Windsor
First Ecclesiastical Society. Records, 1752–1933 (film 0004182).

Land records, 1768–1907 (film 0004159 ff.).
Vital records, 1758–1945 (film 1317066).

Ellington
Vital records, 1754–1856 (film 1319920).

Enfield
First called Fresh Water Plantation and was part of Massachusetts until 1749. The name was changed to Enfield in 1683.
First Congregational Church. Records, 1770–1907 (film 0004145).

Land records, 1750–1906 (film 0004132).
Town records, 1693–1756 (film 0004133).
Town records, 1682–1854 (film 1317124).
Proprietors' records, 1680–1775 (film 0004131).

Fairfield

First Congregational Church. Records, 1694–1806 (film 0004201).
Greenfield Hill Church. Records, 1668–1881 (film 0004199). Established in 1725 as the Northwest Society in Fairfield by division of the First Society.
Stratfield Baptist Church. Records, 1751–1938 (film 0004200).

Land records, 1649–1903 (film 0004245 ff.).
Proprietors' records, 1749–50, and early vital records (film 0004290). The original records are at the State Library in Hartford and the Town Hall in Fairfield.

Farmington

First Congregational Church. Records, 1652–1938 (film 0004241).

Land records, 1645–1905, early vital records (film 0004212).
Vital records extracted from land records, 1643–1850 (film 1315116).

Franklin

Congregational Church. Records, 1718–1934 (film 0004206). Formerly the Second Church in Norwich. Established in 1716 as West Farms Society in Norwich; part was set off in 1761 as Norwich Eighth Society; incorporated in 1786 as Franklin.
Pautipaug Hill Congregational Church. Death records, 1763–1802 (film 1008707). Church formerly known as Norwich Eighth Society.
West Society of Norwich. Ecclesiastical records, 1716–85 (film 0004202). The original records are at the Town Hall in Franklin.

Glastonbury

Congregational Church, Buckingham. Records, 1731–1899 (film 0004394 ff.). Buckingham Society was formerly Eastbury or Second Society in Glastonbury; in 1747 part was set off as the Marlborough Society.
First Congregational Church. Records, 1731–1924 (film 0004393).

Land records, 1690–1904, early town and proprietors' meetings, vital records (film 1316284 ff.).
Vital records, 1680–1905 (film 1316154 ff.).

Goshen

First Congregational Church. Records, 1772–1912 (film 1008709).

Land records, 1739–1958 (film 0004415 ff.).

Greenwich (see also Norwalk)

Baptist Church of Christ at King Street. Records, 1773–1880 (film 2027119). The original records are at the Westchester County Historical Society in Elmsford, New York.

Land records, 1640–1901, early vital records (film 1434424 ff.).
Town records, 1658–1848, vital records, land and property records, 1658–1703 (film 0185372).

Griswold
First Congregational Church. Records, 1720–1887 (film 0004374).

Vital records, 1738–1917 (film 1311196 ff.). The original records are at the Griswold Town Hall in Jewett City.

Groton
Union Baptist Church of Mystic. Records, 1765–1910 (film 1008896 ff.).

Land records, 1705–1908, early vital records (film 1403154 ff.).
Vital records, 1686–1915 (film 1306248 ff.).

Guilford
First Congregational Church and Ecclesiastical Society. Records, 1717–1921 (film 0004369 ff.).
Organized in 1643; the votes of the First Ecclesiastical Society prior to 1717 are recorded among the town acts in the third book of records.
Second Congregational Church at North Guilford. Records, 1720– 1859 (film 0004367).
Christ Episcopal Church. Records, 1744–1909 (film 0004368).
Saint John's Protestant Episcopal Church at North Guilford. Records, 1749–1868 (film 0004366).

Land records, 1645–1903 (film 0004329 ff.).
Vital records, 1639–1905, early court minutes (film 1428110 ff.).

Haddam
First Congregational Church. Records, 1700–1908 (film 0004480).

Land records, 1668–1906, vital records, 1662–1748 (film 0004478 ff.).
Vital records, 1662–1911 (film 1398664).
Earlier vital records taken from land records.

Hamden
First Society. Records, 1764–1812 (film 0003054). Contains vital records of Hamden, 1736–1836. The typescript is at the New Haven Colony Historical Society in New Haven.

Hampton
First Congregational Church. Records, 1723–1879 (film 0004438).
Established in 1717 as Windham Northeast.
Baptist Church. Records, 1770–1853 (film 0004439).

Hartford
First Congregational Church. Records, 1684–1930 (film 1009610 ff.).
Second Ecclesiastical Society. Records, 1767–1920 (film 1010729).

Land records, 1639–1901, early proprietors' records and vital records (film 0004508 ff.).

South Meadow Town Clerk. Proprietors' records, 1659–1929 (film

0004573). The original records are at the State Library in Hartford.

Hartland
First Congregational Church. Records, 1768–1899 (film 1010730). First Ecclesiastical Society and Congregational Church at East Hartland. Records, 1768–1931 (film 0004493).

Land records, 1733–1949 (film 0004490 ff.).
Proprietors' records, 1733–62 (film 0004490).
Vital records, 1772–1935 (film 1317069).

Harwinton
Proprietors' records, 1729–69 (film 0004496).
Land records, 1738–1913, early vital records (film 0004497 ff.).
Family records, 1725–1924 (film 1521829).

Hebron
Gilead Ecclesiastical Society. Records, 1748–1941 (film 0004461). Gilead Society established in 1748 by division of Hebron Society. Gilead Congregational Church. Records, 1752–1943 (film 0004460).

Land records, 1709–1914 (film 0004449 ff.).
Vital records, 1684–1849 (film 1376165 ff.).

Kent
Church of Christ. Records, 1739–1915 (film 0004654).

Land records, 1738–1919, early vital records (film 0004641 ff.).
Vital records, 1723–1903 (film 1516999).

Killingly
Land records, 1709–1907 (film 1450883 ff.). The original records are at the Danielson Town Hall.
Vital records, 1700–1903 (film 1451023 ff.).

Killingworth
First Congregational Church. Records, 1735–1893 (film 0004637). North Parish and Second Parish. Records, 1738–1839 (film 0004620).

Land records, 1664–1904, early vital records (film 0004635 ff.).
Town records, 1692–1849, vital records and land records (film 1378382 ff.).

Lebanon
First Congregational Church. Records, 1700–1883 (film 0004724). Goshen Congregational Church. Records, 1728–1895 (film 0004726). Exeter Congregational Church. Records, 1709–1920 (film 0004726).

Land records, 1695–1922 (film 1451120 ff.).
Vital records, 1700–1915 (film 1312154).

Lisbon

Newent Congregational Church. Records, 1724-1932 (film 0004706). Vital records, 1771-1917 (film 1311198).

Litchfield

First Ecclesiastical Society. Records, 1768-1927 (film 0004766). Earlier records from 1722 destroyed by fire.

Saint Michael's Parish. Records, 1750-1870 (film 0004773). An Episcopal Church was organized in 1745, and four years later the first Saint Michael's Church was built. This also includes some baptisms for Derby, Stratford, Stamford, and Simsbury, 1750-74.

Land records, 1719-1908 (film 004742 ff.).
Proprietors' records, 1723-1807 (film 0004741).
Town records, 1701-1881, early vital records (film 1516502).

Lyme

First Ecclesiastical Society. Records, 1730-1871 (film 1010744). Hadlyme Society in East Haddam and Lyme established in 1742. Hadlyme Ecclesiastical Society and Congregational Church. Records, 1742-1932 (film 0004700 ff.).

Land records, 1664-1929, early vital records (film 0004698 ff.).
Vital records, 1700-1921 (film 1311111).

Madison

North Madison Congregational Church. Records, 1754-1888 (film 1010745).

Vital records, 1763-1853 (film 1420981).

Mansfield

First Congregational Church. Records, 1710-1927 (film 1010746). Second Congregational Church. Records, 1737-1867 (film 0004883 ff.).

Land records, 1702-1912 (film 0004880 ff.).
Vital records, 1686-1901, list of soldiers who served in the Revolutionary War (film 1450838 ff.).

Marlborough

Congregational Church. Records, 1749-1951 (film 1010747).

Town records, 1729-1852, early vital records and militia rolls (film 1318178).

Meriden

First Congregational Church. Records, 1729-1937 (film 0004898).

Vital records, 1761-1908 (film 1403297 ff.).

Middlebury

Congregational Church. Records, 1751-1916 (film 0004915 ff.). Established in 1751 as Middlebury Society by division of Waterbury First Society, Southbury Society, and Woodbury First Society.

Town and vital records, 1734-1855 (film 1412972).

Middletown

Westfield Society was established in 1766 by division of the First and

Second Societies.
First Church of Christ, Congregational. Records, 1668–1871 (film 0004848 ff.).
Third Congregational Church at Westfield. Records, 1773–1929 (film 0004851 ff.).
Church of the Holy Trinity. Records, 1750–1947 (film 0004841 ff.).

Land records, 1654–1909, vital records, 1640–1765 (film 0004788 ff.).
Vital records, 1640–1921 (film 1513707 ff.).

Milford
First Church of Christ. Records, 1639–1964 (film 1012263).
First Ecclesiastical Society. Records, 1760–1830 (film 1010750).
Second Congregational Church. Records, 1747–1930 (film 0004937 ff.).
Saint Peter's Church, Episcopal. Records, 1764–1869 (film 0004938). Records of this parish from 1736 to 1763 are found in those of Christ Church Parish, Stratford.

Land records, 1639–1903, early vital records (film 0004917 ff.).

Monroe
Congregational Church. Records, 1762–1812 (film 0004943). Established in 1762 as New Stratford Society by division of Ripton and North Stratford societies; became New Stratford Second Society in Huntington (now Shelton) in 1789; became New Stratford Society in Monroe on the incorporation from Huntington in 1823; name changed to Monroe Society in 1848.

Montville
Congregational Church. Records, 1722–1909 (film 0004863). Established in 1720 as North Parish in New London; incorporated 1786 as Montville.
First Ecclesiastical Society. Records, 1721–1837 (film 0004863).
Baptist Church. Records, 1749–1827 (film 0960619). The original records are at the Western Reserve Historical Society in Cleveland, Ohio.

Vital records, 1744–1923 (film 1311446 ff.).

New Canaan
Congregational Church. Records, 1733–1899 (film 0004960). Established in 1731 as Canaan Society in Norwalk and Stamford; incorporated in 1801 as New Canaan.

Vital records, 1766–1900 (film 1450629).

New Fairfield
South Congregational Church. Records, 1742–1900 (film 0005351).

New Hartford
Church of Christ. Records, 1739–1877 (film 1010759).

Land records, 1738–1906 (film 0005164 ff.).
Town records, 1718–1864, early vital records (film 1318241).

New Haven

First Church of Christ and Ecclesiastical Society. Records, 1639–1926 (film 0005343). In addition to records, this includes indentures, 1773, leases, 1733–51.
First Ecclesiastical Society. Records, 1715–1937 (film 1010762 ff.).
Congregational Church at White Haven. Records, 1742–1870 (film 1011941).
Fair Haven Church. Records, 1769–1819 (film 1011941).
Trinity Church. Records, 1767–1939 (film 0005341 ff.).

Land records, 1659–1901 (film 0005223 ff.).
Proprietors' records, 1724–71 (film 0005292).
Wills, indentures, etc., 1664–1711 (film 0005292).

Vital records, 1639–1902 (film 1405824 ff.).

New London

First Church of Christ. Records, 1670–1903 (film 0005133 ff.). The First Church believed to have been organized in Gloucester, Massachusetts in 1642 and removed to New London a few years later.
First Congregational Church. Records, 1670–1916 (film 0005131).
Saint James Church, Episcopal. Records, 1725–1874 (film 0005132).

Land records, 1646–1906, vital records, 1646–1724, general court records etc. (film 0005107 ff.).
Vital records, 1644–1922 (film 1312157 ff.).

New Milford

Congregational Church. Records, 1716–1938 (film 1011946).

Land records, 1706–1902, early vital records (film 0005186 ff.).
Vital records, 1702–1902 (film 1516559 ff.).

Newtown

First Congregational Church. Records, 1742–1951 (film 0004991 ff.).
Trinity Church, Episcopal. Records, 1764–1921 (film 0004990). Services were held in Newtown as early as 1722 by missionaries of the Society for the Propagation of the Gospel; organized as a mission in 1732.

Land records, 1712–1911, early vital records (film 0004962 ff.).
Vital records, 1716–1871 (film 1435629).

Norfolk

Church of Christ. Records, 1760–1928 (film 0005182).

Land records, 1758–1905 (film 0005177 ff.).
Vital records, 1740–1917 (film 1503193).

Proprietors' records 1754–72 (film 0005181). The original records are at the State Library in Hartford.

North Branford

Saint Andrew's Church at Northford, Episcopal. Records, 1763– 1899 (film 0005143).

Town and church records, 1769–1885 (film 1420924).

North Haven
Congregational Church. Records, 1716–1910 (film 0005154).
Saint John's Church, Episcopal. Records, 1759–1858 (film 0005153).

Vital records, 1766–1916 (film 1428122).

North Stonington
Congregational Church. Records, 1720–1887 (film 0005081).
North Society. Records, 1720–81 (film 1011949).
Strict Congregational Church. Records, 1746–1822 (film 1011949).
First Baptist Church at Pendleton Hill. Records, 1754–1905 (film 0005079).
Vital records, 1758–1920 (film 1309964).

Norwalk
Saint Paul's' Church, Episcopal. Records, 1741–1925 (film 0005019 ff.).
Church of England. Records, 1742–6 (film 0005815). Includes records for Norwalk, Ridgefield, Stamford, and Greenwich.

Land records, 1652–1915, early vital records (film 0004999 ff.).

Norwich
First Congregational Church. Records, 1660–1928 (film 1011950 ff.). Organized in Saybrook and removed to Norwich in 1660.
Hanover Congregational Church, Sprague. Records, 1761–1915 (film

0005821). Includes the Church of Christ in Norwich.
Christ Church. Records, 1757– 1849 (film 1011950).
Christ Church, Episcopal. Records, 1746–1901 (film 0005064).

Land records, 1660–1907 (film 0005052 ff.).
Vital records, 1640–1921 (film 1311433 ff.).

Oxford
Congregational Church. Records, 1741–1929 (film 0005375). Established in 1741 as Oxford Society in Derby, Waterbury, and Woodbury; incorporated with parts of Derby and Southbury in 1798 as Oxford.
Saint Peter's Church. Records, 1769–1948 (film 1011955).

Vital records, 1743–1848 (film 1420658).

Plainfield
Land records, 1701–1906 (film 0005433 ff.).

Plymouth
First Congregational Church. Records, 1736–1949 (film 1011958). Formerly called Northbury Society of Waterbury.
Saint Matthew's Church, Episcopal. Records 1744–1901 (film 0005411 ff.). Includes the records of the Episcopal Church in New Cambridge (now Bristol).

Vital records, 1745–1938, records of enrolled militia (film 1521827).

Pomfret
Abington Ecclesiastical Society.
Records, 1761–1883 (film 1011965
ff.).

Land records, 1713–1903 (film
0005423 ff.).
Vital records, 1695–1869 (film
1376250 ff.).

Preston
First Congregational Church. Records, 1698–1917 (film 1011968).
Long Society of Preston. Records,
1757–1938 (film 0005393). Formerly called Norwich East Society.
Saint James Church, Poquetanuck.
Records, 1712–1948 (film 1011969).

Land records, 1687–1909 (film
0005392 ff.).
Vital records, 1672–1933 (film
1311194 ff.).

Redding
Congregational Church and Ecclesiastical Society. Records, 1729–
1882 (film 0005481).

Land records, 1767–1910 (film
0005469 ff.).
Vital records, 1726–1902 (film
1435589 ff.).

Ridgefield (see also Norwalk)
First Congregational Church. Records, 1761–1931 (film 0005509).
Ridgebury Congregational Church
and Ecclesiastical Society. Records,
1761–1916 (film 1011971).

Land records, 1708–1901, vital records,
1708–65 (film 0005495 ff.).

Vital records, 1700–1909 (film 1435729
ff.).

Roxbury
Church of Christ. Records, 1743–
1863 (film 1012868).
Congregational Church and Ecclesiastical Society. Records, 1742–
1930 (film 0005494).

Salisbury
Congregational Church. Records,
1744–1941 (film 0005526).

Land records, 1739–1924, early
vital records and proprietors' records (film 0005524 ff.).

Vital and town records, 1740–1848
(film 1509740).

Sharon
First Church of Christ Congregational.
Records, 1755–1879 (film 0005691).

Land records, 1739–1911, early
vital records and proprietors' records (film 0005665 ff.).

Shelton
Huntington Congregational Church
and Ecclesiastical Society. Records,
1717–1946 (film 0005769 ff.).
Ripton Society established in 1717;
name was changed to the Huntington Ecclesiastical Society in
1810; name of the town changed to
Shelton in 1919.
Saint Paul's Church. Records,
1755–1907 (film 0005765).

Huntington Town Clerk. Vital records, 1739–1912 (film 1435632).

Sherman
North Congregational Church. Records, 1744–1921 (film 0005560).

Simsbury (see also Litchfield)
Land records, 1666–1915, vital records, and baptisms, early to 1718 (film 0005640 ff.).
Town records, 1670–1864, vital records, land grants and deeds (film 1314486).

Somers
Part of Massachusetts until 1750.
Congregational Church. Records, 1727–1890 (film 0005717).
Land records, 1750–1923 (film 0005711 ff.). Includes a few earlier deeds originally written when still part of Massachusetts.

Southbury
South Britain Congregational Church. Records, 1766–1884 (film 0005812).
South Britain Society established in 1766; set off from the Church in Southbury in 1769.

Town and vital records, 1752–1878 (film 1420657).

Southington
First Congregational Church. Records, 1728–1876 (film 0005662).

Stafford
First Congregational Church. Records, 1757–1817 (film 1013276).

Land records, 1720–1907, early town and vital records (film 0005728 ff.) The original records are at the Town Hall in Stafford Springs.

Stamford (see also Litchfield and Norwalk)
First Congregational Church. Records, 1747–1907 (film 0005589).

Land records, 1666–1902 (film 0005571 ff.).
Town and vital records, 1640–1806 (film 0005570).
Town records transcript, 1630–1806 (film 0899934 ff.).

Stonington
First Church of Christ. Records, 1720–1869 (film 1013280).
First Congregational Church and Ecclesiastical Society. Records, 1674–1929 (film 0005614 ff.).

Land records, 1664–1907, early vital records and town meetings (film 1403180 ff.).
Town and vital records, 1664–1831 (film 1309871).

Stratford (see also Litchfield)
First Congregational Church. Records, 1688–1927 (film 0005800).

Christ Church and Episcopal Society. Records, 1722–1932 (film 0005799), index to vital records, 1692–1820 (film 0005798).

Land records, 1650–1905, vital records, 1650–1724 (film 0005789 ff.).

Suffield
Before 1749 part of Hampshire

County, Massachusetts. First Congregational Church and Ecclesiastical Society. Records, 1741–1917 (film 1014183 ff.).

Land records, 1747–1978, vital records and marriage intentions (film 0005693 ff.).
Town and proprietors' records, 1677–1725 (film 0005706).
Vital records, 1662–1904 (film 1317067 ff.).

Thompson
Congregational Church. Records, 1728–1930 (film 1003071 ff.).

Vital records, 1733–1904 (film 1376374 ff.).

Tolland
Land records, 1719–1902 (film 0005849 ff.).
Vital records, 1665–1853 (film 1376026).

Torrington
First Congregational Church. Records, 1741–1901 (film 0005848). Torrington Ecclesiastical Society. Records, 1757–1849 (film 0005847).

Land records, 1733–1903, proprietors' records (film 1450656 ff.).
Vital records, 1741–1902 (film 1450834 ff.).

Union
Congregational Church. Records, 1759–1922 (film 0005878).

Land records, 1745–1911, early vital

records, town, and proprietors' records (film 1451122 ff.).
Town records, 1718–49, land records, 1733–44, vital records, 1718–48 (film 0005874).
Vital records, 1731–1863 (film 1319915).

Vernon
First Congregational Church. Records, 1762–1940 (film 0005895). Established 1760 as North Bolton Society in Bolton and Windsor.

Town records, 1758–1876, vital records, 1758–1851(film 1319931).

Voluntown
Voluntown and Sterling Congregational Church, Presbyterian. Records, 1723–1914 (film 0005887 ff.). Later known as the Line Church.

Land records, 1705–1901 (film 0005880 ff.).

Wallingford
First Congregational Church. Records, 1758–1894 (film 0006053).

Land records, 1670–1905, early vital records (film 0006042 ff.).
Vital records, 1762–1903 (film 1405514 ff.).

Warren
Church of Christ. Records, 1750–1931 (film 0005949). Includes East Greenwich Society records. Established in 1750 as the East Greenwich Society of Kent.

Vital records, 1736–1948 (film 1517090).

Washington
First Congregational Church in New Preston. Records, 1757–1845 (film 0006106).
First Congregational Church. Records, 1741–1919 (film 0006105). Established in 1741 as Judea Society in Woodbury.

Vital records, 1742–1854 (film 1517000).

Waterbury
First Church of Christ Ecclesiastical Society and Congregational Society. Records, 1770–1895 (film 1014191).
Saint John's Church, Episcopal. Records, 1761–1927 (film 0006144 ff.). Organized as a mission of the Society for the Propagation of the Gospel in Foreign Parts in 1737.

Land and family records, vital records, 1672–1902 (film 0006108 ff.).
Town records, 1680–1851, early land and vital records (film 1412886 ff.).

Watertown
Vital records, 1753–1850, town records (film 1521444). Includes marriages and deaths from Congregational Church records.

Weston
Norfield Congregational Church and Society. Records, 1757–1941 (film 0006243). Norfield Society in Fairfield and Norwalk established in 1757; this part of Fairfield incorporated as Weston in 1787.

Wethersfield
First Congregational Church. Records, 1694–1846 (film 1014196).

Land records, 1635–1912, early vital records (film 0006012 ff.).
Vital records, 1635–1924 (film 1315118 ff.).

Willington
Congregational Church. Records, 1759–1911 (film 0005981).

Land records, 1727–1916 (film 0005973 ff.).
Town records, 1722–1912 (film 1376043).
Vital records, 1720–1854 (film 1376042 ff.).

Winchester
First Ecclesiastical Society. Records, 1768–1908 (film 0006072 ff.).

Land records, 1744–1903 (film 0006060 ff.).

Town records, 1771–82, vital records, 1756–1818 (film 1503204). The original records are at the Town Hall in Winsted.

Windham
First Congregational Church. Records, 1700–1924 (film 0005942).

Land records, 1686–1923 (film 0005924 ff.).
Vital records, 1692–1893 (film 1376452 ff.). The original records are at the Town Hall in Willimantic.

Windsor
First Congregational Church. Records, 1636-1832 (film 0006208). Organized in 1630 in Plymouth, England; brought to Windsor by the first settlers of the town; a second society established in 1668.
North Windsor Congregational Church. Records, 1761-94 (film 0006209).
Second Congregational Church at Poquonock. Records, 1771-82 (film 0006209).

Land records, 1640-1919 (film 1316290 ff.).
Proprietors' records 1650-1787 (film 0006185).
Vital records, 1638-1925 (film 1316427 ff.).

Woodbury
First Congregational Church and First Ecclesiastical Society. Records, 1670-1911 (film 0006182).
Saint Paul's Church, Episcopal. Records, 1765-1923 (film 0006184). Organized in 1740; services were conducted by ministers of surroun-

ding parishes and Episcopal missionaries until 1771.

Land records, 1659-1922, early vital records (film 0006147 ff.).
Vital records, 1683-1867 (film 1491338).

Woodstock
Settled in 1686 as New Roxbury, Massachusetts, name changed to Woodstock in 1690; annexed to Connecticut in 1749. Records prior to 1731 are in Suffolk County, Massachusetts records. Those from 1741-50 may be in Worcester County, Massachusetts records.

First Congregational Church. Records, 1743-1932 (film 0005967 ff.).
Congregational Church at West Woodstock. Records, 1743-1937 (film 0005970).

Land records, 1749-1908 (film 0005954 ff.).
Vital records, 1686-1929 (film 1376372 ff.).

Suggested Reading

Atwater, Edward E. *History of the Colony of New Haven: To Its Absorption into Connecticut; With Supplementary History and Personnel of the Towns of Branford, Guilford, Milford, Stratford, Norwalk, Southold, Etc.* (Meriden, CT: Journal Publishing Co., 1902, film 0833384).

Bailey, Frederic W. *Early Connecticut Marriages as Found on Ancient Church Records Prior to 1800.* 7 Vols. (1896-1906. Reprint. Baltimore: Genealogical Publishing Co., 1996, film 0924061 ff.).

Cothren, William. *History of Ancient Woodbury, Connecticut: From the First Indian Deed in 1659 ... Including the Present Towns of Washington, Southbury,*

Bethlehem, Roxbury, and a Part of Oxford and Middlebury. 3 Vols. 2nd ed. (Waterbury, CT: William R. Seeley, 1871–9, film 0006181).

Daniels, Bruce C. *The Connecticut Town: Growth and Development, 1635–1790* (Middletown, CT: Wesleyan University Press, 1979).

Ditz, Toby L. *Property and Kinship: Inheritance in Early Connecticut, 1750–1820* (Princeton: Princeton University Press, 1986).

Hinman, Royal R. *A Catalogue of the Names of the First Puritan Settlers of the Colony of Connecticut: With the Time of Their Arrival in the Colony, and Their Standing in Society, Together with Their Place of Residence, as Far as Can Be Discovered by the Records* (1846. Reprint. Baltimore: Clearfield Co., 1996, film 0908908).

Historical Records Survey. *Guide to Vital Statistics in the Church Records of Connecticut* (New Haven: The Survey, 1942, fiche 6051300).

Historical Records Survey. *Inventory of the Church Archives of Connecticut, Protestant Episcopal* (New Haven: The Survey, 1940, film 0908157).

Holbrook, Jay Mack. *Connecticut 1670 Census* (Oxford, MA: Holbrook Research Institute, 1977).

Jacobus, Donald L. *History and Genealogy of the Families of Old Fairfield.* 2 Vols. in 3 (1930–2. Reprint. Baltimore: Genealogical Publishing Co., 1991, film 0599305 ff.).

Jacobus, Donald L. *Families of Ancient New Haven.* 9 Vols. in 3 (1922–32. Reprint. Baltimore: Genealogical Publishing Co., 1997, film 1421640 ff.).

Kemp, Thomas Jay. *Connecticut Researcher's Handbook* (Detroit: Gale Research Co., 1981).

Main, Jackson Turner. *Society and Economy in Colonial Connecticut* (Princeton: Princeton University Press, 1985).

McCain, Diana Ross. *As True as Taxes: An Historian's Guide to Direct Taxation and Tax Records in Connecticut, 1637–1820* (Middletown, CT: Wesleyan University, 1981).

Papers of the New Haven Colony Historical Society (New Haven: The Society,

1865–, film 0421549).

Plimpton, Elizebeth B. *The Vital Records of Saybrook Colony, 1635–1860: Including the Towns of Chester, Deep River, Essex, Old Saybrook, and Westbrook, Connecticut* (Old Saybrook, CT: Saybrook Press, 1985).

Ritter, Kathy A. *Apprentices of Connecticut, 1637–1900* (Salt Lake City: Ancestry Publishing, 1986).

Scott, Kenneth. *Genealogical Data from Colonial New Haven Newspapers* (Baltimore: Genealogical Publishing Co., 1979).

Sperry, Kip. *Connecticut Sources for Family Historians and Genealogists* (Logan, UT: Everton Publishers, 1980).

Taylor, Robert J. *Colonial Connecticut, a History* (Millwood, NY: KTO Press, 1979).

Ullmann, Helen S. *Nutmegger Index . . . to The Connecticut Nutmegger, Volumes 1–28, 1968–1996* (Camden, ME: Picton Press, 1996).

· *Connecticut's First Church, Hartford* ·

Maine

Maine was first settled by English colonists in 1607 on the Sagadhoc Peninsula. The Popham Colony — or Saint George — was the first English colony in New England. This settlement was not permanent. In 1620 most of the area of Maine came under the patent granted to the Plymouth Colony. In 1622 the land between the Merrimac and Kennebec rivers was awarded to the proprietors Gorges and Mason. This province was divided into New Hampshire and New Somersetshire in 1629.

Settlements were made at Monhegan (1622), Saco (1623), and York (1624). In 1639 the Province and County of Maine was chartered. In 1647, Kittery, Gorgeana, Wells, Cape Porpoise, Saco, Casco, and Scarborough were annexed to Massachusetts. In 1653 these settlements sent representatives to the Massachusetts General Court and became freemen of Massachusetts. The County of Yorkshire, Province of Maine was formed in 1658.

The Duke of York was granted the northern portion of Maine in 1664, which became Cornwall County. York and Cornwall were united as Devonshire County in 1674. In 1677 the "Gorges Rights" for Maine were purchased by Massachusetts, and from 1677 all of Maine was generally known as York County. During King Phillip's War (1675–7) many settlements were burned or destroyed and some were deserted. Maine officially became York County, Massachusetts in 1716. In 1760 Lincoln and Cumberland counties were formed. The area became known as the District of Maine, and did not become a separate state until 1820.

Statewide Records and Resources
As all of Maine was at one time part of Massachusetts, court records exist in Maine provincial records, county records, and Massachusetts records.

Province and Court Records of Maine. 6 Vols. (Portland: Maine Historical Society, 1928–75, fiche 6046855). This is a compilation of early provincial

> **SEE ALSO**
> Massachusetts
> New Hampshire

and county records and is organized as follows:
- Vol. 1. Under Sir Ferdinando Gorges, 1636–52, under Ferdinando Gorges the Younger, 1661–5, under the Commissioners of Charles II, 1665–8.
- Vol. 2. York County court records, 1653–79.
- Vol. 3. Province of Maine records, 1680–92.
- Vols. 4–5. York County, Maine, Province of Massachusetts Bay, court records, 1692–1718.
- Vol. 6. Court records of York County, Maine, Province of Massachusetts Bay; the records of the Court of General Sessions of the Peace, 1718–27.

York Deeds [1642–1737]. 18 Vols. (Portland: John T. Hull, 1887–1910, fiche 6046839). Contains royal charters, proprietary grants, Indian deeds, etc.

Suffolk County, Massachusetts court records contain files for the Maine counties of York, Cumberland, Lincoln, Hancock, and Washington, 1734–97 (film 0909879). The records include probate, orphan, oaths of allegiance, bastardy proceedings, etc. The original records are at the Suffolk County Courthouse in Boston.
Maine Land Office.
- Massachusetts Land agent deeds, 1794–1860 (film 0010248 ff.). Includes the deeds of Revolutionary soldiers in Mars Hill area.
- Record of deeds of the Land Office of Maine, 1824–61 (film 0010238 ff.).
The original records are at the State Archives in Augusta.
Maine tax valuations, 1760–1811, various years (film 0959904 ff.) are at the Statehouse in Boston, Massachusetts. The direct tax census of 1798 (film 0940072 ff.) is at the New England Historic Genealogical Society in Boston.
Maine family records: miscellaneous papers and genealogies (film 0010375 ff.). The original records are at the Maine Historical Society in Portland.

Frost, John E. *Maine Probate Abstracts.* 2 Vols. (Camden, ME: Picton Press, 1991, fiche 6332995 ff.). This includes abstracts of wills, administrations, estates, guardianships, etc., 1687–1800.

Sargent, William M. *Maine Wills, 1640–1760* (1887. Reprint. Baltimore: Genealogical Publishing Co., 1972, fiche 6046701).

The *Collections of the Maine Historical Society* (Portland: The Society, 1831–1906) have been compiled in three series:
- First Series. 10 Vols. (film 0844654 ff.).
- Second Series. 10 Vols. (film 0844654 ff.).
- Third Series. 2 Vols. (film 0844659).

This includes papers on Maine in Massachusetts archives.

County Records
Cumberland County
Court of General Sessions of the Peace. Court records, 1761–1857 (film 1683991). From 1761 to 1809 these records were kept by the Court of General Sessions of the Peace, 1809–30 by the Court of Common Pleas or the Court of Sessions, and beginning in 1830 the records were kept by the Court of County Commissioners.

Register of Deeds. Land records, 1760–1902 (film 0010629 ff.).

Index to Cumberland County records from 1760–1886 (film 1711364). Also includes county marriage records.

The original records are at the Cumberland County Courthouse in Portland.

Lincoln County
Register of Deeds.
* Land records, 1760–99 (film 1872354 ff.).
* Record of grants, 1761–1818 (film 1872354). Contains records of lands which are now part of Kennebec County.

The original records are at the Kennebec County Courthouse in Augusta.

Probate Court. Probate records, 1760–1957 (film 0011469 ff.).

Supreme Judicial Court. Marriage records, 1774–1856 (film 1765423). Contains lists of marriage returns sent to the clerks of the Court of General Sessions and the Supreme Judicial Court, from the towns of Lincoln County.

Record of marriages, 1760–1865 (film 1765240 ff.). Marriage records taken from records of the Court of General Sessions, marriage books kept by the Supreme Judicial Court, and other sources.

The original records are at the Lincoln County Courthouse in Wiscasset.

Patterson, William D. *The Probate Records of Lincoln County, Maine, 1760 to 1800* (1895. Reprint. Camden, ME: Picton Press, 1991, fiche 6046983).

York County
County Register of Deeds. Land records, 1642–1860 (film 0012627 ff.).

Probate Court. Probate records, 1687–1860 (film 0012826 ff.).

The original records are at the York County Courthouse in Alfred.

Town and Church Records and Resources
As with other New England colonies, the town was the basic unit of colonial government. Sometimes proprietors' records were recorded separately. Books of vital records are often later transcriptions of births, deaths, and marriages that were recorded along with other records of the town, then abstracted into separate registers for convenience. Town records are also available at the State Archives

in Augusta. Church records that have been filmed are listed under the township where the meetings were held.

Unless otherwise indicated, all of the filmed records are kept at the town or city hall under which they are listed. Unless otherwise noted, all filmed church records are at the State Historical Society in Portland.

Albion
Freetown incorporated as Fairfax in 1804; name changed to Ligonia in 1821 and again to Albion in 1824. Town and vital records, 1750–1891 (film 0010404).

Alfred (see also Waterboro)
Town records, 1796–1895 (film 0010469).

Amherst
Vital records, 1782–1892 (film 0010466).

Appleton
Vital records, 1729–1892 (film 0010405).

Arrowsic
Vital records, 1741–1891 (film 0010407).

Atkinson
Vital records, 1744–1901 (film 0010429).

Auburn
Before 1818 Danville known as Pejebscot; became part of the city of Auburn in 1867.
Danville Town Clerk. Vital records, 1751–1867 (film 0010822 ff.).

General index to vital records: births, 1786–1954 (film 0010409 ff.), marriages, 1786–1954 (film 0010414 ff.), vital records, 1796–1891 (film 0010402 ff.).

Avon
Town and vital records, 1743–1831 (film 0010428). The original records are at the Town Hall in Phillips.

Bangor
Town and vital records, 1775–1891 (film 0010583 ff.).

Bath
Vital records, 1779–1903 (film 0010562).

Belfast
Town and vital records, 1773–1892 (film 0010573 ff.), proprietors' records, 1768–1838 (film 0010572).

Berwick
North Parish Church. Records, 1749–1838 (film 0010554).

Town and vital records, 1701–1891(film 0010552 ff.).

Bethel
Vital records, 1745–1923 (film 0010606).

Biddeford
First Church of Christ. Records, 1742–1872 (film 0010603).

Town and vital records, 1653–1786 (film 0010600). Includes families of Saco.
Vital records, 1779–1895 (film 0010601 ff.).

Bingham
Vital records, 1759–1890 (film 0010566).

Blue Hill
Vital records, 1763–1924 (film 0010608).

Boothbay
Congregational Church. Records, 1797–1838 (film 0010561).
Presbyterian Church. *Church Records, 1766–1780* (n.p., n.d., film 0504282 ff.).

Vital records, 1763–1891 (film 0010560).

Bowdoinham
Vital records, 1777–1891 (film 0010563 ff.).

Bridgton
Vital records, 1785–1892 (film 0010591).

Settlement papers and early history, 1736–1859 (film 0010592). The manuscript material is at the Maine

Historical Society in Portland.

Bristol
Town and vital records, 1765–1900 (film 0010557 ff.).

Brunswick
Town and vital records, 1725–1911 (film 0010595 ff.).

Bucksport
Town and vital records, 1768–1920 (film 0010578).

Burlington
Burlington Town Clerk. Town and vital records, 1769–1893 (film 0010577).

Buxton
Town and vital records, 1773–1891 (film 0010594).

Camden
Town and vital records, 1756–1891 (film 0012046 ff.). Also covers Rockport. The original records are at the Town Hall in Rockport.

Canaan
Vital records, 1776–1910 (film 0010626).

Cape Elizabeth
Set off from Falmouth and incorporated as a district in 1765; became a town in 1775.
Town and vital records, 1734–1900 (film 0010813 ff.). The original records are at the Office of Town Clerk in South Portland.

Castine
Town and vital records, 1727–1892 (film 0010804).

Chesterville
Vital records, 1751–1892 (film 0010792).

China
Town of Harlem annexed to China in 1822. Harlem Town Clerk. Town and vital records, 1775–1864 (film 0010621).

Town and vital records, 1785–1891(film 0010621 ff.).

Clinton
Town and vital records, 1795–1891(film 0010620).

Columbia
Town and vital records, 1752–1860 (film 0010807).

Corinna
Town and vital records, 1797–1891 (film 0010808).

Corinth
Vital records, 1785–1895 (film 0010809). The original records are at the Town Hall in East Corinth.

Cornville
Index of births and marriages, 1772–1953 (film 0010628). The information was extracted from original entry books and on typed cards at the State Board of Health, Division of Vital Statistics, Augusta.

Cumberland
Part of North Yarmouth until 1822. Vital records, 1720–1891 (film 0010812).

Cushing
Town and vital records, 1751–1925 (film 0010623).

Deer Isle
Town, vital, and church records, 1784–1867 (film 1005096 ff.). Proprietors' records, 1795–1822 (film 0599354).

Dennysville
Vital records, 1792–1892 (film 0010828).

Dexter
Town and vital records, 1761–1898 (film 0010830).

Dresden
Town and vital records, 1771–1891 (film 0010820).

Durham
Town and vital records, 1774–1931 (film 0010821).

Eastport
Vital records and marriage intentions, 1760–1930 (film 0010838).

Edgecomb
Town and vital records, 1774–1932 (film 0010845).

Fairfield
Town and vital records, 1788–1867 (film 0010864).

Falmouth
Town and vital records, 1712–1891 (film 0010867).

Farmington

Town and vital records, 1741–1892 (film 0010865).

Fayette

Vital records, 1749–1892 (film 0010862).

Freedom

Town and vital records, 1777–1891 (film 001087).

Friendship

Town and vital records, 1769–1889 (film 0010863).

Fryeburg

Town and vital records, 1776–1891 (film 0010915 ff.). Includes lists of members of First Universal Christian Society, and members of the Baptist religious society.

Georgetown

Town and vital records, 1757–1940 (film 0010919).

Gorham

Proprietors' records, 1733–1807 (film 0010927).
Town and vital records, 1753–1881 (film 0010928 ff).

Gouldsboro

Town and vital records, 1766–1898 (film 0010925).

Gray

Accounts and records of Reverend Samuel Perley, 1767–1818 (film 0010932). Includes list of married couples with fees, 1767–1803. The original records are at the Maine Historical Society in Portland.

Greenbush

Vital records, 1774–1934 (film 0010924).

Greene

Free Baptist Church. Records, 1780–1915 (film 0010921).

Vital records and marriage intentions, 1755–1925 (film 0010920).

Greenwood

Incorporated from Plantation No. 4 in 1816.
Town and vital records, 1797–1920 (film 0859991 ff.).

Hallowell

Town and vital records, 1771–1813 (film 0010934).

Harmony

Town and vital records, 1764–1858 (film 0010937).

Harpswell

Putnam, Eben. *Genealogical Records of the Town of Harpswell, Cumberland County, Maine: Compiled from the Original Town Records with Notes and Additions* (Portland: n.p., 1892, film 0011033). Includes the years 1735–1892.

Hartland

Town and vital records, 1772–1891 (film 0010936).

Hebron

Known as Shepardsfield Plantation until 1792.

Town and vital records, 1786–1893 (film 0011030).

Hope
Vital records, 1776–1896 (film 0010935).

Industry
Vital records, 1732–1891 (film 0011035). The original records are at the Town Hall in Farmington.

Jay
Known as Phipps Canada Plantation until 1795.
Town and vital records, 1779–1891 (film 0011037).

Jefferson
Town and vital records, 1757–1891 (film 0011036).

Kennebunk (see also Wells)
Town and vital records, 1727–1892 (film 0011326).

Kennebunkport
Town and vital records, 1678–1891 (film 0011328). Includes certificates of members of the Baptist and Methodist societies.

Kittery
First Church in Kittery. Records, 1715–97 (film 1035868).
Eliot Congregational Church. Records of the Second Church of Kittery, 1721–1827 (film 0011323).
Third Church in Kittery. Records, 1750–95 (film 0011325).

Town records, 1648–1896 (film 0011319 ff.).

Vital records, 1699–1899 (film 0011322).

Proprietors' records, 1753–82 (film 0011325), land grants in the parish of Unity in Kittery, 1650–1762 (film 0011325), miscellaneous papers, 1760–1806 (film 0011325), The original records are at the Maine Historical Society in Portland.

Lebanon
Town and vital records, 1767–1899 (film 0011536). Includes certificates from members of the Baptist Society.

Leeds
Town and vital records, 1785–1891 (film 0011331).

Levant
Town and vital records 1769–1917 (film 0011530).

Lewiston
Vital records, 1776–1900, town records (film 0011333 ff.).

Vital records, 1764–1889 (film 0223931). The records are at the Androscoggin Historical Society in Auburn.

Limington
Town and vital records, 1792–1899 (film 0011533).

Linneus
Town and vital records, 1784–1892 (film 0011352 ff.).

Lisbon
Known as Thompsonborough until 1802.
Town and vital records, 1782–1891 (film 0011330).

Vital records, 1760–1892 (film 1753679). This DAR typescript is at the Androscoggin Historical Society in Auburn.

Litchfield
Town and vital records, 1740–1892 (film 0011329).

Livermore
Vital and town records, 1762–1910 (film 0011332).

Lovell
Vital records, 1802–91 (film 0011541).

Lyman (see also Waterboro)
Previously known as Waterboro and Coxhall.
Town and vital records, 1783–1893 (film 0011539).

Machias
Town and vital records, 1774–1892 (film 0011562).

Madrid
Births and deaths, 1789–1892 (film 0011553).

Mars Hill
Vital records, 1786–1892 (film 0011559).

Mercer
Vital records, 1804–91 (film 0011552).

Minot (see also Stratham, New Hampshire)
First Congregational Church of Christ. Records, 1784–1977 (film 1753679). The original records are at the Androscoggin Historical Society in Auburn.

Vital records, 1786–1888 (film 0011550).

Monmouth
Town and vital records, 1764–1891 (film 0011546).

Monroe
Vital records, 1778–1891 (film 0011565).

Morrill
Vital records, 1781–1892 (film 0011557).

Moscow
Vital records, 1771–1892 (film 0011551).

Mount Vernon
Town and vital records, 1743–1891 (film 0011547).

New Gloucester
Vital records, 1732–1892 (film 0011586).

Proprietors' records, 1735–1812 (film 1683992). Copy of original papers at the Cumberland County Courthouse in Portland.

Newcastle
Town and vital records, 1754–1891 (film 0011573).

New Portland
Town and vital records, 1770–1891 (film 0011576).

New Sharon
Town and vital records, 1757–1891 (film 0011578).

Nobleboro
Town and vital records, 1788–1891 (film 0011575).

Norridgewock
Town and vital records, 1774–1891 (film 0011577).

Northfield
Town and vital records, 1789–1902 (film 0011581).

North Yarmouth
Vital records, 1701–1898 (film 0011591). The typescript is at the Maine Historical Society in Portland.

Orland
Plantation No. 2 incorporated as Orland in 1800.
Town and vital records, 1765–1892 (film 0011726).

Orrington
Town and vital records, 1788–1893 (film 0011724 ff.).

Paris
Vital records, 1757–1918 (film 0858545 ff.), town records, 1793–1906 (film 0858545 ff.).

Parkman
Vital records, 1782–1892 (film 0011745).

Parsonsfield
Town and vital records, 1762–1897 (film 0012042).

Penobscot
Town and vital records, 1732–1876 (film 0011752).

Perry
Town and vital records, 1780–1895 (film 0011735).

Phillips
Town and vital records, 1756–1891 (film 0011744).

Pittston
Town and vital records, 1788–1891 (film 0011733 ff.).

Poland
Originally called Bakerstown.
Bakerstown Proprietors' records, 1739–98 (film 0011740). Includes a list of proprietors of the township granted to Pike and other officers and soldiers in the Expedition to Canada in 1690. The original records are at the Maine Historical Society in Portland.

Portland
City records, 1786–1882 (film 0012028 ff.).
Births, 1782–1892, index, 1712–1891(film 0012012 ff.).
Deaths, 1800–1910, index, 1720–1910 (film 0012016 ff.).
Marriage intentions, 1837–1891, index, 1733–1886 (film 0012020 ff.).

Marriages and marriage intentions, 1814–1910, index to marriages, 1748–1912 (film 0012025 ff.). The second book of records of the town of Portland, of marriages, births and deaths, 1773–1814 (film 0012011).

Prospect
Vital records, 1756–1890 (film 0011732).

Rangeley
Vital records, 1795–1892 (film 0012050).

Raymond
Vital records, 1745–1918 (film 0012052).

Proprietors' records, 1734–98 (film 0012053). The original records are at the Maine Historical Society in Portland.

Readfield
Town records, 1759–1891 (film 0012043).

Richmond
Town and vital records, 1823–92 (film 0012048).

Rockport
See Camden.

Rome
Town and vital records, 1775–1891 (film 0012044).

Saco
First Church, Pepperrellborough. *First Book of Records of the First Church in Pepperellborough* (Saco, ME: York Institute, 1914, film 1033820).

Saco City Clerk. *First Book of Records of the Town of Pepperellborough, Now the City of Saco* (n.p., 1895, film 0012243).

Sanford
Town and vital records, 1769–1892 (film 0012233 ff.). This includes marriage records from the Congregational Church, 1769–1832.

Proprietors' records, 1661–1782, 1804–26 (film 0012236). The original records are at the Maine Historical Society in Portland.

Scarborough
Black Point Parish. Record of deaths, 1795–1873 (film 0012231).
First Congregational Church. Records, 1728–1876 (film 0012228).
First Parish of Scarborough. Record of deaths, 1795–1899 (film 0012230).
Second Church in Scarborough. Church records, 1744–1830 (film 0012228), parish records, 1759–1865 (film 0012229).

Proprietors' records, 1720–62 (film 0012227).
Miscellaneous papers: judgments, indentures, wills, deeds, depositions, bonds, inventories, etc. (film 0012226).

Town and vital records, 1681–1893 (film 0012221 ff.). The original and typescript records of the above are at the Office of the Town Clerk in Scarborough and the Maine Historical Society in Portland.

Sedgwick
Formed in 1789 from Township No. 4, east of Penobscot River, or Naskeeg.
Town and vital records, 1760–1930 (film 0012248).

Shapleigh
Town and vital records, 1785–1896 (film 0012237 ff.).

Shirley
Vital records, 1797–1883 (film 0012071).

Sidney
Vital records, 1772–1899 (film 0012055).

South Berwick
Town and vital records, 1774–1924 (film 0012240).

South Portland
See Cape Elizabeth.

South Thomaston
Vital records, 1780–1893 (film 0012057).

Standish
Church of Christ. Records, 1769–1859 (film 0012220).

Town and vital records, 1770–1939 (film 0012218).

Strong
Vital records, 1767–1885 (film 0012069).

Sullivan
Incorporated in 1789 from Plantation No. 2 east of Union River.
Town and vital records, 1733–1917 (film 0012217).

Sumner
Vital records, 1733–1891 (film 0012245).

Surry
Vital records, 1750–1940 (film 0012247).

Temple
Vital records, 1773–1896 (film 0012263).

Trenton
Town records, 1738–1891 (film 0012268).

Turner
Vital records, 1740–1955 (film 0012257 ff.).
Town and vital records, 1776–1892 (film 0012255 ff.).

Union
Vital records, 1794–1910 (film 0012269).

Unity
Proprietors' records, 1788, 1791–4 (film 0012271). The original records are at the Maine Historical Society in Portland.

Vassalborough
Town and vital records, 1771–1892 (film 0012273).

Vienna
Vital records, 1752–1893 (film 0012272).

Vinalhaven
Town and vital records, 1785–1892 (film 0012274).

Waldoboro
Town and vital records, 1773–1891 (film 0012307).
Complete copy of old record books, 1714–1892, including cemetery inscriptions (film 0012308).

Wales
Vital records, 1759–1891 (film 0012625).

Warren
Vital records, 1770–1938 (film 0012306).

Waterboro
Town and vital records, 1787–1891 (film 0012326 ff.).

Proprietors' records, 1780–90, from Waterboro and Coxhall (film 0012324). The original records are at the Town Hall in Alfred.

Waterford
Vital records, 1798–1862 (film 0012625).

Wayne
Baptist Church. Records, 1794–1845 (film 1753679). The original records are at the Androscoggin Historical Society in Auburn.

Town and vital records, 1763–1891 (film 0012302).

Weld
Vital records, 1766–1895 (film 0012323).

Wells
First Congregational Church. Records, 1701–1854 (film 0012624). Also known as the First Parish in Wells.
First Congregational Church, Kennebunk. Records, 1750–1887 (film 0011327). Also known as the Second Parish of Wells.

Town and vital records, 1715–1895 (film 0012622 ff.).

Whitefield
Town and vital records, 1791–1924 (film 0012312).

Wilton
Town and vital records, 1760–1891 (film 0012322).

Windham
Known as New Marblehead until 1762.
First Church in Windham. Records, 1762–99 (film 0012620).

Town records, 1762–1896 (film 0012618 ff.).
Proprietors' records, 1735–1804 (film 0012621).
Vital records, 1789–1921 (film 0012617).
The original records are at the Office of Town Clerk in Windham and the Maine Historical Society in Portland.

Winslow
Town and vital records, 1759–1892 (film 0012303).

Winthrop
Town and vital records, 1720–1890 (film 0012299).

Wiscasset
Known as Pownalborough until 1802.
Town and vital records, 1739–1929 (film 0012309).

Woolwich
Town and vital records, 1760–1891 (film 0012314 ff.).

York
Town and vital records, 1717–1889 (film 0012836).

York records: land grants and abstracted minutes of town meetings from about 1641 (film 0012837), from a manuscript in the Bangor Public Library in Bangor.

Suggested Reading

Baxter, James Phinney. *The Baxter Manuscripts.* 24 Vols. (Portland: Maine Historical Society, 1889–1916, film 0599177). Documents relating to the early history of Maine gathered from archives in Massachusetts, and Europe.

Burrage, Henry Sweetser. *Maine at Louisbourg in 1745* (Augusta: Burleigh and Flynt, 1910, film 1035530). Includes correspondence, official reports, lists of officers and men.

Clark, Charles E. *The Eastern Frontier: The Settlement of Northern New England, 1610–1763* (1970. Reprint. Hanover, NH: University Press of New England, 1983).

Frost, John E. *Maine Genealogy: A Bibliographical Guide.* 2nd ed. (Portland: Maine Historical Society, 1985).

Gray, Ruth. *Maine Families In 1790.* 4 Vols. (Camden, ME: Picton Press, 1988–94).

Maine State Archives. *Microfilm List: Maine Town Records and Maine Census Records* (n.p., 1965, film 1036379).

Pope, Charles Henry. *The Pioneers of Maine and New Hampshire 1623 To 1660: A Descriptive List Drawn from Records of the Colonies, Towns, Churches, Courts and Other Contemporary Sources* (1908. Reprint. Baltimore: Genealogical Publishing Co., 1965, fiche 6049825).

Public Record Repositories in Maine (Augusta: Maine State Archives, 1986, film 1036235). A directory to assist the researcher in determining the location and availability of existing municipal and county records.

Spencer, Wilbur D. *Pioneers on Maine Rivers with Lists to 1651* (1930. Reprint. Baltimore: Genealogical Publishing Co., 1973, film 1307614).

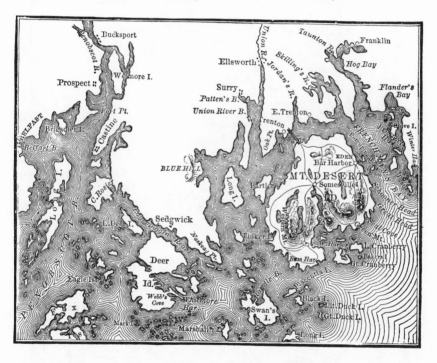

24 Penobscot Bay (Charles Coffin, *Old Times in the Colonies.* 1888)

The South part of New-England, as it is Planted this yeare, 1634.

25 Massachusetts, 1634 (Library of Congress)

Massachusetts

The first settlements in Massachusetts were established at the Plymouth Colony in 1620 and the Massachusetts Bay Colony in 1630. The Bay Colony held jurisdiction over New Hampshire from 1641 until 1679 and over parts of Rhode Island until 1663. In 1647 settlements in southern Maine were annexed to the Bay Colony, and the Province of Maine was formed in 1658. The Bay Colony proclaimed its independence in 1652 and attempted to exercise religious and political sovereignty. In 1684 the English Crown vacated the Massachusetts charter, and it became part of the Dominion of New England from 1686 to 1689. In 1691 the two Massachusetts colonies were united under a new charter, along with parts of Maine and Nova Scotia. The General Court which had been abolished in 1684 was reinstated in 1692. Maine remained part of Massachusetts until 1820.

Statewide Records and Resources

It is important to keep in mind that all official meetings conducted under the Charter of 1629 were deemed to be "courts." Court records are the most important colony-wide colonial resource. The most important of the early courts in Massachusetts were:

- **General Court (1620–84, 1692–1825)**: Held legislative and judicial authority for the entire colony; court of original jurisdiction for criminal cases until 1639, appellate court for Court of Assistants from 1639; court of original jurisdiction in equity cases until 1865. These records are on film for years 1628–1777 (film 0954385 ff.) and include vital records.

- **Court of Assistants (1630–86, 1689–92)**: Appellate court for county and other inferior courts; held jurisdiction for capital crimes and divorce. For a brief period in the 1680s the General Court and the Court of Assistants were replaced by a Governor and Council appointed by the Crown. *Records of the Court of Assistants of the Colony of the Massachusetts Bay, 1630–1692*. 3 Vols. (Boston: County of Suffolk, 1901–28, film 0496679). The surviving Court of Assistants records for the Plymouth Colony are at the Plymouth County Commissioners Office and at the State Archives on microfilm.

SEE ALSO
Connecticut
Great Britain

- **County Courts (1636–92) and Quarter Courts "in the Lawes and Libertyes" (1692–1827)**: Handled probate, orphan dockets, allegiance

243

oaths, bastardy proceedings, etc., but not divorce or capital crimes. See individual counties for records.

- **Superior Court of Judicature (1686–9, 1692–1782)**: Handled appeal cases. See individual counties for records. Renamed the Supreme Judicial Court in 1780.
- **Court of Common Pleas (1692–1827)**: Court of original and general jurisdiction for the trial of issues of fact and law according to the principles of the common law. See individual counties for records.
- **Court of General Sessions of the Peace (1686–1808)**: Justice of the peace courts which handled mainly criminal cases; records contain the proceedings of other courts as well as some civil cases and financial records. See individual counties for records.
- **Vice-Admiralty Court (1714–72, 1692–1775)**: Handled crimes occurring on the high seas; also enforced customs. The court sat at Boston in Suffolk County; court records and account books from 1718–72 have been filmed (film 0902790).
- **County Court of Probate (1692–)**: Handled all matters of probate within a county; located in the county seat or "shiretown"; records were kept in a Registry of Probate. See individual counties for records.
- **Selectmen's courts (1661–)**: Local civil and criminal matters under forty shillings could be judicated by local officials. See specific towns, under town records. There are also some manuscript records at the State Archives in Boston.
- **Stranger's or Courts for Small Causes (1639–84)**: Created by the Court of Assistants. Conducted business of nonresidents engaged in commerce in the colony, or between residents of different towns.
- **Massachusetts Governor and Council.** Divorce records, 1760–86 (film 0946895). This council had jurisdiction for divorces from 1692–1785. Some divorces were filed in other courts after about 1738 and are included in this collection.

The earliest land grants were large tracts of common land given by the General Court to the proprietors, who established the settlements that became towns. Proprietors granted land in the towns, and these transactions were recorded by the town clerks in metes and bounds. Most of these deeds recorded by the town clerks have been filmed and are found under the various townships. After the formation of counties, land transactions were also recorded in the county register of deeds.

Early military records exist as muster lists and are at the State Archives. The years 1643–1774 have been indexed by surname and volume; volumes 69–70 are filmed (film 0543984 ff.); there are also card file indexes for volumes 67–8,

71–80, 91–9, and 286–9 that may not be filmed. The records in volumes 91–9 of have been abstracted in the following:

- Donahue, Mary E. *Massachusetts Officers and Soldiers, 1702–1722: Queen Anne's War to Dummer's War* (Boston: Society of Colonial Wars, 1980).
- Stachiw, Myron O. *Massachusetts Officers and Soldiers, 1723–1743: Dummer's War to the War of Jenkins' Ear* (Boston: Society of Colonial Wars, 1979).
- MacKay, Robert E. *Massachusetts Soldiers in the French and Indian Wars, 1744–1755* (Boston: Society of Colonial Wars, 1978).
- Goss, David. K. *Massachusetts Officers and Soldiers in the French and Indian Wars, 1755–1756* (Boston: Society of Colonial Wars, 1985).
- Voye, Nancy S. *Massachusetts Officers in the French and Indian Wars, 1748–1763* (Boston: Society of Colonial Wars, 1975).

The Revolutionary War muster rolls series begins in 1767 (film 2020564 ff.) and is also at the State Archives.

Massachusetts has a number of published histories of the colonial wars. These and other sources relating to military engagements are:
- Bodge, George, M. *Soldiers in King Philip's War* (1906. Reprint. Baltimore: Genealogical Publishing Co., 1991, fiche 6046769).
- Doreski, Carole. *Massachusetts Officers and Soldiers in the Seventeenth Century Conflicts* (Boston: Society of Colonial Wars, New England Historic Genealogical Society, 1982, film 1320664).
- *Membership Roll of Ancient and Honorable Artillery Company, 1637–1744, Massachusetts Bay Colony* (film 0441442). The original typescript is at the Historical Society of Pennsylvania in Philadelphia.
- Loring, Arthur Greene. *Woburn Men in the Indian and Other Wars Previous to the Year 1754* (Boston: D. Clapp, 1897, fiche 6019383).
- Putnam, Eben. *Soldiers in the French War from Essex County, 1775–1761* . . . (Salem, MA: Historical Society of Essex, 1892, fiche 6019250).

There were a number of newspapers published in Massachusetts in the 1700s. Indexes and abstracts have been published. See:
- Ayer, Mary Farwell. *Checklist of Boston Newspapers, 1704–1780* (Boston: Colonial Society of Massachusetts, 1907, film 0844522).
- *Index of Obituaries in Boston Newspapers, 1704–1800.* 3 Vols. (Boston: G.K. Hall, 1968, film 0823596).

Tax assessments were taken on a state and town level. State tax records are filmed from 1760. See town records for local assessments. The colonial property valuations and taxes, 1760–71 (film 0926471 ff.), at the State Library in Boston cover the towns of Beverly, Boxford, Chelmsford, Danvers, Dedham, Lunenburg, Marblehead, Medford, Middleton, Milton, Needham, Reading, Stoughton, Topsfield, Walpole, Waltham, Wenham, Westford, Woburn, and Wrentham.

Manuscript Collections

Massachusetts State Archives card index, by surname and place (film 0543878 ff.), is an index to a series of volumes containing documents of Massachusetts from its founding in 1629 to the year 1799. These include property valuations, tax records, court records, military records (volumes 69–70), etc., in a total of 328 volumes in the series.

Berkshire Athenaeum, Pittsfield Public Library. Massachusetts family history files, 1550–1990 (film 1711159 ff.). This collection — arranged alphabetically by surname — contains genealogical tables, photos, manuscripts, typescripts, published material, family group sheets, vital records, and newspaper clippings.

Rollin H. Cooke Collection. Also housed at the Berkshire Athenaeum, this is a series of town records in manuscript form. Many of these are listed in this section under individual towns.

Elmer I. Shepard Collection: Massachusetts family group records, 1550–1900 (film 1665846 ff.). Also at the Berkshire Anthenaeum, the Shepard Collection material is from a number of sources, both primary and secondary. Localities included are:

* **Berkshire County towns**: North Adams, Adams, Alford, Becket, Cheshire, Clarksburg, Dalton, Egremont, Florida, Great Barrington, Hancock, Hinsadale, Lanesborough, Lee, Lenox, Monterey, Mount Washington, New Ashford, North Marlborough, Otis, Peru, Pittsfield, Richmond, Sandisfield, Savoy, Sheffield, Stockbridge, Tyringham, Washington, West Stockbridge, Williamstown, Windsor
* **Franklin County towns**: Ashfield, Bernardston, Buckland, Charlement, Colrain, Conway, Deerfield, Halwey, Heath, Greenfield, Gill, Leyden, Monroe, Montague, Northfield, Rowe, Shelburne, Sunderland, Warwick, Whately, Wendell
* **Hampden County towns**: Blandford, Brimfield, Chester, Granville "Bedford," Longmeadow, Monson, Montgomery, Palmer, Russell, Springfield, Tolland, Westfield, West Springfield
* **Hampshire County towns**: Amherst, Belchertown, Chesterfield, Cummington, Easthampton, Goshen, Granby, Hadley, Hatfield, Huntington,

Middlefield, Northampton, Pelham, Plainfield, South Hadley, Southampton, Westhampton, Williamsburg, Worthington
- **Worcester County towns**: Brookfield, Hardwick, New Braintree, Petersham, Phillipston, Spencer, Sturbridge, Warren
- **Michigan pioneers** from western Massachusetts

Walter E. Corbin manuscript collection at the New England Historic Genealogical Society in Boston (film 0928633 ff.). Manuscript collection composed of material generally pertaining to central and western Massachusetts for the period 1650–1850. Contains local records, genealogies, and source notes for:

- **Berkshire County towns**: Cheshire, Great Barrington, Hancock, Lanesborough, Monterey, New Marlborough, Otis, Peru, Pittsfield, Sandisfield, Savoy, Williamstown
- **Bristol County towns**: Dighton
- **Franklin County towns**: Ashfield, Bernardston, Charlemont, Colerain, Hawley, Leverett, Leyden, New Salem, Northfield, Rowe, Shutesbury, South Deerfield, Sunderland, Warwick, Wendell, Whatley
- **Hampden County towns**: Blandford, Brimfield, Chicopee, Hampden, Holland, Holyoke, Ludlow, Monson, Montgomery, Russell, Springfield, Wales, Westfield, West Springfield, Wilbraham
- **Hampshire County towns**: Amherst, Belchertown, Chesterfield, Cummington, Easthampton, Enfield, Florence, Goshen, Granby, Hadley, Hatfield, Haydenville, Huntington, Middlefield, Northampton, Norwich, Pelham, Plainfield, Prescott, South Hadley, Southampton, Ware, Westhampton, Williamsburg
- **Middlesex County towns**: Dunstable, Groton, Pepperell, Shirley, Watertown
- **Norfolk County towns**: Dedham
- **Plymouth County towns**: Hingham, Marshfield, Middleborough
- **Suffolk County towns**: Charlestown, Dorchester
- **Worcester County towns**: Paxton
- **Connecticut towns**: Gilead, Norwalk, Stafford, Stamford, West Stafford, Willington
- **Rhode Island towns**: South Kingstown
- **New Hampshire towns**: Gosport

Bowman, George Ernest. *Massachusetts Society of Mayflower Descendants: The Bowman Files* (Boston: Massachusetts Society of Mayflower Descendants, 1983, fiche 6331448 ff.). These files have been abstracted from primary and secondary source materials. In addition to these original files, abstracts have been printed in:

- Roser, Susan E. *Mayflower Births and Deaths: From the Files of George Ernest Bowman at the Massachusetts Society of Mayflower Descendants* (Baltimore: Genealogical Publishing Co., 1992).
- Roser, Susan E. *Mayflower Marriages: From the Files of George Ernest Bowman at the Massachusetts Society of Mayflower Descendants* (Baltimore: Genealogical Publishing Co., 1990).
- Roser, Susan E. *Mayflower Deeds and Probates: From the Files of George Ernest Bowman at the Massachusetts Society of Mayflower Descendants* (Baltimore: Genealogical Publishing Co., 1994).

The *Mayflower Descendant* is primarily of concern to descendants of the Plymouth Colony; however it should not be overlooked as an alternate source for vital records. Many town records have been transcribed and published. This periodical is also available on CD-ROM (Search and Research Publishers) for volumes published 1899 through the end of 1996.

The Judd Manuscript Collection, 1635–1850 (film 0234515 ff.), at the Forbes Public Library in Northampton, is a ten-volume manuscript series of land town and vital records for Connecticut and Massachusetts. This has been indexed.

The New England Historical and Genealogical Register. This is the most important periodical for general New England research, and it also has many articles on genealogy in other countries, particularly Great Britain. Published since 1847, the complete text of volumes through 148 are available from the Society on CD-ROM (Broderbund), on microfilm, and in hard copy. There are book indexes for volumes 1–100, and the periodicals themselves contain yearly indexes.

Collections of the Massachusetts Historical Society. Printed in several series, the collections include publications of the Winthrop Papers and other colonial records, diaries, journals, etc., including material on other New England states.[19] Several of the original manuscripts that are part of the collection are:
- The Mather papers: the papers of Cotton Mather; the Increase Mather papers (Boston: Massachusetts Historical Society, 1970–81, film 1550843 ff.). The collection is at the State Historical Society and the American Antiquarian Society. The microfilms of both sets of papers serve as original sources for genealogical and family history research, including a manuscript bibliography, diaries, 1659–1724, letters and essays, 1636–1717, etc.
- Winthrop Papers (Ann Arbor, MI: University Microfilms International,

---

[19]For more information, see *Catalog of Manuscripts of the Massachusetts Historical Society.* 7 Vols. (Boston: G.K. Hall, 1969).

1986, film 1490864 ff.). Microfilm of originals at the State Historical Society in Boston. Among the contents are: unbound manuscripts, 1537–1630, Winthrop deeds, commissions, etc., 1577–1801, medical recipes, John Winthrop, history of New England, 1630–49, memoranda of John Winthrop, Jr., Winthrop catalogs and papers relating to Harvard graduates, 1642–1825, etc. See also *The Journal of John Winthrop, 1630–1649* (Cambridge: Harvard University Press, 1996). This has been published in earlier editions as *The History of New England, 1630–1649.*

County Records and Resources

Some county records have and are being transferred to the State Archives. Before planning to visit any repository, please verify the location of the manuscripts in question.

Barnstable County (established 1685 in Plymouth Colony)
Barnstable County Register of Deeds. Index to deeds, 1703–1868 (film 0843118 ff.). Most of the original deeds between 1686–1827 were destroyed by fire.
Barnstable County Probate Court.
• Records, 1686–1894 (film 0904595 ff.).
• Wills, inventories, etc, 1637–85 (film 0904595). Includes a record of Barnstable County references to deeds prior to 1685, in Plymouth records.
The original records are at the Barnstable County Courthouse in Barnstable.

Berkshire County (established 1760 from Hampshire County)
Berkshire County Court of Common Pleas. Records, 1760–1860 (film 0876252 ff.).
Berkshire County Probate Court. Records, 1761–1917 (film 1749904 ff.)
Berkshire County Register of Deeds.
• Colonial records and proprietary plans of the middle, northern (1761–88), and southern (1761–90) districts of Berkshire County (film 0876706 ff.).
• Land records, middle district, 1761–1925 (film 0872066 ff.).
The original records are at the Berkshire County Courthouse in Pittsfield.
• Land records, northern district, 1761–1925 (film 1675879 ff.). The original records are at the Registry of Deeds in Adams.

Bristol County (established 1685 in Plymouth Colony)
Bristol County Court of Common Pleas. Court records 1696–1868 (film 0899093 ff.), 1714–1814 (film 0901268 ff.). Court records of civil cases and some marriages, mostly from the Court of Common Pleas, with some court records from the Court of General Sessions and the Inferior Court of Common Pleas.

Bristol County Court of General Sessions. Court records, 1702–38 (film 0899093). The Court of General Sessions handled mainly criminal cases.

Bristol County Probate Court. Records, 1690–1881 (film 0469935 ff.), 1687–1916 (film 0464527 ff.). The original records are at the Bristol County Courthouse in Taunton.

Bristol County Register of Deeds.

• Deeds, northern district, 1686–1909 (film 0549723 ff.), land records, 1706–13 (film 1405193). The original records are at the Registry of Deeds in Taunton.

• Deeds, southern district, 1686–1904 (film 0577202 ff.). The original records are at the Registry of Deeds in New Bedford.

• Deeds, Fall River district, 1686–1910 (film 0572430 ff.). The original records are at the Registry of Deeds in Fall River.

Dukes County (established in 1683 as a New York county and 1695 as a Massachusetts county)

Dukes County Proprietors' Clerk. Proprietors' records, 1641–1717, index, 1641–1857 (film 0911728 ff.).

Dukes County Probate Court. Records, 1690–1938 (film 0991746 ff.).

Dukes County Register of Deeds. Deeds, 1641–1872 (film 1922707 ff.).

Dukes County Inferior Court of Common Pleas. Court records dating from 1722 have not been filmed.

The original records are at the Edgartown District Court. There are also records of the Superior Court of Judicature at the Suffolk County Courthouse in Boston and other Dukes county papers in the Charles Banks manuscripts at the New England Historic Genealogical Society in Boston.

Essex County (established 1643 in Massachusetts Bay Colony)

Essex County Quarterly Courts. Court records, 1636–41 (film 0877461).

Essex County Court.

• Court records, 1636–94 (film 0877429 ff.).

• Vital records, 1636–1795 (film 0877432 ff.). Vital records were recorded by the County Court until 1692 and by the Court of General Sessions of the Peace thereafter.

Essex County Court of General Sessions of the Peace. Court records, 1692–1796 (film 0877466 ff.).

Essex County Inferior Court of Common Pleas.

• Court records, 1686–1726 (film 0877465 ff.), 1749–82 (film 0877220 ff.).

• Execution records, 1686–1783 (film 0877463 ff.).

Essex County Register of Deeds. Deeds, 1639–1866 (0862800 ff.), unregistered deeds, 1700–1820 (film 0878779). This includes records of Old Norfolk County.

Essex County Probate Court. Records, 1638–91 (film 0876180 ff.), 1638–1881 (0873023 ff.).

Witchcraft papers, 1655–1750 (film 0877465). Cases of persons accused of witchcraft; also records of the Court of Assistants, 1673–92, and the Superior Court of Judicature, 1692–5.

Public notary book, 1723–69 (film 0877434).

The original records are at the Essex County Courthouse in Salem.

(Old) Norfolk County Court. Old Norfolk County (1648–81) contained the towns of Haverhill, Salisbury, Hampton, Exeter, Dover, and Portsmouth (Strawberry Bank). Haverhill and Salisbury became part of Essex County in 1680. The other towns went to New Hampshire.

- Vital records, marriage intentions, earmarks, and strays, 1670–1747 (film 0877468).
- Court records, 1648–81, 1691–2 (film 0877467 ff.).

The original records are at the Essex County Courthouse in Salem.

Records and Files of the Quarterly Courts of Essex County [1636–1686]. 9 Vols. (Salem, MA: Essex Institute, 1911–75, film 0873951 ff.). These courts were held at Salem 1636–41, and at Salem and Ipswich, 1641–92.

Hampshire County (established 1662 from Middlesex County)

Hampshire County Court. Court records, 1677–1728 (film 0886420). Contains records of the County Court, Court of Quarter Sessions, Court of General Sessions of the Peace, and Inferior Court of Common Pleas.

Hampshire County Court of Sessions of the Peace.
- Divorce index cards, 1758–89 (film 2027323).
- Index to marriages, 1758–89 (film 1508791).
- Court records, 1766–71, 1776–90 (film 0886425 ff.).

Hampshire County Inferior Court of Common Pleas. Court records, 1728–83 (film 0886420 ff.). This includes records of the Court of General Sessions of the Peace, 1728–70, and a book for recording executions in the county of Hampshire, 1716–65.

Hampshire County Superior Court. Divorce records index cards, 1758–1960 (film 2027323 ff.).

Hampshire County Probate Court. Index to estate files, 1660–1985 (film 1558627 ff.), records, 1660–1916 (film 1556830 ff.).

The original records are at the Hampshire County Courthouse in Northampton.

Hampden County (established 1812 from Hampshire County)

Although a newer county, the records contain deeds for Hampshire County before 1787 and some court records from 1638.

Hampden County Court of General Sessions of the Peace. Court records, 1638–1812 (film 0905340 ff.).
Hampden County Register of Deeds. Deeds, 1628–1867 (film 0844472 ff.).
The original records are at the Hampden County Courthouse and Register of Deeds in Springfield.

Middlesex County (established 1643 in Massachusetts Bay Colony)
Middlesex County Court. Court records, 1649–99 (film 0892250 ff.).
Middlesex County Court of General Sessions of the Peace.
• Court and session records, 1686–1799 (film 1435716 ff.).
• Court records, 1686–1809 (film 0892252 ff.).
Middlesex County Inferior Court of Common Pleas. Court records, 1699–1783 (film 0892256 ff.). Contains records of the Inferior Court of Common Pleas, 1770–82, and of the Court of Common Pleas, 1782–3.
Middlesex County Supreme Judicial Court. Court records, 1747–1850 (film 0901537 ff.).
Middlesex County Clerk of Courts.
• Card index to births, deaths, wills, and miscellaneous court records, 1600–1799 (film 1420474).
• Colonial county court papers, 1648–1798 (film 0541432 ff.).
Middlesex County Probate Court. Index to probate records, 1648–1871 (film 0385977), records, 1648–1924 (film 0385978 ff.).
Middlesex County Superior Court.
• Folio index cards, 1650–1800 (film 1420472 ff.).
• Vital records, 1651–1793 (film 0892249).
• Vital records, 1671–1745 (film 0892250).
• Middlesex County Register of Deeds. Deeds, southern district, 1649–1900 (film 0532454 ff.). This also contains deeds for Hopkinton and Upton, 1743–1833 (film 0901510 ff.), that were formerly part of Harvard.
The original records are at Middlesex County Courthouse, in Cambridge. There is also a large folio collection of Middlesex County records at the State Archives.

Nantucket County (established 1695 from Dukes County, New York)
Nantucket County Court of Common Pleas. Court records, 1721–1859 (film 0906828 ff.).
Nantucket County Court of General Sessions of the Peace. Court records, 1721–1816 (film 0903862).
Nantucket Proprietors' Clerk. Proprietors' records, 1716–1843 (film 0906226).
Nantucket County Register of Deeds. Deeds, 1659–1866 (film 0906228 ff.).
Nantucket County Probate Court. Records, 1706–1867 (film 0906832 ff.).
The original records are at the Nantucket Town and County Building in Nantucket.

Worth, Henry Barnard. *Nantucket Lands and Landowners*. 2 Vols. (Nantucket, MA: Nantucket Historical Association, 1901-13, film 0896826).

Norfolk County (established 1793 from Suffolk County)
Norfolk County Supreme Judicial Court. Court records, 1764-1859 (film 0878203 ff.).

Plymouth County (established 1685 from Plymouth Colony)
New Plymouth Colony.
* Laws and court records, 1623-76 (film 0912073).
* Records of the colony of New Plymouth, 1643-79 (film 0912074).
Secretary of the Colony, Plymouth.
* Indian deeds, treasurers' accounts, lists of freemen, 1666-82 (film 0567791).
* Court orders, 1633-90 (film 0567792 ff.).
* Deeds, 1620-99 (film 0567788 ff.).
* Wills, 1633-86 (film 0567794 ff.).[20]
Plymouth County Court of Common Pleas. Court records, 1702-1859 (film 0906749 ff.).
Plymouth County Court of General Sessions of the Peace. Court records, 1686-1817 (film 0906746 ff.).
Plymouth County Register of Deeds. Deeds, 1664-99 (film 0912074), 1664-1900 (film 0567747 ff.).
Plymouth County Probate Court. Records, 1686-1903 (film 0549782 ff.).
The original deeds from 1620-92 are at the County Commissioner's Office in Plymouth. Deeds after 1692 are kept at the Registry of Deeds, also in Plymouth. The original records are at the County Commissioner's Office in Plymouth and the Registry of Deeds in Plymouth.

Publications of primary materials and compiled histories are also available:
* Bradford, William. *Bradford's History of Plimoth Plantation: From the Original Manuscript; with a Report of the Proceedings Incident to the Return of the Manuscript to Massachusetts* (Boston: Wright and Potter Printing, 1901, film 0924845).
* Davis, William P. *Genealogical Register of Plymouth Families* (1899. Reprint. Baltimore: Genealogical Publishing Co., 1994).
* Demos, John Putnam. *A Little Commonwealth: Family Life in Plymouth Colony* (New York: Oxford University Press, 1971).
* Shurtleff, Nathaniel B. and David Pulsifer. *Records of the Colony of New Plymouth*. 12 Vols. (Boston: William White, 1855-61, film 0896852 ff.;

---

[20] In 1633, twenty colonists died in an epidemic, generating substantial activity in matters of probate.

Vol. 8 reprinted by Genealogical Publishing Co., 1976). This includes proceedings of the General Court and the Court Assistants, 1633–91, judicial acts 1636–92, miscellaneous records, including vital records, lists of freemen and others, 1633–89, and deeds, 1620–51, reprinted from contemporary sources.

- Simmons, C.H. *Plymouth Colony Records: Wills and Inventories, 1633–1669* (Camden, ME: Picton Press, 1996).
- Stratton, Eugene A. *Plymouth Colony, Its History and Its People, 1620–1691* (Salt Lake City: Ancestry, 1986).
- *Genealogies of Mayflower Families, 1500s–1600s* (Broderbund, 1997). This CD-ROM contains images of *Genealogies of Mayflower Families*. 3 Vols., and *Mayflower Source Records*, published by Genealogical Publishing Company.

Suffolk County (established 1643 in Massachusetts Bay Colony)

Suffolk County Court. Court records, 1680–92 (film 0947731), 1629–1797 (film 0909870 ff.).

Suffolk County Register of Deeds. Deeds, 1639–1855 (film 0579922 ff.).[21]

Suffolk County Court of General Sessions of the Peace. Court records, 1702–80 (film 0946896 ff.).

Suffolk County Court of Common Pleas, 1701–1855 (film 0909525 ff.).

Suffolk County Supreme Judicial Court.

- Partitions and executions, 1694–1856 (film 0947291 ff.). Contains records of the Superior Court of Judicature, 1694–1773, and the Supreme Judicial Court, 1781–1856.
- Records, 1686–1799 (film 0945842 ff.). Records before 1781 were kept by the Superior Court of Judicature.
- Probate records, 1760–1870 (film 0902796).
- Catalogue of records and files in the office of the Clerk of the Supreme Judicial Court for the County of Suffolk (film 0908077).

Suffolk County Probate Court. Records, 1636–1899 (film 0518922 ff.).

Suffolk County miscellaneous papers, 1679–1808 (film 0902791 ff.).

Greenough collection of old court records, 1647–1828 (film 0902795).

The original records are at the Suffolk County Courthouse in Boston.[22]

---

[21] *Suffolk County Deeds (1629–1697)*. 14 Vols. (Boston: Rockwell and Churchill, 1850–1906, fiche 6046903). Suffolk County deeds also include land records in York and Lincoln counties in Maine, Bristol and Newport counties in Rhode Island, and Block Island (before 1663).

[22] From 1686–9, under the Dominion of New England, all estates over £40 had to be probated at Suffolk County. These records have been indexed in *The American Genealogist*, 12:175, 222, 13:98, and 14:34 (film 1425624 ff.).

Aspinwall, William. *A Volume Relating to the Early History of Boston Containing the Aspinwall Notarial Records from 1644 to 1651* (Boston: Municipal Printing Office, 1903, film 1320548).

Historical Records Survey. *Abstract and Index of the Records of the Inferiour Court of Pleas (Suffolk County Court) Held in Boston, 1680–1698* (Boston: Historical Records Survey, 1940, film 0823824).

Suffolk County Wills: Abstracts of the Earliest Wills upon Record in the County of Suffolk, Massachusetts (1848–94. Reprint. Baltimore: Genealogical Publishing Co., 1984, film 1320548).

George, Elijah. *Index to the Probate Records of the County of Suffolk, Massachusetts, from the Year 1636 to and Including the Year 1893*. 3 Vols. (Boston: Rockwell and Churchill, 1895, film 0496888).

Shurtleff, Nathaniel B. *Records of the Governor and Company of the Massachusetts Bay in New England [1628–1686]*. 5 Vols. (Boston: William White, 1853–4, fiche 6046893). Records were also kept on a county level at the county registry of deeds offices.

Worcester County (established 1738 from Suffolk and Middlesex counties)
Worcester County Register of Deeds. Deeds, 1722–1866 (film 0842930 ff.).
Worcester County Inferior Court of Common Pleas. Records, 1732–84 (film 0868526 ff.).
Worcester County Court of General Sessions of the Peace. Records, 1731–1862 (film 0859239 ff.).
Worcester County Probate Court. Records, 1731–1895 (film 0859169 ff.).

Worcester County, Massachusetts Warnings, 1737–1788 (1899. Reprint. Camden, ME: Picton Press, 1992).

Town and Church Records and Resources
Proprietors' records in New England are the recordings of the earliest land grants. Vital records are recorded in the same volumes, mixed in with the deeds. Most of the early town records have been filmed. The records listed below are primarily those that have been filmed. The State Library in Boston has a complete collection of published town vital records and histories, in books and in microform. About eighty percent of the town records in Massachusetts have been published through 1850.

Unless otherwise indicated, all filmed town records are kept at the town hall under which they are listed. Church records are at the original parish or at the town hall, unless another location is given. Please confirm the availability of any record before researching on site.

Abington
Town records, 1712–1860 (film 0904376 ff.).

Acton
First Parish. Records, 1738–1820 (film 0892214).

Town records, 1735–1862 (film 0892201).

Adams
Society of Friends, East Hoosac. Monthly meeting records, 1713–1869 (film 0017331 ff.). The original records are at the Society of Friends Archives in New York City.

Vital records and marriage intentions, 1766–1847 (film 0760652).

Alford
Town and vital records, 1773–1865 (film 0250283).

Amesbury (see also Seabrook, New Hampshire)
Town records and men in the militia, 1642–1861 (film 0893104).

Amherst
Vital and family records, 1600–1891 (film 0186128), vital records, 1739–1891 (film 0186126 ff.). Also includes a list of births in Amherst, Belchertown, Hadley, Pelham, and Shutesbury.

Andover
Town and land records, 1660–1855 (film 0878785 ff.).
Proprietors' records, 1714–1824 (film 0878789).
Tax records, 1678–1865 (film 0878781 ff.).
Selectmen's records, 1715–1970 (film 0887742 ff.).
Vital records, marriage intentions, out-of-town marriages, 1647–1850 (film 0878780 ff.).

Ashburnham
Town records, 1736–1876, proprietors' records, 1736–1839, vital records, deeds (film 0864106 ff.).
Vital records, 1760–1900 (film 0759547).

Ashby
Town records, valuations, 1769–1853 (film 0868699 ff.).
Town records, 1767–1861, deaths, 1755–1862, marriages, 1798–1812 (film 0868698).
Town and vital records, 1755–1863 (film 0763902).
Miscellaneous records, 1750–1850 (film 0868710).

Ashfield
Before 1765 known as Huntstown plantation.
Town and vital records, 1754–1946, church records, 1768–1813 (film 0902896).

Town records, 1762–1854, militia rolls (film 0902897).
Town and vital records, 1750–1916 (film 1901562).

Athol
Proprietors' records, 1734–1824 (film 0864113).
Town and vital records, 1737–1844 (film 0759549).
Town records, 1737–92, vital records (film 0864113).

Attleboro
Town records, 1699–1844, vital records (film 0580658 ff.).
Vital records, 1693–1900 (film 1987017 ff.).
Marriage intentions, 1723–1852 (film 0578844).

Auburn
From 1778 to 1837 Auburn was known as Ward.
Town records, 1773–1867 (film 0863522 ff.).
Vital and town records, 1761–1899 (film 0757001 ff.).

Barnstable
West Parish. Records, 1668–1807 (film 0022364). The original records are at the Rhode Island Historical Society in Providence, Rhode Island.
Proprietors' records, 1703–95 (film 0947064).
Town records, 1640–1855, vital records (film 0947061 ff.).

Barre
Before 1776 known as Hutchinson.
First Parish in Barre, Unitarian. Records, 1767–1937 (film 0859260 ff.).

Proprietors' records, 1686–1770 (film 0840014).
Town records, 1763–1846, vital records, 1749–1895, deeds to pews and other property, 1789–1818 (film 0859256 ff.).
Vital records, 1752–1855 (film 0754012).

Worcester County Historical Society, Barre. Miscellaneous records, 1637–1919 (film 0859261 ff.). Contracts, indentures, receipts, court summonses, military lists, etc.

Beckett
Congregational Church. Records, 1755–1873 (film 0234563).[23]

Bedford
Town records, 1729–1897, military rolls (film 0892216 ff.).
Vital records, 1700–1845 (film 0771074).

Belchertown (see also Amherst)
Congregational Church. Records, 1730–1930 (film 1862889).

Vital records and marriage intentions, 1734–1891 (film 0186139 ff.), index, 1734–1843 (film 1902436 ff.).

---

[23]Cooke Collection.

Bellingham
First Baptist Church. Records, 1737–1891 (film 0901872 ff.).

Town and vital records, 1774–1860 (film 0901871).
Vital records and marriage intentions, 1716–1858 (film 0901871).

Berkley
Town records, 1735–1867, vital records, militia rolls (film 0903401 ff.).

Berlin
Rutland proprietors' records of allotments, 1722–92 (film 0859330).
Vital records, 1739–1896 (film 0751416).

Bernardston
Before 1762 known as the new plantation of Falltown.
Proprietors' records, 1735–1819 (film 0886774).
Town records, vital records, and marriage intentions, 1743–1825 (film 0893958).
Vital records and marriage intentions, 1752–1882 (film 0772617).

Beverly
Before 1668 known as Basse River.
Second Church of Christ. Records, 1715–1862 (film 0864845). The manuscript is at the Beverly Historical Society.
Proprietors of Snake-Hill Pasture, Beverly, records, 1728–1817 (film 0864857).
Town records, 1735–79 (film 0968011).
Town records, 1685–1845 (film 0864846).
Vital records, 1653–1890 (film 0760604 ff.).

Billerica
First Congregational Church. Records, 1663–1870 (film 0901874 ff.).

Town records, 1653–1848 (film 0901876 ff.).
Book of grants, 1678–1786 (film 0901882).
Vital records, 1627–1854 (film 0901881).

Blandford
Town records, early to 1800, vital records, 1737–1890 (film 0186138).

Bolton
Town records, 1771–1848 (film 0858534).
Vital records and marriage intentions, 1738–1868 (film 0771314 ff.).
The Holman papers, 1765–1869 (film 0859191 ff.). Manuscripts for town, church, business, and military records relating to Bolton.

Boston
Baldwin Place Baptist Church. Records, 1769–1881 (film 0856702).
First Church, Boston. Records, 1630–1847 (film 0856693 ff.).
Boston Record Commission. Vol. 9: *First Church Records, 1633–58* (n.p., n.d., film 0165996). The Boston Record Commission published many works in addition to church records.

Brattle Street Church. Records, 1699–1804 (film 0837129).
Christ Church. Records, 1723–1851 (film 0856696 ff.).
Christ Church, Episcopal. Records, 1723–1917 (film 1298903).

Church in Brattle Square. *The Manifesto Church, Records of the Church in Brattle Square, Boston, With Lists of Communicants, Baptisms, Marriages, and Funerals, 1699-1872* (Boston: Benevolent Fraternity of Churches, 1902, film 0547549).

First Baptist Church. Records, 1665-1879 (film 0856702).

First Presbyterian Church. Records, 1730-1865 (film 0856695).

Hanover Street Methodist Episcopal Church. Records, 1736-1875 (film 0856700).

Hollis Street Church. Records, 1732-1887 (film 0856698).

Kings Chapel. Records, 1703-1844 (film 0856698).

New Brick Church. Records, 1722-76 (film 0856701).

New Church. Records, 1714-99 (film 0837130).

New North Church. Records, 1714-1863 (film 0856699 ff.).

New South Church. Records, 1719-1812 (film 0837129).

Old South Church. Records, 1669-1875 (film 0856694).

Second Baptist Church. Records, 1742-87 (film 0837132).

Second Church, Boston. Records, 1676-1816 (film 0856699).

Trinity Church. Records, 1737-1896 (film 1289683 ff.).

West Church. Records, 1737-1880 (film 0856695).

Selectmen's minutes, 1701-1822 (film 0477598 ff.).

Earliest records of the town of Boston (film 0477587 ff.).

Death indexes, records, 1630-1895 (film 0593709 ff.).

Marriages, 1646-1890 (film 0818085 ff.).

Vital records, 1630-1900 (film 0592859 ff.).

Death indexes, 1700-1869 (film 1492778 ff.).

Boxford

First Parish Church, Congregational. Records, 1702-1907 (film 0877752).

Town and vital records, 1681-1859 (film 0877753 ff.).

Boylston

Records of the Second Precinct in Shrewsbury, 1742-86 (film 0859237). The Second or North Precinct of Shrewsbury was incorporated into the township of Boylston in 1785.

Braintree

Before 1640 known as Mount Wollaston.

Town records, 1640-1749 (film 0940976).

Town records, 1731-1850 (film 0931506 ff.).

Selectmen's records, 1688-1847 (film 0940975 ff.).

Treasurers' book, 1744-97 (film 0940976).

Vital records and marriage intentions, 1640-1848 (film 0940974).

Brewster

Births, deaths, 1753-1838 (film 0905414).

Bridgewater

Town and vital records, 1656–1823, land records (film 0902869). Proprietors' records, 1672–1834 (film 0910364). Selectmen's records, 1703–1863 (film 0910366). Town and vital records, 1656–1853 (film 0910359 ff.).

Brimfield

Hampden County Register of Deeds. Land grants from early records of Brimfield, 1731–1824 (film 1502828 ff.). The typescript is from records at the Hampden County Courthouse in Springfield.

Vital records and marriage intentions, 1720–1890 (film 0223943).

Brookfield

First Congregational Church, Unitarian. Records, 1755–1869 (film 0868524).

Proprietors' records, 1687–1804 (film 0868521). Town and vital records, 1768–1847 (film 0763670). Town records, 1719–1853 (film 0868522).

Brookline

Muddy River was established as Brookline in 1705. Town and vital records, 1634–1850 (film 0927366). Town records, 1686–1857 (film 0927367 ff.). *Muddy River and Brookline Records, 1634–1838* (n.p.: J.E. Farwell, 1875, film 0927369).

Burlington

Vital records, 1736–1877 (film 0893876 ff.).

Cambridge

Christ Church, Episcopal. Records, 1760–1909 (film 1289685).

Cambridge City Council. *The Register Book of the Lands and Houses in the New Towne and the Town of Cambridge: With the Records of the Proprietors of the Common Lands Being the Records Generally Called the Proprietors' Records [1634–1829].* 3 Vols. (Cambridge: Harvard University Press, 1896, film 1425544). Reprinted as *Proprietors' Records of Cambridge, 1635–1829* (Bowie, MD: Heritage Books, 1990).

Selectmen's records, 1704–1853 (film 0893857 ff.). Proprietors' records, 1635–1841 (film 0893858). Vital records and marriage intentions, 1694–1820 (film 0893860). Death and burial records, 1632–1886 (film 1434110).

Carlisle

Town records, 1754–1861 (film 0892204 ff.).

Charlemont

Town and vital records, 1749–1864 (film 0953794 ff.). Treasurer's accounts, 1767–1866 (film 0953795).

Charlestown

Annexed to Boston in 1873.
First Church. Records, 1632–1789
(film 0837130).

Town records, 1629–1847 (film 0478190 ff.).
Book of possessions, 1638–1802
(film 0478560).
Vital records, 1629–1843 (film 0740995).
The original records are at the City
Registrar's Office in Boston.

Charlton

Church of Christ, Congregational.
Records, 1761–1836 (film 1421734).

Town records, 1755–1865, militia
rolls, 1755–1857 (film 0860662 ff.).
Vital and town records, 1714–1859
(film 0860661).

Chatham

Vital and town records, 1693–1890
(film 0905410 ff.).

Chelmsford (see also Westford)

First Congregational Church. Records, 1741–1901 (film 0868443 ff.).

Proprietors' records, vital records,
1645–1750 (film 0868436 ff.).
Town records, 1727–79 (film 0968014 ff.).
Vital and town records, 1645–1826
(film 0868434 ff.).

Chelsea

Town records, 1738–1840 (film
0482917). The original records are
at the Suffolk County Courthouse
in Boston.

Vital records, 1738–1900 (film 0482887 ff.).

Cheshire

First Baptist Church. Records, 1769–
1808 (film 0954456). The original
records are at the Statehouse in
Boston.

Chester (see also Westfield)

The town of Murrayfield became
Chester in 1783.
Town records, 1762–1850, proprietors' records, 1762–84, vital records,
1765–1836 (film 0879888 ff.).
Vital and town records, 1765–1864
(film 0879889 ff.)

Chesterfield

Town records, 1762–89, vital records,
1753–97 (film 1871285).
Town records, 1762–1805 (film 0186142).

Chilmark

Town records, 1697–1871 (film 0911738).
Vital records, 1754–1900 (film
1993385). Many records have been
destroyed by fire.

Cohasset

Land grants and mortgages, 1635–
1869 (film 0886771).
Town records, 1717–1864 (film
0886767).
Vital records, 1732–1843 (film 0886766),
1770–1900 (film 0754013).
Marriages and intentions, 1747–
1857 (film 0886769).

Colrain

Vital records, 1740–1900 (film
1888259 ff.).

Concord
Town records, 1650–1930 (film 0964880).

Conway
Congregational Church. Records, 1767–1821 (film 0886876).

Conway
Town and vital records, 1760–1868 (film 0903684).
Town records, 1752–1834 (film 0886878).
Births, deaths, 1750–1849 (film 0766944).

Cummington
Town records, 1762–1860, proprietors' records, vital records (film 0234538).
Vital records and marriage intentions, 1762–1900 (film 1888606).

Dalton
Congregational Church. Church and town records, 1772–1856 (film 0234565).[24]

Danvers
Prior to 1752, when Danvers was set off from Salem, it was known as Salem Village Parish.
Essex County Court of General Sessions of the Peace. List of persons warned from the town of Danvers, 1752–70 (film 0876100).
Salem Village Parish records, 1670–1735, town and vital records (film 0876096).

Tax records, 1766–1856 (film 0876087 ff.).
Strays and lost goods, 1765–1804 (film 0876100).
Overseers of the Poor records, 1774–92 (film 0876100).
Town records, 1755–1841 (film 0876101).
Book of entries, persons coming into the town, 1766–90 (film 0876100).
Vital records, 1652–1880 (film 0758829).
Vital records index, marriage intentions, 1752–1884 (film 0876097 ff.).

Dartmouth (see also Westport)
Society of Friends, New Bedford. Monthly meeting records, 1698–1887 (film 0001337 ff.). Called Dartmouth Monthly Meeting until 1792. The original records are in the Moses Brown Collection at the Rhode Island Historical Society in Providence, Rhode Island.

Land records, 1654–1846 (film 0577962).
Proprietors' records, 1648–1835 (film 0577961 ff.).
Vital records, marriage intentions, miscellaneous town records, 1647–1877 (film 0903381 ff.).
Vital records, 1667–1865 (film 0775496 ff.).

Dedham
First Church. Church records to 1736 (film 0165996). Transcript of original records by the Society of

---

[24]Cooke Collection.

the Daughters of Founders and Patriots of America.

Land and miscellaneous records, 1636-1961(film 0593346 ff.).
Land grants, 1644-1720 (film 0593352).
Town records, 1636-1813 (film 0968024 ff.).
Vital records, 1635-1853 (film 0593353).

Deerfield (see also Hatfield)
Proprietors of the Common Fields. Record book, 1733-1866 (film 0954368). The manuscript is at the Pockumtuck Valley Memorial Association in Deerfield.

Treasurers' accounts, 1737-1807 (film 0954345).
Vital records, 1675-1898 (film 0186146).

Dennis
Second Congregational Church. Records, 1728-1810 (film 0945522).

Town records, 1722-1813 (film 0945519).

Dighton
Proprietors' records, 1672-1795 (film 0905536).
Town records, 1709-1884 (film 0905534 ff.)
Vital records and marriage intentions, 1685-1855 (film 0777615 ff.).

Dorchester
Annexed to Boston in 1870.
First Church. Records, 1636-1845 (film 0856696).

Town records, 1632-1870 (film 0478174 ff.).
Vital records, 1631-1869 (film 0751200 ff.).

Douglas
Town and vital records, 1749-1842 (film 0858543 ff.).

Dracut
Proprietors' records, 1710-21 (film 0868711).
Town and vital records, 1699-1858 (film 0868712).

Dudley
Town records, 1732-1874 (film 0861111).

Dunstable
Until 1740, Dunstable was in Massachusetts, but that year the province line with New Hampshire was drawn so that it split Dunstable between the two colonies. New Hampshire changed the name of Dunstable to Nashua in 1837.
Town and vital records, 1679-1890 (film 0763713 ff.).

Duxbury
Proprietors' records, second division, births by family, 1702-71 (film 0417932). Contains records of the commons of Duxborough and Pembroke for 1709-54.

Town and vital records, land records 1645–1826 (film 0417933 ff.).
Births, 1774–1849 (film 0416800).

Eastham
Became Orleans in 1797.
Town and land records, 1643–1865 (film 0905407 ff.).
Proprietors' records, 1654–1855 (film 0907351).

Town records, 1654–1863, vital records (film 0907350).

Easton
Town records, 1725–1840, militia rolls (film 0946640 ff.).
Vital records by families, 1697–1847 (film 1059951).

Edgartown
Town records, 1657–1873, vital records (film 0911735 ff.).
Proprietors' records, 1718–95 (film 0911737).

Egremont
Church and vital statistics from Berkshire County, 1766–1930 (film 0250319). This includes North Egremont Baptist records, 1797–1866, and other records. The original records are at the Mason Public Library in Great Barrington.

Congregational Church. Records, 1770–1876 (film 0234566).[25]

Fall River
See Swansea.

Falmouth (see also Sandwich)
Proprietors' records, 1661–1891 (film 0904592).
Town and vital records, 1668–1871 (film 0904589 ff.).

Fitchburg
Vital records index, 1753–1873, town and vital records, 1764–1850 (film 0864139 ff.).
Vital and miscellaneous town records, 1751–1865 (film 0756537).

Foxborough
Vital records and marriage intentions, 1753–1856 (film 0769335 ff.).

Framingham
Town and vital records, 1700–1854 (film 0873046 ff.).
Vital records and marriage intentions, 1690–1809 (film 0872797).
Vital records and marriage intentions, 1739–1854 (film 0766527).
Town and vital records, 1700–1854 (film 0873046 ff.).

Franklin
Vital records, 1773–1900 (film 1905558).

Freetown
Town records, 1686–1886, vital records (film 0904379 ff.).

Vital records, 1683–1900 (film 1993524). The manuscript is at the

Old Colony Historical Society in Taunton.

Gardner
Vital records, 1769–1879 (film 0758482).

Gloucester
Deeds, 1708–1914 (film 0876176).
Town records, 1642–1851 (film 0876172 ff.).
Proprietors' records, 1707–1820 (film 0876172 ff.).
Gloucester Fourth Parish. Parish book of records, 1743–1839 (film 0876177).
Selectmen's records, 1699–1874 (film 0876177 ff.).

Vital records and marriage intentions, 1640–1861 (film 0864859 ff.).

Goshen
Town and vital records, 1762–1840 (film 0892564).
Vital records, 1769–1900 (film 1888838 ff.).

Grafton
Hassanamisco Church of Christ. Records, 1731–74 (film 1008687).

Grafton
Proprietors' records, 1728–1861 (film 0855368 ff.).
Town records, 1735–1859 (film 0855365 ff.).
Vital records, 1735–1885 (film 0903642 ff.).

Granby
Part of the town of Hadley and South Hadley until 1768.
Proprietors' records, 1719–1835 (film 0892047). The original records are at the Hampshire County Registry of Deeds in Northampton.

Town and vital records, 1745–1844 (film 0760645).

Granville
Congregational Church, East Granville. Records, 1739–1861 (film 0234566).[26]

Congregational Church. Death records, 1739–1863 (film 0014764). The manuscript is at the Connecticut State Library in Hartford, Connecticut.

Town records, 1751–1858 (film 0185383).
Vital records, 1733–1890 (film 0185380).

Great Barrington
Congregational Church. Records, 1743–1945 (film 0250316). Also includes Sandisfield River and Beach Plain Cemetery records, early court records of Great Barrington from Northampton records, list of taxpayers, 1772, Revolutionary War payroll, births (1762–70), etc.
Miscellaneous land transfers, church records, and vital statistics, 1666–1870 (film 0250316).
The typescripts are at the Mason Public Library in Great Barrington.

---

[26]Cooke Collection.

Vital records, 1761–1900 (film 1905678).

Greenfield
Town and vital records, 1752–1899 (film 0250326 ff.).
Town records, 1752–72, vital records, 1750–1931 (film 1887524 ff.).
Town records, 1772–1865 (film 0886778).

Greenwich
Church of Christ, Congregational. Records, 1760–1935 (film 1871030). The original records were filmed at the County Bank of Ware.

Groton
First Parish Church. Records, 1704–1880, land deeds, 1750–1800 (film 0868733 ff.).

Proprietors' records, 1716–1829 (film 0868722).
Town records, 1655–1896 (film 0868723 ff.).
Town and miscellaneous records, 1691–1873 (film 0763909).
Vital records, 1647–1829 (film 0868721).

Hadley (see also Amherst and Hatfield)
Town records, 1659–1719 (film 0186152).
Vital records, 1660–1882 (film 0186152).

Proprietors' records, 1665–1779 (film 0892047). The manuscript is at the Essex County Courthouse in Salem.

Halifax
Town and vital records, 1734–1856 (film 0904375 ff.).

Hamilton
Originally called the Hamlet and was a part of Ipswich. Hamilton became a separate town in 1793. Congregational Church. Records, 1714–1883 (film 0886035).

Town records, 1712–1848 (film 0878664).

Hancock
Vital records, 1767–1900 (film 1901802).

Hanover
Town records, 1727–99, vital records, 1712–79 (film 0423510).

Hardwick
Records, 1736–86 (film 0868519).
Town and vital records, 1730–1896 (film 0868518 ff.).

Harvard
First Congregational Church, Unitarian. Records, 1773–1909 (film 0859189 ff.).
Town records, 1732–1892 (film 0859185 ff.).
Vital records, 1732–1845 (film 0903680).

Hatfield
Church of Christ, Congregational. Records, 1771–1869 (film 0879900).

Proprietors' records, 1672–1767 (film 0892047). The original records are at the Hampshire County Registry of Deeds in Northampton.

Town records, 1660–1848, men in the militia, 1741–1848 (film 0879898).
Vital records, 1655–1844 (film 0760648).

Also includes some records for Northampton, Hadley, and Deerfield.

Haverhill
Town records, 1654–1861, vital records, 1641–64, 1724–1802 (film 0893120 ff.).

Hawley
Town records, 1730–1855, vital records (film 0886463).
Vital records, 1727–1854 (film 0768339).

Heath
Vital records, 1735–1900 (film 0768340).

Hingham
Vital records, 1635–1880 (film 0423518 ff.).

Holden
Before 1741 known as North Worcester.
Town and vital records, 1741–1850 (film 0721196).
Town records, 1740–1852 (film 0860647).

Holland
Congregational Church. Records, 1765–1862 (film 0887000).
Vital records, 1771–1822 (film 0886999).
The manuscripts of the above are at the Hampden County Courthouse in Springfield.

Holliston
Town records, 1724–1850 (film 0868515 ff.).
Vital records, 1725–1900 (film 0763666).

Hopkinton
First Congregational Church. Records, 1724–1880 (film 0954364).

Middlesex County Register of Deeds. Deeds of Hopkinton and Upton, 1743–1833 (film 0901510 ff.). The original records are at the Middlesex County Registry of Deeds in Cambridge.

Vital records, 1712–1846 (film 0954365).

Hubbardston
Town records, 1767–1856 (film 0864134 ff.).

Hull
Records, 1725–67 (film 0423528).
Town records, 1657–1841, vital and land records (film 0423529).

Ipswich
First Church of Christ. Records, 1739–1805 (film 0476747).
First Church Parish. Records, 1724–56 (film 0476747).
Linebrook Parish. Clerk's book, 1746–1830 (film 0476749).
South Church. Records, 1724–1872 (film 0476747).

Proprietors' records, 1634–1905 (film 0878651 ff.).
Deeds, mortgages, wills, 1639–1965 (film 0873018 ff.).
Town records, 1634–1864 (film 0878651).
Proprietors' records of Turner Hill, 1726–1823 (film 0476752).
Treasury records, 1699–1867 (film 0878653 ff.).

Miscellaneous town records, 1699–1828 (film 0476731 ff.).
Vital records, 1635–1871 (film 0777636 ff.).

Kingston
First Congregational Parish. Records, 1720–1880 (film 0910370).

Town records, 1717–1850 (film 0910369).
Vital records and marriage intentions, 1695–1885 (film 0910367 ff.).

Lancaster (see also Sterling)
Nourse, Henry. *The Birth, Marriage, and Death Register, Church Records and Epitaphs of Lancaster, 1643–1850* (Lancaster, MA: n.p., 1890, film 0547550).

First Church of Christ. Records, 1644–1951 (film 0811848 ff.).

Proprietors' and town records, 1649–1913 (film 0810292 ff.).
Vital records, 1642–1889 (film 0808317 ff.).
Vital records indexes to 1969 (film 0809207 ff.).

Lanesborough
Saint Luke's Episcopal Church. Records, 1767–1900 (film 0861523). The typescript is at the Library, Daughters of the American Revolution, Washington, DC.

Congregational Church. Records, 1764–1875 (film 0234569).
Saint Luke's Church. Records, 1767–1899 (film 0234569).

Town and vital records, 1765–1897 (Oxford, MA: Holbrook Research Institute, 1983, fiche 6334569).

Leicester
Town and vital records, 1714–1887 (film 0858548 ff.).
Index to births, 1706–1897, marriages, 1726–1897, deaths, 1729–1897 (film 0858547).

Lenox
Congregational Church. Records, 1771–1860 (film 0234569).

Town and vital records, 1759–1900 (film 1905888).
Vital records and indexes, 1767–1905 (film 1905888).
Parsons collection of vital statistics, Lenox, 1750–1849 (film 0238335).

Leominster
First Church. Church and society records, 1743–1907 (film 1032649).

Proprietors' records, 1701–1847 (film 0867861).

Leverett
Town records, 1727–1916 (film 0886467 ff.).
Vital records and marriage intentions, 1705–1843 (film 0767314).

Lexington
First Parish, Congregational. Records, 1690–1844 (film 0927926).

Town records, 1692–1861 (film 0927920 ff.).

Vital records, 1683–1844 (film 0927923).

Lincoln
Town and vital records, 1746–1878 (film 0892227).
Vital records and marriage intentions, 1745–1845 (film 0771077).

Littleton
Town records, 1715–1898 (film 0868719 ff.).
Vital records and marriage intentions, 1707–1831 (film 0868718).

Longmeadow
Before 1783 was known as Longmeadow, Springfield.
First Congregational Church. Records, 1741–1923 (film 0185403).

Precinct book of records, 1713–83 (film 0185398).
Account book of records, 1714–83 (film 0185398).
Records of families, 1639–1838 (film 0185400 ff.).

Ludlow
Town and vital records, 1774–1882 (film 0904737). The manuscript is at the Hampden County Courthouse in Springfield.

Lunenburg
Proprietors' meetings, 1729–1833 (film 086413), records, 1730–1833 (film 0861112).
Vital records and marriage intentions, 1765–1848 (film 0758012).
Town records, 1720–1877 (film 0861121 ff).

Vital records, 1719–97 (film 0861119).

Lynn
First Church of Christ. Records, 1763–1929 (film 1288822).

Society of Friends, Lynn. Marriage certificates, 1715–1846 (film 0878648). The manuscript is at the Lynn Historical Society.

Town records, 1691–1868 (film 0877734 ff.).
Vital records and marriage intentions, 1635–1849 (film 0877736 ff.).
Vital records, 1684–1900 (film 1927787 ff.).

Lynnfield
First Congregational Church. Records, 1720–1850 (film 0877218).

Town records, 1711–1808 (film 0877217).
Vital records and marriage intentions, 1763–1848 (film 0760609).

Malden
First Church of Christ. Records, 1770–1887 (film 0893366).
First Congregational Church. Records, 1747–92 (film 0893871).

Town records, 1764–1845 (film 0893872).
Town financial records, 1769–1820 (film 0893870).
Vital records, 1677–1868 (film 0893873 ff.).

Manchester
Town and vital records, 1624–1915 (film 0865432 ff.).
Town records, 1653–1890 (film 0768158).

Mansfield
Town records, 1731–1856 (film 0904374).
Vital records and marriage intentions, 1703–1886 (film 0904373 ff).

Marblehead
First Congregational Church. Records, 1684–1857 (film 0877751).
Saint Michael's Church, Episcopal. Records, 1715–1915 (film 1289696).

Proprietors' records, 1703–1842 (film 0864839).
Town records, 1648–1851 (film 0864833).
Vital records, 1653–1842 (film 0864830 ff.).
Vital records, 1670–1850 (film 0760602).

Marlborough
Church of Christ, Sudbury. Sudbury and Marlboro church records, 1724–43 (film 0185463).

Town records, 1666–1847 (film 0902009 ff.).
Selectmen's records, 1760–1913 (film 0902006 ff.).
Vital records, 1693–1844, indexes, 1661–1860 (film 0771313 ff.).

Marshfield
First Congregational Church. Records, 1669–1920 (film 0417929 ff.).

Town and vital records, 1631–1875 (film 0417925 ff.).

Medfield
Town records, 1649–1788 (film 0832316 ff.).
Vital records, 1652–1900 (film 1887547 ff.).

Medford
First Church of Christ. Records, 1712–1823 (film 0886764).

Town records, 1675–1781 (film 0968005).
Town records, 1673–1864 (film 0886758 ff.). Town records, 1630–70, are missing.
Vital records, 1718–1851 (film 0886761 ff.).

Medway
Second Church of Christ. Records, 1750–1860 (film 0901857).

Town records, 1714–1869 (film 0901854 ff.).
Vital records index, 1713–1849 (film 0901856 ff.).
Vital records, 1740–1900 (film 1887442 ff.).

Mendon
Town records, 1663–1862 (film 0855374).
Vital records and marriage intentions, 1663–1901 (film 0751415 ff.).
Vital records, 1643–1835 (film 0855377).

Methuen
First Church of Christ. Records, 1729-1832 (film 0887750).
First Parish. Records, 1735-1855 (film 0887750).

Town records, 1725-1871, vital records (film 0887745 ff.).
Selectmen's records, 1733-1860 (film 0887747 ff.).
Miscellaneous town records, 1725-1876 (film 0887749 ff.)
Marriages, 1713-1840 (film 0887746).
Vital records, 1716-1876 (film 0760383 ff.).

Middleborough
Before 1669 known as Namassakett.
Town and vital records, 1757-1889 (film 1059954).
Proprietors' records, 1661-1887 (film 0945018).
Vital records and marriage intentions, miscellaneous town records, 1674-1854 (film 0945014 ff.).
Town records, 1658-1705, 1746-1866 (film 0945011 ff.).
Selectmen's records, 1736-1825 (film 0945013 ff.).

Middleton
Evangelical Congregational Church. Records, 1729-1854 (film 0876104).

Town records, 1728-1884 (film 0876102 ff.).
Vital records, 1703-1822 (film 0876103).

Millbury
See Sutton.

Milton
Town records, 1668-1859 (film 0945616 ff.).
Vital records and marriage intentions, 1665-1856 (film 0945618).

Monson
Congregational Church of Christ. Records, 1762-1864 (film 0904741).
Births and deaths, 1755-1837 (film 0904741).
The manuscripts of both of the above are at the Hampden County Courthouse in Springfield.

Montague
Town records, 1719-1859 (film 0886883).
Vital records and marriage intentions, 1715-1866 (film 0766948).

Mount Washington
Vital records, 1745-1900 (film 1902541), birth index, 1745-1987 (film 1769720).

Nantucket
Society of Friends, Nantucket. Monthly meeting records, 1660-1944 (film 0909501 ff.). The original records are at the Nantucket Historical Association.
Monthly meeting records, 1708-1873 (Providence: Rhode Island Historical Society, 1950, film 0014776 ff.). The original records are in the Moses Brown Collection at the Rhode Island Historical Society in Providence, Rhode Island.

Town and vital records, 1695–1852 (film 0906220 ff.).
Vital records, 1662–1827 (film 0906499). Vital records 1754–84 are missing.
Vital records and marriage intentions, 1662–1875 (film 0776073 ff.).

Natick
Miscellaneous town records, 1700–1919 (film 0593458).
Town meeting records, 1745–1967 (film 0593453 ff.).
Vital records, 1720–1890 (film 0593463 ff.).

Needham
Town records, 1711–1862 (film 0901848 ff.).
Vital records, 1711–1900 (film 1940974 ff.).

New Bedford (see also Dartmouth)
Vital records, 1650–1900 (film 1993938 ff.).

New Braintree
Vital records, 1749–1864 (film 0861116 ff.).

New Marlborough
Proprietors' records, 1744 (film 0234570).
Vital records, 1734–1918 (film 0250275).

Newbury
Second Parish of West Newbury. Records, 1731–1869 (film 0890241 ff.).

Record of ear marks, 1715–1880 (film 0886194).

Town records, 1635–1860 (film 0886194 ff.).
Proprietors' records, 1635–1828 (film 0886194 ff.).
Vital records and marriage intentions, 1635–1844 (film 0886202 ff.).

Newburyport
First Presbyterian Church. Records, 1745–1971 (film 0893125 ff.).
Saint Paul's Church, Episcopal. Records, 1714–1930 (film 1290171 ff.).

Town records, 1764–1851 (film 0890253 ff.).
Vital records and marriage intentions, 1740–1875 (film 0767312 ff.).

Newton
Town and vital records, 1674–1849 (film 0844469 ff.).
Vital records, 1626–1852 (film 0745868).
Index to marriages, 1649–1892 (film 0745080).

North Adams
See Adams.

Northampton (see also Hatfield)
First Congregational Church. Records, 1661–1924 (film 0186160).

Proprietors' records, 1653–1731 (film 0892048).
Marriages of residents reported by other cities and towns, 1655–1799 (film 0186164).

Vital records, 1654–1872 (film 0186161 ff.).

Northborough
Town records, 1744–1843 (film 0904751 ff.).
Vital records and marriage intentions, 1761–1887 (film 0775948 ff.).

Northbridge
Town and vital records, 1748–1849 (film 0763664).
Town records, 1733–1935 (film 0868511 ff.).

Northfield
Northfield church records, 1752–94 (film 1888954).
Historic documents, 1671–1835 (film 1888954).
Vital records and marriage intentions, 1713–1839 (film 0886783).

Norton
Congregational Church, Unitarian. Records, 1714–1972 (film 0903392).
Selectmen's records, 1723–1859 (film 0903404).
Town records, 1715–1866 (film 0899109).
Vital records and marriage intentions, 1664–1882 (film 0899107 ff.).
Vital records, 1711–1905 (film 2031210).

Oakham
Evangelical Congregational Church. Records, 1773–1919 (film 0825085).

Town records, 1762–1895 (film 0825075 ff.).

Town and vital records, 1761–1954 (film 0825077 ff.).

Orange
Before 1783 known as the Ervingshire tract.
Births and deaths, 1770–1850 (film 0770464).

Orleans
Before 1797 part of Eastham.
Town records, 1765–1840 (film 0905407).
Town records, 1762–1863 (film 0905409).
Vital records, 1637–1892 (film 0778357 ff.).

Oxford
Births and deaths, 1722–1840 (film 0859253).
Town and vital records, 1713–52 (film 0859252).
Vital records, 1714–1894 (film 0754010 ff.).

Palmer
Before 1752 known as the Elbow Tract.
Proprietors' records, 1732–1824 (film 0947159).
Vital records, 1746–1849 (film 1059952).

Paxton
Town records, 1765–1847 (film 0851570).
Town and vital records, 1749–1852 (film 0851569).

Pelham (see also Amherst)
Town warrants, 1747–1812, (film 1869503).
Town records and marriage intentions, 1743–1830 (film 1863287).

Pew holders in the Pelham Meeting House in 1766 (film 1863562).
Proprietors' records, 1738-67 (film 1863287).

Town records, 1747-1839 (film 1869503).
Town and proprietors' records, 1738-1830, marriage intentions, 1742-1816 (film 0892562 ff.).
Vital records, 1774-1905 (film 1863287).

Pembroke (see also Duxbury)
First Church, Unitarian. Records, 1711-1899 (film 0423501).

Society of Friends, Pembroke. Monthly meeting records, 1676-1876 (film 0001335). Includes records of Sandwich Quarterly Meetings, 1708-80, and sufferings at Plymouth, 1676-80. The original records are in the Moses Brown Collection at the Rhode Island Historical Society in Providence, Rhode Island.

Town and vital records, 1711-1841 (film 0423498 ff.).
Vital records, 1663-1897 (film 0423495), 1694-1844 (film 0423494).

Pepperell
Church of Christ. Records, 1742-1861 (film 0868604).

Town records, 1742-1825 (film 0868715).
Town and vital records, 1655-1919 (film 0868603).

Vital records and marriage intentions, 1727-1867 (film 0763904).

Peru
Incorporated as Partridgefield in 1771. In 1806 the name was changed to Peru. The early name of Peru was Plantation Number 2.
Vital and town records, 1771-1900 (film 1901873).

Petersham
First Congregational Church. Records, 1738-1870 (film 0864102).

Town records, 1733-1888 (film 0864097 ff.).
Vital records, 1735-1839 (film 0864096).

Phillipston
Vital records and marriage intentions, 1764-1851 (film 0763663).

Pittsfield
Before 1761 known as the plantation of Pontoosuck.
Town and vital records, 1761-1890 (film 0234543 ff.).
Vital records, 1772-1900 (film 1902437 ff.).
Death index, 1761-1938 (film 0234546).

Plymouth (see also Plymouth County and Pembroke)
First Parish, Unitarian. Records, 1749-1824 (film 0912071).
Second Church in Plymouth. Records, 1732-1930 (film 0912072).
The manuscripts are at Pilgrim Hall in Plymouth.

Plymouth Colony records, "Scrap Book," 1636–95 (film 0912073). Deeds, inventories of estates, guardian records, bonds, bills of sale, ships' papers, etc.[27] The records have been transcribed in Pope, Charles Henry. *The Plymouth Scrap Book: The Oldest Original Documents Extant in Plymouth Archives* . . . (Boston: C.E. Goodspeed, 1918).

Proprietors' records, 1702–92 (film 0417210).
Notarial records, 1741–1830 (film 0906750).
Vital records, 1699–1886 (film 0416330 ff.).

Records of the Town of Plymouth. 3 Vols. (Plymouth, MA: Avery and Doten, 1889–1903. Reprint. Bowie, MD: Heritage Books, 1989, film 0417211).

Plymouth Church Records, 1620–1859. 2 Vols. (1920–3. Reprint. Baltimore: Genealogical Publishing Co., 1975, fiche 6048992 ff.).

Plympton
Town and vital records, 1695–1924 (film 0910371 ff.).

Princeton
Congregational Church. Records, 1764–1851 (film 0844373).

---

[27] These records are the remnants of the original Plymouth Register of Deeds, which was burned in a fire in 1881.

Town records, 1762–1964 (film 0844374 ff.).
Vital records, 1759–1842 (film 0840015).

Provincetown
Established in 1727; some records of Provincetown have been published in *The Mayflower Descendant*; births have been extracted by the Genealogical Department of The Church of Jesus Christ of Latter-day Saints for 1696–1843 (film 1002750).

Quincy
Christ Church, Episcopal. Records, 1728–1921 (film 1290174 ff.).

First Parish Church. Records, 1688–1848 (film 0845686).

Randolph
Vital records index cards, 1767–1899 (film 1955893 ff.).

Raynham
Town records, 1731–1851 (film 0482212).
Vital records and town records, 1699–1895 (film 1853853 ff.).

Reading
First Church of Christ. Records, 1648–1845 (film 0890239).

Town records, 1638–1847 (film 0886199 ff.).
Selectmen's records, 1663–1852 (film 0886201 ff.).
Vital records and marriage intentions, 1640–1846 (film 0890236).

Rehoboth
Book of orders, notes, receipts, 1749–1856 (film 0562566).
Book of rates, 1671–1712 (film 0562567).
Miscellaneous town records, 1709–64 (film 0562565).
Town records, 1636–1966 (film 0562561 ff.).
Town records, 1648–1966 (film 0562559 ff.).
Vital records, 1720–1900 (film 1987644 ff.).

Proprietors' records, 1641–1849 (film 0550001 ff.). The original records are at the Bristol County Registry of Deeds in Taunton.

Richmond
Church and vital records, 1769–1812 (film 0234573).[28]

Rochester (see also Sandwich)
Town, proprietors', and vital records, 1673–1893 (film 0482220 ff.).

Luce, Joseph. *Proprietors' Records, 1679–1807* (n.p., n.d., film 0482218). Transcription of original records of the towns of Rochester, Mattapoisett, Marion, and Wareham.

Rowe
Vital records and marriage intentions, 1774–1848 (film 0902998).

Rowley
Proprietors' records, 1674–1852,

division of fences, 1756–1910 (film 0887761).
Freeholders' records, 1643–1870 (film 0887760).
Town records, 1648–1872 (film 0887752 ff.).
Selectmen's records, 1758–1864 (film 0887760).
Vital records and marriage intentions, 1636–1835 (film 0887754).
Vital records and marriage intentions, 1715–1860 (film 0761321).

Roxbury
Annexed to Boston in 1867.
Third Parish Church. Records, 1771–1860 (film 0856701).

Town records, 1648–1846, selectmen's records, 1787–1846 (film 0478568 ff.).
Vital records, 1630–1867 (film 0741317 ff.).
The manuscripts are at Boston City Hall.

Royalston
Vital records and marriage intentions, 1772–1843 (film 0759551).
Vital records, 1749–1824 (film 0864124).

Rutland (see also Berlin)
Maps of Surrey plots, 1720–99 (film 0859331).

Miscellaneous town records, 1770–99 (film 0859331).
Town records, 1719–1860 (film 0859328 ff.).
Vital records, 1719–1874 (film 0859332 ff.).

---

[28]Cooke Collection.

Salem
Saint Peter's Church, Episcopal.
Records, 1738–1942 (film 1290176 ff.).

Society of Friends, Salem. Births, deaths, and burials, 1709–1828 (film 0909502). The original records are at the Nantucket Historical Association.

Pierce, Richard D. *The Records of the First Church in Salem, Massachusetts, 1629–1736* (Salem, MA: The Essex Institute, 1974).

Town records, 1634–1836 (film 0877440 ff.).
Vital records, 1650–1865 (film 0761209 ff.), 1644–1870; indexes, 1658–1880 (film 0877447 ff.).

There are additional records at the Essex County Courthouse in Salem:
Notary public records, 1696–1722 (film 0877463).
Tax and valuation lists, 1689–1831(film 0968009 ff.).
Tax records, 1689–1850 (film 0877453 ff.).

Salisbury
Town and proprietors' records, 1638–1858 (film 0890243 ff.).
Vital records and marriage intentions, 1637–1821 (film 0890245).

Sandisfield
(see also Great Barrington)
Congregational Church. Records,

1756–1905 (film 0234572).[29]

Proprietors' records, 1735–61 (film 1728094).
Town and vital records, 1746–1894 (film 1728094 ff.).

Sandwich (see also Pembroke)
Society of Friends, Sandwich. Monthly meeting records, 1646–1850 (film 0001330). This meeting was held in Sandwich, Falmouth, and Rochester. The original records are in the Moses Brown Collection at the Rhode Island Historical Society in Providence, Rhode Island.

Proprietors' records, 1665–1770 (film 0904584).
Town records, 1652–1868 (film 0904582 ff.).
Vital records and marriage intentions, 1640–1886 (film 0904579 ff.).

Savoy
Town records, 1771–1801 (film 0234573).
Vital records, 1736–1900 (film 1902909 ff.).

Scituate
Vital and town records, 1640–1847 (film 0423512 ff.).

Sharon
Before 1783 known as Stoughton and Stoughtonham.

---

[29] Cooke Collection.

First Congregational Church. Records, 1741–1928 (film 0940506).

Valuation records, 1740–1839 (film 0940502 ff.).

Town records, 1753–1856 (film 0940501).
Town records, 1740–1821 (film 0940504).
Vital records, 1764–1848 (film 0777850).

Sheffield
Town records, 1730–1843 (film 0250247).

Shelburne
First Congregational Church. Records, 1772–1870 (film 0886746 ff.).

Town records, 1600–1900 (film 0886786).
Town records, 1768–1849, vital and land records (film 0886748 ff.).
Vital records, 1756–1835 (film 0886747), 1770–1900 (film 1887660 ff.).

Sherborn
Town records, 1674–1861 (film 0872790 ff.).
Town and vital records, 1663–1866 (film 0766581).
Vital records, 1663–1810 (film 0872789).

Shirley
Town and proprietors' records, 1721–1800 (film 0871509).

Town records, 1750–1900 (film 0871509 ff.).
Marriages, 1750–1850 (film 0765406).

Shrewsbury (see also Boylston)
Shrewsbury North Parish became a part of Boylston when the town was incorporated in 1785.
Congregational Church, Boylston. Vital records taken from the Shrewsbury North Parish, 1776–1856 (film 0859237).

Proprietors' records, 1717–1829 (film 0864051).
Town and vital records, 1717–1890 (film 0759526).
Town records, 1719–1857 (film 0864046 ff.).
Vital records, 1730–1810 (film 0864064).

Shutesbury (see also Amherst)
Proprietors' records, 1735–1805 (film 0886454).
Mortgages and attachments, 1772–1851 (film 0886457).
Town records, 1761–1857 (film 0886456).
Vital records, 1763–1900 (film 0768337 ff.).

Somerset
See Swansea.

South Hadley
Town records, 1762–1867 (film 0879895 ff.).

Town and vital records, 1730–1847 (film 0760647).

Southampton
Town and vital records, 1730–1864, proprietors' records, 1730–80 (film 0892587 ff.).

Southborough
Assessors' records, 1740–1887 (film 0861101).
Town records, 1723–1939 (film 0863538 ff.).
Town records, 1727–1868 (film 0861129 ff.).
Vital records, 1718–96 (film 0861127).

Southwick
Congregational Church. Records, 1773–1895 (film 0234575).

Spencer
Congregational Church. Records, 1744–1819 (film 0845609).

Town records, 1744–1879 (film 0845606 ff.).
Vital and town records, 1744–1853 (film 0845608).

Springfield
First Congregational Church. Records, 1736–1878 (film 0185410).

Outward and inward commons land records, 1699–1813 (film 0480833 ff.).
Record of possessions, 1651–99, transcript of grants, 1636–1857 (film 0480833 ff.).
Town records, 1638–1852 (film 0480833 ff.).

Selectmen's records, 1713–1857 (film 0480838), 1636–1857 (film 0886993 ff.).
Town records, 1636–1859 (film 0904746 ff.), 1664–1852 (film 0904748 ff.).
Vital records, 1638–1887 (film 0185411 ff.).

Sterling
First Congregational Church, Unitarian. Records, 1744–1813 (film 0860642). Also known as the Second Church of Lancaster.

Vital records, 1759–1892 (film 0721193).

Stockbridge
Church of Christ, Congregational. Records, 1759–1917 (film 0238336 ff.).

Town records, 1735–1832 (film 0238330).
Vital records, 1737–1900 (film 0238332 ff.).

Stoneham
Town records, 1725–1861 (film 0904951).
Vital records, 1714–1853 (film 0775996 ff.).

Stoughton
Part of Dorchester was established as Stoughton in 1726.
Town and vital records, 1717–1886 (film 0932776).
Town records, 1715–1855 (film 0932777).

Stow
First Parish Church, Unitarian. Records, 1701–1937 (film 0815622).

Town records, 1660–1911 (film 0815616 ff.).
Vital records, 1692–1900 (film 0815612 ff.).

Sturbridge
Before 1738 known as New Medfield.
Congregational Church. Records, 1736–1895 (film 0863530 ff.).
Town records, 1733–1858, proprietors' and vital records, 1733–98 (film 0863527 ff.).
Vital records and marriage intentions, 1734–1861 (film 0757003).
Vital records, 1723–97 (film 0863529).

Sudbury (see also Marlborough)
First Parish Church. Records, 1704–1956 (film 0185464).
West Church. Records, 1772–1800 (film 0185462).

Proprietors' records, 1638–1805, land grants, 1705–1802 (film 0185459 ff.).
Miscellaneous town records, 1700–1850 (film 0185465).
Miscellaneous town records, 1650–1800 (film 0185461).
Town records, 1638–1760 (film 0892225).
Town records, 1639–1800, vital records, 1639–1701 (film 0185453).
Town records, 1640–1884 (film 0185448 ff.).
Vital records, 1663–1857 (film 0185454 ff.).

Sunderland
First Congregational Church. Records, 1749–1849 (film 0886462). The filmed manuscript is at the Franklin County Courthouse in Greenfield.

Town and proprietors' records, 1673–1855 (film 0886459 ff.).
Vital records, 1686–1858 (film 0768338).

Sutton
First Congregational Church, Millbury. Records, 1718–1898 (film 0858539 ff.).

Proprietors' records, 1704–1809 (film 0858540).
Town records, 1732–1835 (film 0858541 ff.).
Vital records and marriage intentions, 1710–1877 (film 0721190).

Swansea (see also Barrington, Rhode Island)
Society of Friends, Swansea. Monthly meeting records, 1720–1891 (film 0001316 ff.). This meeting was held in Somerset and Fall River. The original records are in the Moses Brown Collection at the Rhode Island Historical Society in Providence, Rhode Island.

The Ilston Book: Containing Records of the First Welsh Baptist Church, Ilston, Glamorgan, 1650–1660, and of the Church Which its Pastor, John Miles, Subsequently Founded at Swansea, Massachusetts (Aberystwyth: National Library of Wales, n.d., film

0104833). Records of the Baptist church established at Ilston, near Swansea, in 1649, (the earliest Baptist church in Wales) and of the church established in 1667 in Swansea, copies of letters sent to the church in New England from various "sister" churches in Wales, Ireland, and London.

Town records, 1670-1901 (film 0903396 ff.).
Proprietors' records, 1667-1725 (film 0903396).
Vital records, 1662-1805 (film 0903395).
The above records are at the Bristol County Courthouse in Taunton.

Vital records, 1739-1858 (film 0775499).
Vital records index, 1647-1842 (film 0168996).

Taunton
Saint Thomas' Church, Episcopal. Records, 1742-1921 (film 0899094), 1743-1913 (film 1290178).

Proprietors' records, 1638-1890 (film 0899095 ff.).
Proprietors' records, 1639-1800, vital records, 1648-1786 (film 0899104 ff.).

Proprietors' records of North and South Purchases, 1661-1890 (film 0550006 ff.).
Town records, 1642-1816 (film 0899106 ff.).
Births and marriages, 1648-1905 (film 2047676).

Vital records, 1741-1894 (film 0899100 ff.).

Templeton
Before 1762 known as Narragansett Plantation No. 6.
Town records, 1733-1882, proprietors' records, 1733-1817 (film 0864109 ff.).
Vital records, 1747-1850 (film 0759548).

Tewksbury
Town records, 1734-1860 (film 0892219).
Vital records, 1738-1897 (film 0771075).

Tisbury
Town records, 1673-1884 (film 0911743 ff.).
Vital records and marriage intentions, 1666-1867 (film 0911739 ff.).

Topsfield
Before 1648 known as part of Ipswich called the Village at the New Meadows.
Vital records and marriage intentions, 1645-1833 (film 0887762).
Vital records, 1648-1886 (film 0761323).

Townsend
Proprietors' records, 1719-1822 (film 0868716).
Town and vital records, 1732-1882 (film 0868716 ff.).

Truro
Before 1709 known as the Pawmett tract.

First Congregational Church. Records, 1711–1834 (film 0911762).

Proprietors' records, 1696–1800 (film 0911762).
Town and vital records, 1709–83 (film 0907353).
Town and vital records, 1771–1847 (film 0779027).

Tyringham
Town records, 1737–1840 (film 0234576).
Town records, 1762–82, vital records, 1717–1898 (film 0250272).
Transcripts of marriages, 1771–99 (film 0250272).
Vital records, 1759–1900 (film 1903038 ff.).

Upton (see also Hopkinton)
Town and vital records, 1735–1916 (film 0867868 ff.).
Vital records, 1736–1854 (film 0758483 ff.).

Uxbridge
Church of Christ. Records, 1730–1833 (film 0867876).

Vital records, 1717–1894 (film 0758485 ff.).

Walpole
Town records, 1724–1885 (film 0878208 ff.).

Vital records, 1724–1844 (film 1870925).

Waltham
Town and vital records, 1720–1875 (film 0892245 ff.).

Ware
Town records, 1742–96 (film 0947162), 1742–1864 (film 0879883 ff.).
Vital records and marriage intentions, 1735–1844 (film 0760644).

Wareham (see also Rochester)
Town and vital records, 1739–1876 (film 0482240 ff.).
Vital records, 1738–1893 (film 0482235).

Warren
Before 1834 known as Western.
Town and vital records, 1741–1858 (film 0758011).

Warwick
Vital records, 1739–1900 (film 1888692).

Washington
Town records, 1768–1853 (film 1764060).

Watertown
Vital records, 1630–1851 (film 0745869), 1630–1823 (film 0844471).

Watertown Records [1630–1829].
8 Vols. (Watertown: Historical Society, 1894–1939, film 0014793 ff.).

Wayland

Originally part of Sudbury. In 1780 it was established as East Sudbury, and in 1835 the name was changed from East Sudbury to Wayland. Vital records and marriage intentions, 1676–1844 (film 0892224). Town records, 1638–1908 (film 0892226).

Wellfleet

Town records, 1763–1858 (film 0907352). Vital records, 1734–1875 (film 0779026).

Wendell

Vital records and marriage intentions, 1760–1890 (film 0770463).

Wenham

First Church, Congregational. Records, 1644–55 (film 0878668).

Town records, 1643–1960 (film 0878669). Vital records, 1654–1844 (film 0864290 ff.).

Westborough

Town and vital records, 1678–1867 (film 0867879 ff.). Vital records and marriage intentions, 1694–1864 (film 0758488).

West Boylston

Parts of Boylston, Holden, and Sterling established as West Boylston in 1808. Vital records and marriage intentions, 1752–1850 (film 0754009).

Westfield

First Congregational Church. Records, 1679–1836 (film 0185468 ff.).

Hampden County Register of Deeds. Abstracts of early Westfield and Chester land records, 1667–1830 (film 1502828). The typescript is the Hampden County Registry of Deeds in Springfield.

Vital records, 1669–1854 (film 0185474 ff.).

Westford

First Congregational Church. Records, 1727–1889 (film 0902078). Also known as the Second Church of Chelmsford.

Town records, 1726–1863 (film 0902071 ff.). Births, deaths, 1701–1873, marriages and intentions, 1728–1845 (film 0893381 ff.).

Westhampton

Vital records, 1770–1851 (film 0779551).

Westminster

Proprietors' records, 1728–56, town records, 1759–1894 (film 0864125). Vital records, 1741–1893 (film 0759550), 1747–99 (film 0864125 ff.).

Weston

First Parish Church. Records, 1709–1858 (film 0892235).

Tax records, 1757-1859 (film 0892242 ff.).
Vital records, 1711-1840 (film 0892239 ff.).

Westport
Society of Friends, Westport. Monthly meeting records, 1766-1887 (film 0001339 ff.). Called Acoaxet Monthly Meeting until 1812. The original records are in the Moses Brown Collection at the Rhode Island Historical Society in Providence, Rhode Island.

Vital records and marriage intentions, 1740-1829 (film 0903378).

West Springfield
Vital records, 1774-1856 (film 0186172 ff.).

West Stockbridge
Town records, 1736-1850 (film 0234577).[30]

Weymouth
Proprietors' records, 1642-4 (film 0901867).
Town records, 1636-1860 (film 0901861 ff.).
Vital records, 1633-1905 (film 2031513 ff.).

Whately
Church of Christ, Congregational. Records, 1771-1875 (film 0886750).

Town records, 1771-1850 (film 0959001).
Vital records, 1749-1856 (film 0770462).

Wilbraham
First Congregational Church. Records, 1755-1800 (film 0223923). The manuscript is at the Public Library in Springfield.

Town records, 1773-1844 (film 0904738).
Vital records and marriage intentions, 1770-1826 (film 0904738). The filmed are at the Hampden County Courthouse in Springfield.

Williamsburg
Town records, 1771-1858 (film 0879873 ff.).
Vital records and marriage intentions, 1765-1851 (film 0760643).

Willamstown
Vital records, 1760-1893 (film 0250293).
Town records, 1753-1882 (film 0234577).[31]

Wilmington
Records of taxation, 1731-1872 (film 0887764 ff.).
Town records, 1766-1876 (film 0887763).
Vital records and marriage intentions, 1716-1853 (film 0761324).

---

[30] Cooke Collection.

[31] Cooke Collection.

Winchendon
Town and proprietors' records, 1735–1859 (film 0864129 ff.).

Windsor
Congregational Church. Records, 1773–1870 (film 0234577).

Woburn
Town records, 1673–1852 (film 0893878 ff.).
Selectmen's records, 1673–1775 (film 0968001).
Vital records and marriage intentions, 1641–1849 (film 0859998 ff.).

Worcester
Before 1684 known as Quansigamond plantation.
First Congregational Church. Records, 1747–1892 (film 0851313).

Collections of the Worcester Society of Antiquity [1667–1848]. 15 Vols. (Worcester, MA: The Society, n.d., film 0864091, 0864092 ff., fiche 6050264).

Worthington
Manuscripts and maps of township No. 3, 1762–72 (film 0234522).
Vital records, 1768–1900 (film 1872268 ff.).

Wrentham
Proprietors' and selectmen's records, 1660–1822 (film 0886865).
Town records, 1656–1867 (film 0886861 ff.).
Book of grants, 1663–1767 (film 0886864).
Selectmen's and freeholders' records, 1760–81 (film 0886864).

Yarmouth
Proprietors' records, 1710–87 (film 0945517).
Town records, 1677–1887 (film 0945516). Town records, 1639–76 were destroyed.
Vital records and marriage intentions, 1657–1823 (film 0945511).

Suggested Reading

Bailey, Frederic W. *Early Massachusetts Marriages Prior to 1800: With the Addition of Plymouth County Marriages, 1692–1746.* 3 Vols. in 1 (1896–1906. Reprint. Baltimore: Genealogical Publishing Co., 1991, fiche 6051393).

Banks, Charles Edward. *The English Ancestry and Homes of the Pilgrim Fathers Who Came to New England . . .* (1920. Reprint. Baltimore: Genealogical Publishing Co., 1997).

Banks, Charles Edward. *Planters of the Commonwealth* (1930. Reprint. Baltimore: Genealogical Publishing Co., 1991).

Banks, Charles Edward. *The Winthrop Fleet of 1630: An Account of the Vessels, the Voyage, the Passengers and Their English Home from Original Authorities* (1930. Reprint. Baltimore: Genealogical Publishing Co., 1989, film 1320700).

Collections of the Old Colony Historical Society (Taunton, MA: The Society, 1878–1921, film 1036243).

Colonial Justice in Western Massachusetts, 1639–1702: The Pynchon Court Record, an Original Judge's Diary of the Administration of Justice in the Springfield Courts in the Massachusetts Bay Colony (Cambridge: Harvard University Press, 1961).

Davis, Andrew McFarland. *Papers Relating to the Land Bank of 1740* (Boston: Colonial Society of Massachusetts, 1910, film 0844519). Includes calendar of the papers and records relating to the land bank of 1740, in the State Archives and Suffolk Court files.

Ford, Worthington Chauncey. *Bibliography of the Laws of the Massachusetts Bay, 1641–1776* (Boston: Colonial Society of Massachusetts, 1910, film 0844519).

Historical Records Survey. *Preliminary Edition of Guide to Depositories of Manuscript Collections in Massachusetts* (Boston: The Survey, 1939).

Holbrook, Jay Mack. *Bibliography of Massachusetts Vital Records, 1620–1900: An Inventory of the Original Birth, Marriage, and Death Volumes.* 5th ed. (Oxford, MA: Holbrook Research Institute, 1995, fiche 6344488).

Hutchinson, Thomas. *The History of the Colony of Massachusetts's Bay: From the First Settlement thereof in 1628 Until Its Incorporation with the Colony of Plimouth . . . in 1691.* 2nd ed. (London: M. Richardson, 1765, film 1421670).

Labaree, Benjamin W. *Colonial Massachusetts, a History* (Millwood, NY: KTO Press, 1979).

Longver, Phyllis O. *A Surname Guide to Massachusetts Town Histories* (Bowie, MD: Heritage Books, 1993).

Mayflower Families Through Five Generations. 8 Vols. (Plymouth, MA: General Society of Mayflower Descendants, 1975–, fiche 6049584 ff.).

Menand, Catherine S. *A Research Guide to the Massachusetts Courts and Their Records* (Boston: Massachusetts Supreme Judicial Court, Archives and Records Preservation, 1987).

Northend, William Dummer. *The Bay Colony: A Civil, Religious and Social History of the Massachusetts Colony and Its Settlements from the Landing at Cape Ann in 1624 to the Death of Governor Winthrop in 1650* (Boston: Colonial Press, 1896, film 1486505).

Mayflower Source Records: Primary Data Concerning Southeastern Massachusetts, Cape Cod, and the Islands of Nantucket and Martha's Vineyard (Baltimore: Genealogical Publishing Co., 1986).

Spear, Burton W. *Search for the Passengers of the Mary and John, 1630* (Toledo, OH: The Author, 1985–, fiche 6010908 ff.). Genealogies and records of West country (England) planters in New England.

Wright, Carroll D. *Report on the Custody and Condition of the Public Records of Parishes, Towns, and Counties* (Boston: Wright and Potter, 1889, fiche 6046869).

Seal of Massachusetts Bay
Company.

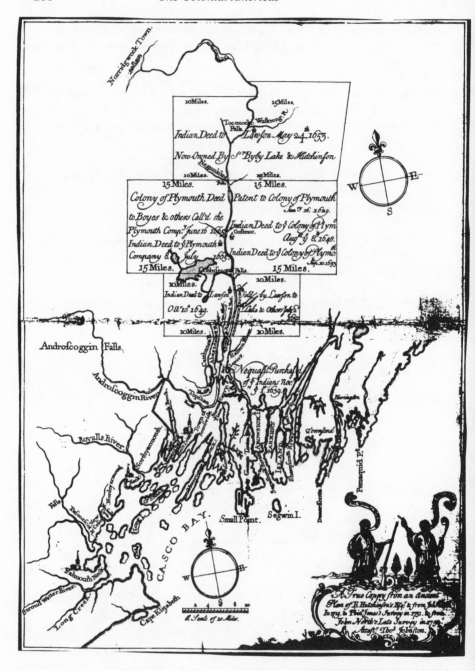

26 Pejepscot Company, Maine (Library of Congress)

New Hampshire

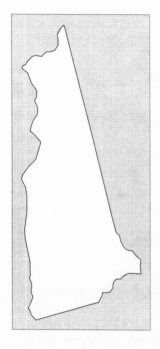

A patent was issued in 1622 for the province of Maine that included all the land between the Merrimack and the Sadahoc rivers. The first settlement in New Hampshire was established at Pascataqua (Rye) in 1623, at the mouth of the Piscataqua River, by merchants from the Plymouth Colony. The second colony was established at Hilton's Point (Dover) in 1628. The Maine province was split in 1629, and the land between the Merrimack and the Piscataqua rivers was granted to Captain John Mason, who named it New Hampshire. He also received a charter for the Laconia Company, which became bankrupt in 1634. The first settlers at Strawberry Banke (Portsmouth) established a trading post in 1632. These early settlements were known as plantations.

By 1640 the settlements at Exeter and Hampton were begun, mostly by people migrating from Massachusetts, some of whom were escaping from the Puritan regime. In 1641 New Hampshire came under the jurisdiction of the General Court (Assembly) of the Massachusetts Bay Colony, and the area was incorporated into the Massachusetts county of Norfolk in 1643.

In 1679 New Hampshire became a Royal province, although it continued to have the same governor as Massachusetts until 1741. During this time there were continual border disputes between the two colonies, which were resolved by about 1741. From 1741 to 1767 the western part of the province was opened for settlement, including some towns in the area of Vermont. The Connecticut River became the western boundary in 1764. The first counties were created in 1769.

Statewide Records and Resources

Most provincial records can be found at the State Archives, the State Library, and the State Historical Society, all in Concord.
Court records at the State Archives are:
Superior Court of Judicature (1699–1771).
* Court minutes, 1699–1771 (film 0980830 ff.). Includes probate minutes, 1707–26.

SEE ALSO
Great Britain
Maine
Massachusetts

- Court records, 1699–1773 (film 0984104 ff.).
Court of General Quarter Sessions (1695–1771).
- Court minutes, 1695–1771 (film 0980828).
- Records, 1730–70 (film 0980937 ff.). This includes the Inferior Court of Common Pleas, 1730 and 1741.
Inferior Court of Common Pleas (1696–1771).
- Court minutes, 1696–1771 (film 0980829).
- Court records, 1729–70 (film 0980938 ff.) Contains some records from the Court of General Quarter Sessions.
New Hampshire Courts, various (1638–1774).
- Courts (various). Court papers, 1659–96 (film 0980932 ff.). Writs, warrants, summonses, verdicts, depositions, testimonies, bonds, etc.
- Court records, 1692–1771(film 0983452 ff.). Includes records of the Court of General Quarter Sessions, Inferior Court of Common Pleas, and the Supreme Court of Judicature.
- Court records, 1714–74 (film 0984105). Contains records for Court of Appeals for years 1714–15 and 1742–74.
- Colonial court records, 1638–1772 (film 1001334 ff.).
Name changes in New Hampshire from state court records, 1699–1899 (film 1598106 ff.).

From 1623 to 1772 all deeds were registered at the Registry of Deeds in Portsmouth. Counties maintained their own registries after this time. There is a card index to New Hampshire Province deeds and probate records from 1623 to 1772 (film 1001345 ff.). The first 100 volumes are at the State Library. Volumes over 100 are in the Rockingham County Court House at Exeter. For records of deeds after 1772, refer to probate offices in the county seats. This index is at the State Historical Society in Concord.

Land and tax records at the State Archives are:
- Proprietors' records, 1748–1846 (film 0983688).
- The Masonian Proprietors' patents are indexed by maps; the maps themselves have also been filmed (film 0980930 ff.).
- Tax books, 1727–88 (film 0983686). Inventories of taxes assessed and received of estates in the towns of New Hampshire Province.

Most of the early records have been published in the series *Provincial and State Papers Published by Authority of the Legislature of New Hampshire.* 40 Vols. (Concord: State Printer, 1867–1943, fiche 6046775). A brief description of the volumes is as follows:

Vols. 1–7 Provincial papers
Vol. 8 State papers, including 1776 enumeration of males over 21
Vol. 9 Town papers
Vol. 10 Provincial and state papers
Vols. 11–13 Town papers
Vols. 14–17 Soldiers, in the Revolutionary War
Vol. 18 Provincial and state papers
Vol. 19 Provincial papers
Vols. 20–2 Early state papers
Vol. 23 Provincial papers (contains a list of the New Hampshire-related documents at the PRO in Kew, Surrey, England. Transcripts are available at the Baker Library, Dartmouth College, in Hanover, and the State Historical Society in

Concord).
Vol. 24 Town charters, including charters granted by Massachusetts to 1740
Vols. 25–6 Town charters
Vols. 27-28 Township grants
Vol. 29 Masonian patents
Vol. 30 Revolutionary documents
Vol.31 Probate records, 1635–1717
Vol. 32 Probate records, 1718–40
Vol. 33 Probate records, 1741–9
Vol. 34 Probate records, 1750–3
Vol. 35 Probate records, 1754–6
Vol. 36 Probate records, 1757–60
Vol. 37 Probate records, 1760–3
Vol. 38 Probate records, 1764–7
Vol. 39 Probate records, 1767–71
Vol. 40 Court records, 1640–92

Volumes 31–9 have been reprinted as *Probate Records of The Province of New Hampshire* [*New Hampshire State Papers*] (Bowie, MD: Heritage Books, 1989–90).

Some of the other records at the State Archives in Concord are:
• Miscellaneous province and state papers, 1641–1800 (film 0983682 ff.).
• Public loan of 1743 (film 0980931). Contains records of indentures made between individuals and trustees appointed by the province, in accordance with the public loan act of 1743.
• Census of New Hampshire, for the years 1767 and 1775 (film 0983687).
• French and Indian Wars and Revolutionary papers: collection of 1880 (film 0983571 ff.).

Early vital records can be searched in the New Hampshire Registrar of Vital Statistics indexes:
• Index to births, early to 1900 (film 1000480 ff.).
• Index to brides, 1640–1900 (film 0975678 ff.). This also includes a name index for the mothers of brides and grooms.
• Index to divorces and annulments prior to 1938 (film 1001323 ff.).
The indexes are at the Registrar of Vital Records and Health Statistics in Concord.

The State Historical Society maintains several surname indexes:
• Card file index to births, deaths, and marriages found in published vital records of Massachusetts, to about 1850 (film 1001443 ff.). Death records

include cards for persons of New Hampshire who died in Massachusetts.
*   Card file index to publishments of marriage intentions prior to 1900 (film 1001439).
*   Card index to genealogies, published and manuscript (film 1001440 ff.). The original records are at the State Historical Society in Concord.

The New Hampshire Society of Genealogists in Portsmouth has compiled the New Hampshire family register, 1623–1910 (film 1532156 ff.), which is a register of families known to have resided in the province or state of New Hampshire prior to 1910.

County Records and Resources
Belknap County
Belknap County Register of Deeds. Copied deeds, 1765–1843 (film 0015596 ff.). The original records area at the Registry of Deeds in Laconia, copied from the land records of Strafford County, and refer to land which is now part of Belknap County.

Cheshire County
Cheshire County Court of Common Pleas. Court records, 1771–1859 (film 1005262 ff.).
Cheshire County Superior Court of Judicature. Court records, 1772–1855 (film 1005277 ff.).
Cheshire County Register of Deeds. Deeds, 1770–1860 (film 0015615 ff.).
Cheshire County Courts. Road and session records, 1772–1901 (film 1005285). The original records are at the Cheshire County Courthouse in Keene.

Index to probate records, Cheshire County, 1769–1800 (film 0167260). The typescript is at the State Historical Society in Concord.

Coos County
Coos County Register of Deeds. Land records, 1772–1902 (film 0015745 ff.). The burnt record volumes contain copies of all records decipherable after being scorched in a fire. The Grafton County volumes contain Coos County records copied from Grafton County, 1772–1804, and some records, 1781–1885. The original records are at the Registry of Deeds in Lancaster.

Grafton County
Grafton County Court of Common Pleas.
*   Court dockets, 1774–5, 1782–1913 (film 1764002 ff.).
*   Court records, 1773–4, 1782–1820, 1840–1859 (film 1763458 ff.).

Grafton County Superior Court of Judicature. Court records and dockets, 1774–1821, 1836–7 (film 1763455 ff.). Includes records of divorce cases.
Grafton County Register of Deeds. Land records, 1773–1902 (film 0015793 ff.).
Grafton County Probate Court. Probate records, 1773–1933 (film 0015897 ff.).
The original records are at the Grafton County Courthouse in Woodsville.

Index to probate records, Grafton County, 1769–1800 (film 0167260). The typescript is at the State Historical Society in Concord.

Hillsborough County
Hillsborough County Superior Court of Judicature. Court records, 1772–1827 (film 1007164 ff.).
Hillsborough County Register of Deeds.
*   Deeds, 1771–6 (film 0016064 ff.).
*   Deed records, 1771–1901 (film 0015914 ff.).
Hillsborough County Probate Court.
*   Probate records and indexes, 1771–1921 (film 0016069 ff.).
*   Register of probate index, 1771–1884 (film 1036181).
The original records are at the Hillsborough County Courthouse in Nashua.

Index to probate records, 1769–1800, Hillsboro County (film 0167260). The typescript is at the State Historical Society in Concord.

Rockingham County (see also Essex County, Massachusetts)
Rockingham County Court of Common Pleas. Court records, 1772–1819 (film 0984389 ff.).
Rockingham County Superior Court of Judicature. Equity records, 1771–1820, 1842–53 (film 0984374 ff.).
Rockingham County Register of Deeds. Deeds, 1770–1852, index, 1643–1882 (film 0016227 ff.). For earlier records, see New Hampshire Province deeds and probate records, 1623–1772.
Rockingham County Probate Court.
*   Estate papers, old series, 1771–1869 (film 1543963 ff.).
*   Probate records, 1771–1969, index, 1660–1894 (film 0016193 ff.).
The original records are at the Rockingham County Courthouse in Exeter.

Index to probate records, Rockingham County, 1753–1800 (film 0167260). The typescript is at the State Historical Society in Concord.

Strafford County
Strafford County Court of Common Pleas. Court records, 1773–1816 (film 0985465 ff.).

Strafford County Superior Court of Judicature. Court records, 1773–1874 (film 0985473 ff.).

Strafford County Register of Deeds. Land records, 1773–1901 (film 0016374 ff.).

Strafford County Probate Court. Probate records and index, 1773–1946 (film 1666743 ff.).

The original records are at the Strafford County Courthouse in Dover.

Index to probate records, Strafford County, 1769–1800 (film 0167260). The typescript is at the State Historical Society in Concord.

Canney, Robert S. *The Early Marriages of Strafford County, New Hampshire, 1630–1860* (Bowie, MD: Heritage Books, 1995).

Town and Church Records and Resources

Town government was the model of government in provincial New Hampshire. Because of the distance from the Bay Colony, both Dover and Portsmouth had separate courts from the Norfolk County Court in Massachusetts.[32] Proprietors' records containing land transactions are included in the town records. The records listed below are primarily those that have been filmed. If vital records are included in the records, it will be so indicated. Several indexes to town records are:

- Index to early town records of New Hampshire, 1639–1910 (film 0014942 ff.). This does not include the town of Exeter. The index is at the State Library in Concord.
- Card index to manuscripts and original town records of New Hampshire in the State Historical Society (film 1001442).
- Warnings out of town, early to 1800, and index (film 1001438 ff.). The original records are at the State Archives in Concord.
- Index to seven towns in New Hampshire: Croydon, Landaff, Lisbon, Meredith, Mount Vernon, New Castle, and Springfield (film 0015374 ff.). The index is at the State Historical Society in Concord.
- Catalogue of town records of New Hampshire (film 0015377). The index is at the State Historical Society in Concord.

Many church records are available in manuscript at the State Historical Society in Concord and have been filmed. For an inventory, see Copeley, William N. *Manuscript Church Records at the New Hampshire Historical Society* (n.p., 1981, fiche 6010549).

---

[32]Jere R. Daniel, *Colonial New Hampshire: A History* (Millwood, NY: KTO Press, 1981) 46.

Unless otherwise indicated, all filmed town records are filmed from typescripts, transcripts, and some original records at the State Archives in Concord. Many of the original records remain in their respective town halls. Unfortunately, due to filming restrictions, most of these films are not allowed to circulate to Family History Centers. They are not available through interlibrary loan from the State Archives. Please check the Family History Library Catalog for restrictions before ordering. Unless otherwise noted, church records —filmed and not filmed —are originals and typescripts at the State Historical Society in Concord.

Acworth
Town records, 1766–1899, vital records (film 1004701).

Alstead
Town records, 1763–1864, vital records, 1751–1842 (film 0015054 ff.).

Amherst
Congregational Church. Records, 1741–1816. These records have not been filmed.

Town records, 1760–1842, vital records, 1739–1849 (film 0015061 ff.).
Monson Town Clerk. 1746–69, vital records (film 0015232).

Andover
Before 1779 known as New Britain.
Town records, 1751–1868, vital records, 1744–1883 (film 0015063 ff.).

Atkinson
Set off from Plaistow 1767.
Congregational Church. Records, 1772–1947 (film 1003435).

Town records, 1767–1842, vital records, 1695–1870 (film 0015064).
Selectmen's records, 1767–1833 (film 0985594). The original records are at the Town Hall in Atkinson.

Barnstead
Town records, 1730–1849, vital records (film 1008244 ff.).

Barrington
Congregational Church. Records, 1771–1923 (film 0987962).

Town and vital records, 1720–1871 (film 0015066).
Town and vital records, 1720–1851 (film 0015553).

Bedford
Town records, 1770–1833, vital records, 1740–1850 (film 0015070 ff.).

Benton
Before 1840 known as Coventry.
Town records, 1764–1846, vital records (film 0015072).

Berlin
Before 1771 known as Maynes-borough.
Town records, 1771–1811 (film 0015072).

Boscawen
Formerly known as Contoocook.
Town records, 1733–1877, vital records, 1735–1806 (film 0015074 ff.).

Bow
Town records, 1767–1885, vital records, 1710–1890 (film 0015076).
Vital records, 1710–1890 (film 0015553). The typescript is at the State Historical Society in Concord.

Brentwood
Congregational Church. Records (film 0015554).

Town records, 1742–1904, vital records, 1699–1830 (film 0015081 ff.).

Bridgewater
See Bristol.

Bristol
Town records, 1770–1837, vital records (film 0015082). This includes New Chester (Hill), Bridgewater, and Bristol prior to the separation of Bristol from those towns.

Brookline
Town records, 1758–1907, vital records, 1740–1923 (film 0015354).

Campton
Town records, 1767–1843, vital records, 1768–1843 (film 0015084 ff.).

Canaan
Town records, 1761–1825, vital records, 1790–1860 (film 0015085 ff.).

Candia
Congregational Church. Records, 1771–1814. These records have not been filmed.

Town records, 1752–1881, vital records, 1728–1881(film 0015087).

Canterbury
Town records, 1727–1864, vital records, 1696–1865 (film 0015088 ff.).

Carroll
Town records, 1772–1865 (film 0015090).

Charlestown
Town records, 1753–1900, vital records, 1729–1878 (film 0015092 ff.).

Chatham
Town records, 1767–1826 (film 0015094 ff.).

Chester
Presbyterian Church. Records, 1738–1842. These records have not been filmed.

Town records, 1720–1869 (film 0015096 ff.).

Chesterfield
Town records, 1770–1831, vital records, 1758–1841 (film 0015098).

Chichester
Town records, 1727–1838, vital records, 1750–1846 (film 0015099). Includes records for Pittsfield.

Claremont
Town records, 1764–1853, vital records, 1750–1865, church records (film 0015100 ff.).

Concord
Concord was known as Rumford. Congregational Church. Records, 1730–1934. These records have not been filmed.

Diaries of Rev. Timothy Walker, the First and Only Minister of Concord, NH, from His Ordination November 18, 1730, to September 1, 1782 (Concord: I.C. Evans, 1889, film 0908590).

Town records, 1725–1864, vital records, 1732–8 (film 0015104 ff.).

Concord Town Records, 1732–1820 [Printed by Authority the City Council] (Concord: Republican Press Association, 1894, film 1415262).

Hammond, Otis G. *Index to Concord Town Records, 1732–1820* (Concord: Rumford Press, 1900, film 1415262).

Conway
Town records, 1763–1861, vital records, 1763–1861 (film 0015106 ff.).

Cornish
Town records, 1767–1837, vital records, 1727–1863 (film 0015108 ff.).

Croydon
Town records, 1763–1829 (film 0015110).

Danbury
Town and vital records, 1775–1847 (film 0015112).

Danville
Before 1836 known as Hawke. Hawke church records, 1764–81 (film 0015582).

Town records, 1760–1848, vital records, 1740–1860 (film 0015113).

Deerfield
Set off from Nottingham in 1766. Congregational Church. Records, 1773–1854. These records have not been filmed.

Town records, 1766–1942, vital records, 1740–1820 (film 0015114 ff.).

Deering
Town records, 1774–1824, vital records, 1760–1840 (film 0015116).

Derry
Presbyterian Church. Records, 1726–1808. These records have not been filmed.

Dorchester
Town and vital records, 1772–1848 (film 0015117).

Dover (see also Essex County, Massachusetts)
First Congregational Church. Records, 1614–1917 (film 0521895 ff.).

Town records, 1647–1838, vital records, 1674–1838 (film 0015118 ff.).

Vital Records of Dover, 1686–1850 [Collections of the Dover Historical Society] (1894. Reprint. Bowie, MD: Heritage Books, 1977, film 1036210).

Dublin
Town records, 1768–1830 (film 0015123 ff.).

Dummer
Town records, 1773–1852 (film 0015123).

Dunbarton
Granted by Massachusetts in 1735 and called Gorham-town; granted by the Masonian Proprietors in 1748 and called Stark's Town; regranted in 1752; incorporated as Dunbarton in 1765.
Town records, 1735–1839, vital records, 1724–1890 (film 0015124).

Dunstable
See Nashua and Hollis.

Durham
Town records, 1739–1936, vital records, 1759–1807 (film 0015125 ff.).

Dodge, Timothy. *Poor Relief in Durham, Lee, and Madbury, New Hampshire, 1732–1891* (Bowie, MD: Heritage Books, 1995).

East Kingston
Congregational Church. Records, 1738–92. These records have not been filmed.

Town records, 1725–1839, vital records, 1720–1876 (film 0015126 ff.).

Effingham
Before 1778 known as Leavitts Town.
Town records, 1748–1852 (film 0015130). Includes some records for Portsmouth.

Ellsworth
Before 1804 known as Trecothick.
Trecothick Town Clerk. Town records, 1769–1806 (film 0015131).

Epping (see also Seabrook)
Set off from Exeter in 1741.
Congregational Church. Records, 1748–1965. These records have not been filmed.

Town and vital records, 1741–1847 (film 0015131 ff.).

Epsom
Congregational Church. Records, 1761–74 (film 0015557).

Town records, 1721–1860, vital records, 1716–1830 (film 0015133 ff.).

Errol
Town records, 1774–1811 (film 0015136).

Exeter
First Congregational Church. Records, 1638–1920 (film 0987081 ff.).
Second Congregational Church. Records, 1755–1920 (film 0987083).
The original records are at the Rockingham County Justice Building in Exeter.

Town records, 1636–1829 (film 0015135 ff.).
Tax records, 1763–1830 (film 0015786 ff.).
Vital records, 1657–1853 (film 0015785). The original records are at the Town Hall in Exeter.

Fitzwilliam
Town records, 1765–1847, vital records, 1769–1886 (film 0015357 ff.).

Francestown
Town records, 1772–1836, vital records, 1730–1875 (film 0015140 ff.).

Fremont
Set off from Brentwood and incorporated as Poplin in 1764; south part set off from Hawke (later Danville) in 1783; name changed to Fremont in 1854.
Town records, 1764–1845, vital records, 1739–1858 (film 0015143 ff.).

Gilmanton
Set off from Belmont in 1812.
Baptist Church. Records, 1773– 1865.
Congregational Church. Records, 1774–1909.
These records have not been filmed.

Town records, 1727–1902, vital records, 1748–1862 (film 0015146 ff.). This includes the proprietors' records for Gilmanton, Gilford, and Belmont. The original records before 1812 are at the Town Hall in Belmont.

Gilsum
Congregational Church. Records, 1772–1872. These records have not been filmed.

Town records, 1752–1847, vital records, 1760–1847 (film 0015148).

Goffstown
Town records, 1749–1843, vital records, 1730–1840 (film 0015359 ff.). Includes some church records.

Gosport
Congregational Church. Records,
1729-74. These records have not
been filmed.

Grantham
Town records, 1767-1850 (film
0015780 ff.).

Greenland
Congregational Church. Records,
1710-67. These records have not
been filmed.

Town records, 1749-1832, vital
records, 1714-1851 (film 0015154
ff.).
Vital records, 1714-1820 (film
0908591). The typescript is at the
State Historical Society in Concord.

Groton (see also Plymouth)
Plymouth was granted in 1763;
portions of Plymouth and Cockermouth (Groton) combined and
incorporated as Hebron in 1792.
Cockermouth changed its name to
Groton in 1796.
Cockermouth Town Clerk. Town
records, 1744-1833, vital records,
1740-1850 (film 0015156).

Hampstead
Congregational Church. Records,
1752-1866 (film 0165996).

Town records, 1746-1867, vital
records, 1730-1870 (film 0015157
ff.).

Hampton (see also Seabrook)
Congregational Church. Records,
1667-1903. These records are

available on film only at the State
Historical Society in Concord.

Town records, 1638-1912, vital
records, 1645-1870 (film 0015159).

Sanborn, George Freeman and Melinde
Lutz Sanborn. *Vital Records of
Hampton, New Hampshire to the End
of the Year 1900* (Boston: New
England Historic Genealogical Society,
1992, fiche 6111014).

Copy of the vital records as
contained in the Jonathan Swain
notebook, together with index of
same, 1726-1848, Hampton and
Hampton Falls (film 0015561). The
typescript is at the State Historical
Society in Concord.

*Historical Sketch of Hampton, NH,
for 250 Years, 1638-1888, and of
the Congregational Church in
Hampton, NH* (Haverhill, MA:
C.C. Morse, 1901, fiche 6017555).

Hampton Falls (see also Hampton
and Seabrook)
Set off from Hampton in 1726.
Kensington was set off from
Hampton Falls in 1768.
Congregational Church. Records,
1712-76 (film 0015560).

Town records, 1677-1899, vital
records, 1645-1845 (film 0015161
ff.).

Hancock
Town records, 1749-1898, vital
records, 1740-1872 (film 0015162
ff.).

Hanover
Town and vital records, 1761–1847 (film 0015163 ff.).

Haverhill
Town records, 1763–1838, vital records, 1700–1840 (film 0015164 ff.).

Hebron (see also Groton)
Town records, 1768–1817, vital records, 1770–1830 (film 0015166).

Henniker
Congregational Church. Records, 1769–1959. These records have not been filmed.

Town records, 1768–1878, vital records, 1730–1860 (film 0016099 ff.).

Hill (see also Bristol)
Formerly known as New Chester.
Town records, 1755–1827 (film 0015170 ff.).

Hillsboro
Town records, 1766–1828, vital records, 1742–1800 (film 0015173 ff.).

Hinsdale
Town and vital records, 1753–1836 (film 0015175).

Holderness
Town records, 1762–1837, vital records, 1770–1840 (film 0015176 ff.).

Hollis (see also Amherst)
Congregational Church. Records, 1750–1939. These records have not been filmed.

Town records, 1673–1887, vital records, 1710–1888 (film 0015361 ff.). Includes some records from Dunstable.

Hopkinton
First Congregational Church. Records, 1757–1846 (film 0015562). Baptist Church. Records, 1768–1899. These records have not been filmed.

Town records, 1735–1800, vital records, 1654–1856 (film 0015180).

Hudson
Before 1790 known as Nottingham West.
First Church of Christ in Nottingham West, 1737–95 (film 0015562).

Town records, 1733–1867, vital records, 1720–1840 (film 0015185 ff.).

Jaffrey
Granted by the Masonian Proprietors in 1749 as Monadnock No. 2, Middle Monadnock, and Middletown; incorporated as Jaffrey in 1773.
Town records, 1749–1886, vital records, 1773–1904 (film 0016102 ff.).

Keene
Town records, 1753–1874, vital records, 1764–1812 (film 0016103 ff.).
Vital records, 1738–1901 (film 1005549 ff.). The transcripts and original records are at the City Clerk's Office in Keene.

Kingston
Second Church of Christ. Records, 1739–72 (film 0015563).

Town records, 1700–1909, vital records, 1680–1921 (film 0015191 ff.).

Vital records, 1681–1823 (film 0015563). The typescript is at the State Historical Society in Concord.

Lancaster
Town records, 1763–1835, vital records (film 0015193 ff.).

Landaff
Town records, 1783–1827, vital records, 1750–1840 (film 0015195).

Lee (see also Durham)
Town records, 1766–1918 (film 0015198 ff.).

Lempster
Town records, 1738–1851, vital records, 1739–1890 (film 0015199 ff.).

Litchfield
Town records, 1734–1839, vital records, 1720–1850 (film 0015204).

Littleton
Part of Cheswich granted in 1764; regranted as Apthorp in 1770. Dalton was set off from Apthorp in 1784, and the remainder of Apthrop was incorporated as Littleton at the same time.
Town records, 1764–1827 (film 0015205).

Londonderry
Presbyterian Church, East Parish. Records, 1742–1837 (film 1638160).
Presbyterian Church, West Parish. Records, 1736–1821 (film 1638159). The original records are at the Presbyterian Historical Society in Philadelphia, Pennsylvania.

Congregational Church. Records, 1740–1875. These records have not been filmed.

Town records, 1719–1869, vital records, 1700–1850 (film 0015206 ff.).

Loudon
Town records, 1763–1839, vital records, 1716–1860 (film 0015210 ff.).

Lyndeborough
Church of Christ. Records, 1756–1916 (film 1006696).

Town records, 1736–1904, vital records, 1720–1892 (film 0015213 ff.).
Vital records, 1763–1905 (film 1006702).

Madbury (see also Durham)
Town records, 1755–1827, vital records, 1686–1802 (film 0015361 ff.).

Manchester
Originally known as Harrytown or Old Harry Town; granted by the Masonian Proprietors in 1735 and the name changed to Tyng's Town; in 1751 incorporated and the name changed to Derryfield. In 1810 the name was changed to Manchester.

Some Manchester church records are indexed in the Loiselle Marriage Index (film 0543721 ff.).

Town records, 1746–1868, vital records, 1722–1834 (film 0015362 ff.).

Proprietors' Records of Tyng Township, 1735–1741 (Manchester: Manchester Historical Association, 1901, film 1415263).

Marlborough
Formerly known as Monadnock No. 5.
Town records, 1751–1825, vital records, 1760–1800 (film 0015217 ff.).

Marlow
Town records, 1761–1865, vital records, 1744–1885 (film 0015219 ff.).

Mason
Congregational Church. Records, 1772–1904. These records have not been filmed.

Town records, 1758–1874, vital records, 1710–1850 (film 0015221).

Meredith
Town records, 1748–1864, vital records, 1748–1812 (film 0015225 ff.).

Merrimack
Town records, 1746–1855, vital records, 1720–1840 (film 0015364 ff.).

Milan
Town records, 1771–1831 (film 0015229).

Milford
See Amherst.

Nashua
(see also Dunstable, Massachusetts)
Before 1836 known as Dunstable.

Town records, 1639–1840, vital records, 1679–1850 (film 0015234 ff.).

Nelson
Previously known as Monadnock No. 6 and Packersfield.
Town records, 1757–1855, vital records, 1731–1858 (film 0015237 ff.).

New Boston
Town records, 1736–1827, vital records, 1740–1840 (film 0015239 ff.).

Newbury
Granted by the Masonian Proprietors as Dantzick in 1753; incorporated as

Fisherfield in 1778; name changed to Newbury in 1837.
Town records, 1753–1827, vital records, 1750–1842 (film 0015268).

New Castle
Town records, 1690–1899 (film 0015240 ff.).
New Castle estates settled in the probate courts of New Hampshire, 1676–1748 (film 0924672).
Fragments of town records, 1696–1899 (film 0985185 ff.).

New Durham
Town and vital records, 1759–1913 (film 0015245 ff.).

Newington
Town records, 1712–1843, vital records, 1700–1853 (film 0015248).

Vital records, 1703–1853 (film 0015568). The typescript is at the State Historical Society in Concord.

New Ipswich
Congregational Church. Records, 1760–1955. These records have not been filmed.

Town records, 1749–1910, vital records, 1743–1892 (film 0015249 ff.).

New London
Town records, 1779–1905, vital records, 1770–99 (film 0015252 ff.).
Vital records, 1765–1876 (film 1003062).

Newmarket
Town records, 1729–1897, vital records, 1740–1830 (film 0015254).
Vital records, 1734–1866 (film 0908586). The typescript is at the State Historical Society in Concord.

Newport
Vital records, 1768–1906 (film 1004705).
Town records, 1761–1900, vital records, 1759–1870 (film 0015255 ff.).
Town records, 1732–1897, vital records, 1700–1890 (film 0015257 ff.).

North Hampton
Set off from Hampton, as North Hill Parish in 1738; incorporated as North Hampton in 1742.

Town records, 1738–1818, vital records, 1723–1830 (film 0015259 ff.).
Selectmen's records, 1749–1811 (film 0985792).

Northumberland
Granted as Stonington in 1761; regranted in 1771; incorporated as Northumberland in 1779.
Town records, 1771–1831 (film 0015260 ff.).

Northwood
Town records, 1773–1865, vital records, 1740–1869 (film 0015261 ff.).

Nottingham
Town records, 1721-1839, vital records, 1730-1877 (film 0015264 ff.).
Vital records, 1734-1877 (film 0908586). The typescript is at the State Historical Society in Concord.

Orford
Congregational Church. Records, 1770-1861 (film 0015569).

Town records, 1761-1832, vital records, 1740-1850 (film 0015271).

Pelham
Congregational Church. Records, 1751-1885 (film 0015570).

Town records, 1746-1844, vital records, 1737-1901 (film 0015273).

Pembroke
Before 1761 known as Suncook and Lovewell.
Congregational Church. Records, 1773-1979. These records have not been filmed.
Presbyterian Church. Records, 1771-1885.
These records have not been filmed.
Town records, 1729-1874, vital records, 1745-1809 (film 0015274).
Vital records, 1714-1829 (film 0908589).

Peterborough
Town records, 1760-1855, vital records, 1730-1850 (film 0015275).

Piermont
Town records, 1765-1825, vital records, 1740-1850 (film 0015276).

Pittsfield (see also Chichester and Seabrook)
Jonathan Perkins' book, 1769: records of deaths and births and marriages (film 0015570). Includes records of deaths in Pittsfield, 1762-1844. The typescript is at the State Historical Society in Concord.

Plainfield
Town records, 1761-1851, vital records, 1746-1860 (film 0015279 ff.).

Plaistow
Town records, 1736-1843, vital records, 1700-1850 (film 0015281).

Vital records, 1726-1871, and other sources, 1652-1905 (film 0015570). The typescript is at the State Historical Society in Concord.

Plymouth
Town records, 1763-1842 (film 0015282 ff.). Includes Groton.
Marriage records and publishments, 1767-1850 (film 0015571). The typescript is at the State Historical Society in Concord.

Portsmouth (see also Effingham)
Third or Independent English Church. Records, 1758-1831 (film 0962800).
Queen's Chapel. Records, 1736-73 (film 0908589).

Church of Christ, Congregational. Records, 1671–1835 (film 0015572). South Church. Records, 1713–1895 (film 0015582). The typescript is at the State Library in Concord.

Town and vital records, 1645–1857 (film 0015284 ff.).
Vital records, 1700–42 (film 0016191).

Book of records kept by Joshua Peirce 1699–1814 (film 0015573). Portsmouth newspaper records, 1761–1861 (film 0015574).

The typescripts and manuscripts of both of the above are at the State Historical Society in Concord.

Raymond
Town records, 1763–1802, vital records, 1745–1829 (film 0015295).

Richmond
Town records, 1770–1852, vital records, 1738–1887 (film 0015296).

Rindge
Granted by Massachusetts in 1736 as Rowley-Canada to inhabitants of Rowley, Massachusetts, who were in the Canada expedition; granted by the Masonian Proprietors in 1749/50 as Monadnock No. 1 or South Monadnock; incorporated as Rindge in 1768.
Congregational Church. Records, 1765–1855. These records have not been filmed.

Town records, 1749–1852, vital records, 1720–1866 (film 0015298 ff.).

Rochester
Town and selectmen's records, 1794–1824, church records, 1756–60 (film 0015301 ff.).
Miscellaneous town papers, 1727–1827 (film 0987951).
Town records, 1737–1801, vital records, 1726–1801(film 0016336).
Copy of town and proprietors' records, 1722–1801, vital records, 1726–1801 (film 0016336).
Transcript of town records, 1722–1801 (film 0015301).

Rumney
Town records, 1767–1848, vital records, 1773–1848 (film 0015304 ff.).

Rye
Church of Christ, Congregational. Records, 1726–1837 (film 0935909).

Town records, 1721–1829, vital records, 1683–1869 (film 0015304 ff.).

Salem
Church records, 1739–1870 (film 0015575).

Town records, 1738–1827, vital records, 1720–1875 (film 0015306 ff.).

Salisbury
Before 1768 known as Stevens Town.
Congregational Church. Records, 1750–1939. These records have not been filmed.

Town records, 1749–1845, vital records, 1739–1864 (film 0015305 ff.).

Sanbornton
Town records, 1748–1824, vital records, 1750–1848 (film 0015309 ff.).

Sandown
Congregational Church, Records 1759–1838 (film 0015575).

Town records, 1759–1864, vital records, 1740–1864 (film 0015311 ff.).

Sandwich
Town records, 1760–1919, vital records, 1760–1874 (film 0015312 ff.).

Seabrook
Seabrook and Hampton Falls Evangelical Congregational Church. Records, 1737–1968 (film 1753354).

Society of Friends, Seabrook. Monthly meeting records, 1701– 1901 (film 0001313 ff.). Called Hampton Monthly Meeting until 1792, then called Seabrook Monthly Meeting. This meeting met at Hampton, Amesbury, Seabrook, Pittsfield, Epping, West Newbury, and Weare.

The original records are in the Moses Brown Collection at the Rhode Island Historical Society in Providence, Rhode Island.

Town records, 1746–1903, vital records, 1746–1824 (film 0015312 ff.).

Somersworth
Formerly known as Rollinsford.
Parish and town records, 1729–1829, vital records, 1730–1830 (film 0015314).

Master Tate's diary: a narrative of events, 1747–78 (film 0015583). Includes vital records for 1747–78. The original records are at the State Library in Concord.

South Hampton
Church of Christ, Congregational. Records, 1743–1800 (film 0015561).

Town and vital records, 1742–68 (film 0015315).

Vital Records of South Hampton, New Hampshire, 1743–1886 (South Hampton, NH: Historical Committee of the Friends of the Library, 1970).

Springfield
Town and vital records, 1765–1880 (film 0016502). The original records are at the Town Hall in Springfield.

Stark
Town records, 1773–1831 (film 0015316).

Stoddard
Town records, 1773–1892, vital
records, 1760–1884 (film 0015317
ff.).
Vital records, 1761–1937 (film
1005559).

Stratham
Congregational Church. Records,
1746–1914 (film 0015577).

Account books of William and Moses
Pottle, 1745–65, 1793–1843 (film
1853971). Accounts for 1745–56 are
from Stratham, New Hampshire, and
accounts for 1793–1843 from Minot,
Maine. The original records are at the
Androscoggin Historical Society in
Auburn, Maine.

Town records, 1716–1846, vital
records, 1700–1870 (film 0015319
ff.).
Vital records, 1700–1867 (film
0015577). The typescript is at the
State Historical Society in Concord.

Surry
Town records, 1763–1827, vital records, 1759–1800 (film 0015326).

Swanzey
Before 1775 known as the Lower
Township on Ashuelot River.
Town records, 1734–1861, vital re-
cords, 1741–1844 (film 0015368
ff.).

Tamworth
Town records, 1760–1918, vital
records, 1753–1874 (film 0015371
ff.).

Unity
Granted as Buckingham in 1753;
regranted and incorporated as Unity
in 1764.
Town records, 1753–1848, vital records, 1725–1851 (film 0015330).

Wakefield
Town records, 1775–1821, vital records, 1753–1834 (film 0015331).

Warner
Granted by Massachusetts in 1735 to
persons from Amesbury, Massachusetts, called New Amesbury;
granted by the Masonian Proprietors
in 1749 to inhabitants of Rye and
called Jenness-town and Rye-town;
incorporated as Warner in 1774.
Town records, 1737–1915, vital
records 1750–1889 (film 0015334
ff.).

Warren
Town records, 1763–1876, vital
records, 1740–1880 (film 0015336).

Washington
Town records, 1777–1896, vital
records, 1767–1848, church records
(film 0015338 ff.).

Weare (see also Seabrook)
Town records, 1749–1858, vital
records, 1764–1800 (film 0015340).

Westmoreland
Town records, 1752–1840, vital
records (film 0015343).

Whitefield
Vital records, 1775–1877 (film 0016507).

Wilton
Town records, 1764–1806, vital records, 1764–1837 (film 0015345). Vital records, 1718–1853 (film 0908590).

Winchester
Granted by Massachusetts in 1733 and called Earlington, then Arlington; incorporated as Winchester in 1753.

Town records, 1732–1849, vital records, 1723–1838 (film 0016505 ff.).

Windham
Town records, 1741–1845, vital records, 1730–1870 (0015347 ff.).

Wolfeboro
Town records, 1770–1831, vital records, 1789–1831 (film 0015352).

Woodstock
Before 1873 known as Peeling. Town records, 1763–1882 (film 0015353).

Suggested Reading

Baxter, J.P. *Trelawney Papers* (Portland, ME: n.p., 1884). Contains correspondence of the Plymouth merchants who received grants in New Hampshire in the 1630s.

Bowles, Ella Shannon. *New Hampshire: Its History, Settlement, and Provincial Periods* (1938. Reprint. Washington, DC: Library of Congress, 1989, film 1704220).

Carpenter, Randall C. *Descriptive Inventory of the New Hampshire Collection* (Salt Lake City: University of Utah Press, 1932, fiche 6075931). Guide to the Family History Library Collection.

Clark, Charles E. *The Eastern Frontier: The Settlement of Northern New England, 1610–1763* (1970. Reprint. Hanover, NH: University Press of New England, 1983).

Copeley, William N. *Index to Genealogies in New Hampshire Town Histories* (Concord: New Hampshire Historical Society, 1988, fiche 6010808).

Daniell, Jere R. *Colonial New Hampshire: A History* (Millwood, NY: KTO Press, 1981).

Duane, James. *State of the Evidence and Argument in Support of the Territorial Rights and Jurisdiction of New York Against the Government of New Hampshire and the Claimants under it and Against the Commonwealth of Massachusetts* (New York: New York Genealogical and Biographical Society, 1871, film 0845285).

Gilmore, George C. *Roll of New Hampshire Men at Louisbourg, Cape Breton, 1745* (Concord: Edward N. Pearson, 1896).

Green, Scott E. *Directory of Repositories of Family History in New Hampshire* (Baltimore: Clearfield Co., 1993).

Hammond, Otis G. *Notices from the New Hampshire Gazette, 1765–1800* (Lambertville, NJ: Hunterdon House, 1970, fiche 6051306).

Historical Records Survey. *Guide to Church Vital Statistics Records in New Hampshire* (Manchester, NH: The Survey, 1942, fiche 6046675).

Historical Records Survey. *Town Government in New Hampshire* (Manchester, NH: The Survey, n.d., fiche 6046846).

Hobrook, Jay Mack. *New Hampshire Residents, 1633–1699* (1979. Reprint. Baltimore: Clearfield Co., 1996).

Jaccaud, Robert D. *Passages to Family History: A Guide to Genealogical Research in the Dartmouth College Library* (Hanover, NH: Dartmouth College Library, 1994).

Jennes, John S. *Transcripts of Original Documents in the English Archives Relating to the Early History of New Hampshire* (New York, 1876).

Lawrence, Robert F. *The New Hampshire Churches: Comprising Histories of the Congregational and Presbyterian Churches in the State, with Notices of Other Denominations; Also Containing Many Interesting Incidents Connected with the First Settlement of Towns* (Claremont, NH: Claremont Manufacturing Co., 1856, fiche 6046841).

Mevers, Frank C. *Guide to Early Documents (1680–1900) at the New Hampshire Records Management and Archives Center* (Concord: The Archives, 1981, fiche 6332691).

Noyes, Sybil, Charles T. Libby, and Walter G. Davis. *Genealogical Dictionary of Maine and New Hampshire* (1928–39. Reprint. Baltimore: Genealogical Publishing Co., 1996).

Potter, Chandler E. *Military History of the State of New Hampshire, 1623–1861* (1866. Reprint. Baltimore: Genealogical Publishing Co., 1972, fiche 6046958)

Sanborn, Edwin D. *History of New Hampshire, from its First Discovery to the Year 1830: With Dissertations upon the Rise of Opinions and Institutions, the Growth of Agriculture and Manufactures, and the Influence of Leading Families and Distinguished Men, to the Year 1874* (Manchester, NH: John B. Clarke, 1875, film 1697738).

Towle, Laird C. *New Hampshire Genealogical Research Guide* (Bowie, MD: Heritage Books, 1983).

Sunday Morning in New Hampshire

Rhode Island

 Rhode Island, known as Aquidneck until 1643, was founded by religious dissenters from the Massachusetts Colony. The first settlements were founded at Providence (Seekonk, 1636) and Portsmouth (Pocasset, 1638). Following this the Proprietors Company for the Providence Plantations was formed and a church organized. This was the beginning of the Providence Baptist movement. Newport was settled in 1639, and a trading post was established at Wickford in 1641 for preaching to everyone who would listen, including the Native Americans. The main distinction that set the church off from the Puritans of Massachusetts and Connecticut was that it did not follow the theocratic practice of using religion to discipline and control the adult population. Warwick (Shawomet) was settled by a group known as the Gortonists who were banished from Massachusetts in 1643.

Providence, Portsmouth, and Newport became the Providence Plantations in the Narragansett Bay in 1643, and shortly thereafter changed the name to Rhode Island. In 1647 the Rhode Island General Assembly called for separation of church and state, and Warwick united with the colony in the same year. In 1663 a royal charter established Rhode Island as a corporate colony; rights to dispose of land and administrate a government were held by the governor and the company of freemen as a corporation. The charter guaranteed religious freedom to "freely and fully have and enjoy his and their own judgments and consciences in matters of religious concernments." The idea of any connection between the secular community and church was rejected. Block Island was admitted as part of the colony in 1664.

Rhode Island became a haven for Quakers from other colonies. In 1656 the Commissioners of the United Colonies of New England passed a law imposing penalties on the master of any ship who landed Quakers within its jurisdiction. The first Quakers from London arrived in Rhode Island, via New Amsterdam, in 1657. In 1658 the General Court of Massachusetts exiled all Quakers from the colony. Monthly meetings were being held in Newport by 1660. The communities of Warwick, Newport, and Portsmouth rapidly became sanctuaries for Quakers from other parts of New

SEE ALSO
Connecticut
Great Britain
Massachusetts
Nova Scotia

313

England. The Seventh-Day Baptist movement began in 1664 in the Westerly area. Converts in nearby New London, Connecticut were known as the Rogerenes (mostly related to the Rogers family). Both Baptists and Quakers allowed women to vote in church meetings. Quakers also admitted women as ministers.

Rhode Island began issuing commissions to privateers in the 1650s. In the eighteenth century it commissioned more privately armed vessels than any other British North American colony.

In the late seventeenth century, around the time of the revocation of the Edict of Nantes in 1685, a group of French Huguenot refugees settled a tract of land called French Town, in East Greenwich. Members of the settlement dispersed to Newport, Kingstown, and Providence.

The first two counties were formed in 1703. Bristol, Cumberland, Little Compton, Tiverton, and Warren were annexed from Massachusetts to Rhode Island in 1747. The first action against the British took place at Newport in 1769, when the sloop *Liberty* was burned. In 1775 the Providence "Tea Party" was carried out by local citizens and members of the Sons of Liberty.

Statewide Records and Resources

Courts met on a colony-wide level until 1730, when the first county courts were created. Probate cases were generally handled on a town level by the town council, until town probate courts were created in the 1790s and 1800s. Unless otherwise specified, the original records are at the Rhode Island Judicial Records Center in Pawtucket or the State Archives in Providence. The important colonial courts in Rhode Island were:

• **General Court of Trials (1647–1729):** First statewide court with criminal and civil jurisdiction, also handled divorce cases.[33] Early records are transcribed in *Rhode Island Court Records: Records of The Court of Trials of The Colony of Providence Plantations, 1647–1670.* 2 Vols. (Providence: Rhode Island Historical Society, 1920–2, film 1035910). Original records that have been filmed are court records, 1671–1730, and fines and recoveries, 1725–8 (film 0945811 ff.). From 1725–8 fines and recoveries were handled by the Court of Trials, after which time they came under the jurisdiction of the Superior Court. The original records may be at the Newport County Courthouse in Newport.

---

[33]These divorces were also usually recorded by the town clerks.

- **Superior Court of Judicature, Court of Assize, and General Gaol Delivery (1729–):** Successor to the General Court of Trials; formed in counties after 1747; it became the Supreme Judicial Court in 1798, which changed to the Supreme Court in 1843. Records are filmed (film 0945811 ff.).

- **Inferior Court of Common Pleas (1729–):** Seat of court in each county; established to handle civil cases formerly heard by the Court of Trials; after 1790 known as the Court of Common Pleas. For records, see under specific counties.

- **Court of Equity (1740–):** Handled equity cases and also some probate. Court records, 1741–3 (film 0954936).

- **General Assembly (1646–1867):** Statewide legislative body which also acted as a court. Proceedings, 1646–1851 (film 0954959 ff.), and petitions to the Assembly, 1725–1867 (film 0934803 ff.), include land transfers, grants, lists of freemen, and some records of the Court of Trials. It also acted as a court of equity after 1705.

- **Court of Admiralty (1726–90):** Admiralty papers, 1726–86 (film 0954917 ff.), and court minute books, 1727–83 (film 0954916) contain maritime-related cases and crimes committed on the high seas. Related papers are found in the maritime papers of Rhode Island, 1723–90 (film 0954931 ff.), which include bonds for masters of vessels, outward and inward entries, letters of marque, colonial wars, 1723–87, etc.

- **Court of Vice-Admiralty (1716–52).** *Records of the Vice-Admiralty Court of Rhode Island: 1716–1752* (1936. Reprint. Millwood, NY: Kraus Reprint, 1975).[34]

- **Governor and Council (1667–1813):** Also known as the Council of Probate, it handled appeals from the lower probate courts from 1667–1813. Minutes and acts of the General Council, 1667–1753 (film 0954936).

- **Town Council and probate courts:** See town records.

Court records from 1636 to 1670 have been published in Bartlett, John R. *Records of the Colony of Rhode Island and Providence Plantations in New England 1636–1792, Printed by Order of the Legislature.* 10 Vols. (Providence: A.C. Green, 1856–65, film 0496842 ff.) This contains early land conveyances and transcriptions from the PRO in Kew, Surrey, England.

Manuscript Collections and Compiled Sources
Some of the materials available at the State Historical Society in Providence are:

---

[34]For more information on admiralty records, see Frederick B. Weiner, "Notes on the Rhode Island Admiralty, 1727–90." *Harvard Law Review* 46 (1932): 43–90.

- Catalog of the Rhode Island Historical Society genealogical records 0022425 ff.).
- Frank T. Calef genealogical index to Rhode Island records (film 0022431 ff.). Index to town vital records, freemen lists, cemetery burials, colonial censuses, etc.
- Moses Brown collection, 1600s–1800s: genealogies, records of the Society of Friends, etc. See individual towns for monthly meeting records.
- Bates collection of genealogical data on Rhode Island families (film 0022268 ff.).
- A census of the freemen of 1747 as found in the supplement to the Rhode Island Colonial manuscripts in the Historical Society in Providence. This has been published in Rider, Sidney. *Supplement to the Rhode Island Colonial Records Comprising a List of the Freemen Admitted from May 1747 to May 1754* (Providence: The Author, 1875, film 0022393). The original records are included in the records of the General Assembly.
- Briggs collection, 1600s–1900s: typescript compilations of records, especially for Coventry, Exeter, and West Greenwich.

Military records at the State Archives in Providence include :
- Military papers: accounts, muster rolls, and correspondence: 1730–65 (film 0954956).
- Card index to military and naval records, 1774–1805 (film 0934758 ff.)
A series on military history and records has been published by the State Historical Society:
- Chapin, Howard M. *A List of Rhode Island Soldiers and Sailors in King George's War: 1740–1748* (Providence: The Society, 1920, film 1425647).
- Chapin, Howard M. *Rhode Island Privateers in King George's War, 1739–1748* (Providence: The Society, 1926, film 1425621).
- Chapin, Howard M. *Rhode Island in the Colonial Wars; A List of Rhode Island Soldiers and Sailors in the Old French and Indian War, 1755–1762* (1918. Reprint. Baltimore: Genealogical Publishing Co., 1994, film 1425576).

The Society of Colonial Wars in the State of Rhode Island has also compiled a related series:
- MacGunnigle, Bruce Campbell. *Red Coats and Yellow Fever: Rhode Island Troops at the Siege of Havana, 1762* (Providence: Webster Press, 1991).
- MacGunnigle, Bruce Campbell. *Canada Must Be Conquered: Rhode Island Troops at the Conquest of Montreal 1760* (Providence: Webster Press, 1990). Muster rolls, billeting rolls, and pay rolls of officers and men involved in the 1760 campaign against Montreal.
- *A Bill of the Albany Hospital for the Care of the Men of the Rhode Island Regiment: Many of Them Wounded in the Unsuccessful Assault on Fort Ticonderoga in July, 1758* (Providence: Roger Williams Press, 1950).

County Records and Resources

The Inferior Court of Common Pleas sat in existing counties after 1729. County superior courts were created in 1747. Town, land, probate, and vital records are not held on a county level. Very few county court records have been filmed but are available at the county courthouses or district courts.

Bristol County (established 1746 from Massachusetts)
See proprietors' records under town of Barrington. Land records prior to 1747 are at the Bristol County Registry of Deeds in Taunton, Massachusetts. Land records prior to 1747 are at the Bristol County Registry of Deeds in Taunton, Massachusetts.

Kent County (established 1750 from Providence County)
Historical Records Survey. *Inventory of the Town and City Archives of Rhode Island: Kent County* (Providence: The Survey, 1942).

Beaman, Alden G. *East Greenwich and West Greenwich, Rhode Island Births from Probate, Grave, and Death Records 1680–1860* (Princeton, MA: The Author, 1980).

Newport County (established 1703)
Newport County Inferior Court of Common Pleas. Court records, 1730–1881 (film 0945813 ff.). After 1789 known as the Court of Common Pleas. The original records are at the Newport County Courthouse in Newport.

Collins, Clarkson A. *A Muster Roll of Newport County Troops Sent Toward Albany in 1757* (Providence: Roger Williams Press, 1961).

Beaman, Alden G. *Newport County, Rhode Island Births, 1751–1860, from Death and Marriage Records* (Princeton, MA: Rhode Island Families Association, 1986).

Beaman, Alden G. *Newport County, Rhode Island Marriages from Probate Records, 1647–1860* (Princeton, MA: Rhode Island Families Association, 1984).

Providence County (established 1703)
Providence County Superior Court. Court records, 1730–1818. The original records are at the County Courthouse in Providence and have not been filmed.

Arnold, James N. *Vital Records of Cranston, Johnston and North Providence, Rhode Island* (1892. Reprint. Lambertville, NJ: Hunterdon House, 1983, fiche 6100964).

Hopkins, Charles Wyman. *The Home Lots of the Early Settlers of the Providence Plantations, with Notes and Plates* (Providence: Providence Press, 1886, film 0547553).

Washington County (established 1729 from Newport County)
Washington Inferior County Court of Common Pleas. Court records, 1731–1880 (film 0937651 ff.). After 1790 known as the Court of Common Pleas. The original records are at the County Courthouse in West Kingston.

Beaman, Alden G. *North Kingstown, South Kingstown, Exeter and Richmond, Rhode Island Marriages from the Probate Records, 1692–1850* (Princeton, MA: n.p., 1975).

Beaman, Alden G. *Washington County, Rhode Island Births from 1685–1860* (Princeton, MA: The Author, 1978).

Beaman, Alden G. *Washington County, Rhode Island Marriages from Probate Records, 1685–1860* (Princeton, MA: The Author, 1978).

Town and Church Records and Resources

Town records include land records and deeds, probate, and vital records. Marriages were required to be recorded in civil records from 1647, but this was not uniformly practiced. Records of the town councils include probate records until the first probate courts were established, sometime after the late 1790s. Probate records include wills, letters of administration, guardian bonds, and related proceedings.

Land records include mortgages, land sold by lottery, and records known as land evidences — similar to deeds — which may contain vital records and family information. Providence and Portsmouth practiced regular recording of deeds and land allotments. Public roads and precise boundaries were laid out. In some areas original shares and sizes of tracts were fixed. Land ownership was patterned after the King's manor in East Greenwich. Full ownership of land was based on paying a tax. The only communities that held large parcels of undivided land after 1715 were Providence and Warwick. In 1718 the General Assembly ruled that towns should accept any new inhabitants who owned £50 of land within their borders. The Assembly drafted a uniform property qualification act in 1724, which further kept towns from keeping out potential new residents. Some miscellaneous sources for land records are:
* Dougine, Genevieve N. Index to Rhode Island land evidences, 1648–96 (film 0022254). The manuscripts are at the New York Genealogical and Biographical Society in New York.

- Worthington, Dorothy. *Rhode Island Land Evidences Vol. I 1648-1696: Abstracts* (Providence: Rhode Island Historical Society, 1921. Reprint. Baltimore: Genealogical Publishing Co., 1970, film 0564389).
- Arnold, James N. *The Records of the Proprietors of the Narragansett: Otherwise Called the Fones Record* (Providence: Narragansett Historical Publishing, 1894, film 1033805). Abstract of colonial land evidences.
- Land and public notary records of Rhode Island, 1648-1795 (film 0947373 ff.). The original records are at the State Archives in Providence.

Unlike other New England colonies, the Congregational Church was not the predominant faith. Early congregations of Baptists and Quakers were also present. The Anglican Church also fared better in Rhode Island than elsewhere in New England, with the first parishes being formed under the Society for the Propagation of the Gospel in Foreign Parts in the early 1700s. One of the first Jewish synagogues in North America was built in Newport in 1763.

Vital and church records were compiled by James N. Arnold in *The Vital Record of Rhode Island [1636-1850]*. 21 Vols. (Providence: Narragansett Historical Publishing, 1891-1912, fiche 6046912). The series contains abstracts of church, vital, military, and newspaper records. There are errors in the transcriptions, however, and the original records should be checked for verification. The description of the volumes is as follows:

Vol. 1 Kent County	1762–1825
Vols. 2–3 Providence County	Vol. 15 *Providence Gazette*, marriages;
Vol. 4 Newport County	*U.S. Chronicle*, deaths
Vol. 5 Washington County	Vol. 16 *U.S. Chronicle*, marriages; *American*
Vol. 6 Bristol County	*Journal, Impartial Observer, Providence*
Vol. 7 Friends and ministers	*Journal*, marriages, deaths; *Providence*
Vol. 8 Episcopal and Congregational	*Semiweekly Journal*, marriages
Vol. 9 Seekonk, Pawtucket, and Newman	Vols. 17–18 *Providence Phenix, Providence*
Congregational Church	*Patriot, Columbian Phenix*, marriages,
Vol. 10 Town and church records	deaths
Vol. 11 Church records	Vol. 19 *Providence Phenix, Providence*
Vol. 12 Revolutionary rolls and newspapers,	*Patriot, Columbian Phenix*, deaths;
including *Providence Journal*, deaths	*Rhode Island American*, marriages
Vol. 13 Deaths, *Providence Journal, Providence*	Vol. 20 *Rhode Island American*, marriages,
Gazette, 1762–1830	deaths
Vol. 14 *Providence Gazette*, deaths, marriages,	Vol. 21 *Rhode Island American*, deaths

A newer work in progress is Beaman, Alden G. *Rhode Island Vital Records, New Series*. 15 Vols. (Princeton, MA: n.p., 1975-), covering Kent, Newport, and Washington counties. See county listings for some of the books in this series.

Unless otherwise stated, all town records are kept at the town or city hall under which they are listed. The State Historical Society in Providence has a complete collection of town records either published or in microform. Unless otherwise noted, church records are believed to be at the original parish, but require verification; Society of Friends records are in the Moses Brown Collection at the State Historical Society in Providence. Copies and original church records are also at the State Historical Society and the John Carter Brown Library, Brown University, both in Providence.

Barrington

Set off from Swansea and incorporated in 1717 in Bristol County, Massachusetts; given to Rhode Island in 1747.

Land evidence records, 1770–1936 (film 0946000 ff.).
Proprietors' records in Swansea (Massachusetts), 1652–1717, Barrington, 1717–97 (film 0945999).
Town records, 1718–1886 (film 0947774 ff.).
Town council and probate records, 1770–1891 (film 0947771 ff.).

Swansea (Massachusetts) Town Clerk. Town and vital records, Swansea, 1663–1798, Barrington, 1733–1846 (film 0022366). The manuscript is at the State Historical Society in Providence.

Bristol

Incorporated in Plymouth Colony, Massachusetts in 1681; annexed to Rhode Island in 1746.
Deeds, wills, inventories, administrations, 1680–1808 (film 0912005). The manuscripts are at the Bristol County Registry of Deeds in Taunton, Massachusetts.

Land evidence records, 1690–1703 (film 0912779).
Deeds, 1690–1893 (film 0912004 ff.).
Books of wills and inventories, 1746–1881(film 0912025 ff.).
Town council records, 1760–1877, probate records, 1760–1836 (film 0912026 ff.).
Town meetings, 1680–1888 (film 0912785 ff.).
Vital records, 1680–1850 (film 0912787).

Charlestown

Society of Friends, Charlestown. Monthly meeting records, 1743–5
Land evidence books, 1738–1931 (film 0931548 ff.).
Land evidence records, 1738–70 (film 0931547).

Town records, 1738–1881, probate records (film 0931554 ff.).

Coventry

(see also East Greenwich)
Land records, 1741–1925 (film 0925117 ff.).
Probate records, 1764–1878 (film 0925617 ff.).

Vital records, 1702-1870 (film 0925615).

Cranston (see also East Greenwich and Providence)
Society of Friends, Cranston. Monthly meeting records, 1705- 1861.

Land records, 1754-1877, index, 1754-1900 (film 0931524 ff.).
Town and vital records, 1722-1868 (film 0931513).
Town council records, 1754-1877 (film 0931508 ff.). Includes records for Smithfield.
Vital records, 1722-1890 (film 0931515 ff.).

Cumberland
Society of Friends, Cumberland. Monthly meeting records, 1750-1888
Deeds, 1692-1891 (film 0955461 ff.).
Earmarks, 1752-1827 (film 0955485).
Probate records, 1746-1916 (film 0955490 ff.).
Town council records, 1746-1878 (film 0955481 ff.).
Vital records, 1734-1858 (film 0955486 ff.).

East Greenwich
Society of Friends, Greenwich. Monthly meeting records, 1699-1900 (film 0001332 ff.). This meeting was held alternately at East Greenwich, Cranston, and Coventry.

Land evidence records, 1677-1927 (film 0927243 ff.).
Mortgages, 1728-1883 (film 0926796 ff.).

Proprietors' records, 1709-1829 (film 0927243).
Probate records, 1715-1910 (film 0926804 ff.).
Town meetings, 1681-1912 (film 0927241 ff.).
Town council records, 1715-1881 (film 0927238 ff.).
Vital records, 1666-1950 (film 0926801 ff.).

Exeter
Land evidence records, 1743-1883 (film 0932341 ff.).
Mortgage deeds, 1743-1801 (film 0932352).
Town council and probate records, 1743-1878 (film 0932359 ff.).
Town and vital records, 1742-1818 (film 0932360 ff.).
Vital records, 1763-1903 (film 0932361).

Glocester
Deed records, 1730-1893, index to deeds, 1730-1856 (film 0941827 ff.).
Probate records, 1731-1900 (film 0941847 ff.).
Town council records, 1731-1892 (film 0941845).
Town meetings, 1730-1865 (film 0941846).
The original records are at the Town Hall in Chepachet.

Hopkinton
(see also South Kingstown)
Rockville Seventh-Day Baptist Church. Marriages, 1706-1903 (film 1872373).
Society of Friends, Hopkinton. Monthly meeting records, 1743- 1880.

Land evidence books, 1757–1875 (film 0931561 ff.).
Town records, 1743–1920, land records, 1743–1861(film 1902556).
Probate records, 1757–1920 (film 0931571 ff.).
Probate index cards, 1757–1993 (film 1877394).

Town and vital records, 1757–1923 (film 0931576 ff.).
Town council records, 1751–1916 (film 0931574 ff.).

Jamestown
Society of Friends, Jamestown. Monthly meeting records, 1684–.

Land evidence records, 1680–1903 (film 0946900 ff.).
Proprietors' and vital records, 1672–1860, town meetings and council records, 1680–1745 (film 0946905 ff.).
Probate and town council records, 1767–1887 (film 0946908 ff.).

Town and probate records, 1744–96, town council records, 1746–66 (film 1728545). The records are at the State Archives in Providence.

Johnston (see also Providence)
Deeds, 1759–1881 (film 0940848 ff.).
Probate records, 1759–1898 (film 0915259 ff.).
Town meetings (film 0940845).
Town council records, 1772–1898 (film 1846319 ff.).
The records are at the City of Providence Archives, City Hall, Providence.

Little Compton
Incorporated as Sakonnet by the Plymouth Colony in 1682; incorporated and annexed from Massachusetts in 1747. Land evidences before 1747 are at the Bristol County registry of deeds in Taunton, Massachusetts.
United Congregational Church. Records, 1704–1932 (film 0902951). The manuscript is at the Town Hall in Little Compton.
Society of Friends, Little Compton. Monthly meeting records, 1700–1900.

Proprietors' records (film 0022387).
Proprietors' records, 1672–1755 (film 0946836).
Land evidence records, 1746–1961 (film 0946830 ff.).
Town records, 1697–1886 (film 0946837 ff.).

Wilbour, Benjamin Franklin. *Little Compton Families.* 2 Vols. 5th ed. (1967. Reprint. Baltimore: Clearfield Co., 1996, film 0844901).

Middletown
Justices' Court. Court records, 1751–85 (film 0946442). Includes some marriages.
Land evidence records, 1743–1939 (film 0946445 ff.).
Mortgage deeds, 1752–1861 (film 0946444).
Proprietors' records, 1712–56 (film 0946444).
Town council and probate records, 1743–1879 (film 0946438 ff.).
Town records and meetings, 1743–1895 (film 0946437).

Vital records, 1700–1870 (film 0946435).

Narragansett

de Forest, L. Effingham. "Records of the French Church at Narragansett, 1686–1691." *New York Genealogical and Biographical Record* 70 (1939): 236.

Updike, Wilkins. *A History of the Episcopal Church in Narragansett Rhode Island Including a History of Other Episcopal Churches in the State:With a Transcript of the Narragansett Parish Register from 1718 to 1774* . . . 3 Vols. 2nd ed. (Boston: D.B. Updike, 1907, film 0908592 ff.).

Potter, Elisha R. *The Early History of Narragansett: With an Appendix of Original Documents, Many of Which Are Now for the First Time Published* (Providence: Marshall, Brown, and Co., 1935).

Newport

Society of Friends, Rhode Island. Monthly meeting records, 1658–1899, manumissions, 1773–98 (film 0022417 ff.). The Rhode Island Monthly Meeting met alternately at Newport and Portsmouth.

Trinity Church, Episcopal. Records, 1709–1925 (film 0954970 ff.).

The original records are at the Newport Historical Society in Newport.

First Baptist Church. Marriage records, 1772–1835 (film 0022422).

Trinity Church. Records, 1709–99 (film 0022422).

The manuscripts are at the State Historical Society in Providence.

Gutstein, Morris A. *The Story of the Jews of Newport: Two and a Half Centuries of Judaism, 1658–1908* (New York: Bloch, 1936).

Notarial records, 1755–98 (film 0947374). Many certificates were the records of Thomas Ward of Newport. The manuscripts are at the State Archives in Providence.

Land evidence records, 1701–76 (film 1000006 ff.).
Mortgages, 1715–45 (film 0945223).
Town meetings, 1682–1776 (film 0941998).
Administration bonds and index, 1728–75 (film 1000010 ff.).
Town council records, index to wills, 1702–76 (film 1000008 ff.).
Inventories, 1721–48 (film 0942000).
Vital records, 1684–1894 (film 0944994 ff.).
Vital records, 1670–1774 (film 0941999 ff.).
The original records are at the Newport Historical Society in Newport.

New Shoreham (Block Island)
Church of Jesus Christ of Latter-day Saints. Genealogical Department. New Shoreham, computer printout: births, 1636– 1850 (film 0933413), marriages, 1636–1850 (film 1002595). These are not original records, but have been extracted from the *Vital Records of Rhode Island, 1636– 1850*. Vol. 4.

Livermore, S.T. *History of Block Island: From its Discovery in 1514 to the Present Time 1876* (Hartford, CT: Case, Lockwood, and Brainard, 1877, film 0022486).

North Kingstown
Land evidence records, 1686–1921 (film 0930952 ff.).
Vital records, 1700–1950 (film 0930980 ff.).
The original records are in the Town Hall in Wickford.

Probate and town council records, 1692–1877 (film 0930979 ff.).
Town council minutes 1696–1870 (film 0930971 ff.).

Bates, Louise Prosser. Peirce manuscripts of North Kingstown land evidences, 1686–1826 (film 0022291 ff.). The manuscripts are in the Bates Collection at the State Historical Society in Providence.

North Providence (see also Providence)
Vital records of North Providence and Pawtucket, 1748–1885, indexes, 1728–1914 (film 0960699 ff.).
Deeds and mortgages, 1765–1871 (film 0959202 ff.).
Town council and probate records, 1765–1874 (film 0960680 ff.).
Town meetings, 1765–1874 (film 0960697).
The original records are at the City Hall in Pawtucket.

Portsmouth (see also Newport)
Land evidence records, 1637–1879 (film 0945374 ff.).

Town council and probate records, 1697–1893 (film 0946796 ff.).
Town records (film 0945383).
Town meetings, 1638–97, vital records, 1638–1799, wills, 1638–1850 (film 0945382).
Town meetings, 1697–1890 (film 0946794).
Vital records, 1684–1853 (film 0946795).

Providence (see also Smithfield)
King, Henry Melville. *Historical Catalogue of the Members of the First Baptist Church in Providence, Rhode Island [1638–1908]* (Providence: F. Townsend, Printer, 1908, film 1697719).

Vital records, 1647–1715, land and court records (film 0915084).
Town council records and wills, 1678–1877 (film 0915006 ff.).
Indian deeds, 1659–62 (film 0915084).
Deeds and mortgages, 1677–1901 (film 0901247 ff.). Includes Cranston and North Providence.
Town meetings, 1677–1832, land records (film 0915877 ff.).

Probate records, index, and docket, 1646–1899 (film 0915020 ff.).
Probate records index, 1700–1996 (film 2033450 ff.).
Town council acts, 1678–1704 (film 0915266).
Town council records, 1692–1877 (film 0915884 ff.). Includes some deaths.
The original records are at the City of Providence Archives, City Hall, Providence.

Providence Record Commissioners. *The Early Records of the Town of Providence.* 21 Vols. (Providence: Snow and Farnham, City Printers, 1892–1915, film 0418109 ff.).

Bowen, Richard L. *Index to the Early Records of the Town of Providence, Volumes I-XXI: Containing Also a Summary of the Contents of the Volumes and an Appendix of Documented Research Data to Date on Providence and Other Early Seventeenth-Century Rhode Island Families* (Providence: Rhode Island Historical Society, 1949, fiche 6051222).

Historical Records Survey. *Ships Documents of Rhode Island.* 2 Vols. (1941. Reprint. Washington, DC: Library of Congress, 1986, film 1486570). Includes indexes of owners and masters of vessels, chronological index, ship registers of Providence, 1773–1939, etc.

Field, Edward. *Index to the Probate Records of the Municipal Court of the City of Providence, Rhode Island: From 1646 to and Including the Year 1899* (1902. Reprint. Washington, DC: Library of Congress, 1989, film 1730824).

Richmond
(see also South Kingstown)
Society of Friends, Richmond. Monthly meeting records, 1743–1844.

Land evidence records, 1747–1895, vital records and town meetings (film 0930837 ff.).
Probate records, 1747–1877 (film 0930847 ff.).
Abstract index to vital records found in land evidence books (film 0930852).
The original records are at the Town Hall in Wyoming. Records before 1747 are at the Town Hall in Westerly.

Scituate
Land evidence records, 1731–1879, vital records, 1731–89 (film 0941131 ff.).
Probate and town council records, 1731–1886 (film 0941155 ff.).
Town meetings, 1731–1906 (film 0941162).
Vital records, 1753–1903 (film 0941154).

Smithfield (see also Cranston)
Central Falls contained the towns of Smithfield and Lincoln. Smithfield became independent in 1871, and Lincoln became independent in 1895.
Society of Friends, Smithfield. Monthly meeting records, 1718–1903 (film 0001308 ff.). This meeting was also held at Providence until 1731.

Deeds, 1731–1874 (film 0959536 ff.).
Probate records, 1733–1879, vital records, 1733–54 (film 0959528 ff.).
Town council records, 1770–1871, probate records, 1770–1845 (film 0959526 ff.).

Town meetings, 1771–1871 (film 0959593).
Vital records of Central Falls, 1725–1948 (film 0959590 ff.).
The original records and manuscripts are at the City Hall in Central Falls.

South Kingstown
Society of Friends, South Kingstown. Monthly meeting records, 1743–1892 (film 0001326 ff.). This meeting was held at South Kingstown, Westerly, Richmond, and Hopkinton. The original records are at the State Historical Society in Providence.

Land evidence records, 1696–1885 (film 0931832 ff.).
Mortgage deeds, 1715–88 (film 0930985 ff.).
Town council records, 1704–1943, probate records, 1704–1886 (film 0931833 ff.).
Tax lists, 1735–1867 (film 0931844 ff.).
The original records from 1674–1723 are at the Town Hall in Wickford. Records after 1723 are at the Town Hall in Wakefield.

Tiverton
Incorporated in Massachusetts in 1694; annexed to Rhode Island in 1747.
Davis, Felix G. and Grace Stafford Durfee. *The History of the Amicable Congregational Church, 1746–1946* (Boston: n.p., n.d., film 0802450). Includes information regarding other churches in Tiverton.

Bristol County Commission, Massachusetts. Deeds in the land records of the town of Tiverton formerly in the town of Tiverton but now in the State of Massachusetts, 1746–1817 (film 0573251 ff.). The manuscripts are at the Bristol County Registry of Deeds in Taunton, Massachusetts.

Land evidence records, 1747–1877 (film 0913067 ff.).
Proprietors' records, 1679–1817 (film 0913078).
Probate and town council records, 1747–1883 (film 0913068 ff.).
Town meetings, 1697–1906, probate records, 1776–89, vital records, 1697–1732 (film 0913075 ff.).
Vital records, 1639–1932, marriage intentions, 1707–46 (film 0913052 ff.).

Warren
Incorporated from parts of Swansea and Rehoboth, Massachusetts in 1747. Land evidences prior to 1747 are at the Bristol County Registry of Deeds in Taunton, Massachusetts.
Deeds, 1744–1895 (film 0902936 ff.).

Mortgages, 1752, 1755, 1786 (film 0902947).
Wills and inventories, 1746–1808 (film 0902950 ff.).
Town meetings, 1746–1881, probate records (film 0902949 ff.).
Vital records, 1730–1856 (film 0947767).

Warwick

Society of Friends, Warwick Monthly meeting records, 1705–1842.

Fuller, Oliver Payson. *The History of Warwick, Rhode Island: Settlement in 1642 to the Present Time; Including Accounts of the Early Settlement and Development of its Several Villages; Sketches of the Origin and Progress of the Different Churches of the Town* (Providence: Angell, Burlingame, Printers, 1875, film 1698060). Separately abstracted from this are marriages by Rev. John Gorton, 1754–92 (film 0022369).

Land evidence records, 1669–1734 (film 0022500 ff.). The manuscripts are at the State Historical Society in Providence.

Town records, 1647–1711, probate and land records (film 0925490). Wills, 1703–1917 (film 0925455 ff.).

Town council and probate records, 1742–1879 (film 0925444 ff.). Town meetings, 1713–1894 (film 0925439 ff.).

Vital records, 1649–1883 (film 0925490 ff.).

Westerly

(see also South Kingstown)
Society of Friends, Westerly. Monthly meeting records, 1743–1800.

Land evidence records, 1661–1903 (film 0940222 ff.). Lottery book, 1751–68 (film 0940222). Land evidence records, 1661–1717, vital records and indentures, 1706–45, town council and probate records, 1699–1719 (film 1901837). Town council and probate records, 1699–1888, town meetings, 1669–94 (film 0930805 ff.). Town and vital records, 1706–1819 (film 0940222 ff.).

West Greenwich

Land evidence records, 1741–1974 (film 1000011 ff.). Mortgages and quit claims, 1742–97 (film 0929547). Probate records, 1743–1893 (film 0925975 ff.). Town council and probate records, 1741–1901 (film 0925979 ff.). Town meetings, 1741–1939 (film 0925981).

Suggested Reading

American Baptist Historical Society. *The Records of American Baptists in Rhode Island and Related Organizations* (Rochester, NY: American Baptist Historical Society, 1982, fiche 6093151).

Arnold, Samuel Greene. *History of the State of Rhode Island and Providence Plantations: 1636–1790.* 2 Vols. (1859. Reprint. Spartanburg, SC: The Reprint Co., 1970, film 1036728).

Austin, John Osborne. *The Genealogical Dictionary of Rhode Island: Comprising Three Generations of Settlers Who Came Before 1690* (1887. Reprint. Baltimore: Genealogical Publishing Co., 1995, film 0022257).

Bartlett, John R. *Census of the Inhabitants of the Colony of Rhode Island and Providence Plantations 1774* (1858. Reprint. Baltimore: Genealogical Publishing Co., 1969, fiche 6046611).

Commerce of Rhode Island: 1726-1800. 2 Vols. (Boston: Massachusetts Historical Society, 1914-15).

Dutch Settlers Society Collection. 7 Vols. (Albany: The Society, 1927-45, film 0532620). Volumes 5 and 6 contain Bible, church, cemetery, and town records from Charlestown, Coventry, East Greenwich, Exeter, Hopkinton, Kent, Narragansett, North Kingstown, Scituate, and South Kingstown.

Genealogies of Rhode Island Families: From Rhode Island Periodicals. 2 Vols. (Baltimore: Genealogical Publishing Co., 1983).

Genealogies of Rhode Island Families: From the New England Historical and Genealogical Register. 2 Vols. (Baltimore: Genealogical Publishing Co., 1989).

James, Sydney V. *Colonial Rhode Island: A History* (New York: Charles Scribner's Sons, 1975).

Parker, J. Carlyle. *Rhode Island Biographical and Genealogical Sketch Index* (Turlock, CA: Marietta Publishing Co., 1991).

Pennington, Edgar L. *The First 100 Years of the Church of England in Rhode Island* (Hartford: Church Missions Publishing Co., 1935).

Potter, Elisha R. *Memoir Concerning the French Settlements and French Settlers in the Colony of Rhode Island* (1879. Reprint. Baltimore: Genealogical Publishing Co., 1968, film 1011237).

Sperry, Kip. *Rhode Island Sources for Family Historians and Genealogists* (Logan, UT: Everton Publishers, 1986).

Taylor, Maureen Alice. *Runaways, Deserters, and Notorious Villains from Rhode Island Newspapers.* Vol. 1. *The Providence Gazette, 1762-1800* (Camden, ME: Picton Press, 1995).

Turner, Henry E. *Settlers of Aquidneck, and Liberty of Conscience* (Newport: Newport Historical Publishing Co., 1880, fiche 6019444.).

FIGHT AT TIVERTON.

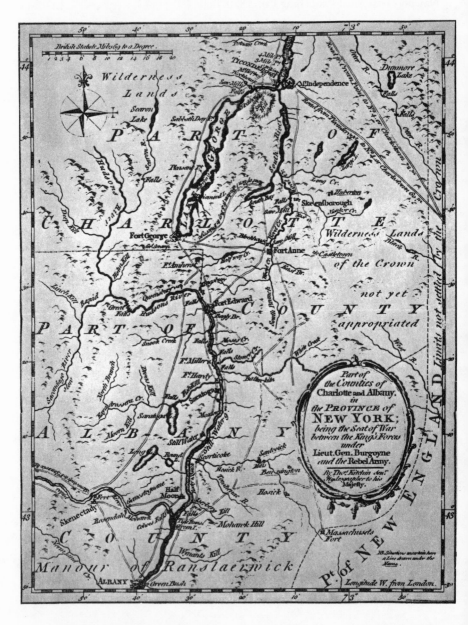

27 Parts of Charlotte and Albany counties, New York, now in Vermont
(*London Magazine*, 1778)

Vermont

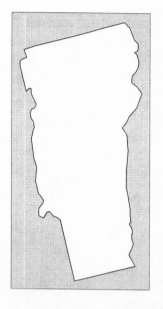

The first permanent British settlement in Vermont was at Fort Dummer (Brattleboro) in 1724, by Massachusetts, to protect its western towns that were subject to Indian attacks. The migration of more settlers did not begin in earnest until after 1760. Because of conflicting land grants issued by other colonies, Vermont was not admitted to the Union until 1791, when it became the fourteenth state.

Grants were issued by Massachusetts from 1672 to 1772, New Hampshire from 1749 to 1764, and New York from 1764 to 1776. By 1764 New Hampshire had issued over 100 grants to land in Vermont. When New York claimed the area as part of Albany County in 1764, grants were issued to lands previously granted by New Hampshire. Settlers mostly from Connecticut and Massachusetts organized the Green Mountain Boys to protect the existing grants. Immigrants from Glasgow, Scotland settled Ryegate and Barnet in 1772. In 1777 Vermont declared itself independent, and was known as New Connecticut for about six months, after which time the name was changed to Vermont.

Statewide Records and Resources

Because of the conflicting jurisdictions during Vermont's colonial period, records may also be found in Connecticut, Massachusetts, New Hampshire, and New York. The first courts established in Vermont were the county courts and the Superior Court (also known as the Supreme Court) in 1777. Records of the Supreme Court and some early county civil and criminal cases are available on microfilm at the Public Records Division Research Center in Middlesex. For a discussion of court records, see county records and resources.

Collections of the Vermont Historical Society. 4 Vols. (Montpelier: The Society, 1870, 1943) includes the following published records:
*   Vol. 1 The Dorset Conventions of inhabitants of the New Hampshire grants in opposition to claims of New York, 1765–77, New York land grants in Vermont, 1765–76.

SEE ALSO
Connecticut
Massachusetts
New Hampshire
New France
New York

331

- Vol. 2 The Haldimand Papers, Vermont, 1783–91.
- Vols. 3–4 Upper Connecticut narratives of settlement.

The *Vermont State Papers* is a series ninety-six manuscript volumes, some published as *Vermont State Papers.* 17 Vols. (Montpelier: Secretary of State, 1918–69). An every name index to *Vermont State Papers, 1740–1850,* is at the State Archives in Montpelier. Descriptions of the volumes are as follows:

Vol. 1 Index to Surveyor General' papers

Vol. 2 Town charters (film 1597817)

Vol. 3 Journals and proceedings of the General Assembly

Vol. 4 Reports to the General Assembly, 1778–1801

Vol. 5 Land petitions, 1778–1811

Vol. 6 Confiscations of Loyalist estates (film 1321236)

Vol. 7 New York land patents, 1688–1786

Vols. 8–11 Land petitions, 1778–99

Vols. 12–16 Laws of Vermont, 1777–99

Vol. 17 Papers of Governor Chittenden

Other relevant state records have been published in Walton, Eliakim Parson. *The Records of the Council of Safety of the State of Vermont, 1775–1836.* 8 Vols. (Montpelier: n.p., 1873–80).

Information on land grants has also been compiled in:
- Denio, Herbert Williams. *Massachusetts Land Grants in Vermont [1672–1772]* (Cambridge: John Wilson and Son, Harvard University Press, 1920, film 0824082).
- Holbrook, Jay Mack. *Vermont Land Grantees, 1749–1803: Vermont Charters and New Hampshire Land Grants* (Oxford, MA: Holbrook Research Institute, 1986, fiche 6044861).
- *New Hampshire State Papers.* Vol. 26. Grants, 1749–64 (Concord: State Printer, 1867–1943, fiche 6046775).

Records of military service have been published in Goodrich, John E. *Rolls of the Soldiers in the Revolutionary War, 1775–1783* (Rutland, VT: Tuttle Co., 1904, fiche 6046670). The Revolutionary War Rolls, 1775–83 (film 083089 ff./M246), contain jackets for Vermont soldiers; however, Vermonters also served in regiments formed in other colonies, also contained in this series.

Records for Vermont can be found in the PRO in Kew, Surrey, England in the following classes, and perhaps others: American Loyalist Claims Commission (AO), Colonial Office Series (CO), War Office Papers (WO). The British Military records, "C" Series, also has information on Loyalist regiments. For more information, see Great Britain and New France.

County Records and Resources

In 1764 all of Vermont became part of Albany County, New York. The area was divided into the counties of Albany (1764–78), Cumberland (1766–78), Gloucester (1770–8), and Charlotte (1773–8). The New York State Library in Albany has Charlotte County records and some for Gloucester County, 1770–4 (published in *Collections of the Vermont Historical Society.* Vols. 3–4).[35] There are also Charlotte County records in the Surrogate Court and Inferior Court of Common Pleas in Albany and Washington counties, New York. Some records for Cumberland County, 1766–77, are available on microfilm at the Vermont Public Records Research Division in Middlesex; the original records are at the Windham County Courthouse (bound with Windham County records, volume 2) in Newfane. Additional Gloucester County records are at the Orange County Courthouse in Chelsea. Most land records were kept on a town level, although a few counties have some early records and also keep records for unorganized towns. County records that begin before 1791 are:

Addison County (established 1785 from Rutland County)
Addison County Clerk. County records including deeds of Middlebury, 1774–
   1870 (film 0865018 ff.). The original records are at the Addison County
   Courthouse in Middlebury.

Bennington County (established 1778 from Charlotte County, New York)
Bennington County Clerk. Land and miscellaneous county records, 1782–1832
   (film 0027962 ff.). Land records, oaths of office, oaths of allegiance,
   warrants, court proceedings, county business, bonds, etc. The original
   records are at the Bennington County Courthouse in Bennington. Earlier
   records are in the records of Washington and Albany counties, New York,
   and were created by the now defunct Charlotte County.

Chittenden County (established 1787 from Addison County)
Land records, 1785–1905 (film 0847974 ff.). The original records are at the
   Chittenden County Courthouse in Burlington.

Essex County (established 1792 from Orange County)
Records for unorganized towns: Averill (1789–1884), Ferdinand (1761–1834),
   and Lewis (1762–98) are also available on microfilm at the Vermont Public
   Records Research Division in Middlesex.

---

[35] Alice Eicholz, *Collecting Vermont Ancestors* (Montpelier, VT: New Trails, 1986), 5–6.

Orange County (established 1781 from Gloucester County, New York)
Deeds, 1771–1832 (film 0028619 ff.), tax records, 1789–1832, and miscellaneous records, 1770–81 (film 0028622). The original records are at the Orange County Courthouse in Chelsea.

Rutland County (established 1781 from Bennington County)
Land records, 1763–1822 (film 0028780 ff.). The original records are at the Rutland Superior Court in Rutland.

Windsor County (established 1781 from Cumberland County, New York)
Land records, 1784–94 (film 0029170). The records are also available on microfilm at the Vermont Public Records Research Division in Middlesex.

Windsor County Court Papers, 1759–1852 (Burlington: University of Vermont, 1983). Inventory of records for the Windsor County Court and the Windsor Supreme Court at the Bailey/Howe Library, University of Vermont, Burlington.

Probate Districts
Vermont probate records are kept by eighteen districts. Those with records that begin before 1791 are:

Bennington District. Probate records, 1778–1851 (film 0027955 ff.). The original records are at the Probate Court in Bennington.

Franklin District. Probate index, 1780–1970 (film 0028197 ff.). The records do not begin until 1796. The original records are at the Probate Court in Saint Albans.

Manchester District. Probate Records, 1779–1851 (film 0027964 ff.). The original records are at the Probate Court in Manchester.

Marlboro District. Probate records, 1781–1850 (film 0029138 ff.). The original records are at the Probate Court in Brattleboro.

Orange District. Probate records, 1792–1854 (film 0028610 ff.), may contain references to extant Gloucester County (New York) records, 1764–81. The original records are at the Orange County Courthouse in Chelsea. In 1994 the Randolph and Bradford districts were consolidated into the Orange District.

Westminster District. Probate records, 1783–1851 (film 0029160 ff.). The original records are at the Probate Court in Bellows Falls.

Windsor District. Probate records, 1787–1850 (film 0029171 ff.). The original records are at the Probate Court in North Springfield.

Probate records before this time can be found in the surrogate court records in Albany and Washington counties, New York, in volumes 31–9 of the *New Hampshire State Papers,* and references to Connecticut families that migrated to Vermont are in some of the Connecticut probate districts, such as Litchfield, Norwich, Salisbury, Windham, and Woodbury.[36]

Town and Church Records and Resources

Proprietor, land, and vital records, along with town business, were kept on a local level. Towns listed here are those having records that begin before 1791 (pre-statehood) and are available on film. Records have been filmed by both the Genealogical Society of Utah and the Vermont Public Records Division. All of the films are also available on site at the Public Records Division Research Center in Middlesex. The State Historical Society Library has an extensive collection of town histories. The earliest town meetings in Vermont were actually held in Connecticut in 1761: Castleton and Salisbury (Salisbury, Connecticut), Norwich and Hartford, Vermont, and Hanover and Lebanon, New Hampshire (Mansfield, Connecticut).[37] The first church was organized at Bennington in 1762.

General index to vital records of Vermont, 1760–1870 (film 0027455 ff.), taken from town vital records. The original index is at the Public Records Division Research Center in Middlesex and is available on film only.

Unless otherwise indicated, all town records are kept at the town hall under which they are listed. Unless otherwise noted, church records are at the original parish.

Addison
Town and vital records, deeds, 1761–1858 (film 0027774 ff.).

Andover
Deeds, 1780–1856 (film 0027784 ff.).

Arlington
Saint James Church, Episcopal. Records from 1772 have not been filmed.

Deeds and vital records, 1780–1860 (film 0027788 ff.).

---

[36]For more information, see Connecticut, New York, and New Hampshire.

[37]Morrow, Rising Lake. *Connecticut Influences in Western Massachusetts and Vermont* (New Haven: Tricentenary Commission, 1936, film 1697313), 14–16.

Athens
Proprietors' records, 1711–1826 (film 0972837).
Land records, 1779–1892 (film 0027795 ff.).
Town records, 1780–1903 (film 0972837).
Vital records, 1775–1867 (film 0027794 ff.).
Averill
Proprietors' records, 1789–1884 (film 0889271).

Barnard
Deeds, 1781–1853 (film 0027937 ff.).
Town and vital records, 1761–1871 (film 0027936 ff.).

Barnet
Associate Reformed Congregation. Session records, 1789–1898 (film 0914061). The original records are at the Presbyterian Historical Society in Philadelphia.

Proprietors' records, 1785–1861 (film 0027865).
Deeds, 1783–1876 (film 0027858 ff.).

Barre
Vital records, 1790–1880 (film 0027905).

Barton
Town records, 1789–1890 (film 0027816 ff.).

Bennington
First Congregational Church. Records from 1762 have not been filmed and are at the Bennington Historical Museum. The years

1762–1862 have been transcribed in J.W. Foley. *Early Settlers of New York State.* 9 Vols. in 2 (1934–42. Reprint. Baltimore: Genealogical Publishing Co., 1993, film 0017044 ff.).

Deeds, 1778–1851, index, 1762–1892 (film 0027801 ff.).
Town and vital records, 1741–1930, deeds, 1741–1809 (film 0027813 ff.).

Benson
Proprietors' records, 1784–6 (film 0027824).
Proprietors' records, 1779–1871 (film 0865373).

Deeds, 1786–1850 (film 0027823 ff.).
Vital records, 1787–1849 (film 0027821).

Berkshire
Deeds, 1794–1852, index, 1789–1950 (film 0027874 ff.).

Berlin
Proprietors' records, 1785–1802 (film 0027846).

Bethel
Christ Church, Episcopal. Records from 1790 have not been filmed.

Land records, 1779–1897 (film 0983521 ff.).
Town records, 1782–1886, vital and land records, 1782–9 (film 0983521 ff.).
Proprietors' records, 1777–1843 (film 0982507).

Vital records, 1780–1882 (film 0027911 ff.). Includes references to records listed in church records.

Bloomfield
Before 1831 known as Minehead. Proprietors' records, 1762–1802 (film 0027852).

Bolton
Proprietors' records, 1763–91 (film 0027882).
Deeds, 1790–1834, index, 1763–1950 (film 0027883 ff.).

Bradford
Deeds and town records, 1775–1852, index, 1762–1876 (film 0027928 ff.).
Town and vital records, 1773–1845 (film 0027935).

Braintree
Deeds, 1780–1849 (film 0027900 ff.).
Proprietors' records, 1780–1801 (film 0027901).
Town and vital records, 1788–1862 (film 0027899).

Brandon
Land records, 1785–1852, vital records, 1750–1809 (film 0027976 ff.).
Index to land records, 1785–1902 (film 0865021).
Vital records, 1750–1909 (film 0027985).

Brattleboro
Deeds, 1783–1851 (film 0027948 ff.).
Town and vital records, 1779–1915, index, 1778–1864 (film 0027944 ff.).

Cabot, Mary R. *Annals of Brattleboro, 1681–1895*. 2 Vols. (Brattleboro, VT: E.L. Hildreth, 1921–2, film 1320918 ff.).

Bridgewater
Deeds, 1781–1894 (film 0027970 ff.).

Bridport
Deeds, 1785–1851 (film 0027833 ff.).

Bristol
Town and vital records, 1790–1867, deeds, 1790–1810 (film 0027845 ff.).

Brookfield
Proprietors' records, 1783–5 (film 0027920).
Deeds, 1786–1850 (film 0027919 ff.).

Brunswick
Proprietors' records, 1786–1825 (film 0027850).
Deeds, 1793–1886, index, 1786–1969 (film 0889279 ff.).

Burlington
Proprietors' records, 1763–1872, deeds, 1778–1850 (film 0027888 ff.).
Vital records, 1789–1909 (film 0027887).

Cabot
Deeds, 1788–1852 (film 0028010 ff.).
Vital records, 1788–1886 (film 0028014).

Calais
Proprietors' records, 1780–8 (film 0028017).
Deeds, 1790–1853 (film 0028017 ff.).

Cambridge
Deeds, 1784–1850 (film 0028026 ff.).
Town and vital records, 1785–1882 (film 0028025).
The original records are at the Town Hall in Jeffersonville.

Canaan
Proprietors' records, Canaan and Norfolk, 1782–1800 (film 0865422).

Castleton
Land records, 1784–1851 (film 0028101 ff.).
Town and vital records, 1784–1847 (film 0028107).

Cavendish
Proprietors' records, 1761–1822, land records, 1789–1880 (film 0028109).
Town charter, 1772 (film 0972843).
Town and vital records, 1776–1885 (film 0028108).

Charleston
Before 1825 known as Navy.
Proprietors' records, 1780–1830 (film 0028006).

Charlotte
Proprietors' records, 1763–1820 (film 0028054).
Land records, 1787–1851, index, 1763–1950 (film 0028054 ff.).

Chelsea
Congregational Church. Records, 1781–1898 (film 0027757). The original records are at the State Historical Society in Montpelier.

Land records, 1784–1878 (film 0028069 ff.).
Town records, 1788–1890 (film 0982532).
Vital records, 1781–1896 (film 0028068 ff.).

Chester
Before 1766 known as New Flamstead.
Proprietors' records, 1763–73 (film 0028087).
Land, town, and vital records, 1763–1867 (film 0028081 ff.).

Chittenden
Land records, 1789–1854, index, 1785–1854 (film 0028095 ff.).

Clarendon
Town records, 1761–1938, vital records, 1778–1868 (film 0028088 ff.).
Proprietors' records, 1761–1821 (film 0982550).

Colchester
Proprietors' records, 1763–1820 (film 0028047).
Deeds, 1774–1851, index, 1763–1851 (film 0028047 ff.).
The original records are at the Town Hall in Winooski.

Concord
Town and vital records, 1784–1856 (film 0027993).

Corinth
Deeds, 1780–1852 (film 0028077 ff.).
Vital records, 1757–1864 (film 0028076).

Cornwall
Surveys, 1774–8 (film 0865390).
Deeds, 1784–1856, vital records, 1785–1845 (film 0028062 ff.).
Land and proprietors' records, 1761–1870 (film 0028061). Includes list of persons buried in the several cemeteries in town, arranged by cemetery, taken in 1919.
Town and vital records, 1790–1855 (film 0028059 ff.).

Craftsbury
Proprietors' records, 1781–1803 (film 0028022).

Danby
Proprietors' records, 1762–91 (film 0028139).
Land, town, and vital records, 1771–1854 (film 0028132 ff.).
Index to vital records, 1771–1925 (film 0028132).

Danville
Land records, 1788–1904, vital records, 1788–1801 (film 1854925 ff.).
Vital records, 1747–1918 (film 0028120 ff.).

Derby
Land records, 1790–1852 (film 0028116 ff.).
Index to vital records, 1790–1905 (film 0028115).

Dorset
Land records, 1770–1852 (film 0028140 ff.).

Dover
Deeds, 1789–1882 (film 0944149 ff.).
Town and vital records, 1789–1856 (film 0028147).
Vital records, 1790–1904 (film 0944152).

Dummerston
Deeds, 1781–1886, index, 1777–1901 (film 0944144 ff.).
Town records, 1771–1972 (film 0944146 ff.).

Vital records, 1761–1911 (film 0028152 ff.).

Duxbury
Land records, 1770–1876 (film 0972867 ff.).
Index to vital records, 1788–1909 (film 0028128).

Elmore
Deeds, 1786–1853 (film 0028163).

Enosburg
Proprietors' records, 1780, 1795–1823 (film 0028169).

Essex
Proprietors' records, 1763–1808 (film 0028178).
Deeds, 1786–1851 (film 0028178 ff.).
Town and vital records, 1786–1861 (film 0028176 ff.).

Fair Haven
Proprietors' records, 1779–1853 (film 0865384).

Fairfax
Deeds, 1763–1850 (film 0028213 ff.).
Town and vital records, 1787–1845 (film 0028213).

Fairfield
Trinity Church, Episcopal. Records from 1789 have not been filmed.

Proprietors' records, 1763–1841, land records, 1791–1851 (film 0028190 ff.).
Town and vital records, 1786–1858 (film 0028189).

Fairlee
Town and vital records, 1787–1875 (film 0028234).

Fayston
Deeds, 1782–1853 (film 0028223 ff.).The original records are at the Town Hall in Moretown.

Ferdinand
Proprietors' records, 1761–1834 (film 0889271).

Ferrisburg
Society of Friends, Ferrisburg. Monthly meeting records, 1755–1891 (film 0028226).

Proprietors' records, 1785–99 (film 0028228).
Deeds, 1787–1852 (film 0028228 ff.).

Town and vital records, 1793–1859, index, 1789–1930 (film 0028227).

Fletcher
Land records, 1790–1877, vital records, 1787–1822 (film 0028185 ff.).
Vital records, 1790–1867 (film 0028184).

Franklin
Town records, 1789–1889 (film 0944190).

Georgia
Proprietors' records, 1763–1808 (film 0028258).

Grafton
Deeds, 1781–1851 (film 0028286 ff.).
Town and vital records, 1781–1865 (film 0028285).

Granby
Land records, 1779–1881 (film 0889288 ff.).

Granville
Proprietors' records, 1782–5 (film 0028280).
Deeds, 1785–1849 (film 0028280 ff.).

Guildhall
Proprietors' records, 1763–83 (film 0889281).
Deeds, 1784–1882, index, 1761–1898 (film 0028246 ff.).

Guilford
Deeds, 1754–1851 (film 0028292).

Town and vital records, 1770–1900 (film 0028290 ff.).

Halifax
Deeds, 1772–1853, town and vital records, 1772–1865 (film 0028361 ff.).

Hartford
Deeds and land records, 1765–1850, vital records, 1787–1812 (film 0028355 ff.).
Proprietors' records, 1765–81 (film 0028355).
Town and vital records, 1764–1863 (film 0028354).
The original records are at the Municipal Building White River Junction.

Hartland
Atwood, Howland Fay. Manuscript collection of history and family records of Hartland (film 0028340 ff.). The original records are at the State Historical Society in Montpelier and include the records of Church of Christ, 1779–1873.

Deeds, 1778–1851 (film 0028347 ff.).

Highgate
Deeds, town and vital records, 1762–1895 (film 0028309 ff.).

Hinesburg
Historical Records Survey. *Inventory of the Church Archives of Vermont: Preprint of Churches of Hinesburg, 1789–1939* (Montpelier, VT: The Survey, 1939, film 0982228).

Land, town, and vital records, 1762–1906 (film 0028317 ff.).

Holland
Deeds, 1780–1859 (film 0028306 ff.).

Hubbardton
Deeds, 1771–1893 (film 0028369 ff.).
Vital records, 1739–1896 (film 0028374 ff.).

Huntington
Proprietors' records, 1763–1808 (film 0028331).
Town and vital records, 1772–1892 (film 0028329).

Hyde Park
Land records, 1790–1876 (film 0972859 ff.).

Ira
Cooper, W.G. *History of the Baptist Church of Ira, Vermont: 1783–1925* . . . (Rutland, VT: Tuttle Co., 1925, film 1597895).

Land records, 1771–1889 (film 0028383 ff.).
Land, town and vital records, 1779–89 (film 0889337).

Jamaica
Deeds and vital records, 1781–1850 (film 0028402 ff.).
Town and vital records, 1790–1880 (film 0028401).

Jay
Town and vital records, 1789–1889 (film 0889331 ff.).

Jericho
Calvary Church, Episcopal. Records from 1788–1909 are at the Bailey/Howe Library, University of Vermont, Burlington.

Proprietors' records, 1785–1802 (film 0028397).
Town and vital records, 1763–1892 (film 0847984 ff.).
Vital records, 1785–1866 (film 0028396).

Johnson
Town ledgers, 1789–1807 (film 0972851 ff.).
Vital records, 1766–1866 (film 0028387).

Leicester
Land and vital records, 1792–1851, index, 1786–1952 (film 0028433 ff.).
Town and vital records, 1786–1862 (film 0028432).

Lemington
Proprietors' records, 1762–1848 (film 0889275).

Lewis
Proprietors' records, 1762–98 (film 0889271).

Lincoln
Society of Friends, Lincoln. Vital records, 1758–1862 (film 0028410). The original records are at the New York State Library in Albany.

Land records, 1782–1854 (film 0028412 ff.).

Londonderry
Land records, 1782–1852, vital and town records, 1782–9 (film 0028440 ff.).

Ludlow
Proprietors' records, 1761–1809 (film 0028447).
Town and vital records, 1768–1873 (film 0028446).

Lunenburg
Deeds, 1781–1853 (film 0028416 ff.).

Maidstone
Proprietors' records, 1761–1829 (film 0028465).

Deeds, 1788–1884 (film 0889286 ff.).

Manchester
Land records, 1766–1850 (film 0028548 ff.).

Marlboro
Deeds and vital records, 1778–1852 (film 0028530 ff.).

Middlebury
Land records, 1786–1877, vital records, 1782–7 (film 1004095 ff.).

Middlesex
Proprietors' records, 1770–84 (film 0865396).
Deeds, 1788–1884 (film 0028476 ff.).
Town and vital records, 1790–1858 (film 0028475).

Middletown Springs
Land records, 1782–1880 (film 0028542 ff.).

Milton
Deeds, 1788–1854, index, 1763–1935 (film 0028497 ff.).

Monkton
Deeds, town and vital records, 1786–1850 (film 0028506 ff.).

Montgomery
Vital records, 1750–1868 (film 0028481).

Montpelier
Deeds, 1788–1853 (film 0028457 ff.).

Moretown
Proprietors' records, 1762–1806 (film 0028492).
Town and vital records, 1777–1921 (film 0028491).

Morgan
Deeds, 1780–1859 (film 0028455 ff.).

Morristown
Proprietors' records, 1784–1800 (film 0028485). The original records are at the Town Hall in Morrisville.

Mount Tabor
Land records, 1788–1879, town and vital records, 1788–1866 (film 0944135 ff.).

New Haven
Deeds, 1786–1857 (film 0028571 ff.).

Town and vital records, 1791–1864 (film 0028578 ff.).

Newbury
Deeds, 1782–1851 (film 0028580 ff.).
Town and vital records, 1745–1855 (film 0028586).

Newfane
Deeds, 1782–1854 (film 0028595 ff.).

Newport
Originally known as Duncansborough.
Proprietors' records, 1789–1835 (film 0028557).

Northfield
Proprietors' records, 1783–7 (film 0028565).
Town charter, 1785 (film 0972858).
Indexes to vital records, 1774–1950 (film 0028563 ff.).

Norwich
Deeds, 1781–1852 (film 0028589 ff.).
Town and vital records, 1761–1890 (film 0028587).

Orange
Proprietors' records, 1781–1812 (film 0028629).

Orwell
Land, town, and vital records, 1784–1887 (film 0028630 ff.).
Town records, 1787–91 (film 0865379).

Panton
Proprietors' records, 1761–1837 (film 0028660).
Deeds, town, and vital records, 1784–1879 (film 0028660 ff.).

Pawlet
Congregational Church. Records, 1781–1900 (film 0972831).

Land records, 1762–1878 (film 0028704 ff.).
Town and vital records, 1762–1896 (film 0972832).
Proprietors' records, 1769–1848 (film 0972832).

Peacham
Proprietors' records, 1780–91 (film 0028654).
Deeds, 1783–1850 (film 0028655 ff.).
Vital records, 1787–1884 (film 0028654).

Peru
Before 1804 known as Bromley.
Proprietors' records, 1761–1856 (film 0028703).

Pittsford
Land records, 1761–1852 (film 0028689 ff.).

Plymouth
Before 1797 known as Saltash.
Land records, 1761–1876, index to land and vital records, 1761–1884 (film 0028681 ff.).
Charter of Saltash, 1761 (film 0972846).

Pomfret
Deeds, 1769–1880 (film 0028666).

Town records, 1773–1914 (film 0889322 ff.).
Vital records, 1770–1903 (film 0028665 ff.).

Pownal
Land records, 1760–1877, proprietors' and vital records, 1760–1800 (film 0028673 ff.).
Town records, 1775–1903, vital records, 1775–1853 (film 0028680 ff.).

Putney
Proprietors' records, 1753–62 (film 0028647).
Deeds, town and vital records, 1770–1851 (film 0028642 ff.).

Randolph
Deeds, 1783–1850 (film 0028727 ff.).
Vital records, 1785–1861 (film 0028726).

Reading
Proprietors' records, 1761–1819 (film 0028808).
Land records, 1760–1851 (film 0028800 ff.).
Town and vital records, 1781–1858 (film 0028798 ff.).

Ripton
Proprietors' records, 1781–1860 (film 0028745).
Town and vital records, 1781–1882 (film 0028747).

Rochester
Land, town, and vital records, 1781–1860 (film 0028740 ff.).

Rockingham

Peck, Thomas Bellows. *Records of the First Church of Rockingham, Vermont: From its Organization, October 27, 1773, to September 25, 1839* (Boston: David Clapp and Son, 1902, film 1597788).

Proprietors' records, 1752–61 (film 0028755).
Deeds, town, and vital records, 1779–1860 (film 0028756 ff.).
The original records are at the Town Hall in Bellows Falls.

Royalton

The Church of Baptised Brethern in Royalton, Vermont: a Record of its Meetings, Conferences and Councils for the Years 1790–1806, from the Original Manuscripts (Woodstock, VT: Elm Tree Press, 1919, fiche 6018922).

Deeds of New York proprietors of Royalton, 1769–70 (film 0982526).
Proprietors' records, 1781–1802 (film 0982526).
Land records, 1784–1881 (film 0028749 ff.).
Town records, 1788–1880 (film 0982526).
Vital records, 1784–1883 (film 0982527 ff.).

Rupert

Proprietors' records, 1765–1882 (film 0944143).
Deeds, 1780–1915 (film 0944139 ff.).

Rutland

Index to deeds, 1766–1857 (film 0865406).

Ryegate

Town and vital records, 1770–1886 (film 0028739 ff.). Includes information on settlers from Glasgow, Scotland, with copies of their certificates.[38]
Deeds, 1781–1849 (film 0028735 ff.).

Saint Albans

Deeds, 1790–1850 (film 0028860 ff.).
Town records, 1785–1891, vital records, 1785–1836 (film 0028859 ff.).

Saint Johnsbury

Land records, 1787–1930 (film 1877405 ff.).
Town and vital records, 1790–1842 (film 0944167).

Salisbury

Deeds, 1786–1859 (film 0028890 ff.).
Town and vital records, 1786–1858 (film 0028889).

Sandgate

Land records, 1775–1854 (film 0028810 ff.).
General index to land records, 1775–1968 (film 0865022).

---

[38] "Testificates" attest to the moral character of a parishioner transferring from one parish to another.

Shaftsbury
Proprietors' records, 1762–1815 (film 0028927).
Deeds, 1779–1851, index, 1765–1917 (film 0028926 ff.).
Town and vital records, 1766–1906 (film 0028923 ff.).

Sharon
Land records, 1761–1855 (film 0028907).
Land records, 1772–1880 (film 0028908 ff.).
Town and vital records, 1768–1943 (film 0028906 ff.).

Shelburne
Deeds, 1786–1849 (film 0028871).
Town and vital records, 1787–1883 (film 0028869).
Land records, 1761–1884, index, 1752–1958 (film 0889325 ff.).

Shoreham
Land records, 1789–1881 (film 0028954 ff.).
Town records, 1783–1900 (film 0865426 ff.).
Town and vital records, 1786–1870 (film 0028960).

Shrewsbury
Land records, 1761, 1782–1879 (film 0028944 ff.).
Town and vital records, 1781–1946 (film 1004081 ff.).

South Hero
Deeds, 1783–1854 (film 0028855 ff.).

Springfield
Proprietors' records, 1761–89 (film 0028963).
Deeds, 1778–1852, index, 1771–1888 (film 0028964 ff.).
Town and vital records, 1730–1880 (film 0028962 ff.).

Stamford
Land records, 1777–1850, vital records, 1777–97 (film 0028915 ff.).

Stockbridge
Proprietors', land, town, and vital records, 1761–1905 (film 0028883 ff.).

Strafford
Proprietors' records, 1761–1831 (film 0028899).
Deeds, 1784–1850 (film 0028900 ff.).
Town and vital records, 1779–1905 (film 0028899).

Stratton
Proprietors' records, 1783–95 (film 0028942).
Land records, 1788–1888 (film 0028940 ff.).
Town charter, 1761(film 0972839).
Town records, 1789–1915 (film 0972840).

Sudbury
Proprietors' records, 1773–1836 (film 0028896).
Deeds, 1783–1852 (film 0028895 ff.).

Sunderland
Copy of proprietors' records, 1763 (film 0028935).

Deeds and vital records, 1760–1857 (film 0028936 ff.).
Original surveys, 1761–1918 (film 0028935).
Vital records index, 1750–1905 (film 0028934).

Swanton
Proprietors' records, 1774–1806 (film 0028837).
Land records, 1790–1890 (film 0028838 ff.).
Town and vital records, 1790–1823 (film 0028837).

Thetford
Deeds, 1778–1850 (film 0028982 ff.).
Vital and town records, 1768–1905 (film 0028981).

Tinmouth
Congregational Church of Christ. Records, 1780–1868 (film 0029001). The original records are at the Town Hall in Tinmouth.

Proprietors' records, 1761–1809 (film 0944196).
Land surveys, 1774–80 (film 0944196).
Deeds, 1771–1886 (film 0944195 ff.).
Town and vital records, 1778–1904 (film 0029000).

Topsham
Land records, 1784–94, 1819–1927 (film 0847986 ff.).

Townshend
Proprietors' records, 1753–1801 (film 0029003).

Deeds and vital records, 1780– 850, index, 1753–1945 (film 0029002 ff.).
Town and vital records, 1786–1869 (film 0029009 ff.).

Tunbridge
Deeds, 1780–1852 (film 0028991 ff.).
Deeds and town records, 1761–87 (film 0028991).

Vernon
Deeds, town, and vital records, 1774–1876 (film 0029029 ff.).

Wallingford
Land records, 1762–1854 (film 0029210 ff.).
Town and vital records, 1778–1904 (film 0029216).

Wardsboro
Deeds, 1787–1850 (film 0029206 ff.).

Waterbury
Proprietors' records, 1763–96 (film 0029073).
Land records, 1790–1850 (film 0029074 ff.).

Weathersfield
Saint John's Church, Episcopal. Records, 1787–1859 may be at the Bailey/Howe Library, University of Vermont, Burlington.

Town and vital records, 1772–1857 (film 0029235).
Proprietors' records, 1761–96 (film 0029245).

Wells
Land records, 1779–1857 (film 0029223 ff.).

Westminster
Land and vital records, 1736–1852, proprietors' records, 1736–67 (film 0029258 ff.).

Weybridge
Proprietors' records, 1762–1811 (film 0029234).
Land records, 1789–1850 (film 0029231 ff.).

Wheelock
Land records, 1785–1852, vital records, 1785–1828 (film 0029049 ff.).

Whiting
Land and vital records, 1783–1863 (film 0029121 ff.).

Whitingham
Deeds and vital records, 1780– 1851, index, 1770–1952 (film 0029201 ff.).
Town and vital records, 1781– 1909, index, 1770–1868 (film 0029193).
The original records are at the Town Hall in Jacksonville.

Williamstown
Proprietors' records, 1781–8 (film 0029109).
Land records, 1782–1880, vital records, 1782–1801 (film 0029109 ff.).

Williston
Proprietors' records, 1763–1804 (film 0029090).
Deeds, 1772–1854 (film 0029090 ff.).
Vital records, 1772–1899 (film 0029089).

Wilmington
Land, town, and vital records, 1766–1875, index, 1752–1935 (film 0029185 ff.).

Windsor
Land records, 1783–1851 (film 0029247 ff.).

Woodbury
Vital records, 1776–1883 (film 0972873 ff.).

Woodstock
Deeds, 1779–1876 (film 0029130 ff.).
Town records, 1773–1904 (film 0889316).

Suggested Reading

Bartley, Scott A. *Vermont Families in 1791* (Camden, ME: Picton Press, 1992).

Bellesiles, Michael A. *Revolutionary Outlaws: Ethan Allen and the Struggle for Independence on the Early American Frontier* (Charlottesville: University of Virginia Press, 1993).

Carleton, Hiram. *Genealogical and Family History of the State of Vermont: A Record of the Achievements of Her People in the Making of a Commonwealth and the Founding of a Nation.* 2 Vols. (New York: Lewis Publishing Co., 1903, fiche 6046680).

Comstock, John Moore. *The Congregational Churches of Vermont and Their Ministry, 1762–1914, Historical and Statistical* (Saint Johnsbury, VT: The Caledonian Co., 1915, fiche 6046853).

Coolidge, Guy. *The French Occupation in the Champlain Valley from 1609 to 1759* (1938. Harrison, NY: Harbor Hill Books, 1979, film 1698225).

Crocker, Henry. *History of the Baptists in Vermont* (Bellows Falls, VT: P.H. Gobie, 1913, fiche 6051223).

Eichholz, Alice. *Collecting Vermont Ancestors* (Montpelier: New Trails, 1986).

Films, Vermont Historical Society (Montpelier: n.p., 1968, film 0824107). Microfilm holdings of the Vermont Historical Society at Montpelier.

Gilman, M.D. *The Bibliography of Vermont, Or, a List of Books and Pamphlets Relating in Any Way to the State: With Biographical and Other Notes* (Burlington, VT: Free Press Association, 1897, film 1425511).

Graffagnino, J. Kevin. *The Shaping of Vermont, 1747–1877* (Rutland, VT: Vermont Heritage Press, 1983).

Hemenway, Abby Maria. *The Vermont Historical Gazetteer: A Magazine Embracing a History of Each Town, Civil, Ecclesiastical, Biographical and Military.* 6 Vols. in 9 (Burlington, VT: The Author, 1868–1923, film 0873674 ff.).

Holbrook, Jay Mack. *Vermont 1771 Census* (Oxford, MA: Holbrook Research Institute, 1982).

Newton, Earle Williams. *Index to the Collections of the Vermont Historical Society.* 10 Vols. (Montpelier: The Society, 1946).

Rollins, Alden. *Vermont Warnings Out, 1779–1817.* 2 Vols. (Camden, ME: Picton Press, 1995–7).

Swift, Esther Munroe. *Vermont Place-Names: Footprints of History* (1977. Reprint. Camden, ME: Picton Press, 1996). Indian, French, and English influences before statehood; name derivations of towns, appendices covering New Hampshire grants, New York patents, and Vermont charters.

Thompson, Zadock. *History of Vermont: Natural, Civil and Statistical in Three Parts, with an Appendix* (Burlington, VT: The Author, 1853, fiche 6046850).

Vermont State Archives. *A Guide to Vermont's Repositories* (Montpelier: The Archives, 1986).

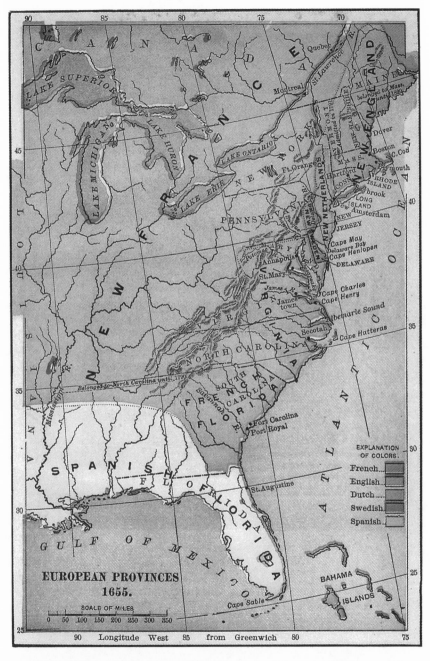

28 The European Provinces, 1655 (Alexander Johnston, *A History of the United States*. New York: Henry Holt, 1892)

29 Maryland, Delaware, and New Jersey (*London Magazine*, 1757)

Delaware

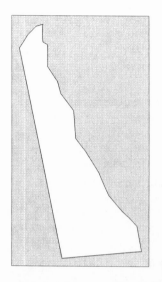

The first permanent settlement in Delaware was established on the Christiana River (Wilmington) by Swedish immigrants in 1638; the first settlement by the Dutch at Zwaanendael (Lewes) was massacred in 1632. New Sweden at its height encompassed both sides of the Delaware river and its tributary streams from the capes as far north as Trenton (except for territory in the vicinity of Fort Nassau). No state lines existed when New Sweden attained its full size, and Delaware, Maryland, New Jersey, and Pennsylvania became separate colonies. The Dutch conquered the area in 1655, and the English in 1664. Quakers arrived in the area in the late 1680s, and the Ulster Scots after 1717. Delaware was under the control of Pennsylvania until it established its own provincial assembly in 1703. From 1682 to 1736, Maryland also claimed large portions of the Delaware Colony.

Statewide Records and Resources

The earliest courts in Delaware are:

- **Chancery Courts (1684–):** County courts of equity.
- **Courts of Common Pleas (1701–):** County courts with civil and criminal jurisdiction; appeals, adoptions, etc.
- **Orphans' Courts (1728–):** County courts with jurisdiction for minors in matters of probate, guardianship, etc.
- **Clerk of The Peace (1642 –):** Prothonotary clerk of the county courts of General Quarter Sessions, Oyer and Terminer, and the Levy Courts (see land and tax records).
- Probate records from 1682 are kept on a county level by the registrar of wills.

For a general inventory see *A Preliminary Inventory of the Older Records in the Delaware Archives* (Dover: Bureau of Archives and Records, 1978, fiche 6331225).

SEE ALSO
Maryland
New Jersey
New York
Pennsylvania
Sweden

Collections of the Genealogical Society of Pennsylvania. Vol. 2. *Philadelphia Administrations, 1683–1744* (Philadelphia: Historical Society of Pennsylvania, n.d., film 0384817). Includes abstracts of original books of letters of administration for Philadelphia city and county. Administrations were also granted for estates of individuals who were residents of Chester County, Bucks County, and the present state of Delaware.

Virdin, Donald Odell. *Colonial Delaware Wills and Estates to 1880: An Index* (Bowie, MD: Heritage Books, 1994).

Land Records

The earliest land grants were given by the Swedes and the Dutch. After the area was acquired by the English, proprietary grants were issued by the Duke of York and can be found in: General Assembly of the State of Delaware. *Land Titles in Delaware Commonly Known as the Duke of York Record: Being an Authorized Transcript from the Official Archives of the State of Delaware, and Comprising the Letters Patent, Permits, Commissions, Surveys, Plats, and Confirmations by the Duke of York and Other High Officials from 1646–1679* (Wilmington: Sunday Star Print, 1903, film 0006616).

From 1682 until the Revolutionary War, land was granted by the Proprietary of William Penn. See *Warrants and Surveys of the Province of Pennsylvania Including the Three Lower Counties, 1759* (1965. Reprint. Knightstown, IN: Bookmark, 1975, film 1036747). See Pennsylvania land records for more information.

In 1682 the Penn Proprietary divided Delaware into "hundreds," an area assumed to be occupied by ten families, for tax purposes. There were originally twelve hundreds: five each in New Castle and Kent counties, and two in Sussex County created in 1692 and 1696). Hundreds were divided and added until 1897, when the total was thirty-seven. The twelve original hundreds were:

Kent County	Saint Jones	New Castle
Duck Creek	**New Castle County**	Saint Georges
Mispillion	Appoquinimink	**Sussex County**
Motherkill	Brandywine	Broadkill
Murderkill	Christiana	Rehoboth

Tax assessments began in 1693: Delaware tax lists for New Castle County, 1693, 1696; Kent County, 1693; Sussex County, 1693; Brandywine Hundred, 1739; Christiana Hundred, 1745 (film 0441413). The original records are at the Historical Society of Pennsylvania in Philadelphia.

The First Tax List for the Province of Pennsylvania and the Three Lower Counties, 1693 (Bedminster, PA: Adams Apple Press, 1994). Philadelphia, Bucks, and Chester counties in Pennsylvania; New Castle, Kent, and Sussex counties in Delaware.

Bendler, Bruce A. *Colonial Delaware Records 1681–1713* (Westminster, MD: Family Line Publications, 1990). Kent and Sussex counties rent rolls, 1681-8, 1693; tax assessment lists of New Castle, Kent, and Sussex counties; Kent County quit rents, 1701-13; Sussex County quit rents, 1702-13.

Delaware Bureau of Archives and Records. *Delaware's Fugitive Records: An Inventory of the Official Land Grant Records Relating to the Present State of Delaware* (Dover: Department of State, Division of Historical and Cultural Affairs, 1980, film 1033995). Guide to Delaware records found in New York and Pennsylvania Archives. See also Gehring, Charles T. *New York Historical Manuscripts, Dutch. Delaware Papers.* 2 Vols. (Baltimore: Genealogical Publishing Co., 1977, 1981).[39]

Records of colonial military service can be found in: Delaware Public Archives Commission. *Delaware Archives.* 5 Vols. (Wilmington: n.p., 1911-, film 0928150 ff.). The volumes contain military and naval records.

Peden, Henry C. *Colonial Delaware Soldiers and Sailors 1638-1776* (Westminster, MD: Family Line Publications, 1995). Alphabetical list of names of servicemen who served in the Delaware area.

The 1693 census of the Swedes on the Delaware was taken to document that there were enough Swedes in America to deserve new pastors and religious books in Swedish. Many had migrated to Maryland and no longer associated with the Swedish churches on the Delaware. The church at Wicaco served Swedes living in the Philadelphia area from Chester County to Marcus Hook and in New Jersey from Pennsauken Creek in Burlington County to the southern boundary of Gloucester County. The church at Crane Hook (Wilmington) served Swedes living in New Castle County, also Cecil County, Maryland, and Salem County, New Jersey.

Craig, Peter Stebbins. *The 1693 Census of the Swedes on the Delaware: Family Histories of the Swedish Lutheran Church Members Residing in Pennsylvania,*

---

[39] For more information, see New York.

Delaware, West New Jersey and Cecil County, Maryland, 1638-1693 (Winter Park, FL: SAG Publications, 1993).

Jackson, Ronald Vern. *Early Delaware Census Records, 1665-1697* (Bountiful, UT: Accelerated Indexing Systems, 1977).

Church and Vital Records
The major religious denominations in Delaware were the Baptists, Protestant Episcopal, Methodist, Presbyterian, and Society of Friends. There is an inventory of all church records available from the 1680s. Almost half of the early church registers were transcribed by the Historical Records Survey and are available on microfilm. The Hall of Records in Dover has a card index of Delaware marriages, baptisms, births, and deaths, 1680-1913 (film 0006416 ff.).

Reynolds, William Morton. *The Swedish Church in America: Discourse Delivered Before the Historical Society of the American Lutheran Church, May 18th, 1848* (Gettysburg, PA: H.C. Neinstedt, 1849, film 1698058). The Swedish church in New Jersey, Delaware, and Pennsylvania.

Historical Records Survey. *Directory of Churches and Religious Organizations in Delaware* (Dover: Public Archives Commission, 1942, film 1036702).

Clark, Raymond B. *Delaware Church Records: A Collection of Baptisms, Marriages, Deaths And Other Records And Tombstone Inscriptions, From 1686-1880* (Saint Michaels, MD: The Author, 1986). Abstracts include Old Drawyers Presbyterian Church, Odessa; Quaker records, Newark; Christ Church, Broad Creek, Sussex County; Little Creek Old Style or Primitive Baptist Church, Sussex County; Saint Peter's Episcopal Churchyard, Lewes.

Wright, F. Edward. *Vital Records of Kent and Sussex Counties, Delaware, 1686-1800* (Westminster, MD: Family Line Publications, 1986). Includes records from various Quaker, Episcopalian, and Presbyterian congregations, as well as information from miscellaneous sources.

County Records and Resources
Kent County (Horrekill District in 1664, Saint Jones County in 1680, renamed in 1682)
Original records at the Kent County Courthouse in Dover are:
Kent County Recorder of Deeds.
* Deed records, 1680-1850, general index, 1680-1873 (film 0006483).
* Land grants, 1680-1743, 1793-1800, miscellaneous deeds and bonds, 1723-30 (film 0006484).

Kent County Levy Court Commissioners. Tax lists, 1726–1850 (film 0006494 ff.).

Kent County Orphans' Court.
* General court records, 1680–1725 (film 0006511).
* Orphans' Court records, 1766–1850 (film 0006439 ff.).
* Wills, 1680–1860 (film 0006492 ff.).

Original records at the Hall of Records in Dover are:
Kent County Recorder of Deeds.
* Land grants and surveys, 1680–1783 (film 0006528)
* Land warrants and surveys, 1683–1774, index cards to land warrants and surveys (film 0006530 ff.).
Kent County Orphans' Court. Guardian accounts (film 0006516 ff.).

Delaware Public Archives Commission. *Calendar of Kent County, Delaware Probate Records, 1680–1800* (Dover: The Commission, 1944, fiche 6051248).

Clark, Raymond B. *Kent County, Delaware Wills and Administrations, 1680–1800: An Index* (Saint Michaels, MD: The Author, 1985).

de Valinger, Leon, Jr. *Court Records of Kent County, Delaware, 1680–1705* (Washington, DC: American Historical Association, 1959).

Church Records
Society of Friends, Duck Creek. Monthly meeting records, 1705–1846 (film 0020390 ff.). Includes manumissions, 1774–92. Meetings were held alternately at Duck Creek and Little Creek, and united in 1830 with Motherkill (Murderkill) Monthly Meeting to form the Camden Monthly Meeting. The original records are at the Friends Historical Library, Swarthmore College, Swarthmore, Pennsylvania.

Historical Records Survey. *Camden Monthly Meeting Formerly the Murderkill Monthly Meeting and Duck Creek Monthly Meeting* (Dover: The Survey, n.d., film 0006321).

New Castle County (area named Niew Amstel by the Dutch in 1657, changed to New Castle by the English in 1664, county established in 1681)
Original records at the New Castle County Courthouse in Wilmington are:
New Castle County Recorder of Deeds.
* Deed books, 1673–1850, general index, 1640–1873 (film 0006610 ff.).
* Land warrants and surveys, 1671–1769 (film 0006614 ff.).

Original records at the Hall of Records in Dover are:
New Castle County Recorder of Deeds.
* Land warrants and surveys; index cards to land warrants and surveys (film 0006617 ff.).
New Castle County Levy Court Commissioners. Tax lists, 1738–1852 (film 0006531 ff.).
New Castle County Orphans' Court.
* Orphans' Court records, 1742–1853 (film 0006553 ff.).
* Wills, 1682–1854 (film 0006545).
Marriage license bonds, New Castle County, 1744–1802 (film 0006301).

Pennsylvania Surveyor General. New Castle County survey notes, 1675–9 (film 1032842). The original records are at the Pennsylvania State Archives in Harrisburg.
New Castle County Court. Court records, 1676–81 (film 0441414). Court, land, and probate records. The manuscript is at the Historical Society of Pennsylvania in Philadelphia. They have also been transcribed in *Records of the Court of New Castle on Delaware, 1676–1681* (Philadelphia: Colonial Society of Pennsylvania, 1904, film 1320671).

Historical Research Committee of the Colonial Dames of Delaware. *A Calendar of Delaware Wills, New Castle County, 1682–1800* (1911. Reprint. Baltimore: Genealogical Publishing Co., 1969, fiche 6051273).

Virdin, Donald Odell. *New Castle County, Delaware, Wills and Estates, 1682–1800: An Index* (n.p.: Raymond B. Clark, 1982).

Church Records
Original Society of Friends records at the Friends Historical Library, Swarthmore College, Swarthmore, Pennsylvania are:
* Wilmington. Monthly meeting records, 1740–1943 (film 0020421). Established 1740 from Newark Monthly Meeting.
* Kennett Square, Philadelphia. Monthly meeting records, 1706–1944 (film 0020401 ff.). Established prior to 1686 and called Newark Monthly Meeting until 1760 when name changed to Kennett Monthly Meeting; has also met at Christiana, Delaware.

Catholic Church, Saint Joseph, Middletown. Records, 1746–1962 (film 1822515). Includes entries for Saint Francis Xavier-Old Bohemia (Warwick, Maryland), and Saint Rose of Lima (Chesapeake City, Maryland). The location of the original records is unknown.

Holy Trinity Church, Wilmington.
- Christina Congregation, Trinity Church. Records, 1750–1889, accounts and indentures, 1687–1747 (film 0006692 ff.). Old Swedes Church is now called Holy Trinity Protestant Episcopal Church. The original records are at the Hall of Records in Wilmington.
- *Holy Trinity Church, Wilmington. The Records of Holy Trinity — Old Swedes — Church, Wilmington, from 1697 to 1773; Catalogue and Errata of the Records of Holy Trinity* (Wilmington: Historical Society of Delaware, 1890, 1919, film 0908217).
- Springer, Courtland B. *Communicant Records, 1713–56, Holy Trinity (Old Swedes) Church* (Wilmington: Historical Society of Delaware, 1953-6, fiche 6089085).
- Springer, Courtland B. *Burial Records, 1713–65, Holy Trinity (Old Swedes) Church* (Wilmington: Historical Society of Delaware, 1953, film 0845765).

Historical Records Survey.
- *Records of the Hanover Presbyterian Church, Wilmington, 1772–1915* (Dover: The Survey, n.d., film 0006308).
- *Records of the Blackwater Presbyterian Church near Frankford, Delaware, 1778–1828* (n.p.: The Survey, n.d., film 0006306).

Carley, Edward B. *Pre-1868 Parish Registers of the Diocese of Wilmington.* 9 Vols. (n.p, 1961–8, film 1846653 ff.). Includes New Castle and Kent County baptisms, 1750–1868.

Historical Society of Delaware. *Welsh Tract Baptist Meeting, New Castle County: Records of the Welsh Tract Baptist Meeting, Pencada Hundred, New Castle County, Delaware, 1701 to 1828, Copied from the Original Records in the Possession of the Meeting Officials* (Wilmington: The Society, 1904, film 0908002).

Lappen, James H. *Presbyterians on Delmarva: The History of the New Castle Presbytery* (n.p.: The Author, 1972, film 0908977).

Holcomb, Thomas. *Sketch of Early Ecclesiastical Affairs in New Castle, Delaware and History of Immanuel Church [1714–1857]* (Wilmington: Delaware Printing Co., 1890, film 1320688).

Wright, F. Edward. *Early Church Records of New Castle County, Delaware [1713–1799].* 2 Vols. (1919. Reprint. Westminster, MD: Family Line Publications, 1994). Congregations included are:

Immanuel Church	Pencader Presbyterian Church
Welsh Tract Baptist Meeting	Asbury Methodist Episcopal Church
Newark Monthly Meeting	Saint Peter's Catholic Church
Wilmington Monthly Meeting	Holy Trinity Church, Wilmington

Weslager, C.A. *The Swedes and the Dutch at New Castle* (Wilmington: Middle Atlantic Press, 1987).

Cope, Gilbert. *A List of Marriage License Bonds, So Far as They Have Been Preserved in New Castle County, Delaware, 1744-1836* (n.p., n.d., film 0441415). The original manuscript is at the Historical Society of Pennsylvania in Philadelphia and includes a few marriages from other counties in Delaware.

Sussex County (established from Deale and Durham counties in Maryland in 1682; part of county annexed to Maryland as Worcester County in 1742)
Original records at the Sussex County Courthouse in Georgetown are:
Sussex County Recorder of Deeds.
• Deed records, 1693–1850 (film 0006623 ff.).
• Land warrants and surveys; index cards of warrants and surveys (film 0006691).
Sussex County Orphans' Court.
• Orphans' Court dockets, 1770–1847, general index, 1728–1847 (film 0006653).
• Wills, 1682–1851, index to wills, 1684–1948 (film 0006618).
Sussex County Court of Chancery. Chancery Court dockets, 1749–1847 (film 0006661).

Original records at the Hall of Records in Dover are:
Sussex County Orphans' Court. Orphans' Court dockets and minute dockets, 1728–1802 (film 0006688).
Court records of Sussex County: proceedings of the Levy Court, County Court,
Court of Common Pleas, Orphans' Court, Court of Quarter Sessions, special courts, 1680–99 (Dover: Bureau of Archives and Records, Division of History and Cultural Affairs, 1979, film 0475648). Includes appointments, commissions, and bonds of officials, records of bridges and roads, taxation, wills, land grants, deeds, births, marriages, apprentice indentures, bounties, etc.
Levy Court Commissioners, Sussex County. Tax lists, 1767–1850 (film 0006674 ff.).

Manuscripts at the Historical Society of Pennsylvania in Philadelphia are:
Sussex County Register of Wills.

- Probate records, 1683–95 (film 0441440).
- Registry of wills, letters of administration, marriages, etc. 1683–95: includes some Kent County probate matters (film 0441423).
- Abstract of wills, 1700s–1800s (film 0441419 ff.).This also includes some records for Worcester and Somerset counties, Maryland, and Bucks County, Pennsylvania.

Clark, Raymond B. *Sussex County, Delaware Wills and Administrations, 1680–1800: An Index* (Saint Michaels, MD: The Author, 1985).

Horle, Craig W. *Records of the Courts of Sussex County, Delaware: 1677–1710.* 2 Vols. (Philadelphia: University of Pennsylvania Press, 1991).

Wright, F. Edward. *Land Records of Sussex County, Delaware, 1769–1782 ...* (Westminster, MD: Family Line Publications, 1994).

Church Records
Historical Records Survey.
- *Records of Deaths, Marriages, and Baptisms of the Lewes Presbyterian Church, Lewes, Delaware, 1737–1856* (n.p.: The Survey, n.d., film 0006306).
- *Records of the Parish of Saint Peter's Church, Lewes, Delaware, 1728–1925* (n.p.: The Survey, n.d., film 0006306)

United Presbyterian Churches of Lewes, Indian River, and Cool Spring. Records, 1756–1855 (film 0441441). The original records are at the Genealogical Society of Pennsylvania in Philadelphia.

Original records at the Presbyterian Historical Society in Philadelphia are:
Protestant Episcopal Church, Saint George's Chapel, Indian River. Records, 1708–1899 (film 0441424).
Presbyterian Church, Broad Creek. Records, 1760–1841 (film 0468373).

Suggested Reading
Acrelius, Israel. *A History of New Sweden, Or, the Settlements on the River Delaware* (1874. Reprint. New York: Arno Press, 1972, film 0982319).

Biographical and Genealogical History of the State of Delaware: Containing Biographical and Genealogical Sketches of Prominent and Representative Citizens, and Many of the Early Settlers. 2 Vols. (1899. Reprint. Tucson, AZ: W. C. Cox, 1974, film 1000155).

Ferris, Benjamin. *A History of the Original Settlements on the Delaware, and a History of Wilmington* (1846. Reprint. Baltimore: Gateway Press, 1987, film 1036276). Covers Delaware and parts of Maryland, New Jersey, Pennsylvania, and New York.

Fisher, Sydney G. *The Quaker Colonies: A Chronicle of the Proprietors of the Delaware* (New Haven: Yale University Press, 1920).

Garber, John P. *The Settlements on the Delaware Prior to the Coming of William Penn* (Philadelphia: City History Society of Philadelphia, 1909, film 1697745).

Governor's Register, State of Delaware: Appointments and Other Transactions by Executives of the State from 1674 to 1851 (Wilmington: Public Archives Commission, 1926, film 1321087).

Historical Records Survey. *Inventory of the County Archives of Delaware: New Castle County* (Dover: The Survey, 1941, fiche 6051279).

A History, Including Genealogical Notes on Families of the Baptist Denomination Who Emigrated from Counties Pembroke and Carmarthen to Delaware and Pennsylvania, 1701 (Aberystwyth: Reproduction Systems, 1970, film 0839693).

Johnson, Amandus. *The Swedish Settlements on the Delaware: Their History and Relation to the Indians, Dutch and English 1638–1664 with an Account of the South, the New Sweden, and the American Companies and the Efforts of Sweden to Regain the Colony* (Philadelphia: University of Pennsylvania, 1911, film 1364768).

Kostiainen, Auvo. *Finnish Identity in America* (Turku, Finland: Institute of History, General History, University of Turku, 1990). Commemoration of the first Finnish settlements in the Delaware River Valley where the Finns and Swedes landed 350 years ago.

Munroe, John A. *Colonial Delaware: A History* (Millwood, NY: KTO Press, 1978).

Pennsylvania Archives. Second Series. Vol 5. *Papers Relating to the Colonies on the Delaware, 1614–1682: Resolution of the States General on the Report of the Discovery of New Netherland* (Harrisburg: C.M. Busch, 1896, film 0823995). Includes information on the boundaries of New York, Pennsylvania,

New Jersey, and probably Delaware. In 1740, the Proprietary Government sent an agent to New York to transcribe documents relating to the settlement of the Dutch on the Delaware River.

Pennsylvania Archives. Second Series. Vol. 9. *Provincial Officers of the Three Lower Counties, New Castle, Kent, and Sussex* (Harrisburg: C.M. Busch, 1896, film 0823996).

Reed, H. Clay. *Delaware, a History of the First State.* 3 Vols. (New York: Lewis Historical Publishing Co., 1947, film 1320666).

Rodney, Richard Seymour. *Early Relations of Delaware and Pennsylvania* (1930. Reprint. Freeport, NY: Books for Libraries Press, 1971, film 1036006).

Turner, Joseph Brown. *Genealogical Collection of Delaware Families* (n.p., n.d., film 0006272 ff.). The original records are at the Hall of Records in Dover.

Ward, Christopher. *The Dutch and Swedes on the Delaware, 1609–64* (Philadelphia: University of Pennsylvania, 1930, fiche 6101604).

Weslager, C.A. *The English on the Delaware, 1610–1682* (New Brunswick: Rutgers University Press, 1967).

Weslager, C.A. *New Sweden on the Delaware, 1638–1655* (Wilmington: Middle Atlantic Press, 1988).

The Swedes in Delaware

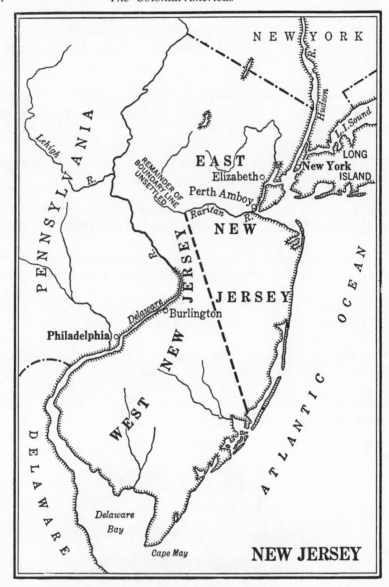

30 East and West Jersey (Oliver P. Chitwood, *A History of Colonial America*. New York: Harper & Bros., 1931)

New Jersey

The first settlement in New Jersey was a Dutch trading post established at Bergen (Jersey City) in 1618. Fort Nassau (Gloucester) was built on the Delaware River in 1623. In 1640 Swedish settlers purchased land in the Cape May-Racoon Creek area from the Lenni-Lenape Indians. A brewery was built at Hoboken in 1642. The first permanent Dutch settlement was founded at Bergen in 1660. After the English conquered New Netherland in 1664, New Jersey was granted to two proprietors, John, Lord Berkeley and Sir George Carteret. In 1676, the province was divided into the proprietorships of East and West Jersey. These were purchased by William Penn and other Quakers between 1672 and 1682.

New Jersey's first colonists were the Swedes and Finns who settled on the Delaware River in 1638, but their first permanent settlement was not until the 1670s. The first Dutch settlement was at Bergen in 1660. The Dutch colonization continued through the seventeenth century, even after the English conquest in 1664.

East Jersey Settlements

In 1664 settlers from the coast of Connecticut, Long Island, and northeastern Massachusetts were granted patents to settle in the new province of East Jersey. The Kill van Kull Patent was granted in 1664, and the Navesink or Monmouth Patent was granted in 1665. The former settled the townships of Elizabethtown, Woodbridge, and Piscataway; the latter founded Middletown and Shrewsbury.

Scots colonists arrived between 1680 and 1750. A large group settled at Perth Amboy between 1683 and 1685. Ulster Scots came by way of Philadelphia and settled in East Jersey after 1725, but a few came as early as 1710. Through 1759, German Lutherans settled along the Raritan River through Monmouth and Somerset counties.

SEE ALSO
Connecticut
Delaware
Germany
Great Britain
The Netherlands
New York
Pennsylvania
Sweden

West Jersey Settlements
West Jersey was settled by a group of English Quakers at Salem in 1675, followed by New Beverly in 1677. Irish Quakers arrived in 1681. The Cape May area was settled by New Englanders from Hartford, the Cape, and Nantucket.

Between 1677 and the early eighteenth century, French Huguenots came from Harlem and Staten Island, New York and settled in the Bergen County area and later in Monmouth, in East Jersey. Palatine Germans came through New York in 1710 and also settled in Bergen County.

The original counties (Burlington and Salem) were established as courts in West Jersey in 1681. Four counties (Bergen, Essex, Middlesex, and Monmouth) were established in East Jersey in 1683. No townships were created until after 1693. The line between East and West Jersey was established between 1687 and 1693. In 1702 New Jersey became a single Royal colony when the two Quaker proprietorships were surrendered to the Crown, although the areas were known for some time as East and West Jersey. In 1769 the long-disputed boundary with New York was settled, and later confirmed in 1773 and 1774.

Statewide Records and Resources
The earliest courts in New Jersey were:
- **Courts of General Quarter Sessions of the Peace (1675–1947):** Organized by county. Jurisdiction: minor criminal cases, civil cases until 1704.
- **Small Cases Courts and Justice's Courts (1675–present):** Justices of the Peace presided over these courts and performed marriages, issued summonses, ruled on minor civil suits, and handled minor criminal cases. Some of these records were turned over to county clerks.
- **Supreme Court of Judicature (1682–present):** Statewide appeals court, had jurisdiction over civil cases, common-law rulings (dower, naturalization, land title, child custody), and capital crimes. Original records of estates and partition of those who died intestate are available for 1712–1866 (film 1902864 ff.). These records are indexed in Supreme Court cases before and after the Revolution, 1709–1842 (film 1028304 ff.), at the State Archives and *Early Index to Burlington Court Minutes, 1681–1709* (Trenton: Historical Records Survey, 1938, film 0016358). Early naturalizations were granted by the legislative Assembly and the Supreme Court of Judicature. There is a card index to the Supreme Court naturalization records for 1761–1860 and records for 1749–1873 (film 1022906 ff.). The original records are in the Mercer County Bureau of Archives and History. The legislative naturalization petitions are found in

an *Index to Naturalization Records, 1703–1862* (film 0913176), a card index at the State Archives. The index is to laws, chancery records, naturalization books, and related items.

- **Court of Chancery (1684–96, 1705–1947):** Statewide court; had jurisdiction over civil and equity cases. These records have been filmed, and include case files indexed by *Alphabetical List of Complaints in Chancery Court Cases, 1743–1824* (films 1032125). For more information on chancery courts, see Miller, George Julius. *The Courts of Chancery in New Jersey, 1684–1696* (1934. Reprint. Washington, DC: Library of Congress, 1990, film 1730855). Chancery court cases from 1743–1850 are at the State Archives in Trenton.
- **Courts of Oyer and Terminer and General Gaol Delivery (1693–1947):** These county courts had jurisdiction over all criminal cases in the county, with the exception of capital offenses (treason and murder). These records are not filmed and are in county clerks' offices.
- **Court of Common Pleas (1700s–1800s):** County courts; records of cases against executors of estates, 1770–4 (film 1028302), and other records are at the State Archives in Trenton. See specific counties for other records that have been filmed.
- **Surrogate's Court (1804–):** County courts of probate; all records have been deposited at the State Archives and are filmed (see specific counties). Records before 1784 were created by the Prerogative Court. The records are indexed in *New Jersey Index to Wills [1705–1830]*. 3 Vols. (Baltimore: Genealogical Publishing Co., 1969, film 1425613). Originally published in 1912 as *State of New Jersey Index of Wills, Inventories, etc. in the Office of the Secretary of State Prior to 1901.*
- **Prerogative Court (1670–1784):** Cases filed for pre-1900 and administrative bonds, 1716–54, and an index to Prerogative court records, sets one and two (film 0542532), are at the State Archives in Trenton.

New Jersey Colony Council. *The Journall of the Procedure of the Governor and Councill of the Province of New Jersey . . . [1682–1703]* (Jersey City: J.H. Lyon, 1872, film 1598334).

The Papers of Lewis Morris, Governor of the Province of New Jersey, from 1738 to 1746 [Collections of the New Jersey Historical Society. Vol. 4] (New York: G.P. Putnam, 1852, fiche 6334110).

Miscellaneous collections containing court records and other documents are:
- Indentures Collection Containing Deeds, Bonds, Commissions, etc. of New Jersey Individuals and Other States, 1600–1900 (film 0849543 ff.). The

original records are at Rutgers University in New Brunswick.

• Clement Papers. Warrants, surveys, and indentures in New Jersey (film 0503314 ff.). The original records are at the Historical Society of Pennsylvania in Philadelphia.

Stevens, Henry. *An Analytical Index to the Colonial Documents of New Jersey, in the State Paper Offices of England* [Collections of the New Jersey Historical Society. Vol. 5] (New York: D. Appleton and Co., 1858, film 1035899).

Hood, John. *Index of Colonial and State Laws: Between the Years 1663 and 1887 Inclusive* (Trenton: State of New Jersey, 1877, film 1320747).

Nelson, William. *The Law and Practice of New Jersey from the Earliest Times: Concerning the Probate of Wills, the Administration of Estates, the Protection of Orphans and Minors, and the Control of Their Estates; the Prerogative Court, the Ordinary, and the Surrogates* [*Archives of the State of New Jersey*. Vol. 13] (Paterson, NJ: Paterson History Club, 1909).

For information on the early occupation of the Delaware by the Dutch and the boundaries of New York, New Jersey, Delaware, and Pennsylvania, see the *Pennsylvania Archives* (Second Series, Vol. 5), *Papers Relating to the Colonies on the Delaware, 1614-1682* . . . (Harrisburg: C.M. Busch, 1896, film 0823995). In 1740, the Proprietary Government of Pennsylvania transcribed documents from the New York Archives relating to the settlement of the Dutch on the Delaware River.

Nelson, William. *Documents Relating to the Colonial History of the State of New Jersey* [*Archives of the State of New Jersey*. First Series, Second Series] 42, 5 Vols. (Newark: The Daily Journal Establishment, 1880-1949, film 0844833 ff.). There is a general index to volumes 1-10 (film 0844833), which has been reprinted as Ricord, Frederick William. *General Index to the Documents Relating to the Colonial History of the State of New Jersey* . . . (1888. Reprint. Baltimore: Genealogical Publishing Co., 1994). The documents include will abstracts, marriage bonds, patents and deeds, newspaper abstracts, and other records. There are many reprints of volumes of these series listed throughout this section.

Land Records
The earliest land grants were during the Dutch period and are included in the New York land records. There are no New Jersey records for that time. The first New Jersey records are of proprietary grants made after 1664. The two provinces of East and West Jersey had separate boards of proprietors.

General indexes to land records and miscellaneous records at the State Archives in Trenton are:

* Grantor and grantee index, East Jersey, 1667–1784, West Jersey, 1677–1854 (film 0539948 ff.).
* Index to powers of attorney, surveyors reports, commissions, etc., referring to deeds, 1703–1856 (film 0542531 ff.).
* Deeds, patents and commissions 1666–1774 (film 0016510).
* Lost deeds, 1685–1870 (film 1903024 ff.).

East and West Jersey records are also indexed in Nelson, William. *Calendar of Records in the Office of the Secretary of State, 1664–1703* [*Archives of the State of New Jersey*. First Series, Vol. 21] (1899, fiche 6051369). This publication has omissions. Reprinted as *Patents and Deeds and Other Early Records of New Jersey, 1664–1703* (Baltimore: Genealogical Publishing Co., 1982).

Records for East Jersey (see also Middlesex County)
The Board of East Jersey Proprietors in Barnegat retains many of the original records that have not been filmed, including petitions, surveys, quit rents, and warrants. Only transactions that were recorded as deeds before 1784 are at the State Archives in Trenton.

Records at the State Archives in Trenton are:
* East Jersey commissions, 1703–1856 (film 0460040 ff.).
* East Jersey deeds, 1667–1783 (film 0522742 ff.). Perth Amboy surveys for East Jersey, 1678–1814 (film 0947881 ff.), are at Surveyor General's Office in Perth Amboy. The Office also holds warrants and surveys from 1719 on.
* East Jersey wills, administrations, and guardianships, 1715–85 (film 05522735 ff.).

Pomfret, John E. *The Province of East New Jersey, 1609–1702* (Princeton: Princeton University Press, 1962).

The Minutes of the Board of Proprietors of the Eastern Division of New Jersey [1685–1794]. 4 Vols. (Perth Amboy, NJ: The Board, 1949–85).

Record of the Governor and Councill in East Jersie, 1682–1703 (1872. Reprint. Bowie, MD: Heritage Books, 1997).

Gardner, Charles Carroll. *Index to Minutes of the Council of East Jersey Proprietors, Liber 1, 1684–1705* (n.p.: n.d., film 0849542).

Cunningham, John T. *The East of Jersey: A History of the General Board of Proprietors of the Eastern Division of New Jersey* (Newark: New Jersey Historical Society, 1992).

Whitehead, William Adee. *East Jersey under the Proprietary Governments: A Narrative of Events Connected with the Settlement and Progress of the Province, until the Surrender of the Government to the Crown in 1703* [Collections of the New Jersey Historical Society, Vol. 1]. 2nd ed. (Newark: Martin R. Dennis, 1875, film 1320732).

Records for West Jersey (see also Salem, Hunterdon, and Gloucester counties) Many West Jersey records have been microfilmed. Most of the original records are at Rutgers University in New Brunswick. Deeds are at the State Archives and some records remain with the West Jersey Proprietors' Office in Burlington.

Records for West Jersey at Rutgers University Library in New Brunswick are:
*   Surveys, 1654–1952 (film 0888803 ff.). The surveys for 1686–1745 include the records of the Corporation for New England Accounts.
*   West Jersey minutes of council meetings, 1688–1951 (film 0888812 ff.)
*   West Jersey warrants, 1717–54 (film 0888815).
*   Council of Proprietors fee book, 1764–1815 (film 0888816).

Records at the State Archives are:
*   West Jersey deeds, 1677–1854 (film 0460045 ff.).
*   West Jersey wills, administrations, and guardianships, 1705–1804 (film 05227148 ff.).

Manuscripts for West Jersey at the Historical Society of Pennsylvania in Philadelphia are:
*   Clement, John. Extracts from minutes of the Council of Proprietors of the western division of the State of New Jersey, from 1687–1859: with additional notes and memoranda (film 0501003).
*   Lee, Francis B. An alphabetical list of names of all persons in the province of West New Jersey in America whose names are to be found upon the pages of *Leaming and Spier's Grants and Concessions*, edition of 1738 (film 0441450).

Pomfret, John E. *The Province of West New Jersey, 1609–1702: A History of the Origins of an American Colony* (Princeton: Princeton University Press, 1956).

Tax Records

Tax assessments began in 1668. Quit rents, paid annually as property taxes to the proprietors, were paid as early as 1670. County tax rateables, listing landowners and other taxables, are filmed in one collection (film 0411287 ff.). The earliest date from 1772 and are arranged by county. An index of these records is available in Jackson, Ronald Vern. *Tax Lists, 1772–1882*. 4 Vols. (Bountiful, UT: Accelerated Indexing Systems, 1981, on microfiche) but is missing large portions of Burlington and Middlesex counties and all of Hunterdon County. The rateable lists that begin before 1775 are as follows:

Burlington County
Burlington City 1773–4
Chester, 1774
Evesham, 1773–4
Little Egg Harbor, 1773
Mansfield, 1774
New Hanover, 1774
North Hampton, 1774
Nottingham, 1773–4
Springfield, 1773–4
Willingboro, 1773–4
Cape May County
Lower, Upper, and
Middle Townships, 1773–4
Cumberland County
Deerfield, 1773–4
Downe, 1773–4
Fairfield, 1773–5
Greenwich, 1773
Hopewell, 1773–4
Maurice River, 1773
Stone Creek, 1773
Gloucester County
Gloucester Township, 1772–4
Great Egg Harbor, 1773

Greenwich 1773–4
Hunterdon County
abstracts, 1773
Middlesex County
New Brunswick, 1772
Salem County
Elsinboro, 1773–4
Lower Alloways Creek, 1773–4
Lower Penns Neck, 1773–4
Mannington, 1773–4
Pilesgrove, 1773–4
Pittsgrove, 1774
Salem, 1774
Upper Alloways Creek, 1773–4
Upper Penns Neck, 1773–4
Sussex County
Greenwich, 1774
Hardyston, 1774
Knowlton, 1773–4
Montague, 1774
Newton, 1774
Oxford, 1774
Sandystone, 1774
Walpack, 1773–4

Quit rents are found in the New Jersey quit rent book, 1683–96 (film 0946001). This is a filming of the manuscripts at the New Jersey Historical Society in Newark. Records include the townships of Elizabeth, Newark, Shrewsbury, Middletown, Piscataway, Woodbridge, and unidentified localities.

The earliest military records for New Jersey are at State Archives and include:
• Military Officers recorded in the Office of the Secretary of State (film 0573334).

* New Jersey, Colonial wars, 1668–1774 (film 0573334).
* Index to colonial period, 1665–1774 (film 0573334).
* French and Indian War records, 1757–64 (film 0573334).

Another source for New Jersey records is the *Annual Report of the State Historian of the State of New York* [Vols. 1 and 2 of the Colonial Series] (Albany: Wynkoop, Hallenbeck Crawford State Printers, 1897, Vol. 1 on film 0924818, Vol. 2 on fiche 6088376). It contains muster rolls for 1673, 1690, and 1715.

Church and Vital Records

The earliest religious denominations established in New Jersey were Reformed Dutch, Congregational, Society of Friends, and Lutheran. At the time of the Revolution, the largest denominations also included Presbyterian, Baptist, and Anglican, as well as Reformed Dutch and Society of Friends.

The Historical Records Survey of the Works Progress Administration prepared a number of inventories of New Jersey church records.

* A general guide can be found in *Guide to Vital Statistics Records in New Jersey.* Vol. 2. *Church Archives* (n.p.: The Survey, 1941, fiche 6051253).
* The inventories are published in ten separate volumes. Some of those that have been filmed are Baptist, Presbyterian, and Protestant Episcopal inventories (all on film 1637446).
* Historical Records Survey. *Inventory of the Church Archives of New Jersey: Congregational Christian Churches* (Newark: The Survey, 1941).

Reformed Dutch records are described in Gasero, Russell L. *Guide to Local Church Records in the Archives of the Reformed Church in America and Genealogical Resources at the Gardiner Sage Library, New Brunswick Theological Seminary* (New Brunswick: Historical Society of the Reformed Church in America, 1979, fiche 6046480).

A guide to determining existing records for all denominations can be found in "Church Records in New Jersey," an article by William Nelson (*Journal of the Presbyterian Historical Society* 2 [March 1904]: 173–88, and 251–66. Reprint. Paterson: Paterson History Club, 1904, fiche 6010550).

Macopin Roman Catholic Church in Echo Lake was the first Catholic Church in New York or New Jersey. It was served by missionaries from Philadelphia. The early records are lost, but some of the marriages may be recorded in the register of Saint Joseph's Church in Philadelphia, published in *Records of the American Catholic Historical Society of Philadelphia* I (1887), II–IV, VIII (1897). There also some records in the Goshenhoppen Registers, 1741–64, in Vols. II and III of this series. Many of these records have been indexed in Dirnberger, Janet Drumm. *New Jersey Catholic Baptismal Records from 1759 to 1781: Index by Surname of Baptisms Performed in the State of New Jersey from 1759 to 1781 by the Catholic Missionaries of Old Saint Joseph's Church in Philadelphia* (Seabrook, TX: Brambles, 1981, film 1033943).

Atkinson, John. *Memorials of Methodism in New Jersey: From the Foundation of the First Society in the State in 1770, to the Completion of the First Twenty Years of its History Containing Sketches of Ministerial Laborers, Distinguished Laymen and Prominent Societies of That Period* (1860. Reprint. Washington, DC: Library of Congress, 1990, film 1730726).

Harmelink, Herman. *The Reformed Church in New Jersey* (Woodcliff-on-Hudson: Synod of New Jersey, 1969, film 1637348).

The first laws for registration of vital records were enacted in 1675 but were not enforced. Most marriages were performed by a justice of the peace. After 1719, a license was required unless banns were published at least three weeks before the marriage. The original bonds are at the State Archives, 1711–1878 (film 0888701 ff.). Marriages are from various counties and are arranged in groups by surname. They are indexed in a bride and groom's card index, 1695–1900 (film 0542553 ff.).

New Jersey Marriage Records, 1665–1800 [*Archives of the State of New Jersey.* Vol. 22] (Baltimore: Genealogical Publishing Co., 1973). These records do not include banns.

The Historical Records Survey abstracted marriage records, 1670–1800 (film 0542538 ff.). The Survey also abstracted early church records, newspaper notices, town records, cemetery headstones, and other records into a card index of birth and death records, 1670–1900 (film 0820014 ff.) Town records, especially the towns in East Jersey that were settled by New Englanders, contain vital records, deeds, freeholder lists, and other documents.

Manuscript Collections

There are many collections available at county historical societies in New Jersey and Pennsylvania (see specific counties). The State Archives has several series of family papers that have been filmed.

The Charles Carroll Gardner collection (film 0941113 ff.) is one of the series available at the New Jersey Historical Society. For more information see Skemer, Don C. *Guide to the Manuscript Collections of the New Jersey Historical Society* (Newark: New Jersey Historical Society, 1979).

Genealogical Society of New Jersey Genealogical Collection (film 0854126 ff.) is at the Rutgers University Library in New Brunswick. For more information see Smith, Herbert F. *A Guide to Manuscript Collections of the Rutgers University Library* (New Brunswick: The Library, 1964).

County Records and Resources
Atlantic County (established 1837 from Gloucester County)
Church Records
Society of Friends, Great Egg Harbor and Cape May, Galloway Township. Monthly meeting records, 1693–1837 (film 0020458). The original records are at the Haverford College Library in Haverford, Pennsylvania.

Bergen County (established 1683 in East Jersey)
Original records at the Passaic County Courthouse in Paterson are:
Bergen County Clerk.
• Deeds, 1715–1838 (film 0946379 ff.).
• Mortgages, 1766–1840 (film 0947502 ff.).
Original records at the Bergen County Courthouse in Hackensack are:
• Deeds, 1713–1901 (film 0893980 ff.).
• Mortgages, 1766–1870 (film 0886387 ff.).
• *Minutes of the Justices and Freeholders of Bergen County, New Jersey, 1715–1795: From the Original in the County Clerk's Office* (n.p.: Bergen County Historical Society, 1924).
Bergen County Surrogate's Court. Probate records, 1714–1962 (film 0910617 ff.).
Records at the State Archives in Trenton are:
• Wills, 1698–1900 (film 0545438 ff.).
• Field book report of the Commissioners for the settling and determining the rights and claims to the common lands of Bergen County (film 1028303).

Church Records
Manuscripts and transcripts at the Holland Society of New York in New York City are:
• Reformed Dutch Church, Hackensack, and the first Reformed Dutch Church of Schraalenburgh. Records, 1724–1858 (film 0016594).
• *Records of the Reformed Dutch Churches of Hackensack and Schraalenburgh, New Jersey, 1686–1802.* 2 Vols. (New York: Holland Society of New York, 1891, film 0016559 ff.). In early times the village of Dumont was known as the village of Schraalenburgh.
• Ramapo Evangelical Lutheran Church, Mahwah. Records, 1749–1817 (film 1019520).
• Reformed Dutch Church, Paramus. Records, 1740–1854 (film 1016881).

Reformed Dutch Church, Dumont. Records, 1747–1854 (film 0888711). The original records are at the Rutgers University Library in New Brunswick.

Taylor, Benjamin Cook. *Annals of Bergen, of the Reformed Dutch Church, and Churches under Its Care: Including the Civil History of the Ancient Township of Bergen, New Jersey* (New York: Board of Publication of the Reformed Protestant Dutch Church, n.d., fiche 6093227, index on fiche 6089193).

Holland Society of New York. *The Reformed Dutch Church of Bergen, New Jersey, 1666–1788* (1913–15. Reprint. Baltimore: Genealogical Publishing Co., 1990).

Burlington County (established 1694 in West Jersey, see also Ocean County) Original records at the Burlington County Courthouse in Trenton are:
Burlington County Clerk.
* Mortgages, 1724–50 (film 0946852).
* Road records, 1762–1950 (film 0848869 ff.).
Burlington County Court of Common Pleas. Court papers, 1730–89 (film 0441453). The original records are at the Historical Society of Pennsylvania in Philadelphia.
Records at the State Archives in Trenton are:
* Burlington County Supreme Court. Index to court minutes, 1681–1842 (film 0016538).
* Burlington County Prerogative Court. Bonds, 1743–75 (film 1028303).
Town records at the State Archives are:
* Burlington Town Clerk. Town records, 1681–1843 (film 0888821).
* Chesterfield Town Clerk. Town meeting minutes, 1692–1712 (film 1024665).
* Mansfield Township Town Clerk. Town records, 1697–1773 (film 0944857).
* New Hanover Town Clerk. Town meeting minutes, 1728–88, 1798–1882, brand markings, 1735–1861 (film 1024665).
* Northampton Town Clerk. Town meeting minutes, 1697–1824 (film 1028306).

Church Records
Saint Mary's Protestant Episcopal Church, Burlington. 1703–1876 (film 0441456). The original records are at the Presbyterian Historical Society in Philadelphia.

Society of Friends records at the Friends Historical Library at Swarthmore College in Swarthmore, Pennsylvania and Haverford College Library in Haverford, Pennsylvania are:

- Burlington. Monthly meeting records, 1675–1897 (film 0020424 ff.).
- Mount Holly. Monthly meeting records, 1678–1942 (film 0020427 ff.). Established 1776 from Burlington Monthly Meeting. Marriages copied from Burlington Monthly Meeting, 1678–1776.
- Chesterfield. Monthly meeting records, 1684–1942 (film 0020382 ff.). Established in 1684 and held in later years at Trenton and Crosswicks.
- Evesham. Monthly meeting records, 1682–1900 (film 0020392 ff.). Established 1760 from Haddonfield Monthly Meeting.
- Medford. Monthly meeting records, 1693–1871 (film 0020483 ff.). Set apart from Evesham Monthly Meeting in 1794.
- Upper Springfield, Mansfield. Monthly meeting records, 1717–1943 (film 0020408 ff.). Established 1783 from Burlington and Chesterfield Monthly Meetings.

Reed, Henry Clay. *The Burlington Court Book: A Record of Quaker Jurisprudence in West New Jersey, 1680–1709* (Washington, DC: American Historical Association, 1944, fiche 6101067).

Camden County (established 1844 from Gloucester County)
Gloucester Town Clerk. Town records, 1747–1808, livestock markings, 1737–1809 (film 1024665). The original records are at the State Archives in Trenton.

Cape May County (established 1692 in West Jersey, see also Cumberland County)
Original records at the Cape May County Courthouse in Cape May are:
Cape May County Clerk.
- Deeds, 1692–1934 (film 0852722 ff.).
- Deeds, wills, and other records, 1692–1734 (film 1289232).
- Mortgages, 1692–1862 (film 0856229).
Cape May County Clerk. Marriages, 1694–1830 (film 0441460). The original records are at the Historical Society of Pennsylvania in Philadelphia.
Records at the State Archives in Trenton are:
- Cape May County Surrogate's Court. Wills, 1704–1900 (film 0528407 ff.).
- Tax rateables, Cape May County, 1773–1822 (film 0865468). Includes the Lower Township, Middle Township, Upper Township, Dennis Township, and abstracts for the county.

Cumberland County (established 1748 from Salem County, see also Salem County)
Cumberland County Clerk. Mortgages, 1766-1861 (film 0853721 ff.). The original records are at the Cumberland County Courthouse in Bridgeton.
Cumberland County Surrogate's Court. Wills, 1747-1900 (film 0528418 ff.). The original records are at the State Archives in Trenton.

Church Records
Deerfield Presbyterian Church. Records, 1746-1904 (film 1509910). A copy of the original record is at the Gloucester County Historical Society in Woodbury.
Fairfield Presbyterian Church, Fairton. Records, 1759-1970 (film 1310562). Also known as First Presbyterian Church of Fairfield. The original records are at the Presbyterian Historical Society in Philadelphia.

Society of Friends original records at the Friends Historical Library, Swarthmore College in Swarthmore, Pennsylvania and Haverford College Library in Haverford, Pennsylvania are:
• Greenwich. Monthly meeting records, 1677-1893 (film 0020415 ff.). Established 1770 from Salem Monthly Meeting.
• Maurice River, Port Elizabeth. Monthly meeting records, 1728-1854 (film 0020418). Established 1804 from Greenwich Monthly Meeting.

Seventh-Day Baptist Church, Shiloh. Records, 1737-1937 (film 0571129).

Essex County (established 1683 in East Jersey)
Original records at the Essex County Hall of Records in Newark are:
Essex County Court of Common Pleas. Court records, 1709-1849 (film 1310991 ff.). Contains records of the Court of Common Pleas, the Court of General Quarter Sessions of the Peace, the Circuit Court, and the Court of Oyer and Terminer and General Gaol Delivery.
Essex County Court of General Quarter Sessions of the Peace. Court minutes, 1760-9 (film 1310991). Contains minutes of the Court of General Quarter Sessions of the Peace, and the Inferior Court of Common Pleas.
Essex County Clerk.
• Road records, 1698-1930 (film 0913954 ff.).
• Mortgage index, 1765-1909 (film 0913088 ff.).
• Deeds, 1688-1901 (film 0912483 ff.).
• Tavern license applications, 1725-1891 (film 0945469 ff.). The courts involved are: General Quarter Sessions of the Peace, Common Pleas, Inferior Court of Common Pleas, and Orphans' Court.

Original records at the Passaic County Courthouse in Paterson are:
Essex County Clerk.

*   Deeds, 1729–1838 (film 0947754 ff.).
*   Mortgages, 1766–1838 (film 0947884 ff.).

Records at the State Archives in Trenton are:

*   Essex County Surrogate's Court. Probate records, 1697–1900 (film 0545455 ff.).
*   Essex County Sheriff. Land records, 1755 (film 1024666). These are freeholders lists arranged alphabetically by township.
*   East New Jersey index to records at Perth Amboy, 1665–1743 (film 1028303). Contains surveys and patents for land in Union, Middlesex, and Essex counties.

Town records at the State Historical Society in Newark are:

*   Newark Town Clerk. Town records, 1666–1836 (film 0944853 ff.).
*   New Jersey quit rent book, 1683–1696 (film 0946001). Records of Elizabeth, Newark, Shrewsbury, Middleton, Piscataway, Woodbridge, and unidentified localities.

Church Records

Church of Jesus Christ at Second River, Belleville. Records, 1727–94 (film 1016878). The transcript is at the Holland Society of New York in New York City.

Trinity Cathedral Episcopal Church, Newark. Records, 1696–1966 (film 0946020 ff.). The original records are at the State Historical Society in Newark.

Gloucester County (established 1683 in West Jersey, see also Salem County)
Original records at the Gloucester County Courthouse in Woodbury are:
Gloucester County Clerk.

*   Mortgages, 1766–1866 (film 0846888 ff.).
*   Board of Chosen Freeholders. Minutes of meetings, 1701–1891 (film 1004243 ff.).
*   Marriage records, 1700–1899 (film 0850324).
*   Roads, 1762–1866 (film 0846907).

Gloucester County Clerk. Ear marks, 1686–1776 (film 0441463). The original records are at the Historical Society of Pennsylvania in Philadelphia.

Records at the State Archives in Trenton are:

*   Gloucester County, record of deeds, 1682–1779 (film 0460077 ff.). These records cover much of West Jersey.
*   Gloucester County Surrogate's Court. Wills, 1691–1900 (film 0533144 ff.).

Stewart, Frank H. *Gloucester County under the Proprietors* (Woodbury, NJ: F.H. Stewart, 1942, fiche 6087793).

Stewart, Frank H. *Notes on Old Gloucester County, New Jersey* (1917–64. Reprint. Baltimore: Genealogical Publishing Co., 1977).

Gloucester County Historical Society, Woodbury.
* Master index to county records (film 1543708 ff.). Included are references to bail bonds, 1688–1871, indictments, 1686–1879, writs and summonses, 1712–1880, affidavits, 1686–1874, recognizances, 1689–1880, tavern petitions, 1713–1899, etc.
* Genealogies and family records from the historical office, 1600–1900s (film 0850326 ff.).
* Card index to births, 1670–1980 (film 1531264 ff.).
* Card index to marriage records, 1670–1980 (film 1543466 ff.).
* Card index to death records, 1670–1900 (film 1543555 ff.). There are not many entries before 1800.
* Early court records (film 1001904 ff.).

Church Records
Moravian Church, West Jersey. Moravian register of births, baptisms, marriages, and deaths in West Jersey, 1742–94, transcribed from the original records in the archives at Bethlehem, Pennsylvania (film 0441451). The manuscript is at the Presbyterian Historical Society in Philadelphia, and includes records for Salem and Gloucester counties.

Saint Peter's Episcopal Church, Clarksboro. Records, 1768–1973 (film 1004994 ff.).
Saint Peter's Episcopal Church, Mount Royal. Records, 1765–1856 (n.p., 1948, film 0848548).

Society of Friends, Woodbury. Monthly meeting records, 1702–1927 (film 0020486). Established in 1785 from Haddonfield Monthly Meeting. The original records are at the Haverford College Library in Haverford, Pennsylvania.

Hudson County (established 1840 from Bergen County)
Hudson County Register of Deeds. Mortgages, 1767–1866 (film 0889697 ff.). The original records are at the Hudson County Courthouse in Jersey City.

Church Records
Reformed Dutch Church, Jersey City. Baptisms, 1666-1788 (film 0855163). The original records are at the Rutgers University Library in New Brunswick.

Winfield, Charles Hardenburg. *History of the Land Titles in Hudson County, New Jersey, 1609-1871* (New York: Wynkoop and Hallenbeck, 1872, film 0874485).

Hunterdon County (established 1714 from Burlington County)
Original records at the Hunterdon County Hall of Records in Flemington are:
Hunterdon County Clerk.
* Hunterdon County Inferior Court of Common Pleas. Miscellaneous court records, loans, etc., 1713-1860 (film 0808067 ff.).
* Affidavits, 1713-1860 (film 0819208 ff.).
* Indictments, 1713-1860 (film 0819111 ff.).
* Recognizances, 1713-1860 (film 0819105 ff.).
* Coroner inquests, 1770-1909 (film 1029981 ff.).
* Index to files including recognizances, indictments, affidavits, appeals, insolvents, and miscellaneous records, 1700-1900 (film 0802468 ff.).
* Mortgages, 1766-1902 (film 0819257 ff.).
* Mortgages, 1733-48 (film 0946855).
* Deeds, 1705-1911 (film 0805487 ff.).
* Early deeds, 1716-30 (film 0818213).
* Special deeds, 1730-1916 (film 0588789 ff.). Land records with special circumstances, such as 99-year leases, conditional sales, etc.
* Record of roads, road openings, 1761-1921 (film 0818210 ff.).
* Petitions for tavern licenses, 1738-1800 (film 0946853 ff.).
* Petitions for peddler licenses, 1763-1879 (film 0807014 ff.).
* Town meetings arranged in alphabetical order by town, 1760-1885 (film 0807016 ff.).
Records at the State Archives in Trenton are:
* Hunterdon County Surrogate's Court. Wills, 1683-1900 (film 0545469 ff.).
* Hunterdon County Court of Common Pleas. Minutes, 1714-1908 (film 1730174 ff.).
* Hunterdon County Loan Office. Account books and mortgages, 1733-48 (film 1028302).

Tewksbury Town Clerk. Town meeting minutes, 1755-1846 (film 1028306). The original records are at the State Library in Trenton.

Hopewell Town Clerk. Minutes, estrays, indentures, etc., 1721–1800 (film 0855160). The original records are at the Rutgers University Library in New Brunswick.

Hunterdon County Historical Society, Flemington. Manuscript collection, 1700–1984 (film 1769166 ff.). This includes slave manumissions, West Jersey Society folders, the Bethlehem Baptist Church register, 1742–1822, etc.

Church Records

Society of Friends, Quakertown. Monthly meeting records, 1703–1921 (film 0020429 ff.). Established as Bethlehem Monthly Meeting in 1744 and name changed to Kingwood in 1747 and to Quakertown 1859. The original records are at the Friends Historical Library, Swarthmore College, and the Haverford College Library in Haverford, Pennsylvania.

Society of Friends, Hardwick and Randolph, Hicksite. Monthly meeting records, 1710–1861 (film 0017352 ff.). Established as Hardwick and Mendham Monthly Meeting in 1797. Records before 1797 copied from Kingwood Monthly Meeting. The original records are at the Society of Friends Archives in New York City and the Haverford College Library in Haverford, Pennsylvania.

Zion Evangelical Lutheran Church, Oldwick. Church records, 1715–1922 (film 0888765 ff.). Also included are some records of Saint Paul's Church of Bedminster, German Valley, Spruce Run, Old Rockaway, Fox Hill, and Leslysland or Leslie's Land. The original records are at the Rutgers University Library in New Brunswick.

Original records at the Archives of the Reformed Church in America in New Brunswick are:
• Reformed Dutch Church, Lebanon. Records, 1768–1966 (film 1927822 ff.).
• Reformed Dutch Church, Readington. Records, 1720–1871 (film 1927824 ff.).

Baptist Church, Hopewell. Records, 1748–1811 (film 0441466). The original records are at the Historical Society of Pennsylvania in Philadelphia.

Mercer County (established 1838 from Burlington, Hunterdon, and Middlesex counties)
Original records at the Mercer County Courthouse in Trenton are:
New Jersey inquisitions on the dead recorded in county coroners' offices, 1688–1798 (film 1023873).
Lawrence Township Town Clerk. Town records, 1716–1928 (film 0888838 ff.).

Nottingham Township, New Jersey Minute Book 1692–1710, 1752–1772 (Trenton: Trenton Historical Society, 1940).

Middlesex County (established 1683 in East Jersey, see also Essex County) Original records at the Middlesex County Courthouse in New Brunswick are: Middlesex County Clerk.

*   Mortgages, 1767–1861 (film 0860021 ff.).
*   Road books, 1773–1930 (film 0861155 ff.).

Original records at the Rutgers University Library in New Brunswick are:

*   Deeds and land conveyances, 1714–22, public road surveys, 1720–75 (film 0851754). Records also cover Somerset County.
*   Miscellaneous records, 1766–1866 (film 0851765). Accounts of tavern licenses, deeds, abstracts of rateables, collectors' bonds, etc.

Records at the State Archives in Trenton are:

*   Middlesex County Court of Common Pleas. Papers, 1741–64 (film 1903112 ff.). Includes papers for the court of quarter sessions.
*   Middlesex County Sheriff. Land records, 1752 (film 1024666). Freeholders' lists arranged alphabetically by township.
*   Middlesex County Surrogate's Court. Wills, 1683–1900 (film 0545469 ff.).

Piscataway Town Clerk. Town records, 1682–1933 (film 0888837). The original records are at the Rutgers University Library in New Brunswick.

Woodbridge Town Clerk. Freeholders' book, 1668–1716 (film 0016596). The original records are in Woodbridge.

Church Records
Original records filmed at the Rutgers University Library in New Brunswick are:

*   First Presbyterian Church, Cranbury. Records, 1739–1954 (film 0888725 ff.).
*   Christ Church, New Brunswick. Records, 1758–1910 (film 0888759).
*   Saint Peter's Church, Spotswood. Records, 1761–1911(film 0016588 ff.).

First Presbyterian Church, Woodbridge. Records, 1707–1954 (film 0468370 ff.). The original records are at the Presbyterian Historical Society in Philadelphia.

Society of Friends original records at the Society of Friends Archives in New York City and the Haverford College Library in Haverford, Pennsylvania are:

*   Rahway and Plainfield, Hicksite. Monthly meeting records, 1686–1894 (film 0017346 ff.). Established in 1686 and met at Amboy, name changed to Woodbridge Monthly Meeting in 1684. Became Rahway, Plainfield, and Woodbridge Monthly Meeting in 1763. Hicksites retained all record books at Separation of 1828.
*   Woodbridge. Monthly meeting records, 1686–1788 (film 0441466 ff.).

Monmouth County (established 1683 in East Jersey, see also Essex County)
Original records at the Monmouth County Courthouse in Freehold are:
Monmouth County Clerk.
- Mortgages, 1766–1859 (film 0592963 ff.).
- Deeds, 1665–1899 (film 0593593 ff.).
Records at the State Archives in Trenton are:
- Monmouth County Surrogate's Court. Wills, 1683–1900 (film 0593593 ff.).
- Monmouth County Sheriff. Land records, 1748, 1755 (film 1024666). Freeholders' lists arranged alphabetically by township.

Upper Freehold Town Clerk. Register of estrays, 1736–1864 (film 0855160). The original records are at the Rutgers University Library in New Brunswick.

Church Records
Reformed Dutch United Congregations of Freehold and Middletown. Records, 1709–1851(film 1298671). The original records are at the Monmouth County Historical Association in Freehold.

Original records at the Rutgers University Library in New Brunswick are:
- First Reformed Church of Freehold, Marlboro Township. Records, 1709–1851 (film 0888745). Also known as the Church of the Navesinks. Includes records of the Dutch congregation of Middletown township.
- Baptist Church, Imlaystown. Records, 1766–1928 (film 0888785). Formerly known as the Upper Freehold Baptist Church.
- Christ Church, Shrewsbury. Baptisms, 1733–1824 (film 0855161).

Society of Friends, Shrewsbury, Hicksite. Monthly meeting records, 1670–1902 (film 0017351 ff.). The original records are at the Society of Friends Archives in New York City.
Society of Friends, Shrewsbury. Monthly meeting records, 1763–1848 (film 0020483). The original records are at the Haverford College Library in Haverford, Pennsylvania.
Salter, Edwin. *History of Monmouth and Ocean Counties . . .* (1890. Reprint. Westminster, MD: Family Line Publications, 1989).

Salter, Edwin and George C. Beekman. *Old Times in Monmouth . . .* (1887. Reprint. Baltimore: Genealogical Publishing Co., 1994).

Morris County (established 1739 from Hunterdon County, see also Hunterdon County)
Original records at the Morris County Courthouse in Morristown are:
Morris County Clerk. Mortgage indexes, 1765–1926 (film 0961290 ff.).

Morris County Court of Common Pleas. Minutes, 1740–1866 (film 0961259 ff.).
Records at the State Archives in Trenton are:
* Morris County Surrogate's Court. Wills, 1740–1900 (film 0550485 ff.).
* Morris County Sheriff. Freeholders' list, 1752 (film 1024666).

Stryker-Rodda, Harriet Mott. *Some Early Records of Morris County, New Jersey, 1740–1799* (New Orleans: Polyanthos, 1975).

Church Records
Original records filmed at the Rutgers University Library in New Brunswick are:
* Zion Lutheran Church, Long Valley. Records, 1775–1940 (film 0888744). Long Valley was known as German Valley until about 1918.
* Reformed Dutch Church, Montville. Records, 1774–1928 (film 0888747).
* First Presbyterian Church, Morristown. Records, 1731–1939 (film 0888748 ff.).
* Presbyterian Church, Parsippany. Records, 1745–1910 (film 0888768).
Presbyterian Church, Madison. Records, 1747–1935 (film 1011094 ff.). The original records are at the Presbyterian Church in Madison.
First Presbyterian Church, Mendham. Records, 1766–1906 (film 0503588 ff.). The original records are at the Presbyterian Historical Society in Philadelphia.
Reformed Dutch Church, Pompton and Pompton Plains. Records, 1713–1871 (film 1016883). The transcript is at the Holland Society of New York in New York City.

Ocean County (established 1850 from Monmouth County)
Little Egg Harbor Town Clerk. Town meeting minutes, 1757–1875 (film 1028306). The original records are at the State Library in Trenton.

Society of Friends, Little Egg Harbor. Monthly meeting records, 1715–1830 (film 0854097). Contains history of the former Little Egg Harbor Township, Burlington County, part of which is now in Ocean County.

Passaic County (established 1837 from Bergen and Essex counties, see also Morris County)
Church Records
Protestant Reformed Dutch Church of Acquackanonk, Passaic. Records, 1726–1944 (film 0888712 ff.). The original records were filmed at the Rutgers University Library in New Brunswick.
Reformed Dutch Old First Church, Passaic. Records, 1726–1895 (film 1927823 ff.). The original records are at the Archives of the Reformed Church in America in New Brunswick.
Totowa Reformed Dutch Church, Paterson. Records, 1756–1869 (film

0946019). The original records are at the State Historical Society in Newark.

Salem County (established 1694 in West Jersey)
Original records at the Salem County Courthouse in Salem are:
Salem County Clerk.
* Mortgages, 1766–1860 (film 0847066 ff.).
* Marriage license index, 1680–1945 (film 1871265).
Salem County Orphans' Court. Docket files, 1748–1804 (film 1293124 ff.).
Records at the State Archives in Trenton are:
* Salem County Surrogate's Court. Wills, 1679–1900 (film 0545493 ff.).
* Salem County surveys, wills, deeds, 1675–1718 (film 0460072 ff.). These records cover much of West Jersey, including Salem town grants, 1678–9, Greenwich town lots, 1686–1704, etc.
Salem County Clerk. Civil marriages, 1682–1703 (film 0441467). The original records are at the Historical Society of Pennsylvania in Philadelphia.

Salem County Historical Society, Salem.
* Salem County survey records, 1684–1786 (film 1763327).
* Salem County unrecorded deeds, 1639–1910 (film 1763329 ff.).
* Salem County Overseers of the Poor, book, upper part of Alloways Creek Precinct, 1749–99 (film 1763327).
* Deeds index, 1726–1900 (film 1543981).
* Salem County lists, 1745–1872 (film 1763328).
* Death index, 1726–1988 (film 1543968 ff.).
* Marriage indexes, 1726–1988 (film 1543982 ff.).
* Marriage records, 1632–1884 (film 1763328).
Salem Town Clerk.
* Estray book, 1738–1847 (film 1763327). The original records are at the Salem County Historical Society in Salem.
* Minutes, 1758–1851 (film 1028307). The original records are at the State Library in Trenton.

Church Records
Original records at the Historical Society of Pennsylvania in Philadelphia are:
* Emmanuel Lutheran Church, Alloway Township. Kirchenbuch, 1744–1838 (film 0441480). Formerly known as Cohansy Lutheran Church.
* Pittsgrove Presbyterian Church, Daretown. Records, 1741–1869 (film 0441480). Organized as Pilesgrove Presbyterian Church.

Trinity Episcopal Church, Swedesboro. Church records, 1713–1915 (film 1004991 ff.). Raccoon Church (now at Swedesboro, Gloucester County) and Penns Neck (now at Churchtown, Salem County) were Swedish Lutheran until about 1789 when they became Protestant Episcopal under the name of Saint George. Film of the original records. Another filming, 1750–91 (film 1364764), is from a photocopy of original records at the Riksarkivet, Stockholm, Sweden.

Federal Writers' Project. *The Records of the Swedish Lutheran Churches at Raccoon and Penns Neck, 1713–1786* (1938. Reprint. Woodbury, NJ: Gloucester Historical Society, 1982, fiche 6117892).

Original records at the Salem County Historical Society in Salem are:
* German Presbyterian Church, Cohansey. Records, 1767–1826 (film 1763327).
* First Baptist Church, Salem. Records, 1755–1859 (film 1763227 ff.).

Society of Friends original records at the Friends Historical Library, Swarthmore College, in Swarthmore, Pennsylvania and the Haverford College Library in Haverford, Pennsylvania are:
* Piles Grove, Woodstown. Monthly meeting records, 1756–1896 (film 0020409 ff.). Established in 1794 from Salem Monthly Meeting.
* Salem. Monthly meeting records, 1686–1947 (film 0020430 ff.).

Somerset County (established 1688 from Middlesex County, see also Hunterdon and Middlesex counties)
Original records at the Somerset County Courthouse in Somerville are:
Somerset County Clerk.
* Mortgages, 1765–1870 (film 0900532 ff.).
* Road books, 1733–1927 (film 0913006 ff.).
* Old road book, 1745–76 (film 0016585).
* Minute book of Board of Chosen Freeholders, 1772–1810 (film 0016585).
Records at the State Archives in Trenton are:
* Somerset County Surrogate's Court. Wills, 1688–1900 (film 0562748 ff.).
* Somerset County Sheriff. Land records, 1753 (film 1024666). List of freeholders.

Franklin Township Town Clerk. Poor book, 1764–1841 (film 0888837). The original records are at the Somerset County Courthouse in Somerville.

Church Records

Transcripts at the Holland Society of New York in New York City are:
- Reformed Dutch Church at Milston, Harlingen. Records, 1727–1802 (film 1016881). Formerly known as Sourland and Milston, or Millstone.
- Reformed Dutch Church, Raritan. Records, 1680–1898 (film 0016584).

Presbyterian Church, Lamington. Records, 1740–1963 (film 0888740 ff.). The original records were filmed at the Rutgers University Library in New Brunswick.

Reformed Dutch Church, Neshanic. Records, 1762–1873 (film 1927823). The original records are at the Archives of the Reformed Church in America in New Brunswick.

Sussex County (established 1753 from Morris County)
Original records at the Sussex County Courthouse in Newton are:
Sussex County Clerk.
- Mortgages, 1766–1868 (film 0959855 ff.).
- Road books, 1761–1924 (film 0961015 ff.).
- Board of chosen freeholders minutes, 1754–1913 (film 0961013 ff.).
Records at the State Archives in Trenton are:
- Sussex County Surrogate's Court. Wills, 1753–1900 (film 0563826 ff.)
- Sussex County Court of Common Pleas. Applications for tavern licenses, 1753–1860 (film 0900372 ff.). Early applications were addressed to the Court of Quarter Sessions of the Peace.
- Unindexed wills of Sussex County, 1760–1850 (film 0589082 ff.).

Stark, Brad. *The Minute Book of Sussex County, New Jersey, Court Records, 1764–1766* (Bowie, MD: Heritage Books, 1993). Contains records of the Court of General Quarter Sessions of the Peace.

Montague Township Town Clerk. Town records, 1734–82 (film 0888797). The original records are at the Sussex County Courthouse in Newton.

Church Records

Reformed Church, Clove. Records, 1700–1835 (film 1927674). The original records are at the Archives of the Reformed Church of America in New Brunswick.

Old Reformed Dutch Church, Walpack Township. Records, 1741–1810 (film 0441481). The original records are at the Presbyterian Historical Society in Philadelphia.

Union County (established 1857 from Essex County, see also Essex County)
Elizabeth Town Clerk. Minutes of town meetings and various other records,
1714–1840 (film 0855160). The original records are at the Rutgers
University Library in New Brunswick.

Church Records
Original records at the Presbyterian Historical Society in Philadelphia are:
• First Presbyterian Church, Elizabeth. Records, 1668–1916 (film 0441482),
subscription ledger, 1772–1810 (film 0912118).
• First Presbyterian Church, Springfield. Records, 1745–1899 (film 0468362).

Original records filmed at the Rutgers University Library in New Brunswick are:
• Baptist Church, Scotch Plains. Records, 1747–1941 (film 0888773 ff.).
• First Presbyterian Church, Westfield. Records, 1727–1958 (film 0888788).

Warren County (established 1824 from Sussex County, see also Hunterdon
County)
Church Records
Saint James Protestant Episcopal Church, Delaware. Records, 1769–1945 (film
0888731). The original records were filmed at the Rutgers University
Library in New Brunswick.
Original records at the Presbyterian Historical Society in Philadelphia are:
• Evangelical Lutheran Church, Greenwich. Records, 1769–1865 (film
0441482).
• Presbyterian Church, Knowlton. Records, 1766–1844 (film 0503575).

Suggested Reading
Acrelius, Israel. *A History of New Sweden, or, The Settlements on the River
Delaware* (1874. Reprint. New York: Arno Press, 1972, film 0982319).

Barber, John Warner. *Historical Collections of New Jersey: Past and Present:
Containing a General Collection of the Most Interesting Facts, Traditions,
Biographical Sketches, Anecdotes, Etc., Relating to the History and Antiquities
with Geographical Descriptions of All Important Places in the State* (1868.
Reprint. Baltimore: Genealogical Publishing Co., 1996, fiche 6050088).

Barker, Bette Marie. *Guide to Family History Sources in the New Jersey State
Archives.* 2nd ed. (Trenton: Division of Archives and Records Management, 1990).

Beekman, George. *Early Dutch Settlers of Monmouth County, New Jersey*
(Freehold, NJ: Moreau, 1901, film 0962197).

Boyer, Carl. *Ship Passenger Lists, New York and New Jersey, 1600–1825* (Newhall, CA: The Author, 1978, fiche 6048671). Contains reprints of passenger lists named in Lancour's *Bibliography of Ship Passenger Lists.*

Chambers, Theodore Frelinghuysen. *The Early Germans of New Jersey: Their History, Churches and Genealogies, with Maps and Illustrations* (Dover, NJ: Dover Printing Co., 1895, film 0016514).

Craven, Wesley Frank. *New Jersey and the English Colonization of North America* (Princeton: D. Van Nostrand Co., 1964).

Federal Writers' Project. *The Swedes and Finns in New Jersey* (1938. Reprint. New York: AMS Press, 1975).

Fisher, Edgar Jacob. *New Jersey as a Royal Province, 1738 to 1776* (New York: Columbia University, 1911, film 1698055).

Historical Records Survey. *Inventory: Classified Research Data, Primary Source Materials, Secondary Source Materials, Special Subject Files, Draft Volumes for Publication, Surplus Publications Relating to: Local, County, State and Federal Historical Subjects* (Newark: The Survey, 1943).

Johnson, Amandus. *The Swedish Settlements on the Delaware . . . 1638–1664* (Philadelphia: University of Pennsylvania, 1911, film 1364768).

Johnson, Robert Gibbon. *An Historical Account of the First Settlement of Salem, in West Jersey: By John Fenwick . . .* (Philadelphia: O. Rogers, 1839, fiche 6048433).

Klett, Joseph R. *Genealogies of New Jersey Families from the Genealogical Magazine of New Jersey.* 2 Vols. (Baltimore: Genealogical Publishing Co., 1996).

Landsman, Ned C. *Scotland and its First American Colony, 1683–1765* (Princeton: Princeton University Press, 1985).

Leiby, Adrian C. *The Early Dutch and Swedish Settlers of New Jersey* (Princeton: D. Van Nostrand, 1964).

Levitt, James H. *For Want of Trade: Shipping and the New Jersey Ports, 1680–1783* (Newark: New Jersey Historical Society, 1981).

Littell, John. *The First Settlers of Passaic Valley* (1852. Reprint. Baltimore: Genealogical Publishing Co., 1981, film 0176652).

Marrin, Richard B. *A Glance Back in Time: Life in Colonial New Jersey (1704–1770) as Depicted in News Accounts of the Day* (Bowie, MD: Heritage Books, 1994).

Monnette, Orra Eugene. *First Settlers of Ye Plantations of Piscataway and Woodbridge, Olde East New Jersey, 1664–1714 . . .* 7 Vols. in 5 (Los Angeles: Leroy Carman Press, 1930, film 0673270 ff.).

Pomfret, John E. *Colonial New Jersey, A History* (New York: Charles Scribner's Sons, 1973).

Shourds, Thomas. *History and Genealogy of Fenwick's Colony* (Bridgeton, NJ: G.F. Nixon, 1876, film 0848551).

Stryker-Rodda, Kenn. *The Early Dutch Settlements in New York and New Jersey: The Dutch Colonial Period in America* (Salt Lake City: Church of Jesus Christ of Latter-day Saints, 1969, fiche 6039405).

Wacker, Peter O. *Land and People: A Cultural Geography of Pre-Industrial New Jersey Origins and Settlement Patterns* (New Brunswick: Rutgers University, 1975).

Ward, Christopher. *The Dutch and Swedes on the Delaware, 1609–1664* (Philadelphia: University of Pennsylvania, 1930, fiche 6101604).

Seal of East Jersey.

FIRST CHURCH IN NEWARK.

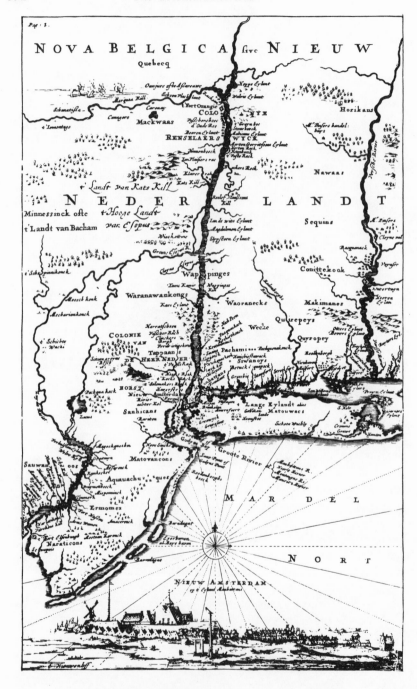

31 New Netherland, 1656 (Library of Congress)

New York

In 1612 the Dutch crews of the ships *Tiger* and *Fortune* built a camp on Manhattan Island. The first permanent European settlement in New York was a Dutch fur trading post at Fort Nassau, near Albany, in 1614. The Dutch West India Company received a charter in 1621, and the first colonists in New Netherland arrived in 1624, establishing settlements on Manhattan Island, called New Amsterdam, and at Fort Orange (Albany). The Dutch landholding systems of patroonship established a manorial system that dominated landownership and leasehold through the time of the Revolution. The patroonship of Rennselaerswyck was founded in 1629 by a grant from the Dutch West India Company and extended over the area of present-day Albany, Columbia, and Rennsselaer counties. Dutch settlements were established at Beverwyck (Albany, 1650) and Esopus (Kingston, 1653).

As part of the New Haven (Connecticut) Colony, a group of English Puritans established Southold, Oyster Bay, and Huntington, Long Island in the 1640s. New Netherland recognized the claim in 1650, but the towns were annexed to New York after 1664. In 1664, the English conquered New Netherland and divided it into the colonies of New York and New Jersey. It was briefly reconquered by the Dutch for one year in 1673.

In 1683 the twelve original counties were established. The English manorial system replaced the patroons, with the granting of a large tract of land by the Governor. The communities established originally as manors were Fox Hall (1667), Livingston (1668), Fordham (1671), Plum Island (1675), Philipsborough (1680), Bentley (1687), Casiltown (1687), Pelham (1687), Saint George (1693), Cortlandt (1697), Morrisania (1697), and Scarsdale (1703).

Immigrants from other countries also settled in New York. French Huguenots founded New Paltz (1677) and New Rochelle (1688). Palatine Germans established Germantown (1708–10) in the Hudson Valley afterwards migrating to the Schoarie Valley and later to the Mohawk Valley. Ulster Scots settled in the area of Orange and Ulster counties in the 1680s.

Boundary disputes plagued the eighteenth century. The boundary between Connecticut and New York

SEE ALSO
Great Britain
Massachusetts
New Jersey
The Netherlands

393

was settled in 1731. The New Jersey boundary was settled in 1769, after a long conflict, and surveyed in 1774. The boundary with Massachusetts was not resolved until 1773.

Statewide Records and Resources

The major New York courts of the colonial period were:

- **Governor and Council (1623–64):** Dutch court of highest jurisdiction; all cases until 1647, after that a court of appeals for the Court of Justice.
- **Court of Justice (1647–1653):** Civil and criminal cases.
- **Courts of Schout, Burgomasters, and Schepens (1653–74):** Dutch courts handling civil and criminal cases. Became the Mayor's Court in New York City. These records are transcribed in O'Callaghan, E.B. *New Netherland Documents. The Records of New Amsterdam from 1653 to 1674 Anno Domini.* 7 Vols. (1897. Reprint. Baltimore: Genealogical Publishing Co., 1976, film 0824405 ff.).
- **Court of Assizes (1665–83):** This court sat at New York City and was the highest provincial court. It had jurisdiction over civil and criminal cases. Records have been printed in Vol. 45 of *The Collections of the New-York Historical Society* (see below) and in the series by Christoph, Peter R. *New York Historical Manuscripts: English* (Baltimore: Genealogical Publishing Co., 1980). The series includes administrative papers of Governors Nichols and Lovelace, 1664–73; Colony of New York records: books of general entries, 1664–73; books of general entries of the colony of New York, 1674–88; records of the Court of Assizes, 1665–82; minutes of the Mayor's Court of New York, 1674–5.
- **Court of Sessions (1685–1846):** See filmed records under specific counties.
- **Court of General Quarter Sessions of the Peace (1665–1895):** Tried criminal cases and probate cases from 1665–83. See New York County and City for filmed records.
- **Mayor's Court (1674–ca 1784):** Handled civil cases, apprenticeships, naturalizations. See New York City for records.
- **Court of Oyer and Terminer and General Gaol Delivery (1683–1895):** Tried capital crimes on a county level.
- **Justice of the Peace Court (1664–):** Also known as small causes courts; local civil matters.
- **Prerogative Court (1686–1778):** Precursor to the Court of Probate (1778–87), which was succeeded by the Surrogate's Court (1787–). See counties under Surrogate's Court. Wills covering the entire colony of New York were recorded with the Prerogative Court and later with the Court of Probate under the first Constitution of the state. A portion of the files are at the State Archives in Albany, at Queens College, and at the New York County Courthouse.

- **Chancery Court (1664–1847):** Records prior to 1823 were created by the Court of Probate. New York Chancery minutes and orders, 1701–1847 (film 0017439 ff.), Surrogate's Court probate records, 1730–86, wills, 1664–83 (film 0478743 ff.). Some have also been abstracted in Scott, Kenneth. *Records of the Chancery Court, Province and State of New York: Guardianships, 1691–1815* (Middletown, NY: Holland Society of New York, 1971, fiche 6088050).
- **Court of Common Pleas (1691–1847):** Handled civil cases and appeals from justice of the peace courts.
- **Supreme Court (1691–):** County court holding original jurisdiction over equity cases. See counties for records. For more information see *Duely and Constantly Kept: A History of the New York Supreme Court, 1691–1847 and an Inventory of its Records (Albany, Utica, and Geneva Offices), 1797–1847* (Albany: New York State Court of Appeals and State Archives, 1991).
- **Court of Vice-Admiralty (1697–1775):** Records of the Vice-Admiralty Court of the Province of New York, 1701–74 (film 1025187/T842) are at the National Archives Northeast Region in New York City. Admiralty courts that existed prior to this time have been transcribed in Christoph, Peter R. *Dongan Papers, 1683–1688: Admiralty Court and Other Records of the Administration of New York Governor, Thomas Dongan* (Syracuse, NY: Holland Society of New York, 1993). Vice-Admiralty records during the occupation of New York City (through 1783) are at the PRO in Kew, Surrey, England (see Great Britain).

Scott, Kenneth. *Genealogical Data from Inventories of New York Estates, 1666–1825* (New York: NYGBS, 1970).[40]

The Colonial Laws of New York from the Year 1664 to the Revolution: Including the Charters to the Duke of York, the Commissions and Instructions to Colonial Governors, the Duke's Laws, the Laws of the Dongan and Leisler Assemblies, the Charters of Albany and New York and the Acts of the Colonial Legislatures from 1691 to 1775 Inclusive. 4 Vols. (Albany: James B. Lyon, State Printer, 1894, film 1421794 ff.).

Complete Index to Colonial Laws and Ordinances of New Netherland and New York, 1638–1775 (Knightstown, IN: Bookmark, 1977, film 1036082).

O'Callaghan, E.B. *Calendar of New York Colonial Commissions, 1680–1770* (New York: New-York Historical Society, 1929).

---

[40] New York Genealogical and Biographical Society, hereinafter known as NYGBS.

Fernow, Berthold. *Calendar of Council Minutes, 1668–1783* (Harrison, NY: Harbor Hill Books, 1987, film 1320694).

Publications to identify the whereabouts of original records are:
- New York Secretary of State. *Annalium Thesaurus, 1629–1767* (n.p., n.d., film 0947119). This is an inventory of records in the Office of the Secretary of State of Dutch records, English colonial records, and state records.
- O'Callaghan, E.B. *Calendar of Historical Manuscripts in the Office of the Secretary of State, Albany, New York.* 2 Vols. (Ridgewood, NJ: Gregg Press, 1968, fiche 6051113). Dutch manuscripts, 1630–64, English manuscripts, 1664–1776.
- Van Laer, Arnold J. F. *Documents Relating to New Netherland, 1624–1626: In the Henry E. Huntington Library* (San Marino, CA: Henry E. Huntington Library and Art Gallery, 1924).
- Gehring, Charles T. *A Guide to Dutch Manuscripts Relating to New Netherland in United States Repositories* (Albany: New York State Library, 1978).

O'Callaghan. E.B. *Documents Relative to the Colonial History of the State of New York: Procured in Holland, England, and France.* 15 Vols. (Albany: Weed, Parsons and Co., 1853–87, film 0824380 ff.). The series includes:

Vols. 1–2 Holland documents
Vols. 3–8 London documents
Vols. 9–10 Paris documents
Vol. 11 General Index to the documents
Vol. 12 Documents relating Dutch and Swedish settlements on the Delaware River

Vol. 13 Document relating to settlements of the towns along the Hudson and Mohawk rivers (with the exception of Albany), 1630–84
Vol. 14 Documents relating to early colonial settlements principally on Long Island
Vol. 15 New York in the Revolution

New York State Historian. *Annual Report* (Albany: Synkoop, Hallenbeck, Crawford, State Printers, n.d., fiche 6088376). Colonial Series Vol. I–II: contains colonial records, 1664–75, and muster rolls, 1664–1775.

A published census collection can be found in *Lists of Inhabitants of Colonial New York: Excerpted from the Documentary History of the State of New York, by Edmund Bailey O'Callaghan* (Baltimore: Genealogical Publishing Co., 1979, fiche 6046723). The original work in its entirety is available as O'Callaghan, E.B. *The Documentary History of the State of New York.* 4 Vols. (Albany: Weed,

Parson, Public Printers, 1849, fiche 6051121). This also contains passenger lists, 1654–64, as found in the New York Colonial Manuscripts (14:83–123), of a Dutch West India Company account book preserved at the State Archives in Albany.[41] A more complete translation of the list is Van Laer, Arnold J.F. "Passengers to New Netherland: List of Passengers, 1654–1664." *Year Book of the Holland Society of New York* (1902): 1–37 (film 0908989).

Land Records
In addition to the manorial grants, many settlers owned their own land. Patents, deeds, grants, and surveys are mostly found at the State Archives in Albany. The earliest patents date from 1630. New England colonists on Long Island and the Connecticut-New York border granted land on a township level. Large tracts of land were granted in western and central New York. Land in Vermont was also granted by the General Assembly of New York from 1764 to 1777.

New York Secretary of State.
- Translation of books of Dutch patents, 1630–74 (film 0947104).
- Land grant application files, 1642–1803. Indexed in:
- *Calendar of New York Colonial Manuscripts, Indorsed Land Papers; in the Office of the Secretary of State of New York, 1643–1803* (1864. Revised Reprint. Harrison, NY: Harbor Hill Books, 1987, 1ˢᵗ ed. on film 0930250).
- Deeds, 1659–1846 (film 0947105 ff.). This includes an index to deeds for land grants in Vermont.
- Land survey field notes, 1665–1927
- Field books and index, 1702–1881
- Escheated land records, 1749–1830 (film 0947117).
- Land patent transcriptions, 1664–1786 (film 0945288 ff.).
- Index to military patents and abstracts, 1764–97 (film 0946418).
- Patents, 1708–1973 (film 0947096 ff.), including the following:

Colonial patent index, 1644–1775
Colonial patent grantee card index, 1638–1780
Arthurboro patent: Brant Lake tract
Canadian and Nova Scotia: Hague tract
Hardenburgh patent: Niagra River tract

North River Head: Onondaga Reservation
Saint Regis Reservation: Townships
Oxbow tract : Roaring Brook tract
Delaware, Massachusetts, New Jersey
Index to patents, 1664–1864
Military patents, 1764–97

Gehring, Charles T. *New York Historical Manuscripts: Dutch. Land Papers, Volumes GG, HH, and II* [1630–1664] (Baltimore: Genealogical Publishing Co., 1980). Also includes New Jersey records.

---

[41] Available on microfilm at the State Archives in Albany, and the New York Public Library and the NYGBS in New York City.

O'Callaghan, E. B. *History of New Netherland, Or, New York under the Dutch.* 2 Vols. (New York: D. Appleton, 1846–8, fiche 6101198 ff.). Includes a list of patents issued by the Dutch government from 1630–64.

Van Laer, Arnold J. *New York Historical Manuscripts: Dutch. Register of the Provincial Secretary, 1638–1660.* 4 Vols. (Baltimore: Genealogical Publishing Co., 1974). Contains land conveyances, 1638–60.

Van Wyck, Frederick. *Select Patents of New York Towns* (Boston: A.A. Beauchamp, 1938, fiche 6088609). Contains discussions of patents of Flushing, (Queens County), Brooklyn (Kings County), and Ulster County.

Bowman, Fred. *Landholders of Northeastern New York, 1739–1802* (Baltimore: Genealogical Publishing Co., 1983, film 1321009).

Christoph, Florence A. *Upstate New York in the 1760s, Tax Lists and Selected Militia Rolls of Old Albany County, 1760–1768* (Camden, ME: Picton Press, 1992).

New-York Historical Society

New-York Historical Society manuscripts were damaged by a fire at the New York Public Library in 1911. Many of the collections have been transcribed or revised and reprinted by Genealogical Publishing Company and Heart of the Lakes Publishing Company. The original series is still available in libraries and on microfilm:

Collections of the New-York Historical Society. 60 Vols. (New York: The Society, 1869–1927, film 0845284 ff.). This series includes:

Vol. 1 Continuation of Chalmers's political annals; The Colden letters on Smith's *History*, 1759–60; Documents relating to the administration of Leisler

Vol. 2 The Clarendon papers; Tracts relating to New York; Gardiner's East Hampton; New York and the New Hampshire grants

Vol. 3 Territorial rights of New York, the New Hampshire grants; Old New York and Trinity Church

Vols. 4–7 The Lee papers

Vol. 8 Official letters

Vols. 9–10 Colden papers

Vols. 11–13 Revolutionary and other papers

Vols. 14 The Montresor journals

Vol. 15 Revolutionary War journals

Vols. 16–17 The Kemble papers

Vol. 18 The Burghers of New Amsterdam and the freemen of New York, 1675–1866

Vols. 19–23 The Deane papers

Vol. 24 Muster rolls of New York provincial troops, 1755–64

Vols. 25–41 Abstracts of wills on file, Surrogate's Office, City of New York, 1665–1801

Vol. 42 Chamberlain's Office, Corporation

of the City of New York, 1691–9;
Indentures of apprentices, 1718–27
Vols. 43–4 Tax lists, City of New York,
1695–9
Vol. 45 Proceedings of the General Court of
Assizes held in the City of New York,
1680–2
Vol. 46 Original book of New York deeds,
1672/3 –5
Vols. 47–8 Muster and pay rolls of the War
of the Revolution, 1775–83

Vol. 49 Proceedings of a board of general
officers of the British Army at New
York, 1781
Vols. 50–1 Letters and papers of
Cadwallader Colden, 1711–42
Vols. 57–8 Minutes of the Committee for
Detecting Defeating Conspiracies in
the State of New York, 1776–8
Vols. 59–60 Papers of the Lloyd family of
the manor of Queens Village, Lloyd'
Neck, Long Island, 1654–1826

Collections of the New-York Historical Society. Second Series (New York: The Society, 1841–, film 0845305). This series includes the following:

Verrazano's voyage, 1524
Indian tradition of the first arrival of the
Dutch on Manhattan Island
Lambrechtsen's *History of New Netherland*
Van der Donck's description of New Netherland
Extracts from the voyages of De Vries
Extracts from De Laet's *New World*
Juet's journal of Hudson's voyage
Argall's expedition, 1613
Correspondence between New Netherland
and New Plymouth, 1627
Charter of liberties and other documents
Catalogue of Dutch Church members, 1686
New Sweden history
Voyages from Holland to America, 1632–44

Short sketch of the Mohawk Indians in New
Netherland
The Jogues papers
Extract: Castell's *Discoverie of America*, 1644
Broad advice to the United Netherland
Province
Extract from Wagenaar's *Beschryving van
Amsterdam*
Seven articles from the Church of Leyden,
1617
Negotiations between New England and
Canada, 1648–51
Proceedings of the first Assembly of
Virginia, 1619

Van Laer, Arnold J. *New York Historical Manuscripts: Dutch. Register of the Provincial Secretary, 1638–1660.* 4 Vols. (Baltimore: Genealogical Publishing Co., 1974). Contains the most basic Dutch records.

Gehring, Charles T. *New York Historical Manuscripts: Dutch. Council Minutes, 1652–1654* (Baltimore: Genealogical Publishing Co., 1983).

Gehring, Charles T. *New York Historical Manuscripts: Dutch. Delaware Papers.* (Dutch Period) (Baltimore: Genealogical Publishing Co., 1981). Documents pertaining the regulation of affairs on the South River of New Netherland, 1648–64.

Gehring, Charles T. *New York Historical Manuscripts: Dutch. Delaware Papers* (English Period) (Baltimore: Genealogical Publishing Co., 1977). Documents pertaining to the regulation of affairs on the Delaware, 1664–82.

Church Records

The first religious denominations in New York were the Reformed Dutch, French Protestant, and Lutheran churches. Society of Friends meetings were held in the 1650s. The first Jews arrived from Brazil in 1654, but a synagogue was not built until 1730. A Lutheran parish was organized in Albany in 1669. Huguenots established a French Protestant Church in 1685, and an Anglican Church was founded in 1697. Baptists were on Long Island before 1700.

An inventory to the New York records is *Guide to Vital Statistics in the Records of Churches in New York State* (Albany: Historical Records Survey, 1942, fiche 6046729) and *Inventory of the Church Archives in the City of New York.* 9 Vols. (New York: Historical Records Survey, 1942, see denomination for film number). Some of the denominations covered are Protestant Episcopal (fiche 6011785), Presbyterian (film 1036716), Lutheran (film 1036522), Reformed (film 1035526), and Society of Friends (film 0017255).

Also useful in finding Reformed Church records is Gasero, Russell L. *Guide to Local Church Records in Archives of the Reformed Church of America and to Genealogical Resources in the Gardiner Sage Library, New Brunswick Theological Seminary* (New Brunswick: Historical Society of the Reformed Church in America, 1979, fiche 6046480).

There are many collections of New York church records that have been filmed, including the Reformed Dutch Church Collection, the Vosburgh Collection of New York Church Records, and the Society of Friends Archives. See New York County for more information.

Holland Society of New York.
* Compiled genealogies (film 1016510 ff.). Files include records of compiled family genealogies, Bibles, cemeteries, etc.
* Manuscript and historical genealogical collection (film 1013471 ff.). Alphabetically arranged files contain records of correspondence, genealogy, family records, Bible records, church records, cemeteries, etc.
* *Inventory and Digest of Early Church Records in the Library of the Holland Society of New York* (New York: Holland Society of New York, 1912, film 1421917). Covers churches in New York, New Jersey, and Pennsylvania.

Vosburgh, Royden Woodward. New York Church Records: Vosburgh Collection (film 0017441 ff.) The transcribed records that begin before 1775 are:

Albany, First Lutheran Church, 1774–1901

Canaan, Congregational Church of New Canaan, 1740–1884

Claverack, Saint Thomas' Evangelical Lutheran Church, Churchtown, 1705–1905

Germantown, Christ's Evangelical Lutheran Church, 1746–1877

Ghent, Reformed Dutch Church called Christ Church, 1775–1919

Kinderhook, Reformed Dutch Church, 1716–1864

Livingston, Saint John's Evangelical Lutheran Church, Manorton, 1765–1848

Pine Plains, Round Top Lutheran Church, 1760–88

Florida, United Presbyterian Church, 1743–1861

Catskill, Reformed Dutch Church, 1732–1833

Coxsackie, First Reformed Dutch Church, 1738–1918

German Flats, Reformed Protestant Dutch Church, 1753–1848

Fonda, Reformed Protestant Dutch Church of Caughnawaga, now the Reformed Church of Fonda, 1758–1858

Palatine, Lutheran Trinity Church of Stone Arabia, 1751–1866

Palatine, Reformed Dutch Church of Stone Arabia, 1739–1911

Schodack, Reformed Dutch Church at Muitzeskill, 1770–1846

Stillwater, First Congregational Church, 1752–1852

Schoharie, Reformed Church, 1728–1892

Schoharie, Saint Paul's Evangelical Lutheran Church, 1728–1882

New York Secretary of State. *New York Marriages Previous to 1784: A Reprint of the Original Edition of 1860 with Additions and Corrections Including: Supplementary List of Marriage Licenses; New York Marriage Licenses* (1860. Reprint. Baltimore: Genealogical Publishing Co., 1968).

Marriage Index: Selected Areas of New York, 1639–1916 (Broderbund, 1996). This CD-ROM contains marriage information from selected areas of New York for approximately 152,000 individuals. It includes some of the earliest known church and government marriage information, from 1639, and continues through the eighteenth and nineteenth centuries.

County Records and Resources

The original twelve counties were formed in 1683: Albany, Cornwall, Dukes (annexed to Massachusetts in 1695), Dutchess, Kings, New York, Orange, Queens, Richmond, Suffolk, Ulster, and Westchester.

Albany County (established 1683)

Albany County Clerk.

- Treasurer records, 1702–12 (film 0463369).
- Court minutes, 1652–1782 0463361 ff.).

- Proceedings, justices of the peace, 1665–85 (film 0463368).
- Proceedings of commissioners, 1676–80, notarial papers, 1660–95 (film 0463366 ff.).
- Index to deeds, 1630–1966 (film 0464896 ff.).
- Mortgages, 1652–60, 1765–1830; indexes, 1630–1894 (film 0466856 ff.).
- Wills, 1691–1835 (film 0463364).

Albany County Supreme Court.
- Index to maps, 1630–1904 (film 0466871).
- Hamlin, P.M. and C.E. Baker. *Supreme Court of Judicature of the Province of New York, 1691–1704* (Charlottesville: University of Virginia, 1975).

Albany County Chancery Court. Index to Court of Chancery records, plaintiff and defendant, 1600s–1800s (film 0501159).

Albany County Surrogate's Court.
- Original records of administrations of estates, 1700–1825, and inventories and accounts, 1600s–1700s (film 0504477 ff.).
- Record of wills, 1629–1802 (film 0481435 ff.).

Published records include:

Fernow, Berthold. *Calendar of Wills on File and Recorded in the Offices of the Clerk of the Court of Appeals, of the County Clerk at Albany and of the Secretary of State, 1626–1836* (New York: Colonial Dames of the State of New York, 1896, fiche 6046668).

Van Laer, Arnold J.F. *Minutes of the Court of Fort Orange and Beverwyck, 1652–1660.* 2 Vols. (Albany: University of the State of New York, 1920–3, film 1321279). Reprinted as Gehring, Charles T. *New Netherland, Inferior Court of Justice, Beverwyck. Fort Orange Court Minutes, 1652–1660* (Syracuse, NY: Holland Society of New York, 1990).

Van Laer, Arnold J.F. *Minutes of the Court of Rensselaerswyck, 1648–1652* (Albany: University of the State of New York, 1922, film 1321474).

Van Laer, Arnold J.F. *Minutes of the Court of Albany, Rensselaerswyck, and Schenectady, 1668–1673, 1675–1685.* 3 Vols. (Albany: University of the State of New York, 1926–32).

Gehring, Charles T. *New Netherland Laws and Writs of Appeal, 1647–1663* (Syracuse, NY: Syracuse University Press, 1991).

Van Laer, Arnold J.F. *Early Records of the City and County of Albany and Colony of Resselaerswyck.* 4 Vols. (Albany: University of the State of New York, 1869–1919, film 0924668). Includes deeds, 1656–1704, notarial papers, 1660–6, mortgages, 1658, and wills, 1681–1765.

Van Rensselaer Manor papers (film 1697716). Manuscript maps of portions of the East Manor and the West Manor, field notes and surveys of all the towns of the East Manor and of Berne (including the present town of Knox) in the West Manor, leases, miscellaneous papers and documents, deeds, mortgages, agreements, and covenants; ledgers and books of record of the proprietor of the Manor showing the accounts between the patron and the tenants and giving the chain of title for much of the land in Albany and Rensselaer counties.

Church Records

Some of the manuscripts and original records at the State Library in Albany are:

*   Saint Peter's Episcopal Church, Albany. Records, 1756–1883 (film 0017506).

*   Albany Lutheran Society Baptisms, 1704–23, at Albany and Loonenburg (Athens); Newtown and Kisketamesy baptisms, 1725–39, deaths, 1710–12, 1726–9 (film 0529185).

*   Madison Avenue Reformed Church, Albany. Records, 1683–1913 (film 0534205).

*   First Reformed Church at Albany. Records, 1718–1825 (film 0017507 ff.).

Reformed Dutch Church at Albany. Records, 1683–1909 (film 1016557 ff.). The transcript is at the Holland Society of New York in New York City. Also published as *Records of the Reformed Dutch Church of Albany, New York, 1683–1809: Marriages, Baptisms, Members, Etc. Excerpted from the Year Books of The Holland Society of New York* (Baltimore: Genealogical Publishing, 1978).

Evangelical Lutheran Church called Ebenezer, Albany. Index to records, 1774–1842 (film 1293950). The manuscript is at the Montgomery County Department of History and Archives in Fonda.

Reformed Dutch Church of the Beaver Dam, Berne. Records, 1763–1877 (film 0017528). Also known as the First Reformed Dutch Church of Berne. The transcript is at the NYGBS in New York City.

Church of Jesus Christ, Albany. *Names of the Members of the Church of Jesus Christ at New Albany, at the End of the Year 1683, and Afterward* (n.p., n.d., film 0823764).

Society of Friends, Coeymans. Monthly meeting records, 1761–1867 (film 0017387 ff.) Coeymans Meeting was located in the town of New Baltimore, Greene County. The original records are at the Society of Friends Archives in New York City.

Bronx County

See Westchester County.

Columbia County (established 1786 from Albany County)

List of debts due by Palatines living in the four villages in the Manor of Livingston, 1709–26: includes one list of debtors from other places,

1709–10 (film 0017137). Records, 1717–26, are for the villages of Hunterstown, Kingsberry, Annsberry, and Haysberry within Livingston Manor. Records, 1709–10, are for all the manors along the Hudson River. The Livingston manuscripts are in the Johnston Livingston Redmont estate papers at the New York Public Library in New York City.

Church Records

Some original records at the Archives of the Reformed Church in America in New Brunswick, New Jersey are:

• Reformed Dutch Church, Gallatin. Records, 1748–1900 (film 0963011 ff.). Originated in 1748 as Reformed Protestant Dutch Church in the Town of Ancram and rebuilt in 1823 as Gallatin Reformed Church. Also known as Stissing, Livingston Manor, Greenbush, and Vedder. These records include Dutchess County.

• Reformed Protestant Dutch Church of Linlithgo at Livingston. Records, 1722–1964 (film 1928066).

Some records and manuscripts at the State Library in Albany are:

• First Reformed Church of Germantown. Records, 1728–1884 (film 0532617). Formerly known as the German Reformed Church of The Camp.

• Reformed Dutch Church of Kinderhook. Records, 1716–1864 (film 0534198 ff.).

• Saint John's Evangelical Lutheran Church at Manorton, Livingston. Records, 1732–1875 (film 0534200).

• Saint Thomas Evangelical Lutheran Church, Churchtown, Claverack District. Records, 1760–1864 (film 0534192).

Reformed Dutch Church of Claverack. Records, 1726–1801(film 1016559). The transcript is at the Holland Society of New York in New York City.

Christ Evangelical Lutheran Church at Germantown. Records, 1764–1864 (film 1293950). The manuscript is at the Montgomery County Department of History and Archives in Fonda.

Dutchess County (established 1683)

Original records at the Dutchess County Courthouse in Poughkeepsie are:
Dutchess County Board of Supervisors.

• *Book of Supervisors and Old Miscellaneous Records of Dutchess County.* 3 Vols. (Poughkeepsie, NY: Vassar Brothers' Institute, 1907–11, film 1036811).

• Tax lists, 1717–79, supervisors' records, 1771–94 (film 0925907 ff.).

Dutchess County Clerk.

• Docket of declarations, 1768–1808 (film 0925899).

• Dockets of writs and executions, 1758–72 (film 0925057).

- Record of roads, 1744–88 (film 0923908).
- Declarations, pleas, records of the Court of General Sessions and Common Pleas, 1721–1864 (film 0565226 ff.).
- Ancient documents, 1721–1862 (film 0931616 ff.). Probate records, warrants for arrest, court cases, statements of debt, bonds, etc.
- Deed records, 1718–1901 (film 0565253 ff.).
- Mortgages, 1754–1857 (film 0565278 ff.).
- Loan office minutes, 1771–9, accounts, 1771–7 (film 0925900 ff.).
- Records of the loan office, 1771–1882 (film 0565219 ff.).
- Index of deeds deposited with the loan commissioners, 1771–1861 (film 0925056).

Dutchess County Surrogate's Court.
- Land records, 1697–1907 (film 0940248).
- Wills, 1751–1903 (film 0913658 ff.).

Buck, Clifford and William McDermott. *Eighteenth Century Documents of the Nine Partners Patent, Dutchess County, New York* (Baltimore: Gateway Press, 1979, fiche 6088543).

Original records and transcripts at the Adriance Memorial Library in Poughkeepsie are:
- Collection and indexes (film 0931498 ff.). Includes appointments to public office, 1744–1872, court proceedings, 1718–1927, deeds, surveys, 1739–1913, appointments to and removal from public office, 1752–1847, miscellaneous family and county records.
- Extracts of mortgages, 1754–99 (film 0940239).
- Miscellaneous records of roads, wills, precinct allowances, and charges, 1742–70 (film 0940240).
- Land and tax records, 1718–42 (film 0940240).
- Dutchess County precincts, 1738–99: Crum Elbow Precinct, Charlotte Precinct, Clinton Precinct (film 0940279).
- Deeds, town of Fishkill (Rambout Precinct), 1720–92 (film 0940241).
- Fishkill will extracts, 1766–85 (film 0940239).
- Tax lists, 1757–71, 1786 (film 0940242).
- Christ's Church, Poughkeepsie, Episcopal. Records, 1734–1855 (film 0940278).
- First Reformed Church, Poughkeepsie. Records, 1716–1824 (film 0940278).
- Poughkeepsie Town Clerk. Town records, 1769–1850 (film 0930250).
- Beekman Town Clerk. Town records, 1772–1827, covering towns of Beekman, La Grange (Greedom), and Unionvale (film 0929819).

Church Records (see also Adriance Memorial Library, above)
Koehler, Linda. *Dutchess County, New York, Churches and Their Records, an Historical Directory* (Rhinebeck, NY: Kinship, 1994).

Some records and transcripts at the NYGBS in New York City are:
- Amenia Presbyterian Church. Records, 1756–1864 (film 0931485).
- Old Red Meeting House, Amenia. Baptisms, 1749–1815 (film 0017517).
- Trinity Church, Fishkill. Records, 1733–1808 (film 0017636).
- Round Top Lutheran Church, Pine Plains. Records, 1760–88 (film 0017828 ff.).
- Reformed Dutch Church, Kingston. Records, 1663–1881 (film 0017734). Also known as Wiltwyck or Esopus Church. Records also include Ulster County.

Some records and transcripts at the State Library in Albany are:
- First Baptist Church of Christ, Dover. Records, 1757–1844 (film 0529189).
- Dover First Baptist Church, Wingdale. Records, 1758–1922 (film 0931486).
- Flatts Reformed Dutch Church, Rhinebeck. Records, 1731–98 (film 0533474).
- Saint Peter's Lutheran Church, Rhinebeck. Records, 1733–1806 (film 0533473).
- Presbyterian Church of South Amenia. Records, 1759–85 (film 0017961).
- Saint Paul's Lutheran Church, Wurtemburg. Records, 1760–1874 (film 0533475). The village of Wurtemburg was located in the in the town of Rhinebeck.

Some transcripts at the Montgomery County Department of History and Archives in Fonda are:
- Reformed Dutch Church of Fishkill. Records, 1717–1850 (film 0514682).
- Red Church of Tivoli (Old Red Hook Church). Baptisms, 1766–1813 (film 1293951).

Reformed Dutch Church, New Hackensack, New York: Records, 1757–1906 (Poughkeepsie, NY: Dutchess County Historical Society, 1932, film 1206459).

Some original records at the Society of Friends Archives in New York City are:
- Society of Friends, Nine Partners, Washington. Monthly meeting records, 1769–1862 (film 0017306 ff.). Includes manumission of slaves, 1769–98.
- Society of Friends, Nine Partners, Washington. Hicksite. Monthly meeting records, 1769–1898 (film 0017307 ff.).
- Society of Friends, Oblong, Quaker Hill, Hicksite. Monthly meeting records, 1745–1893 (film 0017313 ff.).

Records and transcripts at the Holland Society of New York in New York City are:

- Congregation of Roode Hoek (Red Hook) Records, 1766–1814 (film 1016878).
- Reformed Church at Reyn Beek (Rhinebeck). Records, 1730–1803 (film 1016871).
- Hopewell Dutch Church. Records, 1766–1811 (film 1016562).

Saint John's Reformed Dutch Church, Upper Red Hook. Records, 1766–1900 (film 1928067). The original records are at the Archives of the Reformed Church in America, New Brunswick, New Jersey.

Fulton County (established 1838 from Montgomery County)
Fulton County Clerk. Deeds, 1772–1908 (film 0513920 ff.). The original records are at the Fulton County Courthouse in Johnston.

Saint John's Episcopal Church, Johnstown. Records, 1772–1900 (film 0533498). The transcript is at the State Library in Albany.

Kings County (established 1683, see also New York County)
Kings County Clerk. Conveyances, 1683–1950 (film 1413114 ff.)
Kings County Surrogate's Court. Record of inventories, 1723–1923 (film 1553447).
The original records are at the City Registrar's Office in Brooklyn and the Municipal Building in New York City.

Church Records (see also New York County)
Original records of the above are at the Archives of the Reformed Church in America, New Brunswick, New Jersey are:
- Flatlands Reformed Dutch Church, Brooklyn. Records, 1673–1881 (film 0888716).
- Reformed Dutch First Church, Brooklyn. Records, 1660–99 (film 1927966).
- Reformed Dutch New Utrecht Church, Brooklyn. Records, 1718–1922 (film 1927967).

Reformed Dutch Church of Jesus Christ gathered at Gravesend. Records, 1715–1805 (film 1016877). The transcript is at the Holland Society of New York in New York City.

Dutch Reformed Church, Brooklyn. Index to the First Book of Records, 1660–1719 (New York: n.p., 1957, film 0823735).

Montgomery County (established as Tryon County in 1772, renamed in 1784; see also Washington County)
Montgomery County Court of General Sessions. Minutes of General Sessions and Court of Common Pleas, 1772–1806 (film 0513997). The records are at the Montgomery County Department of History and Archives in Fonda.

Penrose, M. Barton. *Mohawk Valley Land Records: Abstracts, 1738–1788* (Franklin Park, NJ: Liberty Bell Associates, 1985).

Church Records

United Presbyterian Church, Florida. Records, 1743–1933 (film 0533498). The transcript is at the State Library in Albany.
Reformed Dutch Church of Fonda. Records, 1758–1803 (film 1016561). Also known as the Reformed Dutch Protestant Church of Cauhnawaga. The transcript is at the Holland Society of New York in New York City.

New York County and City (county established 1683)
Prior to 1787, probate records in New York County included records from most counties in the province. Wills covering the entire colony of New York were recorded with the Prerogative Court and later with the Court of Probate under the first Constitution of the state.

Original records and manuscripts at the New York County Courthouse in New York City and the State Archives in Albany are:
New York County Chancery Court.
* Minutes, 1711–1847 (film 0590388 ff.).
* Index to records, 1700–1848 (film 1204888).
* Index to chancery decrees, 1764–1847 (film 1017477).
New York County Court of General Sessions.
* Minute books, 1683–1731 (film 0497558).
* Minutes, 1705–14, 1722–42 (film 1021265). Includes Mayor's Court records, 1733–42, for New York City.
New York County Court of Oyer and Terminer. Minutes, 1716–17, for various counties (film 1021265).
New York County Supreme Court.
* Minute books, 1704–1847 (film 1018632 ff.).
* Index to pleadings, 1754–1910 (film 1204906 ff.).
New York County Courts.
* Index to parchments, 1686–1847 (film 1204976 ff.).
* Miscellaneous court and civil records, 1767–1889 (film 0497581 ff.).
* Conveyances, 1654–1866 (film 0888232 ff.).
* Index to conveyances, 1680–1941 (film 1413946 ff.).
* Mortgages, 1754–1851 (film 0888287 ff.).

New York County Surrogate's Court.
* Wills, 1665–1916, index, 1662–1923 (film 0872164 ff.).
* Will libers, New York City, 1662–1927 (film 0501139 ff.).
* Administration bonds, 1753–1866 (film 0907917 ff.).
* Letters of administration, 1768–1866, index, 1743–1871 (film 0872170 ff.).
* Wills and administrations, 1680–1804 (film 0497592 ff.).

Original records and manuscripts at the Municipal Archives in New York City are:
City of New York.
* Almshouse records of admissions, discharges, and deaths, 1759–1861 (film 1311487 ff.).
* Mayor's Court council minutes, 1731–8 (film 1021264).
* Mayor's Court minutes, 1674–1821 (film 1021714 ff.).
* New York City Assessor. Assessment roll, 1699–1782 (film 0484033).

Collections of the New-York Historical Society:[42]
* *Proceedings of the General Court of Assizes Held in the City of New York October 6, 1680 to October 6, 1682; Minutes of the Supreme Court of Judicature, April 4, 1693 to April 1, 1701* (New York: The Society, 1913, film 0845302). The General Court of Assizes had original jurisdiction in all criminal matters and civil cases of over twenty pounds.
* *Original Book of New York Deeds, January 1st 1672/3 to October 19th, 1675* (New York: The Society, 1914, film 0845303). Also includes miscellaneous documents relating to the City of New York and Long Island, 1642–96; Melyn papers, 1640–99 (relating to Staten Island).
* *Tax Lists of the City of New York, December 1695 to July 15th, 1699; Assessment of the Real and Personal Property of the East Ward, City of New York, June 24, 1791.* 2 Vols. (New York: The Society, 1911, film 0845302).
* *Abstracts of Wills on File in the Surrogate's Office, City of New York, 1665–1801.* 17 Vols. (New York: The Society, 1893–1909, fiche 6046928).
* *New York Bureau of City Chamberlain: Ledger Number I, Chamberlain's Office, Corporation of the City of New York, May 11, 1691, to November 12, 1699; Indentures of Apprentices, October 21, 1718, to August 7, 1727* (New York: The Society, 1910, film 0845302).

Other published records include:
Fernow, Berthold. *Minutes of the Orphanmasters of New Amsterdam, 1655 to 1663* (1902. Reprint. Washington, DC: Library of Congress, 1975, film 1730415).

---

[42] See the section on state records for a complete list.

Fernow, Berthold. *The Records of New Amsterdam from 1653 to 1674 Anno Domini*. 7 Vols. (1897. Reprint. Baltimore: Genealogical Publishing Co., 1976, film 0982184 ff.).

Scott, Kenneth. *New York City Court Records, 1684–1760: Genealogical Data from the Court of Quarter Sessions* (Washington, DC: National Genealogical Society, 1982).

Scott, Kenneth. *New York City Court Records, 1760–1797: Genealogical Data from the Court of Quarter Sessions* (Washington, DC: National Genealogical Society, 1983).

O'Callaghan, E.B. *The Register of Salomon Lachaire, Notary Public of New Amsterdam, 1661–1662: Translated from the Original Dutch Manuscript in the Office of the Clerk of the Common Council of New York* (Baltimore: Genealogical Publishing Co., 1978).

Church Records

New York Genealogical and Biographical Society, New York City. Collection of transcripts of church records by various individuals:

*   Reformed Dutch Church, New York City. Burial register, 1726–1804 (film 0017777).
*   Reformed Dutch Church, New York City. Records, 1649–1810 (film 0017778).
*   Reformed Dutch Church in New Amsterdam and New York City. Marriages, 1639–1801 (fiche 6016529 ff.).
*   Reformed Protestant Dutch Church, Flatbush, Kings County. Records, 1677–1872 (film 0017663). Flatbush is now part of metropolitan New York.
*   New Dorp, Richmond County. Cemetery and church records, 1742–1892 (film 0017902).
*   Reformed Dutch Church, Port Richmond. Baptisms, 1696–1772 (film 0476226).
*   United Brethren Congregation (Moravian). Records, 1749–1863 (film 0476226).
*   Saint Andrews' Church, Richmond. Records, 1752–1808 (film 0476226).
*   First Moravian Church, New York City. Records, 1707–1890 (film 0017783).
*   First Presbyterian Church, New York City. Records, 1769–1809 (film 0017783).
*   First Presbyterian Church, New York City. Records, 1717–1977 (film 1017607 ff.). Organized in 1716 as Wall Street Congregation.
*   Marriages (before the Revolutionary War) and baptisms (prior to 1720) of the Dutch Church in New York: also list of early immigrants to New Netherland (film 0162019).

Moravian Church, Staten Island. Church records, 1749–1965 (film 0514669). The original and typewritten records are at the United Brethren Church, New Dorp.

Reformed Dutch Church of New York City. Records, 1639–1774 (film 1927968). The original records are at the Archives of the Reformed Church in America, New Brunswick, New Jersey.

Original records and transcripts at the Society of Friends Archives in New York City are:
- Monthly meeting records, 1762–1887 (film 0017378 ff.). Established as Flushing Monthly Meeting in 1695, and name changed to New York Monthly Meeting in 1795. At various times has met alternately in Flushing, New York, and Newtown.
- Hicksite Monthly Meeting records, 1640–1904 (film 0017376 ff.).
- New York Friends, 1671–1792 (film 0017256). Includes Westbury quarterly minutes, 1671–1702, Flushing monthly minutes, 1685–1703, and New York yearly minutes, 1696–1792.
- New York Yearly Meeting. Memorials of New York Yearly Meeting deceased Friends, 1707–1820 (film 0017353).

Lutheran Church records at Saint Matthew's Lutheran Church in New York City are:
- Trinity Lutheran Church, New York City. Church records, 1704–83 (film 1901794 ff.). A congregation was founded in Manhattan in 1664; in 1729 Trinity Lutheran Church grew out of the Manhattan congregations. Trinity Church was destroyed by fire in 1776.
- Christ Lutheran Church, New York City. Church records, 1752–1814 (film 1901794 ff.). The church was organized in Manhattan in 1749 by German members of Trinity Lutheran, eventually merging in 1784 as the United German Lutheran Churches.

The Holland Society of New York in New York City has a collection of Reformed Dutch church records, mostly transcriptions. All of the following are Reformed Dutch records:
- Church at Flatlands, Long Island. Baptisms, 1747–1802 (film 0017637).
- Church at New Utrecht, Kings County. Baptisms, 1718–41 (film 1016562).
- Church at Flatbush, Kings County. Records, 1677–1757 (film 1016562).
- Church at Breukelen (Brooklyn). Records, 1660–1710 (film 1016558).
- Church at Port Richmond, Staten Island. Records, 1696–1849 (film 1016876).
- Church at Jamaica, Long Island. Records, 1702–1805 (film 1016558).
- Church at New Town, Long Island. Records, 1731–1845 (film 1016878).
- Church at New York City. Records, 1698–1850 (film 1016869).
- First Church at Jamaica, Long Island. Records, 1702–1863 (film 1019523).

Wittmeyer, Alfred Victor. *Registers of the Births, Marriages and Deaths of the 'Eglise Françoise À La Nouvelle York,' from 1688–1804* (New York: Huguenot Society of America, 1886. Reprint. Baltimore: Genealogical Publishing Co., 1968, film 1033670).

Orange County
Original records at the Orange County Courthouse in Goshen are:
Orange County Court of Common Pleas. Court minutes, 1727–1856 (film 0830706 ff.).
Orange County Clerk.
* Deeds, 1703–1900 (film 0826917 ff.).
* Mortgages, 1754–1851, index, 1703–1869 (film 0829315 ff.).

Early Orange County Wills, 1731–1830 (Goshen, NY: Orange County Genealogical Society, 1991, fiche 6117875). Abstracts of wills, 1731–88, Surrogate's Office, City of New York; abstracts of wills, 1787–1830, Orange County Surrogate's Office.

Historical Records Survey. *Minutes of the Town Courts of Newtown, 1656–1690* (New York: The Survey, 1940, fiche 6104134).

Church Records
Reformed Dutch Church Records in Ulster and Orange County (n.p., n.d., film 1405479). Includes baptisms and marriages in Kingston 1766–76, Catsbaan 1730–60, and later records.

Some transcripts of church records at the NYGBS in New York City are:
* Reformed Dutch Church of Machackemeck, Deerpark. Records, 1716–1827 (film 0017859).
* Minisink Valley Reformed Dutch Church. Records, 1716–1830 (film 0599307).
* German Reformed Church of Montgomery. Records, 1734–1849 (film 0017751). This church was also called Brick Reformed Church.
* Reformed Dutch Church, Deerpark. Records, 1737–1816 (film 0016563).

New Windsor Presbyterian Church. Records, 1774–96 (film 0529189). The transcript is at the State Library in Albany.

Queens County (established 1683, see also Suffolk County)
Queens County originally included parts of what are now Nassau and Suffolk counties. Many records were destroyed in 1790.
Queens County Chancery Court. Orders in chancery, Province of New York, 1701–1802 (film 0481384 ff.). The original records are at Queens College Library in Flushing.

Queens County Clerk. Conveyances and indexes, 1686–1951 (film 1414443 ff.). The original records are at the City Registrar's Office in Jamaica.
Jamaica Town Clerk. Records of Jamaica, 1661–1855 (film 0484029).

Published records include:
Gritman, Charles T. *An Index to Land Records of Queens County, Long Island, New York, Libers A–H, 1656–1903* (n.p., n.d., film 0017870). Includes most of the conveyances to be found in the Jamaica town records and many of those in the records of the towns of Hempstead, Flushing, Newtown, and Oyster Bay.
Historical Records Survey. *Abstracts of Early Wills of Queens County, New York: Recorded in Libers A and C of Deeds Now in the Registrar's Office at Jamaica, New York, 1683–1744* (n.p., n.d., film 0017872).
Eardeley, William A.D. *Records in the Office of the County Clerk at Jamaica, Long Island, 1680–1781: Wills and Administrations, Guardians, and Inventories* (n.p., n.d., film 0017715).
Meyers, Carol M. *Rate Lists of Long Island, 1675, 1676, 1683* (Saugus, CA: RAM Publishers, 1967, fiche 6117045).

Rensselaer County
See Albany County.

Richmond County (established 1683, see also New York County)
Original records at the Richmond County Courthouse in Saint George are:
Richmond County Clerk.
* Deeds, 1683–1901, index, 1630–1972 (film 0932059 ff.).
* Mortgages, 1756–1851 (film 0944669 ff.).
* Staten Island record book, 1680–1760 (film 0514661).
Richmond County Superintendent of Highways. Record of roads, 1758–1888 (film 0481429). The original records are at the Queens College Library in Flushing.
Miscellaneous genealogical records, wills, deeds, 1649–1925 (film 0514658). The manuscript may be at the Staten Island Historical Society Library in Staten Island.
Richmond County Surrogate's Court. Probate records, 1664–1866 (film 0509190 ff.).

Historical Records Survey. *Transcriptions of Early Town Records of New York: the Earliest Volume of Staten Island Records, 1678–1813* (New York: The Survey, 1942, film 0860298).

Rockland County (established 1798 from Orange County)
Rockland County Clerk. Mortgages, 1703–1857 (film 0557589 ff.). The original records are at the Rockland County Courthouse in New City.

Saratoga County (established 1791 from Albany County)
Saratoaga County Clerk. Deeds, 1774–1901 (film 0557456 ff.). The original
records are at the Saratoga County Courthouse in Ballston Spa.

Suffolk County (established 1683, see also New York and Queens counties)
Original records and manuscripts at the Suffolk County Courthouse in Riverhead
are:
Suffolk County Clerk.
* Copy of sessions, 1669–84 (film 1928014). Court of Sessions records,
  including wills, inventories, deeds, and other land records.
* Deeds, 1660–1926 (film 1870010 ff.).

Cooper, Thomas W. *The Records of the Court of Sessions of Suffolk County in
the Province of New York, 1670–1688* (Bowie, MD: Heritage Books, 1993).

Early wills of Riverhead, 1669–87 (film 0017117). Includes early wills at
  Riverhead, Suffolk County, Lester Will book, and abstracts of Queens
  County wills, and Liber A of Deeds of Jamaica. The manuscript is at the
  Holland Society of New York in New York City.

Pelletreau, William Smith. *Early Long Island Wills of Suffolk County, 1691–
1703: An Unabridged Copy of the Manuscript Volume Known as "The Lester
Will Book," Being the Record of the Prerogative Court of the County of Suffolk,
New York; with Genealogical and Historical Notes* (New York: F.P. Harper,
1897, film 0833370).

*Records of the Town of Brookhaven, Suffolk County, New York, 1655–1885:
Copied from the Original Records . . .* 3 Vols. (Patchogue, NY: Town of
Brookhaven, 1880–93, film 1033944).

*Records of the Town of East Hampton, Long Island, Suffolk County, New York:
With Other Ancient Documents of Historic Value.* 2 Vols. (Sag Harbor, NY: J.H.
Hunt, 1887–1905, fiche 6049864 ff.).

Huntington Town Clerk.
* *Huntington Court Records, 1657–1700 and the Duke's Law, 1664* (Huntington,
  NY: Town Board, 1994).
* *Huntington-Babylon Land Deeds, 1663–1797.* 6 Vols. (Huntington, NY: Town
  of Huntington, 1985, fiche 6101273 ff.).
* *Town of Huntington, Ear Marks and Stray Sheep, 1745–1831* (Huntington, NY:
  Town of Huntington, 1989).

* *Town of Huntington Highway Books, 1724–1872 with Name Index* (Huntington, NY: Town of Huntington, 1982, fiche 6088398 ff.).
* *Town of Huntington Land Grants by Trustees, 1688–1802* (Huntington, NY: Town of Huntington, 1986, film 1321262).
* *Town of Huntington Surveys of Land Grants, 1697–1787* (Huntington, NY: Town of Huntington, 1986, film 1321262).
* *Town of Huntington, Records of the Overseers of the Poor: Part 1, 1752–1804, Index; Part 2, 1805–1861, Index* (Huntington, NY: Town of Huntington, 1986, film 1321326).
* *Town of Huntington, Records of the Overseers of the Poor: Addendum, 1729–1843* (Huntington, NY: Town of Huntington, 1992, 1697772).
* *Huntington Town Records, Including Babylon, Long Island [1653–1914].* 5 Vols. (Huntington, NY: Towns of Huntington and Babylon, 1887-9, 1989, film 1697444). Babylon formed a part of Huntington until it was made a separate town in 1872.

Book One of the Minutes of Town Meetings and Register of Animal Ear Marks of the Town of Islip 1720–1851 (Islip, NY: Town of Islip, 1982).

Contents of Court of Sessions book, Riverhead, 1669–84 (film 0017903). Abstract of original Court of Sessions records, containing wills, inventories, deeds, and other land records. The typescript is at the NYGBS in New York City.

Records of the Town of Smithtown, Long Island, New York: with Other Ancient Documents of Historic Value (Smithtown, NY: Town of Smithtown, 1898, film 1033665).

Contents of the "Small Book of Deeds" from Southampton Town Clerk's Office... 1661–1678 (n.p.: G.B. Ackerly, 1879, film 0017929).

Southold Town Clerk. *Southold Town Records, 1651–1787.* 2 Vols. (New York: Towns of Southold and Riverhead, 1882-4, film 0896629).

Genealogies of Long Island Families (Broderbund, 1997). This CD-ROM contains images of *Genealogies of Long Island Families* and *Long Island Source Records*, published by Genealogical Publishing Company.

Church Records (see also New York County)
Records of the First Church of Southold, 1749–1823 (Shippensburg, PA: Overton Publications, 1984). The First Church of Southold, Long Island, New York, was established in 1640.

Parish registers of Mattituck and Aquebogue, 1751–1809 (film 0547576). From *History of Mattituck*, by Rev. Charles E. Craven (1906).

Presbyterian Church, Newtown. Records, 1687–1902 (film 0497549).
Presbyterian Church, Smithtown. Records, 1751–1867 (film 1320970).

Ulster County (established 1683, see also Orange County)
Original records and manuscripts at the Ulster County Courthouse in Kingston are:.
Ulster County Court of Common Pleas. Court records, 1693–1877 (film 0497536 ff.).
Ulster County Court of Sessions. Minutes, 1693–8 (film 0497536).
Ulster County Justices' Court. Court records, 1693–8 (film 0497536).
Ulster County Clerk.
• Court and civil records, 1681–1775 (film 0497639 ff.).
• Miscellaneous papers, accounts, and agreements, 1718–1814 (film 0497561).
• Deeds, 1685–1902 (film 0941822 ff.).
• Mortgages, 1767–1851, index, 1755–1899 (film 0841150 ff.).
• Denomination and description of lands, 1666–1750 (film 0930120).
• County assessment lists by towns, 1711–29 (film 0497536).
• Record of roads laid out, 1722–95 (film 0497536).
Ulster County Surrogate's Court.
• Probate records, 1707–1921 (film 0941437 ff.).
• Probate court records, wills, and administrations, 1662–1783, 1787–1822 (film 0481433).
Anjou, Gustave. *Ulster County, New York Probate Records in the Office of the Surrogate and in the County Clerk's Office at Kingston, New York . . . Abstract and Translation of the Dutch and English Wills, Letters of Administration after Intestates, and Inventories from 1665.* 2 Vols. (1906. Reprint. Baltimore: Clearfield Co., 1996, film 0908531).

Historical Records Survey.
• *Minutes of the Board of Supervisors of Ulster County, 1710/1 to 1730/1* (Albany: The Survey, 1939, film 0908039).
• *Records of the Road Commissioners of Ulster County, 1722–1795.* 2 Vols. (Albany: The Survey, 1940, film 1697993).

Kingston Court. Translations of the Dutch records, court minutes and secretary's papers, 1661–84 (film 0945990). An index to these records may be found in Albany County Court Clerk, index to the public records (film 0464896). Also published as Versteeg, Dingman. *New York Historical Manuscripts: Dutch. Kingston Papers.* 2 Vols. (Baltimore: Genealogical Publishing Co., 1976).

Town of Kingston. Trustees records, 1688–1764, 1767–1816 and minutes, 1736–1818 (film 0941793 ff.). Records include conveyances of property deeded.

Town of Marbletown. Accounts, 1717–85 (film 0497536).

Attorney Papers; Clinton, Livingston, 1767–1791 (New York: n.p., n.d., film 0497537).

Church Records (see also Dutchess and Orange counties)
Hasbrouck, Kenneth E. *Church Records from 1700: Churches of Alligerville, Accord, Crawford, Galeville, Kerhonkson, Kripple Bush, Modena, Newburgh, New Paltz, Platterkill, Pine Bush, Pine Hill, Rossville, Stone Ridge* (n.p., n.d., film 0514680).

Hasbrouck, Kenneth E. *Church Records from 1730: Churches of Dashville, Flatbush, Gardiner, Guilford, High Falls-Cove, Hurley, Kaatskaan, Kingston, Marbleton, Montgomery, New Hurley, New Paltz, New Rochester, Rochester, Rosendale, Shawangunk, Wallkill, Wawarsing, West Hurley, Woodstock* (n.p., n.d., film 0514676).

Kelly, Arthur C. M. *Marriage Record of the Lutheran Churches of Athens and West Camp, New York, 1705–1899* (Rhineback, NY: The Author, 1976).

Some original records at the Archives of the Reformed Church in America, New Brunswick, New Jersey are:
• Reformed Dutch Church at Marbletown, Stone Ridge. Church records, 1746–1871(film 1928069).
• Reformed Church of Shawangunk, Wallkill. Tombstone inscriptions, 1752–1872 (film 1928069).

Some transcripts of church records at the NYGBS in New York City are:
• Catsbaan (Kaatsbaan), now Saugerties, Reformed Church. Records, 1730–1841 (film 0017722).
• Reformed Church at New Paltz. Records, 1677–1816 (film 0017822). Also known as the Reformed Protestant Dutch Church of New Paltz. Includes miscellaneous lists of residents of the town of Rochester, 1677–1715 and 1769–80.
• Reformed Dutch Church of Rochester. Records, 1736–1855 (film 0017885).

Transcripts at the Holland Society of New York in New York City are:
• Reformed Dutch Church of Shawangunk. Records, 1667–1863 (film 1016566 ff.).

- Reformed Dutch Church of Wawarsing Records 1745–1803 (film 1016566 ff.).
- Reformed Dutch Church at New Hurley. Records, 1770–1923 (film 1016566 ff.).

Society of Friends, Plains, Rosendale. Monthly meeting records, 1750–1876 (film 0017389 ff.). The original records are at the Society of Friends Archives in New York City.

Saint Paul's Evangelical Lutheran Church, West Camp. Records, 1708–1891 (film 0533475). The transcript is at the State Library in Albany.

Washington County (established 1772 as Charlotte County, including part of Vermont; name changed in 1784)

Later records for Washington County have been included because pre-statehood records for Vermont (when it was part of New York) can be found here. Charlotte County became Washington County; Tryon County became Montgomery County.

Washington County Clerk.

- Deeds, 1774–1816 (film 0475436 ff.), 1774–1930 (film 0553339 ff.). Unrecorded conveyances, 1742–1820, are also at the County Archives in Fort Edward.
- Mortgages, 1773–1816 (film 0475437 ff.), 1773–1861 (film 0553336 ff.).

Washington County Surrogate's Court.

- Probate records, 1788–1916 (film 0513861 ff.).
- *Washington County Surrogate Court History and Surrogate Records Inventory* (Fort Edward, NY: Washington County Archives, 1990).

The Washington County Clerk is in Hudson Falls; the Surrogate's Court is in Salem.

Burleigh, H. C. *Confiscations, Albany, Charlotte, and Tryon Counties, New York* (Toronto, ON: United Empire Loyalists' Association of Canada, 1970, film 1321358). The original document is at the State Library in Albany.

Westchester County (established 1683)

Original records at the Westchester County Courthouse in White Plains are:

Westchester County Clerk

- Deeds, 1684–1902 (film 0579022 ff.).
- Mortgages, 1755–1851 (film 0579046 ff.).

Westchester County Surrogate's Court. Estate tax files, 1775–1900 (film 0597819 ff.).

Westchester County Registry. Certified copies of Westchester County deeds, now Bronx County, 1657–1895 (film 1413001 ff.).

Fox, Dixon Ryan. *The Minutes of the Court of Sessions (1657–1696) Westchester County, New York* (White Plains, NY: Westchester County Historical Society, 1924, film 0017998).

Historical Records, 1680–1899. 6 Vols. (Bedford Hills, NY: Town of Bedford, 1966–80). Town meetings and land records.

Records of the Town of Eastchester, New York, 1665–1865. 11 Vols. (Eastchester, NY: Eastchester Historical Society, 1964, film 0824106 ff.).

English, Mary O'Connor. *Early Town Records of Mamaroneck, 1697–1881* (Mamaroneck, NY: Town of Mamaroneck, 1979, fiche 6048678).

North Castle/New Castle Historical Records [1736–1850]. 3 Vols. (Chappaqua, NY: Town of New Castle, 1975–86).

Forbes, Jeanne A. *Records of the Town of New Rochelle, 1699–1828* (New Rochelle, NY: The Author, 1916, film 1598230).

Church Records (see also New York County)
Records of The Combined Parish of Westchester (Bronx), Eastchester, New Rochelle, Yonkers, Pelham, Morris Anna, 1702–1720 (Eastchester, NY: Eastchester Historical Society, 1975, film 6111141). This combined parish was one of the earliest in New York (1690s–1797).

Reformed Dutch Church, Cortlandt. Records, 1741–1894 (film 1928067). The original records are at the Archives of the Reformed Church in America, New Brunswick, New Jersey.

Transcripts at the Holland Society of New York in New York City are:
• French Reformed Church of New Rochelle. Records, 1726–65 (film 1019517).
• Reformed Dutch Church, Tarrytown. Records, 1697–1791 (film 1016877).

Original records at the Society of Friends Archives in New York City are:
• Purchase Monthly Meeting, Hicksite. Monthly meeting records, 1724–1931 (film 0017292 ff.).
• Purchase Monthly Meeting. Monthly meeting records, 1725–1919 (film 0017292 ff.).

South Salem Church. Records, 1765–1823 (film 0982332).

First Presbyterian Church, Yorktown. Congregational annual meeting minutes and reports, 1761–1873 (film 0913463). The original records are at the Presbyterian Historical Society in Philadelphia.

The Journal of the Reverend Silas Constant, Pastor of the Presbyterian Church at Yorktown, New York: With Some of the Records of the Church and a List of His Marriages, 1784–1825, Together with Notes on the Nelson, Van Cortlandt, Warren, and Some Other Families Mentioned in the Journal (Philadelphia: J.B. Lippincott, 1903, fiche 6087249).

Suggested Reading

Cameron, Viola Root. *Scotch Emigrants to New York 1774–1775* (Baltimore: Genealogical Publishing Co., 1966, film 0962167).

Chester, Alden. *Courts and Lawyers of New York: A History, 1609–1925* (New York: American Historical Society, 1925, fiche 6100435 ff.).

Coolidge, Guy. *The French Occupation in the Champlain Valley from 1609 to 1759* (1938. Reprint. Harrison, NY: Harbor Hill Books, 1979, film 1698225).

Dern, John P. *The Albany Protocol, Wilhelm Christoph Berkenmeyer's Chronicle of Lutheran Affairs in New York Colony, 1731–1750* (1971. Reprint. Camden, ME: Picton Press, 1992).

Epperson, Gwen F. *New Netherland Roots* (Baltimore: Genealogical Publishing Co., 1994).

Gehring, Charles T. *[New Netherland Documents] Curacao Papers, 1640–1665* (Interlaken, NY: Heart of the Lakes Publishing, 1987). Manuscripts reflecting Petrus Stuyvesant's interest and responsibilities in the Caribbean, including the names of refugees from Brazil.

Hershkowitz, Leo. *Wills of Early New York Jews [1704–1799]* (New York: American Jewish Historical Society, 1967).

Janvier, Thomas A. *The Dutch Founding of New York* (New York: Harper and Brothers, 1903, fiche 6048339).

Jones, Henry Z. *The Palatine Families of New York: A Study of The German Immigrants Who Arrived in Colonial New York in 1710*. 2 Vols. (Universal City, CA: The Author, 1985).

Jones, Henry Z. *More Palatine Families: Some Immigrants to the Middle Colonies 1717–1776 and Their European Origins plus New Discoveries on*

German Families Who Arrived in Colonial New York in 1710 (Universal City, CA: The Author, 1991).

Kammen, Michael G. *Colonial New York: A History* (White Plains, NY: KTO Press, 1987).

Kim, Sung Bok. *Landlord and Tenant in Colonial New York: Manorial Society, 1664–1775* (Chapel Hill: University of North Carolina Press, 1978).

Lefevre, Ralph. *History of New Paltz, New York, and Its Old Families, from 1678 to 1820, Including the Huguenot Pioneers . . .* (1903. Reprint. Baltimore: Genealogical Publishing Co., 1973).

Meyers, Carol M. *Early New York State Census Records, 1663–1772* (Gardena, CA: RAM Publishers, 1965, fiche 6111479).

Narrett, David. *Inheritance and Family Life in Colonial New York* (Ithaca, NY: Cornell University Press, 1992).

New York State Archives. *Guide to Records in the New York State Archives.* 2nd ed. (Albany: The Archives, 1993).

New York State Archives. *List of Pre-1847 Court Records in the State Archives* (Albany: Office of Cultural Education, 1984).

New York State Archives. *Local Records on Microfilm in the New York State Archives* (Albany: The Archives, 1979).

Onondaga Historical Association. *Moravian Journals Relating to Central New York, 1745–1766* (Syracuse, NY: Dehler Press, 1916, film 1421705).

Richards, Matthias Henry. *The German Emigration from New York Province into Pennsylvania* (Lancaster, PA: Pennsylvania German Society, 1899, film 0924110).

Schweitzer, George K. *New York Genealogical Research* (Knoxville, TN: The Author, 1995).

Zimm, Louise Hasbrouck. *Southeastern New York: A History of the Counties of Ulster, Dutchess, Orange, Rockland and Putnam* (New York: Lewis Historical Publishing, 1946, fiche 6046834).

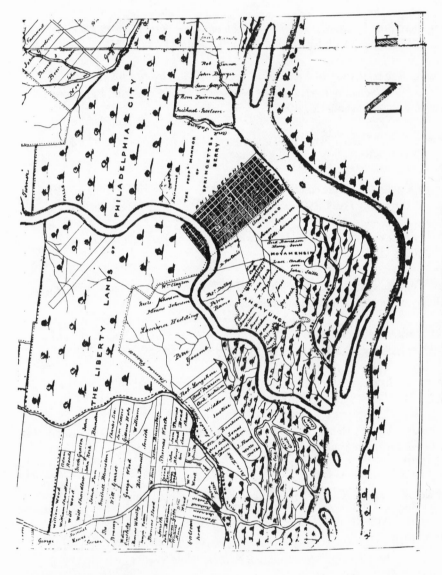

32 Pennsylvania, 1681 (Library of Congress)

Pennsylvania

Dutch settlers founded the first European settlement in Pennsylvania on Delaware Bay in 1623. In 1634 a group of Virginians built a small fort on the mouth of the Schuylkill River (near Philadelphia). Swedish settlers founded a settlement on Tincum Island (Essington) in 1643. This colony was taken over by the Dutch in 1655 and by England in 1664. In 1681 the proprietary rights for the area were granted to William Penn, and the first English Quakers arrived in 1682. The original counties of Bucks, Chester, and Philadelphia were established the same year. The Penn Proprietary was founded as a "holy experiment," based on the principle of liberty of conscience. Diverse religious groups were encouraged to emigrate from Europe and to establish communities that would live in peace and harmony with each other.

German Mennonites from Krefeld in the Rhineland settled in the area of Germantown in 1683. Welsh Baptists arrived in 1688. The settlement of large groups of the so-called "Pennsylvania Dutch" from Alsace-Lorraine, Baden, Wurttemburg, the Rhineland, and Switzerland began after 1708. Scotch-Irish from Ulster began to arrive at Philadelphia in 1717. The first Moravians resettled in the 1730s, migrating from their original settlement in Georgia.

As settlement advanced westward, new counties were created: Lancaster (1729), York (1749), Berks (1752), and Northampton (1752). The French, who claimed this land and all the land to the west, began to build a series of forts, including Fort Duquesne (Pittsburgh) in 1753. The initial battles of the French and Indian Wars took place in 1754 when the French besieged and captured a British expeditionary force sent to destroy French forts along the western frontier. British troops captured Fort Duquesne in 1758 and renamed it Fort Pitt. Indians continued to attack British settlements but were defeated in 1763.

The years prior to the Revolution were marked by conflicting land claims from lands in Pennsylvania granted by the colonies of Maryland, Virginia, and Connecticut. The disputed border with Maryland was settled with the establishment of the Mason-Dixon Line. The disputes with Connecticut and Virginia were not resolved until 1782 and 1786, respectively.

SEE ALSO
Delaware
Germany
Great Britain
New Jersey
New York

423

Statewide Records and Resources

In colonial times Quaker church courts also settled civil disputes and cases of immorality at their monthly meetings. Most cases in colonial times were heard on a county level. The clerk of the court was known as a prothonotary.

* **County Courts of the Quarter Sessions and Justice of the Peace (1682–):** Held general jurisdiction for civil and criminal cases, presided over by a justice of the peace. It also issued court writs directing sheriffs to partition decedent's real estate among heirs giving date, parties, land to be partitioned, and sheriffs' return listing date, jurors who determined the partition, etc. See individual counties for records.

* **Court of Common Pleas (1707–):** County courts with criminal and civil jurisdiction. It also kept records of roads, appointments of civil officials, and tavern and peddlers' licenses issued. See individual counties for records.

* **Orphans' Courts (1716–):** County courts which handled cases involving estates and administrations with minors. See individual counties for records.

* **Provincial Court (1683–1707):** Served as an appellate court for the county courts, published in *Minutes of the Provincial Council of Pennsylvania from the Organization to the Termination of the Proprietary Government [1683–1775]*. 10 Vols. (Philadelphia: State Printer, 1851–2, films 0844501 ff.). See also *Guide to the Microfilm of the Records of the Provincial Council, 1682–1776, in the Pennsylvania State Archives* (Harrisburg: Pennsylvania Historical and Museum Commission, 1966).

* **Supreme Court (1707–):** Succeeded Provincial Court as appellate court of last resort for the colony, held original jurisdiction over capital crimes, functioned as a trial court until 1874. Some records have been filmed: records for the Eastern District, 1736–1896 (film 1017076 ff.), include habeas corpus for Negro slaves, 1771–3, 1775, 1785–7. The original records are at the State Archives in Harrisburg.

* **Chancery Court (1720–36):** Court of equity, which only functioned for sixteen years. Registrar book, 1720–39 (film 1032845). Also published in *The Registrar's Book of Governor Keith's Court of Chancery of the Province of Pennsylvania, 1720–1735* (Harrisburg: Pennsylvania Bar Association, 1941). The original records are at the State Archives in Harrisburg.

Published Records

Two important series of records have been published by the state of Pennsylvania. The first, *Colonial Records,* contains mostly court and public records. The second, *Pennsylvania Archives,* is actually nine separate series, which include land, church, military, naval, maritime, public, and other records; they also include records copied from other archives. They are great finding aids, but do contain errors and omissions. Whenever possible it is best to use original records.

Colonial Records. 16 Vols. (Philadelphia and Harrisburg, 1851–3, film 0844506 ff.), contain the minutes of the Provincial Council (1683–1776), of the Council of Safety, and of the Supreme Executive Council of Pennsylvania (1776–90); see also Pennsylvania Provincial Council, minutes.

- Dunn, Mary. *Index to Pennsylvania's Colonial Records Series* (Baltimore: Genealogical Publishing Co., 1992).
- Hazard, Samuel. *General Index to the Colonial Records in 16 Volumes* (Philadelphia: Joseph Sevens and Co., 1860, film 0844501).

Pennsylvania Archives. 135 Vols. (Philadelphia: J. Severns, 1852–6, 1874–1935, fiche 6051521 ff.). A collection of nine series of documents supplementing the *Colonial Records* series. There have been numerous reprints of selected volumes by contemporary publishers. Please note that this list refers only to documents prior to 1775; there are many additional records contained in these series.

First Series (12 Vols. 1852–6)
Colonial Records
Vols. 1–2 1664–1756
Vols. 3–4 1756–76
Vols. 5–6 1776–8
Vols. 7–8 1778–81
Vols. 9–10 1781–6
Vols. 11–12 1786–90 and appendix
Second Series (19 Vols. 1896–9)
Vol. 1 Officers and men of the Pennsylvania Navy, 1775–81; British prisoners in Pennsylvania
Vol. 2 Persons for whom marriage licenses were issued previous to 1790; persons naturalized in the province of Pennsylvania, 1740–73; officers and soldiers in the service of the province of Pennsylvania, 1744–64; Indian traders, Mediterranean passes, letters of marque and ships' registers, 1743–76, papers relating to the province of Pennsylvania prior to the Revolution
Vol. 3 Resolves of the Committee for the Province, 1774, proceedings of the convention for the Province of Pennsylvania, 1775

Vol. 5 Colonies on the Delaware, 1614–82, copied in 1740 from the Colonial Documents of New York
Vol. 6 French occupation in western Pennsylvania, 1631–1764
Vol. 7 Provincial affairs in Pennsylvania, 1682–1750, papers relating to the boundary dispute between Pennsylvania and Maryland, 1734–60; journal kept at Fort Augusta, 1763; Dutch and Swedish settlements on the Delaware River
Vol. 8 Record of Pennsylvania marriages (churches except where noted):
- Registrar General of the Province, 1685–9
- Christ, Philadelphia, 1709–1806
- Swedes, Philadelphia, 1750–1810
- Saint Paul's Episcopal, Chester, 1704–33
- Reformed, Falkner Swamp, 1748– 1800
- Lutheran, New Hanover, 1745–1809
- German Reformed, Philadelphia, 1748–1802
- First Baptist, Philadelphia, 1761–1803
- Paxtang and Derry, 1741–1810
Vol. 9 Officers of the colonies on the Delaware,

1614–81, officers of the Province of Pennsylvania, 1681–1776, provincial officers of the three lower counties, New Castle, Kent, and Sussex, provincial officers for the three original counties, Chester, Philadelphia, and Bucks, 1682–1776, provincial officers for additional counties, 1729–76; marriage records:

- First Presbyterian, Philadelphia, 1702–45, 1760–1803
- Moravian, Bethlehem, 1742–1800
- Moravian, Nazareth, 1742–1800
- Moravian Church, Litiz, 1743–1800
- Moravian, Philadelphia, 1743–1800
- Moravian, Emmaus, 1758–1800
- Abington Presbyterian, 1716–1821
- Philadelphia Monthly Meeting, 1682–1756
- Middletown Monthly Meeting, 1685–1810
- Falls Monthly Meeting, 1700–1800
- Buckingham Monthly Meeting, 1730–1810
- Quakertown Monthly Meeting, 1752–1810
- Wrightstown Monthly Meeting, 1744–1809
- Saint Michael's and Zion, Philadelphia, 1745–1800
- Saint Paul's, Philadelphia, 1759–1806
- Presbyterian Church, Churchville, 1738–1810
- Second Presbyterian, Philadelphia, 1763–1812

Vols. 10–11 Pennsylvania battalions and line, 1775–83

Vols. 13–14 Pennsylvania associated battalions and militia, 1775–83

Vol. 15 Journals with lists of officers and soldiers, 1775–83

Vol. 16 The Breviate in the boundary dispute between Pennsylvania and Maryland

Vol. 17 Names of foreigners who took the oath of allegiance to the province of Pennsylvania, 1727–75

Vol. 18 Documents relating to the Connecticut settlement in the Wyoming Valley: minutes of the Susquehanna Company claiming lands in Wyoming, 1753–1801, Connecticut claim to lands in Pennsylvania, 1774, Dutch records of New Netherland in connection with the boundaries of Connecticut, book of the fifteen townships, miscellaneous papers relating to the Wyoming controversy, 1769–1808

Vol. 19 Minutes of the Board of Property of the province of Pennsylvania, early Pennsylvania land records, minute books, 1686–1739

Third Series (30 Vols. 1894–99)

Vol. 1 Minutes of the Board of Property and other references to lands in Pennsylvania, 1681–1791; Minutes of Welsh purchases, 1681; Minute book, 1732–41; Minutes of Board of Property, 1765–95

Vol. 2 Minutes of the Board of Property and other references to lands in Pennsylvania, including proprietary (old) rights Caveat books, 1748–84

Vol. 4 Draughts of the proprietary manors in the Province of Pennsylvania, as preserved in the Land Department of the commonwealth

Vol. 8 Commissions with official proclamations, 1733–52

Vol. 9 Commissions with official proclamations, 1752–66

Vol. 10 Commissions with official proclamations, 1766–90

Vols. 11–12 Proprietary tax lists of the county of Chester

Vols. 14–16 Proprietary, supply, and state tax lists of the city and county of Philadelphia

Vol. 17 Proprietary and state tax lists of the county of Lancaster for the years 1771–3

Vol. 18 Proprietary and state tax lists of the county of Berks, 1767–85, various years

Vol. 19 Proprietary, supply, and state tax

lists of the counties of Northampton and Northumberland, 1772–87

Vol. 22 Returns of taxables for the counties of Bedford, 1773–84

Vol. 23 Muster rolls of the Navy and Line, Militia and Rangers, 1775–83

Vol. 24 Warrantees of land: Philadelphia, 1733–1866, Chester, 1733–1858, Bucks, 1733–1889, Lancaster, 1733–1896, Cumberland, 1750–1874

Vol. 25 Warrantees of Northumberland, 1772–1892

Vol. 26 Warrantees of land: Northampton, 1752–1886, Westmoreland, 1773–1892

Vol. 27 Indexes and tables of contents, Vols. 1–26 index, Vols. 11–26

Vols. 28–30 index, Vols. 11–26

Fourth Series (12 Vols. 1900–2)

Papers of the governors, 1681–1902

Vol. 1 The charter of the province; the laws agreed upon in England; admini-strations of the governors, 1681–1747

Vol. 2 Administrations of the governors, 1747–59; papers of the Proprietaries, 1718–76

Vol. 3 Administrations of the governors, 1759–76; Committee of Safety, 1775–6

Vol. 12 General index to Fourth Series

Fifth Series (8 Vols. 1906)

Vol. 1 Officers and soldiers in the service of the Province of Pennsylvania, 1744–65; Indian traders, 1743–75; Ships' registers, 1762–76

Vols. 2, 3, and part of 4 are corrected versions of most records found in Second Series, Vols. 10–11, and 13–14.

Sixth Series (15 Vols. 1906–7)

Vol. 6 Records of Egypt Reformed Church, 1734–84; Records of Rev. John Wad-schmidt, Lancaster County, 1752–86

Vol. 15 General index to Fifth Series

Seventh Series (5 Vols. 1914)

Vols. 1–5 Index to Sixth Series

Weikel, Sally A. *Genealogical Research in the Published Pennsylvania Archives* (Harrisburg: State Library of Pennsylvania, 1974, film 1036613).

Eddy, Henry Howard. *Guide to the Published Archives of Pennsylvania Covering the 138 Volumes of Colonial Records and Pennsylvania Archives, Series I–IX* (Harrisburg: Pennsylvania Historical and Museum Commission, 1949, 1976, film 1036386).

Land Records

Land records are available on both the state and county levels. It is advisable to search the county deeds first before using the records at the State Archives. Land records at the State Archives, Division of the Bureau of Land Records in Harrisburg, include:

- Warrant registers, 1682–1950 (film 1003194 ff.). Index to the surveys, warrants, and patents. Registers prior to 1733 are in list form. For an index to these records see the index to the "Old Rights" surveys, 1682–1761 (film 0986897).
- Original warrants (film 1028662 ff.).
- Applications for warrants, 1734–1865 (film 0984123 ff.), 1755–1866 (film 0988263 ff.).
- Original surveys, 1682–1920 (film 1003388 ff.).

- Patent books, 1676–1960 (film 1028673 ff.). The patent index includes names of patentees who did not also receive the warrant. For all other cases after 1733 use the warrant registers.
- Proprietary papers, 1682–1850 (film 1006521 ff.).
- Board of Property papers, 1682–1850 (film 0988274 ff.).
- Board of Property petitions, undated, 1682–1815 (film 0988269 ff.).
- Loan Office mortgage books, 1774–88 (film 1032593 ff.).
- Mortgages and valuations for Bedford, Chester, Cumberland, Philadelphia, and York counties (film 032650 ff.).
- Rent rolls and quit rent books, 1703–44 (film 1035090 ff.).
- Land office journal, 1738–73 (film 1032840 ff.).
- Proprietary towns, 1751–1829 (film 1003200). Includes Bedford, Carlisle, Easton, Indiana, Reading, Sunbury, and York.
- Caveats, 1699–1890 (film 0986599 ff.). Caveats against the acceptance of surveys of land, or patents, until the survey can be reevaluated or corrected.
- Depositions, 1683–1881 (film 0986869 ff.).
- Island records (sales, surveys, appraisals, etc.), 1757–1865 (film 0987838 ff.).
- Mortgage records, 1687–1820 (film 0987914 ff.).
- Nicholson lands commissioner's return of sale, 1769–1843 (film 0986898).
- Original purchases, 1683–1702 (film 1028678).
- County surveys, 1683–1859 (film 0986891 ff.).
- East and West side applications, 1765–9 (film 0986894).
- Record of land surveyed by the Deputy Surveyors, 1683–1859 (film 0986885 ff.).
- Philadelphia city lots, 1682–1790 (film 0988268).

Pennsylvania Provincial Assembly. *Warrants and Surveys of the Province of Pennsylvania, 1682–1759 . . .* 9 Vols. (Philadelphia: Department of Records, 1962, film 0981096 ff.). The original manuscripts are at the Philadelphia City Archives, Department of Records in Philadelphia.

Vol. 1 Surveys of "Old Rights" (lists warrants and surveys prior to 1730s) for Philadelphia City and County, surveys for Bucks and Chester counties

Vol. 2 Philadelphia City, 1682–92, and new returns, 1735–59, returns for Philadelphia, Bucks, Chester, and Lancaster counties

Vol. 3 General returns of the Society of Free Traders; entries for Philadelphia City and County and counties of Bucks, Chester, Kent, and Newcastle for 1682–98

Vol. 4: Surveyor General's returns, 1700, entries for Philadelphia City and County and counties of Bucks, Chester, Kent, and Newcastle

Vol. 5 Surveyor General's returns, 1733, entries for Philadelphia City and County and counties of Bucks, Chester, Kent, Lancaster, Newcastle, and Sussex

Vol. 6 Philadelphia County 1684–1713, Bucks County new returns, 1734–58

Vol. 7 General returns, 1735–41, entries for Philadelphia City and County and counties of Bucks, Chester, Kent, Lancaster, Newcastle, and Sussex

Vol. 8 General returns, 1752–9, entries for Philadelphia City and County and counties of Berks, Bucks, Chester,

Cumberland, Kent, Lancaster, Newcastle, Northampton, and York, and for the towns of Carlisle, Easton, Reading, and Yorktown

Vol. 9 Philadelphia County new returns, 1734–5

Records of land granted from Connecticut are at the Connecticut State Library in Hartford:

* Susquehanna Settlers Western lands, 1642–1819 (film 0003622 ff.).
* Boyd, Julian P. and Robert Joseph Taylor. *Susquehannah Company. The Susquehannah Company Papers [1750–1898].* 11 Vols. (Ithaca, NY: Cornell University Press, 1930–71).

Records of land granted from Virginia are at the Virginia State Library in Richmond:

* Virginia Land Office, county abstracts, 1623–1923, containing abstracts of patent and grant books, including the Yohogania area in Pennsylvania (Vol. 43, film 0029317).
* "Virginia Land Grants in Pennsylvania." *Virginia Genealogist* 7 (1963).

Important finding aids for land records are:

➤ Munger, Donna B. *Pennsylvania Land Records, A History and Guide for Research* (Wilmington, DE: Scholarly Resources, 1991).

➤ Dructor, Robert. *A Guide to Genealogical Sources at the Pennsylvania State Archives* (Harrisburg: Pennsylvania Historical and Museum Commission, 1980). In 1967 the State Archives became the Division of Archives and Manuscripts in the Pennsylvania Historical and Museum Commission. The Archives guides for record groups and manuscripts are also very useful.

➤ Duffin, James M. *Guide to the Mortgages of the General Loan Office of the Province of Pennsylvania, 1724–1756* (Philadelphia: Genealogical Society of Pennsylvania, 1995).

➤ Crumrine, Boyd. *Virginia Court Records in Southwestern Pennsylvania* (1902–5. Reprint. Baltimore: Genealogical Publishing Co., 1981).

Sergeant, Thomas. *View of the Land Laws of Pennsylvania* (Laughlin: Southwest Pennsylvania Genealogical Services, 1992).

Manuscripts

Historical Society of Pennsylvania. *Guide to the Manuscript Collections of the Historical Society of Pennsylvania.* 3rd ed. (Philadelphia: The Society, 1991).

Historical Records Survey. *Guide to Depositories of Manuscript Collections in*

Pennsylvania (Harrisburg: Pennsylvania Historical Commission, 1939, film 0982367).

State Library of Pennsylvania. Genealogical surname card index (film 1002825 ff.). Catalog cards listing the genealogical collection at the State Library in Harrisburg.

In addition to the state societies and archives there are many manuscript collections at county historical societies. One that has been filmed is the Albert Cook Myers manuscripts at the Chester County Historical Society, West Chester:

* Notes on immigrants to Pennsylvania, 1681–1737 (film 0567010 ff.).
* Notes on English Quakers in Pennsylvania, late seventeenth and early eighteenth centuries (film 0567024 ff.).
* See also Myers, Albert Cook. *Immigration of the Irish Quakers into Pennsylvania, 1682–1750, with Their Early History in Ireland* (1902. Baltimore: Genealogical Publishing Co., 1969, film 1036555). Contains list of certificates of removal from Ireland, received at the Monthly Meeting of Friends in Pennsylvania.

Church Records
Many important denominational repositories or societies are located in Pennsylvania. Some of the most notable are:
➢ The Evangelical and Reformed Historical Society, Phillip Schaff Library, Franklin and Marshall College, Lancaster
➢ The Presbyterian Historical Society, Philadelphia
➢ The American Catholic Historical Society, Philadelphia
➢ Friends Historical Association, Haverford College Library, Haverford
➢ Friends Historical Library, Swarthmore College, Swarthmore
➢ Lutheran Archives Center, Krauth Memorial Library, Philadelphia
➢ Archives of the Moravian Church, Bethlehem
➢ Schwenkfelder Library, Pennsburg
➢ United Methodist Church Commission on Archives and History (Western Pennsylvania Conference), Mount Pleasant
➢ Eastern Baptist Theological Seminary, Philadelphia

Two projects by the Historical Records Survey are somewhat outdated but still useful:
* *Inventory of the Church Archives of Pennsylvania Presbyterian Churches* (Philadelphia: n.p., 1936–40, film 0899326 ff.).
* *Inventory of Church Archives in Pennsylvania* (film 1014729 ff.).

Hinke, William John. *Reformed Church Records in Pennsylvania Arranged*

According to Their Age, 1731–1880 (n.p., n.d., film 0940406). List of churches giving the name, township, county, and dates.

Original records and manuscripts at the Evangelical and Reformed Historical Society, Schaff Library, Franklin and Marshall College, in Lancaster, include:
Pastoral and church records of the Reformed Church in the collection of the
   Historical Society of the Evangelical and Reformed Church (film 0562985).
Zacharias, George Merle de Fere. Moravian (death) records (film 0020364).
   Includes:

Lancaster County:
Donegal, 1748–59
Lancaster, 1749–53
Berks County:
Heidelberg, 1748–60

Oley, 1746–59
Lehigh County:
Lynn, 1751–9
York County:
York, 1749–60

Maryland:
Frederick County
Manakasie, 1747–60

Pastor's records, John Casper Stoever, 1729–98 (film 0020436). Pastor Stoever served in the following areas:

Philadelphia: 1733–5
Adams County:
Conewago, 1735–42
Berks County:
Reed's, 1735–40s
Little Tulpehocken, 1742–60s and 1774–9
Northkill, Blue Mountain, Atolheo, 1746–57
Dauphin County:
Hill/Maxe, Hummelstown, Middletown, 1768–70
Lancaster County:
Conestoga 1735–43
Muddy Creek, 1735–59
Earl, 1733–44
Lancaster, 1733–42
Warwick, 1743–54 and 1777–9

Bishop's 1768–70
York County:
Codorus, 1741–3
Lebanon County:
Quitopahilla, 1740–79
Bindnagel, 1745–79
Fredericksburg ,1766–74
Jonestown, 1765–79
Ziegel, 1765–74
Maryland:
Frederick County
Monocacy, 1735–42
Virginia:
Madison County
Hebron, 1735–42

Schumacher, Daniel. Baptisms by the Rev. Daniel Schumacher, pastor of the Lutheran congregations in Berks, Lehigh, and Northampton counties, Pennsylvania, 1754–74 (film 0385062). These registers have been published in Weiser, Frederick S. *The Record Book of Daniel Schumacher, 1754–1773: Containing Registers of Baptisms and Comfirmations in Berks, Lehigh, Northampton, and Schulykill Counties, Pennsylvania* (Camden, ME: Picton Press, 1993). Includes the following:

Berks County:
Trinity Lutheran, Reading, 1754–5, 1758
Alsace Church, Alsace, 1754–8
Schwarzwald, Exeter, 1754–8
Saint Paul's, Windsor, 1754–7, 1760–1, 1764–
    5, 1771–5
Jerusalem or Allemangel, 1755–70
New Allemangel or Friedens, Albany, 1770–7
Bern Church, Bern, 1755–7
Zion or Northkill, Upper Tulpehocken, 1756–8
New Jerusalem, Dunkel's, or Ontelauncee,
    Greenwich, 1761–2, 1764–5
Saint Michael's, Tilden, 1771–3
Saint John's or Maxatawny, Kutztown, 1756,
    1758, 1766–7, 1770
Oley Hills, 1756–60, 1771–2
Tulpehocken near Stouchsburg, 1757–8
Rosenthal near Eckville, 1763
Long Swamp, Longswamp Township, 1768
Lehigh County:
Weisenberg, 1757–75 and Ziegel, Weisenberg
    1765–70

Jerusalem, Western Salisbury, 1758–63,
    1766–8
Ebenezer, New Tripoli, 1759–63
Jerusalem, Eastern Salisbury, 1759–63,
    1766–8
Egypt, Whitehall Township, 1760–5
Saint Paul's, Indianland, 1760–2, 1770–1
Heidelberg, Heidelberg, 1762–9
Great Swamp Church, Lower Milford, 1759
Lehigh or Zion, Lower Macungie, 1759–60,
    1769
Upper Milford, 1766–8 and Macungie, Old
    Zionsville, 1767–8, 1771
Schuylkill County:
Zion or "Across the Blue Mountains," West
    Brunswick, 1755–7, 1770–81
Northampton County:
Williams Township, 1758
Dryland Church, Lower Nazareth, 1758
New Jersey:
Phillipsburg, Warren County, 1758

Records of the American Catholic Historical Society of Philadelphia. 29 Vols.
(Philadelphia: The Society, 1887–1912, first eleven volumes on film 1698288
ff.). Contains documents relating to the history of the Catholic Church in the
United States with some articles on Canada, and a cumulative index. Some of the
accounts that begin before 1775 are:

Account of the society called "Sisters of Jesus
    and Mary"
French refugee Trappists in the United States
Catholics in the three lower counties (Delaware)
Sketch of the history of Saint Augustine's
    Church, Philadelphia
Ursuline nuns in America
Baptisms registered at Saint Joseph's Church,
    Philadelphia, 1758–75
Expedition down the Allegheny and Ohio
    Rivers, 1740
Early days of Catholics in Pittsburgh
French in early western Pennsylvania
Register of baptisms and interments, Fort
    Duquesne, 1753–6
Acadians in Philadelphia
Detroit in early times
Catholic annals of Saint Louis, 1770–6

Bodies buried in the Catholic grave yard,
    Natchez, Mississippi
Spanish documents relating to founding of the
    church at Natchez
History of the Menominee Indians of Wiscon-
    sin and the Catholic missions
Churches founded in Pennsylvania in the
    1700s and earliest dates known for visits of
    missionaries
Names of Roman Catholics in New York City,
    June 1696
Scenes of the Huron missions
Missions of upper California and the date of
    foundation
Missions settled by Jesuits in California, 1702
The Catholic religion in the western states of
    North America
Memoirs of the Roman Catholic Church, 1750:

North Carolina, Ohio, Jesuit mission to
the Illinois
Narrative of upper Washington Territory, 1659

Origin of the Maryland mission
Early missionaries among the Iroquois in the
Province of New York

Ziegler, Warren J. *Catholic Goshenhoppen Registers, Nos. 1 and 2* (Milford, NJ: The Author, 1983, film 1421958). Contains Father Schneider's Goshenhoppen registers, 1741–64, and Goshenhoppen registers, 1765–85. These records cover several counties in Pennsylvania (Bucks, Berks, Montgomery, Philadelphia, Northampton, and the area that became Lehigh County), and Hunterdon County, New Jersey. These are the oldest Catholic records known to exist for the places and the time period covered.

Irish, Donna R. *Pennsylvania German Marriages: Marriages and Marriage Evidence in Pennsylvania German Churches* (Baltimore: Genealogical Publishing Co., 1982).

Newspapers
Published abstracts of newspapers include:
Scott, Kenneth. *Genealogical Abstracts from the American Weekly Mercury, 1719–1746* (Baltimore: Genealogical Publishing Co., 1974).
Hocker, Edward W. *Genealogical Data Relating to the German Settlers of Pennsylvania and Adjacent Territory from Advertisements in German Newspapers Published in Philadelphia and Germantown, 1743–1800* (1935. Reprint. Baltimore: Genealogical Publishing Co., 1980, film 0021591). Also includes Conococheague (Maryland) and Anweil (New Jersey). Advertisements came from: *Pennsylvanische Geschichts-Schreiber,* 1743–62, *Wochentlicher Pennsylvanischer Staatsbote,* 1767–79, *Philadelphische Zeitung* 1756–7, *Philadelphische Correspondenz,* 1781–1800, *Germantauner Zeitung,* 1785–90
Grubb, Farley. *Runaway Servants, Convicts, and Apprentices Advertised in the Pennsylvania Gazette, 1728–1796* (Baltimore: Genealogical Publishing Co., 1992).
Scott, Kenneth. *Abstracts from Ben Franklin's Pennsylvania Gazette, 1728–1748* (Baltimore: Genealogical Publishing Co., 1975).
Scott, Kenneth and J.R. Clarke. *Abstracts from The Pennsylvania Gazette, 1748–1755* (Baltimore: Genealogical Publishing Co., 1977).
Smith, Frances Schive. *Abstracts from Benjamin Franklin's Pennsylvania Gazette, April 17, 1755 to December 27, 1764.* 3 Vols. (Magnolia, NJ: A.W. Smith, 1990).
Scott, Kenneth. *Genealogical Data from the Pennsylvania Chronicle, 1767–1774* (Washington, DC: National Genealogical Society, 1971, film 1035770). Includes persons from Pennsylvania, New Jersey, Maryland, the three lower counties of Delaware, New England, Virginia, the Carolinas, New York, Georgia, and East Florida.

Salisbury, Ruth. *Pennsylvania Newspapers: A Bibliography and Union List* (Pittsburgh: Pennsylvania Library Association, 1969, fiche 6087742).

County Records and Resources

State Library of Pennsylvania. County records card file, 1651–1977 (film 1002825). Contains cards concerning the counties of Pennsylvania in alphabetical order by the name of the county.

Information at the State Archives in Harrisburg includes:
Some county tax lists, tax and exoneration lists, by county, 1762–1801 (film 0295759 ff.).
Historical Records Survey. Inventory of the county archives of Pennsylvania (film 1014724 ff.).

Bedford County (established 1771 from Cumberland County)
Bedford County Orphans' Court.
* Orphans' Court dockets, records of requests and appointments of guardians for minors, 1772–1900 (film 0331335 ff.).
* Wills, 1771–1906 (film 0331357 ff.).
Bedford County Recorder of Deeds. Deed books, 1771–1905 (film 0331362 ff.).
Tax lists, 1772–1850 (film 1449350 ff.).

Berks County (established 1752 from Philadelphia County)
Berks County Recorder of Deeds.
* Deeds, 1734–1866 (film 0020739 ff.).
* Miscellaneous records, 1752–1869, grantor and grantee indexes, 1752–1936 (film 0929936 ff.).
* Mortgage records, 1752–1822 (film 0929921 ff.).
* Unrecorded deeds (indentures), 1717–1867 (film 0020825).
Berks County Register of Wills.
* Administration books, 1752–1822 (film 0020531).
* Register of wills, estate files, 1752–1850 (film 1644017 ff.).
* Unrecorded wills, 1753–79 (film 0020821 ff.).
* Wills, 1752–1860 (film 0020722 ff.)
Berks County Orphans' Court.
* Miscellaneous deeds, 1755–84 (film 1643803).
* Administration letters and bonds, 1752–1851 (film 0020812 ff.).
* Orphans' Court proceedings, 1752–1857 (film 0020731 ff.).
The original records are at the Berks County Courthouse in Reading.

Tax lists, 1752–1856 (film 0020826 ff.), at the Historical Society of Berks County in Reading are from the following townships (lists that begin after 1775 are not included here):

Albany	District	Oley
Alsace	Douglas	Reading
Amity	Exeter	Richmond
Bern	Greenwich	Robeson
Bethel Township	Heidelberg	Rockland
Brecknock	Hereford	Ruscombmanor
Brunswick	Longswamp	Tulpehocken
Caermarvon	Maiden Creek	Union
Colebrookdale	Maxatawny	Windsor
Cumru		

Original records at the State Historical Society in Philadelphia are:
Pennsylvania General Assembly. "Registers of all persons residing within the
County of Berks, as well as freemen and servants, and the time of the said
servants freedome and wages, 1681–9 (film 0020452)."
Taxables and tax lists, 1753–69 (film 0385040 ff.).

Church Records
Original records and transcripts at the Evangelical and Reformed Historical
Society in Lancaster include:
Epler's near Reading (film 0020362)
Bern Reformed, Berneville (film 0020362)
Spiess' Schwartzwald, Berne (film 0020362)
Oley (Salem) Reformed (film 0020362)
Huguenots from Oley (film 0020362)
Goshenhoppen Reformed, 1731–63 (film 1305840 ff.)

Records at the State Historical Society in Philadelphia include:
Records of Goshenhoppen Church, 1741–1818 (film 0385057).
Saint Gabriel's Protestant Episcopal Church. Records of Amity Township,
1735–1856 (film 0385065).

Berks County, Pennsylvania Marriages, 1730–1800. 2 Vols. (Reading, PA: HP
Publishing, 1986, film 1697680). Abstracts from:

Berks County Lutheran and Reformed	New Bethel (Zion) Lutheran, Grimville
Christ Lutheran, Stouchsburg	Saint Gabriel's Episcopal, Douglassville
Christ (Little Tulpehocken) Lutheran, Jefferson	Saint Joseph's (Hill) Union, Pike
Christ (Mertz) Lutheran, Rockland	Saint Paul's Union, Amityville
Exeter Friends Meeting House, Exeter	Trinity Tulpehocken Reformed
Most Blessed Sacrament Roman Catholic, Bally	Zion (Moselem) Lutheran, Richmond

Bucks County (established 1682, see also Philadelphia County)
Records at the Bucks County Historical Society in Doylestown include (court of
common pleas and quarter sessions have not been filmed):
Marriage license bonds, 1772–82 (film 0172925).

Bucks County Coroner's views and inquisitions, 1710–1906 (film 0941417 ff.).
Bucks County Recorder of Deeds.
* Deeds, 1684–1866 (film 0172829 ff.)
* Mortgages, 1782–1821, index, 1684–1919 (film 0905877 ff.).
Bucks County Register of Wills. Wills, 1713–1906, index, 1682–1939 (film 0387828 ff.).

Records at the State Historical Society in Philadelphia include:
Extracts from Common Pleas and Quarter sessions courts and abstracts from justice docket of Buckingham: indentures of servants and marriages, 1684–1805 (film 0387839).
Welsh settlers of Hilltown and New Britain, 1700–1899 (film 0388544).
Tax lists, 1693, proposal to settle upon Susquehannah (film 0441413).
Bucks County Court of Common Pleas and Quarter Sessions. Petitions for roads, 1721–1801 (film 0388567).
Bucks County Board of County Commissioners. Treasurer's accounts, 1747–96 (film 1429872).

Records of the Courts of Quarter Sessions and Common Pleas of Bucks County, Pennsylvania, 1684–1700 (Meadville: Colonial Society of Pennsylvania, 1943, film 0173018).

Historical Records Survey. *Records of the Courts of Quarter Sessions and Common Pleas of Bucks County, Pennsylvania, 1700–1730* (Doylestown, PA: Bucks County Historical Society, 1946, film 0173019).

Williams, Richard T. *Index of Bucks County, Pennsylvania Wills and Administration Records, 1684–1850* (Danboro, PA: The Author, 1971, film 0845444).

Church Records (see also *Pennsylvania Archives*)
Humphrey, John T. *Pennsylvania Births, Bucks County, 1682–1800* (Washington, DC: Humphrey Publications, 1993). Contains the church records of:

Falls Friends Monthly Meeting
Middletown Friends Monthly Meeting
Wrightstown Friends Monthly Meeting
Richland Friends Monthly Meeting
Buckingham Friends Monthly Meeting
Southampton Baptist
Tinicum Presbyterian (Red Hill)
Neshaminy Presbyterian,
  Hartsville, Warwick
Newtown Presbyterian, Newtown
Reformed Low Dutch, Southampton and

Northampton
Dutch Reformed, Bensalem
Tohickon Reformed, Bedminister
Christ Evangelical Lutheran (Tinicum Lutheran), Tinicum
Tohickon Lutheran, Bedminister
Christ Reformed, Trumbauersville, Milford
Springfield Lutheran, Springfield
Saint Matthew's (Keller's) Evangelical Lutheran, Bedminister
Springfield Reformed, Springfield

Evangelical Lutheran, Nockamixon
Saint Luke's Reformed, Ferndale,
  Nockamixon
Christ Evangelical Lutheran,

Trumbauersville, Milford
Journal of John Dyer, Plumsteadville,
Plumstead, beginning in 1769

Original records at the American Baptist Historical Society in Rochester, New York include:
"Records of the Redstone Baptist Church: being an account of the gathering, settling, order, and continuance of the church of Baptized Believers inhabiting in the counties of Philadelphia and Bucks, in the province of Pennsylvania and in the town and county of Burlington in the Province of New Jersey" (film 0020721).
Baptist Church, New Britain. Records, 1754–1888 (film 0021679).

Society of Friends records at the Friends Historical Library, Swarthmore College, in Swarthmore include:
* Falls, Fallsington. Monthly meeting records, 1683–1788 (film 0020459).
* Wrightstown. Monthly meeting records, 1716–1916 (film 0020710).
* Buckingham. Monthly meeting records, 1693–1947 (film 0387851 ff.).
* Middletown, Langhorne. Monthly meeting records, 1664–1806 (film 0020707), 1671–1947 (film 1120711).
* Richland, Quakertown. Monthly meeting records, 1742–1925 (film 0020406 ff.), 1715–1948 (film 0020708).

Original records at the Presbyterian Historical Society in Philadelphia are:
Great Swamp Reformed Church, Lower Milford Township, Lehigh County. Records, 1736–1822 (film 0388547), one mile from Spinnerstown in Bucks County.
Church records in the Van Vlecq journal, 1710–37 (film 0501928). Includes the following churches: Low Dutch Presbyterian, Bensalem, and Sammeny; Low Dutch, Sammeny; English Presbyterian, Bensalem; Low Dutch, Whitemarsh, Mongomery County; Low Dutch, Six Mile Run, New Jersey (now Franklin Park).
North and Southampton Reformed Dutch Church, Churchville. Records, 1704–1899 (film 0915001 ff.).
Presbyterian Church, Deep Run. Records, 1761–1901 (film 0501950 ff.). In 1726 it was Upper Congregation of Neshaminy; in 1738 it was organized as Deep Run.
Presbyterian Church, Doylestown. Records, 1732–1928 (film 0503546 ff.).
Neshaminy Presbyterian Church, Hartsville. Records, 1743–1901 (film 0503604 ff.).

Newtown Presbyterian Church, Newtown. Records, 1769–1889 (film 1313850 ff.).

Original records at the Lutheran Archives in Philadelphia include:
Keller's Lutheran Church, Bedminster Township. Records, 1751–1921 (film 1312361).
Tohickon Lutheran Church, Hagersville, Bedminster Township. Records, 1750–1880 (film 0022076).

Original records at the Evangelical and Reformed Historical Society in Lancaster are:
Springfield Reformed Church, Springfield Township. Records, 1755–1957 (film 1671298 ff.).
Nockamixon Reformed Church, Nockamixon Township. Records, 1773–1943 (film 1294882 ff.).

Saint Luke's Union Church, Ferndale. Records, 1773–1897 (film 0388546). The original records are at the State Historical Society in Philadelphia.
Springfield Lutheran Church, Springfield Township. Records, 1751–1913 (film 1671313 ff.). The original records are at Trinity Lutheran Church in Quakerstown.

Chester County (established 1682)
Probate records prior to 1714 were recorded in Philadelphia County. Land records before 1761 are indexed in the old rights of Philadelphia County (film 0986897). All other county records prior to 1775 are at the Chester County Archives and Records Services in West Chester (joint operation of the Chester County Historical Society and county government):
Chester County Surveyor. Warrants and surveys, 1701–27 (film 0020886).
Chester County Recorder of Deeds.
• Deeds, 1688–1903 (film 0020874 ff.).
• Petitions, 1720–50 (film 0571146).
• Mortgage records, 1774–1852, index, 1628–1920 (film 0556709 ff.).
• Miscellaneous deeds (film 0571144).
Chester County Court of Common Pleas.
• Sheriffs' deeds index for 1773–1876, and Sheriffs' deed books, 1773–1850 (film 0020888).
• Court records, 1681–1712 (film 0020887).
Chester County Court of Private Sessions. Appointments of Overseers of the Poor, Supervisors of Roads, Constables, 1718–1800 (film 0566524).
Chester County Court of Quarter Sessions.
• Docket, 1714–1906 (film 0558038 ff.).
• Tavern petitions and index, 1700–1800 (film 0567051 ff.).

Chester County Register of Wills.
* Estate papers, 1700–1810 (film 1429155 ff.).
* Wills, 1713–1854 (film 0020839 ff.).
Chester County Orphans' Court.
* Records, 1716–1850; index to minors' estates and decedents' estates, 1716–1885 (film 0020889 ff.).
* Decedents' estate papers, 1716–1810 (film 1429174 ff.)
* Minors' estate papers, 1717–1820 (film 1429185 ff.).
Miscellaneous court records, 1697–1788 (film 0571145).
Chester County Treasurer. Book of levies, 1699–1749 (film 0567076).
Chester County Board of Commissioners. Tax records, 1715–1820 (film 1449233 ff.). These include the following townships in Chester and Delaware counties:
* Provincial tax records: rates, 1715, 1757–64 (various years), assessments, 1765–7
* Lower Darby returns and assessments, 1768
* New Garden rates, 1769
* Aston, Chester, East Fallowfield, and Sadsbury: returns, 1770, assessments, 1770–6, county tax rates, 1718–25 (various years)
* Thornbury returns, 1726, rates, 1726–75 (various years)
Tax lists to 1900 (film 0570720 ff.).
Radnor tax records, including minutes, relief of the poor, etc., 1765–1810 (film 0570719)

Records at the State Archives in Harrisburg include Chester County tax and exoneration lists, 1764–88 (film 0295763 ff.).
Records at the State Historical Society in Philadelphia include tax lists for Chester County, 1693–1774 (film 0387952 ff.).

Records at the Chester County Historical Society in West Chester include:
Minutes of the Provincial Court and Provincial taxes, 1756–78 (film 0020896).
William Pim, book of records for the town of Whiteland, 1739–51 (film 0020994). Includes marriages, servants assigned [bound], and cash paid for the relief of the poor of the town.
West Bradford Township Treasurer. Account book, 1740–1800 (film 0567076).

Naturalization records for Philadelphia, Chester, Lancaster, and Bucks counties for April 11–13, 1743, have been abstracted from the records of the Supreme Court at Philadelphia County (film 0020361). The manuscript is at the Franklin and Marshall College Library in Lancaster.

Anderson, Bart. *Index to Chester County, Pennsylvania, Wills and Intestate Records, 1713–1850* (Danboro, PA: Richard T. and Mildred C. Williams, 1970, film 0496936).

Catanese, Lynn Ann. *Guide to Records of the Court of Quarter Sessions, Chester County, Pennsylvania, 1681–1969: Records of the Clerk of Courts, Records of the Court of Oyer and Terminer and General Jail Delivery, Criminal Records of the Sheriff* (West Chester, PA: Chester County Historical Society, 1988).

Catanese, Lynn Ann. *Guide to Records of the Court of Common Pleas, Chester County, Pennsylvania, 1681–1900: Records of the Prothonotary, Civil Records of the Sheriff, Select Civil Records of the Circuit Court of Chester County and the Supreme Court of Pennsylvania* (West Chester, PA: Chester County Historical Society, 1987).

Church Records

Records at the Chester County Historical Society in West Chester include:
- Cemetery and church records, 1700–1968 (film 0568056 ff.).
- Complete index to church records of the Society of Friends, Goshen area (film 0571401).

Vincent Baptist Church, Chester Springs, West Vincent Township. Minutes, 1746–1882 (film 0022075).

Saint David's Church, Radnor Township, Episcopal. Records, 1706–1859 (film 0432018).

Records at the State Historical Society in Philadelphia are:

Society of Friends, Western Quarterly Meeting. Minutes, 1758–79 (film 0389410).

Brandywine Baptist Church, Delaware County. Baptisms and burials, 1697–9, 1715–1848 (film 0432015).

Society of Friends, Chester. Manuscript records of Darby, Sadbury, Nottingham, Goshen, Little Britain, London Grove and New Garden, 1682–1868 (film 0389402 ff.).

Society of Friends, Nottingham. Women's and men's minutes, 1730–78 (film 0389414).

Original records at the Presbyterian Historical Society in Philadelphia are:

Forks of the Brandywine Presbyterian Church. Records, 1761–81 (film 0503559).

New Londonderry Presbyterian Church, Faggs Manor. Records, 1740–1890 (film 0525750 ff.).

Presbyterian Church, Oxford. Session records, 1760–1914 (film 1314171 ff.).

Original records at the American Baptist Historical Society in Rochester, New York include:

Glen Run Baptist Church. Minutes and membership lists (film 0021341).

Great Valley Baptist Church, Tredyffrin Township. Records, 1740–1942 (film 0986477 ff.).

Records at the Lutheran Archives in Philadelphia are:
Saint Peter's Lutheran Church, West Pikeland Township. Records, 1771–1880 (film 0021718 ff.).
Zion Lutheran Church, East Pikeland Township. Records, 1760–1883 (film 1312361 ff.).
Brownback's Reformed Church, East Coventry Township. Records, 1756–1889 (film 0021329 ff.).

Original records at the Friends Historical Library, Swarthmore College, in Swathmore are:
- Bradford, Marshallton. Monthly meeting records, 1726–1909 (film 0020454).
- Goshen. Monthly meeting records, 1705–1930 (film 0020398 ff.), 1722–1938 (film 0021336 ff.).
- Kennett, Kennett Square. Monthly meeting records, 1706–1944 (film 0020401 ff.). Established prior to 1686 and called Newark Monthly Meeting until 1760 when name changed to Kennett Monthly Meeting. Meeting has also met at Christiana, Delaware.
- New Garden. Monthly meeting records, 1682–1903 (film 0020465 ff.).
- Uwchlan. Monthly meeting records, 1752–1894 (film 0020484).

Humphrey, John T. *Pennsylvania Births, Chester County, 1682–1800* (Washington, DC: Humphrey Publications, 1994). Includes:

Quaker records from Kennett, Bradford, Goshen, Nottingham, New Garden, Sadsbury, Uwchlan, Londongrove, Birmingham, and Fallowfield	East Vincent Reformed, Vincent Brownbacks German Reformed, Coventry Forks of the Brandywine Presbyterian Faggs Manor Presbyterian
Zion's Lutheran, Pikeland	Records of Rev. John Casper Stoever

Cumberland County (established 1750 from Lancaster County)
Original records in the Cumberland County Courthouse in Carlisle are:
Cumberland County Court of Common Pleas. Appearance dockets, 1769–1905, adsecturm index, 1750–1894 (film 1010167 ff.).
Cumberland County Court of Quarter Sessions. Docket, 1750–1909 (film 1011065 ff.). Includes Court of Oyer and Terminer and General Gaol Delivery.
Cumberland County Recorder of Deeds. Deeds and miscellaneous records, 1750–1866 (film 0021029 ff.).
Cumberland County Surveyor. Land drafts and warrants, 1738–1890 (film 1010322 ff.).

Land papers from Board of Property, 1753–1868 (film 1010326).

Cumberland County Register of Wills. Wills, 1750–1908, administrators' books, 1750–1906 (film 0021075 ff.).

Cumberland County Orphans' Court. Court docket, 1751–1906 (film 1010105 ff.).

Cumberland County Board of Commissioners. Tax lists, 1750–1850 (film 0021087 ff.).

Original records at the State Archives in Harrisburg are:
Cumberland County Prothonotary of the Court of Common Pleas.
* Continuance dockets, 1750–1851 (film 1449384 ff.).
* Appearance dockets, 1765–1807 (film 1433964 ff.).

Church Records
The following are films of original records. Their location is unknown:
Carlisle Presbytery, Carlisle. Minutes, 1765–1877 (film 0450467).
Zoar Lutheran Church, Dauphin County. Records, 1754–1820 (film 0021533).

Original records at the Evangelical and Reformed Archives in Lancaster are:
Evangelical Lutheran and Reformed Church, Shippensburg. Records, 1770–1921 (film 1486703 ff.).
Bucher, John Conrad. Pastoral records, 1763–9 (film 1294885). Rev. Bucher performed baptisms and marriages in the following localities:
* Cumberland County: Carlisle, 1763–9, Shippensburg, 1764–9
* Dauphin County: Middletown, 1765–8, Hummelstown, 1765–8
* Franklin County: Chambersburg, 1765–8
* Western Pennsylvania, 1764–8

Lancaster County (established 1729 from Chester County)
Land records from 1729 are at the Office of Records and Archives Services, Old Court House, Lancaster. Records prior to this time are at the Chester County Archives in West Chester.

Original records at the Lancaster County Courthouse in Lancaster are:
Lancaster County Orphans' Court. Miscellaneous books, 1742–1867 (film 0021368 ff.).
Lancaster County Recorder of Deeds.
* Deeds, 1729–1867 (film 0021439 ff.).
* Mortgage index, 1729–1940 (film 0941084 ff.).
Lancaster County Register of Wills. Wills, 1729–1908 (film 0383290 ff.).
Lancaster County Board of Commissioners. Tax lists, 1750–1814 (film 0021448 ff).

Bethel Township, 1751–83
Derry Township, 1754–82
Hanover Township, 1750–83
Heidelberg Township, 1751–88

Londonderry Township, 1769–83
Paxton Township, 1750–82
Upper Paxton Township, 1769–83

Lancaster County tax records, 1748–1855 (film 1449193 ff.) at the Lancaster County Historical Society in Lancaster are:

Lebanon Township, 1750–83
Bart Township, 1750–1834
Brecknock Township, 1750–1846
Caernarvon Township, 1754–1845
Cocalico Township, 1751–1808
Colerain Township, 1751–1846
Conestoga Township, 1751–1855
Donegal Township, 1750–1816
Drumore Township, 1751–1831
Earl Township, 1750–1812
Elizabeth Township, 1757–1825
Hempfield Township, 1751–1818
Lampeter Township, 1751–1821

Lancaster Township, 1750–1828
Lancaster Borough, 1750–87
Leacock Township, 1757–1825
Little Britain Township, 1754–1846
Manheim Township, 1751–1846
Manor Township, 1751–1825
Martic Township, 1751–1831
Mount Joy Township, 1759–1825
Rapho Township, 1751–1825
Sadsbury Township, 1750–1840
Strassburg Township, 1751–1814
Warwick Township, 1751–1825

Original records at the State Archives in Harrisburg include Lancaster County tax and exoneration lists, 1772–86 (film 1027051 ff.).

Fulton, Eleanore Jane. *An Index to the Will Books and Intestate Records of Lancaster County, Pennsylvania, 1729–1850: With an Historical Sketch and Classified Bibliography* (Lancaster: Intelligencer Printing Co., 1936, film 0207681).

Church Records
Original records at the Lutheran Archives in Philadelphia are:
Diary of Frederich August Conrad Muhlenberg, 1770–4 (film 0022036). Muhlenberg served as pastor in Heidelbergtown or Schaefferstown in Lebanon County; Manheim, Warwick, and White Oaks in Lancaster.
Christ Evangelical Lutheran Church, Elizabethtown. Records, 1771–1870 (film 0021325 ff.).
Saint Michael's Lutheran Church, Strasburg. Records, 1749–1869 (film 1428446 ff.). The first church was built in 1746 and called Beaver Creek; also known as Stoutzenberger Church and Bethelhaus.
Trinity Lutheran Church, Lancaster. Records, 1724–1850 (film 0021450). Some records transcribed in Braun, Fritz. *Trauungen aus dem Kirchenbuch der Evangelical Lutheran Church of the Holy Trinity in Lancaster, Pennsylvanien, 1748–1767: Mit Zahlreichen Deutschen Herkunftsangaben* (Kaiserslautern: Heimatstelle Pfalz, 1973, fiche 6000937). Marriages performed at the Evangelical

Lutheran Church of the Holy Trinity in Lancaster, 1748–67, including places of emigrant origin in Germany.

Saint John's Evangelical Lutheran Church, Maytown. Records, 1767–1915 (film 1730900 ff.).

Original records at the Presbyterian Historical Society in Philadelphia are:

Presbyterian Church, Seltenreich. Records, 1766–1800 (film 0504290).

Presbyterian Church, Cocalico. Record book of Rev. John Waldeschmidt, 1752–94 (film 0504290).

Saint James' Episcopal Church, Lancaster. Marriages, 1755–74 (film 0504290).

Presbytery of Lancaster. Minutes, 1765–6 (film 0450467).

Original records at the State Historical Society in Philadelphia are:

Saint James' Episcopal Church, Lancaster. Church and burial records, 1755–1856 (film 0383295).

Evangelical Lutheran Church, Brickerville. Records, 1730–1896 (film 0383301 ff.).

Trinity Evangelical Lutheran Church, New Holland. Records, 1730–1949 (film 0021705 ff.).

Moravian Church, Lancaster. Records, 1730–1821 (film 1029744). A photocopy of the original records is at the State Library in Harrisburg.

Bangor Church, Churchtown, Episcopal. Records, 1730–1950 (film 0500734 ff.). The original records are at the parish in Churchtown.

Records at the Evangelical and Reformed Historical Society in Lancaster include:

Zion Lutheran Church, Manheim. Records, 1771–1849 (film 1305845).

Evangelisch-Reformierte Kirche Warwick. Almosenbuch, 1763–1818 (film 0020365). Record of alms or charity at the Warwick Evangelical Reformed Church.

Maytown Reformed Church, Maytown. Records, 1765–1947 (film 1428178 ff.).

Pequea Reformed Church, Strasburg Township. Records, 1744–1942 (film 1432885 ff.).

White Oaks Reformed Church, Penn Township. Records, 1754–1898 (film 0940435 ff.).

Reyer's Reformed Church, Elizabeth Township. Records, 1773–87 (film 0020363 ff.).

Muddy Creek Lutheran Church, East Cocalico Township. Records, 1728–45 (film 0020358 ff.).

Muddy Creek Reformed Church, East Cocalico Township. Records, 1743–1916 (film 1434437 ff.).

First Reformed Church, Lancaster. Records, 1736–1947 (film 0021452 ff.).

Society of Friends, Sadsbury. Monthly meeting records, 1770–1902 (film 0020420 ff.). The original records are at the Friends Historical Library, Swarthmore College, in Swarthmore.

Humphrey, John T. *Pennsylvania Births, Lancaster County, 1723–1777* (Washington, DC: Humphrey Publications, 1997). Contains records from the following churches:

Sadsbury Monthly Meeting, Sadsbury	Christ Lutheran, Elizabethtown
Little Britain Monthly Meeting, Little Britain	Saint Michael's Lutheran, Strasburg
Saint James' Protestant Episcopal, Lancaster	Swamp Reformed, West ocalico
Muddy Creek Lutheran, East Cocalico	Zion Reformed, Elizabeth
Old Warwick Lutheran Lutheran, Elizabeth	Blasser Reformed, West Donegal
Holy Trinity Lutheran, Lancaster	White Oak Lutheran and Reformed, Penn
Moravian, Lancaster	Zeltenreich/Seltenreich Reformed, Earl
First Reformed, Lancaster	Maytown Reformed, East Donegal
Trinity Lutheran, New Holland	Saint Paul's Reformed, Manheim
Saint Mary's Roman Catholic, Lancaster	Pequea Reformed, Strasburg
Zion Lutheran Church, Manheim	Maytown Lutheran, East Donegal
Muddy Creek Reformed, East Cocalico	Cocalico Reformed, Ephrata
Bangor Protestant Episcopal, Caenarfon	Records of Rev. John Casper Stoever, Jr
Bergstrasse Lutheran, Ephrata	Moravian, Lititz
Records of Rev. John Waldschmidt	

Rineer, A. Hunter. *Churches and Cemeteries of Lancaster County, Pennsylvania: A Complete Guide* (Lancaster: Lancaster County Historical Society, 1993).

Weiser, Frederick S. *Parochial Registers for Lutheran Congregations in Lancaster County, Pennsylvania, 1730–1982: A Guide to Genealogical Resources in the Parish Records of Baptisms, Marriages, and Burials, as Well as to Translations and Copies in Print and in Public Institutions.* Rev. ed. (New Oxford, PA: The Author, 1982, 1st ed. on film 0940406).

Northampton County (established 1752 from Bucks County)
Original records at the Northampton County Courthouse in Easton include:
Northampton County Recorder of Deeds.
• Deeds, 1752–1866 (film 0947056 ff.).
• Mortgage index, 1752–1922 (film 0953667 ff.).
Northampton County Register of Wills. Wills, 1752–1907 (film 0945722 ff.).
Northampton County Orphans' Court. Court records and index, 1752–1882 (film 0946983 ff.).
Northampton County Board of Commissioners. Tax lists, 1761–93, assessments, 1761–1815 (film 0021682 ff.).

Records at the State Historical Society in Philadelphia include:

Papers, warrants, surveys, wills, accounts, bonds and agreements, minutes, etc. (film 0021686 ff.).

Deeds, wills, correspondence, treasurers' accounts, 1727–1851 (film 0021680 ff.).

Original records at the State Archives in Harrisburg include tax and exoneration lists for Northampton County, 1772–90 (film 1027055 ff.).

Church Records

Records at the Lutheran Archives in Philadelphia are:

Zion Lutheran Church, Allen Township. Records, 1773–1907 (film 0021346 ff.).

Saint John's Lutheran Church, Easton. Records, 1769–1912 (film 0021327 ff.).

Lower Saucon Reformed Church, Lower Saucon Township. Records, 1747–1931 (film 1671325 ff.).

Saucon Lutheran Church, Williams Township. Records, 1740–1881 (film 1312467 ff.).

Presbyterian Church, Allen Township. Records, 1749–1898 (film 0501916). The original records are at the Presbyterian Historical Society in Philadelphia.

Emanuel Lutheran and Reformed Church, Moore Township. Records, 1755–1955 (film 1671321 ff.). The original records are at Emmanuel Lutheran Church in Bath.

Zion Reformed Church, Allen Township. Records, 1771–1949 (film 1651940 ff.). The original records are at Zion's Stone United Church of Christ in Northampton.

First Reformed Church, Easton. Records, 1760–1913 (film 1671306 ff.). The original records are at the First United Church of Christ in Easton.

Few Moravian records have been filmed. Some have been abstracted in the *Pennsylvania Archives*, such as the marriage registers of the Moravian Church in Bethlehem, 1742–1800 (Second Series, 9:106–28, film 0823996), and Nazareth, 1742–1800 (Second Series, 9:129–35, film 0823996). The Archives of the Moravian Church is the official depository of the Northern Province of the Moravian Church in America and the Moravian Congregation of Bethlehem. For more information see *The Archives of the Moravian Church, Bethlehem, Pennsylvania* (Bethlehem: The Archives, 1983, fiche 6019434).

Original records at the Evangelical and Reformed Church Historical Society in Lancaster are:

Egypt Reformed Church, Whitehall. Records, 1736–1965 (film 1888054 ff.). Includes Heidelberg and Jordan for 1752–3.

Saint Paul's Lutheran Church, Indianland. Record extracts, 1757–1861 (film 1428443).

Salem Lutheran and Reformed Church, Moorestown. Records, 1774–96 (film 0020361 ff.).

Mount Bethel Lutheran and Reformed Church, Upper Mount Bethel Township. Records, 1774–1813 (film 0020361 ff.).

Transcripts of original records of twenty-eight churches (film 1029737 ff.), including a few churches in Berks and Bucks counties, are available in the Easton Public Library. Some volumes were compiled by the Historical Records Survey. Transcripts beginning before 1775 include:

Surname index to records
Saint Luke's Union (Nockamixon)
Durham and Riegelsville
German Evangelical Lutheran, Easton
Saint James Lutheran, Greenwich, New Jersey (Straw Church)
Plainfield Reformed
Emmanuel Petersville, Moore
Reformed, Lower Saucon
Evangelical, Moorestown

Lutheran and Reformed, Mount Bethel
Lutheran and Reformed, Stone Church near Kreidersville
United Protestant Lutheran and Reformed, Frieden's Church (New Allemangel)
Trinity Lutheran and Dryland Reformed, Hecktown
Albany Lutheran, Allemangel
Rosenthal, New Bethel, or Corner Church, Albany

Humphrey, John T. *Pennsylvania Births, Northampton County, 1733–1800* (Baltimore: Gateway Press, 1991).

Williams Township Congregation
Nazareth Moravian Congregation including congregations of Gnadenthal, Friedensthal, and Niskey
Reformed Congregation, Lower Saucon
Emanuel Petersville, Moore
Reformed and Lutheran, Lower Nazareth
First Reformed, Easton
Moravian Congregation, Schoeneck, Upper Nazareth

Saint Peter's Union Lutheran and Reformed, Plainfield Township
German Evangelical Lutheran, Easton
Lutheran and Reformed, Stone Church near Kreidersville, Allen
Salem Lutheran and Reformed, Moore
Mount Bethel Lutheran and Reformed, Upper Mount Bethel
Bethlehem Moravian
Daniel Schumacher's baptismal register

Northumberland County (established 1772 from Bedford, Berks, Cumberland, Lancaster, and Northampton counties)

Original records in the Northumberland County Courthouse in Sunbury include:

Northumberland County Orphans' Court. Orphans' Court docket, 1772–1868 (film 0961029 ff.).

Northumberland County Recorder of Deeds.

- Deeds, 1770–1866 (film 0961183 ff.).
- Mortgage index, 1772–1974 (film 0961102 ff.).

Northumberland County Register of Wills. Wills, 1772–1907 (film 0961020 ff.).

Records at the State Archives in Harrisburg include:
Northumberland County Board of Commissioners. Tax records, 1774–1843 (film 1449342 ff.), for the following townships:
* Augusta Township and County, 1774–96
* Lower Bald Eagle Township and County, 1774–94
* Lycoming Township and County, 1775–1811
* Muncy Township and County, 1773–97

Philadelphia County (established 1682)
Philadelphia probate records also include wills for Chester County before 1714; there are also numerous wills recorded for residents of Bucks County and the "three lower counties" of Kent, New Castle, and Sussex, Delaware. The original wills are at the City Archives. Inventory records and administrations are only available on microfilm at the City Archives.
Original records at the Philadelphia City Archives include:
Philadelphia County Recorder of Deeds.
* Deeds, 1683–1886 (film 1318501 ff.).
* Exemplification record, patent books, 1667–1839 (film 0021869 ff.). Transactions between recipients of original land patents and those to whom they sold land.
Philadelphia County Court of Quarter Sessions.
* Court docket, 1753–1879 (film 0965370 ff.).
* Road docket, 1685–1870 (film 0966339 ff.). Petitions for laying out or opening of roads, streets, and bridges specifying desired routes and names of petitioners, reports of court appointed road viewers, etc.
* Road petitions, 1699–1800 (film 0968419 ff.). Papers in re-opening of streets, roads, bridges, parks, filed by location; court's appointment of viewers and their reports, etc.
Philadelphia County Court of Common Pleas.
* Partition deeds, 1740–1869 (film 0963394).
* Sheriffs' deeds, 1736–1851 (film 0965344 ff.).
* Defendant and purchaser indexes to sheriffs'deeds, 1736–1905 (film 0963395 ff.).
Philadelphia County Registrar of Wills. Wills, 1682–1916 (film 1311039 ff.).
Philadelphia Constables. Constables' returns to tax assessors, 1762–80 (film 0981095 ff.). Entries list householder's name and occupation, house landlord and rent, grounded landlord and rent, inmates, hired and bond servants, children, Negroes. Includes returns for:
* Upper Delaware, Lower Delaware, South, Chestnut, High Street, Mulberry, North, Middle, Walnut, and Dock wards, 1775
* Walnut ward, 1762

- High and East Mulberry wards, 1770
- Middle and South Dock wards, 1775

Records at the State Archives in Harrisburg include:

Index to old rights in Philadelphia County, 1682–1748, and Bucks and Chester counties, 1682–1761 (film 0986897).

Tax and exoneration lists for Philadelphia County, 1762–94 (film 1027056 ff.).

Records from the State Historical Society in Philadelphia include:

Philadelphia County Orphans' Court. Minutes of court records and probate actions, 1716–55 (film 0384827).

Philadelphia County Recorder of Deeds. Immigration lists, oaths of allegiance in Philadelphia, 1728–75 (film 0020446).

Indexes to wills (1681–1859) and administrations (1683–1842) by the Registrar of Wills for the city and county of Pennsylvania (film 0384803 ff.).

Abstracts of Philadelphia administrations granted for estates of residents of Chester and Bucks counties and Delaware, 1683–1744 (film 0384817). Includes abstracts for original books A–E of letters of administration for Philadelphia city and county.

The First Tax List for the Province of Pennsylvania and the Three Lower Counties, 1693 (Bedminster, PA: Adams Apple Press, 1994). Contains Philadelphia County, Bucks County, and Chester County in Pennsylvania; New Castle, Kent, and Sussex counties in Delaware.

Church Records

Original records in the Presbyterian Historical Society in Philadelphia are:

German Reformed Church, Germantown. Records, 1750–1900 (film 0503613 ff.).

Trinity Protestant Episcopal Church, Philadelphia, Oxford. Records, 1711–1855 (film 0441386).

First Presbyterian Church, Philadelphia. Records, 1701–1946 (film 0468374 ff.).

Second Presbyterian Church, Philadelphia. Records, 1744–1914 (film 0973460 ff.).

Third Presbyterian Church, Philadelphia. Records, 1773–1899 (film 0901397 ff.).

Scots Presbyterian Church, Philadelphia. Records, 1768–1924 (film 0504371 ff.).

Presbytery of Philadelphia. Minutes, 1758–81 (film 0450467).

Original records at the Lutheran Archives in Philadelphia are:

Saint Michael's Lutheran Church, Germantown. Records, 1741–1922 (film 1312443 ff.).

Saint Michael's and Zion Lutheran Church, Philadelphia. Records, 1745–1927 (film 1312256 ff.).

Muhlenberg, Henry Melchior. Memorandum book, 1765–70 (film 1312366).

Records and transcripts at the State Historical Society in Philadelphia are:
First and Second Universalist Church. Records, 1755–1933 (film 0387903).
First Baptist Church and Pennepack Baptist Church. Records, 1687–1859 (film 0382736).
Moravian Church, Philadelphia. Extracts from the records, 1743–61 (film 0020438).
Church of the Brethren, Germantown. Records, 1766–1860 (film 0941583).

Original records that are believed to be at the original parishes are:
First Baptist Church, Philadelphia. Records, 1691–1900 (film 0986466 ff.).
First Reformed Church, Philadelphia. Records, 1748–1993 (film 1905870 ff.).
Gloria Dei Church, Philadelphia, Episcopal. Records, 1636–1967 (film 0511804 ff.).
Saint Paul's Church, Philadelphia, Episcopal, 3rd Street and Walnut and Spruce. Records, 1759–1903 (film 1731981 ff.).
Saint Peter's Church, Philadelphia, Episcopal, 3rd and Pine Streets. Records, 1771–1831 (film 1490580 ff.).

Society of Friends original records in the Friends Historical Library, Swarthmore College, in Swarthmore are:
• Philadelphia. Monthly meeting records, 1672–1949 (film 0020467 ff.).
• Spruce Street, Philadelphia. Monthly meeting records, 1686–1902 (film 0020405).
• Byberry. Monthly meeting records, 1736–1886 (film 0020410 ff.).
• Northern District, Philadelphia. Monthly meeting records, 1772–1914 (film 0020473 ff.).
• Southern District, Philadelphia. Monthly meeting records, 1772–1872 (film 0020476 ff.).

Humphrey, John T. *Pennsylvania Births, Philadelphia County, 1644–1780.* 2 Vols. (Washington, DC: Humphrey Publications, 1994).

Gloria Dei, Old Swedes, or Wicaco
Philadelphia Friends Monthly Meeting
Christ Church
First Presbyterian
Second Presbyterian
Pennypack Baptist, Lower Dublin Township
First Moravian
Saint Michael's and Zion Lutheran, Philadelphia
First Reformed, Philadelphia
Saint Michael's Lutheran, Germantown
German Reformed, Germantown

Saint Joseph's Roman Catholic
Trinity Episcopal, Oxford Township
First Baptist, Philadelphia
Friends Monthly Meeting, Pine and Orange Streets
Scots Presbyterian
Register of Rev. Blackwell
Northern District Monthly Meeting
Southern District Monthly Meeting
Saint Paul's Protestant Episcopal
Saint George's Methodist Episcopal

Westmoreland County (established 1773 from Bedford County)
Original records at the Westmoreland County Courthouse in Greensburg are:
Westmoreland County Recorder of Deeds. Deeds, 1773–1897 (film 0929096 ff.).
Westmoreland County Register of Wills. Wills, 1773–1917 (film 1316409 ff.).
Orphans' Court. General index, register's office (film 1316398 ff.).

Church Records
Ruff, Paul Miller. *The German Church Records of Westmoreland County, Pennsylvania [1772–1820].* 4 Vols. (Aliquippa, PA: The Author, 1989).

Ruff, Paul Miller. *Baptism and Confirmation Index, the German Church Records of Westmoreland County, Lutheran and Reformed, 1772–1804* (Aliquippa, PA: The Author, 1982, film 1597536).

York County (established 1749 from Lancaster County)
Original records at the York County Courthouse in York include:
York County Orphans' Court. Court dockets, 1749–1881 (film 0022150 ff.).
York County Recorder of Deeds. Deeds, 1749–1859 (film 0022085 ff.).
York County Register of Wills. Wills, 1749–1882 (film 0022130 ff.).

Original records at the State Archives in Harrisburg include:
York County Court of Quarter Sessions.
* Dockets, 1749–94 (film 1449257 ff.). Index to road docket, 1750–85, appointments of township constables, overseers of the poor, supervisors of the highways and town clerks, etc.
* Road papers, 1742–1868 (film 1449146 ff.).
York County Board of Commissioners. Township assessment lists, 1762–1849 (film 0022234 ff.). Adams County was formed from York County in 1800 and took all or parts of the following townships: Berwick, Cumberland, Franklin, Germany, Hamilton Bann, Huntington, Menallen, Mount Joy, Mount Pleasant, Reading, Straban, and Tyrone. Townships with lists 1775 and earlier are:

Berwick	Huntington	Paradise
Chanceford	Manchester	Reading
Cumberland	Manheim	Shrewsberry
Dover	Menallen	Straban
Fawn	Monaghan	Tyrone
Germany	Mount Joy	Warrington
Hamilton's Bann	Mount Pleasant	Windsor
Hellam	Newberry	York
Hopewell		

Gross, Patricia A. *An Everyname Index to Orphans' Court Book A (1749–1762) plus Introductory Text* (York: South Central Pennsylvania Genealogical Society, 1993).

Church Records

Original records and transcripts at the York County Historical Society in York are:
Church records surname index of Adams and York counties (film 0022174 ff.).
Abstracts of York County church records (film 0022203 ff.).

Warrington Monthly Meetings, 1747–63
Warrington births and deaths, 1731–1876
Reformed Church, Kreutz Creek, 1757–1855
Christ Episcopal, Huntingdon, 1760–1880
Lower Bermudian Union, 1745–1864
Books of attendance records of schoolmasters

in Cumberland and York counties, 1771–74
Christ Lutheran, York, 1733–1801
Saint Jacob's (Stone) Union Church, Brodbeck, 1756–1858
Trinity and First Reformed, York, 1744–1852
German Reformed, York, 1734–1843

First Moravian Church, York County. Records, 1751–1900 (film 0022188 ff.).
Christ Lutheran Church, York. Manuscript of church records, 1733–1921 (film 0020491 ff.)
Emanuel Reformed Church, Hanover. Records, 1770–1856 (film 0022193).
Saint David's Lutheran Church, West Manheim Township. Records, 1763–1869 (film 0022193 ff.).
Canadochly Lutheran Church, Lower Windsor Township. Records, 1755–1873 (film 0022192).
Saint Matthew's Lutheran Church, Hanover. Records, 1740–1865 (film 0020499).
Strayer's (Salem) Lutheran and Reformed Church, Dover Township. Records, 1762–1873 (film 0022193 ff.).
Stehley's Lutheran and Reformed Church, Chanceford Township. Records, 1772–1943 (film 0022202 ff.).

Society of Friends, Menallen. Monthly meeting records, 1727–1908 (film 0020701 ff.). The manuscript and photocopy of original records are at the Historical Society of Adams County in Gettysburg.
Original records at the Presbyterian Historical Society in Philadelphia include:
Zion's Lutheran and Reformed (Quickel's Church), Conewago Township. Records, 1765–1833 (film 0387942).
Guinston United Presbyterian Church, Chanceford Township. Records, 1772–1970 (film 1977238 ff.).
Saint Paul's (Wolf's) Lutheran and Reformed Church, West Manchester Township. Records, 1764–1930 (film 0387951).

Society of Friends, Warrington Monthly Meeting. Marriage registers, 1748–1849 (film 0441389). The manuscript is at the State Historical Society in Philadelphia.

Original records at the Evangelical and Reformed Historical Society in Lancaster include:

Blymire's Lutheran and Reformed Church, York Township. Records, 1767–1890 (film 1433083 ff.).

Saint Paul's Reformed Church, Manheim. Transcript of records, 1751–1868 (film 0020364 ff.).

Kreutz Creek Reformed Church, Hellam Township. Records, 1757–1855 (film 0020348).

Reformed Church baptisms including Kreutz Creek, Conewago, and Bromutsch, 1744–66 (film 0020365).

Saint Jacob's Lutheran and Reformed Church, Codorus Township. Records, 1756–1955 (film 1414855 ff.).

Lischy, Jacob. Pastor's record, 1744–1801: Reformed churches in York and Adams counties, and Carroll and Baltimore counties, Maryland (film 1888121). Jacob Lischy served the following congregations:

York County
First Reformed, York 1744–61
Kreutz Creek (Trinity Reformed), Hellam, 1745–7
Saint David's, West Manheim, 1753–61
Canadochly, Lower Windsor, 1753–61
Codorus or Lischy's (Saint Peter's), North Codorus (Spring Grove), 1753–69
Codorus or Jacob's, Codorus near
    Brodbeck, 1756–69
Reformed (Strayer's), Dover, 1757–69
Saint Paul's Reformed, West Manchester, 1763–9
Reformed, Hanover, 1765–9
Quickel's, Conewago, 1765–9
Shuster's, Springfield, 1768–70
Adams County
Bermudia (Mount Olivet Reformed),
    Latimore, 1745–69
Conewago (Christ Reformed), German Township (Littlestown), 1745–52
Maryland
Baltimore County Zion Reformed, 1758–69
Carroll County
Saint Mary's Reformed, Silver Run, 1762–9
Pipe Creek (Benjamin Reformed), 1762–5
Reformed Church, Taneytown, 1763–9

Suggested Reading

Adams, Edmund J. *Catholic Trails West: The Founding Catholic Families of Pennsylvania* (Baltimore: Genealogical Publishing Co., 1988).

Brecht, Samuel Kriebel. *The Genealogical Record of the Schwenkfelder Families: Seekers of Religious Liberty Who Fled from Silesia to Saxony and Thence to Pennsylvania in the Years 1731 to 1737* (New York: Rand McNally, 1923, film 1266718).

Burgert, Annette Kunselman. *Eighteenth-Century Emigrants from German- Speaking Lands to North America.* 2 Vols. (Breinigsville: Pennsylvania German Society, 1986). Emigrants are mainly from northern Kraichgau and the western Palatinate.

Books on CD-ROM

Several CD-ROMs from Broderbund's *Family Archives* collection contain images of books published by Genealogical Publishing Company. The first two CDs are from articles in *The Pennsylvania Genealogical Magazine* and *The Pennsylvania Magazine of History and Biography*.

➢ *Genealogies of Pennsylvania Families*
➢ *Pennsylvania Vital Records [1701–1882]*
➢ *Pennsylvania German Church Records, 1729–1870* (from *Pennsylvania German Church Records*).

Burgert, Annette Kunselman and Henry Z. Jones. *Westerwald to America: Some Eighteenth-Century German Immigrants* (Camden, ME: Picton Press, 1989).

Diffenderffer, Frank R. *The German Immigration into Pennsylvania Through the Port of Philadelphia from 1700 to 1775: Part 2, The Redemptioners* (Lancaster: Pennsylvania German Society, 1900, film 0924111).

Dubbs, Joseph Henry. *The Reformed Church in Pennsylvania* (Lancaster: Pennsylvania German Society, 1902, film 0924111).

Dunaway, Wayland F. *The Scotch-Irish of Colonial Pennsylvania* (Chapel Hill: University of North Carolina Press, 1944, fiche 6046742).

Eastman, Frank Marshall. *Courts and Lawyers of Pennsylvania: A History, 1623–1923.* 3 Vols. (New York: American Historical Society, 1922, fiche 6089143 ff.).

Glatfelter, Charles H. *Pastors and People: German Lutheran and Reformed Churches in the Pennsylvania Field, 1717–1793.* 2 Vols. (Breinigsville: Pennsylvania German Society, 1980). Includes information for the District of Columbia, Maryland, New Jersey, New York, Pennsylvania, Tennessee, Virginia, and West Virginia.

Glenn, Thomas Allen. *Welsh Founders of Pennsylvania* (1911. Reprint. Baltimore: Genealogical Publishing Co., 1970, film 0496948).

Graeff, Arthur D. *The Relations Between the Pennsylvania Germans and the British Authorities, 1750–1776* (Norristown, PA: Norristown Herald, 1939).

Heisey, John W. *Pennsylvania Genealogical Library Guide* (Elverson, PA: Olde Springfield Shoppe, 1994).

Illick, Joseph E. *Colonial Pennsylvania: A History* (New York: Charles Scribner's Sons, 1976).

Jones, David. *Memorial Volume of Welsh Congregationalists in Pennsylvania: Their Churches, Periodical Convocations, Clergy and Prominent Lay Members* (n.p., 1934, film 0823832).

Klett, Guy Soulliard. *Presbyterians in Colonial Pennsylvania* (Philadelphia: University of Pennsylvania Press, 1937, fiche 6093723).

Kuhns, Levi Oscar. *The German and Swiss Settlements of Colonial Pennsylvania: A Study of the So-Called Pennsylvania Dutch* (1901. Reprint. Detroit: Gale Research, 1979, film 1320513).

Miller, Daniel. *Early History of the Reformed Church in Pennsylvania* (Reading, PA: The Author, 1906, fiche 6089088).

Reichel, Levin Theodore. *The Early History of the Church of the United Brethren (Unitas Fratrum), Commonly Called Moravians, in North America, A.D. 1734–1748* (Nazareth, PA: Moravian Historical Society, 1888, film 0928125).

Rupp, Israel Daniel. *A Collection of Upwards of Thirty Thousand Names of German, Swiss, Dutch, French and Other Immigrants in Pennsylvania from 1727 to 1776 . . . Containing Lists of More than One Thousand German and French Names in New York Prior to 1712* (1876. Reprint. Baltimore:

Genealogical Publishing Co., 1965, film 1421791). Also includes names of first Palatines in North Carolina and names of Salzburger settlers in Georgia, 1734–41.

Schmauk, Theodore E.A. *History of the Lutheran Church in Pennsylvania, 1638–1820, from Original Sources.* 2 Vols. (Lancaster: Pennsylvania German Society, 1903, film 0924112).

Sheppard, Walter Lee. *Passengers and Ships Prior to 1684: Reprints of Articles with Corrections, Additions and New Materials* (Baltimore: Genealogical Publishing Co., 1970, film 0962561).

South Central Pennsylvania Genealogical Society. *Abstracts and Identifications of Entries Giving European Origins in Church Records of South Central Pennsylvania* . . . (York: The Society, 1990).

State Library of Pennsylvania. *A Guide to the Genealogy/Local History Section of the State Library of Pennsylvania* (Harrisburg: The Library, 1985, film 1320564).

Strassburger, Ralph Beaver. *Pennsylvania German Pioneers: A Publication of the Original Lists of Arrivals In the Port of Philadelphia From 1727 to 1808.* 2 Vols. (1934. Reprint. Baltimore: Genealogical Publishing Co., 1966, fiche 6051507 ff.).

Tepper, Michael. *Emigrants to Pennsylvania, 1641–1819: A Consolidation of Ship Passenger Lists from The Pennsylvania Magazine of History and Biography* (Baltimore: Genealogical Publishing Co., 1975).

Yoder, Don. *Pennsylvania German Immigrants, 1709–1786: Lists Consolidated from Yearbooks of The Pennsylvania German Folklore Society* (Baltimore: Genealogical Publishing Co., 1980).

THE PENN SEAL.

Maryland

 aryland's charter as a proprietary colony was granted in 1632 to Cecilius Calvert, the second Lord Baltimore. His father, George, had converted to Catholicism in 1625, and had originally been granted the charter. Saint Mary's City was established in 1634 by a group of English settlers arriving at Chesapeake Bay on the ships *Ark* and *Dove*. A conflicting claim by colonists on Kent Island resulted in four years of armed conflict.

In 1645 a group of Puritans overthrew Lord Baltimore, who regained control of the colony in 1647 and appointed a Protestant governor. At this time a group of Puritans from Virginia, fleeing from the laws of conformity, settled in Maryland. Puritans again took control in 1654 and repealed the Act of Toleration which had been passed by the Maryland Assembly in 1649. Later, Lord Baltimore regained control and restored religious tolerance in 1657.

Many of the first colonists were convicts and indentured servants from England. The first Quakers arrived in 1657, followed by Germans in the 1670s. Scotch-Irish began to emigrate to Maryland in the 1680s. Until Crown currency was introduced in 1683, tobacco was the only legal tender in the colony and it continued to be used as currency for some time afterward.

In 1689 the Protestants again overthrew Lord Baltimore and requested a royal governor. From 1691 to 1715 Maryland reverted to the Crown. The Anglican Church was made the official church of the colony in 1692. In 1715 the current Lord Baltimore converted to Anglicanism, resulting in the restoration of the proprietary. In 1718 all Quakers and Catholics were disenfranchised and prohibited from practicing their religion.

Border disputes with Virginia were resolved in 1732, at which time much land was ceded to Virginia. The border between Maryland and Pennsylvania was established as the Mason-Dixon Line between 1763 and 1767. During the period prior to the Revolutionary War, many settlers began developing the western lands of the colony.

SEE ALSO
Acadia
Delaware
Great Britain
Pennsylvania
Virginia

Statewide Records and Resources

All records listed below are kept at the Hall of Records in Annapolis.

Provincial Court (1637–1805): Statewide jurisdiction, handled capital crimes, land disputes, and other civil matters. Court judgments, 1679–1778 (Annapolis: Hall of Records, 1947, film 0012941 ff.). There is a card index to Provincial Court records at the Hall of Records. See also *Archives of Maryland* and the *Calvert Papers*.

Chancery Court (1668–1851): Colony-wide jurisdiction, handled equity cases, such as divorces, name changes, mortgages, foreclosures, civil damage suits, and guardianships. See also *Archives of Maryland* and the *Calvert Papers*.

Prerogative Court (1635–1777): Probates were conducted on a province level until 1776. Counties also began handling probates in the 1690s. See also *Archives of Maryland* and the *Calvert Papers*.

- Inventories and accounts of estates, 1674–1718 (Annapolis: Hall of Records, 1947, film 0012918 ff.).
- Accounts of estates, 1718–77 (Annapolis: Hall of Records, 1947, film 0012899 ff.).
- Inventories of estates, 1718–77 (Annapolis: Hall of Records, 1947, film 0012862 ff.).
- Testamentary proceedings, 1657–1777 (Annapolis: Hall of Records, 1947, film 0012930 ff.).
- Will books, 1635–1777 (Annapolis: Hall of Records, 1947, film 0012841 ff.).
- Probate accounts, 1752–8 (film 0901271).
- Index to inventories and accounts, 1674–1718 (Annapolis: Hall of Records, 1947, film 0012929).
- Index to balances of final distribution books, 1751–75 (Annapolis: Hall of Records, 1947, film 0012860).
- Index to inventories of estates, 1718–77 (Annapolis: Hall of Records, 1947, film 0012898).

Court of Appeals, General Assembly (1635–50), Governor and Council (1650–1776): Colony-wide court of last resort of appeals. *Proceedings of the Maryland Court of Appeals, 1695–1729* (1933. Reprint. Millwood, NY: Kraus Reprint, 1975).

County Circuit Courts (1637–): County, district, and orphans' courts are found under specific counties.

Vice-Admiralty Court: see Great Britain.

All land was originally owned by the Calvert family. Headrights, or land grants, were issued to settlers from 1633 to 1683 in return for providing transport for themselves and others to Maryland. By 1683, cash land sales had replaced the headright system. Settlers were charged a fee, known as caution money. Documentation was comprised of a warrant, a survey, and a patent. The grantee had to pay a tax called a quit rent. These are also found in the *Calvert Papers*. The original land office records are in the patents series, under the Maryland Land Office. The patents series, 1636–1852 (film 0013063 ff.), also contain some other land records and some proprietary and court records for the same period. The original records are at the Hall of Records in Annapolis.

The Maryland State Papers contain a series of records known as the "Rainbow Series." Most of the series concerns the Revolutionary War, but the "Black Books" contain colonial records. Proprietary papers, 1701–85 (Annapolis: Hall of Records, 1947, film 0012969 ff.), church vestry papers (Annapolis: Hall of Records, 1947, film 0012975). The original records are at the Hall of Records.

Calvert Papers (Baltimore: Maryland Historical Society, 1973). Some of the records have been published in the *Archives of Maryland*. The original manuscripts are at the Maryland Historical Society.

Calvert family papers
family wills, 1598–1783
other wills, 1716–45
marriage settlements, 1584–1725
marriage settlements, 1725–61
English land documents
Dorset: East Pulham, 1653–8
Durham: Billingham, 1762–4
Hampshire: Southampton, Christ Church, 1602–55
Huntingdon: Chesterton, 1731–6
Middlesex: Saint Giles in the Fields, 1696–1704
Surrey: Ebbisham, 1681–1765
Wiltshire:
Semly, 1566–1655
Tishbury, 1582–1639
Yorkshire:
Kiplint, 1596–1678
Moulton, 1618–76
Danby Wiske, 1599–1695
Heraldry papers (1622–1783)
Colonial ventures
Avalon, 1623–1756
Virginia, 1623–1765
Maryland, 1633–1765

Land records with Land Office accounts, 1736–61
Muster rolls, Fort Cumberland, 1757–8 (film 0013158).
Land grants
Anne Arundel County, 1701–38
Baltimore County, 1722
Calvert County, 1636–69
Cecil County, 1721–54
Charles County, 1636–59
Dorchester County, 1663–83
Kent County, 1744
Prince George's County, 1729–45
Saint Mary's County, 1636–81
Talbot County, 1679–84
Miscellaneous land grants, 1633–99
Land warrants, 1720–1
Alienation fines, 1753
Quit rents (film 0013151 ff., most counties filmed only through the 1720s).
Anne Arundel County, 1651–1762
Baltimore County, 1658–1761
Calvert County, 1651–1759
Cecil County, 1658–1762
Charles County, 1642–1762
Dorchester County, 1659–1761

Frederick County, 1760–1
Kent County, 1638–1761
Prince George's County, 1650–1761
Queen Anne's County, 1640–1761
Saint Mary's, 1639–1761
Somerset and Worcester counties, 1659–
    1761
Worcester County, 1663–1761
Talbot County, 1658–1761
Financial records
Revenues of the Lords Baltimore, 1731–61
Naval officers' records (1756–61)
Annapolis
Oxford
Patuxent
Pocomoke
Potomac
Debt books (1750)
Anne Arundel County
Baltimore County
Charles County

Prince George's County
Frederick County
Government records
Lower House journals, 1716–63
Upper House journals, 1718–63
Official printed session laws, 1727–63
Legislative acts, 1638–1757
Council records, 1638–1760
Provincial Court records, 1670–1760
Chancery Court records, 1716–21
Paper Currency Office, 1739–46
Political commissions, 1633–1761
Petitions and printed documents of the Lords
    Baltimore, 1653–1754
Maryland-Pennsylvania boundary dispute,
    1680–1769
Correspondence
from the Lords Baltimore 1616–1767
from the Principal Secretaries 1725–65
to the Principal Secretaries 1719–68

Ellis, Donna M. *The Calvert Papers: Calendar and Guide to the Microfilm Edition* (Baltimore: Maryland Historical Society, 1989, film 1685848 ff.).

Published Records
Archives of Maryland. 72 Vols. (Baltimore: Maryland Historical Society, 1883–1972). This series contains original records from both the Hall of Records in Annapolis and the Calvert Papers at the Maryland Historical Society in Baltimore. Some county records have also been published (see counties).

• *Proceedings of the Court of Chancery of Maryland* [*Archives of Maryland*. Vol. 51. Court Series 5] (film 0908320).

• *Judicial and Testamentary Business of the Provincial Court, 1637–1683*. 11 Vols. [*Archives of Maryland*. Court Series 1–4, 8, 10–15] (film 0924323).

• *Proceedings of the Council of Maryland, 1636–1770*. 11 Vols. [*Archives of Maryland*. Vols. 3, 5, 8, 15] (film 0430292 ff.).

• *Proceedings and Acts of the General Assembly of Maryland, January 1637/38–April 1774*. 32 Vols. [*Archives of Maryland*. Vols. 1–2, 7, 13, 19, 22, 24, 26–7, 29, 30, 33–40, 42, 46, 50, 55–6, 58–9, 61–4] (film 0924322 ff.).

Finding Aids

Some of the inventories, calendars, and abstracts of court and public records include:

- Baldwin, Jane. *The Maryland Calendar of Wills [1635–1774].* 14 Vols. (Baltimore: Genealogical Publishing Co., 1968–, fiche 6046924).
- Magruder, James C. *Index of Maryland Colonial Wills, 1634–1777* (1933. Reprint. Baltimore: Genealogical Publishing Co., 1986).
- Meade, Elizabeth W. *Calendar of Maryland State Papers: No. 1. The Black Books* (1943. Reprint. Baltimore: Genealogical Publishing Co., 1967, fiche 6050087).
- Eden, Henry C. *Maryland Deponents, 1634–1799* (Westminster, MD: Family Line Publications, 1991), and Eden, Henry C. *More Maryland Deponents, 1716–1799* (Westminster, MD: Family Line Publications, 1992).
- Skinner, V.L. *Abstracts of the Inventories and Accounts of the Prerogative Court of Maryland [1674–1718]* (Westminster, MD: Family Line Publications, 1992–).
- Skinner, V.L. *Abstracts of the Inventories of the Prerogative Court of Maryland [1718–1777]* (Westminster, MD: Family Line Publications, 1981–8).
- Skinner, V.L. *Abstracts of the Balance Books of the Prerogative Court of Maryland [1755–1777]* (Westminster, MD: Family Line Publications, 1995).
- Hooper, Debbie. *Abstracts of Chancery Court Records of Maryland, 1669–1782* (Westminster, MD: Family Line Publications, 1996).
- Skordas, Gust. *The Early Settlers of Maryland: An Index to Names of Immigrants Compiled from Records of Land Patents, 1633–1680, in the Hall of Records, Annapolis, Maryland* (Baltimore: Genealogical Publishing Co., 1968).
- Hartsook, Elisabeth. *Land Office and Prerogative Court Records of Colonial Maryland* (1946. Reprint. Baltimore: Genealogical Publishing Co., 1968, fiche 6117897).

Some of the record indexes at the Hall of Records in Annapolis include:

- Hodges Marriage reference card file, 1674–1851. Evidences taken from land evidences and other records.
- Marriage licences, etc., 1650–95. Posting of marriage banns was required from 1640.
- Births, and deaths, 1649–1715. Some vital records were recorded in county land records before 1720.
- Colonial muster and pay rolls, 1732–72

- Provincial naturalizations, 1634–1776
- County land records for Anne Arundel, Baltimore, Calvert, Cecil, Charles, Dorchester, Queen Anne's, Somerset, Talbot, and Worcester
- Rent rolls, 1639–1776

Brumbaugh, Gaius M. *Maryland Records: Colonial, Revolutionary, County and Church from Original Sources.* 2 Vols. (1928. Reprint. Baltimore: Genealogical Publishing Co, 1975, fiche 6046943).

Passano, Eleanor Phillips. *An Index to the Source Records of Maryland: Genealogical, Biographical, and Historical* (1940. Reprint: Genealogical Publishing Co., 1994).

Church Records
The records of Catholics and Quakers are few prior to the Revolutionary War, as they were disenfranchised in 1718. Many records created prior to this time were destroyed. The Anglican Church was established as the official church from 1692 until 1776.

The Maryland Historical Society has microfilm copies of the Evangelical and Reformed Church records that are in Pennsylvania archives. Most original Presbyterian records are at the Presbyterian Historical Society in Philadelphia. The Hall of Records in Annapolis has many Methodist and Quaker records on microfilm. Some original Methodist records are at the United Methodist Historical Society in Baltimore. Roman Catholic records are kept at individual parishes, the Diocese of Wilmington in Greenville, Delaware, and are on film at the Hall of Records in Annapolis. Some of the early Jesuit Province of Maryland records are available at Georgetown University in Washington, DC. Baptist Church records are kept at local congregations; some have been filmed by the Southern Baptist Historical Library and Archives in Nashville, Tennessee.

The church records and manuscripts at the Maryland Historical Society in Baltimore are indexed in the Norris Harris Church Register File available on-site. There are also several indexes to church records at the Hall of Records in Annapolis.

Kanely, Edna A. *Directory of Maryland Church Records* (Westminster, MD: Family Line Publications, 1987). Most recent guide to locating Maryland church records; replaces WPA surveys.

Jacobsen, Phebe R. *Quaker Records in Maryland* (Annapolis: Hall of Records, 1966).

Carroll, Kenneth Lane. *Quakerism on the Eastern Shore* (Baltimore: Maryland Historical Society, 1970).

Henry, J. Maurice. *History of the Church of the Brethren in Maryland* (Elgin, IL: Brethren Publishing, 1936, fiche 6100195).

Eby, Lela. *Every Name Index: History of the Church of the Brethren in Maryland by J. Maurice Henry, 1936* (Mill Valley, CA: The Author, 1975, fiche 6104839).

McIlvain, James William. *Early Presbyterianism in Maryland* (1890. New York: Johnson Reprint, 1973).

Skirven, Percy Granger. *The First Parishes of the Province of Maryland: Wherein Are Given Historical Sketches of the Ten Counties and of the Thirty Parishes in the Province at the Time of the Establishment of the Church of England in Maryland in 1692; Also a Short Treatise on the Religious Situation Before the Establishment* (Baltimore: Norman Remington Co., 1923, film 1321223).

Middleton, Arthur Pierce. *Anglican Maryland, 1632–1792* (Virginia Beach, VA: Donning Co., 1992).

Wright, F. Edward. *Vital Records of the Jesuit Missions of the Eastern Shore, 1760–1800* (Westminster, MD: Family Line Publications, 1986).

Eden, Henry C. *Quaker Records of Northern Maryland: Births, Deaths, Marriages and Abstracts from the Minutes, 1716–1800* (Westminster, MD: Family Line Publications, 1993).

Eden, Henry C. *Quaker Records of Southern Maryland: Births, Deaths, Marriages and Abstracts from the Minutes, 1658–1800* (Westminster, MD: Family Line Publications, 1992).

Treacy, William P. *Old Catholic Maryland and its Early Jesuit Missionaries* (Swedesboro, NJ: n.p., 1889).

County Records and Resources

Anne Arundel County (established 1650)
Original records at the Hall of Records in Annapolis are:
Anne Arundel County Clerk of the Circuit Court. Land records, 1653–1850 (film 0013241 ff.). The volumes before 1699 were destroyed, and the records before this date are reconstructions.

Church Records

Manuscripts of records at the Maryland Historical Society in Baltimore are:
Saint James' Parish, Episcopal. Records, 1682–1869 (film 0013280).
Saint Margaret's, Protestant Episcopal. Records, 1673–1885 (film 0013279).
Saint Anne's Parish, Annapolis, Episcopal. Records, 1687–1848 (film 0013281).
All Hallows Parish, Davidsonville, Episcopal. Records, 1685–1899 (film 0013279).
Saint George's Parish. Records, 1681–1850 (film 0014132).

Baltimore County (established 1659)
Original records at the Hall of Records in Annapolis are:
Baltimore County Clerk of the Circuit Court. Deeds, 1653–1849 (film 0013572 ff.).
Original records at the Baltimore City Courthouse in Baltimore are:
Baltimore County Orphans' Court.
* Administration accounts, 1631–1850 (film 0013602 ff.).
* Administrators' bonds, 1721–1852 (film 0013645 ff.).
* Inventories, 1666–1850 (film 0013654 ff.).
* Wills, 1666–1851 (film 0013589 ff.).

Church Records

Manuscripts at the Maryland Historical Society in Baltimore are:
* Saint John's Parish and Reisterstown Parish. Records, 1694–1891 (film 0014451).
* Saint Thomas Parish, Garrison. Records, 1728–1891 (film 0014450).
* First Presbyterian Church, Baltimore. Records, 1767–1879 (film 0013699).
* Saint Paul's Protestant Episcopal Church, Baltimore. Parish registers, 1710–1837 (film 0013696).

Original records at the Evangelical and Reformed Historical Society in Lancaster, Pennsylvania are:
First German Reformed Church, Baltimore. Records, 1701–1877 (film 0941096).
"Vital Records of the First and Saint Stephen's United Church of Christ of Baltimore, Maryland: Baptismal and Birth Records [1768–1838]."

Maryland Genealogical Society Bulletin 15 (1–4), 16 (1–3), 19 (1–3), 20 (3–4) (film 1428443).

Richards, Lewis. *Marriage Records, Reverend Lewis Richards, Pastor of the First Baptist Church, Baltimore City.* 2 Vols. (n.p.: Daughters of the American Colonists, Cecilius Calvert Chapter, n.d.). This church was organized in 1742. The original records are at the American Baptist Historical Society in Rochester, New York.

Boulden, J.E.P. *The Presbyterians of Baltimore: Their Churches and Historic Grave-Yards* (Baltimore: William K. Boyle, 1875, fiche 6099926).

Calvert County (established as Old Charles County in 1650, became Calvert County in 1654)
Church Records
Manuscripts at the Maryland Historical Society in Baltimore are:
Christ Church Parish. Records, 1688–1847 (film 0013888).
All Saint's Parish. Vestry proceedings, 1702–53 (film 0013888).

Caroline County (established 1773 from Dorchester and Queen Anne's counties)
Original records at the Caroline County Courthouse in Denton are:
Caroline County Orphans' Court.
• Land records, 1774–1851 (film 0013766 ff.).
• Administration accounts, 1703–1850 (film 0013784 ff.).
• Administrators' bonds, 1679–1851 (film 0013787 ff.). Contains bonds for slaves.
• Inventories, 1680–1856 (film 0013790 ff.).
• Wills, 1688–1899 (film 0013783 ff.).

Church Records
Saint John's Parish, Protestant Episcopal, Hillsborro. Records, 1749–1858 (film 0014144). The manuscript is at the Maryland Historical Society in Baltimore.

Cecil County (established 1674 from Kent and Baltimore counties)
Original records at the Cecil County Courthouse in Elkton are:
Cecil County Clerk of the Circuit Court. Land records, 1674–1850 (film 0013819 ff.).
Cecil County Orphans' Court.
• Administrators' and guardian bonds, 1674–1859 (film 0013879 ff.).
• Inventories, 1675–1850 (film 0013870 ff.).
• Wills, 1675–1853 (film 0013867 ff.).

Church Records (see also Kent County)
Saint Mary Ann's Parish, Protestant Episcopal. Records, 1718–99 (film 0013887).
    The manuscript is at the Maryland Historical Society in Baltimore.
Saint Stephen's North Sassafras Parish. Parish register, 1695–1817 (film
    0441446). Sassafras is on the border between Cecil and Kent counties. The
    original records are at the Presbyterian Historical Society in Philadelphia.

Saint Joseph Catholic Church, Middletown. Records, 1746–1962 (film
    1822515). This also contains entries for Saint Francis Xavier-Old Bohemia,
    Warwick, and Saint Rose of Lima, Chesapeake City. Film of original
    records.

Charles County (established 1658)
Original records at the Hall of Records in Annapolis are:
Charles County Circuit Court. Land records, 1658–1770 (film 0013746 ff.).
    Contains vital records, 1654–1706, land commissions, 1716–21, laws to
    1692, probate records, 1698–1792, and court records through 1780.
Original records at the Charles County Courthouse in La Plata are:
Charles County Orphans' Court.
* Administration accounts, 1708–1806 (film 0013725 ff.).
* Inventories, 1673–1852 (film 0013740 ff.).
* Wills, 1629–1947 (film 0013722 ff.).
Charles County Court.
* *Proceedings of the County Court of Charles County, 1658–1666 and Manor
    Court of Saint Clement's Manor, 1659–1672* [*Archives of Maryland*. Vol.
    53. Court Series 6] (Baltimore: Maryland Historical Society, 1936, film
    0908321).
* *Proceedings of the County Court of Charles County: 1666–1674* [*Archives
    of Maryland*. Vol. 60. Court Series 9] (Baltimore: Maryland Historical
    Society, 1943, film 0908324).

Church Records
Original records and manuscripts at the Library of Congress in Washington, DC
include:
Durham Parish, Episcopal. Records, 1774–1824 (film 0013201).
Trinity Parish, Newport, Episcopal. Records, 1729–1857 (film 0013203 ff.).

Dorchester County (established 1668, see also Caroline County)
Original records at the Hall of Records in Annapolis and the Dorchester County
Courthouse in Cambridge are:
Dorchester County Circuit Court. Land records, 1669–1851 (film 0013900 ff.).

Frederick County (established 1748 from Baltimore and Prince George's counties)

Manuscripts at the Frederick County Courthouse in Frederick and the Hall of Records in Annapolis are:

Frederick County Clerk of the Circuit Court. Land records, 1748–1851 (film 0013951 ff.).

Original records at the Frederick County Courthouse in Frederick are:

Frederick County Orphans' Court.

* Administration accounts, 1750–1852 (film 0014040 ff.).
* Inventories, 1749–1851 (film 0014046 ff.).
* Wills, 1737–1854 (film 0014025 ff.).

Church Records

Original records at the Evangelical and Reformed Historical Society in Lancaster, Pennsylvania are:

Apple's Lutheran and Reformed Church, Thurmont. Records, 1773–1886 (film 0940421 ff.).

Monocacy Reformed Church. Records, 1742–87 (film 0020365).

Evangelical Lutheran Church, Frederick City. Church record extracts, 1748–1887 (film 0013933).

Reformed Church, Glade Charge. Records, 1768–1857 (film 1294818).

Reformed Church, Frederick. Records, 1747–58 (film 0020365), 1749–1801 (film 0013931).

Christ Reformed Church, Middletown. Records, 1770–1840 (film 1888286).

Evangelical Lutheran Church, Frederick. Records, 1742–1910 (film 0020487 ff.). Includes Frederick Lutheran and Monocacy Reformed Churches. The original records are at the Lutheran Theological Seminary, Gettysburg, Pennsylvania.

Moravian Church, Graceham. Family registers, 1759–1871 (film 0020503). The manuscript is at York County Historical Society in York, Pennsylvania.

Harford County (established 1773 from Baltimore County)

Original records at the Harford County Courthouse in Bel Air are:

Harford County Clerk of the Circuit Court. Land records, 1773–1850 (film 0014084 ff.).

Harford County Orphans' Court.

* Administrators' bonds, 1774–1820 (film 0014131).
* Wills, 1774–1948 (film 0014117 ff.).

Church Records

Manuscripts at the Maryland Historical Society in Baltimore are:

Saint George's Parish, Perryman, Protestant Episcopal. Records, 1681–1850 (film 0014132).

Saint John's Parish, Joppa and Saint George's Parish, Perryman, Protestant Episcopal. Vestry records, 1735–82 (film 0014132).

Kent County (established 1642, see also Cecil County)

Land records after 1790 and probate records from 1798 are at the Kent County Courthouse in Chestertown. Earlier records are at the Hall of Records in Annapolis.

Original records at the Hall of Records in Annapolis are:

Kent County Clerk of the Circuit Court. Land records, 1648–1790, births, 1701–5 (film 0014148 ff.).

Kent County Orphans' Court.

- Administration accounts, 1709–89 (film 0014162 ff.).
- Administrators' bonds, 1664–1789 (film 0014160 ff.).

Index to Kent County Court records, 1656–62 (film 0014206). The manuscript is at the Maryland Historical Society in Baltimore.

Kent County Court. *Proceedings of the County Courts of Kent (1648–1676), Talbot (1662–1674), and Somerset (1665–1668) Counties [Archives of Maryland.* Vol. 54. Court Series 6] (Baltimore: Maryland Historical Society, 1937, film 0908321).

Church Records

Society of Friends, Cecil. Monthly meeting records, 1698–1913 (film 0020377 ff.). Also covers Cecil County. The original records are at the Friends Historical Library, Swarthmore College, Swarthmore, Pennsylvania.

Prince George's County (established 1695 from Calvert and Charles counties)

Original records at the Prince George's County Courthouse in Upper Marlboro and the Hall of Records in Annapolis are:

Prince George's County Clerk of the Circuit Court. Land records, 1696–1884, court records for 1696–9, strays (film 0014277 ff.).

Original records at the Prince George's County Courthouse in Upper Marlboro are:

Prince George's County Orphans' Court.

- Probate records, 1703–1858 (film 0014293 ff.).
- Inventories, 1696–1854 (film 0014282 ff).
- Administration accounts, 1698–1948 (film 0014302 ff.).
- Bonds, 1698–1847 (film 0014296 ff.).

• Wills, 1698–1948 (film 0014281 ff.).

Church Records
Manuscripts at the Library of Congress in Washington, DC are:
Queen Anne Parish, Episcopal. Records, 1705–73 (film 0013206).
Saint Paul's Parish, Baden, Episcopal. Records, 1733–1819 (film 0013201).

Piscataway Parish, Accokeek. Vestry minutes from 1693 (film 0014303). The
manuscript is at the Maryland Historical Society in Baltimore.

Queen Anne's County (established 1706 from Talbot, Kent, and Dorchester
counties)
Original records at the Queen Anne's County Courthouse in Centerville and the
Hall of Records in Annapolis are:
Queen Anne's County Clerk of the Circuit Court. Deeds, 1707–1873 (film
0014342 ff.).
Queen Anne's County Orphans' Court.
• Administration accounts, 1741–1855 (film 0014315 ff.).
• Bonds, 1774–1857 (film 0014314 ff.).
• Inventories, 1739–1851 (film 0014317 ff.).
• Wills, 1706–1945 (film 0014320 ff.).

Church Records
Saint Luke's Parish. Records, 1722–1847 (film 0013890). The manuscript is at
the Maryland Historical Society in Baltimore.

Saint Mary's County (established 1637)
Original records at the Saint Mary's County Courthouse in Leonardtown are:
Saint Mary's County Orphans' Court. Wills, 1658–1946 (film 0014427 ff.).

Church Records
Original records and manuscripts at the Library of Congress in Washington, DC
are:
All Faith Parish, Huntersville, Episcopal. Records, 1692–1820 (film 0013207).
Includes chapels of ease at Four Mile Run Church, Red Church, and Dent
Memorial Chapel.

Saint Andrew's Parish, Episcopal, Leonardtown. Records, 1700s–1900s (film
0985192).

Somerset County (established 1666, see also Kent and Worcester counties)
Original records at the Hall of Records in Annapolis and the Somerset County
Courthouse in Princess Anne are:

Somerset County Clerk of the Circuit Court. Land records, 1665–1850 (film
    0014372). Also includes court proceedings, 1665–1715 (various years),
    births, marriages, and burials, 1649–1722 (various years), and cattle marks,
    1666–1723.
Original records at the Somerset County Courthouse in Princess Anne are:
Somerset County Orphans' Court.
• Administration accounts, 1685–1858 (film 0014398 ff.).
• Inventories, 1725–1850 (film 0014403 ff.).
• Probate records, 1664–1948 (film 0014393 ff.).

Somerset County Deputy Surveyor. Land warrant book, 1670–85 (film
    0020449). Includes a few records from the Provincial Court involving fines
    levied. The original records are at the Historical Society of Pennsylvania in
    Philadelphia.

Church Records
Original records at the Presbyterian Historical Society in Philadelphia are:
Coventry Parish, Rehobeth, Protestant Episcopal. Records, 1700–1800 (film
    0441447), 1709–1831 (film 0441448).
Somerset Parish, Protestant Episcopal. Records, 1650–1825 (film 0441446).

Talbot County (established 1662 from Kent County, see also Kent County)
Original records at the Talbot County Courthouse in Easton and the Hall of
Records in Annapolis are:
Talbot County Clerk of the Circuit Court. Land records, 1662–1850 (film
    0014491 ff.). Includes court proceedings for 1662–1708 (various years), and
    vital records, 1657–91, including baptisms.

Original records at the Talbot County Courthouse in Easton are:
Talbot County Orphans' Court.
• Bonds, 1664–1852 (film 0014474 ff.).
• Probate records, 1668–1851 (film 0014478 ff.).
• Administration accounts, 1674–1960 (film 0014464 ff.).
• Wills, 1668–1900 (film 0014457 ff.).

Church Records
Society of Friends. Third Haven. Monthly meeting records, 1675–1941 (film
    0013144 ff.). Includes Nicholite records, 1760–1820. The original records
    are at the Friends Historical Library, Swarthmore College, Swarthmore,
    Pennsylvania.

Carley, Edward B. *Pre-1868 Parish Registers of the Diocese of Wilmington.* 9
Vols. (n.p., 1961–86, film 1846653 ff.). Contains:

- Saint Francis Xavier-Old Bohemia, Warwick. Baptisms, 1750–1868: covers Kent, Queen Anne's, Caroline, Talbot, and Dorchester counties in Maryland and New Castle and Kent counties, Delaware.
- Saint Joseph, Cordova. Burials, 1767–1802
- Saint Francis Xavier-Old Bohemia, Warwick. Marriages, 1775–1874

Worcester County (established 1742 from Somerset County)
Original records at the Worcester County Courthouse in Snow Hill and the Hall of Records in Annapolis are:
Worcester County Clerk of the Circuit Court. Land records, 1742–1868 (film 0014565 ff.). Includes mortgages, 1742–1921, chattel records, 1742–1921 (with slave manumissions), indentures, 1742–1855, bonds, 1742–1901, appraisals of orphans' property, 1742–75, plats, 1742–1915, oaths of office, 1742–84.
Worcester County Orphans' Court.
- Bonds, 1667–1844 (film 0014530 ff.).
- General index, 1742–1850 (film 0014569).
- Probate records, 1688–1851 (film 0014533 ff.). Includes Somerset County inventories, 1688–1742, and accounts, 1687–1719.
- Wills, 1665–1850 (film 0014528 ff.).

Suggested Reading

Barnes, Robert W. *Baltimore County Families* (Baltimore: Genealogical Publishing Co., 1988).

Barnes, Robert W. *Gleanings from Maryland Newspapers, 1727–1790*. 3 Vols. (Lutherville, MD: Bettie Carothers, 1975, film 0928166).

Barnes, Robert W. *Marriages and Deaths from the Maryland Gazette, 1727–1839* (Baltimore: Genealogical Publishing Co., 1973).

Barnes, Robert W. *Maryland Marriages [1634–1820]*. 3 Vols. (Baltimore: Genealogical Publishing Co., 1975).

Brugger, Robert J. *Maryland: A Middle Temperament, 1634–1980* (Baltimore: Johns Hopkins University Press, 1988).

Coldham, Peter Wilson. *Settlers of Maryland [1679–1783]*. 5 Vols. (Baltimore: Genealogical Publishing Co., 1995-6).

Cunz, Dieter. *The Maryland Germans: A History* (Princeton: Princeton University Press, 1948, fiche 6048035).

Dobson, David. *Scots on the Chesapeake, 1607–1830* (Baltimore: Genealogical Publishing Co., 1992). Scots in Virginia and Maryland from sources in Great Britain and North America, such as probate records, court records, indenture agreements, jail registers, family papers, contemporary newspapers and magazines, naturalization papers, Loyalist claims, church registers, militia papers, gravestone inscriptions, government documents, and census returns.

Gambrall, Theodore C. *Church Life in Colonial Maryland* (1885. Reprint. Washington, DC: Library of Congress, 1987, film 1490395).

Green, Karen Mauer. *The Maryland Gazette, 1727–1761: Genealogical and Historical Abstracts* (Galveston, TX: Frontier Press, 1989).

Harris, Ernest Lloyd. *Church and State in the Maryland Colony* (1894. Washington, DC: Library of Congress, 1987, film 1550159).

Hayward, Mary Ellen. *Maryland's Maritime Heritage: A Guide to the Collections of the Radcliffe Maritime Museum, Museum and Library of Maryland History, the Maryland Historical Society* (Baltimore: The Society, 1984).

Land, Aubrey C. *Colonial Maryland, A History* (Millwood, NY: KTO Press, 1981).

Main, Gloria L. *Tobacco Colony: Life in Early Maryland, 1650–1720* (Princeton: Princeton University Press, 1983).

Maryland State Archives. *A Guide to Government Records at the Maryland State Archives: A Comprehensive List by Agency and Record Series* (Annapolis: The Archives, 1992).

Meyer, Mary K. *Divorces and Names Changed in Maryland: By Act of the Legislature, 1634–1867* (Mount Airy, MD: Pipe Creek Publications, 1991).

Newman, Harry Wright. *The Flowering of the Maryland Palatinate: An Intimate and Objective History of the Province of Maryland to the Overthrow of Proprietary Rule in 1654, with Accounts of Lord Baltimore's Settlement at Avalon* (1961. Reprint. Baltimore: Genealogical Publishing Co., 1973).

Newman, Harry Wright. *Seigniory in Early Maryland: With a List of Manors and Manor Lords* (1949. Reprint. Baltimore: Genealogical Publishing Co., 1985, film 0989407).

Newman, Harry Wright. *To Maryland from Overseas* (1982. Reprint. Baltimore: Genealogical Publishing Co., 1984). Digest of the Jacobite Loyalists sold into white slavery in Maryland, and the British and Continental background of approximately 1400 Maryland settlers from 1634 to the early federal period.

Neill, Edward D. *The Founders of Maryland: As Portrayed in Manuscripts, Provincial Records, and Early Documents* (Albany: Joel Munsell, 1876, film 1425713).

Papenfuse, Edward C. *A Guide to the Maryland Hall of Records: Local, Judicial and Administrative Records on Microform* (Annapolis: Archives Division, Hall of Records, 1978, fiche 6049468).

Pedley, Avril J.M. *The Manuscript Collections of the Maryland Historical Society* (Baltimore: The Society, 1968).

Radoff, Morris Leon. *The County Courthouses and Records of Maryland: Part Two: The Records* (Annapolis: Hall of Records, 1963, fiche 6054101).

Russell, William T. *Maryland: The Land of Sanctuary: A History of Religious Toleration in Maryland from the First Settlement until the American Revolution.* 2nd ed. (Baltimore: J.H. Furst, 1908).

Semmes, Raphael. *Crime and Punishment in Colonial Maryland* (Baltimore: Johns Hopkins University Press, 1938, 1995).

Sioussat, Annie Middleton. *Old Manors in the Colony of Maryland.* 2 Vols. (Baltimore: Lord Baltimore Press, 1911, fiche 6048081).

Spencer, Richard Henry. *Genealogical and Memorial Encyclopedia of the State of Maryland: A Record of the Achievements of Her People in the Making of a Commonwealth and the Founding of a Nation.* 2 Vols. (New York: American Historical Society, 1919, fiche 6046929).

Steiner, Bernard Christian. *Maryland under the Commonwealth: A Chronicle of the Years, 1649–1658* (1911. Reprint. New York: AMS Press, 1971).

Tate, Thad W. and David L. Ammerman. *The Chesapeake in the Seventeenth Century: Essays on Anglo-American Society* (New York: W.W. Norton, 1979).

Wright, F. Edward. *Citizens of the Eastern Shore of Maryland, 1659–1750* (Westminster, MD: Family Line Publications, 1986). Listings of taxables, petitioners, bounty recipients, overseers of roads, militiamen, cattle mark registrants, charity cases, persons reimbursed by the court and persons fined.

Wright, F. Edward. *Maryland Eastern Shore Vital Records: 1648–1825.* 5 Vols. (Westminster, MD: Family Line Publications, 1982).

Maryland Shilling.

Virginia

T he First European settlement in Virginia was a temporary one: Jesuit missionaries from Nueva España (Mexico) founded a Chesapeake mission from 1570 to 1572, when the area was considered Northern Florida. The first permanent settlement in Virginia was made in 1607 at Jamestown by a trading corporation of settlers from the southern and midland counties of England, called the Virginia Company of London. The Company received a charter in 1609 and created a governor and council. The first African slaves were transported to Virginia by the Dutch in 1619.

The earliest private land grants were made in 1617 at Smith's Hundred, followed by Martin's Hundred in 1618, and then sold in fifty-acre parcels through the headright system. The House of Burgesses first met in 1619. The colony was divided into four corporations or plantations: James City, Charles City, Henrico, and Kiccowtan. The Virginia Company was dissolved in 1624, and Virginia was established as a Royal colony. Eight shires were created in 1634, becoming counties in 1643. In addition to the county government, the local parishes of the Anglican Church also functioned as part of the civil government, even writing bylaws until 1679.

Bacon's Rebellion began in 1676 when Nathaniel Bacon organized an illegal militia of Indian fighters. Receiving some popular support, he challenged the governor of the colony and burned down Jamestown. The rebellion ended after Bacon's death early the following year.

French Huguenots arrived in the early 1700s and settled near Richmond in Monocan. In 1714 the first large group of Germans, from the Seigen area of Westphalia, built a fort called Germanna on the Rappahanock River, and established the first German Reformed congregation in Virginia. Other German settlements were established in 1725 in the Robinson River Valley, the Valley of Virginia (Shenandoah) in 1728, and Jeffersonton /Little Fork (Culpeper County) in 1734. By the 1730s colonists began entering the Shenandoah Valley area from Pennsylvania and New Jersey. These included Ulster Scots and Germans.

SEE ALSO
Germany
Great Britain
Kentucky
Maryland
Ohio
Pennsylvania

In 1749 the Virginia Council issued grants to over one million acres of land in the Ohio Valley. From 1750 until the 1780s the Ohio Company of Virginia settled in those lands beyond the Allegheny mountains. The Wilderness Road was opened in the 1770s, giving Virginians access across the Cumberland Gap into Kentucky.

Statewide Records and Resources

The earliest courts in Virginia were:

*   **Governor and Council (1609–1775), General Assembly, and Court (1661–1851):** Handled all civil and criminal cases, and appeals from county courts; primarily an appeals court after 1634. The quarterly court of the council became the General Court, or General Assembly, in 1661 and was an elected legislature. The House of Burgesses was the other house of the General Assembly; it initiated legislation, controlled taxes, and had oversight over local affairs. Up until 1689, members of the House of Burgesses were also members of the county courts. See the records of the Virginia Company of London, and:

McIlwaine, H.R. *Minutes of the Council and General Court of Colonial Virginia: 1620–1632, 1670–1676* . . . (1924. Reprint. Richmond: VSL, 1979, film 1035450).[43]

Virginia Council. *Executive Journals of the Council of Colonial Virginia [1680–1775].* 6 Vols. (1925. Reprint. Richmond: VSL, 1966–78, film 0599302).

Barton, R.T. Virginia *Colonial Decisions: The Reports by Sir John Randolph and Edward Barradall of the Decisions of the General Court of Virginia, 1728–1741.* 2 Vols. Boston: n.p., 1909).

Kennedy, John Pendleton and Henry Reed McIlwaine. *The Journals of the House of Burgesses of Virginia, 1619–1776.* 13 Vols. (1905–15. Reprint. Richmond: VSL and Scholarly Resources, 1985, film 1486518 ff.).

*   **Monthly Courts (1619–43) and County Courts (1642–1902):** Handled minor civil and criminal cases, equity, probate, and orphan dockets. Probate records were kept at the county level. For a general reference, consult Torrence, Clayton. *Virginia Wills and Administrations, 1632–1800* (1930. Reprint. Baltimore: Genealogical Publishing Co., 1965, film 0844943). There is a card catalog supplement at the VSL. See county records for more information.

Palmer, William P. *Calendar of Virginia State Papers and Other Manuscripts [1652–1879].* 11 Vols. (Richmond: n.p., 1875–93, fiche 6046648). Records of land patents, state papers, petitions, licenses, acts, and proceedings.

---

[43] Records of the General Court were destroyed during the Civil War, except for one book, 1670–6. "VSL" is the Virginia State Library and Archives in Richmond.

Billings, Warren M. *The Old Dominion in the Seventeenth Century: A Documentary History of Virginia, 1606–1689* (Chapel Hill: University of North Carolina Press, 1975).

Early statute law and legislative records have been published in:

Hening, William Waller. *Statutes at Large, Being a Collection of All the Laws of Virginia from the First Session of the Legislature in the Year 1619.* 13 Vols. (1819–23. Reprint. Charlottesville: University Press of Virginia, 1969, fiche 6051115).

Winfree, Waverly K. *The Laws of Virginia: Being a Supplement to Hening's Statutes at Large, 1700–1750* (Richmond: VSL, 1971, film 1320665).

Casey, Joseph J. *Personal Names in Hening's Statutes at Large of Virginia, and Shepherd's Continuation* (1896. Reprint. Baltimore: Clearfield Co., 1977, fiche 6051115).

The Virginia Company of London was the governing body until 1624. Records are found in:

Fleet, Beverley. *Virginia Company of London, 1607–1624* [*Virginia Colonial Abstracts.* Series 2. Vol. 3] (Washington, DC: L.O. Duvall, 1955, film 0850107).

Kingsbury, Susan Myra. *An Introduction to the Records of the Virginia Company of London, with a Bibliographical List of the Extant Documents* (1905. Reprint. Fort Wayne, IN: Allen County Public Library, 1990).

Kingsbury, Susan Myra. *The Records of the Virginia Company of London.* 3 Vols. (Washington, DC: GPO, 1906–35, film 0962288 ff.). The Council and General Court of Virginia was both an elected assembly and a court of appeals.

Colonial Records of Virginia (1874. Reprint. Baltimore: Genealogical Publishing Co., 1964).

Proceedings of the First Assembly of Virginia, 1619	Number of men, women and children, several counties, 1634
List of living and dead in Virginia, 1623	Letter from Charles II, 1668
Brief declaration of the plantation of Virginia, first twelve years	List of parishes in Virginia, 1680

Land Records

The first grants of land were issued by the Virginia Company in 1617/18. The original patents, 1623–1774, are filmed, including a few issued under the authority of the Virginia Company of London, presented for re-recording in order to affirm title. Records after the initial grant are recorded on a county level. Records of the Virginia Land Office:

• Index and abstracts of county patents and grants, 1623–1774 (Richmond: VSL, 1949, film 0029308 ff.). Abstracts of patent and grant books recorded by county in the Land Office since 1818, although abstracts were made of earlier books.

* Index to land patents and grants, 1623–1774 (film 1854108 ff.). Taken from the county abstracts and arranged by name of patentee: shows date of patent (grant), county, number of acres, brief description, and volume and beginning page.
* French and Indian War: military and importation warrants, land bounty certificates, land bounty books (Richmond: VSL, 1949, film 0029634 ff.). Index gives the warrantee's name, rank and unit if known, number of acres, and warrant number. Warrantee may not be the person who served in the war and no cross reference was made to the soldier when the warrantee was an assignee. Certificates and warrants contain warrantee's name, quantity of acres, name of person for whose service the warrant was issued, rank and length of service, date warrant was issued, and sometimes other information.

The Northern Neck Proprietary was issued by patent in 1649 but not developed until 1690. It lay between the Potomac and the Rappahannock rivers and existed until 1781. The proprietors "were to possess all the rights of any court baron of England . . . they could build towns, castles, and forts, could create and endow colleges and schools . . . enjoy the patronage of churches . . . (establish) court(s) authorized by the patent . . (convey) lands sold or leased . . .," and collect quit rents.[44]

The heaviest concentrations of slaves were on the Northern Neck plantations. Large tracts of lands remained in the hands of a few Virginia families, such as Carter, Culpeper, Fairfax, Custis, Fitzhugh, Lee, Mason, and Washington. The farmers on the land held it by tenancy only, and 75 percent lacked title up to the time of the Revolution.[45] Northern Neck land lay in the counties of Lancaster, Richmond, Northumberland, King George, Westmoreland, Stafford, Prince William, Fauquier, Loudoun, and Fairfax, and may also include the counties of Frederick, Culpeper, Shenandoah, Rappahannock, Clarke, Warren, Page, and part of West Virginia. See the records of the Virginia Land Office, and also:

* Northern Neck survey register, index to surveys (film 0029508).
* Northern Neck grants and index, 1690–1874 (Richmond: VSL, 1949, film 0029508 ff.).
* Gray, G.E. *Virginia Northern Neck Land Grants [1694–1862].* 4 Vols.

---

[44] Quoted from the appendix "Northern Neck Proprietary to 1745," in Douglas Southall Freeman, *George Washington: A Biography.* Vol. 1. *Young Washington, 1732–1754* (New York: Charles Scribner's Sons, 1948), 451.

[45] Warren M. Billings, et al., *Colonial Virginia, A History* (New York: KTO Press, 1986), 211.

(Baltimore: Genealogical Publishing Co., 1987–93).

Published land records include:

Nugent, Nell Marion. *Cavaliers and Pioneers: Abstracts of Virginia Land Patents and Grants [1623–1749]*. 5 Vols. (Richmond: Dietz Printing Co., VSL, Virginia Genealogical Society, 1934, 1963, 1977–9, 1994, Vol. 1 on film 1320779).

Robinson, W. Stitt. *Mother Earth: Land Grants in Virginia, 1607–1699* (Williamsburg, VA: 350th Anniversary Celebration Corporation, 1957).

The Acts of Naturalization were passed in Virginia in 1658, 1671, and 1680 and affected those who were not subjects of England. After petitioning the General Assembly of Virginia and taking certain oaths of allegiance and supremacy, an act would be passed investing the petitioner with the rights of a native-born subject. The 1680 Act stated that the governor would then issue a public document declaring the alien naturalized. Naturalizations are found in both the records of the General Assembly (see Hening's *Statutes at Large*), and county courts.

Colonial militia records have been abstracted in:

* Crozier, William Armstrong. *Virginia Colonial Militia, 1651–1776* (1905. Reprint. Baltimore: Southern Book Co., 1954, fiche 6048997).
* Eckenrode, H.J. *List of Colonial Soldiers of Virginia: Special Report of the Department of Archives and History for 1913* (1917. Reprint. Baltimore: Genealogical Publishing Co., 1974, fiche 6046993).
* Bockstruck, Lloyd DeWitt. *Virginia's Colonial Soldiers* (Baltimore: Genealogical Publishing Co., 1988).

Church Records

The Church of England was the established church from 1624 to 1786. Other major religious denominations in Virginia were Baptist, Methodist Episcopal, and Presbyterian. Marriages from 1631 were by bond or bann, and most early marriages are found in church registers or Bible records. From 1705, if the parties lived in two different parishes, the banns were published in both places. This act also required that the minister of each parish keep an exact record of births and deaths. A few marriage bonds can be found in county court order books, but this was not a required practice until 1780.

Axelson, Edith F. *A Guide to Episcopal Church Records in Virginia* (Athens, GA: Iberian Publishing Co., 1988).

Brock, Henry Irving. *Colonial Churches in Virginia* (Richmond: The Dale Press, 1930).

Brydon, George MacLaren. *Virginia's Mother Church and the Political*

Conditions under Which it Grew. 2 Vols. (Richmond: Virginia Historical Society, 1947–52).

Cassell, C.W. *History of the Lutheran Church in Virginia and East Tennessee* (Strasburg, VA: Shenandoah Publishing House, 1930, fiche 6049862).

Clark, Jewell T. *A Guide to Church Records in the Archives Branch, Virginia State Library* (Richmond: VSL, 1981).

Colonial Churches: A Series of Sketches of Churches in the Original Colony of Virginia: with Pictures of Each Church (1907. Reprint. Fort Wayne, IN: Allen County Public Library, 1990).

Goodwin, Edward Lewis. *The Colonial Church in Virginia: With Biographical Sketches of the First Six Bishops of the Diocese of Virginia, and Other Historical Papers, Together with Brief Biographical Sketches of the Colonial Clergy of Virginia* (Milwaukee: Morehouse Publishing Co., 1927, film 6088014).

Hart, Lyndon H. *A Guide to Bible Records in the Archives Branch, Virginia State Library* (Richmond: VSL, 1985).

Mason, George Carrington. *Colonial Churches of Tidewater, Virginia* (Richmond: Whittet and Shepperson, 1945, film 0973026). Covers counties of Surrey, Sussex, James City, Charles City, Prince George, Dinwiddie, Elizabeth City, Warwick, Princess Anne, Norfolk, Nansemond, Isle of Wight, Southampton, York, Gloucester, Mathews, Middlesex, King and Queen, King William, Accomack, and Northampton.

Meade, William. *Old Churches, Ministers and Families of Virginia, Reprinted with Digested Index and Genealogical Guide Compiled by Jennings Cropper Wise.* 2 Vols. (1857, 1910. Reprint. Baltimore: Genealogical Publishing Co., 1966, fiche 6087788 ff.).

Worrall, Jay, Jr. *The Friendly Virginians: America's First Quakers* (Athens, GA: Iberian Publishing Co., 1994).

Manuscript Collections
Major manuscript collections for Virginia are at the VSL and the State Historical Society in Richmond, the Alderman Library, University of Virginia, Charlottesville, The Colonial Williamsburg Foundation, and Earl Swem Library, College of William and Mary, in Williamsburg, the Library of Congress, and other university and historical society libraries in Virginia. See the section on Africa for a description of some of the plantation paper manuscripts that have

been filmed.

The William Blathwayt Papers at Colonial Williamsburg, 1661–1722 (Frederick, MD: University Publications of America, 1989, film 1843294). The original papers are at the PRO in Kew, Surrey, England (CO 1/48), and copies at the Colonial Williamsburg Foundation in Williamsburg. William Blathwayt was an English official from 1681 to 1704. The collection contains his correspondence with many leading American and English administrators for that time period. Topics include:

➤ Boundary disputes with the French
➤ King William's War
➤ Indian attacks
➤ Illegal colonial trade
➤ Trade and fishing in Newfoundland
➤ Attacks upon the charter of Massachusetts Bay
➤ Captain Kidd, Sir Henry Morgan, and piracy in the Caribbean
➤ Tobacco trade in Virginia
➤ Wars with the French and Spanish in Jamaica
➤ Slavery in the Leeward Islands
➤ Governors and Assembly in Bermuda

Vol. 1 New England, 1683–90

Vol. 2 New York, New England, Virginia, Ireland, Maryland, Pennsylvania, Carolina, Bermuda, 1690–1700

Vol. 3 Flanders, Massachusetts, New Hampshire, Maine, Connecticut, Rhode Island, New Jersey, New York, 1669, 1679–80, 1686–98

Vol. 4 Massachusetts, Connecticut, Plymouth, Rhode Island, New York, New Hampshire, Maine, Maryland, New Jersey, West Indies, 1680–91

Vol. 5 Massachusetts, Rhode Island, New Hampshire, Bermuda, New York, 1683–98

Vol. 6 Massachusetts, New Hampshire, New England, Pennsylvania, New York, Plymouth, Narragansett, Rhode Island, Connecticut, New Plymouth, 1679–1700

Vol. 7 Pennsylvania, New Jersey, pirates, 1680–1702

Vols. 8–10 New York, 1685–1710

Vol. 11 New York, Rhode Island, 1679–99

Vol. 12 New Hampshire, Barbados, 1675–99

Vols. 13–14 Virginia, 1676–1715

Vol. 15 Virginia, Maryland, New England, New York, 1686–1715

Vols. 16–17 Virginia, 1657–1715

Vol. 18 Maryland, Virginia, Carolina, 1678–99

Vol. 19 New France, Newfoundland, 1674–99

Vol. 20 Plantation Office papers and accounts, 1680–99

Vol. 21 Jamaica, 1683–1700

Vol. 22 Jamaica, Barbados, 1678–95

Vols. 23–8 Jamaica, 1661–1712

Vols. 29–35 Barbados, 1655–1715

Vol. 36 Bermuda, 1684–1702

Vols. 37–9 Leeward Islands, 1677–1714

Vol. 40 Sir Henry Morgan, West Indies, 1680–3

Vol. 41 Plantation Office papers, accounts, 1681–1722

Ingram, John E. *William Blathwayt Papers at Colonial Williamsburg, 1631–1722: Guide to the Microfilm Collection* (Bethesda, MD: UPA Academic Editions, 1989).

County Records and Resources

Eight shires were created in 1634 which became the first counties. They are: Accawmacke (Northampton), Charles City, Charles River (York), Elizabeth City, James City, Warrosquake (Isle of Wight), Warwick River (Warwick), and Henrico. Five of these original eight have had some or most of their records destroyed. The county court was sometimes known as the court of quarterly session, court of monthly sessions, and court of oyer and terminer, and they were the most important instruments of record keeping, along with the church vestry books. The cities that were incorporated before 1775 were Williamsburg in 1722 (from James City and York counties) and Norfolk in 1737 (from Norfolk County).

Burned Counties

Many Virginia county records have been burned or destroyed in times of war or during a courthouse fire. Missing records can sometimes be substituted with vestry records and Chancery Court records. Counties with records beginning before 1775 that were burned will be so indicated below. Published works that can be used to identify missing records include works such as:

Woodson, Robert F. and Isobel B. Woodson. *Virginia Tithables from Burned Record Counties: Buckingham, 1773–1774, Gloucester, 1770–1771, 1774–1775, Hanover, 1763 and 1770, James City, 1768–1769, Stafford, 1768 and 1773* (Richmond: The Authors, 1970).

Fleet, Beverley. *Virginia Colonial Abstracts*. 34 Vols. in 3 (1937–49. Reprint. Baltimore: Genealogical Publishing Co., 1988).

Accomack County, 1632–40	Essex County, 1703–6
Lancaster County, 1652–66	King and Queen County, 1700s
Richmond County, 1692–1724	York County, 1633–57
Northumberland County, 1652–1810	Charles City County, 1655–96
Northumbria Collectanea, 1645–1720	Henrico County, 1736
Westmoreland County, 1653–7	Lower Norfolk County, 1651–4
Essex County, 1711–17	Huntington Library data, 1607–1850

des Cognets, Louis. *English Duplicates of Lost Virginia Records* (1958. Reprint. Baltimore: Genealogical Publishing Co., 1981). County officers, land records, rent rolls, court records, shipping records, etc.

Keys to County Records

The following descriptions are essential to understanding where to look for information in Virginia county records. There is some overlap between ecclesiastical and civil records.

➢ *Court order books and minute books:* Order books are sometimes called common law (judicial decisions based on custom and precedent) order books. Orders are judgments based on these laws and involved writs, estate appraisements, guardianships, wills, deeds, etc. Virtually all early orders and minutes are missing for Buckingham, Gloucester, James City, King and Queen, King William, and New Kent counties.

➢ *Vestry books:* Until 1785, the parish vestry was required by law to perform many civil governmental functions. Vestry books recorded orders to settle land boundary disputes and orders regarding land processioning, care of the poor, repairs to the church, accounting of funds, pew allotments, apprenticeships and guardianships of orphans, levying of taxes, indentures, and other civil matters.

➢ *Processioners returns:* Approximately every four years, land owners would walk or ride along the boundaries of their land. Surveyors, or processioners, would accompany the owners to determine the legal boundaries and record the description of the boundary markers. Sometimes the vestry or the county court would have to settle the disputes. The records include dates, land owners, description and marks of corners, persons present, and lands not processioned.

➢ *Levy books:* The levy was collected for public or county claims. The County Court would assess a levy on the tithables to pay the claims. County claims included salaries of certain persons performing duties for the county, such as prison watchman, county sheriff, county clerk, ferryman, etc. Public claims included grievances and propositions held for the county, such as reimbursing a slave owner for a slave executed by the county, paying the sheriff for care of prisoners in jail, care and upkeep of public buildings, etc. The record gives names, reasons for claim, amounts of claim, and amounts to be collected from tithables in the county.

➢ *Surveyors' books:* Sometimes called processioners records, surveyors' records contain plat maps and property descriptions.

➢ *Marriage returns, licenses, and bonds:* A marriage register contains abstracts of the original marriage bonds and papers connected with them and may be helpful in finding original marriage bonds and ministers' returns. Original bonds give names of parties, amount and date of the bond, names of sureties, etc. Original licenses give date and place of marriage, names of parties, their ages, marital status, race, birthplaces, parents' names, and husband's occupation.

➤ *Tithables and quit rents:* Tithables (taxes) were collected on the personal property of male residents over twenty-one years of age. Quit rent lists name those who owed taxes for proprietary land grants or grants from the Royal Governor. Some are abstracted in Smith, Annie Laurie Wright. *The Quit Rents of Virginia: Copy of the Rent Rolls of the Several Counties in Virginia for the Year 1704* (1957. Reprint. Baltimore: Genealogical Publishing Co., 1975, film 1035761).

➤ *Dead papers:* Dead papers are suits brought to conclusion.

Accomack County (established 1663 from Northampton County, see also Northampton County)
Original records at the Accomack County Courthouse in Accomac are:
Accomack County Court and Clerk.
- Land causes and complete cases, 1727–1805 (film 0030017).
- Order books, 1676–1860 (film 0030111 ff.).
- Orphan accounts, 1741–1850 (film 0030108 ff.).
- Wills, deeds, and orders, 1663–1881 (film 0029993 ff.). Also includes appraisements, administrators' or executors' accounts, accounts of sales, and list of tithables, 1678–95.
- Deed records, 1737–1902, indexes, 1663–1969 (film 0029994 ff.).
- Processioners returns, 1764–1895 (film 0030110 ff.).
- Marriage licenses and bonds, 1733, 1774–1917 (film 0030012 ff.).
Original records at the VSL in Richmond are:
Accomack Parish, Episcopal. Vestry orders, 1723–84 (Richmond: VSL, 1946, film 0030107).
Saint George's Parish, Episcopal. Vestry book, 1763–87 (film 0033853).

Dorman, John Frederick. "A Guide to the Counties of Virginia: Accomack." *The Virginia Genealogist* 3 1(January–March 1959): 38–42.

Nottingham, Stratton. *Accomack Tithables (Tax Lists) 1663–1695* (1931. Reprint. Westminster, MD: Family Line Publications, 1987, fiche 6017851).

Albemarle County (established 1744 from Goochland and Louisa counties)
Original records at the Albemarle County Courthouse in Charlottesville are:
Albemarle County Court and Clerk.
- Order books, 1744–1831 (film 0030255 ff.).
- Deeds, 1758–1902, indexes, 1748–1917 (film 0030223 ff.).
- Wills, 1748–1919 (film 0030210 ff.). Includes some deeds, 1748–52.
- Surveyors' books, 1750–55, 1791–1853 (film 1889151).

Fredericksville Parish, Episcopal. Vestry book, 1742–87 (film 0031332). Fredericksville Parish was established in 1742 and covered most of Louisa County from 1742–57. From 1757–1845 it covered part of Albemarle and Louisa counties. The original records are at the Bishop Payne Library, Virginia Theological Seminary, Alexandria.

Saint Ann's Parish, Episcopal. Vestry book, 1772–85, and overseers of the poor accounts, 1786–1809 (film 0033852). The original manuscripts are at the Henry E. Huntington Library, San Marino, California.

Tabor Presbyterian Church. Records, 1747–1959 (film 1490913 ff.). The original records are at the Presbyterian Church Archives, Union Theological Seminary, Richmond.

Dorman, John Frederick. "A Guide to the Counties of Virginia: Albemarle." *The Virginia Genealogist* 3 2 (January–March 1959): 86–90.

Pawlett, Nathaniel Mason. *Albemarle County Road Orders, 1744–1748* (Charlottesville: Virginia Highway and Transportation Research Council, 1975, fiche 6049582).

Amelia County (established 1734 from Prince George and Brunswick counties)
Original records at the Amelia County Courthouse in Amelia are:
Amelia County Court and Clerk.
- Court order books, 1735–1866 (film 0030459 ff.).
- Deeds, 1734–1869 (film 0030422 ff.).
- Wills, 1734–1865 (film 0030449 ff.).
- Marriage bonds and registers, 1735–1918 (film 0030474).

Dorman, John Frederick. "A Guide to the Counties of Virginia: Amelia." *The Virginia Genealogist* 3 4 (October–December 1959): 171–4.

Williams, Kathleen B. *Marriages of Amelia County, Virginia, 1735–1815* (1961. Reprint. Baltimore: Genealogical Publishing Co., 1979).

Amherst County (established 1761 from Albemarle County)
Original records at the Amherst County Courthouse in Amherst are:
Amherst County Court and Clerk.
- Court records, 1766–1868 (film 0030299 ff.).
- Deeds, 1761–1865 (film 0030283 ff.).
- Wills, 1761–1870 (film 0030274 ff.).
- Marriage registers, 1763–1900 (film 0030273 ff.).

Dorman, John Frederick. "A Guide to the Counties of Virginia: Amherst." *The Virginia Genealogist* 4 1 (January–March 1960): 38–40.

Augusta County (established 1745 from Orange County)
Original records at the Augusta County Courthouse in Staunton are:
Augusta County Court and Clerk.
• Court order books, 1745–1867 (film 0030374 ff.).
• File index to loose papers, 1745–1952 (film 0030420).
• Deeds, 1745–1866 (film 0030334 ff.).
• Surveyors' records, 1744–1906 (film 0030418 ff.).
• Wills, 1745–1871 (film 0030314 ff.).
Virginia Militia, Augusta County, Court of Inquiry. Militia court records of the 32nd regiment, 1756–1812 (film 0030421). Contains courts martial, rosters, copies of orders, minutes of councils of war, lists of fines, and other regimental records.
Augusta Parish, Episcopal. Vestry book, 1746–80 (film 0030165).

Original records at the Presbyterian Church Archives, Union Theological Seminary, Richmond are:
Tinkling Spring Presbyterian Church, Fishersville. Records, 1741–1963 (film 1490915 ff.). The church was organized 1740. Includes a commissioner's book, south side of Triple Forks of Shenando Congregation, 1741–67.
Hebron Presbyterian Church, Staunton. Records, 1766–1941 (Richmond: VSL, 1960, film 1490432). The church's founding date is considered to be 1746 under the name of Brown's Meeting House Church.
Bethany Lutheran Church, Waynesboro. Register, 1771–1845 (film 0373150).

Chalkley, Lyman. *Chronicles of the Scotch-Irish Settlement of Virginia: Extracted from the Original Court Records of Augusta County, 1754–1800.* 3 Vols. (1912. Baltimore: Genealogical Publishing Co., 1980, film 0162043 ff.).

Dorman, John Frederick. "A Guide to the Counties of Virginia: Augusta." *The Virginia Genealogist* 4 2 (April–June 1960): 80–6.

Bedford County (established 1754 from Lunenburg and Albemarle counties)
Original records at the Bedford County Courthouse in Bedford are:
Bedford County Court and Clerk.
• Order books, 1754–1904 (film 0030573 ff.).
• Deeds, 1754–1901 (Richmond: VSL, 1976-7, film 1941016 ff.).
• Wills, 1763–1914, indexes, 1754–1976 (Richmond: VSL, 1977, film 1940727 ff.).

- Surveyors' records, 1754–1881 (film 0030572).
- Ministers' returns, 1785–1853, indexes to bonds, licenses, and returns, 1754–1870 (film 0030592 ff.).
- Sheriffs' bonds and tax receipts, 1755–1851

Bedford County, Virginia, Index of Wills from 1754 to 1830 (Baltimore: Genealogical Publishing Co., 1964).

Dorman, John Frederick. "A Guide to the Counties of Virginia: Bedford." *The Virginia Genealogist* 4 4 (October–December 1960): 171–5.

Botetourt County (established 1769 from Augusta and Rockbridge counties) Original records at the Botetourt County Courthouse in Fincastle and the VSL in Richmond are:
Botetourt County Court and Clerk.
- Order books, 1770–1904 (film 0030722 ff.).
- Deeds, 1770–1869 (film 0030701 ff.).
- Wills, 1770–1869 (film 0030694 ff.).
- Lists of tithables, 1770–89 (Richmond: VSL, 1973, film 1906467).
- Surveyors' records, 1774–1914 (film 0030720 ff.).
- Register of marriages, 1770–1853 (film 0030733 ff.).

Dorman, John Frederick. "A Guide to the Counties of Virginia: Botetourt." *The Virginia Genealogist* 5 3 (July–September 1961): 131–4.

Vogt, John and William Kethley, Jr. *Botetourt County Marriages, 1770–1853.* 2 Vols. (Athens, GA: Iberian Publishing Co., 1987).

Brunswick County (established 1732 from Prince George, Surry, and Isle of Wight counties)
Original records at the Brunswick County Courthouse in Lawrenceville are:
Brunswick County Court and Clerk.
- Court order books, 1732–1864 (film 0030662 ff.).
- Orphan and guardian records, 1740–1860, index to guardian accounts, 1732–1948 (film 0030678 ff.).
- Deeds, 1732–1869 (film 0030632 ff.).
- Wills, 1732–1865 (film 0030632 ff.).
- Marriage records, 1750–1948 (film 0030658 ff.).
Saint Andrew's Parish, Episcopal. Vestry book, 1732–98 (film 0030681).

Dorman, John Frederick. "A Guide to the Counties of Virginia: Brunswick." *The Virginia Genealogist* 6 1 (January–March 1962): 34–8.

Pawlett, Nathanile Mason. *Brunswick County Road Orders, 1732–1746* (Charlottesville: Virginia Highway and Transportation Research Council, 1988).

Buckingham County (established 1761 from Albemarle County)

Fire destroyed most of the records in 1869. Original records at the Buckingham County Court House in Buckingham are:

Buckingham County Court and Clerk.

*   Surveyors' books, 1762–1848 (film 1907144 ff.).
*   Lists of tithables, 1773–4 (film 0030684).

Dorman, John Frederick. "A Guide to the Counties of Virginia: Buckingham." *The Virginia Genealogist* 6 3 (July–September 1962): 121–4.

Stinson, Jeanne. *Early Buckingham County, Virginia, Legal Papers: Volume 1, 1765–1806: Accounts and Legals Transcribed from the Austin-Twyman Collection of the Earl Gregg Swem Library, College of William and Mary* (Athens, GA: Iberian Publishing Co., 1993).

Warren, Mary B. *Buckingham County, Virginia, Church and Marriage Records, 1764–1822* (Athens, GA: Heritage Papers, 1993). Contains church records and marriages from Tillotson Parish (Anglican), 1764 county tax list, Buckingham Baptism Church, diary of Rev. Rene Chastain, Jr., Buckingham County marriage bonds, and other records.

Caroline County (established 1728 from Essex, King and Queen, and King William counties)

Fires during the Civil War destroyed many records. Original records at the Caroline County Courthouse in Bowling Green are:

Caroline County Court and Clerk.

*   Minute books, 1770–1899 (film 0030843 ff.).
*   Order books, 1732–1824, index to wills, inventories, administrations, 1732–1800 (film 0030842 ff.).

Original records at the VSL in Richmond include:

*   Survey book, 1729–62 (film 0030828). Photocopy of original that was located at the Campbell County, Kentucky Clerk's Office in 1923. Contains surveys of lands in Saint Margaret's, Drysdale, and Saint Mary's parishes.

Caroline County Committee of Safety. Proceedings, 1774–6 (film 0030830). Published in *Proceedings of the Committees of Safety of Caroline and Southampton Counties, Virginia, 1774–6* (Richmond: Division of Purchase and Printing, 1929, film 0908190).

Virginia Chancery Court.

*   Caroline County deeds, 1758–1845 (film 0030830).

- Caroline County wills, 1742, 1762–1830, and plats, 1777–1847 (film 0030828).

Dorman, John Frederick. "A Guide to the Counties of Virginia: Caroline." *The Virginia Genealogist* 7 1 (January–March 1963): 30–3.

Sparacio, Ruth Trickey. *Abstracts of the Account Books of Edward Dixon, Merchant of Port Royal, Virginia [1747–1752].* 2 Vols. (McLean, VA: Antient Press, 1990). Includes list of persons who purchased tea, and list of names, birth dates, and mothers of slave children.

Charles City County (established as shire 1634, see also Prince George County)
Fires during the Civil War destroyed many records. Original records at the Charles City County Courthouse in Charles City and the VSL in Richmond are:
Charles City County Court and Clerk.
- Minute books, 1762–1860 (film 0031004 ff.).
- Order books, 1655–1762 (film 0030989 ff.).
- Deeds, wills, and estate accounts, 1689–90, 1763–4, 1766–74 (film 0031010).
- Marriage bonds, 1762–1931 (film 0031011).
- Refunding bonds, 1760–1834
- Replevy and stay bonds, 1767–1844
- Sheriffs' bonds, 1760–1889, warrants, 1770–1820
- Coroners' inquests, 1771–1893
- Grist mill and water papers, 1772–1817

Dorman, John Frederick. "A Guide to the Counties of Virginia: Charles City County." *The Virginia Genealogist* 7 2 (April–June 1963): 75–7.

Saunders, Kirkland. *Westover Church and its Environs* (1937. Reprint. Washington, DC: Library of Congress, 1993, film 1843195).

Weisinger, Benjamin B. *Charles City County, Virginia Records, 1737–1774: With Several Seventeenth-Century Fragments* (Richmond: The Author, 1986, film 1697900).

Charlotte County (established 1765 from Lunenburg County)
Original records at Charlotte County Courthouse at Charlotte Court House are:
Charlotte County Court and Clerk.
- Order books, 1765–1868 (film 0030796 ff.).

- Deeds, 1765–1870 (film 0030781 ff.).
- Guardian accounts, 1765–1880 (film 0030812 ff.).
- Wills, inventories, and accounts, 1765–1867 (film 0030776 ff.).

Cub Creek Presbyterian Church, Charlotte Court House. Records, 1738–1938 (film 1445934 ff.). The original records are at the Presbyterian Church Archives, Union Theological Seminary, Richmond.

Dorman, John Frederick. "A Guide to the Counties of Virginia: Charlotte." *The Virginia Genealogist* 7 3 (July–September 1963): 115–17.

Chesterfield County (established 1749 from Henrico County)
Original records at the Chesterfield County Courthouse in Chesterfield are:
Chesterfield County Court and Clerk.

- Order books, 1749–1865 (film 0030908 ff.).
- Deeds, 1749–1866 (film 0030883 ff.).
- Wills, 1749–1873 (film 0030870 ff.).
- Marriage bonds and records, 1771–1860 (film 0030869 ff.).
- Court martial minutes, 1760

Original records at the VSL in Richmond are:
Dale Parish, Episcopal. Lists of tithables and insolvents, 1747–1821 (Richmond: VSL, 1986, film 1929611). Tithes, 1747–78, were taken for the parishes of Dale, Manchester, and King William.

Dorman, John Frederick. "A Guide to the Counties of Virginia: Chesterfield." *The Virginia Genealogist* 7 4 (October–December 1963): 174–6.

Lutz, Francis Earle. *Chesterfield: An Old Virginia County* (Richmond: The William Byrd Press, 1954).

Culpeper County (established 1748 from Orange County)
Original records at the Culpeper County Courthouse in Culpeper are:
Culpeper County Court and Clerk.

- Court minute books, 1763–1823 (film 0030970 ff.).
- Deeds, 1749–1913 (film 0030939 ff.).
- Mixed probate records, 1749–1870 (film 0030931 ff.).

Original records at the VSL in Richmond are:
Saint Mark's Episcopal Church. Vestry book, 1730–53, levies, 1731–85, parish records, 1730–97 (film 0033856 ff.).

Dorman, John Frederick. "A Guide to the Counties of Virginia: Culpeper." *The Virginia Genealogist* 8 2 (April–June 1964): 63–6.

Cumberland County (established 1749 from Goochland County)
Original records at the Cumberland County Courthouse in Cumberland are:
Cumberland County Court and Clerk.
* Court orders, 1749–1869 (film 0030759 ff.).
* Causes determined, 1773–1800
* Fee books, 1752–4
* Deeds, 1749–1868 (film 0030743 ff.).
* Guardian accounts, 1766–1860 (film 0030773).
* Wills, inventories, and accounts, 1749–1887 (film 0030737 ff.).
* Marriage bonds, 1749–1866 (on film at the VSL only).

Dorman, John Frederick. "A Guide to the Counties of Virginia: Cumberland."
The Virginia Genealogist 8 3 (July–September 1964): 122–4.

Elliott, Katherine B. *Marriage Records, 1749–1840, Cumberland County, Virginia* (1969. Reprint. Easley, SC: Southern Historical Press, 1983, film 0496620).

Dinwiddie County (established 1752 from Prince George County, see also Prince George County)
A fire in 1864 destroyed most records prior to 1833. Records at the VSL in Richmond are:
Dinwiddie County Clerk.
* Surveyors' book, 1755–1865 (film 0031090).
* Deeds, 1755–6, 1774
* Wills, 1755–1865, copies, 35 items
* Miscellaneous papers, 1704–1869, copies, 36 items

Dorman, John Frederick. "A Guide to the Counties of Virginia: Dinwiddie." *The Virginia Genealogist* 8 4 (October–December 1964): 170–3.

Hughes, Thomas. P. *Dinwiddie County, Virginia Data, 1752–1865* (Memphis, TN: The Author, 1975).

Dunmore County (established 1772 from Frederick County, name changed to Shenandoah in 1778)
See Shenandoah County.

Elizabeth City County (established as a shire in 1634, abolished 1952 and incorporated 1954 as the independent city of Hampton)
Fires during the Revolutionary War, War of 1812, and Civil War destroyed many records. Original records at the Circuit Court of the City of Hampton and the VSL in Richmond are:

Elizabeth City County Court and Clerk.
- Court order books, 1721–3 (film 0031119), 1731–47, 1755–69 (film 0031126 ff.), 1747–55, 1784–8, 1798–1802, 1808–16 (film 0031131 ff.).
- Court records, wills, deeds, inventories, ejectments, court orders, and bonds, 1648–1799 (film 0031120 ff.).
- Guardian accounts, 1737–48 (film 0031150).
- Surveys and plats, 1761–1883 (film 0031153).
- Deeds, wills, and settlements of estates, 1721–23 (film 0031119).
- Index to deeds and wills, 1759–1899, mixed probate and land records, 1642–1859 (film 0031142 ff.).
Saint John's Episcopal Church. Vestry book, 1751–1883 (film 0031759).

Mero, James C. *Elizabeth City County, Virginia (now City of Hampton): A Guide for Research in Elizabeth City County Records* (Hampton, VA: Genealogical Society of Tidewater, Virginia, 1984).

Neal, Rosemary C. *Elizabeth City County, Virginia: Deeds, Wills, Court Orders, 1715–1721* (Bowie, MD: Heritage Books, 1988).

Essex County (established 1692 from Old Rappahannock County [abolished])
Records at the Essex County Courthouse in Tappahannock are:
Essex County Court and Clerk.
- Court order books, 1716–23 (film 0031270).
- Deeds, 1702–1867, mixed deed and probate records, 1692–1868, indexes to deeds and wills, 1654–1903 (film 0031158 ff.). Includes deeds, wills, bonds, indentures, guardianship records, estate accounts, plats, and land trials.
- Guardian accounts, 1731–1867 (film 0031170 ff.).
Records at the VSL in Richmond are:
- Court order books, 1723–1801 (film 0031209 ff.).
- Land trials, 1706–60, 1790–1818 (film 0031208).
Old Rappahannock County deeds and probate records, 1656–92 (film 0033647 ff.).
South Farnham Episcopal Church. Vestry book, 1739–1876 (film 0033934).

Dorman, John Frederick. "A Guide to the Counties of Virginia: Essex." *The Virginia Genealogist* 9 2 (April–June 1965): 175–8.

Wilkerson, Eva Eubank. *Index to Marriages of Old Rappahannock and Essex Counties, Virginia, 1655–1900* (Richmond: Whittet and Shepperson, 1953, film 0873775).

Fairfax County (established 1752 from Prince William County)
Original records at the Fairfax County Courthouse in Fairfax are:
Fairfax County Court and Clerk.

- Court order books and minute books, 1749–1867 (film 0031321 ff.).
- Deeds, 1742–1866 (film 0031293 ff.).
- Record of surveys, 1742–1856 (film 0031320 ff.).
- Land causes, 1742–70, 1788–1832 (film 0031320 ff.).
- Administrators' bonds, 1752-1782 (film 0031330).
- Wills, 1742–1866 (film 0031283 ff.).

Fairfax County History Commission.

- *Fairfax County Court Order Book, 1765–1766, Surveys, 1742–1856, Land Records of Long Standing, 1742–1770, Land Causes, 1788–1832* (Cleveland: Bloch and Co., 1982, fiche 6331436).
- A *Cumulative Subject Index to the Court Order Books of Fairfax County, Virginia, 1749–1802* (n.p., 1976, fiche 6330001 ff.).
- A *Surname and Subject Index of the Minute and Order Books of the County Court, Fairfax County, Virginia, 1749–1800* (n.p., 1976, fiche 6330125 ff.).

Dorman, John Frederick. "A Guide to the Counties of Virginia: Fairfax." *The Virginia Genealogist* 9 3 (July–September 1965): 124-7.

Hopkins, Margaret L. *Cameron Parish in Colonial Virginia* (n.p.: The Author, 1988). Also includes Loudoun County.

Truro Parish, Episcopal. *Minutes of Vestry, Truro Parish, Virginia, 1732–1785* (1974. Reprint. Washington, DC: Library of Congress, 1985, film 1421477). The original records are at Pohick Episcopal Church in Lorton. Also published in Liddle, Chester A. *Families of Pohick Church, Virginia, Truro Parish, Fairfax County, Virginia* (Baltimore: Gateway Press, 1991).

Fauquier County (established 1759 from Prince William County, see also Prince William County)
Original records at the Fauquier County Courthouse in Warrenton are:
Fauquier County Court and Clerk.

- Miscellaneous court records, 1759–1807 (film 0031610).
- Court minute and order books, 1759–1865 (film 0031613 ff.).
- Deeds, 1759–1866 (film 0031579 ff.).
- Mixed probate records, 1759–1865 (film 0031565 ff.).
- Marriage bonds and returns, 1759–1853 (film 0031632 ff.).

Dorman, John Frederick. "A Guide to the Counties of Virginia: Fauquier." *The Virginia Genealogist* 9 4 (October–December 1965): 176-9.

Gott, John K. *Abstracts of Fauquier County, Virginia Wills, Inventories, and Accounts, 1759–1800* (Marceline, MO: Walsworth Publishing Co., 1976). "Minutes of the Broad Run Baptist Church near Warrenton, Fauquier County, Virginia 1762–1872." *Genealogical Record* (Houston Genealogical Forum) 7 3 (September 1965) to 9 4 (December 1967).

Fincastle County (established from Botetourt County 1772, abolished when divided into Montgomery, Washington, and Kentucky counties at the end of 1776) See Montgomery County.

Frederick County (established 1743 from Orange County)
Original records at the Frederick-Winchester Judicial Center in Winchester are: Frederick County Court and Clerk.
- Court order books, 1743–1806 (film 0031416 ff.).
- Deeds, 1743–1867 (film 0031366 ff.).
- Land record books, 1762–1830 (film 0031362 ff.).
- Surveys, 1736–58, 1782–1808 (film 0031415).
- Court martial records, 1755–61 (film 0031376).
- Mixed probate records, 1743–1917 (film 0031347 ff.).
- Marriage bonds, 1773–1850 (film 0031456 ff.).
- Marriage registers, 1774–1907 (film 0031459).

Society of Friends, Hopewell. Monthly meeting records, 1748–1869 (film 0441486). The original records are at the Friends Historical Library, Swarthmore College, Swarthmore, Pennsylvania and have been published in *Hopewell Friends History, 1734–1934, Frederick County, Virginia: Records of Hopewell Monthly Meetings and Meetings Reporting to Hopewell, Two Hundred Years of History and Genealogy* (1936. Reprint. Baltimore: Genealogical Publishing Co., 1975, film 0908975).
Frederick Parish Episcopal Church. Vestry book, 1764–1818 (film 0031331). The original records are at the Bishop Payne Library, Virginia Theological Seminary, Alexandria.
Cedar Creek Presbyterian Church, Cedar Creek. Records, 1755–1937 (film 1577704). The church was organized in 1736. The original records are at the Presbyterian Church Archives, Union Theological Seminary, Richmond.

Dorman, John Frederick. "A Guide to the Counties of Virginia: Frederick." *The Virginia Genealogist* 10 4 (October–December 1966): 174–8.

 Gloucester County (established 1651 from York County)
Fires in 1821 and 1865 destroyed many records. Original records at the VSL in Richmond are:
Gloucester County Clerk.

* Surveyors' books, 1733–1810 (film 0031638).
* Tax accounts, 1770–1 (film 1955385).

Abingdon Parish, Episcopal. Parish register, 1678–1761 (film 0030159). Includes christenings for slaves.

Petsworth Parish, Episcopal. Vestry book, 1677–1793 (film 0033050).

Boddie, Charles A. and William H. Seiner. *A Guide to Gloucester County, Virginia Historical Manuscripts, 1651–1865* (Richmond: VSL, 1976).

Matheny, Emma Robertson. *Kingston Parish Register, Gloucester and Mathews Counties, 1749–1827* (Richmond: E.R. Matheny and H.K. Yates, 1963).

Goochland County (established 1728 from Henrico County)
Original records at the Goochland County Courthouse in Goochland are:
Goochland County Court and Clerk.
* Court order and minute books, 1728–1871 (film 0031671 ff.).
* Deeds, wills, and inventories, 1728–1868 (film 0031651 ff.).
Original records at the VSL in Richmond are:
* Marriage register, 1730–1853 (film 0031650).
Saint James Northam Parish, Episcopal. Vestry book, 1744–1850 (film 0033855).

Dorman, John Frederick. "A Guide to the Counties of Virginia: Goochland." *The Virginia Genealogist* 11 3 (July–September 1967): 132–4.

Douglas, William. *The Douglas Register: Being a Detailed Record of Births, Marriages, and Deaths Together with Other Interesting Notes, as Kept by the Rev. William Douglas, from 1750 to 1797: An Index of Goochland Wills, Notes on the French-Huguenot Refugees Who Lived in Manakin-Town* (1928. Reprint. Baltimore: Genealogical Publishing Co., 1977, film 0031690).

Vestry Book of King William Parish, Virginia, 1707–50 (1906. Reprint. Midlothian, VA: Manakin Episcopal Church, 1966, film 0873785).

Halifax County (established 1752 from Lunenburg County)
Original records at the Halifax County Courthouse in Halifax are:
Halifax County Court and Clerk.
* Court orders, 1752–1821 (film 0031919 ff.).
* Deeds, 1752–1867 (film 0031875 ff.).
* Land surveys, south district of Lunenberg, 1746–1901 (film 0031940).
* Mixed probate records, 1753–1865 (film 0031857 ff.).
* Marriage records, 1753–1949 (film 0031910 ff.).

Antrim Parish, Episcopal. Vestry book, 1752–1817 (film 0030163). The original records are at the Bishop Payne Library, Virginia Theological Seminary, Alexandria.

Dorman, John Frederick. "A Guide to the Counties of Virginia: Halifax." *The Virginia Genealogist* 12 4 (October–December 1968): 184–7.

 Hanover County (established 1720 from New Kent County)
A fire in 1865 destroyed many records. Original records at the VSL in Richmond are:
Hanover County Court and Clerk. Miscellaneous probate and land records, 1733–92 (film 0031942 ff.).
Saint Paul's Episcopal Church. Vestry book and land overseers' records, 1706–85 (film 0033858).

Dorman, John Frederick. "A Guide to the Counties of Virginia: Hanover." *The Virginia Genealogist* 13 3 (July–September 1969): 125–8.

Glazebrook, Eugenia G. and Preston G. Glazebrook. *Virginia Migrations, Hanover County, Volume I, 1723–1850, Wills, Deeds, Depositions, Invoices, Letters, Other Documents of Historical and Genealogical Interest* (Richmond: The Authors, 1954).

Reynolds, William W. "Records of a Hanover County, Virginia, Day Book, 1751–1757." *The Virginia Genealogist* 29 4 (October–December 1985): 289–93.

 Henrico County (established as a shire 1634)
A fire during the Revolutionary War destroyed some records. Original records at the VSL in Richmond are:
Henrico County Court and Clerk.
- Court records, deeds, wills, and settlements of estates, 1677–1787 (film 0031763 ff.).
- Deeds, wills, and settlements of estates, 1677–1739 (film 0031769 ff.).
- Court order and minute books, 1650–1807 (film 0031772 ff.). Wills, deeds, estate inventories, accounts, and indentures.
Saint John's Episcopal Church. Vestry book, parish records, 1730–1860, 1785–1887 (film 0031761).
Society of Friends, White Oak Swamp. Monthly meeting records, 1757–1831 (film 0031779).
Society of Friends, Henrico County. Monthly meeting records, 1699–1834 (film 0031762).

Bockstruck, Lloyd D. "Henrico County, Virginia Orphans' Court Records, 1755–1762." *The Virginia Genealogist* 34 2 (April–June 1990): 120–6.

Henrico County, Virginia: Proceedings of Commission Re. Its Records Destroyed by British, 1774–1782 (n.p., n.d., film 0850092). Contains transcript of documents brought before the county court to replace documents destroyed by the British during the Revolutionary War.

Isle of Wight County (established as the shire of Warrosquoyoake 1634, name changed to Isle of Wight 1637)
Original records at the Isle of Wight County Courthouse in Isle of Wight are:
Isle of Wight County Court and Clerk.
* Deeds, 1688–1866, wills, 1715–26, court orders, 1755–7 (film 0032000 ff.).
* Court order books, 1746–1866 (film 0032033 ff.).
* Guardian accounts, 1767–1861 (film 0032042 ff.).
* Mixed probate records, 1643–1866 (film 0032021 ff.).
Records at the VSL in Richmond include:
* Marriage bonds, 1772–1850, ministers' returns, 1789–1852 (film 0031998).
Mill Swamp Baptist Church. Minute book, 1774–90 (film 0833056).
Newport Parish Episcopal Church. Vestry book, 1723–72 (film 0032635).

Blunt, William. Account books for Poplar Hill Plantation, 1751–1844 (film 1753000 ff.). May include some slave births. The original records were filmed at the Smithfield Branch of the Isle of Wight Library in Smithfield.

Boddie, John Bennett. *Seventeenth Century Isle of Wight County, Virginia: A History of the County of Isle of Wight, Virginia, During the Seventeenth Century, Including Abstracts of the County Records* (1938. Reprint. Baltimore: Genealogical Publishing Co., 1973, film 1033862).

White, Miles. *Early Quaker Records in Virginia* (1902. Reprint. Baltimore: Genealogical Publishing Co., 1977). Earliest records of Friends in Nansemond and Isle of Wight counties, 1668–1768.

James City County (established as a shire 1634, see also New Kent and York counties)
A fire in 1865 destroyed most of the records. Original records and manuscripts at the VSL in Richmond are:
James City County Clerk. Tax books for James City and Williamsburg, 1768–9, also transcribed in "James City County, Virginia Sheriff's Tax Book, 1768." *The Virginia Genealogist* 1 1 (January–March 1957) 18–22.

Middletown Parish Episcopal Church. Bruton and Middletown parish register, 1662–1797 (film 0034219).
James City and James City Island land owners, 1619–1779 (film 0032047).

Cappon, Lester J. and Stella F. Duff. *Virginia Gazette Index, 1736–1780.* 2 Vols. (Williamsburg, VA: Institute of Early American History and Culture, 1950, fiche 6051225). Not complete for all issues.

Crozier, William Armstrong. *Williamsburg Wills: Being Transcriptions from the Original Files at the Chancery Court of Williamsburg* (1906. Reprint. Baltimore: Genealogical Publishing Co., 1973, film 0823832).

Duvall, Lindsay. *James City County, Virginia, 1634–1904: Abstracts of Genealogical Contents of Manuscript Volumes in the Manuscript Division, Library of Congress, and Archives Division, Virginia State Library* (Washington, DC: The Author, n.d., film 0850107).

Gardner, Virginia D. *Index to Wills and Estate Settlements Commencing 1608, Williamsburg, James City, York County, Virginia* (Williamsburg, VA: The Author, 1977).

Goodwin, William. *Historical Sketch of Bruton Church, Williamsburg, Virginia* (Petersburg, VA: Franklin Press, 1903, fiche 6104247).

Goodwin, William. *The Record of Bruton Parish Church [Williamsburg]* (1907. Reprint. Baltimore: Clearfield Co., 1997, fiche 6101647).

Noël Hume, Ivor. *Martin's Hundred: The Discovery of a Lost Colonial Virginia Settlement* (New York: Dell, 1982). Early history of Wolstenholme Towne.

Virginia Gazette, Williamsburg, 1736–1780 (Williamsburg, VA: The Institute of Early American History and Culture, 1950, film 0029718 ff.).

King and Queen County (established 1691 from New Kent County) A fire in 1864 destroyed all earlier records. Original records at the VSL in Richmond are:
King and Queen County Clerk. Court records, 1763–1868, copies, and deed, 1719
Stratton Major Parish, Episcopal. Vestry book, 1729–83 (film 0033935).

Dorman, John Frederick. "A Guide to the Counties of Virginia: King and Queen." *The Virginia Genealogist* 15 3 (July–September 1971): 191–3.

Fleet, Beverley. *King and Queen County Records Concerning Eighteenth-Century Persons: First–Ninth Collections* [*Virginia Colonial Abstracts*. Vols. 4–7, 14–15, 27–8, 33] (1938–48. Reprint. Baltimore: Genealogical Publishing Co., 1961 film 0850103 ff.).

King George County (established 1721 from Richmond and Westmoreland counties)
Original records at King George County Courthouse in King George are:
King George County Court and Clerk.
* Administrator, guardian, executor, inspection, surveyor, and sheriff bonds, 1765–1874 (film 0032087 ff.).
* Court orders and minute books, 1721–1869 (film 0032054 ff.).
* Miscellaneous probate records, 1721–1921 (film 0032071 ff.).
* Deeds, 1721–1868, inventories and appointments, 1745–84 (film 0032060 ff.).
* Wills, 1752–1901 (film 0032058 ff.).
Original records at the VSL in Richmond are:
Saint Paul's Episcopal Church. Parish register, 1716–93 (film 0033859).

Dorman, John Frederick. "A Guide to the Counties of Virginia: King George." *The Virginia Genealogist* 15 3 (July–September 1971): 193–5.

King William County
A fire in 1885 burned most of the records. Original records at the King William County Courthouse in King William are:
King William County Court and Clerk.
* Miscellaneous records and index, 1701–1884 (film 0032109 ff.). Wills, inventories, bonds, deeds, trust deeds, powers of attorney for the sale of property, estate sales of property, leases, mortgages, surveys, etc. Most documents are badly damaged.

Clarke, Peyton. *Old King William Homes and Families: An Account of Some of the Old Homesteads and Families of King William County, Virginia from Its Earliest Settlements* (Louisville, KY: J.P. Morton, 1897).

Dorman, John Frederick. "Guide to the Counties of Virginia: King William." *The Virginia Genealogist* 15 3 (July–September 1971): 195–7.

Lancaster County (established 1651 from Northumberland County)
Original records at the Lancaster County Courthouse in Lancaster are:
Lancaster County Court and Clerk.

- Court orders, 1655–1854 (film 0032140 ff.).
- Deeds, wills, settlements of estates, and inventories, 1650–1795, general index to records, 1652–1881 (film 0032130 ff.).
- General index to wills, 1669–1950 (film 0032181 ff.).
- Marriage registers, 1715–1852 (film 0032129).

Original records at the VSL in Richmond are:
Christ Church Parish, Episcopal. Vestry books, 1739–1870 (film 0030820).

Lee, Ida J. *Abstracts, Lancaster County, Virginia Wills, 1653–1800* (1959. Reprint. Baltimore: Genealogical Publishing Co., 1973).

Lee, Ida J. *Lancaster County, Virginia Marriage Bonds, 1652–1850* (Baltimore: Genealogical Publishing Co., 1972).

Loudoun County (established 1757 from Fairfax County, see also Fairfax County)
Original records at the Loudoun County Courthouse in Leesburg are:
Loudoun County Court and Clerk.

- Miscellaneous county records, 1757–1845 (film 0032346 ff.).
- Court order books, 1757–1812 (film 0032347 ff.).
- Guardian accounts, 1759–1870 (film 0032370 ff.).
- Deeds, 1757–1865 (film 0032294 ff.).
- Mixed probate records, 1757–1866 (film 0032274 ff.).

Society of Friends, Fairfax Monthly Meeting, Waterford. Marriage extracts, 1766–1892 (film 0032373).
Cameron Parish, Episcopal. Tithables, 1758–99 (film 0031052).
Ebenezer Baptist Church. Church book, no dates (film 0032378).

Loudoun County Court and Clerk. Land surveys, deeds, indentures, and court decisions, 1757–1850 (film 0032377). The original records are at the Frederick-Winchester Judicial Center in Winchester.
German Reformed Church. Records, 1764–1859 (film 1428440 ff.). The original records are at the Evangelical and Reformed Historical Society in Lancaster, Pennsylvania.
Shelburne Episcopal Church, Leesburg. Vestry book, 1771–1805 (film 0033932). The original records are at the VSL in Richmond.
Catoctin Presbyterian Church, Waterford. Records, 1769–1967 (film 1550287 ff.). The original records are at the Presbyterian Church Archives, Union Theological Seminary, Richmond.

Head, James W. *History and Comprehensive Description of Loudoun County, Virginia* (1908. Reprint. Baltimore: Clearfield Co., 1989).

Hiatt, Marty. *Early Church Records of Loudoun County [1745–1800]* (Westminster, MD: Family Line Publications, 1995). Contains records from:

Fairfax Monthly Meeting
Goose Creek Monthly Meeting
New Jerusalem Lutheran Church
Shelburne Parish

Reformed Church, Loudoun County
Frying Pan Baptist Church
Ketoctin Baptist Church
North Fork Primitive Baptist Church

Louisa County (established 1742 from Hanover County)
Original records at the Louisa County Courthouse in Louisa are:
Louisa County Court and Clerk.
* Inventory book, 1743–90 (film 0032232).
* Court order and minute books, 1742–1860 (film 0032218 ff.).
* Mixed probate records, 1745–1901 (film 0032191 ff.).
* Guardian bonds and accounts, 1767–1819 (film 0032231).
* Deeds, 1742–1865 (film 0032199 ff.).
Original records at the VSL in Richmond are:
* Marriage registers, 1766–1861 (film 0032190).
* Tithables, 1676–84

Fredericksville Parish, Episcopal. Vestry book, 1742–87 (film 0031332). The original records are at the Bishop Payne Library, Virginia Theological Seminary, Alexandria.

Bell, John C. *Louisa County Records You Probably Never Saw of 18th Century Virginia* (Nashville: The Author, 1983).

Pawlett, Nathaniel Mason. *Louisa County Road Orders, 1742–1748* (Charlottesville: Virginia Highway and Transportation Research Council, 1975).

Lunenburg County (established 1746 from Brunswick County)
Original records at the Lunenburg County Courthouse in Lunenburg are:
Lunenburg County Court and Clerk.
* Court order books, 1746–1865 (film 0032403 ff.).
* Deeds, 1746–1869 (film 0032386 ff.).
* Mixed probate records and index, 1746–1904 (film 0032379 ff.).
* Marriage registers and bonds, 1746–1929 (film 0032421).
Original records at the VSL in Richmond are:
Cumberland Parish Episcopal Church. Vestry book, 1747–1831 (film 0030824).

Dorman, John Frederick. "A Guide to the Counties of Virginia: Lunenburg." *The Virginia Genealogist* 16 3 (July–September 1972): 219–21.

Matheny, Emma R. and Helen K. Yates. *Marriages of Lunenburg County, Virginia, 1746–1853* (1967. Reprint. Baltimore: Genealogical Publishing Co., 1979).

Mecklenburg County (established 1765 from Lunenburg County)
Original records at the Mecklenburg County Courthouse in Boydton are:
Mecklenburg County Court and Clerk.
- Court order books, 1765–1904 (film 0032552 ff.).
- Fiduciary book, 1765–1885 (film 0032567).
- Guardian account books, 1766–1879 (film 0032565 ff.).
- Guardian bond book, 1765–1850 (film 0032567).
- Deeds, 1765–1905 (film 0032528 ff.).
- Wills, 1765–1922 (film 0032517 ff.).
Original records at the VSL in Richmond are:
- Marriage bonds, 1765–1912 (film 1870761 ff.).

Bracey, Susan L. *Life by the Roaring Roanoke: A History of Mecklenburg County, Virginia* (Mecklenburg: Mecklenburg County Bicentennial Committee, 1977).

Vogt, John and T. William Kethley, Jr. *Mecklenburg County Marriages, 1765–1853* (Athens, GA: Iberian Publishing Co., 1989).

Middlesex County (established 1669 from Lancaster County)
Original records at the Middlesex County Courthouse in Saluda and at the VSL in Richmond are:
Middlesex County Court and Clerk.
- Court order books, 1673–1795 (film 0032449 ff.).
- Miscellaneous land and property records, 1679–1831 (film 0032444 ff.).
- Guardianships, estate inventories, and orphan accounts, 1760–1820 (film 0032460).
- Mixed probate records, 1675–1890 (film 0032502 ff.).
- Administrators' bonds, 1767–1810 (film 0032461).
- Marriage bonds and register, 1740–1854 (film 0032443).
- Register of marriages, 1663–1715, 1754–63 (film 0032507).
- Militia records, 1678/9–82
- Slave records, 1764–1800
Christ Church Parish, Episcopal.
- Parish register, 1653–1814 (film 0030821).
- Vestry book, 1663–1767 (film 0030822).

Hopkins, William Lindsay. *Middlesex County, Virginia Wills and Inventories, 1673–1812, and Other Court Papers* (Richmond: The Author, 1989).

Montgomery County (established 1776–7 from Fincastle [abolished 1777], Botetourt, and Pulaski counties)
Original records at the Montgomery County Courthouse in Christiansburg are:
Montgomery County Court and Clerk.

* Index to mixed probate records, 1773–1953 (film 0032598 ff.).
* Deeds, 1773–1868, wills, 1773–97 (film 0032604 ff.). Includes some Fincastle County deeds, 1773–7.
* Court order books, 1773–1867 (film 0032621 ff.). Includes some court orders from Fincastle County, 1773–6.
* Surveyors' records, 1773–1890 (film 0032617 ff.).

Worrell, Anne Lowry. *A Brief of Wills and Marriages in Montgomery and Fincaslte Counties, Virginia, 1733–1831* (1932. Reprint. Baltimore: Genealogical Publishing Co., 1976).

Nansemond County (established 1637 as Upper Norfolk County, name changed to Nansemond 1642, abolished 1972, became independent city of Suffolk 1974, see also Isle of Wight County)
A fire in 1866 destroyed most records. Original records at the VSL in Richmond are:
Suffolk Parish, Episcopal. Vestry book, 1749–1856 (film 0033936).
Upper Nansemond Parish Episcopal Church. Vestry book, 1744–93 (film 0034215).

Society of Friends, Chuckatuck. Monthly meeting records, 1651–1755 (film 0441485). The original records are at the Friends Historical Library, Swarthmore College, Swarthmore, Pennsylvania.

Burton, A. *History of Suffolk and Nansemond County* (Suffolk, VA: Phelps Ideas, 1970).

Dorman, John Frederick. "A Guide to the Counties of Virginia: Nansemond." *The Virginia Genealogist* 19 1 (January–March 1975): 59–61.

New Kent County (established 1654 from York County)
Fires in 1787 and 1865 destroyed most of the records. Original records and copies at the VSL in Richmond are: New Kent County Court and Clerk. Deeds, 1697–1827, and grants, 1674, 1679
Records at the Bishop Payne Library, Virginia Theological Seminary, Alexandria are:
Blisland Parish, Episcopal. Vestry book, 1721–86 (film 0030624). Includes James City County.

Saint Peter's Church, Episcopal. Vestry book, 1685–1758, parish register, 1733–78 (film 0033860 ff.). Also includes James City County.

Providence Forge Presbyterian Church, Providence Forge. Records, 1750–1967 (film 1490377 ff.). First known as the New Kent Church. The original records are at the Presbyterian Church Archives, Union Theological Seminary, Richmond.

Harris, Malcolm H. *Old New Kent County: Some Account of the Planters, Plantations, and Places in New Kent County.* 2 Vols. (West Point, VA: The Author, 1977).

Norfolk County (established 1691 from Lower Norfolk County, abolished 1963 when it became part of the independent cities of Chesapeake, Norfolk, and Portsmouth, see also Warwick County)
Original records at the Chesapeake City Courthouse in Chesapeake are:
Norfolk County Court and Clerk.
- Order books, 1754–61 (Richmond: VSL, 1975, film 1941623).
- Order books, 1675–86, 1719–34, 1742–75, 1783–1801 (film 0032807 ff.).
- Guardian bonds, 1751–75, 1785–1850 (film 0032899 ff.).
- Deeds and wills, 1637–1900 (film 0032821 ff.).
- Administrators' bonds, 1722–7 (Richmond: VSL, 1975, film 1941629).
- Appraisements, inventories, and accounts, 1755–1884 (film 0032882 ff.).
- Audits, 1755–1874 (film 0032889 ff.).
- Inventory book, 1755–91 (film 0032820).
- Wills, 1693–1821 (Richmond: VSL, 1975, film 1941624 ff.).
- Wills, 1755–1868 (film 0032902 ff.).
- Tithables, 1730–85 (Richmond: VSL, 1975, film 1941615).
- Levy book, 1753–68 (Richmond: VSL, 1975, film 1941615).
- Marriage bonds, 1706–1819 (Richmond: VSL, 1975, film 1941614 ff.).
Original records at the Norfolk City Courthouse in Norfolk are:
Norfolk Hustings Court. Order books, 1761–1850 (film 0032958 ff.).
Norfolk Borough register (film 0032985). Deed of Norfolk Borough, 1682; Act confirming titles to town lands and an Act for ports, 1705, "hire of the parish Negroes, 1789."
Original records at the VSL in Richmond are:
Elizabeth River Parish, Episcopal. Vestry book, 1749–61 (film 0031118). Elizabeth River Parish was dissolved in 1761 when it was divided into three parishes.

First Presbyterian Church, Norfolk. Records, 1683–1934 (film 1549223 ff.). The original records are at the Presbyterian Church Archives, Union Theological Seminary, Richmond.

Cross, Charles Brinson. *The County Court, 1637–1904, Norfolk County, Virginia* (Portsmouth, VA: Printcraft Press, 1964).

Northampton County (established as the shire of Accawmacke 1634, name changed to Northampton 1642)
Original records at the Northampton County Courthouse in Eastville and the VSL in Richmond are:
Northampton County Court and Clerk.
* Deeds, wills, and court orders, 1632–1867 (film 0032794 ff.).
* Land causes, 1754–71 (film 0032782).
* Court order and minute books, 1655–1865 (film 0032740 ff.).
* Surveyors' records, 1764–1833 (film 0032741).
* Orphan accounts, 1731–1813 (film 0032783).
* Probate records, 1632–1792 (film 0032793 ff.).
* Tithables, 1662-4, 1675-7 (film 0032736).
* Marriage register, 1702–1853 (film 0032735).
Hungars Parish Church. Vestry book, 1758–82 (film 0032800).

Ames, Susie M. *County Court Records of Accomack-Northampton, Virginia, 1632–1640* (1954. Reprint. Millwood, NY: Kraus Reprint Co., 1975).

Ames, Susie M. *County Court Records of Accomack-Northampton, Virginia, 1640–1645* (Charlottesville: University Press of Virginia, 1973).

Dorman, John Frederick. "A Guide to the Counties of Virginia: Accawmack." *The Virginia Genealogist* 3 1 (January–March 1959): 38.

Fleet, Beverley. *Acchawmacke, 1632–1637* [*Virginia Colonial Abstracts*. Vol. 18] (1943. Reprint. Baltimore: Genealogical Publishing Co., 1961, film 0850105).

Fleet, Beverley. *Accomacke County, 1637–1640* [*Virginia Colonial Abstracts*. Vol. 32] (1948. Reprint. Baltimore: Genealogical Publishing Co., 1961, film 0908181).

 **Northumberland County** (established 1648 from Indian District of Chichacoan)
A fire in 1701 destroyed many earlier records. Original records at the VSL in Richmond are:
Northumberland County Court and Clerk.
* Court order books and deeds, 1649–52 (film 0032641), 1652–1756 (film 0032648 ff.).
* Court order books, 1756–97 (film 0032670 ff.).

- Wills, inventories, deeds, and powers of attorney, 1652–1749 (film 0032638 ff.), 1749–1839 (film 0032672 ff.).

Wicomico Parish Episcopal Church. Vestry book, 1703–95 (film 0034216).

Miscellaneous church records, 1650–1810 (film 0032641). Includes parishes of Saint Stephen's, Chichacoan, Fairfield, and Boutracy.

Haynie, W. Preston. *Records of Indentured Servants and of Certificates for Land, Northumberland County, Virginia, 1650–1795* (Bowie, MD: Heritage Books, 1996).

Old Rappahannock County (established 1656 from Lancaster County, abolished 1692 when divided into Essex and Richmond counties)
See Essex County.

Orange County (established 1734 from Spotsylvania County)
Original records at the Orange County Courthouse in Orange are:
Orange County Court and Clerk.

- Deeds, 1734–1865, court records, 1734–60, marriage and birth records, 1751–78 (film 0033009 ff.). Many Germans from the Robinson Colony were naturalized in the Orange County Court, January–February, 1742/3.
- Court order and minute books, 1734–1867 (film 0033033 ff.).
- Wills, 1735–1906 (film 0033002 ff.).
- Marriage registers, 1757–1938 (film 1869574 ff.).

Original records at the VSL in Richmond are:

- Judgments and other court papers, 1735–1911 (Richmond: VSL, 1976, film 1863092 ff.).
- Tithables, 1736–82 (Richmond: VSL, 1976, film 1869674).

Pittsylvania County (established 1767 from Halifax County)
Original records at the Pittsylvania County Courthouse in Chatham are:
Pittsylvania County Court and Clerk.

- Court orders, 1767–1866 (film 0033304).
- Mixed probate records, 1767–1949 (film 0033292 ff.).
- Surveyors' records, 1746–1863 (film 0033324).
- Mixed deeds and wills, 1767–1948 (film 0033258 ff.).
- Marriage bonds, 1767–1862 (film 0033326).

Camden Parish Episcopal Church. Vestry book, 1767–1852 (film 0030818).

White, Elizabeth Tunstall. *Military Records of Pittsylvania County, Virginia, 1767–1783* . . . (Danville, VA: VA-NC Piedmont Genealogical Society, 1983).

Prince Edward County (established 1754 from Amelia County)
Original records at the Prince Edward County Courthouse in Farmville are:
Prince Edward County Court and Clerk.
* Court order books, 1754–1869 (film 0033236 ff.).
* Wills, 1754–1899 (film 0033216 ff.).
* Marriage bonds, 1754–1850 (film 0033254).
Original records at the VSL in Richmond are:
Saint Patrick's Parish, Episcopal. Vestry book and processioners returns, 1755–
74 (film 0033857).

Dorman, John Frederick. "A Guide to the Counties of Virginia: Prince Edward."
The Virginia Genealogist 20 4 (October–December 1976): 291–4.

Prince George County (established 1703 from Charles City County)
Fires during the Civil War destroyed many records. Original records at
the Prince George County Courthouse in Prince George and at VSL are:
Prince George County Court and Clerk.
* Court order book 1714–20, and minute books, 1737–40 (film 0033055).
* Surveyors' books, deeds, wills, inventories, and settlements of estates,
1711–92 (film 0033051 ff.).
Bristol Parish, Episcopal. Parish register, 1701–97, vestry book, 1720–89 (film
0030625). Records also published in Slaughter, Philip. *A History of Bristol
Parish: with Genealogies of Families Connected Therewith, and Historical
Illustrations*. 2nd ed. (Richmond: J.W. Randolph and English, 1879, film
0982350). Published records include baptisms, 1689–1794. Also covers
Dinwiddie County.

Robbins, Gus. *Merchants' Hope Church: Erected in 1657, Oldest Protestant
Church Still Standing in America and Used as a House of Worship* (n.p.: The
Author, 1975). Divided from Westover Parish (Charles City County) in 1657
and called Jordan Parish.

Prince William County (established 1731 from Stafford and King
George counties)
Fires during the Revolutionary and Civil wars destroyed many earlier
records. Original records at Prince William County Courthouse in Manassas are:
Prince William County Court and Clerk.
* Court minute and order books, 1752–1869 (film 0033129 ff.).
* Deeds, 1731–1869 (film 0033104 ff.).
* Bond book, executors of wills, 1753–86 (film 0033137).
* Wills, inventories, and accounts, 1734–1872 (film 0033119 ff.).

Original records at the VSL in Richmond are:
Dettingen Parish, Episcopal. Vestry book, 1745–1802 (film 0031089), list of
tithables, 1747 (film 0033138). Includes Fauquier County.

Federal Writers' Program. *Prince William: The Story of Its People and Places*
(Richmond: Whittet and Shepperson, 1941).

Princess Anne County (established 1691 from Lower Norfolk County [abo-
lished], dissolved 1952 and incorporated as the independent city of Virginia
Beach, see also Warwick County)
Original records at the Virginia Beach Circuit Court and the VSL in Richmond
are:
Princess Anne County Court and Clerk.
• Mixed land and probate records, 1691–1865 (film 0033186 ff.).
• Court minute books, 1709–1861 (film 0033173 ff.).
• Court orders and minute books, 1717–69 (film 0033150 ff.).
• Court order books, 1691–1714 (film 0033172).
• Guardian accounts, 1736–1871 (film 0033206 ff.).
Lynnhaven Parish, Episcopal. Vestry book, 1723–1892 (film 0032128).

Maling, Anne E. *Princess Anne County, Virginia Land and Probate Records
Abstracted from Deed Books One to Seven, 1691–1755* (Bowie, MD: Heritage
Books, 1992).

Richmond County (established 1692 from old Rappahannock County)
Original records at the Richmond County Courthouse in Warsaw and the VSL
in Richmond are:
Richmond County Court and Clerk.
• Account books, 1724–1866 (film 0033679 ff.).
• Fines, examination of criminals, "tryalls" of slaves, from March 1710 to
  1754 (film 0033687). Published in Scott, William B. *Criminal Proceedings
  in Colonial Virginia: Fines, Examination of Criminals, Trials of Slaves,
  Etc., from March 1710 to 1754* (Athens: University of Georgia Press, 1984).
• Miscellaneous records, 1699–1724 (film 0033705).
• Court order books, 1692–1871 (film 0033741 ff.).
• Deeds, 1692–1869 (film 0033738 ff.).
• Deeds, 1714–20 (film 0033678).
• Wills and inventories, 1699–1879 (film 0033737 ff.).
North Farnham Parish, Episcopal. Parish register, 1672–1800 (film 0032637).

"A list of Negroes instructed and baptized by John Garzia, minister of the Parish
of North Farnham, 1724" (film 1955385). The original records are at the
Earl Gregg Swem Library, College of William and Mary, Williamsburg.

Headley, Robert K., Jr. *Wills of Richmond County, Virginia, 1699–1800* (Baltimore: Genealogical Publishing Co., 1983).

Rockbridge County (established 1778 from Augusta and Botetourt counties, independent city of Lexington is county seat)
New Monmouth Presbyterian Church, Lexington. Records, 1771–1965 (film 1490448 ff.). The church was organized in 1746 as Forks of the James Church. The original records are at the Presbyterian Church Archives, Union Theological Seminary, Richmond.

Dorman, John Frederick. "A Guide to the Counties of Virginia: Rockbridge." *The Virginia Genealogist* 21 3 (July–September 1977): 222–4.

 Rockingham County (established 1778 from Augusta County)
A fire in 1864 destroyed many records. Original records at the Rockingham County Courthouse in Harrisonburg are:
Rockingham County Court and Clerk. Survey books, 1761–1876, survey entry books, 1776–1880 (film 0033477 ff.0.

Linvill Creek Baptist Church. Minute book, 1742–1844 (film 0441485).The original records are at the Presbyterian Historical Society in Philadelphia.
Roeder's Church, Lutheran, Timberline. Records, 1764–1834 (film 0020366). The manuscript is at the Evangelical and Reformed Historical Society in Lancaster, Pennsylvania.

Dorman, John Frederick. "A Guide to the Counties of Virginia: Rockingham." *The Virginia Genealogist* 22 1 (January–March 1978): 54–7.

Shenandoah County (established as Dunmore County from Frederick County 1772, name changed to Shenandoah 1778)
Original records at the Shenandoah County Courthouse and Archives in Woodstock are:
Shenandoah County Court and Clerk.
• Court order and minute books, 1772–1865 (film 0033916 ff.).
• Deeds, 1772–1867 (film 0033884 ff.).
• Wills, 1772–1866 (film 0033865 ff.).
• Marriage bonds, 1772–1850 (film 0033930).
Archives Collection #11, 1723–1965 (film 1548900 ff.). Miscellaneous records, including deeds, wills, accounts of Indian massacres, copies of the registers from Reformed Zion Church, Friedens Church, Fort Valley Church, Evangelical Lutheran Church in Frederick-Town, Dunmore County census records, 1775, etc.

Dorman, John Frederick. "A Guide to the Counties of Virginia: Shenandoah." *The Virginia Genealogist* 22 3 (July–September 1978): 210–13.

Southampton County (established 1749 from Isle of Wight and Namsemond counties)
Original records at the Southampton County Courthouse in Courtland are:
Southampton County Court and Clerk.
* Court order and minute books, 1749–1870 (film 0034018 ff.).
* Deeds, 1749–1870 (film 0034003 ff.).
* Wills, inventories, and accounts, 1749–1896 (film 0033994 ff.).
* Marriage records, 1750–1853 (film 0033993).

Chapman, Blanch Adams. *Wills and Administrations of Southampton County, Virginia, 1749–1800* (1947–58. Reprint. Baltimore: Genealogical Publishing Co., 1980).

Spotsylvania County (established 1721 from Essex, King William, and King and Queen counties)
Original records at the Spotsylvania County Courthouse in Spotsylvania are:
Spotsylvania County Court and Clerk.
* Court order and minute books, 1724–1871 (film 0034087 ff.).
* Record of executions, 1756–71 (film 0034043).
* Deeds, 1722–1922 (film 0034066 ff.).
* Wills, inventories, and accounts, 1722–1876 (film 0034055 ff.).
Saint George's Parish Episcopal Church, Fredericksburg. Vestry books, 1726–1817 (film 0031564).

Pawlett, Nathaniel Mason. *Spotsylvania County Road Orders, 1722–1734* (Charlottesville: Virginia Highway and Transportation Research Council, 1985).

 Stafford County (established 1664 from Westmoreland County)
Fire destroyed many records prior to the Civil War. Original records at the VSL in Richmond are:
Stafford County Court and Clerk.
* Court records, 1680 (film 0033956). Wills, assignments, surveys, sale of land, depositions, inventories, bonds, earmarks, agreements, etc.
* General index of deeds, deeds of trust, release deeds and wills, 1664–1914, deeds, 1699–1709, 1722–64, 1780–6, court records, 1664–8, 1689–93 (film 0033940 ff.).
* Court order book, 1686–94 (film 1445833).
* Rent rolls, 1723, 1729, 1768, 1773
Town of Falmouth. Proceedings, 1764–1868

Overwharton Parish, Episcopal. Parish register, 1724–74, and vestry book, 1815–20 (film 0032998).

Vogt, John and T. William Kethley, Jr. *Stafford County, Virginia Quit Rents, Personal Property Taxes, and Related Lists and Petitions, 1723–1790.* 2 Vols. (Athens, GA: Iberian Publishing Co., 1990).

Surry County (established 1652 from James City County)
Original records at the Surry County Courthouse in Surry are:
Surry County Court and Clerk.
* Guardian and fiduciary accounts, 1672–1865 (film 0034143 ff.).
* Court order books, 1671–1877 (film 0034128 ff.).
* Deeds, 1741–1873 (film 0034113 ff.).
* Wills and deeds, 1652–1754, wills, 1754–1875 (film 0034099 ff.).
Original records at the VSL in Richmond are:
* Deeds, wills, and inventories, 1645–86 (film 0034098).
* Marriage register, 1768–1853 (film 0034097).

Albemarle Parish, Episcopal, Surry and Sussex counties. Vestry book, 1742–87 (film 0030162), parish register, 1739–78 (film 0030161). Includes separate register for births of "negro and mulatto slaves," 1730–58, and deaths of "negroes," 1739–78. The original records are at the Bishop Payne Library, Virginia Theological Seminary, Alexandria.

Boddie, John B. *Colonial Surry* (1948. Reprint. Baltimore: Genealogical Publishing Co., 1959).

Sussex County (established 1754 from Surry County, see also Surry County)
Original records at the Sussex County Courthouse in Sussex are:
Sussex County Court and Clerk.
* Court order and minute books, 1754–1864 (film 0034175 ff.).
* Deeds, 1754–1864 (film 0034163 ff.).
* Wills, 1754–1864 (film 0034155 ff.).
* Marriage records, 1754–1853 (film 0034154).

Knorr, Catherine L. *Marriage Bonds and Ministers; Returns of Sussex County, Virginia, 1754–1810* (Pine Bluff, AR: The Author, 1952).

 Warwick County (established 1634 as the Warwick River shire, name changed to Warwick 1642, abolished 1952, incorporated into independent city of Newport News 1957)
Fires during the Civil War destroyed most records. Original records at the VSL in Richmond are: Warwick County Court and Clerk. Court minute books, 1748–62 (film 0034220).

Rollings, Virginia H. *Warwick, Virginia, 1713 Rent Roll* (Newport News, VA: n.p., 1990, film 1728878).

Walter, Alice Granbery. *Virginia Land Patents of the Counties of Norfolk, Princess Anne and Warwick from Patent Books . . . 1666-1679* (Lawrence, NY: The Author, 1972). Source of records not given: abstracts for Norfolk (now independent city of Chesapeake), Princess Anne (now independent city of Virginia Beach), and Warwick (now independent city of Newport News) counties.

"Warwick County, Virginia Court Orders, 1647." *The Virginia Genealogist* 18 4 (October–December 1974): 285-7.

Westmoreland County (established 1653 from Northumberland County)
Original records at the Westmoreland County Courthouse in Montross and the VSL in Richmond are:
Westmoreland County Court and Clerk.
* Court order books, 1662–1873 (film 0034264 ff.).
* Fiduciary book, 1742–89 (film 0034290).
* Index to fiduciary accounts, 1723–1917 (film 0034331).
* Mixed deeds, wills, and court orders, 1653–1859 (film 0034267 ff.).
* Records and inventories of estates, 1723–46, 1752–6, 1767–76, 1790–1867 (film 0034332 ff.).
* Miscellaneous land and probate records, 1654–1790 (film 0034260 ff.)
* Rent roll, 1740
* Delinquent tax roll, Cople Parish, 1724

Dorman, John Frederick. *Westmoreland County, Virginia Records, 1658–1661* (Washington, DC: The Author, 1991).

Harwell, Richard Barksdale. *The Committees of Safety of Westmoreland and Fincastle: Proceedings of the County Committees, 1774–1776* (Richmond: VSL, 1974).

York County (established as shire of Charles River 1634, name changed to York 1642, see also James City County)
Original records at the York County Courthouse in Yorktown are:
York County Court and Clerk.
* Deeds and bonds, 1691–1729, deeds, 1729–77 (film 0034419 ff.).
* Deeds, orders, and wills, 1633–1710, orders and wills, 1709–32, wills and inventories, 1732–1811 (film 0034402 ff.).
* Judgment and order books, 1746–1851 (film 0034430 ff.).
* Land causes and pleas, 1746–69, 1795–1854 (film 0034429).

- Guardian accounts, 1736–1846 (film 0034418).
- Quit rents, 1704 (film 1064761).
- Marriage bonds and consents, 1772–1849 (film 0034443).

Charles Parish, Episcopal. Parish register, 1648–1800 (film 0030819). Known as York-Hampton Parish Episcopal Church after 1789. The original records are at the Bishop Payne Library, Virginia Theological Seminary, Alexandria.

Dorman, John Frederick. "A Guide to the Counties of Virginia: York Prince Edward." *The Virginia Genealogist* 20 4 (October–December 1976): 291–4.

Suggested Reading

Bailey, Kent. *A Guide to Seventeenth-Century Virginia Court Handwriting* (Richmond: Association for Preservation of Virginia Antiquities, 1980).

Barbour, Philip. L. *The Complete Works of Captain John Smith.* 3 Vols. (Chapel Hill: University of North Carolina Press, 1986).

Billings, Warren, John Selby, and Thad Tate. *Colonial Virginia, a History* (White Plains, NY: KTO Press, 1986).

Bly, Daniel W. *From the Rhine to the Shenandoah: Eighteenth-Century Swiss and German Pioneer Families in the Central Shenandoah Valley of Virginia and their European Origins* (Baltimore: Gateway Press, 1993).

Boddie, John Bennet. *Historical Southern Families.* 23 Vols. (1957. Reprint. Baltimore: Genealogical Publishing Co., 1967–80).

Brock, R.A. *Documents, Chiefly Unpublished, Relating to the Huguenot Emigration to Virginia and to the Settlement at Manakin-Town . . . with "List of Refugees,"1700* (1886. Reprint. Baltimore: Genealogical Publishing Co., 1979, fiche 6049042).

Currer-Briggs, Noel. *Virginia Settlers and English Adventurers: Abstracts of Wills, 1484–1798, and Legal Proceedings, 1560–1700, Relating to Early Virginia Families.* 3 Vols. in 1 (Baltimore: Genealogical Publishing Co., 1970).

Daniel, R.R. *A Hornbook of Virginia History.* 3rd ed. (Richmond: VSL, 1983).

Davis, Virginia Lee. *Tidewater Virginia Families* (Baltimore: Genealogical Publishing Co., 1989).

Dorman, John Frederick and Virginia M. Meyer. *Adventurers of Purse and Person, Virginia, 1607–1624/5.* 3rd ed. (Richmond: Dietz Press 1987).

Foley, Louise. *Early Virginia Families Along the James River* . . . 3 Vols. (Baltimore: Genealogical Publishing Co., 1979, 1980, 1990, fiche 6046679). Abstracts from land records and quit rent rolls for the counties of Charles City, Henrico, Goochland, Prince George, James City, and Surry.

Greer, George Cabell. *Early Virginia Immigrants, 1623–1666* (1912. Reprint. Baltimore: Genealogical Publishing Co., 1960).

Hamlin, Charles Hughes. *They Went Thataway.* 3 Vols. (1964–6. Reprint. Baltimore: Genealogical Publishing Co., 1985).

Hamlin, Charles Hughes. *Virginia Ancestors and Adventurers.* 3 Vols. in 1 (1967–73. Reprint. Baltimore: Genealogical Publishing Co., 1975).

Records on CD-ROM

Virginia Vital Records (Broderbund, 1997), contains images of the pages of the following six books originally published by Genealogical Publishing Company, which originally appeared in *The Virginia Magazine of History and Biography, The William and Mary College Quarterly,* and *Tyler's Quarterly*:

- *Virginia Tax Records* (1983)
- *Virginia Will Records* (1982)
- *Virginia Land Records* (1982)
- *Virginia Marriage Records* (1984)
- *Virginia Military Records* (1983)
- *Virginia Vital Records* (1984)

Also on CD-ROM:

- *Genealogies of Virginia Families from The Virginia Magazine of History and Biography* (5 Vols.) (Broderbund, 1996).
- *Genealogies of Virginia Families from the William and Mary College Quarterly* (5 Vols.) and *Genealogies of Virginia Families from Tyler's Quarterly* (4 Vols.) (Broderbund, 1997).

Hatch, Charles. *The First Seventeen Years, Virginia, 1607–1624* (Williamsburg, VA: Virginia 350th Anniversary Celebration Corporation, 1957).

Haws, Charles H. *Scots in the Old Dominion, 1685–1800* (Edinburgh: John Dunlop, 1980, fiche 6087317).

Hughes, Sarah S. *Surveyors and Statesmen: Land Measuring in Colonial Virginia* (Richmond: Virginia Surveyors Foundation, 1979).

Hume, Robert. *Early Child Immigrants to Virginia, 1618–1642: Copied from the Records of Bridewell Royal Hospital* (Baltimore: Magna Carta Book Co., 1986).

A Key to Survey Reports and Microfilm of the Virginia Colonial Records Project. 2 Vols. (Richmond: VSL, 1990).

Lewis, Clifford M. and Albert J. Lewis. *The Spanish Jesuit Mission in Virginia, 1570–1572* (Chapel Hill: University of North Carolina Press, 1953).

McGinnis, Carol. *Virginia Genealogy: Sources & Resources* (Baltimore: Genealogical Publishing Co., 1993).

The Muster of the Inhabitants in Virginia Taken the 23ʳᵈ January 1624/25: Transcribed from the Original in the State Paper Office American and West Indies, Vol. 447 (Washington, DC: n.p., 1848–9, film 0844901).

Stanard, Mary Mann P.N. *The Story of Virginia's First Century* (Philadelphia: J.B. Lippincott, 1928, film 1697525).

Stanard, Mary Mann P.N. *Colonial Virginia: Its People and Customs* (Detroit: Singing Tree Press, 1970).

Stanard, William G. *Some Emigrants to Virginia: Memoranda in Regard to Several Hundred Emigrants to Virginia During the Colonial Period Whose Parentage Is Shown or Former Residence Indicated by Authentic Records* (1915. Reprint. Baltimore: Genealogical Publishing Co., 1979, film 0845113).

Stone, Kathryn Crossley. *Research Aids for the Colonial Period, Emphasis on Virginia: A Dictionary-Encyclopedia for Genealogical Research* (Boulder, CO: Empire Printing, 1976).

Summers, Lewis Preston. *Annals of Southwest Virginia, 1769–1800.* 2 Vols. (Baltimore: Genealogical Publishing Co., 1970).

True, Ransom B. *Biographical Dictionary of Early Virginia, 1607–1660* (Richmond: Association for the Preservation of Virginia Antiquities, 1984, fiche 6332718).

Virginia in 1740: A Reconstructed Census (Miami Beach: TLC Genealogy, 1992, film 1697799). Based on deeds, wills, tax lists, order books, etc.

Wayland, John W. *The German Element of the Shenandoah Valley of Virginia* (1907. Reprint. Bridgewater, VA: C.J. Carrier Co., 1964, film 1597906).

Weaver, Glenn. *The Italian Presence in Colonial Virginia* (New York: Center for Migration Studies, 1988).

Wulfeck, Dorothy Ford. *Marriages of Some Virginia Residents, 1607–1800.* 7 Vols. in 2 (1961–7. Reprint. Baltimore: Genealogical Publishing Co., 1986, film 1321057 ff.).

Wurst, Klaus. *Virginia Germans* (Charlottesville: University Press of Virginia, 1969).

An Indian Village at the Roanoke Settlement.

North Carolina

North Carolina's first colonists migrated from Virginia in 1653 and settled on the northern coast of Albemarle Sound (Chowan County). The Carolina area (named in 1629) was granted to eight proprietors in 1663. In 1665 the Concessions and Agreements of Albemarle Province were written (for information on the settlement at Charleston, see South Carolina). In 1691 the Albemarle area was renamed North Carolina. In 1705 Huguenots established the town of Bath. New Bern was founded by Swiss and Germans in 1710. In 1706 the Privy Council declared the Carolina charter null and void. The Crown appointed governors in 1712 and separated Carolina into two provinces, North and South. Over the next decade, the coastal area of North Carolina was prey to pirates, some operating from the Bahamas, and some from Jamaica.

In 1719 South Carolina declared a provisional government, no longer recognized the authority of the proprietors, and became a Royal colony. When the Carolina charter was officially surrendered in 1729 and the palatine court was abolished, North Carolina also became a Royal colony. Ulster Scots first arrived in 1730 and settled in the Cape Fear area. Migrations on the Great Philadelphia Wagon Road brought more Germans and Ulster Scots to settle the Piedmont area. A back country group in both North and South Carolina known as the Regulators rebelled against the provincial government but were defeated in battle in 1771.

Statewide Records and Resources

During the eighteenth century, North Carolina courts frequently changed in jurisdiction and name. A summary of the earliest courts in North Carolina is:

- **General Court (1670–1754):**Comprised of the Governor and Council, was an appellate criminal court, court of original jurisdiction over capital crimes, sat at Edenton.
- **Palatine Court (1669–1729):** Proprietary court that was abolished when North Carolina became royalized.
- **County Courts (1663–1868):** Also called precinct and magistrate courts; criminal cases except for capital crimes.
- **District Superior Courts (1754–72, 1778–ca 1829):** Court with jurisdiction over more than one county; usually sat at a county seat; was an extension of the General Court.

Cooke, Charles S. *The Governor, Council, and*

SEE ALSO
Great Britain
South Carolina
Virginia

Assembly in Royal North Carolina (Chapel Hill: North Carolina University, 1912, fiche 6048317).

Index to the Colonial and State Records of North Carolina, Covering Volumes I–XXV, Published under the Supervision of the Trustees of the Public Libraries, by Order of the General Assembly. 2 Vols. (1886. Reprint. Wilmington, NC: Broadfoot Publishing, 1993).

Saunders, William. *The Colonial Records of North Carolina, 1662–1790.* 30 Vols. (1886. Reprint. Wilmington, NC: Broadfoot Publishing, 1993, fiche 6078231). Includes court records, military records, public records, and law and legislation.

The office of the Secretary of State was the official repository for wills and estates during colonial times. In about 1760, it was ordered that wills would be filed with clerks of court, but some wills continued to be filed with the Secretary of State until 1789. From 1760 to 1868 wills were kept by the County Court of Pleas and Quarter Sessions; from 1868 to 1966 wills were kept by the Superior Court. Original records at the State Archives in Raleigh are:

- Colonial estate papers, 1669–1759 (film 2047891).
- Wills and estate papers, 1663–1978 (film 1605076 ff.).
- Wills and court records, 1679–1775 (film 0018054 ff.). Includes wills, council minutes, inventories, Court of Chancery minutes, commissions and powers of attorney, and other miscellaneous records.

Grimes, John Bryan. *North Carolina Wills and Inventories Copied from Original and Recorded Wills and Inventories in the Office of the Secretary of State* (Raleigh: Edwards and Broughton, 1912, fiche 6051125).

Mitchell, Thornton W. *North Carolina Wills: A Testator Index, 1665–1900* (Baltimore: Genealogical Publishing Co., 1992).

Olds, Fred A. *An Abstract of North Carolina Wills from about 1760 to about 1800: Supplementing Grimes' Abstract of North Carolina Wills 1663 to 1760* (Baltimore: Genealogical Publishing Co., 1965, fiche 6019970).

Ratcliff, Clarence E. *North Carolina Taxpayers, [1679–1790].* 2 Vols. (Baltimore: Genealogical Publishing Co., 1987–9).

Land Records
Land was first granted under the Proprietors from 1663. After 1727 land grants were issued by the royal government of North Carolina. There were still some proprietary grants issued in what was known as the Granville District through

1763. Records at the State Archives in Raleigh are:
Secretary of State.
* List of warrants for various counties of North Carolina, 1769–71 (film 0018065).
* Court of claims of land records, 1755–74 (film 0018070).
* Land grants, land entries and warrants and list of grants for various counties, 1764–1853 (film 0018062).
* Land records, 1600–1800s (film 1942606 ff.).

Bradley, Stephen E. *Early Records of North Carolina: From the Secretary of State Papers, 1677–1794* (Keysville, VA: The Author, 1992).

Hofmann, Margaret M. *Province of North Carolina, 1663–1729, Abstracts of Land Patents* (Roanoke Rapids, NC: The Author, 1983).

Hofmann, Margaret M. *Colony of North Carolina, Abstracts of Land Patents [1735–1775]*. 2 Vols. (Roanoke Rapids, NC: The Author, 1982).

Hofmann, Margaret M. *The Granville District of North Carolina, 1748–1763: Abstracts of Land Grants* (Weldon, NC: Roanoke News, 1986). There is also a Granville grant card file at the State Archives.

Holcomb, Brent H. *Deed Abstracts of Tryon, Lincoln And Rutherford Counties, North Carolina, 1769–1786: Tryon County Wills And Estates* (Easley, SC: Southern Historical Press, 1977).

Holcomb, Brent H. *North Carolina Land Grants in South Carolina [1749–1773]* (Clinton, SC: The Author, 1975). Includes Anson and Mecklenburg counties.

Morgan, Lawrence. *Land Tenure in Proprietary North Carolina* (Chapel Hill: North Carolina University, 1912, fiche 6048317).

Powell, William Stevens. *The Proprietors of Carolina* (1963. Raleigh: Department of Archives and History, 1968, film 0896978).

Manuscript Collections
Some of the major manuscript collections in North Carolina are:
➤ Blosser, Susan Sokol. *The Southern Historical Collection: A Guide to Manuscripts* (Chapel Hill: University of North Carolina Library, 1970).
➤ Cain, Barbara T. *Guide to Private Manuscript Collections in the North Carolina State Archives.* 3rd ed. (Raleigh: North Carolina Department of Cultural Resources, Division of Archives and History, 1981).
➤ *Guide to Research Materials in the North Carolina State Archives: Section B,*

County Records. 10th ed. (Raleigh: Division of Archives and History, 1988).
➤ Historical Records Survey. *List of the Papeles Procedentes De Cuba (Cuban Papers) in the Archives of the North Carolina Historical Commission* (Raleigh: The Survey, 1942).
➤ McCubbins Collection at the Rowan County Library (film 0019828 ff.). Records of Rowan County and counties formed from Rowan County.
➤ Smith, Everard H. *The Southern Historical Collection: Supplementary Guide to Manuscripts, 1970-1975* (Chapel Hill: University of North Carolina Library, 1976).
➤ Trilley, Nannie M. *Guide to the Manuscript Collections in the Duke University Library* (Durham: Duke University Press, 1947, film 1425564).

Church Records

Original records at the State Archives in Raleigh (see also under specific counties) are:
Church of England. Letters from North and South Carolina to England regarding the conditions of the Church of England, 1712-81 (film 0239273).
Society of Friends, North Carolina.
•   Eastern Quarterly Meetings. Minutes, 1762-1934 (film 0317020).
•   Yearly Meeting. Minutes and standing committee, 1704-1846 (film 0371250).

There are also 620 manuscript volumes of Society of Friends records from 1680 at the Guilford College Library in Greensboro. For more information, see *Genealogical Resources in the Guilford College Library* (Greenville, NC: The Library, 1977).

Bjorkman, Gwen Boyer. *Quaker Marriage Certificates: Pasquotank, Perquimans, Piney Woods, and Suttons Creek Monthly Meetings, North Carolina, 1677-1800* (Bowie, MD: Heritage Books, 1988).

Moravian records are kept at the archives of the Southern Province of the Moravian Church in America at Winston-Salem. Many of the records have been published in *Records of the Moravians in North Carolina, 1752-1879*. 11 Vols. (Raleigh: Edwards and Broughton, 1922-69, film 1321198 ff.). This includes congregational diaries, church registers, account books, minute books, personal diaries, memoirs, and letters.

Bernheim, G.D. *History of the German Settlements and of the Lutheran Church in North and South Carolina: From the Earliest Period of the Colonization of the Dutch, German and Swiss Settlers to the Close of the First Half of the Present Century* (Philadelphia: Lutheran Book Store, 1872, film 0874034).

Chreitzberg, A.M. *Early Methodism in the Carolinas* (1897. Reprint. Spartanburg, SC: The Reprint Co., 1972, film 0897452).

London, Lawrence and Sarah Lemmon. *The Episcopal Church in North Carolina, 1701-1959* (Raleigh: Episcopal Diocese of North Carolina, 1987).

Oliver, David Dickson. *The Society for the Propagation of the Gospel in the Province of North Carolina and Correspondence of John Rust Eaton* (Raleigh: James Sprunt, 1910).

Paschal, George. *History of North Carolina Baptists*. 2 Vols. (Raleigh: General Board, North Carolina Baptist State Convention, 1930–55, fiche 6049246 ff.).

Reformed Church, Classis of North Carolina. *Historic Sketch of the Reformed Church in North Carolina* (Philadelphia: Publication Board of the Reformed Church in the United States, 1908).

United Evangelical Lutheran Synod of North Carolina. *History of the Lutheran Church in North Carolina* (n.p.: The Synod, 1953).

County Records and Resources

North Carolina's first civil divisions were four precincts (later to become counties) created in 1670: Currituck, Pasquotank, Chowan, and Perquimans.

Apprentice bonds and records, 1716–1921 (film 2027751 ff.).

Bertie County, 1750–1866	Martin County, 1774
Bute County, 1764–79	Mecklenburg County, 1772–1904
Carteret County, 1756–1897	Onslow County, 1757–1907
Chowan County, 1737–1811	Pasquotank County, 1716–1881
Craven County, 1748–1835	Perquimans County, 1737–1866
Granville County, 1749–1809	Tyrell County, 1742–1886
Hyde County, 1771–1892	Wake County, 1770–1903

Bastardy bonds and records, 1736–1957 (film 2030782 ff.).

Bertie County, 1739–1880	Hyde County, 1740–1896
Bute County, 1769–79	Onslow County, 1764–1909
Carteret County, 1771–1838	Pasquotank County, 1740–1917
Chowan County, 1736–1869	Perquimans County, 1756–1905
Cumberland County, 1760–1910	Rowan County, 1757–1821
Edgecombe County, 1771–1909	Wake County, 1772–1937
Granville County, 1746–1803	

Tax lists (film 0018071).

Anson County, 1763	Granville County, 1769
Beaufort County, 1764	Onslow County, 1769–70
Bladen County, 1763	Pasquotank County, 1754, 1769
Brunswick County, 1769	Pitt County, 1762
Craven County, 1720, 1769	

Tax lists (film 0018072).

Beaufort County, 1755	New Hanover County, 1755
Cumberland County, 1755	Orange County, 1755
Currituck County, 1755	Tyrrell County, 1755
Granville County, 1755	

District Courts

Jurisdictional divisions, called districts, were established in 1760. Each district court covered more than one county. Records created before 1760 were kept with the circuit courts, which preceded the district courts. Counties included in districts before 1775 were:

Edenton District

Edenton District Superior Court covered the following counties: Hertford, Bertie, Tyrrell, Chowan, Perquimans, Pasquotank, and Currituck.
* Wills and estate papers, 1756–1806 (film 1905429).
* Prosecution docket, 1765–87 (film 0018519).

Halifax District

Halifax District Superior Court covered the following counties: Bute, Edgecombe; Edgecombe District of the Halifax District Superior Court (1767–1806) covered Edgecombe and Northampton.
* Minutes, papers, and petitions, 1763–1808

Hillsboro District

Hillsboro District Superior Court covered the following counties: Chatham, Wake, Granville, Orange (1767–1806), and Caswell.
Hillsboro District Superior Court.
* Court minutes, 1768–1806 (film 1486563).
* Wills and estate papers, 1772–1806 (film 1906925 ff.).

New Bern District

New Bern District Superior Court covered the following counties: Craven, Beaufort, Carteret, Dobbs, Hyde, Johnston, and Pitt.
* Dockets, trials, and minutes, 1755–88
*

Salisbury District

Salisbury District Superior Court covered the following counties: Anson, Guilford, Mecklenburg, Orange (1760–7), Rowan, Surry, and Tryon. The jurisdiction extended to the Tennessee counties of Washington (1778–82) and Sullivan (1779–82).
* Court minutes, 1756–1809 (film 1486561 ff.).

Wilmington District
Wilmington District Superior Court covered the following counties: Bladen, Brunswick, Cumberland, New Hanover, and Onslow.
* Dockets, minutes, and papers, 1755–1808

Morgan District
Morgan was formed as a military/judicial district in 1782 and included parts of Tennessee in addition to North Carolina. The Tennessee counties that were part of the military district of Morgan were: Sullivan (1782–4), Washington (1782–4, before it became the separate Washington District), Greene (1783–4), and Davidson (1783–4).

County Records
Records under a county titled "wills and estate papers" from the State Archives in Raleigh include three types of records:
➢ County records that have left official government custody and whose validity cannot be proved
➢ Wills that were filed with the Secretary of State, 1760–89, and later
➢ Files of loose estate papers arranged alphabetically by county, including administrators' bonds, guardian bonds, inventories, accounts of sales, annual accounts, allotments of year's provisions, settlements, divisions, bills, and receipts
There appears to be an extensive amount of duplicate filming of North Carolina county records. Because of ambiguities in cataloging, it has been impossible to identify all the records that have been repeated.

Albemarle County (established 1663, abolished 1668 when divided into Chowan, Currituck, Pasquotank, and Periqumans precincts)
See Pasquotank County.

Anson County (established 1750 from Bladen County)
A fire in 1868 destroyed many records. Original records at the Anson County Courthouse in Wadesboro and the State Archives in Raleigh are: Anson County Court of Pleas and Quarter Sessions.
* Court minutes, 1771–7 (film 0018165).
* Deeds, 1749–1926 (film 0018126 ff.).
* Will records, 1751–1962 (film 0018158 ff.)
Wills and estate papers (film 1547862 ff.).

Medley, Mary L. *History of Anson County, North Carolina, 1750–1976* (Wadesboro, NC: Anson County Historical Society, 1976).

Archdale County (established before 1696, name changed to Bath in 1696, name changed to Craven in 1712)
See Craven County.

Bath County (established 1696, abolished 1705 when divided into Archdale, Pampetocough, and Wickham precincts)
See Beaufort County.

Beaufort County (established 1705 as Pamptecough Precinct in Bath County, name changed to Beaufort in 1712)
Original records at the Beaufort County Courthouse in Edenton and the State Archives in Raleigh are:
Beaufort County Court of Pleas and Quarter Sessions.
* Court minutes, 1756–1868 (film 0018193 ff.).
* Minutes, appearance, prosecution, and trial docket, 1756–61 (film 0234248).
* Partitions and divisions, 1736–1878 (film 0234276).
* Index to real estate conveyances, 1696–1868, deeds and mortgages, 1700–1868 (film 0416377 ff.).
* Wills, 1720–1960 (film 0234280 ff.).
Beaufort County General Court. Court dockets, 1744–5 (film 0018516).
Wills and estate papers (film 1547987 ff.).

Beaufort County Genealogical Society. *Beaufort County, North Carolina, Will Abstracts, 1720–1868* (Baltimore: Gateway Press, 1990).

Bertie County (established 1722 from Chowan County)
Original records at the Bertie County Courthouse in Windsor and the State Archives in Raleigh are:
Bertie County Court of Pleas and Quarter Sessions.
* Guardian bonds, 1753–1831 (film 0018217).
* Deeds, 1732–1847, deeds, land grants, and disputed entries, 1714–20 (film 0018215).
* Deeds 1722–1857 (film 0018229 ff.).
* Bonds, 1762–9 (film 0018214).
* Wills, 1761–1942 (film 0018220 ff.).
* Court minutes, 1770–1877 (film 0018211).
* Inventories and sales of estates, 1728–1871 (film 0018209 ff.).
* Wills, 1749–1844 (film 0018202 ff.).
Wills and estate papers (film 1547987 ff.).
Sandy Run Baptist Church. Records, 1773–1807 (Nashville: Historical Commission of the Southern Baptist Convention, n.d., film 0986271).

Bell, Mary Best. *Colonial Bertie County, North Carolina Deed Books A–H, 1720–1757* (Easley, SC: Southern Historical Press, 1977).

The Episcopal Church in Bertie County, 1701–1990: From its Anglican Roots to the Twentieth Century (Windsor, NC: Saint Thomas' Episcopal Church, 1990).

 Bladen County (established 1734 from New Hanover County)
Fires in 1800 and 1893 destroyed many records. Original records at the Bladen County Courthouse in Elizabethtown and the State Archives in Raleigh are:
Bladen County Court of Pleas and Quarter Sessions.
• Deeds, 1738–79 (film 0018271).
• Deeds 1770–1869 (film 0018277 ff.).
• Wills, 1766–1961 (film 0018272 ff.).
Wills and estate papers (film 1673281 ff.).

 Brunswick County (established 1764 from Bladen and New Hanover counties)
A fire in 1865 destroyed many records. Original records at the Brunswick County Courthouse in Bolivia and the State Archives in Raleigh re:
Brunswick County Court of Pleas and Quarter Sessions.
• Deeds, 1764–1952 (film 0018317 ff.)
• Cross index to wills, 1764–1946 (film 0018321).
Wills and estate papers (film 1547991 ff.).

Roussos, Joseph A.G. *The Argyll Colony: The Last Clan Gathering* (Fayetteville, NC: The Author, 1992). Scottish immigration information and history, land ownership records, and church history of the Cape Fear area.

Bute County (established 1764 from Granville County, abolished 1779 when divided into Franklin and Warren counties)
Original records at the State Archives in Raleigh are: Bute County land and probate records, 1760–1800 (film 0018348).

Carteret County (established 1772 from Craven County)
Original records at the Carteret County Courthouse at Beaufort and the State Archives in Raleigh are:
Carteret County Court of Pleas and Quarter Sessions.
• Court minutes, 1723–47 (film 0018407).
• Wills and inventories, 1750–1807, grants, powers of attorney, official bonds, inventories, taxable property, wills, and bonds, 1717–1844 (film 0018381).

- Deeds, 1721–1931 (film 0262353 ff.).
- Wills, 1745–1961 (film 0018408 ff.).
- Wills, inventories, and sales and settlements of estates, 1741–1887 (film 0018378 ff.).

Wills and estate papers (film 1548323 ff.).

Saint John's Parish, Beaufort. Vestry book, 1742–1843 (film 0368570).

Davis, Pat and Kathy Hamilton. *The Heritage of Carteret County, North Carolina* (Beaufort, NC: Carteret County Historical Research Association, 1982).

Chatham County (established 1771 from Orange County)
Some records have been destroyed, cause unknown. Original records at the Chatham County Courthouse in Pittsboro and the State Archives in Raleigh are:
Chatham County Court of Pleas and Quarter Sessions.

- Minutes, 1774–1861 (film 0590299 ff.).
- Deeds, 1771–1902 (film 0018452 ff.).
- Wills, 1770–1931 (film 0018448 ff.).

Wills and estate papers (film 1689169 ff.).

Sandy Creek Baptist Church. Records, 1773–1845 (Nashville, TN: Historical Commission of the Southern Baptist Convention, n.d., film 0986269).

Chowan County (established 1668 as Shaftsbury Precinct in Albemarle County, renamed Chowan in 1685)
Some records were destroyed in 1848, possibly by the Clerk of Court.
Original records at the Chowan County Courthouse in Edenton and the State Archives in Raleigh are:
Chowan County Court of Pleas and Quarter Sessions.

- Court minutes, 1730–1868 (film 0478498 ff.).
- Minutes, 1735–8, 1762–1801 (film 0018507 ff.).
- Miscellaneous court records, 1724–1866 (film 0018484). Wills, administrators' bonds, accounts, inventories, sales of estates, court minutes and papers, and procession dockets.
- Accounts of sales of estates, 1745–1808 (film 0018551 ff.).
- Petitions, 1770–1887 (film 0018531 ff.).
- Returns, 1764–1805 (film 0018542).
- Processioners records, 1756, 1795–1808 (film 1730368).[46]
- Orphans' court docket, 1767–75 (film 1730360).
- Mixed guardian and probate records, 1740–1916 (film 0018517 ff.).
- Wills, 1694–1808 (film 0018476 ff.).

---

[46] See Virginia county records for a description of processioners records.

- Administrators' bonds, 1748–1903 (film 0018533 ff.).
- Division of estates, 1700s–1831 (film 0018543).
- Record of estates, 1745–1820 (film 0018545).

Chowan County General Court.
- Suits dismissed and miscellaneous court papers, 1687–1783 (film 0018558 ff.).
- Civil suits and bonds in General Court and Court of Admiralty, 1706–62 (film 0018539 ff.).
- Crown prosecutions, 1722–47 (film 0018552 ff.).
- Depositions, 1726 (film 0018542).
- General court docket, 1724–45, assize court records, 1741–6 (film 0018514 ff.).
- Executions, 1729–46 (film 0018556 ff.).

Wills and estate papers (film 1548452 ff.).
Saint Paul's Episcopal Church, Edenton. Vestry and parish records, 1701–1957 (film 0259399 ff.).

Clarendon County (established 1664, settlement abandoned)
See New Hanover County.

Craven County (established 1705 as Archdale Precinct in Bath County, name changed to Craven in 1712)
Original records at the Craven County Courthouse in New Bern and the State Archives in Raleigh are:
Craven County Court of Pleas and Quarter Sessions.
- Deeds and wills, 1744–89, inventories, accounts of sales and deeds, inventories of estates, administrators' accounts (film 0018602 ff.).
- Deeds and mortgages, 1708–1918 (film 0018628 f.).
- Grants, surveys, and land entries, 1716–78 (film 0018616).
- Land entries, 1770–1959 (film 0018679).
- Land grants, 1710–1835 (film 0018677).
- Land records, 1745–59 (film 0018601). Includes deeds, powers of attorney, bonds, and inventories.
- Mixed court records, 1737–1891 (film 0018597 ff.).
- Patent records, 1738–1936 (film 0288282 ff.).
- Wills, 1700–1960 (film 0018617 ff.).
- Loose wills and estate papers, 1746–1890 (film 0288343 ff.).
- Wills, 1755–1860 (film 0018594).
- Wills and estate papers, 1736–1865 (film 0288332 ff.).

Wills and estate papers (film 1548458 ff.).

Cumberland County (established 1754 from Bladen County)
Original records at the Cumberland County Courthouse in Fayetteville and the

State Archives in Raleigh are:
Cumberland County Court of Pleas and Quarter Sessions.
* Minutes, 1755–1868 (film 0316819 ff.).
* Miscellaneous records: court papers, 1766–1837, deeds, 1757–1815, and inventories and wills, 1759–92 (film 0018682).
* Real estate conveyances, 1733–92 (film 1689454 ff.).
* index to grants, 1774–1927 (film 0316905).
* Deeds, 1754–1947 (film 0316608 ff.).
* Wills, 1761–1942 (film 0018726 ff.).
* Wills, 1757–1869 (film 0018680 ff.).
Wills and estate papers (film 1548506 ff.).

Myrover, James H. *Short History of Cumberland County and the Cape Fear Section* (Fayetteville: Baptist Publishing Co., 1905).

Currituck County (established 1670 from Albemarle County)
Many records are missing, cause unknown. Original records at the Currituck County Courthouse in Currituck and the State Archives in Raleigh are:
Currituck County Court of Pleas and Quarter Sessions.
* Miscellaneous probate records, 1772–1845 (film 0018750). Administrators' accounts, entry and trial docket, inventory key, lists of guardian bonds, and orphans' docket, 1772–1827.
* Deeds, 1719–1918 (film 0018756 ff.).
* Wills, 1761–1960 (film 0018751 ff.).
Wills and estate papers (film 1548672 ff.).

Bennett, William Doub. *Currituck County, North Carolina, Eighteenth Century Tax and Militia Records* (Baltimore: Genealogical Publishing Co., 1994).

Dobbs County (established 1758 from Johnston County, abolished 1791 when divided into Glasgow and Lenoir counties)
Original records at the State Archives in Raleigh are:
Dobbs County Court of Pleas and Quarter Sessions.
* Wills, deeds, and minutes, 1765–9 (film 0018802).
* Tax list, 1769 (film 0018072).
Wills and estate papers (film 1548853).

Duplin County (established 1750 from New Hanover County)
Records are missing, cause unknown. Original records at the Duplin County Courthouse in Kenansville and the State Archives in Raleigh are:
Duplin County Court of Pleas and Quarter Sessions.
* Inventories, divisions of estates, and wills, 1761–1804 (film 0018803).
* Deeds, 1754–1927 (film 0018821 ff.).

- Loose papers, 1769–1880 (film 0018846 ff.).
- Wills, 1760–1962 (film 0018812 ff.).
Wills and estate papers (film 1548853 ff.).

Edgecombe County (established 1741 from Bertie County, see also Halifax County)
Original records at the Edgecombe County Courthouse in Tarboro and the State Archives in Raleigh are:
Edgecombe County Court of Pleas and Quarter Sessions.
- Court minutes, 1744–1868 (film 1014864 ff.).
- Deeds, 1732–1931 (film 0018873 ff.).
- Probate records, 1730–1961 (film 0018851 ff.).
- Marriage bonds, 1741–1868 (film 0296815 ff.).
Wills and estate papers (film 1548855 ff.).

Gates County (established 1779 from Chowan, Hertford, and Perquimans counties)
Original records at the Gates County Courthouse in Gatesville and the State Archives in Raleigh are:
Gates County Court of Pleas and Quarter Sessions.
- Wills, 1762–1805 (film 0018945).
Wills and estate papers (film 1571507 ff).

Granville County (established 1746 from Edgecombe County)
Original records at the Granville County Courthouse in Oxford and the State Archives in Raleigh are:
Granville County Court of Pleas and Quarter Sessions.
- Wills, 1749–1943 (film 0018968 ff.).
- Deeds, 1746–1923 (film 0306108 ff.).
- Loose wills, 1749–71 (film 0306193).
- Wills, 1749–71 (film 0306801 ff.).
- Tax lists, 1755–1935 (film 1758774 ff.).
Wills and estate papers (film 1571510).

A History of Granville County, North Carolina (Chapel Hill: University of North Carolina, 1950).

Guilford County (established 1770 from Rowan and Orange counties) A fire in 1872 destroyed some records. Original records at the Guilford County Courthouse in Greensboro and the State Archives in Raleigh are:
Guilford County Court of Pleas and Quarter Sessions.
- Deeds, 1771–1957 (film 0019042 ff.).
- Wills, 1771–1943 (film 0502409 ff.).

- Probate records, 1771–1968 (film 0833264 ff.).
- Marriage bonds, 1770–1868 (film 0536823 ff.).

Wills and estate papers (film 1571681 ff.)
Brick German Reformed Church. Records, 1772–1854 (film 0478489).
Society of Friends, New Garden. Monthly meeting minutes, 1740–1803 (film 0371252).

Halifax County (established 1758 from Edgecombe County)
Some records are missing, cause unknown. Original records at the Halifax County Courthouse in Halifax and the State Archives in Raleigh are:
Halifax County Court of Pleas and Quarter Sessions.

- Miscellaneous legal papers, 1772 (film 0019082).
- Deeds, 1732–1934 (film 0317023 ff.).
- Inventories of estates, 1773–9 (film 0019082).
- Wills, 1759–1943 (film 0019083 ff.).
- Wills, 1755–1854 (film 0019080 ff.).
- Marriage bonds, 1758–1868 (film 1002774 ff.).

Wills and estate papers (film 1571686 ff.).

Hertford County (established 1759 from Bertie, Chowan, Northampton, and Gates counties)
Fires in 1830 and 1862 destroyed most records. Original records at the State Archives in Raleigh are wills and estate papers (film 1571819 ff.).

Hyde County (established 1705 as Wickham Precinct of Bath County, name changed to Hyde 1712)
A fire in 1789 destroyed some records. Original records at the Hyde County Courthouse at Swanquarter and the State Archives in Raleigh are:
Hyde County Court of Pleas and Quarter Sessions.

- Court minutes, 1736–97 (film 1758969).
- Orphans' book docket, 1756–62 (film 1758972).
- Deeds, 1716–1917 (film 0260359 ff.).
- Wills, 1764–1960 (film 1759000 ff.).
- Wills, inventories, and sales, 1765–1802 (film 1758987 ff.).

Wills and estate papers (film 1571820 ff.).

Johnston County (established 1746 from Craven County)
Original records at the Johnston County Courthouse in Smithfield and the State Archives in Raleigh are:
Johnston County Court of Pleas and Quarter Sessions.

- Deeds and land grants, 1749–1936 (film 0019225 ff.).
- Wills, 1759–1863 (film 0019194 ff.). Also includes some deeds, court martial minutes, inventories, settlements of estates, guardian accounts, etc.

- Wills, 1760–1830 (film 0019192 ff.).
- Marriage bonds, 1768–1868 (film 0546455 ff.).
- Marriage register, 1764–1961 (film 0295111 ff.).
Wills and estate papers (film 1571952 ff.).

Lincoln County (established 1778 from Tryon County)
Some records are missing, cause unknown. Original records at the Lincoln County Courthouse in Lincolnton and the State Archives in Raleigh are:
Lincoln County Court of Pleas and Quarter Sessions.
- Court minutes of Tryon and Lincoln counties, 1769–82 (film 0833297).
- Court minutes of Tryon County, 1769–79 (film 0019979).
- Tryon County deeds, 1769–79 (film 0833298).
- Real estate conveyances, 1769–1911 (film 1760458 ff.).
- Wills, 1765–79 (film 0018678).
Tryon County wills and estate papers (film 1579717).
Lincoln County wills and estate papers (film 1571956 ff.).

Martin County (established 1774 from Halifax and Tyrell counties)
A fire in 1884 destroyed some records. Original records at the Martin County Courthouse in Williamston and the State Archives in Raleigh are:
Martin County Court of Pleas and Quarter Sessions.
- Deeds, 1771–1867 (film 0019315 ff.).
- Wills, 1774–1867 (film 0019324).
Wills and estate papers (film 1572065 ff.).

Mecklenburg County (established 1762 from Anson County)
Original records at the Mecklenburg County Courthouse in Charlotte and the State Archives in Raleigh are:
Mecklenburg County Court of Pleas and Quarter Sessions.
- Court minutes, 1774–85 (film 0019310).
- Deeds, 1755–1959 (film 0497471 ff.).
- Wills, 1749–1869 (film 0019275 ff.).
- Wills, 1763–1930 (film 0019301 ff.).
Wills and estate papers (film 1561631 ff.).

Philbeck, Miles S. *Mecklenburg County, North Carolina, Index to Land Surveys, 1763–1768* (Chapel Hill: The Author, 1988). Most Mecklenburg County grants through 1768 lie in present-day Cleveland, Gaston, Lincoln, Mecklenburg, Polk, Rutherford, and Union counties in North Carolina and in present-day Cherokee, Chester, Lancaster, Spartanburg, Union, and York counties in South Carolina.

New Hanover County (established 1729 from Craven County)
Fires in 1798, 1819, and 1840 destroyed some records. Original records
at the New Hanover County Courthouse in Wilmington and the State
Archives in Raleigh are:
New Hanover County Court of Pleas and Quarter Sessions.
* Court minutes, 1737–1868 (film 0276157 ff.).
* Probate records, 1746–1858 (film 0019359 ff.).
* Deeds, 1734–1939 (film 0019376 ff.).
* Wills, 1732–1864 (film 0019357 ff.).
* Wills, 1735–1961 (film 0019375 ff.).
Wills and estate papers (film 1577514 ff.).

Lennon, Donald. *The Wilmington Town Book, 1743–1778* (Raleigh: Department
of Archives and History, 1973).

Northampton County (established 1741 from Bertie County)
Original records at the Northampton County Courthouse in Jackson and the State
Archives in Raleigh are:
Northampton County Court of Pleas and Quarter Sessions.
* Deeds, 1741–1932 (film 0275832 ff.).
* Wills, 1760–1871 (film 0019433 ff.).
* Wills, 1770–1808 (film 0019417 ff.).
* Wills, 1760–92 (film 0019416).
Wills and estate papers (film 1577612 ff.).

Onslow County (established 1734 from New Hanover County)
Records were lost due to storms in 1752 and 1786. Original records at the
Onslow County Courthouse in Jacksonville and the State Archives in Raleigh
are:
Onslow County Court of Pleas and Quarter Sessions.
* Guardian accounts, 1754–1867, land entries, 1778–96 (film 0019441 ff.).
* Deeds, 1734–1925 (film 0267572 ff.).
* Wills, 1746–1863 (film 0019437 ff.).
* Wills, 1760–1961 (film 0019443 ff.).
* Tax lists 1769–71 (film 0267618).
Wills and estate papers (film 1577754 ff.).
North Carolina Secretary of State. Land grants, 1705–1928 (film 0267585 ff.).

Orange County (established 1752 from Bladen, Granville, and Johnston counties)
Original records at the Orange County Courthouse in Hillsboro and the State
Archives in Raleigh are:
Orange County Court of Pleas and Quarter Sessions.
* Deeds, 1753–93 (film 0019473 ff.).

- Deeds, 1764–5 (film 0019491).
- Deeds, 1755–1961 (film 0305917 ff.).
- Minutes, 1752-1868 (film 0306043 ff.).
- Wills, 1753–1865 (film 0019467 ff.).

Wills and estate papers, 1754–1954 (film 1577756 ff.).

Society of Friends, Cane Creek. Monthly meeting records, 1755–1840 (film 0371251).

Pasquotank County (established 1670 as a precinct in Albemarle County)

A fire in 1862 destroyed many records. Original records at the Pasquotank County Courthouse in Elizabeth City and the State Archives in Raleigh are:

Pasquotank County Court of Pleas and Quarter Sessions

- Orphans' Court minutes, 1757–85, deeds, 1759–62 (film 0019502).
- Deed records, 1700–1910 (film 0019527 ff.). Also contains records for Albemarle County.
- Vital records, 1691–1822 (film 0019496).
- Wills, 1720–1941 (film 0019494 ff.).

Wills and estate papers (film 1577995 ff.).

State papers, letters of administration, and land patents (film 0018123).

Ray, Worth S. *Old Albemarle and its Absentee Landlords* (1947. Reprint. Baltimore: Genealogical Publishing Co., 1968, film 1033558).

Haun, Weynette Parks. *Old Albemarle County, North Carolina, Book of Land Warrants and Surveys, 1681-1706* (Durham, NC: W.P. Haun, 1984).

Perquimans County (established 1670 as a precinct in Albemarle County)

Original records at the Periquimans County Courthouse in Hertford and the State Archives in Raleigh are:

Perquimans County Precinct Court.

- Minutes, probate, and land records, 1688–1738 (film 0350400).
- Deeds, 1681–1919 (film 0019564 ff.).
- Land records, plat books, sales and resales under mortgagees and trustees, records of marks and brands, 1759–1959 (film 0370654 ff.).
- Estate divisions, 1736–1805 (film 0019546 ff.).
- Will records, 1711–1800 (film 0019544).
- Will records, 1762–1960 (film 0019549 ff.)
- Court minutes, 1738–1827 (film 0350398 ff.).

Wills and estate papers (film 1578099 ff.).

Society of Friends, Perquimans County. Monthly meeting minutes, 1680–1802 (film 0371247).

Pitt County (established 1760 from Beaufort County)
A fire in 1857 destroyed some records. Original records at the Pitt
County Courthouse in Greenville and the State Archives in Raleigh are:
Pitt County Court of Pleas and Quarter Sessions.

* Miscellaneous papers, 1762–1851 (film 0019614 ff.).
* Deeds, 1762–1946 (film 0340064 ff.).
* Probate records, 1663–1978 (film 1578102 ff.).

Methodist Church, Bethel. Church history, 1734–1939 (film 0361881).

 Rowan County (established 1753 from Anson County)
A fire or Union troops destroyed some records in 1865. Original records
at the Rowan County courthouse in Salisbury and the State Archives in
Raleigh are:
Rowan County Court of Pleas and Quarter Sessions.

* Minutes, 1753–1868 (film 0313775 ff.). Includes list of taxables, 1759–
  1869, settlement of estates, 1756–1845.
* Guardian bonds, 1764–1952 (film 0019823 ff.).
* Deeds, 1753–1962 (film 0313505 ff.).
* Administrators' bonds, 1753–1830 (film 0019826).
* Wills and list of early settlers, 1743–1868 (film 0019720 ff.).
* Wills, 1757–1942 (film 0019731 ff.).
* Marriage records, 1759–1868 (film 0317002 ff.).
* Historical records (film 1760536 ff.). Includes cemetery inscriptions, tax
  lists for 1761–1845, etc.

Wills and estate papers (film 1578691 ff.).
Organ Lutheran Church. Membership lists and church records, 1772–1913 (film
0175422).

Linn, Jo White. *Rowan County, North Carolina Tax Lists, 1757–1800:
Annotated Transcriptions* (Salisbury, NC: The Author, 1995).

Surry County (established 1770 from Rowan County)
Original records at the Surry County Courthouse in Dobson and the State
Archives in Raleigh are:
Surry County Court of Pleas and Quarter Sessions.

* Deeds, 1771–1951, index to estate records, 1771–1937 (film 0344615 ff.).
* Wills, 1771–1963 (film 0344609 ff.).

Tryon County (established 1768 from Mecklenburg County, abolished 1779
when divided into Lincoln and Rutherford counties)
See Lincoln County.

Tyrrell County (established 1729 from Bertie, Chowan, Currituck, and Pasquotank counties)
Original records at the Tyrrell County Courthouse at Columbia and the State Archives in Raleigh are:
Tyrrell County Court of Pleas and Quarter Sessions.
• Guardian bonds, 1739–1871 (film 0019983).
• Deeds, 1736–1920 (film 0260481 ff.).
• Register of land, 1747–8 (film 0019981 ff.).
• Administrators' accounts and inventories, 1758–75 (film 0019981).
• Wills, 1750–1961 (film 0260504 ff.).
• Wills, 1744–1836 (film 0019980 ff.).
• Marriage bonds, 1752–1862 (film 0296809 ff.).
Wills and estate papers (film 1579717 ff.).

Wake County (established 1771 from Cumberland, Johnston, and Orange counties)
A fire in 1832 destroyed some records. Original records at the Wake County Courthouse in Raleigh and the State Archives in Raleigh are:
Wake County Court of Pleas and Quarter Sessions. Record books of wills, inventories, and settlements of estates, 1771–1902, indexes to wills and divisions of land, 1770–1946 (film 0020021 ff.).
Wills and estate papers (film 1602610 ff.).

Suggested Reading

Briceland, Alan Vance. *Westward from Virginia: The Exploration of the Virginia-Carolina Frontier, 1650–1710* (Charlottesville: University Press of Virginia, 1987).

Clemens, William M. *North and South Carolina Marriage Records: From the Earliest Colonial Days to the Civil War* (1927. Reprint. Baltimore: Genealogical Publishing Co., 1981).

Hakluyt, Richard. *Explorations, Descriptions, and Attempted Settlements of Carolina, 1584–1590.* Rev. ed. (Raleigh: Department of Archives and History, 1953, film 0908689).

Hehir, Donald M. *Carolina Families: A Bibliography of Books about North and South Carolina Families* (Bowie, MD: Heritage Books, 1994).

Leary, Helen and Maurice Stirewalt. *North Carolina Research: Genealogy and Local History* (Raleigh: North Carolina Genealogical Society, 1980).

Lee, Enoch Lawrence. *Indian Wars in North Carolina, 1663–1763* (Raleigh: Department of Archives and History, 1968, film 0897236).

Lefler, Hugh Talmage. *Colonial North Carolina, a History* (New York: Charles Scribner's Sons, 1973).

McCain, Paul M. *The County Court in North Carolina Before 1750* (1954. Reprint. New York: AMS Press, 1970).

Meyer, Duane. *The Highland Scots of North Carolina, 1732–1776* (Chapel Hill: University of North Carolina Press, 1966).

Newsome, Albert Ray. *Records of Emigrants from England and Scotland to North Carolina, 1774–1775* (Raleigh: Department of Archives and History, 1962, film 0908208).

Powell, William Stevens. *The Regulators in North Carolina: A Documentary History, 1759–1776* (Raleigh: Department of Archives and History, 1971, film 6048874).

Rankin, Hugh F. *The Pirates of Colonial North Carolina* (Raleigh: Department of Archives and History, 1972, film 0908717).

Ray, Worth S. *The Mecklenburg Signers and Their Neighbors* (1947. Reprint. Baltimore: Genealogical Publishing Co, 1966).

Salley, A.S. *Narratives of Early Carolina, 1650–1708* (New York: Charles Scribner's Sons, 1911, film 1698055).

Spindel, Donna J. *Crime and Society in North Carolina, 1663–1776* (Baton Rouge: Louisiana State University Press, 1989).

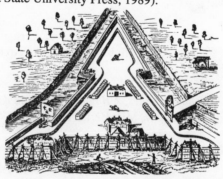

Fort Carolina on the River of May.

South Carolina

In 1563 French Huguenots attempted to settle on Parris Island, but returned to France. Spain established a settlement at Santa Elena (Hilton Head) in 1566. The first permanent settlement was at Charles Town in 1669 by English settlers, mostly from Barbados, at Albemarle Point (the colony moved to Oyster Point in 1680). The constitution or Fundamental Orders was written in 1669, making the Anglican Church the official church. The first Dutch settlers migrated from New York in 1671. Huguenot refugees began to arrive from England in 1680. Scottish Covenanters founded Stuart's Town in 1686. The Province was divided into twelve parishes in 1706. In 1712 Carolina was divided into the two provinces of North and South Carolina and received separate governors. A group of Jacobite prisoners from Scotland were transported to South Carolina in 1715. During the Yamassee War in 1715 a number of settlers were massacred at Pocataligo and at Port Royal.

In 1719 South Carolina officially became a separate Royal colony. By the Township Act of 1731, nine townships were laid out, extending settlement to the west. Germans began settling the Dutch Fork area near the Broad and Saluda rivers in Newberry and Lexington counties. Scotch-Irish migrated from Pennsylvania to the Abbeville County area in the 1750s. The border between North and South Carolina was not resolved until 1772, resulting in some confusion in the recording of land on the bordering counties and districts.

Statewide Records and Resources

The earliest court records in South Carolina were:

- **Court of Chancery (1671–1790):** Held jurisdiction over entire colony, handled equity cases involving land inheritance. Records have been published in Gregorie, Anne King. *Records of the Court of Chancery of South Carolina, 1671–1779* (Washington, DC: American Historical Association, 1950, fiche 6051256).
- **Court of General Session (1767–76):** Province-wide court with criminal jurisdiction.
- **Court of Vice-Admiralty.** Court records, 1716–32 (film 1025189/T309), 1716–89 (film 1549526 ff./M1180). The original records are at

SEE ALSO
Barbados
Great Britain
North Carolina
Virginia

the National Archives in Washington, DC. This was the local court of the British High Admiralty Court. There are also records at the PRO in Kew, Surrey, England. See the section on Great Britain for more infor-mation on Admiralty records.

* **Court of Common Pleas (1703–):** Became a district court in 1785; before that time the court sat at Charleston. Handled civil cases and guardianships.

Combined alphabetical index, 1695–1925: consolidated index and "spindex" (Columbia: Department of Archives and History, 1992, film 1690458 ff.). Available on film only at the Department of Archives and at the Family History Library in Salt Lake City. Some of the series (an ongoing project) indexed with records that begin before 1775 are:

➤ South Carolina Court of Common Pleas, judgment rolls, 1703–90, renunciation of dower, 1726–75
➤ South Carolina Court of Chancery, petitions to practice law, 1752–88
➤ Secretary of State, bills of sale, 1773–1840
➤ Public register, land conveyances, 1719–76
➤ Auditor General, land memorials, 1731–75
➤ Colonial Series, Royal land grants, 1694–76, 1731–76 (uncopied)
➤ Secretary of State, township grants, 1735–61
➤ Charleston County plat collection, 1680–1926
➤ Surveyor General, unrecorded plats for land not granted, 1730–1855

The original records of the province are at the Department of Archives and History in Columbia, under South Carolina Secretary of the Province. Colonial records, 1671–1754 (film 0022715 ff.).

Commissions and Instructions from the Lords Proprietors of Carolina to Public Officials of South Carolina, 1685–1715 (Columbia: n.p., 1916).

Grimke, John Faucheraud. *The Public Laws of the State of South Carolina, from its First Establishment as a British Province to the Year 1790, Inclusive* (1790. Reprint. Woodbridge, CT: Research Publications, 1978, film 0944131).

Moore, Caroline T. *Records of the Secretary of the Province of South Carolina, 1692–1721* (Columbia: R.L. Bryan Co., 1978).

Salley, A.S. *Records of the Secretary of the Province and the Register of the Province of South Carolina, 1671–1675* (Columbia: Historical Commission of South Carolina, 1944, film 1425662).

South Carolina Assembly. *The Journal of the Commons House of Assembly [1736–1754]* [The Colonial Records of South Carolina] (Columbia: Historical Commission of South Carolina, 1951, fiche 6051246).

Trott, Nicholas. *The Laws of the Province of South Carolina, in Two Parts* (1736. Reprint. Woodbridge, CT: Research Publications, 1978, film 0944132).

Warren, Mary B. *South Carolina Jury Lists, 1718–1783* (Danielsville, GA: Heritage Papers, 1977).

Published will and probate records include:
Holcomb, Brent H. *Probate Records of South Carolina [1746–1821]*. 3 Vols. (Easley, SC: Southern Historical Press, 1977). Includes records of the Court of Ordinary.

Houston, Martha Lou. *Indexes to the County Wills of South Carolina [1766–1864]* (1939. Reprint. Baltimore: Genealogical Publishing Co., 1964, fiche 6046877).

Lesser, Charles H. *South Carolina Begins: The Records of a Proprietary Colony, 1663–1721* (Columbia: Department of Archives and History, 1995). Includes decedent index to probate records, 1671–21.

Moore, Caroline T. *Abstracts of the Wills of the State of South Carolina*. 3 Vols. (Columbia, SC: R.L. Bryan Co., 1960–9, fiche 6051514).

Land Records
The earliest land transactions are the proprietary grants made by the Lords Proprietor between 1670 and 1719. These have been published in Salley, A.S. *Warrants for Land in South Carolina, 1672–1711* (1910. Reprint. Columbia: University of South Carolina Press, 1973, film 0845162 ff.). The original records are in the books of the Grand Council, found in the proceedings of the Secretary of the Province (see above) and contain deeds, wills, etc. Records of early memorials and registration of land grants, 1704–75 (film 0023297 ff.), are at the Department of Archives and History in Columbia.[47]

After 1719 Royal grants were issued, and the lands of the proprietors were purchased by the Crown in 1729. The proprietors still retained rights to the land,

---

[47] For additional information on land ownership in South Carolina, see the introduction to the Thirteen Colonies.

however, and received quit rent payments. These records, 1733–74, are available at the Department of Archives and History in Columbia. Other records at the Archives are:

South Carolina Secretary of State.

* Miscellaneous records, 1771–1868 (film 0022521 ff.). Includes bonds, mortgages, bills of sale (including slaves), manumissions, powers of attorney, and other miscellaneous records.
* Mortgage records, 1734–1860, index, 1709–1840 (film 0022627 ff.). Predominantly "mortgages of negroes." Includes sale of land, bonds, furniture, livestock, and miscellaneous property.

South Carolina Surveyor General.

* Land plats, 1731–1861, indexes, 1688–1872 (film 0022598 ff.).
* Memorials of seventeenth- and eighteenth-century land titles and index to auditor general memorials, 1731–75 (film 1412520).

Published abstracts and transcripts of land records include:

Esker, Katie-Prince Ward. *South Carolina Memorials, 1731–1776: Abstracts of Selected Land Records from a Collection in the Department of Archives and History, Columbia, South Carolina.* 2 Vols. (New Orleans: Polyanthos, 1973–7).

Holcomb, Brent H. *North Carolina Grants in South Carolina, 1745–1773* (Greenville, SC: n.p., 1980).

Langley, Clara A. *South Carolina Deed Abstracts, 1719–1772.* 4 Vols. (Easley, SC: Southern Historical Press, 1983).

Royal Land Grants in South Carolina, Book XX, 1763–1764 (Columbia: Department of Archives and History, 1962, film 0361873).

Manuscript Collections

In addition to the department of Archives and History in Columbia, the major repositories for manuscript collections are:

➢ The South Carolina Historical Society in Charleston, including the Motte Alston Read collection of colonial families of South Carolina (film 0022750 ff.).
➢ The South Caroliniana Library, University of South Carolina, Columbia, has an extensive collection, including the plantation papers that are described in the section in this book on Africa and the New World. For more information, consult Stokes, Alan H. *A Guide to the Manuscript Collection of the South Caroliniana Library* (Columbia: The Library, 1982).
➢ *Sources of Genealogical Research in the Winthrop College Archives and Special Collections* (Rock Hill, SC: Dacus Library, n.d., film 1321375).

➤ Charleston Library Society, originally founded in 1748, holds pamphlets, eighteenth-century newspapers, and information on South Carolina history.
➤ For more information on locations of other records, see Côté, Richard N. *Local and Family History in South Carolina, a Bibliography* (Easley, SC: Southern Historical Press, 1981).
➤ *Records in the British Public Record Office Relating to South Carolina, 1663–1710.* 5 Vols. (Atlanta: Foote and Davies Co., 1928–47, film 0944131). These records are also available at the Department of Archives and History in Columbia and on microfilm at the Family History Library in Salt Lake City (film 0929234 ff.).
➤ Leonardo Andrea Collection (film 0954524 ff.), correspondence (film 0954255 ff.), and miscellaneous data (film 0954253 ff.). Available only on microfilm.

Church Records

Collection of miscellaneous cemetery and church records (film 0022791 ff.). The records are at the South Caroliniana Library in Charleston. Includes:

Episcopal Church, James Island, 1769–1936	Jacksonboro, 1718–1856
Presbyterian Church, James Island, 1766–1950	Burnt Church, Colleton County, 1705–1841
Episcopal Church, Orangeburg, 1735–1914	Saint Thomas and Saint Denis, Berkeley, 1712–1872
Saint Bartholomew Parish (Burnt Church, Pon Pon Chapel of Ease), Colleton County, 1706–1841	Saint Stephen's Parish vestry book, 1754–1858
Inscriptions, Isaac Hayne Plantation, near	Miscellaneous records from plantations and churches

Extracts from the Urlsperger nachrichten, 1735–52: relating to Reformed churches and pastors in South Carolina and Georgia (film 0020360). The original records are at the Evangelical and Reformed Historical Society in Lancaster, Pennsylvania.

Records at the Presbyterian Historical Society, in Philadelphia, are inventoried in: Historical Records Survey. *Inventory of the Church Archives of South Carolina Presbyterian Churches* (film 0505562 ff.) and *Inventory of the Church Archives of South Carolina Presbyterian Churches: 1969 Arrangement with Indexes* (film 0906117 ff.).

Bernheim, Gotthardt. *History of the German Settlements and of the Lutheran Church in North and South Carolina: From the Earliest Period of the Colonization of the Dutch, German and Swiss Settlers to the Close of the First Half of the Present Century* (Philadelphia: Lutheran Book Store, 1872, film 0874034).

Dalcho, Frederick. *An Historical Account of the Protestant Episcopal Church in South Carolina: From the First Settlement of the Province, to the War of the Revolution; with Notices of the Present State of the Church in Each Parish and Some Account of the Early Civil History of Carolina, Never Before Published* (Charleston: E. Thayer, 1820, film 0022657).

Howe, George. *History of the Presbyterian Church in South Carolina*. 3 Vols. (Columbia: Duffie and Chapman, 1870, fiche 6110643).

Lawrence, Harold. *[Francis] Asbury's South Carolina Visits: Abstracted from His Journal* (Tignall, GA: Boyd Publishing, 1988). Early Methodism.

Marshall, Thomas W. *Early Quaker Records of South Carolina, 1750–1815* (1933. Reprint. Nashville, TN: Historical Commission of the Southern Baptist Convention, n.d., film 0984338). Includes some Quaker records from McDuffie County, Georgia.

Shipp, Albert Micajah. *History of Methodism in South Carolina* (Nashville, TN: Southern Methodist Publishing House, 1884, film 0908353).

Townsend, Leah. *South Carolina Baptists, 1670–1805* (Florence, SC: Florence Printing Co., 1935, fiche 6101031).

County Records and Resources

The first regional divisions were the four colonial counties of Berkeley, Craven, Colleton, and Granville, but they did not keep records. The first jurisdictional divisions in South Carolina were the seven districts established in 1769, each with a district court.

Record keeping in colonial South Carolina was very centralized. Most of the records originated in Charleston until 1785 and are recorded in the Charleston County records. Records listed under other counties are primarily of churches. Because of the geographical disparity between Charleston and the inland and northern parts of the province, few records exist for these areas, except in some vestry records.

Beaufort County (established 1769 as district)
A fire destroyed most records in 1865.
Saint Helena's Parish, Protestant Episcopal. Parish registers and
        minutes, 1726–1914 (fiche 6016804 ff.). The original records are at the
State Historical Society in Charleston.

Berkeley County (established 1882 from Charleston District)
Clute, Robert F. *The Annals and Parish Register of Saint Thomas and Saint Denis Parish in South Carolina from 1680 to 1884* (1884. Reprint. Baltimore: Genealogical Publishing Co., 1974, film 0908766).

Calhoun County (established 1908 from Lexington County)
Salley, A.S. *Minutes of the Vestry of Saint Matthew's Parish, South Carolina, 1767–1838* (Columbia: The State Co., 1939, film 0954252). The greater part of Saint Matthew's Parish is located in Calhoun County.

Charleston County (established 1769 as district)
Original records filmed at the Charleston County Courthouse in Charleston are:
Charleston County Register of Mesne Conveyance.
* Charleston City, Charleston County, and South Carolina miscellaneous land records, 1719–1873 (film 0023494 ff.).
* Public register, 1735–1916 (film 1429860 ff.).
Charleston District Court of Equity.
* Indexes, bills of complaint, 1721–1868 (film 0023862).
* Estate inventories, 1732–1844 (film 0194630 ff.).
Charleston County Probate Court.
* Miscellaneous probate records, 1696–1792 (film 0194642 ff.).
* Transcript of wills and miscellaneous probate records, 1671–1868 (film 0023493 ff.).
* Wills and related probate matters, 1671, 1692–1868 (film 0023452 ff.).

South Carolina Department of Archives and History. Transcript of Charleston County Common Pleas court records containing renunciation of dowers, land, probate, and miscellaneous court actions, 1740–87 (film 0370945 ff.).

Church Records
Records of the Protestant Episcopal (Anglican) Church at the original parishes and the South Carolina Historical Society in Charleston are:
Christ Church, Protestant Episcopal. Records, 1694–1936 (film 0022741 ff.).
Church of the Redeemer, Orangeburg Township, Protestant Episcopal. Records, 1739–1885 (film 0022742 ff.). Includes the Church of the Redeemer in Orangeburg County.
Saint Andrew's Parish, Charleston, Protestant Episcopal. Records, 1719–83 (film 0022659).
Saint Michael's Protestant Episcopal Church, Charleston. Records, 1759–1869 (film 0022742 ff.).
Saint Philip's Protestant Episcopal Church, Charleston. Records, 1713–1940 (film 0023339 ff.). Some records published in Salley, A.S. *Register of Saint*

Philip's Parish, Charles Town, South Carolina, 1720–1758 (Charleston: Walker, Evans and Cogswell, 1904, film 0845161).
Society for the relief of widows and orphans of the clergy of the Protestant Episcopal Church in South Carolina, 1762–1861 (film 0023346 ff.).

Other church records at the Charleston Historical Society and parishes in Charleston are:
Congregational Church, Charleston. Records, 1732–1872 (film 0023356), typescript of records, 1695–1935 (film 0023353 ff.). Also known as the Circular Church or Independent Church of Charleston.
Evangelisch Lutherische Kirche (Saint John's Lutheran Church), Charleston. Records, 1765–87 (film 0023357), translation of records, 1763–87 (film 0203237).
Fellowship Society, Charleston. Roll of members and rules, 1700–1862 (film 0023347).

Ashley River Baptist Church. Records, 1736–69 (Nashville, TN: Historical Commission of the Southern Baptist Convention, n.d., film 0984623).

Society of Friends, Charleston. Monthly meeting records, 1708–86 (film 0020457). The original records are at the Friends Historical Library, Swarthmore College, Swarthmore, Pennsylvania.

Cheraws District (established 1769, abolished 1785 when divided into the counties of Chesterfield, Darlington, Florence, Georgetown, Horry, Marion, Marlboro, and Williamsburg)
Saint David's Parish, Protestant Episcopal. Records, 1768–1827 (film 0022742).

Greeg, Alexander. *History of Old Cheraws* (1924. Reprint. Baltimore: Clearfield Co., 1994).

Chester County (established 1785 from Camden District)
Union Associate Reformed Presbyterian Church. Records, 1752–1939 (film 0023336).

 Colleton County (established 1785 from Charleston District)
Fires in 1805 and 1865 destroyed many records.
Saint John's Parish, Protestant Episcopal. Records, 1738–1917 (film 0024514). Also includes Saint John's Church on John's Island. The original records are at the Diocesan House Headquarters, Episcopal Diocese of South Carolina, Bishop's Office, Charleston.

Darlington County (established 1785 from Cheraws District)
A fire in 1806 destroyed many records.
Cashaway Baptist Church, Craven County. Records, 1767–1805 (film
0022813). Includes Mechanicville Baptist Church and Mount
Pleasant Baptist Church. The original records are at the Baptist
Historical Collection at Furman University in Greenville.

Laurens County (established 1785 from the Ninety-Six District)
Original records at the Laurens County Courthouse in Laurens are: Laurens
County Register of Mesne Conveyance. Index to deeds, 1774–1903 (film
1028916).

Motes, Jesse Hogan. *Laurens and Newberry Counties, South Carolina: Saluda
and Little Rivers Settlements, 1749–1775: Neighborhood Maps and Abstracts
of Colonial Surveys and Memorials of Land Titles; Including a Case Study:
Jonathan Mote, 1727–1763, Migration to Little River* (Easley, SC: Southern
Historical Press, 1994).

 Orangeburg County (established 1769 as district, see also Charleston
County)
A fire destroyed most records in 1865.
Salley, A.S. *History of Orangeburg County* (1898. Reprint. Baltimore:
Clearfield Co., 1994). Includes transcriptions of the Giessendanner records,
1737–61.

Williamsburg County (established 1785 from Georgetown District)
Williamsburg District Court of Common Pleas. Deeds, plats, grants, bonds, etc.,
1730–1866 (film 0317637). Includes Georgetown District and Craven
County. The original records are at the Williamsburg County Courthouse in
Kingstree.

Historical Records Survey. Prince Frederick Winyah, 1729–63 (film 0022740).
Protestant Episcopal parish register transcripts pertaining to Prince
Frederick and Prince George parishes, including the present-day counties
of Williamsburg, Florence, Marion, Dillon, Horry, and Georgetown.

York County (established 1785 from Camden District)
Langdon, Barbara R. *York County Marriages, 1770–1869, Implied in York
County, South Carolina Probate Records* (Aiken, SC: The Author, 1983).

Suggested Reading
Andrea, Leonardo. *South Carolina Colonial Soldiers and Patriots* (Columbia:
R.L. Bryan, 1952, film 1320504).

Baldwin, Agnes Leland. *First Settlers of South Carolina, 1670–1680* (Columbia: University of South Carolina Press, 1969, film 2055168).

Brown, Richard Maxwell. *The South Carolina Regulators* (Cambridge: Belknap Press of Harvard University Press, 1963).

Carroll, Bartholomew Rivers. *Historical Collections of South Carolina: Embracing Many Rare and Valuable Pamphlets, and Other Documents Relating to the History of That State, from its First Discovery to its Independence, in the Year 1776.* 2 Vols. (New York: Harper and Brothers, 1836, film 1033914).

Dobson, David. *Directory of Scots in the Carolinas, 1680–1830* (Baltimore: Genealogical Publishing Co., 1986).

Draine, Tony. *South Carolina Tax List, 1733–1742* (Columbia: Congaree Publications, 1986).

Dubose, Samuel and Frederick A. Porcher. *A Contribution to the History of the Huguenots of South Carolina, Consisting of Pamphlets* (New York: Knickerbocker Press, 1887 film 1036613).

Helsley, Alexia J. and Michael E. Stauffer. *South Carolina Court Records: An Introduction for Genealogists* (Columbia: Department of Archives and History, 1993).

Hirsch, Arthur Henry. *The Huguenots of Colonial South Carolina* (Durham: Duke University Press, 1928, fiche 6048233).

Ivers, Larry E. *Colonial Forts of South Carolina, 1670–1775* (Columbia: University of South Carolina Press, 1970).

McKown, Bryan F. *Destroyed County Records in South Carolina* (Columbia: Department of Archives and History, 1996).

Porcher, Frederick A. *Upper Beat of Saint John's Berkeley, a Memoir* (n.p.: Huguenot Society of South Carolina, 1906, film 1036613).

Ravenel, Daniel. *Liste des Francois et Suisses* (New York: Knickerbocker Press, 1888, film 1036613). From manuscript list of French and Swiss Protestants settled in Charleston, on the Santee and at the Orange Quarter in Carolina who desired naturalization, prepared about 1695-6.

Salley, A.S. *Marriage Notices in the South Carolina and American General Gazette from May 30, 1766, to February 28, 1781, and in its Successor the Royal Gazette (1781–1782)* (Columbia: State Co., 1914, film 0928193).

Salley, A.S. *Marriage Notices in the South Carolina Gazette and its Successors, 1732–1801* (1902. Reprint. Baltimore: Genealogical Publishing Co., 1976, fiche 6048428).

Salley, A.S. *Narratives of Early Carolina, 1650–1708* (New York: Charles Scribner's Sons, 1911, film 1698055).

Simmons, M. Eugene. *Colonial South Carolina: A Political History, 1663–1763* (Chapel Hill: University of North Carolina Press, 1966). Especially useful in tracing migrations from Barbados to Carolina.

Seal of the Proprietors of Carolina.

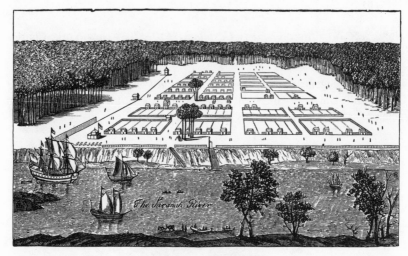

Savannah, from a Print of 1741.

Georgia

Spain's settlements on Santa Catalina Island in 1566 were the first European colonies in Georgia. In 1573 some Franciscans established a mission on Cumberland Island. The first British settlement was in 1721 at Fort King George (Darien). In 1732 the British Crown granted a charter for the colony of Georgia as a place of refuge for former convicts, English poor and indigent, and those fleeing from religious intolerance. The earliest colonial settlers came from the Carolinas, Virginia, or directly from England.

The first permanent colonists arrived at Yamcraw Bluff (Savannah) in 1733. A Jewish colony in Savannah was begun the same year. Groups of Protestants came from Europe, including French, Germans, Moravians, and Swiss. In 1734, German Salzburgers immigrated and settled at Ebenezer (Effingham County). Augusta was founded in 1735. In 1736 Scots Highlanders settled along the Savannah and Ogeechee rivers and founded New Inverness (Darien). The Battle of Bloody Marsh was fought against the encroaching Spanish from Florida in 1742.

South Carolinians from Dorchester migrated to Georgia in 1751. Slavery became legal in Georgia in 1749, having been banned by the trustees of the colony from 1732. Georgia was chartered as a Royal province in 1752. That year a group of 350 Puritans from South Carolina, along with 1,500 slaves, settled the area known as the Midway District and founded the town of Sunbury in 1758.

Statewide Records and Resources

Georgia's earliest court records were kept by the Common Council in England and the governor and council in Georgia. Few early court records survive, and many have been transcribed from British records.
The earliest county records date from 1777, when the first real counties were formed. From 1741 to 1743 Georgia was divided into the counties of Savannah and Frederica, but no records were kept. Eight Anglican parishes were established in 1758, and an additional four in 1765. The parish vestries also kept some civil records.

SEE ALSO
Germany
Great Britain
Pennsylvania
South Carolina

549

Original probate records at the State Archives in Atlanta are:
Early colonial records, 1754–78 (film 0158964 ff.).
- Wills, 1754–77
- Letters of administration, 1755–71
- Inventories of estates, 1754–70
- Letters of guardianship, 1757–77
- Probate, administration, letters, minutes, appraisements, 1771–5
- Inventories, probate, 1776–8
Original colonial wills, 1751–88 (film 0840408).

Some published records of wills and estates are:
Abstracts of Colonial Wills of the State of Georgia, 1733–1777 (1962. Reprint. Spartanburg, SC: The Reprint Co., 1981).
Brooke, Ted O. *In the Name of God, Amen: Georgia Wills, 1733–1860, an Index of Testators to Wills of Georgia Recorded in Colonial Will Books and in Loose Will Collections, 1733–1777 and Wills Recorded or on File in County and State Offices, 1777–1860* (Atlanta: Pilgrim Press, 1976, film 1036842).
Index to Probate Records of Colonial Georgia, 1733–1778 (Atlanta: R.J. Taylor, Jr. Foundation, 1983).

Land Records
Initially, from 1732 to 1755, Georgia was neither a corporate, proprietary, nor Royal colony, but a trusteeship in which land was allotted to males and their heirs. After 1755 these restrictions were lifted. After 1756 land was distributed in the eastern quarter by headright and bounty grants.

Original land records at the State Archives in Atlanta are:
Colonial records of Georgia, 1750–1829 (film 0158965 ff.).
- Commission books, 1754–1827
- Conveyances, 1750–98
- Mortgages, 1755–85
- Proclamations, 1754–94
- Bonds, bills of sale, deeds of gift, powers of attorney, 1755–62
- Fiats for grants, 1755–76
- Entry of claims, 1755, 1762–5
- Miscellaneous records, 1765–77
Marks and brands, 1755–93 (film 0158972).
Georgia Surveyor General.
- Entry of land claims, 1755–8 (film 0488183).
- Headright surveys, 1748–73 (film 0465059). Copied and recorded in 1798.
- Headrights and registers of land grants, 1756–1939 (film 0465071 ff.). Includes list of wharf lots and town lots in the town of Brunswick.

- Headright surveys, 1753–67, and undated (film 0464998 ff.).
- Land Office records index, 1767–1908 (film 0465173 ff.).
Telamon Cuyler collection of colonial records (film 0214742). Includes deeds, inventories, bonds, powers of attorney, etc.

Published land records include:
Aldridge, Christine. *Early Miscellaneous Land Records of Georgia* (Nacodoches, TX: Partin, 1994). Contains Augusta land petitions, 1744–73, and list of Saint Paul parish land owners, 1747–77.

Beckemeyer, Frances Howell. *Abstracts of Georgia Colonial Conveyance Book, C-1, 1750–1761* (Atlanta: R.J. Taylor, Jr., Foundation, 1975).

Bryant, Pat. *Entry of Claims for Georgia Landholders, 1733–1755* (Atlanta: State Printing Office, 1975).

An Index to English Crown Grants in Georgia (Spartanburg, SC: The Reprint Co., 1989).

An Index to Georgia Colonial Conveyances and Confiscated Lands Records, 1750–1804 (Atlanta: R.J. Taylor, Jr. Foundation, 1981).

Index to the Headright and Bounty Grants of Georgia, 1756–1909 (Vidalia, GA: Genealogical Reprints, 1970).

Walker, George Fuller. *Abstracts of Georgia Colonial Book J, 1755–1762* (Atlanta: R.J. Taylor, Jr. Foundation, 1978). Affidavits, bills of sale, bonds, deeds, letters, marriage records, etc.

Weeks, Eve Bondurant Warren. *Georgia Land Owner's Memorials: 1758–1776* (Danielsville, GA: Heritage Papers, 1988).

For information on colonial laws, see:
The Earliest Printed Laws of the Province of Georgia, 1755–1770. 2 Vols. (Wilmington, DE: Michael Glazier, 1978).
Marbury, Horatio and William H. Crawford. *Digest of the Laws of the State of Georgia: From its Settlement as a British Province in 1755 to the Session of the General Assembly in 1800 Inclusive...With a Copious Index to the Whole* (Savannah, GA: Seymour, Woolhopter and Stebbins, 1802, film 0203234).

The published records for Georgia are in the series *The Colonial Records of the State of Georgia*. 32 Vols. (Atlanta: Franklin Printing, 1904–16, except where indicated). There is a general index to all thirty-nine (some only in manuscript at this time) volumes at the State Archives in Atlanta. The contents are:

- Vol. 1 *Journal of the Trustees for Establishing the Colony of Georgia in America [1732–1752]* (film 0944117).
- Vol. 2 *The Minutes of the Common Council for the Trustees for Establishing the Colony of Georgia in America [1732–1752]* (film 0944117).
- Vol. 3 *The General Account of All Monies ... Received and Expended by the Trustees for Establishing the Colony of Georgia in America: for the Carrying on the Good Purposes of Their Trust for One Whole Year ...Exhibited by the Said Corporation, Pursuant to the Directions of Their Charter... [1732–1739]* (film 0944117).
- Vol. 4 *Journal of Colonel William Stephens, Secretary to the Board of Trustees at Savannah: Supplement to Volume IV, Containing All of His Journal Not Embraced in Volume IV of this Compilation [1740–1741]* (0944118).
- Vol. 5 *Journal of the Earl of Egmont, First President of the Board of Trustees, from June 14, 1738 to May 25, 1744* (film 0944118).
- Vol. 6 *Proceedings of the President and Assistants from October 12, 1741 to October 30, 1754* (film 0944119).
- Vols. 7–12 *Proceedings and Minutes of the Governor and Council [1754–1782]* (film 0944119 ff.).
- Vols. 13–15 *Journal of the Commons House of Assembly [1755–1782]* (film 0944122 ff.).
- Vols. 16–17 *Journal of the Upper House of Assembly [1755–1774]* (film 0944123 ff.).
- Vol. 18 *Statutes Enacted by the Royal Legislature of Georgia from its First Session in 1754 to 1768* (film 2055215).
- Vol. 19 *Statutes, Colonial and Revolutionary [1768–1805]* (film 0944125 ff.).
- Vol. 20 *Original Papers, Correspondence to the Trustees, James Oglethorpe, and Others, 1732–1735* (Athens: University of Georgia Press, 1982).
- Vols. 21–5 *Original Papers, Correspondence, Trustees, General Oglethorpe and Others [1735–1750]* (film 0944125 ff.).
- Vol. 26 *Original Papers, Trustees, President and Assistants and Others, 1750–1752* (film 0944127).
- Vol. 27 *Original Papers of Governor John Reynolds, 1754–1756* (Athens: University of Georgia Press, 1977).

- Vol. 28. Pt. 1 *Original Papers of Governors Reynolds, Ellis, Wright, and Others, 1757–1763* (Athens: University of Georgia Press, 1976).
- Vol. 28. Pt. 2 *Original Papers of Governor Wright, President Habersham, and Others, 1764–1782* (Athens: University of Georgia Press, 1979). Correspondence with the Board of Trade in London.
- Vols. 29–31 *Trustees' Letter Book [1732–1752]* (Athens: University of Georgia Press, 1985–6).
- Vol. 32 *Entry Books of Commissions, Powers, Instructions, Leases, Grants of Land, etc., by the Trustees, 1732–1738* (Athens: University of Georgia Press, 1989).
- Vols. 33 to 39 will be published in the future.

Church Records
There were few churches in Georgia before 1775 that have surviving records. The earliest denominations were Baptist, Methodist, Lutheran, Quaker, Anglican, Reformed, and Congregational.

Midway Congregational Church (Liberty County). Church and index of names, 1754–1898 (film 0203209 ff.). The manuscript is at the State Historical Society in Savannah. See also Stacy, James. *History and Published Records of the Midway Congregational Church, Liberty County, Georgia* (1903. Spartanburg, SC: The Reprint Co., 1979).

St. Andrew's Episcopal Church, Darien (McIntosh County). Church records, 1759–1958 (film 0184506). The original records may be at the original parish in Darien.

Records at the Episcopal Diocese of Georgia at Savannah are:
Episcopal Church Diocese of Georgia. Church histories and assorted papers, 1758–1946 (film 0177520).
History of Saint Paul's Episcopal Church, Augusta, 1750–1945 (film 0177489).

Society of Friends, Wrightsboro (McDuffie County). Monthly meeting records, 1772–1893. These records have been abstracted in Marshall, Thomas W. *Early Quaker Records of South Carolina, 1750–1815* (1933. Reprint. Nashville, TN: Historical Commission of the Southern Baptist Convention, n.d., film 0984338). The original records may be at the Friends Historical Library, Swarthmore College, Swarthmore, Pennsylvania.

Extracts from the Urlsperger nachrichten, 1735–52: relating to Reformed churches and pastors in South Carolina and Georgia (film 0020360). The pastors, Boltzius and Gronau, kept a daily register of emigrants. The original records are at the Evangelical and Reformed Historical Society in Lancaster, Pennsylvania. See also Urlsperger, Samuel. *Detailed Reports on the Salzburger Emigrants Who Settled in America.* 17 Vols. (Athens: University of Georgia Press, 1968).

Jones, George F. and Sheryl Exley. *Ebenezer Record Book, 1754–1781: Births, Baptisms, Marriages and Burials of Jerusalem Evangelical Lutheran Church of Effingham, Georgia, More Commonly Known as Ebenezer Church* (Baltimore: Genealogical Publishing Co., 1991). The original manuscript may be at the Library of Congress in Washington, DC.

Jones, George Fenwick. *Henry Newman's Salzburger Letterbooks* (Athens: University of Georgia Press, 1966). Letters relating to emigrants from Salzburg who settled in Georgia.

Dotson, Flora Belnap. *History of Kiokee Baptist Church, Columbia County, Georgia: History and Records of Big Stephens Creek Church, Edgefield County, South Carolina* (n.p., n.d., film 0982072).

Campbell, J.H. *Georgia Baptists: Historical and Biographical* (Macon, GA: J. W. Burke and Co., 1874, film 1033617).

Malone, Henry Thompson. *The Episcopal Church in Georgia, 1733–1957* (Atlanta: Protestant Episcopal Church in the Diocese of Atlanta, 1960).

Warlick, Roger K. *As Grain Once Scattered: The History of Christ Church, Savannah, Georgia, 1733–1983* (Columbia, SC: The State Printing Co., 1987).

Lawrence, Harold. *A Bibliography of Georgia Methodism* (Tignall, GA: Boyd Publishing Co., 1981).

Boyd, John Wright. *A Brief History of Early Methodist Societies and Meeting Houses in the Broad River Valley of Georgia* (Washington, GA: Wilkes Publishing Co. 1986, fiche 6100452).

Stacy, James. *A History of the Presbyterian Church in Georgia* (Elverton, GA: Press of the State, 1912, fiche 6103873).

Peeler, Banks J. *A Story of the Southern Synod of the Evangelical and Reformed Church, 1740–1968* (Salisbury, NC: Southern Synod of the Evangelical and Reformed Church, 1968).

Fries, Adelaide L. *The Moravians in Georgia, 1735–1740* (1905. Reprint. Baltimore: Genealogical Publishing Co., 1967, film 1425607).

Manuscript Collections

Some of the major manuscript collections in Georgia are:

➢ The State Archives in Atlanta. See *A Preliminary Guide to Eighteenth-Century Records Held by the Georgia Department of Archives and History* (Atlanta: The Department, 1976, fiche 6100334).

➢ The State Historical Society in Savannah. See Hawes, Lilla M. *Checklist of Eighteenth-Century Manuscripts in the Georgia Historical Society* (Savannah: The Society, 1976).

➢ The R.J. Taylor, Jr. Foundation in Atlanta. See *The Leon S. Hollingsworth Genealogical Card File: An Introduction and Inventory* (Atlanta: The Foundation, 1980).

➢ Hargrett Rare Book and Manuscript Library, University of Georgia, Athens.

➢ Washington Memorial Library, Stevens-Davis Memorial Collection, Macon.

➢ Robert W. Woodruff Library, Emory University, Atlanta.

Suggested Reading

Aldridge, Christine. *Early Miscellaneous Georgia Records* (Nacogdoches, TX: Partin, 1994). Earliest records listed are for Bethesda Orphanage, 1739–46.

Austin, Jeannette H. *Emigrants from Great Britain to the Georgia Colony* (Riverdale, GA: The Author, 1970, film 1597743). Alphabetical listing of people who emigrated from Great Britain on the *Britannica* to Georgia in 1772 and those who emigrated beginning in 1733.

Austin, Jeannette H. *The Georgians: Genealogies of Pioneer Settlers* (Baltimore: Genealogical Publishing Co., 1984).

Bolton, Herbert E. *Arredondo's Historical Proof of Spain's Title to Georgia: A Contribution to the History of the Spanish Borderlands* (Berkeley: University of California Press, 1925).

Coulter, E. Merton and Albert B. Saye. *A List of the Early Settlers of Georgia* (1949. Reprint. Baltimore: Genealogical Publishing Co., 1983, film 1421844). Indexed in Buss, Karen. *An Every Name Index to "A List of the Early Settlers of Georgia"* (Burbank: Southern California Genealogical Society, 1992).

Davis, Harold E. *The Fledgling Province: Social and Cultural Life in Colonial Georgia, 1733–1776* (Chapel Hill: University of North Carolina Press, 1976).

Dorsey, James Edwards. *Georgia Genealogy and Local History: A Bibliography* (Spartanburg, SC: The Reprint Co., 1983).

Dumont, William H. *Colonial Georgia Genealogical Data, 1748–1783* (Washington, DC: National Genealogical Society, 1971). Contains marriage agreements, administrations of colonial estates, guardianships, grants, genealogical data, supplement to genealogical data from deed books, and stock owners, 1755–78.

Huxford, Folks. *Genealogical Material from Legal Notices in Early Georgia Newspapers* (Easley, SC: Southern Historical Press, 1989).

Jones, George Fenwick. *The Georgia Dutch: From the Rhine and Danube to the Savannah, 1733–1783* (Athens: University of Georgia Press, 1992). History of the German-speaking settlers who emigrated to the Georgia colony from Germany, Alsace, Switzerland, Austria, and adjacent regions, known collectively as the Georgia Dutch.

Jones, George Fenwick. *The Germans of Colonial Georgia, 1733–1783* (Baltimore: Genealogical Publishing Co., 1986).

Lanning, John Tate. *The Spanish Missions of Georgia* (Chapel Hill: University of North Carolina Press, 1935).

Smith, George G. *The Story of Georgia and the Georgia People, 1732–1860.* 2nd ed. (1901. Reprint. Baltimore: Genealogical Publishing Co., 1968, film 0908502).

Wylly, Charles Spalding. *The Seed That Was Sown in the Colony of Georgia: The Harvest and the Aftermath, 1740–1870* (1910. Reprint. Washington, DC: Library of Congress, 1983, film 0929227).

Part Five

*Other U.S. States
with settlements prior
to the American Revolution*

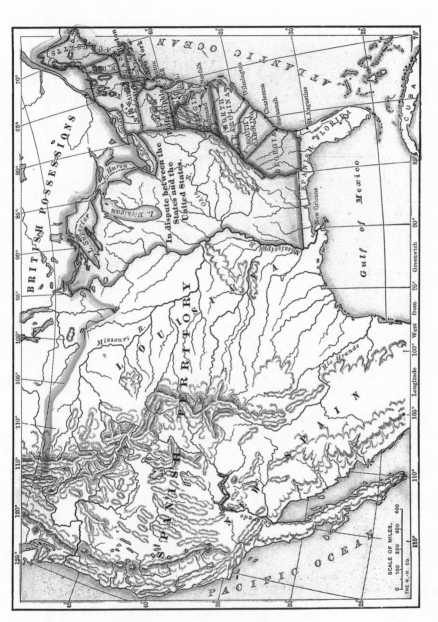

33 The United States in 1783 (Edward Channing, *A Short History of the United States.* New York: Macmillan & Co., 1911)

Alabama

Tristan de Luna established a settlement on Mobile Bay in 1559, which was abandoned in 1561. Spanish Franciscans established missions in the Alabama area, moving northward and eastward from Saint Augustine, Florida after 1573. France claimed the region in 1699 and founded Fort Conde (Mobile) in 1702 and Fort Toulouse in 1717. The first African slaves arrived in 1719. Mobile was devastated by a hurricane in 1733. The area remained under French control until 1763. From 1763 until 1783 it was governed by Great Britain as a part of West Florida. Another hurricane hit Mobile in 1772.

In 1783 Mobile was ceded to Spain, and the rest of Alabama became part of Georgia. The border between them was established in 1787. In 1798 Alabama was incorporated into the Mississippi Territory. The Spanish settlement of Tombeebé was abandoned in 1799. Mobile was taken by the United States in 1813 during the War of 1812. The Alabama Territory was organized in 1817.

Ecclesiastical and Civil Records and Sources
Early French censuses for 1706, 1721, and 1725 have been abstracted in the *Deep South Genealogical Quarterly* 1 (August 1963).

De Ville, Winston. *Mobile Funerals, 1726–1764: Alabama Church Records of the French Province of Louisiana* (Ville Platte, LA: Smith, 1994). Includes marriages from the present-day area of Mobile, Alabama when Alabama was part of Louisiana, taken from the records of the Cathedral of the Immaculate Conception.

Suggested Reading
Badger, R. Reid and Lawrence A. Clayton. *Alabama and the Borderlands from Prehistory to Statehood* (Tuscaloosa: University of Alabama Press, 1985).

Dodd, Donald B. *Historical Atlas of Alabama* (Tuscaloosa: University of Alabama Press, 1974).

Hamilton, Peter Joseph. *Colonial Mobile* (1897. Reprint. Tuscaloosa: University of Alabama Press, 1976).

SEE ALSO
Florida
Georgia
Louisiana
Mississippi

Holmes, Jack D.L. "Alabama's Forgotten Settlers: Notes on the Spanish Mobile District, 1780–1813." *Alabama Historical Quarterly* 33 (Summer 1974): 87–97, fiche 6334262.

Saunders, James E. and Elizabeth S. Blair. *Early Settlers of Alabama.* 2 Vols. (1899. Reprint. Baltimore: Genealogical Publishing Co., 1969, fiche 6051449).

Thomas, Daniel H. *Fort Toulouse: The French Outpost at the Alabamas on the Coosa* (Tuscaloosa: University of Alabama Press, 1989).

Arizona

The first Spanish missions in Arizona were founded by the Franciscans for the Hopi in the northeastern area in 1629. Jesuits established missions for Pima in the southeast in 1692. This expanded to a chain of missions on the Arizona-Sonora frontier, known as the *Pimería Alta* of Nueva España, at Guevavi (near Nogales) in 1701 and at San Xavier del Bac (near Tucson). Tubac was founded as a *visita* in 1726. After a rebellion by the Pima Indians in 1751, Spain built a presidio at Tubac in 1751, and at Tucson in 1776. Arizona became part of Mexico in 1810, and did not become a U.S. territory until the mid-nineteenth century.

Ecclesiastical Records and Sources

Church records can be found in parish archives in Sonora, Mexico, the Provincias Internas Collection at the Archivo General de la Nación in Mexico City, and the Pimería Alta Mission Records, Bancroft Library, University of California, Berkeley; there are copies on microfilm at the Arizona Historical Society, Arizona State University, the University of New Mexico, Albuquerque, the Library of Congress, and Saint Louis University, Saint Louis, Missouri.

Records for Tucson, 1793–1849, are available on microfilm at the University of Arizona in Tucson. There are also records for Tucson at the Magdalena parish archives, Sonora, Mexico that date from 1684. Parish registers for San José de Tumacácori (near Tubac), 1768–1825, are on microfilm at the Arizona Historical Society in Tucson.

Radding de Murrieta, Cynthia and María Lourdes Torres Chavéz. *Catálogo Archivo Histórico de Estado Sonora.* 4 Vols. (Hermosilla, Mexico: Centro Regional de Noroeste, 1974–7). Holdings of parish archives, including records for Arizona.

Radding de Murrieta, Cynthia and María Lourdes Torres Chavéz. *Catálogo de Archivo de las Parroquia de la Purisima Concepcion de los Alamos, 1685–1900* (Hermosilla, Mexico: Centro Regional de Noroeste, 1976). These registers are available on microfilm at Arizona State University, Tempe.

SEE ALSO
California
Latin America
Mexico
New Mexico
Spain

Colley, Charles C. *Documents of Southwestern History: A Guide to the Manuscript Collections of the Arizona Historical Society* (Tucson: Arizona Historical Society, 1972).

Kessell, John L. *Friars, Soldiers, and Reformers: Hispanic Arizona and the Sonora Mission Frontier, 1767–1856* (Tucson: University of Arizona Press, 1976).

McCarty, Kieran. *A Spanish Frontier in the Enlightened Age: Franciscan Beginnings in Sonora and Arizona* (Washington, DC: Academy of American Franciscan History, 1981).

Smith, Watson. *Seventeenth-Century Spanish Missions of the Western Pueblo Area* (Tucson: Tucson Corral of the Westerners, 1970). The Western Pueblo area is composed of the modern states of Arizona and New Mexico and the area of northern Mexico.

Civil Records and Sources

Colonial *padrones* (censuses) at the Archivo General de la Nación in Mexico City include:
*   San Xavier del Bac, 1766, 1768, 1801
*   Tubac, 1767
*   Tucson, 1766, 1797

Records on microfilm at the University of Arizona in Tucson include:
*   Pimería Alta, 1801
*   San José de Tumacácori, 1796, 1801

Dobyns, Henry F. *Spanish Colonial Tucson* (Tucson: University of Arizona Press, 1976). This includes *padrones* for San Xavier del Bac, 1801, military troop lists for Tucson, 1775, and *padrones* for Tucson, 1767–1818.

Sierras, Eugene L. *Mexican Census Pre-Territorial: Pimería Alta, 1801* (Tucson: Arizona State Genealogical Society, 1986).

Records of Spanish land grants are available on microfilm, and the originals are at the U.S. Bureau of Land Management, Santa Fe, New Mexico. For more information, see New Mexico.

Suggested Reading

Bancroft, Hubert Howe. *History of the Pacific States of North America: Arizona and New Mexico 1538–1888* (1888. Reprint. Tucson: W.C. Cox, 1974, film 0934827).

Beers, Henry Putney. *Spanish and Mexican Records of the American Southwest* (Tucson: University of Arizona Press, 1979). This includes Arizona, California, New Mexico, Texas, and Mexico.

Harrison, John P. *Materials in the National Archives Relating to the Mexican States of Sonora, Sinaloa, and Baja California* (Washington, DC: The National Archives, 1952).

Lockwood, Frank C. *Pioneer Days in Arizona from the Spanish Occupation to Statehood* (New York: Macmillan & Co., 1932).

McCarthy, Kieran. *Desert Documentary: The Spanish Years, 1767–1821* (Tucson: Arizona Historical Society, 1976).

Officer, James E. *Hispanic Arizona, 1536–1856* (Tucson: University of Arizona Press, 1987).

Roca, Paul M. *Paths of the Padres Through Sonora: An Illustrated History and Guide to Its Spanish Churches* (Tucson: Pioneers' Historical Society, 1967).

Temple, Thomas Workman. *Sources for Tracing Spanish-American Pedigrees in the Southwestern United States: California and Arizona* (Salt Lake City: Genealogical Society of the Church of Jesus Christ of Latter-day Saints, 1969, fiche 6039366).

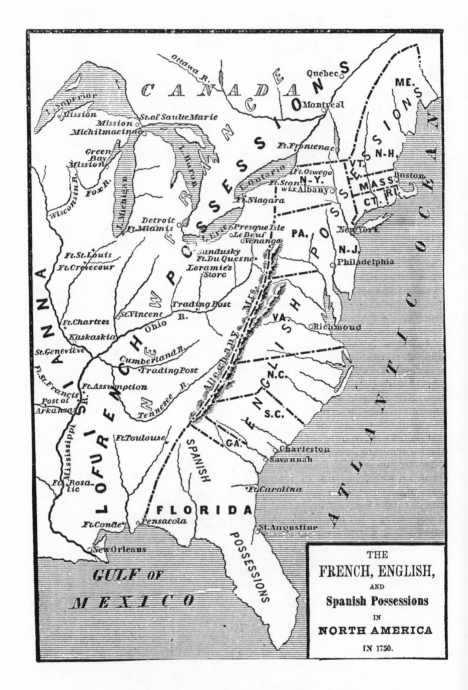

34 North America, 1750 (*The Great West*, 1860)

Arkansas

The Arkansas Post was established by French traders from Louisiana in 1686. This area, known as Upper Louisiana, was ceded to Spain in 1763 but was returned to France in 1800 and acquired by the United States in the Louisiana Purchase of 1803. It was incorporated into the newly formed Missouri Territory in 1812 and established as a separate territory in 1819.

Suggested Reading

Arnold, Morris S. *Arkansas Colonials, a Collection of French and Spanish Records Listing Early Europeans in the Arkansas, 1686–1804* (Gillett, AR: Grand Prairie Historical Society, 1986).

Arnold, Morris. *Unequal Laws unto a Savage Race: European Legal Traditions in Arkansas, 1686–1836* (Fayetteville: University of Arkansas Press, 1985).

A Baptismal Record of the Parishes Along the Arkansas River: August 5, 1796 to July 16, 1802 (Pine Bluff, AR: Pine Bluff Jefferson County Historical Society, 1982).

Clark, Mrs. Larry P. *Arkansas Pioneers and Allied Families* (Little Rock: The Author, fiche 6051363).

Core, Dorothy Jones. *Abstract of the Catholic Register of Arkansas [1764–1858]* (Gillett, AR: Grand Prairie Historical Society, 1976). This work is compiled from the Myra McAlmont Vaughn collection held by the Arkansas History Commission.

Dinn, Gilbert. C. "Arkansas Post in the American Revolution." *Arkansas Historical Quarterly* 40 (Spring 1981): 3–10.

Williams, C. Fred. *A Documentary History of Arkansas* (Fayetteville: University of Arkansas Press, 1984).

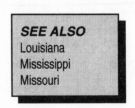

SEE ALSO
Louisiana
Mississippi
Missouri

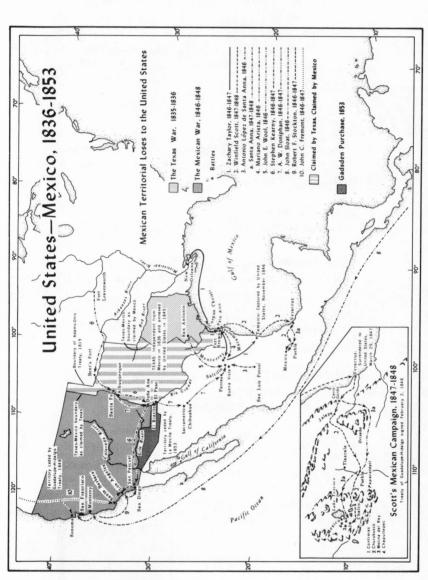

35 United States-Mexico, 1836 to 1853 (Cathryn L. Lombardi, et al., *Latin American History: A Teaching Atlas*. Madison: University of Wisconsin Press, 1983)

California

From 1542 until the beginning of the nineteenth century, various claims were made to California by Spain, Mexico, England, and Russia. The first permanent settlement by Spain was not made until 1769, when the Mision San Diego de Alcalá was founded at San Diego Bay. Over the next twelve years, the following settlements were established:

- Monterrey, a mission in 1770
- San Antonio de Padua, a mission and presidio in 1771
- San Gabriel, a mission in 1771
- San Luis Obispo, a mission in 1772
- San Francisco, a mission and a presidio in 1776
- San José, a mission in 1777
- Los Angeles, a town in 1781
- Santa Barbara, a mission and a presidio in 1782

In 1822 California became part of Mexico. It was annexed by the United States in 1850.

Ecclesiastical Records and Sources

Many of the missions still in existence maintain archives that include parish registers, *padrones*, and other records. The Bancroft Library at the University of California, Berkeley also holds originals and copies of many original records.

Catholic Church. Mission San Luis Obispo de Tolosa. Mission registers, 1772–1906 (film 0913300). The original records are at the Diocesan Pastoral Office, Monterey and at the California State Archives in Sacramento.

Berger, John A. *The Franciscan Missions of California* (New York: G.P. Putnam's Sons, 1941).

Bowman, J.N. "The Parochial Books of the California Missions." *Historical Society of Southern California Quarterly* 43 (September 1961): n.p.n.

Doyle, John T. *The Missions of Alta California* (1896. Reprint. Santa Barbara, CA: W.T. Genns, 1991).

SEE ALSO
Arizona
Latin America
Mexico
New Mexico
Spain

Engelhardt, Zephyrin. *The Missions and Missionaries of California.* 2 Vols. (Santa Barbara, CA: Mission Santa Barbara, 1929–30).

Hildrup, Jesse S. *The Missions of California and the Old Southwest* (1912. Reprint. Salt Lake City: Genealogical Society of Utah, 1995). Contains histories of the early missions and churches, as well as a history of the introduction of Christianity to the native Indians of California and the southwest. Includes California, Texas, New Mexico, Arizona, and Lower (Baja) California.

Keys, James M. *Las Misiones Españolas de California* (Madrid: Consejo Superior de Investigaciones Científicas, Instituto Juan, 1950). Spanish missions of California.

Corral, Ralph Francis. *Index to Baptismal Records, Santa Clara Mission, 1777–1855* (n.p., 1979, film 1036271).

Geiger, Maynard J. *Calendar of Documents in the Santa Barbara Mission Archives* (Washington, DC: Academy of American Franciscan History, 1947).

Civil Records and Sources
Some of the early *padrones* are kept at mission archives, such as the Santa Barbara Mission and the San Juan Bautista Mission in Monterrey.

1790 Padron of California. (n.p., n.d., film 1036747). This has been copied from "Las Familias de California" section of *Southern California Historical Society Quarterly.*

Temple, Thomas Workman. "The First Census of Los Angeles." *Historical Society of Southern California Quarterly* 16 (1931): 148–9.

Ramo de Californias: 1582–1842 (film 1857189 ff.). The Californias document series in the Archivo General de la Nación in Mexico City comprises historical materials from the Viceroyalty of Nueva that deal with both Lower and Upper California. This includes records for the settlement of the Pueblo de Los Angeles, 1781, military lists, 1748, 1769–74, and records of the Inquisition. The original records are at the Archivo General de al Nación in Mexico City.

California, Surveyor-General's Office. Spanish Archives, 1833–45 (film 0978888 ff.). Land records. The original records are at the State Archives in Sacramento.

Cowan, Robert Granniss. *Ranchos of California: A List of Spanish Concessions, 1775–1822, and Mexican Grants, 1822–1846* (Fresno, CA: Academy Library Guild, 1956).

Shumway, Burgess McK. *California Ranchos: Patented Private Land Grants Listed by County* (San Bernardino, CA: Borgo Press, 1988). Lists name of rancho and to whom the patent was granted, including date and description of the location.

Bowman, J. N. *Index to the Spanish-Mexican Private Land Grant Records and Cases of California* (1958. Reprint. Berkeley: Bancroft Library, University of California, 1970, film 0833343).

Sánchez, Joseph P. *Spanish Bluecoats, the Catalonian Volunteers in Northwestern New Spain, 1767–1810* (Albuquerque: University of New Mexico Press, 1990). Includes history and maps of the Spanish claims to Mexico, California, and Alaska.

Suggested Reading

Beers, Henry Putney. *Spanish and Mexican Records of the American Southwest* (Tucson: University of Arizona Press, 1979). The states included are Arizona, California, New Mexico, Texas, and Mexico.

Brackett, Robert W. *The History of San Diego County Ranchos: The Spanish, Mexican and American Occupation of San Diego County and the Story of the Ownership of Land Grants Therein* (1939. Reprint. San Diego: Union Title Insurance Co., 1960).

Buglio, Rudecinda Lo. *Survey of Pre-Statehood Records: A New Look at Spanish and Mexican-Californian Genealogical Records* (Salt Lake City: Corporation of the President, 1980, fiche 6085820).

California Gazetteer (Wilmington, DE: American Historical Publications, 1985, fiche 6088199).

Chapman, Charles E. *Catalogue of Materials in the Archivo General de Indias for the History of the Pacific Coast and the American Southwest* (Berkeley: University of California Press, 1919).

Chapman, Charles E. *The Founding of Spanish California: The Northwest Expansion of New Spain, 1687–1783* (New York: Macmillan & Co., 1916).

Chapman, Charles E. *A History of California: The Spanish Period* (New York: Macmillan & Co., 1921, fiche 6051216).

Denis, Albert Johnston. *Spanish Alta California* (New York: Macmillan & Co., 1927, film 1697423).

Derkum, Adam C. *Spanish Families of Southern California.* 38 Vols. (n.p., 1967, film 1597975 ff.).

Guide to American Historical Manuscripts in the Huntington Library (San Marion, CA: The Library, 1979). The Library's diverse collection includes holdings for Latin America and the Caribbean, the Dutch settlement of New Netherland, and French and Indian War records, such as regimental records for Pennsylvania (1758), Connecticut (1761), and New York (1759).

Hatch, Flora Faith. *The Russian Advance into California* (Berkeley: University of California, 1922. Reprint. San Francisco: R & E Research Associates, 1971, fiche 6039366). This covers California and Arizona.

The Illustrated Atlas and History of Yole County, California: Containing a History of California from 1513 to 1850, History of Yole County from 1825 to 1880, and the Official County Map (1879. Reprint. Woodbridge, CT: Research Publications, Inc., 1968, film 0468752).

Index to Genealogical Tables of Spanish and Mexican Families of California (Berkeley, CA: Bancroft Library, 1959, film 0874197).

Mathes, W. Michael. *A Brief History of the Calafia: The Californians, 1533–1795* (San Diego: n.p., 1974).

Nasatir, Abraham Phineas. *French Activities in California: An Archival Calendar-Guide* (Stanford: Stanford University Press, 1945). Includes summaries and extracts of French activities in California prior to statehood and a guide to the materials relating to California in the Archives of France.

Northrup, Marie, C. *Spanish Mexican Families of Early California: 1769–1850* (New Orleans: Polyanthos, 1976).

Nunis, Doyce B. and Gloria Ricci Lothrop. *A Guide to the History of California* (New York: Greenwood Press, 1989).

Richman, Irving Berdine. *California under Spain and Mexico, 1535–1847: A Contribution Toward the History of the Pacific Coast of the United States, Based on Original Sources (Chiefly Manuscript) in the Spanish and Mexican Archives and Other Repositories* (1911. Reprint. New York: Cooper Square Publishing, 1965, film 0897366).

Sanchez, Nellie Van de Grift. *Spanish and Indian Place Names of California, Their Meaning and Their Romance* (San Francisco: A.M. Robertson, 1930, film 1320727).

Shinn, Charles Howard. *Pioneer Spanish Families in California* (1896. Reprint. Santa Barbara, CA: W.T. Genns, 1991).

Society of California Archivists. *Directory of Archival and Manuscript Repositories in California.* 3rd ed. (San Marino: The Society, 1991, 1st ed. on film 1036038).

Strong, Gary E. *Local History and Genealogy Resources of the California State Library*. Rev. ed. (Sacramento: California State Library Foundation, 1991).

Winther, Oscar O. *The Story of San José: California's First Pueblo, 1777–1869* (San Francisco: California Historical Society, 1935).

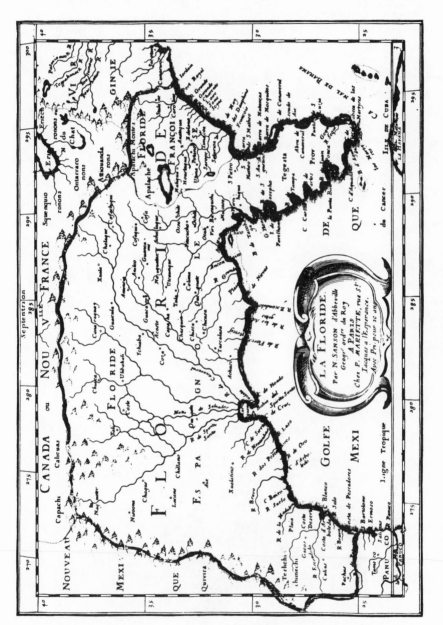

36 Florida, 1657 (Library of Congress)

Florida

Florida was the site of the first permanent settlement in the United States. Spain established the presidio of Saint Augustine in 1565 with a group of colonists and soldiers from Cuba. French Huguenots had built Fort Caroline on the Saint Johns River the previous year but were attacked by the Spanish, and were eventually all killed. Spanish Jesuit missionaries arrived the following year. Their missions were taken over by the Franciscans in 1572. The English attacked and burned Saint Augustine in 1586, which had been rebuilt by Spain. The next major settlement was at Pensacola in 1698.

Originally Florida was considered to include all the territory of Alabama, Florida, Georgia, and South Carolina. As the English colonies of South Carolina — and then Georgia — grew, Spain's hold on the area weakened. In 1763 it was ceded to Britain and divided into East and West Florida. Most of the Spanish subjects in Saint Augustine moved to Cuba, and those in Pensacola moved to Veracruz, Mexico. In 1768 colonists from Italy, Greece, and Spain settled in British East Florida to work as indentured servants on the indigo plantations. In 1784 Florida was returned to Spain. Parts of West Florida were annexed to Louisiana and Mississippi in 1812, and Spain ceded the rest of Florida to the U.S. in 1819.

Ecclesiastical Records and Sources

Many copies of the early Catholic parish registers are at the Historical Society in Saint Augustine, and the original records are at the Diocese of Havana in Havana, Cuba. Records of the Diocese of Louisiana and the Floridas, established in 1793, are at the Notre Dame Archives, Notre Dame University, South Bend, Indiana.

Historical Society Library, Saint Augustine. Chronological document files, 1766–1930 (film 1019970 ff.). Includes land records, probate records, census records, letters, parish records from 1594, copies of documents from Spanish, Cuban, and British archives, surname card index, and other records. The original files are at the Historical Society Library in

SEE ALSO
Bahamas
Caribbean
Cuba
Great Britain
Latin America
Louisiana
Mississippi
New France
Spain

Saint Augustine.

McAvoy, Thomas Timothy. *Guide to the Microfilm Edition of the Records of the Diocese of Louisiana and the Floridas, 1576–1803* (South Bend: University of Notre Dame Archives, 1967).

Curley, Michael Joseph. *Church and State in the Spanish Floridas, 1783–1822* (New York: AMS Press, 1974, fiche 6104719).

Gannon, Michael V. *The Cross in the Sand: The Early Catholic Church in Florida, 1513–1870* (Gainesville: University of Florida Press, 1965).

Thomas, David H. *Missions of Spanish Florida* (New York: Garland, 1991).

O'Daniel, V.F. *Dominicans in Early Florida* (1930. Reprint. Berkeley: University of California, 1992, film 1862235).

Historical Records Survey. *The Spanish Missions of Florida* (n.p.: The Survey, 1940, film 0908063).

Vargas Ugarte, Rubén. *Los Mártires de la Florida, 1566–1572* (Lima, 1940. Reprint. Washington, DC: The Library of Congress, 1975, film 1688882). Study of Spanish Jesuit missionary activities in Florida.

De Ville, Winston. *British Burials and Births on the Gulf Coast: Records of the Church of England in West Florida, 1768–1770* (Ville Platte, LA: The Author, 1986).

Civil Records and Sources
Administrative records for Florida are spread through many archives in different countries.

Spanish Dominion
Records of the Spanish colonial government can be found at:
- Archivo General de Indias in Seville, Spain: *Papeles de Cuba* and *Papeles de Santo Domingo*.
- Mitchell Library, Louisiana State University in Baton Rouge (copies of Cuban papers).
- Tilton Library, Tulane University, New Orleans (copies of Cuban papers).
- Loyola University Library, New Orleans (copies of Santo Domingo papers).
- Pace Library, University of West Florida, Pensacola (copies of Cuban papers and Panton Leslie Papers, 1738–1853, on microfilm).

- Archivo General de Cuba in Havana.
- Saint Augustine Historical Society (copies of records from Havana).
- Mississippi State Archives in Jackson (Spanish series, Provincial Archives).
- State Archives in Tallahassee. Spanish land grant archives, 1764–1844 (film 1020288 ff.). Miscellaneous land grants, deeds, wills, bills of sale, etc.
- The P.K. Yonge Library, University of Florida, in Gainesville.

Historical Records Survey. *Spanish Land Grants in Florida: Brief Translations from the Archives of the Board of Commissioners for Ascertaining Claims and Titles to Land in the Territory of Florida.* 5 Vols. (Tallahassee: State Library Board, 1940, film 0897334 ff.). This provides an index to the above records.

Spanish Florida land records, 1764–1849 (film 1905943 ff.). The Board of Land Commissioners, established in 1822 to settle all Spanish land grants, ascertained validity of titles and private claims in East and West Florida. This includes documents of private claims of individuals, abstracts of claims to lots in Pensacola, and records related to claims in West Florida, land surveys, and correspondence. The original records are at the State Archives in Tallahassee.

Connor, Jeanette Thurber. *Colonial Records of Spanish Florida [1570–1580].* 2 Vols. (DeLand: Florida State Historical Society, 1925–30).

The records for Spanish East Florida, 1783–1821, are at the Manuscript Division of the Library of Congress in Washington, DC. There is a card index and an unpublished analytical index to the series. The original records are also available on microfilm at the division. For more information, see Manning, Mabel W. "The East Florida Papers in the Library of Congress." *Hispanic American Historical Review* X No. 3 (August 1930), 392–7. Some records have been published in Lockey, Joseph Byrne. *East Florida, 1783–1785: A File of Documents Assembled and Many of Them Translated* (Berkeley: University of California Press, 1949).

Snider, Billie Ford. *Spanish Plat Book of Land Records of the District of Pensacola, Province of West Florida, British and Spanish Land Grants, 1763–1821* (1895. Reprint. Pensacola: Antique Compiling, 1994).

Arthur, Stanely Clisby. *Index to the Archives of Spanish West Florida, 1782–1810* (New Orleans: Polyanthos, 1975).

British Dominion

Records of the British period in East Florida are at the PRO in Kew, Surrey,

England and copies are at the P.K. Yonge Library, University of Florida, in Gainesville. The PRO records include:

- East Florida Claims Commission, 1763–89 (film 1020205 ff. /T 77).
- Loyalist birth, marriage, and death records, 1755–1908 (film 0857997 ff/ WO 42).
- Land grants (CO 5), American Loyalist Claims, series II (AO 13).
- Documents relating to refugees, 1780–1856 (T 50).
- List and Index Society. *List of the Records of the Treasury, Paymaster General's Office, the Exchequer and Audit Department, and the Board of Trade to 1837.* Vol. 46 (1921. Reprint. New York: Kraus Reprint Co., 1963). This indexes claimants in the East Florida Claims Commission (T 77).

For more information, see Great Britain and New France. Copies of many of the PRO records are available on microfilm at the Manuscript Division of the Library of Congress in Washington, DC.

Materials for British West Florida can be found at:

- ➤ Lelia Abercrombie Historical Library in Pensacola.
- ➤ Pace Library, University of West Florida, Pensacola.
- ➤ Library of Congress, Washington, DC (Oliver Pollock Papers).
- ➤ Mississippi State Archives (copies of PRO records).

West Florida. "A State of All Grants of Land Which Have Passed the Great Seal of the Province of West Florida on Family Right and Purchase since the Arrival: Of His Excellency Governor Chester at Pensacola on the 10th Day of August, 1770 to the 4th Day of November, 1773." *Mississippi Provincial Archives, 1763–1783, English Dominion* 6 (Jackson: Department of Archives and History, film 0899983): 83–9. For more information, see Mississippi.

De Ville, Winston. *English Land Grants in West Florida: A Register for the States of Alabama, Mississippi, and Parts of Florida and Louisiana, 1766–1776* (Ville Platte, LA: The Author, 1986).

Siebert, Wilbur Henry. *Loyalists in East Florida, 1774 to 1785: The Most Important Documents Pertaining Thereto.* 2 Vols. (1929. Reprint. Boston: Grogg Press, 1972). Transcript of PRO class T 77; this contains errors and omissions.

Suggested Reading

Bolton, Herbert E. *The Spanish Borderlands: A Chronicle of Old Florida and the Southwest* (New Haven: Yale University Press, 1921).

Catalog of the Florida State Archives (Tallahassee: Department of State, 1975).

Catalog of the P.K. Younge Library of Florida History. 4 Vols. (Boston: G.K. Hall, 1977).

Coker, William S. and Douglas Ingles. *The Spanish Censuses of Pensacola, 1784–1820: Genealogical Guide to Spanish Pensacola* (Pensacola: Perdido Bay Press, 1980).

Johnson, Cecil. *British West Florida, 1763–1769* (New Haven: Yale University Press, 1943).

Mowatt, Charles L. *East Florida as a British Province, 1763–1784* (Berkeley: University of California Press, 1943).

Panagopoulos, E.P. *New Smyrna, an Eighteenth Century Greek Odyssey* (Gainesville: University of Florida Press, 1966).

Peters, Thelma. "The Loyalist Migration from East Florida to the Bahama Islands." *Florida Historical Society Quarterly* 40:226–40.

Proctor, Samuel. *Eighteenth-Century Florida and the Caribbean* (Gainesville: University of Florida Press, 1976).

Roselli, Bruno. *The Italians in Colonial Florida: A Repertory of Italian Families Settled in Florida under the Spanish and British Regimes; with a Brief Historical Outline and an Appendix on the Contemporary Colonial Press* (Miami: n.p., 1940, film 1035661).

Servies, James. *A Bibliography of West Florida.* 4 Vols. (Pensacola: John C. Pace Library, 1981–).

Siebert, Wilbur Henry. *Loyalists in East Florida, 1774 to 1785.* 2 Vols. (Deland: Florida State Historical Society, 1929).

Tebeau, Charlton. *A History of Florida* (Coral Gables: University of Miami Press, 1971).

TePaske, John Jay. *The Governorship of Spanish Florida, 1700–1763* (Durham: Duke University Press, 1964).

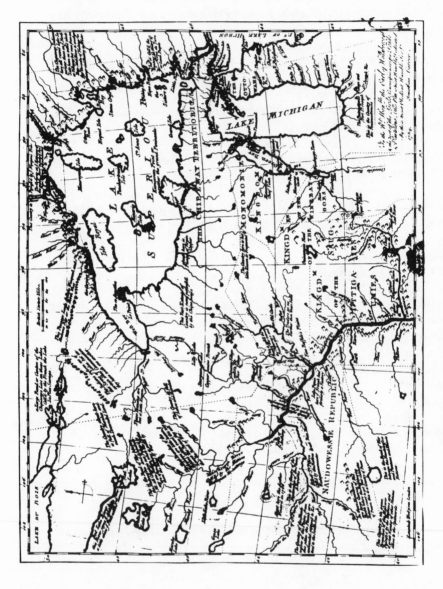

37 North Central states, 1769 (Library of Congress)

Illinois

The first settlements in Illinois were French missions founded at Fort Crevecoeur (Peoria) in 1680, at Cahokia in 1699, and another at Kaskaskia in 1703. This area — known as Upper Louisiana, or the Illinois Country — remained under French control until 1763, when it was ceded to Great Britain. From 1778 to 1784 Illinois was a county of Virginia and included all of Illinois, Indiana, Michigan, Ohio, and Wisconsin. Illinois became part of the Northwest Territory in 1787 and a separate territory in 1809.

Ecclesiastical Records and Sources

Copies of some parish registers of the Illinois Mission are at the National Archives of Canada in Ottawa, Ontario and originals are at the French National Archives, Section Outre-Mer, Paris. For the records of the part of Illinois that was in the Diocese of Vincennes, see Indiana. For Kaskaskia parish registers, see Louisiana.

Civil Records and Sources

The National Archives in Washington, DC has a series of private land claims relating to Kaskaskia, 1723–1809, many of which are copies of files from the recorder's office at Kaskaskia. These can be found in the Bureau of Land Management Records (RG 49.12) and have not been filmed.

Hammes, Raymond H. Consolidated index for the Raymond H. Hammes Collection at the Illinois State Genealogical Society, land records, 1678–1814 (film 1543598). The records include:

- Cahokia land records, 1790–97 (film 1543598). Entries made between 1790 and 1795 pertain to all the Illinois villages then in existence along the Mississippi River: Kaskaskia, Prairie du Rocher, Fort Chartres, Prairie du Pont, and Cahokia.
- Kaskaskia land records, 1804–14, Randolph County land records, 1768–1815 (film 1543598). Kaskaskia was the county seat of Randolph County, including all or parts of the present-day counties of Randolph, Perry, Franklin, Jackson,

SEE ALSO
France
Indiana
Louisiana
Michigan
Missouri
New France
Wisconsin

Williamson, Union, Johnson, Alexander, Pulaski, and Massac.

- Cahokia land records, 1800–20, historical material, 1671–1819 (film 1543598). All entries pertain to Saint Clair County and to the inhabitants of the villages then within its borders: Cahokia, the county seat, Prairie du Pont, Harrison, Prairie du Chien, Peoria, Michillimackinac, and Bellefontaine.
- Illinois land transaction typescripts/printouts, 1720–1866 (film 1535995).
- Miscellaneous land records: insinuations, grants, confirmations, lists of inhabitants, lists of militia men entitled to land, etc., 1722–1812 (film 1543598). Marriage contracts and insinuations, some probate-related material, land transmittals, militia lists, etc.

Illinois and Wabash land company minutes, 1778–1812 (film 0020445). The original records are at the Historical Society of Pennsylvania in Philadelphia. They cover Pennsylvania, Illinois, and Indiana.

Harding, Margery Heberling. *George Rogers Clark and His Men, Military Records, 1778–1784* (Frankfort: The Kentucky Historical Society, 1981, film 6050443). Part of the collection known as the Illinois Papers or Clark Papers is housed at the Virginia State Library. These records cover Kentucky and Illinois.

Suggested Reading

Alvord, Clarence Walworth. *The Illinois Country, 1673–1818* (1920. Reprint. Urbana: University of Illinois Press, 1987).

Bateman, Newton. *Historical Encyclopedia of Illinois* (1906. Reprint. Wooster, OH: Micro Photo Division, Bell and Howell Co., n.d., film 0825561).

Beers, Henry Putney. *The French and Spanish in the Old Northwest: A Bibliographical Guide to Archive and Manuscript Sources* (Detroit: Wayne State University, 1964). Covers the Illinois Country, Michigan, Quebec, and Ontario.

Carter, Clarence Edwin. *Great Britain and the Illinois Country, 1763–1774* (Washington, DC: The American Historical Association, 1910, film 1597561). This also covers Ohio, Indiana, Michigan, and Wisconsin.

Clark, George Rogers. *The Conquest of the Illinois* (n.p.: R.R. Donnelly and Sons, 1920, film 1597594). Description of the region between the Ohio River and the Great Lakes, the Alleghenies, and the Mississippi. This also covers Ohio, Indiana, Michigan, and Wisconsin.

Davidson, Alexander. *A Complete History of Illinois from 1673 to 1884: Embracing the Physical Features of the County, Its Early Explorations, Aboriginal Inhabitants* (Springfield, IL: H.W. Rokker, 1884, fiche 6051133).

Historical Records Survey. *Guide to Depositories of Manuscript Collections in Illinois* (Chicago: The Survey, 1940).

Pease, Theodore Calvin. *Illinois on the Eve of the Seven Years' War, 1747–1755* (Springfield: Trustees of the Illinois State Historical Library, 1940).

38 Trans-Alleghany region, 1775 to 1782 (Oliver P. Chitwood, *A History of Colonial America*. New York: Harper & Bros, 1931)

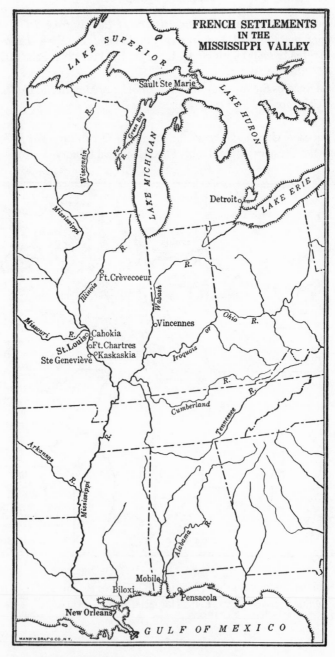

39 French settlements in the Mississippi Valley (Oliver P. Chitwood, *A History of Colonial America*. New York: Harper & Bros, 1931)

Indiana

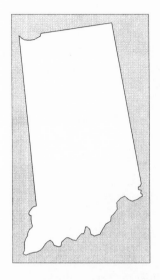

T hree trading posts were established by the French along the Waubash-Maumee trade route between 1700 and 1735. These posts became the present-day cities of Fort Wayne (Fort Miami), Lafayette (Ouiatenon), and Vincennes. In 1763, at the close of the French and Indian War, France ceded the Indiana area to Great Britain. Indiana became part of the Northwest Territory in 1784 and a separate territory in 1800.

Ecclesiastical Records and Sources

The Diocese of Vincennes covered both Indiana and Illinois. Saint Francis Xavier was the first Catholic Church erected in Indiana.

Catholic Church. Saint François Xavier de Ouabache.

- Parish registers, 1749–86 (Ottawa: Natonal Archives, 1967, film 1026606). Includes baptisms, marriages, and burials of the French and Indians. The transcripts of the original records are at the National Archives of Canada in Ottawa, Ontario. The original records are at the French National Archives, Section Outre-Mer, Paris.
- Parish registers, 1780–1960 (film 1433361 ff.). The original records are at Saint Francis Xavier Church in Vincennes.

Alerding, Herman Joseph. *A History of the Catholic Church in the Diocese of Vincennes* (Indianapolis: Carlon and Hollenbeck, 1883, film 0928082). This also covers Illinois.

Walker, Fintan Glenn. *The Catholic Church in the Meeting of Two Frontiers* (New York: AMS Press, 1974).

Civil Records and Sources

Census of Indiana Territory for 1807 (Indianapolis: Indiana Historical Society, 1980, film 1033927). The Indiana Territory included Saint Clair and Randolph counties of Illinois. This is a facsimile of

SEE ALSO
Illinois
Michigan
Wisconsin

the original manuscript.

Dunn, Jacob Piatt. *Documents Relating to the French Settlements on the Wabash* (Indianapolis: Bowen-Merrill, 1894, film 1320754).

Suggested Reading

Barnhart, John Donald. *Indiana to 1816: The Colonial Period* (Indianapolis: Indiana Historical Bureau and Indiana Historical Society, 1971).

Cauthorn, Henry Sullivan. *A History of the City of Vincennes, Indiana, from 1702 to 1901* (Vincennes: M.C. Cauthorn, 1902, film 0934909).

Dillon, John Brown. *A History of Indiana: From Its Earliest Exploration by Europeans to the Close of the Territorial Government, in 1816; Comprehending a History of the Discovery Settlement and Civil and Military Affairs of the Territory of the U.S. Northwest of the River Ohio and a General View of the Progress of Public Affairs in Indiana, from 1816 to 1856* (Indianapolis: Bingham and Doughty, 1859, fiche 6051127).

Law, John. *The Colonial History of Vincennes: Under the French, British, and American Governments, from its First Settlement down to the Territorial Administration of General William Henry Harrison* . . . (1858. Reprint. Fort Wayne: Allen County Public Library, 1987).

Smith, Hubbard Madison. *Historical Sketch of Old Vicennes, Founded in 1732: Its Institutions and Churches, Embracing Collateral Incidents, and Biographical Sketches of Many Persons and Events Connected Therewith* (1902. Reprint. Vincennes: Vincennes Historical and Antiquarian Society, n.d., fiche 6019139).

Thompson, Donald E. *Preliminary Checklist of Archives and Manuscripts in Indiana Repositories* (Indianapolis: Indiana Historical Society, 1980).

Kentucky

Kentucky's first settlement was a trading village on the Ohio River, established by the French in 1736. In 1774 a land company called the Transylvania Company purchased the rights to land in all of Kentucky and part of Tennessee. The first British settlements were at Harrodsburg in 1774 and at Fort Boonesborough in 1775, made by settlers from Virginia who came across the Wilderness Road through the Cumberland Gap. Kentucky County, Virginia was created in 1776. Boonesboro (1779) was the first town created by the Virginia Assembly, followed by Louisville (1780), Lexington (1781), and Harrodsburg (1785). Also in 1779 the Assembly passed an act to open a road through the Cumberland Mountains. The Kentucky District was part of Virginia until 1792.

Civil Records and Sources

Kentucky County was established from Fincastle County, Virginia in 1776. It was divided into Fayette and Lincoln counties in the Kentucky District (as the original county came to be known). County courts were established as the counties were formed. The Superior Court of the Kentucky district was created in 1782 and functioned as a supreme court of judicature. Due to a lack of clergy, county courts were authorized to solemnize marriages in 1783. Madison County, Virginia and the Kentucky District were part of Virginia that became Kentucky in 1792 when the state was created.

Kentucky State Land Office. Virginia land grant surveys in Kentucky, 1774–96 (film 0272939 ff.). The original and typescript copies are at the State Land Office in Frankfort.

Virginia Land Office. Commonwealth grants or patents, 1779–94, 1801 now in Kentucky (Richmond: Virginia State Library, 1949, film 0007811). The original records are at the State Land Office in Richmond.

Indexes to Court Records, Madison County, Kentucky: 1787–1852 (Frankfort: Kentucky Public Records Division, 1981, film 1534019). The records include indexes for the Virginia Supreme Court for the district of Kentucky, 1787–92; Madison County Court, Virginia, 1787–92; Madison County Court of Quarter Sessions, 1792–1802; Madison County Circuit Court, 1803–52; and general cross index to

SEE ALSO
Illinois
Ohio
Tennessee
Virginia
Wisconsin

civil and criminal case files, 1787–52. The original records are at the Madison County Courthouse in Richmond.

Brookes-Smith, Joan E. *Master Index, Virginia Surveys and Grants 1774–1791* (Frankfort: Kentucky Historical Society, 1976, film 1320833).

Cook, Michael L. *Fincastle and Kentucky County, Virginia-Kentucky Records and History* (Evansville, IN: Cook Publishing, 1987).

Cook, Michael L. *Virginia Supreme Court; District of Kentucky, Order Books, 1783–1792* (Evansville, IN: Cook Publishing, 1988).

Fothergill, Augusta B. *Virginia Tax Payers, 1782–1787, Other than Those Published by the United States Census Bureau* (Baltimore: Genealogical Publishing Co., 1974). Includes Fayette and Lincoln counties, Kentucky.

Hammon, Neal O. *Early Kentucky Land Records, 1773–1780* (Louisville: Filson Club, 1992).

Harwell, Richard Barksdale. *The Committees of Safety of Westmoreland and Fincastle: Proceedings of the County Committees, 1774–1776* (Richmond: Virginia State Library, 1974).

Kegley, Mary B. *Soldiers of Fincastle County, Virginia, 1774* (Dublin, VA: The Author, 1974). The records are copied from the Auditor's accounts for Dunmore's War at the Virginia State Library in Richmond. Fincastle County was divided into Montgomery, Washington, and Kentucky counties at the end of 1776. These records also cover Tennessee.

Robertson, James R. *Petitions of the Early Inhabitants of Kentucky to the General Assembly of Virginia, 1769 to 1792* (1915. Reprint. New York: Arno Press, 1971, film 1425691). Contains records of petitions for towns, land courts, etc., recorded in Hening's *Statutes at Large* (see Virginia).

Suggested Reading

Chinn, George Morgan. *Kentucky, Settlement and Statehood, 1750–1800* (Frankfort: Kentucky Historical Society, 1975).

Ely, William. *The Big Sandy Valley: A History of the People and Country from the Earliest Settlement to the Present Time* (Baltimore: Genealogical Publishing Co., 1969).

McDonald, Cecil D. *Some Kentucky Marriages, 1775–1799* (n.p., n.d., film 1036829).

Nowlin, William Dudley. *Kentucky Baptist History, 1770–1922* (Louisville: Baptist Book Concern, 1922, fiche 6087434).

Peden, Henry C. *Marylanders to Kentucky, 1775–1825* (Westminster, MD: Family Line Publications, 1991).

Speed, Thomas. *The Wilderness Road: A Description of the Routes of Travel by Which the Pioneers and Early Settlers First Came to Kentucky* (1886. Reprint. New York: Burt Franklin, 1971, film 0897452).

Spencer, John H. *A History of Kentucky Baptists: From 1769 to 1885, Including More than 800 Biographical Sketches.* 2 Vols. (Cincinnati: J.R. Baumes, 1886, film 0896971).

Louisiana

Louisiana, at the mouth of the Mississippi River, was claimed by France in 1682 and named for King Louis XIV. Fort Mississippi was built in 1699, about thirty miles below the future city of New Orleans. Little progress was made at the settlement until after the end of Queen Anne's War (the War of the Spanish Succession) in 1713. From 1712 to 1731, Louisiana was owned by private companies. The first permanent settlement was made at Natchitoches in 1714, some colonists coming directly from France and others from Quebec. German settlers from Alsace and the Rhine Valley arrived shortly thereafter and settled Allemands, near New Orleans. Forced migration from France brought in more settlers between 1717 and 1721. The city of Nouvelle Orléans (New Orleans) was founded in 1718. "Casket Girls" were imported in 1728 to offset the shortage of females in the colony (so-called because of the dress in a casket they received as an emigration gift). The colony reverted to the French Crown in 1731. In 1762 France ceded Upper and Lower Louisiana west of the Mississippi to Spain. The remainder of Louisiana east of the Mississippi went to Great Britain, which formed the colonies of East and West Florida.

In 1780 Britain returned the Floridas to Spain. Spanish West Florida was that section of Louisiana that is east of the Mississippi River, south of the Mississippi state line, and north of Pontchartrain and Maurepas lakes, extending to the Peal River. It was technically part of the Viceroyalty of Nueva España but was administered by the Captaincy General of Cuba, where some of the records still remain. During the Spanish period the largest groups of immigrants were from the Canary Islands in the 1770s and French refugees from Haiti in the 1790s, but the largest group was the Acadians.

In 1802 Spain ceded Louisiana back to France, which in turn sold it to the United States in 1803.

Ecclesiastical Records and Sources

The first Catholic Church was founded in 1700. The earliest church records begin in 1720. The Catholic

SEE ALSO
Acadia
The Bahamas
Caribbean
Cuba
Florida
France
Latin America
Mississippi
Missouri
New France
Nova Scotia
Quebec
Spain
Texas

Diocese of New Orleans — known initially as the Diocese of Louisiana and the Floridas — was established in 1793. The original diocese extended from the Canadian border to the Gulf of Mexico, from Spanish Texas to the Mississippi River and southern tip of Florida. The original documents are at the Notre Dame Archives, Notre Dame University in South Bend, Indiana, and the Archivo Nacional de Cuba in Havana. There are original duplicates of earlier records — from the French administration — at the French National Archives, Section Outre-Mer, Paris. There are copies of the French records at the National Archives of Canada in Ottawa, Ontario.

Église Catholique. Paroisse de Nouvelle-Orléans. Registres paroissiaux, 1720–34 (film 0959147). Parish registers of baptisms, marriages, and burials for New Orleans, 1724–30; Biloxi, Mississippi, 1720–2; and Kaskaskia, Illinois, 1723–4. The original records are at the French National Archives, Section Outre-Mer, Paris.

McAvoy, Thomas Timothy. *Guide to the Microfilm Edition of the Records of the Diocese of Louisiana and the Floridas, 1576–1803* (South Bend: University of Notre Dame Archives, 1967). This guide also covers Florida.

Bourquard, Shirley Chaisson. *Marriage Dispensations in the Diocese of Louisiana and the Floridas, 1786–1803* (New Orleans: Polyanthos, 1980). The documents also include Texas. The original records are at the Notre Dame Archives, Notre Dame University in South Bend, Indiana.

Diocese of Baton Rouge, Catholic Church Records: 1707–1882. 15 Vols. (Baton Rouge: Diocese of Baton Rouge, Department of Archives, 1978, fiche 6093541 ff.).

Woods, Earl C. *Sacramental Records of the Roman Catholic Church of the Archdiocese of New Orleans [1718–1912]* (New Orleans: Archdiocese of New Orleans, 1987–95).

Hebert, Donald J. *A Guide to Church Records in Louisiana, 1720–1975* (Eunice, LA: n.p., 1975, fiche 6051420 ff.). Includes indexes to Catholic, Protestant, and Jewish congregations.

Mills, Elizabeth Shown. *Natchitoches: Abstracts of the Catholic Registers . . . 1729–1803* (New Orleans: Polyanthos, 1977).

Civil Records and Sources

Military and local censuses were taken in Louisiana between 1699 and 1805. The original records are at the Archivo General de Indias in Seville, Spain, the

French National Archives, Section Outre-Mer, Paris, and the Archivo Nacional de Cuba in Havana. Copies of many of these records are available at the Louisiana State Archives in Baton Rouge.

Gouverneur-Général, Louisiane. Recensements et correspondance général, 1696-1781 (film 108000 ff.). General correspondence, passenger lists, censuses, and land grants during French administration of Louisiana. The original records are at the French National Archives, Section Outre-Mer, Paris.

The following works, all authored by Winston De Ville:

The Acadian Coast in 1779: Settlers of Cabanocey and La Fourche in the Spanish Province of Louisiana During the American Revolution (Ville Platte, LA: The Author, 1993). The original records are in the *Papeles Procedentes de Cuba*, at the Archivo General de Indias in Seville.

Rapides Post on Red River: Census and Military Documents for Central Louisiana, 1769-1800 (Ville Platte, LA: The Author, 1985).

Southwest Louisiana Families in 1785: The Spanish Census of the Posts of Attakapas and Opelousas (Ville Platte, LA: The Author, 1991).

Attakapas Post, the Census of 1771 (Ville Platte, LA: The Author, 1986).

Southwest Louisiana Families in 1777: Census Records of Attakapas and Opelousas Posts (Ville Platte, LA: The Author 1987).

Valenzuela in the Province of Louisiana: A Census of 1784 (Ville Platte, LA: The Author, 1987). The settlers, natives of the Canary Islands, arrived between 1778 and 1783.

New Feliciana in the Province of Louisiana: A Guide to the Census of 1793 (Ville Platte, LA: The Author, 1987).

Rapides Post, 1799: A Brief Study in Genealogy and Local History (Baltimore: Genealogical Publishing Co., 1968).

Maduell, Charles René. *The Census Tables for the French Colony of Louisiana from 1699 Through 1732* (Baltimore: Genealogical Publishing Co., 1972).

Robichaux, Albert J. *Louisiana Census and Militia Lists, 1770-1798.* 2 Vols. (Harvey, LA: The Author, 1974). The records cover the German coast, New Orleans, below New Orleans and along Bayou Lafourche.

From 1679 to 1769 (and some records through 1803) Louisiana was governed by the French Consiel Superior. The Spanish Cabildo governed from 1769 to 1804. Both European countries were predominately Catholic, and ecclesiastical and notarial record keeping was similar in both administrations.

Information on both dominions can be found in:

- Historical Records Survey. *English Language Summaries of the Records of the French Superior Council and the Judicial Records of the Spanish Cabildo, 1714–1800* (n.p., n.d., film 1292541 ff.). Records are at the Louisiana Historical Center in New Orleans.
- Name card index to records of the French Superior Council and judicial records of the Spanish Cabildo (film 1276244 ff.).

The original records are at the Louisiana Historical Center in New Orleans. For the Mississippi Provincial Archives, see Mississippi.

French Dominion

Gouverneur-Général, Louisiane. Recensements et correspondance général, 1696–1781 (film 0108000 ff.). General correspondence, passenger lists, censuses, and land grants during the French administration of Louisiana. The original records are at the French National Archives, Section Outre-Mer, Paris.

Louisiane passages 1718–24 (film 1305374, index on film 1292185 ff.). Arrivals by ship in Louisiana. The original records are at the Louisiana Historical Center in New Orleans, and there may be copies of records at the French National Archives, Section Outre-Mer, Paris. The records also include emigrants to Arkansas.

O'Neill, Charles Edwards. *Church and State in French Colonial Louisiana: Policy and Politics to 1732* (New Haven: Yale University Press, 1966).

Rowland, Dunbar. *General Correspondence of Louisiana: 1678–1763* (1907. Reprint. New Orleans: Polyanthos, 1976).

Dart, Henry P. *Marriage Contracts of French Colonial Louisiana* (n.p.: Louisiana Historical Quarterly, 1934, film 1421730).

Forsyth, Alice D. *Louisiana Marriage Contracts: A Compilation of Abstracts from Records of the Superior Council of Louisiana During the French Regime, 1725–1769.* 2 Vols. (New Orleans: Polyanthos, 1980). The original Superior Council Records of French Louisiana are at in the Louisiana Historical Center in New Orleans.

De Ville, Winston. *The New Orleans French, 1720–1733: A Collection of Marriage Records Relating to the First Colonists of the Louisiana Province* (Baltimore: Genealogical Publishing Co., 1973).

Forsyth, Alice D. *German "Pest Ships," 1720–1721* (New Orleans: New Orleans Genealogical Research Society, 1969, fiche 6094099). This contains the names of immigrants sent to Louisiana.

Deiler, J. Hanno. *The Settlement on the German Coast of Louisiana and the Creoles of German Descent* (Baltimore: Genealogical Publishing Co., 1970). Names of the Germans enumerated in the 1724 French census.

Spanish Dominion

The Spanish Cabildo consisted of *alcaldes* (judges), an *alguacil mayor* (high sheriff), an *escribano* (clerk), and other officers. The proceedings included all types of cases, especially land transactions and settlements of debts.

Cabildo, Province of Louisiana.
* Acts and deliberations of the Cabildo, 1769–1803 (film 1309934 ff.).
* Inventory of the records of the French Superior Council and judicial records of the Spanish Cabildo 1702–1803 (film 1306185).
* Judicial records, 1769–1804 (film 1031280 ff.).
* Petitions, decrees, and letters of the Spanish Cabildo, 1770–1803 (film 1309932 ff.)

The original records are at the Louisiana Historical Center in New Orleans.

Court of Louisiana. Law suits, 1790–1804 (film 0906355). The text of the suits is in Spanish and French with synopsis in English. The original records are at the New Orleans Public Library.

Archives of the Spanish government of West Florida (film 0327823 ff.). The records include probate, land, and notarial records, 1782–1810. The translated records are at the records room of the Nineteenth Judicial Court in Baton Rouge. The original records are at the Library of Congress in Washington, DC.

Arthur, Stanley Clisby. *Index to the Archives of Spanish West Florida, 1782–1810* (New Orleans: Polyanthos, 1975).

De Ville, Winston. *Louisiana and Mississippi Lands: A Guide to Spanish Land Grants at the University of Michigan* (Ville Platte, LA: Evangeline Genealogical and Historical Society, 1985). Includes properties at Ascension, Attakapas, Baton Rouge, Chapitoulas, Concordia, Feliciana, Galveztown, Opelousas, Pointe Coupee, Rapides, Saint Bernard, Saint Charles, and Valenzuela in Louisiana, and at Natchez in Mississippi.

De Ville, Winston. *Marriage Contracts of the Attakapas Post, 1760–1803* (Saint Martinville, LA: Attakapas Historical Association, 1966).

Din, Gilbert C. *The Canary Islanders of Louisiana* (Baton Rouge: Louisiana State University Press, 1988, fiche 6100657).

Villeré, Sidney Louis. *The Canary Islands Migration to Louisiana, 1778–1783: The History and Passenger Lists of the Islenos Volunteer Recruits and Their Families* (Baltimore: Genealogical Publishing Co., 1972). The villages allocated to the Canary Islanders were San Bernardo de Galvez (Saint Bernard Parish), Galveztown (Iberville Parish), Valenzuela (Assumption Parish), and Nueva Iberia (Iberia Parish).

Other Records

Orleans Parish, First Judicial District. Case papers, 1813–1846 (film 1710492 ff.). Selected suits, including interdictions, divorces, authorizations, separations of bed and board, successions, emancipations, separations of property, and tutorships. The original records are at the Orleans District Court in New Orleans.

Saint Charles Parish Notary. Actes notaries, 1811–53, index, 1850–90 (film 0392483 ff.). Notarial records. The original records are at the Saint Charles Parish Courthouse in Hahnville.

Bureau of Land Management. Bound Records of the General Land Office Relating to Private Lands Claims in Louisiana, 1767–1892 (M1382 ff.). According to the inventory of these records, roll 1 also contains land claims in Alabama, 1715–1812.

U.S. District Land Office, Saint Helena, Louisiana. Greensburg claim papers, 1770–1880 (film 1319543 ff.). Greensburg papers are documents of claims of land obtained previous to the American period that by law had to be proved during the early 1800s. The original records are at the Division of State Land Office in Baton Rouge.

De Ville, Winston. *English Land Grants in West Florida: A Register for the States of Alabama, Mississippi, and Parts of Florida and Louisiana, 1766–1776* (Ville Platte, LA: The Author, 1986). Entries list date of grant, grantee, amount of acres, purchase price, and date quit rents began to be collected.

The following works are authored by Donna Burge Adams:
Trades and Professions in the Florida Parishes of Louisiana (Baton Rouge: The Author, 1989). Excerpts from court records, news clippings, and letters containing genealogical information regarding businessmen and women from 1780 to 1919. Includes information for Mississippi.

Schooners and Scows in the Florida Parishes of Louisiana. 2 Vols. (Baton Rouge: The Author, 1988). Contains information taken from probate and other court records, letters, news clippings, oral traditions, and census reports about people involved in navigation. Includes business records, slavery records, some genealogies, marriages, and deaths dating from 1770 to about 1920 for Louisiana and Mississippi.

Women in the Florida Parishes of Louisiana. 5 Vols. (Baton Rouge: The Author, 1985–91). Abstracts from court records, probate records, vital records, newspaper clippings, deeds and other land records, oral traditions, and correspondence about women residing in Louisiana and Mississippi, 1780–1971.

Pre-Civil War Military Records of the Florida Parishes (Baton Rouge: The Author, 1990). This also covers Florida, Mississippi, and Texas.

Military records can be found at the Archivo General de Indias in Seville, Spain, the Archivo General de Simancas in Valladolid, Spain, the French National Archives, Section Outre-Mer, Paris, the Texas State Archives in Austin, and the National Archives in Washington, DC.

The following military compilations were written by Winston De Ville:

Louisiana Colonials: Soldiers and Vagabonds (Mobile, AL: The Author, 1963). Descriptive lists for 1719–20, from originals at the French National Archives, Section Outre-Mer, Paris.

Louisiana Recruits, 1752–1758: Ship Lists of Troops from the Independent Companies of the Navy Destined for Service in the French Colony of Louisiana (Cottonport, LA: Polyanthos, 1973).

Louisiana Troops, 1720–1770 (Fort Worth: American Reference Publishers, 1965).

Historical Records Survey. *An Account of Louisiana: Louisiana Militia Records [1712–1908]* (Philadelphia: The Survey, 1937, film 1673097 ff.).

Historical Records Survey. *Louisiana Militia Under Don Bernardo De Galvez, 1770–1797* (n.p.: The Survey, 1937, film 1704157).

Suggested Reading

Baudier, Roger. *The Catholic Church in Louisiana* (New Orleans: Louisiana Library Association, 1972, film 1425652).

Beers, Henry Putney. *French and Spanish Records of Louisiana: A Bibliographical Guide to Archive and Manuscript Sources* (Baton Rouge: Louisiana State University Press, 1989). Contains history of land records, military records, parish records, ecclesiastical records, birth registers, marriage, and death records from what are now known as the states of Louisiana, Mississippi, Alabama, Missouri, and Arkansas; provides a description of these records and their past as well as current locations.

Blume, Helmut. *The German Coast During the Colonial Era, 1722–1803: The Evolution of a Distinct Cultural Landscape in the Lower Mississippi Delta During the Colonial Era; with Special Reference to the Development of Louisiana's German Coast* (1956. Reprint. Destrehan, LA: German-Acadian Coast Historical and Genealogical Society, 1990).

Cummins, Light Townsend and Glen Jeansonne. *A Guide to the History of Louisiana* (Westport, CT: Greenwood Press, 1982).

Delanglez, Jean. *The French Jesuits in Lower Louisiana, 1700–1763* (1922. Reprint. New York: AMS Press, 1974).

De Ville, Winston. *Gulf Coast Colonials: A Compendium of French Families in Early Eighteenth Century Louisiana* (Baltimore: Genealogical Publishing Co., 1968).

De Ville, Winston. *The Natchez Ledgers, 1790–1791: A Finding Aid for Anglo-Americans in Pre-Territorial Mississippi* (Ville Platte, LA: The Author, 1994).

De Ville, Winston. *The Sainte Catherine Colonists, 1719–1720: Early Settlers of Natchez and Pointe Coupée in the French Province of Louisiana* (Ville Platte, LA: Smith Books, 1991). Includes a list of the victims of the 1729 massacre at Natchez.

French, Benjamin Franklin. *Historical Collections of Louisiana: Embracing Many Rare and Valuable Documents Relating to the Natural, Civil and Political History of That State, Compiled with Historical and Biographical Notes . . . 1678 to 1691* (New York: Wiley and Putnam, 1846, fiche 6100290).

Giraud, Marcel. *Histoire de la Louisiana Française*. 3 Vols. (Paris: Presses Universitaires de France, 1953. Reprint. Baton Rouge: Louisiana State University Press, 1974). History of French Louisiana.

Goins, Charles Robert. *Historical Atlas of Louisiana* (Norman: University of Oklahoma, 1995)

Hefly, Sue. *Resources in Louisiana Libraries: Public, Academic, Special and in Media Centers; Preliminary Checking Edition* (Baton Rouge: Louisiana State Library, 1971, fiche 6019941).

Historical Records Survey. *Guide to the Manuscript Collections in Louisiana, the Department of Archives, Louisiana State University* (Baton Rouge: Louisiana State University, 1940).

Holmes, Jack D.L. *A Guide to Spanish Louisiana, 1762–1806* (New Orleans: The Author, 1970).

Inventory of the Louisiana Historical Association Collection: On Deposit in the Howard-Tilton Memorial Library Tulane University, New Orleans, Louisiana (New Orleans: Louisiana Historical Association, 1983).

Louisiana State Archives and Records Commission. *Calendar of Louisiana Colonial Documents*. 3 Vols. (n.p.: The Commission, 1961–7, film 0496718).

Margry, Pierre. *Découverte par Mer des Bouches du Mississipi et Établissements de Lemoyne de'Iberville Sur le Golfe du Mexique, 1694–1703* (1879. Reprint. New York: AMS Press, 1974, film 1036107). The discovery of the mouth of the Mississippi by sea and the establishment of Lemoy ne D'Iberville on the Gulf of Mexico.

McDermott, John Francis. *Frenchmen and French Ways in the Mississippi Valley* (Urbana: University of Illinois Press, 1965).

McDermott, John Francis. *The Spanish in the Mississippi Valley, 1762–1804* (Urbana: University of Illinois Press, 1974).

Moore, John Preston. *Revolt in Louisiana: The Spanish Occupation, 1766–1770* (Baton Rouge: Louisiana State University Press, 1976).

Smith, Judith Dinkel. *Searching for Your Ancestors on Microfilm* (Baton Rouge: State Library, 1990, film 1697866). Contains a list of microfilm in the State Library that is available through inter-library loan, including records of census, church, land, military, court, newspapers, emigration, immigration, and census of Indian tribes.

Spillman, Barbara Comeaux. *Louisiana Genealogical, Historical Societies and Libraries* (Baton Rouge: Ancestor Research and Analysis, 1994).

Toups, Neil J. *Mississippi Valley Pioneers* (Lafayette: Neilson Publishing Co., 1970).

University of Southwestern Louisiana. *Guide to Southwestern Archives and Manuscripts Collection* (Lafayette: University of Southwestern Louisiana, 1968, film 0824284).

Vogel, Claude Lawrence. *The Capuchins in French Louisiana, 1722–1766* (1922. Reprint. New York: AMS Press, 1974).

West, Robert Cooper. *An Atlas of Louisiana Surnames of French and Spanish Origin* (Baton Rouge: Geoscience Publishing, Louisiana State University, 1986, fiche 6088326).

Willie, Leroy Ellis. *The History of Spanish West Florida and the Rebellion of 1810, and Philemon Thomas, Patriot* (Baton Rouge: Sons of the American Revolution, 1991). West Florida became part of the states of Mississippi, Louisiana, and Alabama.

New Orleans in 1719.

Michigan

Michigan's first permanent settlement was founded by Canadian French at Sault Sainte Marie in 1668. Fort Saint Joseph (present-day Niles) was founded in 1691, and Fort Ponchartrain (Detroit) was founded in 1701. In 1763 the area was ceded by France to Great Britain. Most of Michigan became part of the Northwest Territory in 1787. A separate territory was organized in 1805.

Ecclesiastical Records and Sources

Catholic Church.

* L'Assomption de la Pointe-de-Montréal, Detroit. Registre de la Paroisse, 1761–99 (Ottawa: National Archives of Canada, 1967, film 1026603 ff.). Parish registers, 1761–99.
* Sainte Anne, Detroit. Registre de la Paroisse, 1704–1800 (Ottawa: National Archives of Canada, 1967, film 1026602 ff.). Registers of Fort Ponchartrain, now Detroit, Michigan.

Copies of the original records are at the National Archives of Canada in Ottawa, Ontario.

There are eighteenth-century parish and city maps and church sacramental registers from 1704 at the Archdiocese of Detroit in Detroit.

Paré, George. *The Catholic Church in Detroit, 1701–1888* (Detroit: Gabriel Richard Press, 1951).

Civil Records and Sources

Records from the U.S. Land Office at Detroit contain land grants and claims in the Detroit area, 1707–1825. The French land grants begin in 1707; British grants begin in 1781. These records are in the Bureau of Land Management record group (RG 49.13) at the National Archives in Washington, DC.

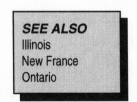

SEE ALSO
Illinois
New France
Ontario

Suggested Reading

Denissen, Christian. *Genealogy of the French Families of the Detroit River Region, 1701–1936.* 2 Vols. (Detroit: Detroit Society for Genealogical Research, 1987). The Detroit River region includes the boundary between Michigan and Ontario from the Saint Clair River, through Lake Saint Clair, then west along the Detroit River to Lake Erie. This includes the genealogies of the early settlers of French descent along the Detroit River on both sides of the river, in Michigan and Ontario.

History of the Upper Peninsula of Michigan Containing a Full Account of its Early Settlement (1883. Reprint. New Haven, CT: Research Publications, 1973, film 0485331).

Jacobson, Judy. *Detroit River Connections: Historical and Biographical Sketches of the Eastern Great Lakes Border Region* (Baltimore: Clearfield Co., 1994).

McGinnis, Carol. *Michigan Genealogy: Sources and Resources* (Baltimore: Genealogical Publishing Co., 1987).

Newton, Stanley D. *The Story of Sault Sainte Marie and Chippewa County* (1923. Reprint. Grand Rapids, MI: Black Letter Press, 1975).

Peyser, Joseph L. *Letters from New France, the Upper Country, 1686–1783* (Urbana: University of Illinois Press, 1992). Collection of historical documents from archival repositories in Canada, France, and the United States dealing with French-colonial military, religious, and mercantile life.

Russell, Donna Valley. *Michigan Censuses, 1710–1830, under the French, British and Americans* (Detroit: Detroit Society for Genealogical Research, 1982).

Sprenger, Bernice Cox. *Guide to the Manuscripts in the Burton Historical Collection* (Detroit: Burton Historical Collection, Detroit Public Library, 1985).

Stuart, Donna Valley. *Michigan Censuses, 1710–1830: Under the French, British, and Americans* (Detroit: Detroit Society for Genealogical Research, 1982).

Warner, Robert M. *Guide to Manuscripts in the Michigan Historical Collections of the University of Michigan* (Ann Arbor: n.p., 1963, film 0874197).

Williams, Ethel W. *Tracing Your Ancestors in Michigan* (Salt Lake City: Genealogical Society of the Church of Jesus Christ of Latter-day Saints, 1969, fiche 6039418).

Minnesota

Minnesota was claimed by France in 1671. French fur traders established a chain of forts in the Minnesota area between 1686 and 1762. That year France ceded the area to Spain, which turned it over to Great Britain the following year. From 1763 until 1819 it was controlled by British fur traders of the Northwest Company, except for the portion that was ceded to the United States in 1783. Part of Minnesota was acquired by the U.S. in the Louisiana Purchase of 1803.

Suggested Reading

Pope, Wiley R. *Tracing Your Ancestors in Minnesota, French and Canadian: A Brief Outline* (Saint Paul: The Pope Family Association, 1979, fiche 6105012).

Hubbard, Lucius F., William P. Murray, and James H. Baker. *Minnesota in Three Centuries, 1655–1908* (New York: Publication Society of Minnesota, 1908, film 1036696).

Neill, Edward D. *The History of Minnesota from the Earliest French Explorations to the Present Time* (Philadelphia: J.B. Lippincott, 1858, film 1036190).

Upham, Warren and Rose Barteau Dunlap. *Minnesota Biographies, 1655–1912. Collections of the Minnesota Historical Society.* Vol. XIV (Saint Paul: Minnesota Historical Society, 1912).

White, Bruce M. *The Fur Trade in Minnesota: An Introductory Guide to Manuscript Sources* (Saint Paul: Minnesota Historical Society, 1977).

SEE ALSO
Illinois
Rupert's Land

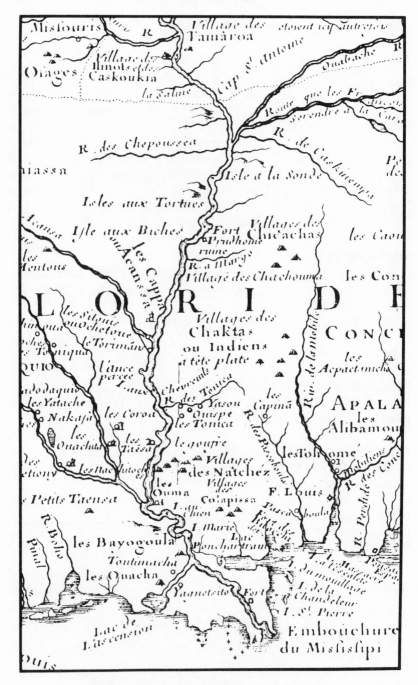

40 The Lower Mississippi (*Delisle Atlas*, 1703)

Mississippi

Fort Maurepas was founded on Biloxi Bay by the French in 1699, and Fort Rosalie (Natchez) in 1716. The area east of the Mississippi River was ceded by France to Great Britain in 1763. It was administered with British West Florida, which had been ceded by Spain to Britain the same year. The Louisiana area west of the Mississippi was ceded from France to Spain the same year. In 1783 the coastal area of Mississippi, Alabama, and the Floridas was ceded to Spain by Britain. The rest of Mississippi and Alabama was claimed by Georgia until 1795. From 1789 to 1794 the legislature of Georgia engaged in the Yazoo land sales in Mississippi. The Mississippi Territory was organized in 1798, and the Spanish fort at Nogales (Vicksburg) was evacuated by Spanish troops. The U.S. acquired the coastal area from Spain during the War of 1812. The Alabama territory was organized from Mississippi in 1817.

Ecclesiastical and Civil Records and Sources

The Mississippi Provincial Archives are three series of transcribed documents collected from European archives by Dunbar Rowland. The series are:

* *Mississippi Provincial Archives: French Dominion, 1612–1763.* 6 Vols. (Jackson: Department of Archives and History, 1968, film 0899957 ff.). Transcripts of the French National Archives relating to the lower Mississippi Valley area. This also covers Louisiana.
* *Mississippi Provincial Archives: French Dominion, 1701–1743.* 3 Vols. (Jackson: Department of Archives and History, 1927–32, film 0904441 ff.). This also covers Louisiana.
* *Mississippi Provincial Archives: French Dominion, 1729–1763.* 5 Vols. (Jackson: Department of Archives and History, 1984, film 1305386 ff.). This also covers Louisiana.
* *Mississippi Provincial Archives, Spanish Dominion, 1757–1820.* 4 Vols. (Jackson: Department of Archives and History, 1969, film 0899972 ff.). Transcripts of Spanish Provincial Archives relating to the Gulf Coast,

SEE ALSO
Acadia
Florida
Georgia
Louisiana
Nova Scotia

copied from original documents in the Archivo General de Indias in Seville, Spain. This also covers Louisiana, Florida, and Georgia.

*   *Mississippi Provincial Archives: English Dominion 1763–1783* (Jackson: Department of Archives and History, 1969, film 0899981 ff.). Military and government correspondence and documents relating to British colonies in the province of West Florida. Includes a list of the inhabitants of Mobile, 1764; registers of births, christenings, burials in Pensacola, 1768–71; grants of land in West Florida, 1770–3; land surveyed on the Mississippi River, 1767–77; and land grants and deeds, 1765–83. This also covers Florida, Alabama, and Louisiana. The records are transcripts of archives in the PRO in Kew, Surrey, England.

The original transcriptions are at the State Archives and History in Jackson.

Work Projects Administration. *Mississippi Provincial Archives; Spanish Dominion.* 4 Vols. (n.p., 1942, film 0904443 ff.). English translations of the original records.

Mississippi territorial land and court records, 1798–1817 (film 0904447 ff.). The original records are at the State Archives in Jackson.

First Settlers of the Mississippi Territory (Nacogdoches, TX: Ericson Books, n.d., fiche 6051448). Grants taken from the American State Papers, Class VIII, Public Lands, 1789–1809. The Mississippi Territory covered a large area, most of present-day Georgia, Alabama, and Mississippi.

King, J. Estelle Stewart. *Mississippi Court Records, 1799–1835* (Beverly Hills, CA: n.p., 1936, film 0547551).

McBee, May Wilson. *The Natchez Court Records: Abstracts of Early Records, 1767–1805* (Greenwood, MS: The Author, 1954).

Strickland, Jean. *Residents of Mississippi Territory.* 2 Vols. (Moss Point, MS: The Author, 1995). Contains miscellaneous records such as court records, land and property records, censuses, maps, passports, tax rolls, etc.

Suggested Reading

Boyd, Sandra E. *Mississippi's Historical Heritage: A Directory of Libraries, Archives, and Organizations* (Hattiesburg: Mississippi Historical Society, 1990).

Gillis, Norman. *Early Inhabitants of the Natchez District* (Baton Rouge: The Author, 1963).

Greenwell, Dale. *Twelve Flags: Triumphs and Tragedies.* 3 Vols. (Ocean Springs, MS: The Author, 1968).

Lipscomb, Anne S. *Tracing Your Mississippi Ancestors* (Jackson: University Press of Mississippi, 1994).

Research in the Mississippi Department of Archives and History (n.p., n.d., film 0908063).

Rowland, Eron Opha Moore. *Mississippi Territory in the War of 1812* (Baltimore: Genealogical Publishing Co., 1968, film 1036243).

RICE PLANTATION.

41 New Madrid, 1796 (Library of Congress)

Missouri

Missouri was part of the area known as Upper Louisiana, or the Illinois Country. The first settlement was planted at Sainte Genevieve by French lead miners in 1735. The area was ceded by France to Spain in 1763. The following year, French fur traders founded Saint Louis. Spain founded New Madrid in 1789, near the confluence of the Ohio and Mississippi rivers. The area was ceded back to France in 1800, who sold it to the United States in the Louisiana Purchase of 1803. Missouri was part of the Louisiana Territory until 1812, when a separate territory was created.

Ecclesiastical Records and Sources

The first Catholic Church was established at Saint Genevieve in 1752.

Catholic Church. Basilica of Saint Louis, King of France. Church records, 1766–1993 (fiche 6075777 ff.). Baptisms, marriages, burials, and indexes for the Saint Louis Cathedral, 1765–1839. The original records are at the Pius XII Memorial Library, Saint Louis University, in Saint Louis.

Catholic Baptisms, Saint Louis, Missouri, 1765–1840 (Saint Louis: Saint Louis Genealogical Society, 1982, fiche 6111225).

Rothensteiner, John Ernest. *History of the Archdiocese of Saint Louis: In Its Various Stages of Development from A.D. 1673 to 1928.* 2 Vols. (Saint Louis: Blackwell Wielandy, 1928). This also includes Illinois.

Civil Records and Sources

Saint Louis Archival Library. *French and Spanish Archives, 1766–1816* (Saint Louis: City of Saint Louis, 1962, film 0981650 ff.).

Louisiana Territory, Recorder of Land Titles. *Record Books, 1795–1808; Index to French and Spanish Land Grants, 1795–1812* (Jefferson City: State of Missouri, 1970, film 0984777). The original records are at the State Archives in Jefferson City.

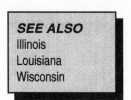

SEE ALSO
Illinois
Louisiana
Wisconsin

Houck, Louis. *The Spanish Regime in Missouri: A Collection of Papers and Documents Relating to Upper Louisiana Principally Within the Present Limits of Missouri During the Dominion of Spain, from the Archives of the Indies at Seville* (1909. Reprint. Washington, DC: Library of Congress, 1990, film 1723770).

Lee, Grace. *From Arpents to Acres: French and Spanish Land Grants at the Missouri State Archives* (Jefferson City: Secretary of State, Roy D. Blunt, 1992). The French and Spanish land records from 1770 through the 1830s.

Williams, Betty H. *Index to French and Spanish Land Grants, Recorded in Registers of Land Titles in Missouri . . .* (Warrensburg, MO: The Author, 1977). The index was prepared by the staff at the State Archives in Jefferson City.

Suggested Reading

Billon, Frederic L. *Annals of Saint Louis in Its Early Days under the French and Spanish Domination* (1886. Reprint. Bowie, MD: Heritage Books, 1997).

Bishop, Beverly D. *A List of Manuscript Collections in the Archives of the Missouri Historical Society* (Saint Louis: Missouri Historical Society, 1982).

Conard, Howard Louis. *Encyclopedia of the History of Missouri: A Compendium of History and Biography for Ready Reference.* 6 Vols. (New York: Southern History Co., 1901, fiche 6051492).

Foley, William E. *The Genesis of Missouri: From Wilderness Outpost to Statehood* (Columbia: University of Missouri Press, 1989).

Gerlach, Russell L. *Settlement Patterns in Missouri, a Study of Population Origins, with a Wall Map* (Columbia: University of Missouri Press, 1986).

Western Historical Manuscripts Collection. *Guide to the Western Historical Manuscripts Collection* (Columbia: University of Missouri, 1957).

New Mexico

The first settlement in New Mexico was the colony of San Juan de los Caballeros, founded in 1598 by Spanish soldiers, families, and Indian servants. Santa Fe was established as the capital of New Mexico in 1610. The colony included the pueblos of the Hopi Indians. Small settlements, called *estancias,* were established along the Rio del Norte. All the settlers were driven out during the Pueblo Revolt of 1680, when they took refuge at the mission of Guadeloupe del Paso. The settlers returned in 1693, bringing additional colonists. Albuquerque was founded in 1706. New Mexico became a province of Mexico in 1821 and was ceded to the United States in 1848.

Ecclesiastical Records and Sources

Parish registers and other ecclesiastical records can be found in parish archives and the following repositories:

➤ University of New Mexico, Albuquerque: holds the archives of the Archdiocese of Santa Fe.

➤ Archivo General de Indias in Seville, Spain. The papers also include notarial records. Photocopies are at the Coronado Library, University of New Mexico, Santa Fe.

➤ The Ayer Collection, Newberry Library, Chicago.

➤ Bancroft Library, University of California, Berkeley.

➤ The Old Mission, Ciudad Juarez, Mexico.

➤ Biblioteca Nacional de México in Mexico City.

➤ Huntington Library, San Marino, California.

➤ The Historical Society of New Mexico, Santa Fe.

➤ Archives Division, New Mexico Records Center, Santa Fe.

Catholic Church. San Juan de los Caballeros. Church records, 1726–1956 (El Paso, TX: Golightly, 1956, film 0016981). The original records are at the San Juan de los Caballeros Church, San Juan, New Mexico.

Brugge, David M. *Navajos in the Catholic Church Records of New Mexico, 1694–1875* (Window Rock, AZ: Parks and Recreation Department, 1968).

SEE ALSO
Arizona
California
Latin America
Mexico
Spain
Texas

Chávez, Angélico. *New Mexico Roots Ltd.: A Demographic Perspective from Genealogical, Historical, and Geographical Data Found in the Diligencias Matrimoniales or Pre-Nuptial Investigations (1678–1869) of the Archives of the Archdiocese of Santa Fe.* 11 Vols. (Santa Fe: n.p., 1982, fiche 6051367).

Chávez, Angélico. *Archives of the Archdiocese of Santa Fe, 1678–1900* (Washington, DC: Academy of American Franciscan History, 1957).

Dominguez, Francisco Atanasio. *The Missions of New Mexico, 1776: A Description, with Other Contemporary Documents* (Albuquerque: University of New Mexico Press, 1956).

Martinez, Thomas D. *Santa Fe Baptisms, 1747–1851: Baptism Database of Archives Held by the Archdiocese of Santa Fe and the State Archives of New Mexico* (San Jose, CA: n.p., 1993).

Ocaranza, Fernando. *Establececimientos Franciscanos en el Misterioso Reino del Nuevo México* (Mexico: n.p., 1934).

Smith, Watson. *Seventeenth-Century Spanish Missions of the Western Pueblo Area* (Tucson: Tucson Corral of the Westerners, 1970). The Western Pueblo area is composed of present-day Arizona, New Mexico, and northern Mexico.

Civil Records and Sources

Spanish archives of New Mexico, 1621–1821 (Santa Fe: State Records Center, 1967, film 0581463). This is a microfilm project sponsored by the National Historical Publications Commission. A selection of the types of manuscripts in the archives are:

- Military activities against Indian attacks, reports from the Villa of Albuquerque, 1707–14
- Indian campaigns, French intrusion into Spanish territory, and Pueblo Indian rights, 1715–22
- Civil and criminal suits of Spanish residents, government records, 1733–40
- Civil and criminal court proceedings, 1741–55
- Civil and criminal petitions, proceedings, and suits, 1756–66
- Local governmental affairs and administration of frontier areas, 1767–79
- Military records, 1780–7
- Census records of 1790, defensive efforts against hostile Indians, 1788–91
- Civil documents, 1792–6
- Correspondence on Indian difficulties, 1797–1802
- Military records of Comanche relations, documents on importation of Mexican weavers, 1803–5

- U.S. Pike expedition and French interference on northern borders, 1806–9
- Civil and service records, 1815–17
- Navajo campaigns, Pueblo Indian matters, 1818–19
- Last documents of Spanish sovereignty, 1820–1

The original records are at the New Mexico Records Center and Archives in Santa Fe.

New Mexico State Records Center and Archives. *Guide to the Microfilm of the Spanish Archives of New Mexico, 1621–1821, in the Archives Division of the State of New Mexico Records Center* (Santa Fe: The Center and Archives, film 0928111).

New Mexico State Records Center and Archives. *Guide to the Microfilm of the Spanish Archives of New Mexico, 1697–1821* (Santa Fe: The Center and Archives, 1967, film 0468381 ff.).

Jenkins, Myra Ellen. *Calendar of the Microfilm Edition of the Mexican Archives of New Mexico, 1821–1846* (Sante Fe: The Center and Archives, 1970, film 0962164). Extant official administrative records of New Mexico under the sovereignty of the Mexican national government from the signing of the Treaty of Córdova, 1821, to the occupation of Santa Fe by United States forces, 1846. The original records are at the New Mexico Records Center and Archives in Santa Fe.

Twitchell, Ralph E. *The Spanish Archives of New Mexico: Compiled and Chronologically Arranged with Historical, Genealogical, Geographical, and Other Annotations, by Authority of the State of New Mexico*. 2 Vols. (Cedar Rapids, IO: Torch Press, 1914, film 0845276).

Land records of the Spanish dominion are at the U.S. Bureau of Land Management in Santa Fe. New Mexico Territory included Colorado until 1861, and Arizona until 1863. The records on film include:
- U.S. Surveyor General, New Mexico. Pueblo grants, 1523–1903 (Albuquerque: University of New Mexico Library, 1955–7, film 1016946). Includes land grants and patents, surveys, and Acoma Pueblo Indians' land dispute.
- Miscellaneous archives relating to New Mexico land grants, 1695–1842 (Albuquerque: University of New Mexico Library, 1955, film 1016947 ff.).
- Twitchell, Ralph E. *The Twitchell Archives, 1685–1898* (Albuquerque: University of New Mexico Library, 1955, film 1016940 ff.). Includes Spanish records in the office of the Surveyor-General, Santa Fe, New Mexico, land grant requests, land disputes, appeals, land grants, wills, judgments, mine claims, inventories, and municipal ordinances.

* Vigil, Donaciano. Vigil's index, 1681–1846 (Albuquerque: University of New Mexico Library, 1955–7, film 1016949). General index of all the documents from the time of the Spanish and Mexican governments until the year 1846.

The original records of the above are at the U.S. Bureau of Land Management in Santa Fe.

Lista de revista de las compañías de Nuevo México, Nueva Vizcaya y Sonora: correspondientes a los meses de Mayo a Diciembre de 1818 (film 1149545). Troop lists for Chihuahua, Durango, and Coahuila, Mexico, and New Mexico. The original records are at the Archivo General de la Nación in Mexico City. For other military records, see Spain.

Diaz, Albert James. *A Guide to the Microfilm of Papers Relating to New Mexico Land Grants* (Albuquerque: University of New Mexico Press, 1960).

Spanish and Mexican Land Grants in New Mexico and Colorado (Manhattan, KS: AG Press, 1980).

Westphall, Victor. *Mercedes Reales: Hispanic Land Grants of the Upper Rio Grande Region* (Albuquerque: University of New Mexico Press, 1983). Area covered is in New Mexico and Colorado.

Olmsted, Virginia Langham. *Spanish and Mexican Censuses of New Mexico, 1750–1830* (Albuquerque: New Mexico Genealogical Society, 1981).

Ortiz, Roxanne Dunbar. "The Roots of Resistance: Pueblo Land Tenure and Spanish Colonization." *International Migration Review* XI (Winter 1975): 4.

Vigil, Julián Josué. *Early Taos Censuses and Historical Sources* (Sante Fe: State Records Center and Archives, 1983, fiche 6331382). This includes a 1790 census for Taos, militia muster rolls of 1806 for Taos, and an 1841 census for Taos; also covered are Taos genealogical materials in the archives of the Archdiocese of Sante Fe, the Huntington Library, San Marino, California, and the Bancroft Library, University of California, Berkeley.

Suggested Reading

Chávez, Thomas E. and Fray Angélico Chávez. *Origins of New Mexico Families: A Genealogy of the Spanish Colonial Period* (Santa Fe: Historical Society of New Mexico, 1954. Reprint. Santa Fe: Museum of New Mexico Press, 1992).

Cruz, Gilberto Rafael. *Let There Be Towns: Spanish Municipal Origins in the American Southwest, 1610–1810* (College Station: Texas A & M University Press, 1988). This includes Arizona, Texas, New Mexico, and California.

Hackett, Charles Wilson. *Historical Documents Relating to New Mexico, Nueva Viscaya, and Approaches Thereto, to 1773* (Washington, DC: Carnegie Institute, 1937).

Hackett, Charles Wilson. *Revolt of the Pueblo Indians of New Mexico and Otermin's Attempted Reconquest, 1680–1682.* 2 Vols. (Albuquerque: University of New Mexico Press, 1942).

Jenkins, Myra Ellen. *Tracing Spanish-American Pedigrees in the Southwestern United States: New Mexico, Texas, Colorado* (Salt Lake City: Genealogical Society of the Church of Jesus Christ of Latter-day Saints, 1969, fiche 6039366).

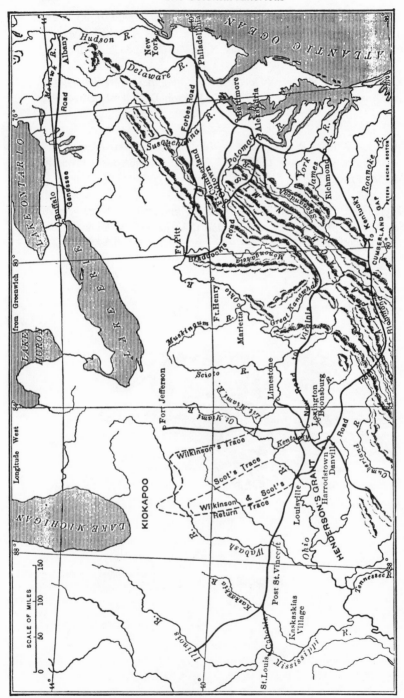

42 Early post roads and canals (Katherine Coman, *The Industrial History of the United States*. New York: Macmillan & Co., 1911)

Ohio

The earliest European claims to the Ohio Valley were made by the French. In 1749 an expedition actually traveled through the area, planting lead markers attesting to that claim. That same year the Ohio Company of Virginia received a charter to land claimed by the British, French, and the Iroquois Confederacy. In 1752 French forces destroyed the British post of Pickawillany (Piqua) and captured Fort Necessity in 1753. In 1763, at the close of the French and Indian War, the area was ceded to Great Britain, and the Ohio Valley was reopened for settlement. A Moravian community was founded in 1772 near the site of present-day New Philadelphia. Ohio was incorporated into the Northwest Territory in 1787 and was part of the U.S. Military District, the Virginia Military District, and was also claimed by Connecticut and Pennsylvania.

U.S. Department of State. Territorial Papers southwest of the River Ohio, 1790–95 (film 1578870/ M0471). The original records are at the National Archives in Washington, DC.

Suggested Reading

Beers, Henry Putney. *The French and British in the Old Northwest: A Bibliographical and Manuscript Source* (Baton Rouge: Louisiana State University Press, 1957).

Belote, Theodore Thomas. *The Scioto Speculation and the French Settlement at Gallipolis* (1907. Reprint. Fort Wayne, IN: Allen County Public Library, n.d., fiche 6048082).

Drake, Samuel Adams. *The Making of the Ohio Valley States, 1660–1837* (1916. Reprint. Fairborn, OH: Cincinnati Branch Library, 1973, film 0925037). This also covers Kentucky, Illinois, Pennsylvania, Indiana, and West Virginia.

SEE ALSO
Illinois
Michigan
New France
Virginia

Green, Karen Mauer. *Pioneer Ohio Newspapers, 1793–1810: Genealogical and Historical Abstracts* (Galveston, TX: Frontier Press, 1986). Contains abstracts of genealogical and historical material from *The*

Centinel of the North-Western Territory; *Freeman's Journal*; *The Western Spy and Hamilton Gazette*; *Freeman's Journal and Chillicothe Advertiser*; and *Scioto Gazette and Chillicothe Advertiser*.

Houck, George Francis. *History of Catholicity in Northern Ohio and in the Diocese of Cleveland from 1749 to December 31, 1900*. 2 Vols. (1903. Reprint. Fort Wayne, IN: Allen County Public Library, 1983, fiche 6048435 ff.).

Ohio Country Missionary: The Diary of David McClure, 1748–1820 (1899. Reprint. Camden, ME: Penobscot Press, 1996).

Ohio Vital Records, 1750–1880s (Broderbund, 1997). This CD-ROM contains images from *Ohio Cemetery Records, Ohio Source Records*, and *Ohio Marriages*, published by Genealogical Publishing Company. The material was originally published in *The Old Northwest Genealogical Quarterly* and the *Ohio Genealogical Quarterly*.

Scamyhorn, Richard and John Steinle. *Stockades in the Wilderness: The Frontier Defenses and Settlements of Southwestern Ohio, 1788–1795* (Dayton, OH: Landfall Press, 1986).

Taylor, James Wickes. *History of the State of Ohio: First Period, 1650–1787* (Cincinnati: H.W. Derby, 1854, film 0940920).

Zeisberger, David. *Diary of David Zeisberger: A Moravian Missionary Among the Indians of Ohio*. 2 Vols. (1885 Reprint. Saint Clair Shores, MI: Scholarly Press, 1972, film 1697367). The localities include Ohio, Michigan, and Ontario.

Tennessee

 In 1682 the French built a trading post at Fort Prud'homme, situated on the confluence of the Hatchie and Mississippi rivers. French soldiers were garrisoned at Fort Assumption (Memphis), built in 1739. The British built Fort Loudon in 1759, but all the inhabitants were massacred in 1760. After 1763 the French ceded all land claims in the area to Great Britain,

In 1769 settlers from North Carolina and Virginia established the first permanent settlement in the Watauga Valley, including a group of Regulators from Orange County (North Carolina). The Watauga settlement became the Washington District of North Carolina in 1776, and a county by that name in 1777 (and also part of Rowan County). In 1784 the state of Franklin was laid out by land ceded from South Carolina, but North Carolina refused to recognize the new state. Tennessee was ceded to the U.S. in 1790 and became part of the Southwest Territory. In 1795 Spain built Fort San Fernando de las Barrancas on the Chickasaw Bluffs, site of present-day Memphis.

Civil Records and Sources

Early records in Tennessee are in the North Carolina and Tennessee state archives and in the county courthouses.

Secretary of State, North Carolina. List of North Carolina land grants in Tennessee 1778-91 (film 10024541/ M0068). The original records are at the National Archives in Washington, DC.

Governor, Tennessee. Land grants, 1775–1905 (Nashville: State Library and Archives, 1976, film 1002725 ff). The land that is now Tennessee was part of North Carolina until 1790. The original records are at the Tennessee State Library and Archives in Nashville.

Burgner, Goldene Fillers. *North Carolina Land Grants in Tennessee, 1778–1791* (Easley, SC: Southern Historical Press, 1981).

McCown, Mary Hardin. *The Wataugah Purchase, March 19, 1775 at Sycamore Shoals of Wataugah River: The Cherokee Indians to Charles Robertson, Trustee for the Wataugah Settlers, an Index of the Wataugah Purchase, the North Carolina Land Grants and Deeds Through 1782* (Johnson City, TN: Overmountain Press, 1976, film 1036062).

SEE ALSO
Kentucky
North Carolina
Virginia

Pruitt, Albert Bruce. *Spartanburg County/District, South Carolina, Deed Abstracts . . . 1785–1827* (Easley, SC: Southern Historical Press, 1988). The deeds in this book were recorded in books from 1785 to 1827; the money changed hands from 1752 to 1827. The localities include South Carolina, North Carolina, Georgia, and Tennessee.

McGhee, Lucy Kate. *Partial Census of 1787 to 1791 of Tennessee as Taken from the North Carolina Land Grants* (Washington, DC: The Author, n.d., film 1728882 ff.).

Davidson County (established 1783 from Washington County)
Original records at the Davidson County Courthouse in Nashville are:
* Daily minutes and court minutes, 1783–1929 (film 0205435 ff.).
* Deeds, 1784–1946 (film 0392082 ff.).
* Wills, 1784–1941 (film 0200252 ff.).
* Marriage licenses and bonds, 1789–1886 (film 1994117 ff.).

Greene County (established 1783 from Washington County)
Original records at the Greene County Courthouse in Greeneville are:
* Court minutes, 1783–1908 (film 0944389).
* Deeds, 1785–1887 (film 0944411 ff.).
* Marriages, 1780–1947 (film 0944386 ff.).

Burgner, Goldene Fillers. *North Carolina Land Grants Recorded in Greene County, Tennessee* (Easley, SC: Southern Historical Press, 1981).

Burgner, Goldene Fillers. *Greene County, Tennessee, Wills, 1783–1890* (Easley, SC: Southern Historical Press, 1981).

Hawkins County (established 1787 from Sullivan County)
Original records at the Hawkins County Courthouse in Rogersville are:
* Deeds, 1787–1894 (film 0972798 ff.).

Bell, Annie W.B. *Hawkins County, Tennessee Marriages and Wills, 1786–1851* (n.p., 1934, film 0896967).

Hawkins County Genealogical and Historical Society. *Hawkins County, Tennessee, Marriage Records, 1789–1866: Bride and Groom Index* (Rogersville, TN: The Society, 1994, fiche 6126140).

Sullivan County (established 1779 from Washington County)
Original records at the Sullivan County Courthouse in Blountsville are:
* Deeds, 1775–1894 (film 0972701 ff.).

Sumner County (established 1787 from Davidson County)
Original records at the State Library and Archives in Nashville are:
* Deeds, 1783–1967, land plat books, 1786–1833 (film 0467510 ff.).
* Tax list, 1787–94, Sumner County, Tennessee (film 0024839).
* County Court minutes, 1787–1805 (film 0024837).
Original records at the Sumner County Courthouse in Gallatin are:
* Marriage records, 1787–1915 (film 0969843 ff.).
* Will books, 1789–1967 (film 0467505 ff.).

Tennessee County (established 1788 from Davidson County, abolished 1796)
Original records at the State Library and Archives in Nashville are:
* Montgomery County Register of Deeds. Index to deeds, 1786–1869 (film 0320851), deeds 1789–1805 (film 0320857). There are also Tennessee County records at the Montgomery County Courthouse in Clarksville.

Washington County (established 1777 from Washington District)
Original records at the Washington County Courthouse in Jonesboro are:
* Court minute books, 1778–1913 (film 0825510 ff.).
* Deeds, 1782–1887 (film 0825522 ff.).
* Wills and inventories, 1778–1889 (film 0825521 ff.).
* Tax books, 1778–1885 (film 0825545 ff.).
* Marriage records, 1787–1962 (film 0825502 ff.).

Suggested Reading

Coker, C.F. *Records Relating to Tennessee in the North Carolina State Archives* (Raleigh: The Archives, 1980).

Durham, Walter T. *Before Tennessee: The Southwest Territory, 1790–1796, a Narrative History of the Territory of the United States South of the River Ohio* (Piney Flats, TN: Rocky Mount Historical Association, 1990, fiche 6101361).

Garrett, W. R. *History of the South Carolina Cession and the Northern Boundary of Tennessee* (Nashville: Southern Methodist Publishing House, 1884, fiche 6101131).

Hamer, Philip May. *Tennessee, a History, 1673–1932* (1933. Reprint. Tucson, AZ: W.C. Cox, 1974, film 1000311).

Norton, Herman A. *Religion in Tennessee, 1777–1945* (Knoxville: University of Tennessee Press, 1981).

Ramsey, James Gettys McGready. *The Annals of Tennessee to the End of the Eighteenth Century: Comprising its Settlement, as the Watauga Association, from 1769 to 1777; a Part of North Carolina, from 1777 to 1784; the State of Franklin, from 1788 to 1790; the Territory of the U.S., South of the Ohio, from 1790 to 1796; the State of Tennessee, from 1796 to 1800* (Charleston, SC: Walker and James, 1853. Reprint. n.p., 1967, film 0024525).

Williams, Samuel Cole. *History of the Lost State of Franklin* (New York: Press of the Pioneers, 1933, film 1000311).

Texas

Spanish settlements in Texas usually began as a mission, progressing to a presidio (military post), and then a pueblo (civil settlement). The first settlement in Texas was a Franciscan mission in the El Paso area in 1659, and the first permanent was a presidio at El Paso in 1682. French established the rival settlement of Fort Saint Louis on Matagordo Bay in 1685. It was destroyed by the Karankawas tribe in 1689.

The missions of San Francisco de los Tejas and Santísimo Nombre de Mária were founded on the Neches River in 1690. A Spanish governor was appointed to administer Texas as an interior province of Nuevo España (Mexico) in 1691. The Hasinai tribe, also known as the Tejas, drove the missionaries out in 1693. The next mission founded was San Juan Bautista in 1700. The presidios of San Francisco de los Dolores, San Miguel de los Adaes, and Dolores de los Ais were founded in 1716. The presidio of San Antonio de Bejár was built in 1718. In 1731 Canary Islanders from Tenerife arrived at San Antonio. Laredo was founded in 1749 and Nacogdoches in 1779.

In 1803 the United States considered Texas to be part of the Louisiana Purchase. A force of Americans and Mexicans captured San Antonio in 1813 and proclaimed Texas an independent nation, but the rebellion was crushed. Royalist forces were defeated in 1821, and the Republic of Mexico was proclaimed in 1822. Texas became a separate republic in 1836 and was annexed by the U.S. in 1845.

Ecclesiastical Records and Sources

Parish registers can be found in parish, diocesan, and archdiocesan archives in Texas and Mexico. Examples are:

Catholic Church.
- San Fernando Cathedral Missions, San Antonio. Parish registers, 1731–1860 (El Paso: Golightly Co., 1957, film 0025433 ff.). This includes Misión de la Purisima Concepcion, Misión de la San Jose, San Juan y San Francisco, and Misión de San Antonio de Valero.

SEE ALSO
California
Louisiana
Mexico
New Mexico
Spain

621

- San Fernando Cathedral, San Antonio. Parish registers, 1703–1957 (El Paso: Golightly Co., 1957, film 0025438 ff.).

The original records are at the Archdiocese of San Antonio.

Guerra, Raul J., Nadine M. Vasquez, and Baldomero Vela. *Index to the Marriage Investigations of the Diocese of Guadalajara Pertaining to the Former Provinces of Coahuila, Nuevo León, Nuevo Santander, and Téxas* (Edinburg, TX: The Authors, 1989). Printed in cooperation with the Rio Grande Valley Historical Collection, this also includes Coahuila, Nuevo León, Nayarit, and Jalisco, Mexico.

Habig, Marion Alphonse. *The Alamo Chain of Missions: A History of San Antonio's Five Old Missions* (Chicago: Franciscan Herald Press, 1968).

Civil Records and Sources
Records for Texas can be found at archives in Spain, national and state archives in Mexico, archives in Texas, Louisiana, the Bancroft Library at the University of California, Berkeley, and the University of New Mexico, Albuquerque.

There are early census records at the Archivo General de Indias in Seville, Spain. They have been abstracted in:
- Salazar, J. Richard. *El Paso Census, 1684* (Albuquerque: The Author, 1992).
- Salazar, J. Richard. *1692 Population Census of El Paso* (Albuquerque: The Author, 1992).

The Bexar Archives of the Province of Texas and the Mexican State of Coahuila y Texas, for the years, 1717–1836, are at the Texas History Center, University of Texas at Austin, and at the Bexar County Archives in San Antonio. The former have been filmed and are described in Benavides, Adán. *The Bexar Archives, 1717–1836* (San Antonio: University of Texas at Austin, 1989). Localities documented in the records also cover La Bahía, Nacogdoches, and the Texas- Louisiana border. The records taken from the papers of the viceroys of New Spain and the governors of Texas include census records, deeds, slave sales, trade reports, tax lists, judicial records, mission records, militia reports and pay lists, soldiers' petitions for marriage, arrest warrants, marriage records, and wills and estates.

Kielman, Chester Valls. *Guide to the Microfilm Edition of the Bexar Archives.* 3 Vols. (Austin: University of Texas, 1967–71). The microfilmed records cover the years 1717–1836.

De Mézièeres, Athanase. *Athanase de Mézièeres and the Louisiana-Texas Frontier, 1768–1780: Documents Published for the First Time, from the Original Spanish and French Manuscripts, Chiefly in the Archives of Mexico and Spain.* 2 Vols. (1914. Reprint. New York: Kraus Reprint, 1970).

Mauro, Garry. *Guide to Spanish and Mexican Land Grants in South Texas* (Austin: Texas General Land Office, 1988).

Miller, Thomas Lloyd. *The Public Lands of Texas, 1519–1970* (Norman: University of Oklahoma Press, 1972).

Taylor, Virginia H. *Index to Spanish and Mexican Land Grants in Texas* (Austin: Lone Star Press, 1974).

Suggested Reading

Almaráz, Félix D., Jr. *The San Antonio Missions and Their System of Land Tenure* (Austin: University of Texas Press, 1989).

Bancroft, Hubert Howe. *History of the North Mexican States and Texas, 1531–1889.* 2 Vols. (1889. Reprint. New York: Arno Press, 1967, film 0982471).

Chipman, Donald E. *Spanish Texas, 1519–1821* (Austin: University of Texas Press, 1992).

Corbin, John. *Catalog of Genealogical Materials in Texas Libraries* (Austin: Texas State Library and Historical Commission, 1965, fiche 6051116).

Cruz, Gilberto Rafael. *Let There Be Towns: Spanish Municipal Origins in the American Southwest, 1610–1810* (College Station: Texas A & M University Press, 1988). This also includes New Mexico and California.

Duaine, Carl Laurence. *Caverns of Oblivion* (Corpus Christi, TX: The Author, 1971). Commentary and English translations of writings concerning the Spanish settlement of Northern Mexico and Texas in the sixteenth and seventeenth centuries.

Fish, Jean Y. *José Vasquez Borrego and la Hacienda de Nuestra Señora de Dolores* (Zapata, TX: Zapata County Historical Society, n.d., fiche 6105007). Nuestra Señora de Dolores was created in 1750 and no longer exists.

Gómez Canedo, Lino. *Primeras Exploraciones y Poblamiento de Texas, 1686–1694* (Monterrey, Mexico: Instituto Tecnológico y de Estudios Superiores de Monterrey, 1968). Early exploration and colonization of Texas.

Ladrón de Guevara, Antonio. *Noticias de los Poblados de que se Componen el Nuevo Reino de León, Provincia de Coahuila, Nueva-Extremadura, y la de Téxas* (Monterrey, Mexico: Instituto Tecnológico y de Estudios Superiores de Monterrey, 1969, film 1224515). Geographical and historical information about localities in the northeastern frontier region of the Viceroyalty of New Spain in the eighteenth century.

López Jiménez, Eucario. *Cedulario de la Nueva Galicia* (Guadalajara, Mexico: Editorial Lex, 1971, film 0873667). Decrees of Nueva Galicia, which once comprised the present states of Texas, Jalisco, Zacatecas, Aguascalientes, Durango, San Luis Potisí, Nuevo León, Coahuila, Tamaulipas, Guanajuato, and Nayarit.

Picazo Muntaner, Antoni. *Mallorquines en la Colonización de Téxas* (Palma de Mallorca, Spain: El Tall Edition, 1993). Majorcans in the colonization of Texas in the late seventeenth and early eighteenth centuries.

Sturmberg, Robert. *History of San Antonio and of the Early Days in Texas* (San Antonio: Saint Joseph's Society, 1920).

SCENE IN TEXAS.

Wisconsin

Wisconsin's first European settlers were Jesuits who established a mission at De Pere in 1672. French fur traders from Canada built a trading post at Green Bay in 1684. In 1763 the area was ceded by France to Great Britain. Wisconsin became part of the Northwest Territory in 1787 and the Michigan Territory in 1818.

Ecclesiastical and Civil Records and Sources

Draper, Lyman Copeland. *Draper Manuscript Collection, 1600–1883* (Chicago: University of Chicago Library, n.d., film 0889097 ff.). The papers cover Kentucky, New York, Illinois, Indiana, Virginia, Tennessee, and Wisconsin. The original records are at the State Historical Society of Wisconsin in Madison.

State Historical Society of Wisconsin. *Descriptive List of Manuscript Collections of the State Historical Society of Wisconsin Together with Reports on Other Collections of Manuscript Material for American History in Adjacent States* (Madison: The Society, 1906, film 0368687).

Suggested Reading

Kellogg, Louise P. *The French Régime in Wisconsin and the Northeast* (Madison: State Historical Society of Wisconsin, 1925).

Lareau, Paul L. and Elmer Courteau. *French-Canadian Families of the North Central States: A Genealogical Dictionary.* 8 Vols. (Saint Paul: Northwest Territory French and Canadian Heritage Institute, 1980, fiche 6010503-11).

Quaife, Milo Milton. *Wisconsin: Its History and its People 1634–1924.* 4 Vols. (Chicago: S.J. Clarke Publishing Co., 1924, fiche 6046726).

Rentmeester, Les. *The Wisconsin Fur-Trade People* (Melbourne, FL: The Author, 1991, film 1750767).

Thwaites, Reuben Gold and Louise Phelps Kellogg. *Documentary History of Dunmore's War, 1774* (Madison: State Historical Society of Wisconsin, 1905, film 0564367).

SEE ALSO
Illinois
New France
Rupert's Land

Compiled from the Draper Manuscripts at the library of the State Historical Society of Wisconsin.

Part Six

Canada

43 New France (*Delisle Atlas*, 1703)

New France

Two separate French colonies were the first permanent settlements in New France: Acadia in 1605 and Quebec in 1608. In 1534 French explorers arrived at the Gulf of Saint Lawrence. A colony was briefly established there in 1541. The first fur trading expeditions began in 1581. From 1600 to 1607 a French trading post operated on the Saguenay River. Quebec was founded by French fur traders in 1608 on the Saint Lawrence River. These were the only permanent settlements in New France for twenty-six years (Acadia was a separate colony). A viceroyalty was instituted in 1613. The first Recollects (Franciscan missionaries) arrived in 1615. Jesuits joined the missionary effort in 1625 and received a land grant at Notre-Dame-des-Agnes. The *Compagnie de Cens Associes* (Company of One Hundred Associates) was organized in 1627 and purchased the rights to grant land and control the fur trade in New France. The colony was captured by the English in 1629 but returned to France by treaty in 1632.

Trois Rivières (Three Rivers) and Montréal were established as trading posts in 1634. From 1646 to 1649 fur trading and efforts of the missionaries were continually hampered by Indian wars and attacks. The charter of the *Compagnie de Cens Associes* was revoked in 1663, and Quebec was declared a Royal province. The English established trading posts on James Bay and Hudson Bay in 1670. The French built Fort-de-la-Baie-des-Puants (Green Bay, Wisconsin) the same year, and two forts on Lake Ontario: Fort Frontenac (1673), and Fort Niagara (1676). Over the next three years the French fur trade expanded to a series of posts on the Illinois River. Fur trade into the interior of Canada was legalized by France in 1681.

By the Treaty of Utrecht in 1713, France recognized Great Britain's claims on the Hudson Bay. The British built their first fort on the Great Lakes: Fort Oswego (New York) in 1725. The French built Fort Bourbon on Lake Winnipeg in 1739. British troops seized Quebec in 1759 and burned many farms in the area. A British military government was established in 1763 when France ceded the colony to Great Britain. The Quebec Act in 1774 established the boundaries of Quebec northward to include Labrador, southward to the Ohio River, and westward to the

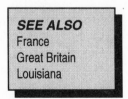

SEE ALSO
France
Great Britain
Louisiana

Mississippi River. French common law was continued, except in cases of criminal proceedings or the settlement of an English will. The seigneurial land system was also left in place, and Catholics were allowed to practice their beliefs, subject to the King of Great Britain. A group of Loyalists settled along the Richelieu River in 1783.

In 1783 the Treaty of Paris established the boundary between the United States and British North America. Most of the United Empire Loyalists settled in Nova Scotia, the western shore of the Saint Lawrence River, and the area that became known as Upper Canada. Some of these Loyalists were instrumental in creating the Province of New Brunswick in 1784. Cape Breton Island also became a province. The Constitutional or Canada Act was passed by the British Parliament in 1791, dividing Quebec into the provinces of Upper and Lower Canada. Lower Canada retained French civil law and the seigneurial system for previously titled land; Upper Canada received British law and freehold land tenure.

Rebellions in Lower Canada in 1837 and in Upper Canada in 1836 did not succeed in establishing a government that would be more democratic in form. British Parliament passed the Act of Union in 1841, creating the United Province of Canada. Lower and Upper Canada were now called Canada East and Canada West. In 1842 the boundary was settled between Maine and New Brunswick and in 1846 between Oregon and the Hudson's Bay Company. In 1867 the British North America Act created the Dominion of Canada, comprising the provinces of Quebec, Ontario, Nova Scotia, and New Brunswick.

Canada a.k.a. (also known as) what?

One of the most confusing aspects of research in Canada is keeping track of the changes of place names from the sixteenth through twentieth centuries.[48] Some of the most important are:

Canada: New France (also included North America south to Louisiana); Province of Quebec, British North America, Upper and Lower Canada, Province of Canada, Dominion of Canada.

Province of Alberta: Rupert's Land, Northwest Territories, Athabasca District (part), Alberta District (part), Mackenzie District (part).

Province of British Columbia: Rupert's Land, New Caledonia, Columbia, Colony of British Columbia, Colony of Vancouver Island (part).

---

[48]For more information see Donald G. Kerr, *Historical Atlas of Canada*. (Don Mills, ON: Thomas Nelson and Sons, 1975).

Province of Manitoba: Rupert's Land, Red River settlement.

Province of New Brunswick: Acadia, Acadie, Nouveau-Brunswick, Province of Nova Scotia, Atlantic Canada, The Maritimes.

Province of Newfoundland and Labrador: Terre-Neuve, The Colony of Newfoundland and Labrador, Atlantic Canada.

Province of Nova Scotia: Acadia, Acadie, Port Royal, Île-Royale (Cape Breton), New Scotland, Colony of Cape Breton (part), Atlantic Canada, The Maritimes.

Province of Ontario: Québec, Upper Canada, Canada West, Keewatin District (part).

Province of Prince Edward Island: Acadia, Acadie, Île-Saint-Jean, Island of Saint John, Province of Nova Scotia, Atlantic Canada, The Maritimes.

Province of Quebec: Québec, Saint Lawrence Valley, Eastern Townships (part), Lower Canada, Canada East, Ungava District (part).

Province of Saskatchewan: Rupert's Land, Northwest Territories, Saskatchewan District, Assiniboia District (part), Athabasca District (part), Mackenzie District (part).

Northwest Territories: Rupert's Land.

Yukon Territory: Rupert's Land, Northwest Territories.

Military Records and Sources
French Records
Some military records of the French dominion are at the National Archives in Ottawa. They are in manuscript form and on film:

* *Troupes de colonies*, 1627–1758: colonial troop lists.
* *Personnel militaire et civil*, 1685–1765: civil officers, military officers, clergy, etc.
* *Dossiers personnels*, 1626–1816: salaries, promotions, pensions, service records, land grants, vital records, and notarial records.

Records of the French soldiers who served in America during the French and Indian War (*Guerie de Sept Ans*) from 1758–63, are at the Archives Nationales du Québec in Sainte-Foy. The most famous of the French regiments is the Carignan-Salières Regiment, which was sent to Canada in 1665 to secure the colony from Mohawk and Iroquois attacks. About a third of the soldiers remained in Canada permanently.

Roy, Régis. *Le Régiment de Carignan, Son Organisation et Son Expédition au Canada (1665–1668), Officiers et Soldats qui s'Établirent en Canada* (Montreal: G. Ducharme, 1925, film 1320669). The Carignan regiment, its organization and its expedition into Canada, including the officers and soldiers who established themselves in Canada.

Verney, Jack. *The Good Regiment: The Carignan-Salières Regiment in Canada, 1665–1668* (Montreal: McGill-Queen's University Press, 1991).

Gallup, Andrew. *La Marine: The French Colonial Soldier in Canada, 1745–1761* (Bowie, MD: Heritage Books, 1992).

Sulte, Benjamin. *Histoire de la Milice Canadienne-Française, 1760–1897* (Montreal: Desbarats, 1897). History of the French-Canadian militia, 1760–1897.

British Records

The records of British forces in North America — including American Loyalist regiments — at the National Archives in Ottawa, Ontario are known as the "C" Series. These are original records of the British Army that were left behind when the last of the British garrisons were removed from Canada in 1873. The records contain correspondence of the Military Secretary of the Commander of the Forces, 1767–1870, records of the Canadian Command, 1785–1883, records of the Nova Scotia Command, 1762–1899, some American Loyalist regiment muster rolls, 1777–83, records of some Canadian militia units from the War of 1812, the Rebellions of 1837–8, and other miscellaneous military records, 1757–1896. Two important record groups in the "C" Series for this time period are the records of Department of Militia and Defence, (RG 9), and the records of British forces in Canada (RG 8). Royal Navy and Royal Marine records, 1813–67, are also in the "C" Series.

Army, Great Britain. Muster rolls, 1777–83 (Ottawa: National Archives, 1969 film 1689400 ff.). The rolls pertain to British forces, including American Loyalist regiments, in North America during the Revolutionary War. The original records are part of the "C" Series (RG 8) at the National Archives in Ottawa, Ontario. The units included in this series are:

American Legion	Loyal New Englanders
British Legion	Maryland Loyalists
Chasseurs	Nassau Blues
Delancey's Brigade	New Jersey Volunteers
Guides and Pioneers	New York Volunteers
Light Dragoons	Pennsylvania Loyalists
King's American Dragoons	Philadelphia Dragoons
King's American Regiment	Provincial Light Infantry
King's Orange Raiders	Prince of Wales American Regiment
Kingston Naval Depot	Roman Catholic Volunteers
Loyal American Regiment	Royal American Reformers
Loyal Foresters	Royal Fencible American Regiment

Royal Garrison Battalion
Queen's Rangers
South Carolina Dragoons
South Carolina Rangers

South Carolina Royalists
Volunteers of Ireland
Volunteers of New England

British forces in Canada, 1815–62 (Ottawa: National Archives, 1969, film 0928947). The original records in Series "C" (RG 8) are at the National Archives in Ottawa, Ontario.

The British military records, "C" Series, 1757–1896 have been indexed (film 1683760 ff.). Each entry has a "C" number following the catalog description. They are the National Archives of Canada film numbers. The "C" numbers listed on the index cards are the volume numbers of the "C" Series.

The records of the British Army, 1760–1900 (film 0868535 ff.), also known as the "Regular Soldiers' Documents," are only for soldiers who were pensioned out, not those who died in service. They contain information on age, birthplace, and trade or occupation on enlistment, and a record of service, including any decorations and the reason for discharge to pension. They are arranged by the number or name of the regiment. Many of these records are for regiments that served in North America. The original records are in the War Office Papers (WO 97) at the PRO in Kew, Surrey, England. Film copies of the North American regiments only are at the National Archives in Ottawa, Ontario and the Archives of Ontario in Toronto. The regiments in this series (except for the African regiments) are:

Battalion Rifle Brigade
County Militia
Foot Guards
Life Guards
Garrison Battalion
Garrison Company
King's German Legion
King's German Legion, Hussars
Regiments of Foot (105 regiments)
Royal Battalion of Veterans
Royal Newfoundland Companies

Royal Regiment of Fencibles
Royal Regiment of Veterans
Royal Regiment of Wagon Train
Royal Sappers and Miners
Royal Staff Corps (recruiting staffs)
Royal West India Rangers Regiment of
    Infantry
Royal York Rangers Regiment of Infantry
Saint Helena Regiment of Foot
York Light Infantry
Miscellaneous regiments

These records have been published by the List and Index Society, in Volume 201, *War Office: Regular Army Soldiers' Documents, 1760–1913* (London: Swifts Printers, 1983).

Kitzmiller, John M. *In Search of the Forlorn Hope: A Comprehensive Guide to Locating British Regiments and Their Records, 1640–WWI.* 2 Vols. Supp. (Salt Lake City: Manuscript Publishing Foundation, 1988).

Crowder, Norman J. *British Army Pensioners Abroad, 1772–1899* (Baltimore: Genealogical Publishing Co., 1993). This work indexes the Chelsea regimental pension registers of British veterans who settled abroad on an army pension. They have been abstracted from the War Office Papers (WO 120) at the PRO in Kew, Surrey, England.

Perkins, Roger. *Regiments: Regiments and Corps of the British Empire and Commonwealth, 1758–1993, a Critical Bibliography of Their Published Histories* (Newton Abbot, Devon: The Author, 1994).

Stewart, Charles H. *The Service of British Regiments in Canada and North America: A Resumé* (Ottawa: Department of National Defence, 1962). This identifies the British regiments that served in North America and where they were posted.

Whitfield, Carol M. *Tommy Atkins: The British Soldier in Canada, 1759–1870* (Ottawa: National Historic Parks and Sites Branch, 1981).

Five battalions of German mercenaries, "Hessians," that served in the British Army during the American Revolution claimed land grants in Canada at the end of the war.

DeMarce, Virginia. *An Annotated List of 317 Former German Soldiers Who Chose to Remain in Canada after the American Revolution* (n.p., 1981, fiche 6101457). The names were taken from Lower Canada land petitions (RG 1).

DeMarce, Virginia. *German Military Settlers in Canada, After the American Revolution* (Sparta, WI: Joy Reisinger, 1984).

Smith, Clifford Neal. *British and German Deserters, Dischargees, and Prisoners of War Who May Have Remained in Canada and the United States* (McNeal, AZ: Westland Publications, 1988). The names have been taken from the War Office Papers (WO 12) muster rolls at the PRO in Kew, Surrey, England for the period beginning about 1774 (if the military unit was already stationed in America) to 1783, when the British units were withdrawn from American soil at the end of the Revolution.

Merz, Johannes Helmut. *Register of German Military Men Who Remained in Canada after the American Revolution* (Hamilton, ON: German Canadian Historical Book Publishers, 1993, film 1697953).

Wihelmy, Jean-Pierre. *German Mercenaries in Canada* (Quebec: La Maison des Mots, 1985).

Cruikshank, E. A. *Inventory of the Military Documents in the Canadian Archives* (Ottawa: Government Printing Bureau, 1910, film 1421600).

A Compilation of Things Naval and Military (Hamilton, ON: Hamilton Branch, OGS, n.d.). Muster rolls, nominal lists, sleigh lists, reserve militia rolls, and oaths of allegiance.

Canadian volunteers also served in British forces in the War of 1812. Their records are included in the filmed War Office Papers at the PRO in Kew, Surrey, England and the National Archives in Ottawa, Ontario.

Jonasson, Eric. *Canadian Veterans of the War of 1812* (Winnipeg, MB: Wheatfield Press, 1981).

Militia Records
Militia in Upper Canada were organized in the eighteenth century by county regiment. Annual muster rolls were taken. Most of the early muster rolls are at the National Archives in Ottawa, Ontario.

Elliott, Bruce S., Dan Walker, and Fawne Stratford-Devai. *Men of Upper Canada: Militia Nominal Rolls, 1828–1829* (Toronto: Ontario Genealogical Society, 1995). The returns are at the National Archives in Ottawa, Ontario Series "C," among other militia nominal rolls (RG 9, I-B-2, Vols. 29–31), but have not been filmed.

Files, Angela. *Militia Roll, Upper Canada Gazette, May 11, 1826* (Brantford, ON: Brant County Branch, OGS, 1989). Soldiers who died or were disabled in 1812–15, from various districts in Ontario.

Index des Miliciens, 1812–14 (Sainte-Foy, PQ: Ministère des Affaires Culturelles, Archives Nationales du Québec, 1983, fiche 6334280). Index of the militia of the War of 1812. The original records are at the Archives Nationales du Québec in Sainte-Foy.

United Empire Loyalists (UE)
American colonials who remained loyal to the King sought refuge in other British colonies both during and after the American Revolution. The majority of them went to Nova Scotia and New Brunswick (30,000), and the Province of Quebec in Upper Canada and the Bay of Quinte (10,000). Some refugees also emigrated to the West Indies and Bermuda.

Loyalist Lists

In 1796 an attempt was made to create a definitive list of Loyalists entitled to free Crown land. Such a list was compiled by the Commissioner of Crown Lands: it included names, residences, and also the names of descendants of the Loyalists. The original list is at the Archives of Ontario in Toronto; a second list is at the National Archives in Ottawa, Ontario. The lists are known as the District Rolls and the UE Lists (Executive Council UE list and Crown Lands list; Old UE list). For lists of Loyalists in the Bahamas (Colonial Office Papers, CO 23/25), see the Bahamas.

United Empire Loyalist Centennial Committee, Toronto. *The Centennial of the Settlement of Upper Canada by the United Empire Loyalists, 1784–1884: The Celebrations at Adolphustown, Toronto and Niagara, with an Appendix Containing a Copy of the U.E. List, Preserved in the Crown Lands Department at Toronto* (Toronto: Rose Publishing Co., film 0924058). This has been republished under the title, *The Old United Empire Loyalists List* (Baltimore: Genealogical Publishing Co., 1969).

Fitzgerald, E. Keith. *Lieutenant Governor John Graves Simcoe's District Loyalist Rolls, 1796–1803* (n.p. 1985, fiche 6104008). The rolls include the following districts: Eastern, Midland (1796, includes British soldiers and discharged German soldiers), Home or Niagara (1797), Home (1796, 1797), Western (1796); and provisions list, Loyalists setters at Niagara, 1784–5. These are transcriptions of material at National Archives in Ottawa, Ontario.

Fitzgerald, E. Keith. *Loyalist Lists: Over 2,000 Loyalist Names and Families from the Haldimand Papers* (Toronto: Ontario Genealogical Society, 1984).

Fitzgerald, E. Keith. *Ontario People, 1796–1803* (Baltimore: Genealogical Publishing Co., 1993). The files are usually called the District Loyalist Rolls of 1796. A proclamation issued on 6 April 1796 required Loyalists to surrender their land certificates in exchange for title deeds and to make a statement under oath in the district court as to their right to hold them. These rolls were made by local Justices of the Peace.

Pringle, Jacob Farrand. *Lunenburgh, Or, the Old Eastern District, its Settlement and Early Progress: With Personal Recollections of the Town of Cornwall, from 1824, to Which Are Added a History of the King's Royal Regiment of New York and Other Corps, the Names of All Those Who Drew Lands in the Counties of Stormont, Dundas and Glengarry* (Cornwall, ON: Standard Printing House, 1890, film 0874425).

Loyalist Claims

Those who remained loyal to the King submitted claims for losses suffered during the American Revolution. The records are in the Audit Series (AO) at the PRO in Kew, Surrey, England. One series (AO 12) describes the claims for losses. Another series (AO 13) is the evidence presented by the claimants. For Loyalist claims of the East Florida Claims Commission, Treasury Office Papers (T 77), see Florida. Treasury Office Papers also contain claims for Jamaica and the Bahamas, 1780–1835 (T 50), 1777–1841(T 77), 1776–1831 (AO 12), and 1780–1835 (AO 13).

The American Loyalist Claims Commission reviewed claims of British subjects who remained loyal to the Crown during the American Revolution. Records of claims (memorials, certificates, accounts, and vouchers) submitted by British citizens in America, the Bahamas, and Canada for losses sustained during the American Revolution have been filmed in two series. The localities included in these claims are: the Bahamas, Connecticut, Florida, Georgia, Maryland, Massachusetts, New Brunswick, New Hampshire, New Jersey, New York, North Carolina, Nova Scotia, Pennsylvania, Rhode Island, South Carolina, Vermont, and Virginia.[49]

- American Loyalist claims (AO 12), 1776–1831, Series I (London: PRO, 1972, film 1401498 ff.). This series is indexed by name of the claimants.
- American Loyalist claims (AO 13), 1730–1835, Series II (London: PRO, 1960-2 (film 0944044 ff.).
- American Loyalist claims, 1777–1841 (T 79). Duplication of papers in the AO series, and lists of papers of claimants, 1777–1804.

Coldham, Peter W. *American Loyalist Claims, Volume I, Abstracted from the Public Record Office Audit Series (AO 13), Bundles 1–35, and 37* (Washington, DC: National Genealogical Society, 1980, fiche 6051361 ff.).

Dwyer, Clifford S. *Index to Series II of American Loyalist Claims [1730–1835]* (DeFuniak Springs, FL: Ram Publishing, 1985, film 1698293).

Antliff, W. Bruce. *Loyalist Settlements, 1783–1789: New Evidence of Canadian Loyalist Claims* (Toronto: Ministry of Citizenship and Culture, 1985, fiche 6101708). Information is transcribed from records found at the PRO in Kew, Surrey, England and the Library of Congress in Washington, DC. The records concern Nova Scotia, New Brunswick, Quebec, and Ontario.

---

[49]For additional information on Loyalist claims in Nova Scotia and Florida, see the respective sections in this book.

Crowder, Norman Kenneth. *Early Ontario Settlers: A Source Book* (Baltimore: Genealogical Publishing Co., 1993). Compilation of a number of official documents about people who settled in Ontario in the 1780s: discharged British and German servicemen, American Loyalists who served in provincial regiments or who aided the British cause in various ways, and some refugees; includes provisioning lists for 1784 and 1786.

Fryer, Mary Beacock. *King's Men: The Soldier Founders of Ontario* (Toronto: Dundurn Press, 1980).

Holmes, Theodore C. *Loyalists to Canada: The 1783 Settlement of Quakers and Others at Passamaquoddy* (Camden, ME: Picton Press, 1992). Loyalists' settlements around Passamaquoddy Bay, Charlotte County, New Brunswick.

Nominal Rolls (Military)

The Nominal rolls in the "C" Series at the National Archives in Ottawa, Ontario and the War Office Papers (WO 28) at the PRO in Kew, Surrey, England contain muster rolls and pay lists of Loyalist regiments. Other military records can be found in the Haldimand Papers (1758–85) and the Bouquet Papers (1757–65), available on film at the National Archives in Ottawa, Ontario and the Archives of Ontario in Toronto; the original papers are at the National Archives. The Carleton Papers (1775–83), also known as the British Headquarters Papers (WO 28/PRO 30/55) are at the PRO in Kew, Surrey, England and on film at the archives in Toronto and Ottawa. There is also a slip index to the Carleton Papers at the British Library in London, in what is known as the Stevens Transcripts.

War Office, Great Britain. Pensions for widows and children of Loyalist officers, 1755–1908 (film 0857997 ff.). These records are from the War Office Papers (WO 42) and include applications from Ontario, Quebec, New Brunswick, Nova Scotia, and East Florida. The original records are at the PRO in Kew, Surrey, England.

Loyalists in Canada Required to Give Proof of Military Service for the British (film 0823683). The original manuscript, dated 1804, is at the Archives of Ontario in Toronto.

Loyalist Finding Aids

Allen, Robert S. *Loyalist Literature: An Annotated Bibliographic Guide to the Writings on the Loyalists of the American Revolution* (Toronto: Dundurn Press, 1982).

Bunnell, Paul J. *Research Guide to Loyalist Ancestors: A Directory to Archives, Manuscripts, and Published Sources* (Bowie, MD: Heritage Books, 1990). Sources for Loyalist research in Canada and the United States, including England, the Bahamas, Bermuda, Sierra Leone, Jamaica, Dominica, and Saint Vincent.

Cruikshank, Ernest Alexander. *The Settlement of the United Empire Loyalists on the Upper Saint Lawrence and Bay of Quinte in 1784: A Documentary Record* (1934. Reprint. Toronto: Ontario Historical Society, 1966, film 0897095).

Palmer, Gregory. *A Bibliography of Loyalist Source Material in the United States, Canada, and Great Britain* (Westport, CT: Meckler Publishing, 1982). Also includes material from Loyalist newspapers, 1763–83.

National Archives of Canada, Ottawa, Ontario

The National Archives (NAC) was formerly known as the Public Archives of Canada. Some finding aids for the Archives are:

Anderson, W.J. *The Archives of Canada* (1872. Reprint. Washington, DC: Library of Congress, 1990, film 1688892).

Atherton, James J. *Records of Genealogical Interest in the Public Archives of Canada* (Salt Lake City: Genealogical Society of the Church of Jesus Christ of Latter-day Saints, 1969, fiche 6039426).

Campeau, Marielle and Patricia Kennedy. *Checklist of Parish Registers* (Ottawa: National Archives, 1975). Parish registers at the National Archives, including: Arkansas, Canada, French Guiana, Illinois, Indiana, Louisiana, Massachusetts, Michigan, New York, Ohio, and Saint-Pierre-et-Miquelon.

Catalogue of Pamphlets, Journals and Reports in the Dominion Archives, 1611–1867, with Index (Ottawa: Government Printing Bureau, 1911, film 0897033).

Coderre, John E. *List of Parish Registers Held at the Public Archives of Canada* (Ottawa: Ontario Genealogical Society, 1980, film 1036008).

National Archives of Canada, Manuscript Division. Main entry catalogue (Ottawa: The Archives, 1987, fiche 6333985 ff.).

Public Archives of Canada, Manuscript Division, Preliminary Inventory. 30 Vols. (Ottawa: Queen's Printer, 1951–67).

Suggested Reading

Bailey, Thomas Melville. *Traces, Places and Faces: Links Between Canada and Scotland* (Hamilton, ON: Walsh Printing Service, 1957, fiche 6019780).

Baxter, Angus. *In Search of Your Canadian Roots.* 2nd ed. (Baltimore: Genealogical Publishing Co., 1994, 1st ed. on fiche 6051392).

Beers, Henry Putney. *The French and British in the Old Northwest: A Bibliographical Guide to Archive and Manuscript Sources* (Detroit: Wayne State University Press, 1964). Historical account of the acquisition, preservation, and publication by American and Canadian institutions of the original records created by French and British officials in the Old Northwest.

Bercuson, David Jay. *Dictionary of Canadian Military History* (Toronto: Oxford University Press, 1992).

Carrington, Philip. *The Anglican Church in Canada: A History* (Toronto: Collins, 1963).

Eccles, W.J. *The Canadian Frontier, 1534–1750.* Rev. ed. (Albuquerque: University of New Mexico Press, 1983).

Fiske, John. *New France and New England* (Boston: Houghton, Mifflin, 1902).

Guide des Surces de l'Histoire du Canada Conservées en France (Ottawa: National Archives, 1982). A guide to sources relating to Canadian history held in French archives.

Harrison, Michael. *Canada's Huguenot Heritage* (Toronto: Huguenot Society of Canada, 1987).

Konrad, J. *French and French-Canadian Family Research* (Munroe Falls, OH: Summit Publications, 1985, fiche 6049408).

Lehmann, Heinz. *The German Canadians, 1750–1937: Immigration, Settlement and Culture* (Saint John's, NF: Jesperson Press, 1986).

Massicotte, E. Z. *Canadian Passports, 1681–1752* (1921. Reprint. New Orleans: Polyanthos, 1975, film 1036799).

Miscellaneous Records on Emigration from England and Scotland to Canada Located in the Public Archives of Canada (Ottawa: National Archives, n.d., film

0393997). The extracts are entries that pertain to those who emigrated from England to Canada, particularly to Nova Scotia, Quebec, and Prince Edward Island, with a few entries for Newfoundland, from the Treasury Papers and Colonial Office Papers, 1773–1808.

Reaman, George Elmore. *The Trail of the Black Walnut* (Scottdale, PA: Herald Press, 1957). History of the Pennsylvania Germans and their role in the settlement of Ontario, including Quakers, Lutherans, Dunkards, Seventh-Day Baptists, Brethren in Christ, Huguenots, Amish, Moravians, Schwenkfelders, and Hutterite Brethren.

Sulte, Benjamin. *Histoire de Canadiens Français*. 8 Vols. (1882. Reprint. Montreal: Editions Elysée, 1977). Comprehensive history of Canada.

Thwaites, Reuben Gold. *Jesuit Relations and Allied Documents: Travels and Explorations of the French Jesuit Missionaries among the Indians of Canada and the Northern and North-Western States of the United States, 1610–1791, with Numerous Historical, Geographical and Ethnological Notes, etc., and an Analytical Index* (1895. Reprint. Washington, DC: The Microcard Foundation, 1960, fiche 6082091 ff.). The records cover Acadia, Quebec, Hudson Bay, Lower Canada, Illinois, the Mississippi Valley, and Louisiana.

Turk, Marion G. *The Quiet Adventurers in Canada* (Detroit: Harlow Press, 1979, fiche 6089090). Genealogical and historical information about immigrants from the Channel Islands to Canada.

Vachon, André. *Dreams of Empire: Canada Before 1700* (Ottawa: Public Archives Canada, 1982).

Vaillancourt, Emile. *La Conquête du Canada par les Normands, Biographie de la Première Génération Normande du Canada*. 2nd ed. (Montreal: G. Ducharme, 1933, fiche 6050123). The conquest of Canada by the Normans, biography of the first generation.

Weaver, Jack W. and DeeGee Lester. *Immigrants from Great Britain and Ireland: A Guide to Archival and Manuscript Sources in North America* (Westport, CT: Greenwood Press, 1986).

Whyte, Donald. *A Dictionary of Scottish Emigrants to Canada Before Confederation.* 2 Vols. (Toronto: Ontario Genealogical Society, 1986–95).

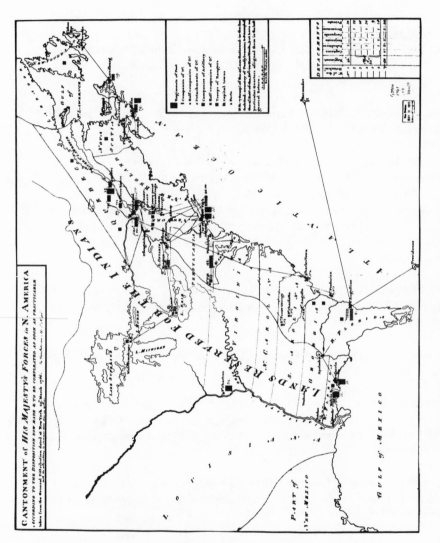

44 British forces in North America, 1766 (Library of Congress)

Quebec

Quebec's first permanent French settlement was in 1608. After the end of the French and Indian War in 1763, France ceded the colony to Great Britain. In 1774 the Province of Quebec was created by Great Britain. The Province of Quebec was divided into the provinces of Upper Canada (Ontario) and Lower Canada (Quebec) in 1791 (the Canada Act). They were reunited in 1841 as the Province of Canada (the Act of Union) and divided into Canada East (Quebec) and Canada West (Ontario). The Province of Ontario was not created until 1867.

Church Records, Civil Registration, and Notarial Records

Catholic parish registers begin in 1621. The parish priest, or *curé*, began to submit all records in duplicate to civil archives called the Palais de Justice in 1679. These were recorded by protonotaries. Examples of parish registers are:

Église Catholique, Archidiocèse de Québec. Registres paroissiaux, 1662–1848 (film 1311432). Baptisms, marriages, burials, confirmations and abjurations, including Nova Scotia, New Brunswick, Labrador, and Newfoundland, and the Church of Notre-Dame de Québec. The original records are at l'Archives de l'Archidiocèse de Québec.

Église Catholique, Mission Saint-Joseph-de-Sillery. Registres paroissiaux, 1638–90 (film 1290490). Baptisms and confirmations. The original records are at the Presbytère de la Mission in Sillery.

Église Catholique, Notre-Dame-de-Québec. Registres paroissiaux, 1621–1876 (film 1289658). Baptisms, marriages, and burials. The original records are at the Presbytère de Notre-Dame.

Église Catholique, La Purification-de-Repentigny. Registres paroissiaux, 1679–1876 (film 1018261 ff.). Baptisms, marriages, and burials. The original records are at the Presbytère de La-Purification and l'Archives de la Chancellerie del'Archevêché de Montréal.

Église Catholique, Sainte-Anne-de-Ristigouche (Cross Point). Registres paroissiaux, 1759–95, 1842–76 (film 1029863 ff.). Baptisms, marriages, and burials, including New Brunswick and Nova Scotia. The original records are at the Presbytère de Sainte-Anne.

SEE ALSO
France
Great Britain
Louisiana
New France
Ontario
Wisconsin

Église Catholique, Sainte-Famille-de-Boucherville. Registres paroissiaux, 1668–1877 (film 1288825 ff.). Baptisms, marriages, and burials. The original records are at the Presbytère de Sainte- Famille-de-Boucherville.

Église Catholique, Saint-Joseph-de-Beauce. Registres paroissiaux, 1738–1876 (film 1294970 ff.). Baptisms, marriages, burials, and confirmations. The original records are at the Presbytère de Saint-Joseph.

The Loiselle Index and the Rivest Index

Two important indexes provide a general catalog to Quebec parish records and civil registration:

* Loiselle, Antonin. *Loiselle Card Index to Many Marriages of the Province of Québec and Adjacent Areas* (Montreal: Covent des Dominicans, n.d., film 0543721 ff.). The records also cover Manchester, New Hampshire, and Madawaska, New Brunswick.

* *Index Alphabétique des Mariages de Certaines Paroisses du Québec: Supplément a Collection Loiselle* (Montreal: Ville de Montréal, 1988, film 1571024 ff.). Alphabetical index of marriages of certain parishes of Quebec. This also contains civil registration. The original records are at the Convent of the Dominicans in Montreal.

* Rivest, Lucien. Index to Marriages of Quebec and Adjacent Areas, 1670–1964 (film 0933142). The marriage records are from the counties of Berthier, Joliette, L'Assomption, Montcalm, Argenteuil, Deux-Montagnes, Terrebonne, Gatineau, Labelle, Yamaska, Richelieu, Laval, and Drummondville.

The book, *Guide to Quebec Catholic Parishes and Published Parish Marriage Records* (Baltimore: Genealogical Publishing Co., 1993), by Jeanne Sauve White, describes which counties and parishes are included in the Loiselle and Rivest marriage indexes.

The Fabien Marriage File at the National Archives in Ottawa, Ontario indexes marriage records in Outaouais, the counties around Montreal, and Prince Edward Island.

Mariages de Québec: Comtés de Drummond, Sherbrooke, Stanstead, Richmond, Wolfe, Compton, Nicolet, Arthabaska, Mégantic et Frontenac (film 1381846 ff.). Contains transcriptions of marriages performed at Catholic churches in several Quebec counties from the beginning of the records through 1970. The original records are at the Société de Généalogie des Cantons de l'Est, Sherbrooke.

Québec registres paroissiaux, marriages (film 0105969). Copies of parish registers: L'Islet County, 1679–1760 and 1840–53, Saint-Antoine-de-Tilly, 1765–1826, Sainte-Croix, 1768–1841, Saint-Gilles, and Saint-Louis-de-Lotbinière, 1764–1804. The location of the original manuscript is unknown.

Bangsberg, Tara N. La Londe. *A List of the Catholic Churches in the Province of Québec Established Prior to 1890 and the Year in Which They Were Established* (Puyallup, WA: The Author, 1995, fiche 6334769).

Belanger, Pauline and Yves Landry. *Inventaire des Registres Paroissiaux Catholiques du Québec, 1621–1876* (Montreal: Les Presses de l'Universite de Montréal, 1990).

Emard, Michel. *Le Registre de Ristigouche, 1759–95, Baie des Chaleurs et Acadie, Historique, Transcription et Index* (Paris: The Author, 1980, fiche 6088773). Baptisms, marriages, and burials transcribed and indexed from a photocopy of the original register of Sainte-Anne-de-Ristigouche (Cross Point), Restigouche, the Comtés de Bonaventure and Gaspé-Est, and l'Acadie (Nova Scotia and New Brunswick).

Fortin, Francine. *Guide to Québec's Parishes and Civil Registers, 1621–1993* (Lachine, PQ: The Author, 1993, fiche 6075969).

Index of Irish Marriages. 2 Vols. (n.p., 1973, film 0962398). Index of Irish marriages, an extract from the register of Notre Dame de Québec, Saint Coulombe de Sillery, and Saint Gabriel de Valcartier, including English and Scottish marriages for 1760–1900.

Magnan, Hormisdas. *Dictionnaire Historique et Géographique des Paroisses, Missions et Municipalities de la Province de Québec* (Arthabaska, PQ: Imprimerie d'Arthabaska, 1925, fiche 6016524 ff.). Geographical and historical dictionary of parishes, missions, and municipalities of Quebec.

Notarial Records

Acte notariés (notarial records) may contain transactions as diverse as marriage contracts, inheritance records, land rents, grants, and purchases, pensions paid to parents for the use of land, indenture agreements, livestock purchases, and many other documents.[50] Some of the available records on microfilm are:

Notariat,Québec.
- Actes de notaire, 1702–59 (film 0963359). Notarial records for Quebec.
- Noms des notaires de Québec (film 0963357 ff.). Notarial records: wills, marriage settlements, etc.

The original records are at the French National Archives, Section Outre-Mer, Paris.

---

[50] For more information on notarial records, see France.

Notariat, Montréal, Québec, District Judiciaire.
*   Actes de notaire, 1746–1800 (film 1420438 ff.).
*   Actes de notaire, 1657–99 (film 1419832 ff.).
*   Actes de notaire, 1709–44 (film 1420140 ff.).
*   Actes de notaire, 1685–90 (film 1420327 ff.).
*   Actes de notaire, 1648–57 (film 1430223).

Notariat, Trois-Rivières, Québec, District Judiciaire. Actes de notaire, 1636–1828 (Sainte-Foy, PQ: Archives Nationales du Québec, 1985, film 1430753).

The original records of the above are at the Archives Nationales du Québec in Sainte-Foy.

National Archives of Canada.
*   Lower Canada marriage bonds (film 1309916 ff.). The marriage bonds were originally issued by various protonotary districts throughout Quebec, 1799–1844.
*   Nominal card index for the Lower Canada marriage bonds (film 1276179 ff.). Contains card index for Quebec marriage bonds, 1779–1860.

The original records are at the National Archives in Ottawa, Ontario.

Harris, Richard Colebrook. *The Seigneurial System in Early Canada: A Geographical Study* (Madison: University of Wisconsin Press, 1966).

Instruments de Recherches des Registres Notariaux (Sainte-Foy, PQ: Ministère des Affaires Culturelles, Archives Nationales du Québec, 1981–4, fiche 6333604 ff.). Finding aids for notarial records. Contains chronological lists and/or indexes for many of the notarial records in the province of Quebec. The original records are at the Archives Nationales du Québec in Sainte-Foy.

Inventaire des Contrats de Mariage Déposés aux Archives Nationales de Trois-Rivières, 1647–1918. 8 Vols. (Trois-Rivières, PQ: Société de Généalogie de la Mauricie et des Bois-Francs, 1995). Listing of 28,363 marriage contracts and inventories found in the notarial files at Trois-Rivières.

Lafortune, Hélène. *Parchemin s'Explique: Guide de Dépouillement des Actes Notariés du Québec Ancien* (Montreal: Société de Recherche Historique Archiv-Histo, 1989). Finding aids for notarial records, with alphabetical lists of notaries in Quebec before 1900.

Laliberté, J. M. *Index des Greffes des Notaires Décédés, 1645–1948* (Quebec: B. Pontbriand, 1967, fiche 6046554). Index of deceased notaries of French Canada.

Laliberté, J. M. *Marriages of Québec Province, Canada, 1682–1960.* 2 Vols. (n.p., 1966–7, film 0928003 ff.). Some of the earliest entries include Batiscan, 1682–1850, and Sault au Récollet, 1720–1850.

Martel, Jules. *Index des Actes Notariés du Régime Français à Trois-Rivières, 1634–1760* (n.p., 1974). Index of notarial records under the French regime at Trois-Rivières, 1634–1760.

Munro, William Bennett. *The Seigniorial System in Canada: A Study in French Colonial Policy* (1907. Reprint. Washington, DC: Library of Congress, 1990, film 1723750).

Quintin, Robert J. *The Notaries of French-Canada, 1626–1900: Alphabetically, Chronologically, by Area Served* (Pawtucket, RI: The Author, 1994, film 1750788).

Roy, Jean-Guy. *Répertoire des Mariages, Comté de Kamouraska, 1685–1990* (Quebec: Société de Généalogie de Québec, 1993).

Roy, Pierre-Georges. *Les Letters de Naturalité Sous le Regime Français* (1924. Reprint. Quebec: Laval University, n.d., film 0982147). Letters of naturalization under the French regime. Abstracts from the letters of naturalization from Quebec and also in the French National Archives, Section Outre-Mer, Paris, which pertain to French Canada.

Census Records and Sources

Nouvelle-France. Recensements: 1666–81 (Ottawa: National Archives, 1966, film 1375924). Contains censuses for 1666, 1667, and 1681 for New France. The original records are at the National Archives in Ottawa, Ontario and the French National Archives, Section Outre-Mer, Paris. For information on the original records and other French censuses, see France.

Charbonneau, Hubert et Jacques *Légaré. Répertoire des Actes de Baptême, Mariage, Sépulture et des Recensements du Québec Ancien [1621–1765].* 47 Vols. (Montreal: Presses de l'Université de Montréal, 1980–90). Contains mostly information transcribed from parish registers, with some information taken from censuses and other public archives, including Quebec, Trois-Rivières, Montréal, Île d'Orléans, l'Île Dupas, Île Jésus, and others.

Le Premier Recensement de la Nouvelle-France (1935. Reprint. Ottawa: National Archives, 1960, film 0281228). Contains first census for Quebec, 1666.

Bangsberg, Tara N. La Londe. *An Every Name Index to the 1666 Census of Québec Province* (Puyallup, WA: The Author, 1991, fiche 6334759).

Bangsberg, Tara N. La Londe. *A Census Inventory, 1640–1851: A List of One Hundred Thirty Three Early Census Returns for Canada, Nouvelle France or the Province of Québec Area and How to Gain Access to Them* (Puyallup, WA: The Author, 1993, fiche 6334772).

Bangsberg, Tara N. La Londe. *An Index to the 1760–1762 Census of the Trois-Rivières Area of the Province of Québec, Canada* (Puyallup, WA: The Author, 1994, fiche 6334761). The district of Trois-Rivières includes the following counties: Champlain, Maskinongé, Nicolet, and Saint-Maurice.

Aveu et Dénombrement de Montréal (Quebec: Archives de la Province de Québec, 1943). Census of Montreal Island, 1731, with indexes of heads of families, streets, and places.

Court Records and Sources
French Records
The earliest court records of the French dominion begin in 1651. Copies of most court proceedings are recorded in the notarial records. The courts of New France were:
* *plaidoyers communs* (court of common pleas), 1651– ca. 1760
* *Conseil Supérieur* (superior court), 1663– ca. 1760
* *cours seigneuriales* (seigneurial courts), 1662– ca. 1760
* *registres du baillage* (bailiff's court), 1651– ca. 1760

The early court records are kept at the *Archives Judiciaires de Québec* (Judicial Archives) at the Archives Nationales du Québec in Sainte-Foy. Some of the records that have been indexed on film are:
* *Index des Dossiers Criminels de la Cour Supérieure du District Judiciaire de Québec, 1765–1925* (Sainte-Foy, PQ: Ministère des Affaires Culturelles, Archives Nationales du Québec, 1984, fiche 6334285). Index of Superior Court criminal documents of the Judicial District of Quebec, 1765–1925.
* *Index des Dossiers de la Cour des Plaidoyers Communs et de la Cour du Banc du Roi, District de Québec, 1765–1808* (Sainte-Foy, PQ: Ministère des Affaires Culturelles, Archives Nationales du Québec, 1984, fiche 6334284). Index of counsels' speeches, 1765–1808, for both the defendants and the plaintiffs for Lévis Lotbinière, Montmorency No. 1, Montmorency No. 2, Portneuf, and Bellechasse.
* *Index des Dossiers du Coroner de la Cour Supérieure du District Judiciaire de Québec, 1765–1930* (Sainte-Foy, PQ: Ministère des Affaires Culturelles,

Archives Nationales du Québec, 1984, fiche 6334286). Index of superior court coroner documents of the Judicial District of Quebec, 1765-1930.

A series of finding aids to the Judicial Archives of Quebec has been written by Pierre-Georges Roy:

* *Inventaire des Jugements et Délibérations du Conseil Supérieur de la Nouvelle-France de 1717 à 1760.* 7 Vols. (Beauceville, PQ: L'Eclaireur, 1932-5, fiche 6017995). Inventory of the judgments and deliberations of the Conseil Supérieur of New France.

* *Inventaire des Testaments, Donations et Inventaires du Regime Français Conservés aux Archives Judiciaires de Québec.* 3 Vols. (Quebec: n.p., 1941, fiche 6046878). List of wills, gifts, and inventories of the French regime preserved in the Judicial Archives of Quebec.

* *Inventaire des Contrats de Mariage du Régime Français Conservés aux Archives Judiciaires de Québec.* 6 Vols. (Quebec: n.p., 1937-8, fiche 6019961). Inventory of marriage contracts of the French regime held in the Judicial Archives of Quebec.

* *Inventaire des Testaments, Donations et Inventaires du Regime Français Conservés aux Archives Judiciaire de Québec.* 3 Vols. (Quebec: n.p., 1941, fiche 6046878). List of wills, gifts, and inventories of the French regime preserved in the Judicial Archives of Quebec.

British Records

The earliest courts of the British are the provincial courts, which began in 1765. These records can be found at the National Archives in Ottawa, Ontario.

* Superior Court, Court of King's (Queen's) Bench, 1765-1867, civil and criminal trials.

* Superior Court, Court of Appeals, 1765-1832, court of last instance for appeals of civil and criminal cases from the Superior Court and lower courts.

* Court of Chancery, 1765-1867, equity cases involving civil litigation.

* Court of Common Pleas, 1781-91, minor civil and criminal cases.

There is also a collection of bonds, licenses, and certificates, 1763-1867, and a series of miscellaneous records known as the "S" Series (RG 4), which contain some court records.

Land Records

The Compagnie made its first seigneurial grants near Quebec in 1634, mostly to nobility, religious groups, and merchants. After 1663 *augmentations* (extensions) of some segneuries were granted and *arrière-fiefs* (sub-seigneuries) were created. The holders paid an annual rent known as a *concession* or *habitation*. A *concession* could be subdivided into *lots*. The residents were known as *habitants.* The taxes paid on seigneurial land sales, *lods et ventes,* can be found in notarial records. The unit of measure used in land records was an *arpent,* equal to about five-sixths of an acre. Most farm lots were between sixty and one hundred and twenty *arpents.*[51] These settlements began to form into villages near the end of the eighteenth century. In 1763 the British Crown accepted the titles of the previously granted seigneurial lands, but claimed ownership of all unoccupied territory. Beginning in 1764 British Crown land grants were issued in Quebec.[52]

Original Records
Assemblée Législative, Législature, Québec Province.
* *Seigniories, Land Grants of 1674–1760, Québec* (Quebec: Secretary's Office, 1853, fiche 6046787).
* Land records for the Province of Québec, 1788–1867 (Sainte-Foy, PQ: Archives Nationales du Québec, 1990, film 1723570 ff.).
* *Inventaire de la Série Domaine de la Couronne, Cencive de Québec, du Fonds Ministère des Terres et Frêts, 1667–1875* (Sainte-Foy, PQ: Ministère des Affaires Culturelles, Archives Nationales du Québec, 1983, fiche 6334278). Inventory of Crown land records of the city of Quebec and neighboring areas, 1667–1875.

The original records of the above are at the Archives Nationales du Québec in Sainte-Foy.

Executive Council, Land Committee, Lower Canada. Land petitions and related records, 1637–1842 (Ottawa: National Archives, 1965–95, film 1831844). Documents relating to the settlement of lands that became part of Upper Canada in 1791 are included in this set of records. After 1841, petitions relating to land that had been Lower Canada are preserved with the Upper Canada Land Petitions. The original records are at the National Archives in Ottawa, Ontario.

Secondary Sources
Bouchette, Joseph. *A Topographical Description of the Province of Lower Canada, with Remarks Upon Upper Canada and the Relative Connexion of Both Provinces with the United States of America* (London: W. Faden, 1815, fiche 6016343 ff.). Appendix contains extracts from title concessions of land grants in Quebec.

---

[51] R. Cole Harris, *Historical Atlas of Canada.* Vol 1. *From the Beginning to 1800* (Toronto: University of Toronto Press, 1987), 115.

[52] For a description of Crown lands and Heir and Devisee records, see Ontario.

Mathieu, Jacques and Alain Laberge. *L'Occupation des Terres dans la Vallée du Saint-Laurent: Les Aveux et Dénombrements, 1723–1745* (Sillery, PQ: Les Éditions du Septentrion, 1991). Land records of the Saint Lawrence River Valley in Quebec.

Roy, Léon. *Les Terres de l'Île d'Orléans, 1650–1725* (Montreal: Editions Bergeron et Fils, 1978). Land owners of l'Île d'Orléans (Montmorency No. 2) comprising the following municipalities: Saint-Pierre, Sainte-Famille, Saint-François, Saint-Jean, and Saint-Laurent.

Roy, Pierre-Georges. *Papier Terrier de la Compagnie des Indes Occidentales, 1667–1668* (Beauceville, PQ: L'Eclaireur, 1931).Transcripts of land records (fealty and homage, and avowals and enumerations) of the West Indies Company, which include names of seigneurs and the inhabitants of their lands, 1667–8.

Trudel, Marcel. *Le Terrier du Saint-Laurent en 1663* (Ottawa: Editions de l'Université d'Ottawa, 1973). A description of the seigniories along the Saint Lawrence River in 1663, including maps and a description of each and its subdivisions. One of these extends from the river to the Atlantic, extending through part of the eastern United States.

Research Guide for Lower Canada Land Records Index (Regina, SK: Saskatchewan Genealogical Society, 1995, film 1698253). Brief description of the Lower Canada index to land petitions, 1737–1867, and the index to the grantees of lands granted in Quebec by the Crown, 1763–1890.

Roy, Pierre-Georges. *Inventaire des Concessions en Fief et Seigneurie, Fois et Hommages et Aveux et Dénombrements Conservés aux Archives de la Province de Québec.* 6 Vols. (Beauceville, PQ: L'Eclaireur, 1927–9, fiche 6046791).

Suggested Reading

Archives Nationales du Québec. *État Général des Archives Publiques et Privées* (Quebec: Ministère des Affaires Culturelles, 1968, fiche 6046879).

Bangsberg, Tara N. La Londe. *A List of Libraries, Historical Societies and Museums in the Province of Québec and Throughout Canada and the U.S. with French-Canadian or Acadiana (Cajun) Historical or Genealogical Collections and How to Obtain Your Genealogy from Them by Mail or Interlibrary Loan* (Puyallup, WA: The Author, 1993, fiche 6334771).

Beauregard, Marthe Faribault. *La Généalogie: Retrouver Ses Ancêtres* (Quebec: Les Editions de l'Homme, 1987). Guide to genealogical research in Quebec.

Biggar, Henry P. *The Early Trading Companies of New France* (Toronto: University of Toronto Studies on History, 1901).

Bosher, J. F. *Men and Ships in the Canada Trade, 1660–1760: A Biographical Dictionary* (Ottawa: National Historic Sites, Parks Services, Environment Canada, 1992). Alphabetical list of merchants and an alphabetical list of ships bound for Quebec or the Saint Lawrence, or occasionally for Louisbourg or Acadia. When Canada was a French colony, between 1608 and 1760, it depended on shipping from France. This contains facts about the vessels that crossed the Atlantic during the colony's last century and the people who owned, managed, or used them.

Day, Mrs. C. M. *Pioneers of the Eastern Townships: A Work Containing Official and Reliable Information Respecting the Formation of Settlements; with Incidents in Their Early History, and Details of Adventures, Perils and Deliverances* (Montreal: John Lovell, 1863, film 0564367).

Dumas, Silvio. *Les Filles du Roi en Nouvelle-France Étude Historique avec Répertoire Biographique* (Quebec: Société Historique de Québec, 1972, film 1421670).

Godbout, Archange. *Les Passagers du Saint-André: La Recrue de 1659* (Montreal: Société Généalogique Canadienne-Française, 1964).

Landry, Yves. Orphelines en France, *Pionnières au Canada: Les Filles du Roi au XVIIe Siècle Suivi d'un Répertoire Biographique des Filles du Roi* (Montreal: Leméac Editeur, 1992). Women immigrants from France who agreed to travel to the new lands in Quebec and marry settlers there in exchange for a dowry from the French King, 1663–73. The first part concerns historical demography and social history. The second part consists of brief biographies of the "daughters" of the King.

Ministère des Affaires Culturelles, Québec. *Etat Sommaire des Archives Nationales du Québec à Montréal* (Quebec: Editeur Official, 1972, film 0908697). Inventory of the National Archives of Quebec in Montréal.

Quintin, Robert J. *French-Canadian Surnames: Aliases, Adulterations and Anglicizations* (Pawtucket, RI: The Author, 1993, film 1698288).

Quebec in 1730—F.om an old Print.

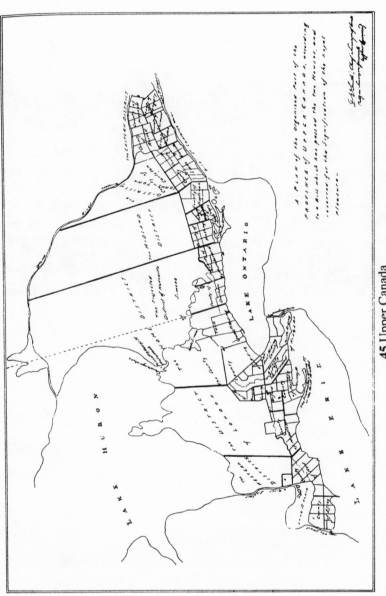

45 Upper Canada

Ontario

Ontario was originally part of Quebec; the northern portion was in the territory of the Hudson's Bay Company. One of the earliest settlements was at Sainte-Maire-Among-the-Hurons, (present-day Midland, Ontario) in 1693[53]. In 1774 Ontario was part of the Province of Quebec. The districts of Hesse, Lunenburg, Mecklenburg, and Nassau — in what became southern Ontario — were created in 1788. The Province of Quebec was divided into the provinces of Upper Canada (Ontario) and Lower Canada (Quebec) in 1791 (the Canada Act). They were reunited in 1841 as the Province of Canada (the Act of Union) and divided into Canada East (Quebec) and Canada West (Ontario). The Province of Ontario was not created until 1867.

Knowing when districts were created, names changed, and counties formed is essential to research in Ontario. The first districts were changed by name in 1793: Hesse to Western, Lunenburg to Eastern, Mecklenburg to Midland, Nassau to Home. In 1793 the first counties were created. After this time, as new districts and counties were formed, they did not always parallel the boundaries of the previously existing political division.

A finding aid for many types of Ontario records is a biographical and genealogical card index, 1780–1869 (film 1544194 ff.). This is a card index of personal names extracted from the following types of records: agreements (apprenticeship papers, promissory notes, etc.), baptismal records, biographical sketches, cemetery records, commissions, land records, family histories, funeral notices, obituaries, genealogical records, litigations, marriage records, Rebellion losses name cards, United Empire Loyalists cards, and wills. The original card index is at the Archives of Ontario in Toronto.

Church Records and Civil Registration
Civil Registration
The earliest civil registrations are the district marriage registrations, some of which began in 1800. Between 1754 and 1793 only Anglican and Roman Catholic

SEE ALSO
Great Britain
Michigan
New France
New York
Quebec

---

[53]Brenda Dougall Merriman, *Genealogy in Ontario: Searching the Records.* 3rd ed. (Toronto: Ontario Genealogical Society, 1996), 9.

clergy could legally perform marriages. In 1793 district clerks were also allowed to perform and record marriages. Clergy from the Calvinist, Church of Scotland, and Lutheran denominations were added to the approved group in 1798. In 1831 Methodist, Baptist, and Presbyterian clergy were also authorized to perform marriages. Marriages were required to be registered with the district clerk; for those who chose to be married only by bond (license), there would only be a record in the civil district register.

There is a nominal card index for the Upper Canada marriage bonds, 1803–45 (film 1276180 ff.). The original records are at the National Archives in Ottawa, Ontario.

The original marriage returns are — unless otherwise indicated — at the Archives of Ontario in Toronto. The district marriage registers in this series that begin before 1850 are:

- Bathurst, 1831–48 (Lanark, and parts of Carleton and Renfrew counties, film 1030051 ff.).
- Brock, 1839–58 (Oxford and Brant counties, film 1030051 ff.).
- Colborne, 1843–58 (listed under Colborne County, film 1030051 ff.).
- Dahlousie, registers are missing.
- Eastern, 1831–65 (Ottawa: National Archives, 1967, film 0928968). The original registers are at the National Archives in Ottawa, Ontario.
- Gore, 1842–55 (Halton, Wentworth, Brant, and part of Haldimand County, film 1030051 ff.).
- Home, 1816–30 (Presbyterian), and baptisms, 1823–8; marriages, 1831–57 (Ontario, York, Peel, Simcoe, and part of Grey County, film 1030051 ff.).
- Huron, 1841–9 (parts of Huron, Perth, and Middlesex counties, film 1030051 ff.).
- Johnstown, 1801–51 (Leeds, Grenville, Lanark, Renfrew, and part of Carleton County, film 1030051 ff.).
- London, 1784–1834 (Ottawa: National Archives, 1965, film 0477532). The original registers are at the National Archives in Ottawa, Ontario.
- London, 1833–55 (Middlesex and Elgin counties); 1851–7 (listed under Elgin and Middlesex counties, film 1030051 ff.).
- Midland, registers are missing.
- Newcastle, 1810–55. The original registers are at Trent University in Peterborough, Ontario. These records have not been filmed.
- Newcastle, 1839–54 (Northumberland and Durham counties, film 1030051 ff.).
- Niagara, registers are missing.
- Ottawa, 1816–53 (film 1030051 ff.).
- Prince Edward, 1833–46 (Prince Edward County, film 1030051 ff.).

- Simcoe, 1842–58 (listed under Simcoe County, film 1030051 ff.).[54]
- Talbot, 1838–57 (Norfolk and Haldimand counties, film 1030051 ff.).
- Victoria, 1839–58 (Victoria and Hastings counties, film 1030051 ff.).
- Wellington, registers are missing.
- Western, 1795–1857; baptisms, 1826–49 (available at the Archives of Ontario on film MS 205, reel 13).

Roman Catholic marriage registers:
- Saint Paul's Parish (Toronto), 1833–56 (film 1030051 ff.).
- Saint Paul's Parish (Toronto), 1846–56 (film 1030051 ff.).
- Saint Gregory Mission, 1844–56 (includes Oshawa, Whitby, Pickering, and Brock, film 1030051 ff.).
- Townships above Toronto, 1830–52 (film 1030051 ff.).
- Niagara-on-the-Lake, 1828–69 (film 1030051 ff.).
- Gore Mission, 1834–69 (film 1030051 ff.).

Church Records

Pineau, Dora. *The Marriage Register of the Western District, 1796–1856* (Windsor, ON: Essex County Branch, OGS, 1993). Compiled and prepared from a microfilm copy of the original register.

Examples of early parish registers that have been filmed are:
Williamstown Presbyterian Church. Church records, 1779–1817 (Ottawa: National Archives, 1955, film 0272356). Registers kept by Rev. John Bethune for the counties of Glengarry and Stormont and elsewhere in the Province of Upper Canada. The original records are at the National Archives in Ottawa, Ontario.
Society of Friends. Yonge Street Monthly Meeting. Hicksite registry of births, 1803–6, and deaths, 1811–75, Yonge Street (Toronto: Archives of Ontario, 1988, film 1482975). Includes names of people who died before the Hicksite movement began in 1828. Residences listed are primarily in York County, with some in Ontario County and surrounding areas. The original records are at the Archives of Ontario in Toronto.
Catholic Church, Assumption, Windsor. Parish registers, 1761–1910 (film 1312030 ff.). The original records are at the Diocese of London Archives and the Assumption Rectory. These records have been compiled in Chiasson, Germaine. *Mariages, Paroisse l'Assomption de Windsor, Ontario, 1700–1985* (Ottawa: Société Franco-Ontarienne d'Histoire et de Généalogie, 1985).

---

[54]The descriptions of the districts of Colborne, London, and Simcoe, incorrectly listed in the finding aid for this series, have been corrected by Brenda Dougall Merriman, *Genealogy In Ontario: Searching the Records.* 3rd ed. (Toronto: Ontario Genealogical Society, 1996), 67.

Église Catholique, Saint-François-Régis, Québec. Registres paroissiaux, 1762–1876 (film 1031635 ff.). Baptisms, marriages, burials, and confirmations in southern Quebec, Haut-Canada (Ontario), and northern New York. The original records are at the Chancellerie de Valleyfield, Valleyfield, Quebec.

Methodist Church, Canada. Baptismal registers, 1825–1910 (Scarborough, ON: Standard Microfilm Reproduction Co., Ltd., n.d., film 1759292 ff.). This also includes records of the Wesleyan Methodist Church in Canada and the Methodist Church of Canada. The original records are at the Archives of the United Church of Canada, Victoria University, Toronto.

Secondary Sources

Alexis de Barbezieux. *Histoire de la Province Écclesiastique d'Ottawa et de la Colonisation dans la Vallée de l'Ottawa* (Ottawa: La Cie d'Imprimerie d'Ottawa, 1897, film 0833356).

Archivists of the Ecclesiastical Province of Ontario. *Guide to the Holdings of the Archives of the Ecclesiastical Province of Ontario* (Agincourt, ON: Generation Press, 1990). Complete holdings of the seven dioceses in the Ecclesiastical Province of Ontario, the Anglican Church of Canada, along with holdings pertaining to the Ecclesiastical Province and the Diocese of Moosonee held at the General Synod Archives in Toronto. Selected holdings held in the archives of Wycliff College and Trinity College are also included.

Champagne, Joseph-Étienne. *Les Missions Catholiques dans l'Ouest Canadien, 1818–1875* (Ottawa: Editions de l'Université, 1949). History of Catholic missions in Canada West.

Harris, W.R. *History of the Early Missions in Western Canada* (Toronto: Hunter, Rose and Co., 1893, film 1698151). History of Catholic missions in Ontario.

Power, Michael. A *History of the Roman Catholic Church in the Niagara Peninsula, 1615–1815* (Saint Catharines, ON: Roman Catholic Diocese, 1983).

Robbins, Douglas A. *Early Marriages in Ontario's Eastern Townships* (Saint Catharines, ON: The Author, 1991). Records cover the counties of Stormont, Dundas, Glengarry, Prescott, and Russell, taken from church records and civil records published in *The Ontario Register* and *The Glengarrian*.

Wanamaker, Loral R. *Anglican Registers, 1787–1814: Rev. John Langhorn, Rector of Ernestown, Upper Canada* (Kingston, ON: Ontario Genealogical Society, 1980). The parish extended from Kingston to the western shore of Prince Edward County.

Wanamaker, Loral R. *Early Church Records of Rev. John Langhorn and Rev. Robert McDowall* (n.p., 1976, film 1421873). The registers of Rev. Langhorn are at the Synod Office of the Anglican Church in Kingston. The register of Rev. Robert McDowall are at the Douglas Library of Queen's University in Kingston.

Wilson, Thomas B. *Marriage Bonds of Ontario, 1803–1834* (Lambertville, NJ: Hunterdon House, 1985). Abstraction of part of the National Archives marriage bonds for Upper and Lower Canada.

Wilson, Thomas B. *Ontario Marriage Notices [1830–1856]* (Lambertville, NJ: Hunterdon House, 1982).

Zeisberger, David. *Diary of David Zeisberger: A Moravian Missionary Among the Indians of Ohio.* 2 Vols. (1885. Reprint. Saint Clair Shores, MI: Scholarly Press, 1972, film 1697367). Contains church history with some church records for Indians in Ohio, Michigan, and Ontario, including baptisms, marriages, and deaths.

Census Records and Sources

For censuses before 1790, see Quebec. The earliest census records in Upper Canada were taken in 1796, Augusta, Grenville County. The early district censuses and assessments, which are filmed and available at the Archives of Ontario in Toronto, are as follows:

Gore District, 1816–50	Niagara District, 1828–49
Johnstown District, 1796–1850	Ottawa District, 1822–50
Newcastle District, 1802–50	Western District, 1813–50

Census of Augusta township, Ontario, 1796, 1806, 1813, 1823, 1824 (film 0393998). The original records are at the National Archives in Ottawa, Ontario.

Hillman, Thomas. *Catalogue to Census Returns on Microfilm, 1666–1891* (Ottawa: National Archives, 1987). This includes township, county, and district censuses and assessments.

Johnston, Lorna. *Some Early Censuses, Augusta Township, Grenville County, Ontario* (Brockville, ON: Leeds and Grenville Branch, OGS, 1994).

Beettam, Margaret. *Gore District Census and Assessment, 1816–1850* (Oakville, ON: Halton-Peel Branch, OGS, 1990).

Beettam, Margaret. *Newcastle District Census and Assessment, 1803–1850* (Oakville, ON: Halton-Peel Branch, OGS, 1990). Covers townships in the counties of Victoria, Peterborough, Durham, and Northumberland.

Beettam, Margaret. *Ottawa District Census and Assessment, 1822–1850* (Oakville, ON: Halton-Peel Branch, OGS, 1990). Covers the counties of Prescott and Russell and two townships in Carleton County.

Court and Probate Records and Sources

Prerogative courts had jurisdiction over probate until 1793. The files were kept in district registers, and the few surviving documents are at the National Archives in Ottawa, Ontario. Courts of Justice were created in 1789. The Province of Upper Canada was a single probate district in 1793, and surrogate courts were established in the four districts. The Court of Probate was a central court located in the provincial capital and had jurisdiction over estates where the deceased possessed goods to the value of five pounds and the property was in two or more districts. Other cases could also be filed in the district Surrogate Courts or Court of Probate. In 1827 the authority of the court was expanded to include guardianship cases. The district Surrogate Courts were abolished in 1858 and replaced by county courts.

Court of Probate, Upper Canada. Probate registers, 1793–1858, estate files, 1793–1859 (film 1312312 ff.). The original records are at the Archives of Ontario in Toronto.

Surrogate Court, Eastern District. Register, 1787–1830 (Ottawa: National Archives, 1965, film 0477530 ff.). Wills and other probate records. The original records are at the National Archives in Ottawa, Ontario.

Surrogate Court, Johnstown District. Minutes of the Surrogate Court, 1795–1847 (film 0466942). The original records are at the Grenville County Courthouse in Brockville.

Surrogate Court, London District. Register, 1800–39. The original records are at the University of Western Ontario in London, Ontario. They are available on microfilm by interlibrary loan, through the D.B. Weldon Library at the University.

Some of the county probate registers that have been filmed are:
Surrogate Court, United Counties of Leeds and Grenville.
• Probate records, 1786–1885 (film 1312272 ff.). The original records are at the Archives of Ontario in Toronto.
• Probate records, 1789–1901 (film 0466944 ff.). The original records are at the Grenville County Courthouse in Brockville.
The United Counties of Leeds and Grenville area was historically known as Johnstown District.

Surrogate Court, Essex County. Probate records, 1785–1903, index, 1785–1969 (film 0589000 ff.). The original records are at the Essex County Courthouse in Windsor.

Surrogate Court, Norfolk County. Probate records, 1800–1903, index, 1842–1967 (film 0501181 ff.). The original records are at the Norfolk County Courthouse in Simcoe.

Surrogate Court, United Counties of Stormont, Dundas, and Glengarry. Probate records, 1800–1930 (film 0862333 ff.). Probate registers and the original estate files from which the registers were compiled, containing wills, petitions, letters of administration, etc. The original records are at the Archives of Ontario in Toronto.

Probate Records Finding Aids

Shepard, Catherine. *Surrogate Court Records Index, 1793–1858* (Toronto: Ontario Genealogical Society, n.d., fiche 6334160). Compiled from surrogate court sources: estate files, estate filings, registers, and guardianship files.

Speirs, B. *Court Records: Probate Court Records, 1793–1859* (Toronto: Department of Public Records and Archives, 1970, film 13123120).

Wanamaker, Loral R. and Mildred Wanamaker. *Abstracts of Surrogate Court Wills, Kingston and Vicinity, 1790–1858* (Kingston, ON: Kingston Branch, OGS, 1982, fiche 6101583).

Yeager, William R. *Wills of the London District, 1800–1839: An Abstract and Index Guide to the London District Surrogate Registry Registers, Wills and Testamentary Documents* (Simcoe, ON: Norfolk Historical Society, 1979).

Shepard, Catherine. *Surrogate Court Records at the Archives of Ontario: A Genealogical Research Guide* (Toronto: Ontario Genealogical Society, 1984). Includes a history of the records and holdings of the archives.

Zuefelt, Bill. *Court of Probate: Registers and Estate Files at the Archives of Ontario: An Index of Genealogical Research* (Toronto: Ontario Genealogical Society, 1986). Contains an alphabetical list of estate files, 1793–1859 (Series 155), handled in the Court of Probate.

Other Court Records

The Court of King's (Queen's) Bench, 1796–1849, issued bonds, licenses, and certificates, 1803–17, and kept records of fines levied, 1798–1867, and handled some civil and criminal cases. Records from 1796–1849 are at the Archives of Ontario in Toronto. There are also other records of this court at the University of Western Ontario in London, Ontario:

Court of King's (Queen's) Bench, Ontario. Court records, 1828–81 (film 0851369 ff.). Judgment dockets of the Court of Queen's Bench and the Court of Common Pleas.

Land Records and Sources

All land in Ontario was originally owned by the British Crown. Most Crown land grants were made after 1783. Four District Land Boards were established in 1788. The first major settlement in Ontario was by United Empire Loyalists—settlers from the British North American colonies who chose to remain loyal to the King — in 1783, at Kingston.[55] Free grants were made between 1783 and 1826 to United Empire Loyalists, their children, and certain groups of settlers. After 1826 only Loyalists or those with military service received free grants. Crown lands could be purchased after 1827 by other settlers. Land was also obtained through the Canada Company, mostly in the Huron District.

Types of Records

* Land petitions or memorials: the initial step in the process to acquire Crown land. Land books recorded when a petition was received.
* Land Boards: established in 1788 to grant certificates of location to settlers in the area to be known as Upper Canada; abolished in 1794. They include documents that predate the establishment of the Land Boards, presented to support applications for grants, etc.
* Patents: the document confirming ownership of Crown land. Any conveyances made after issue of patent are registered in the local Registry Office.
* Abstract indexes to deed: transfers of land after the initial grant was made; found in county and district registry offices.
* Township Papers: contain records of local property disputes; arranged by concession and lot number; in loose files at the Archives of Ontario in Toronto. Orders-in-Council, location certificates of settlement duties, copies of receipts, some correspondence, copies of Surveyor-General's descriptions, etc.
* Upper Canada Sundries files: correspondence, petitions, reports, returns and schedules, certificates, accounts, warrants, legal opinions, instructions and regulations, proclamations, and other documents received by the Civil and Provincial Secretaries of Upper Canada, 1791–1841. Many letters concern land and military matters.
* *Ontario Archives Land Record Index* (n.p.: Computrex Centre Ltd., 1979, fiche 6049631 ff.). The information is derived from three groups of records: the Crown Lands Papers, the Canada Company Papers, and the Peter Robinson Papers. The Index to Land Patents is not incorporated into this

---

[55] For more information on Loyalists, see New France.

system, and the Land Board records from 1819–25 must be used separately. The data ranges from the 1780s to the beginning of World War I.

- Heir and Devisee Commission: issued rulings on land titles before patents were issued, especially for those who had not exchanged their Crown land certificates for a patent. Sometimes an heir to the original nominee had to complete the process.
- Concessions: see Quebec.

Provincial Records

Crown Lands Department, Ontario.
- Land records, 1792–1876 (film 1316141 ff.).
- Township Papers, 1783–1870s (Toronto: Archives of Ontario, 1982, film 1319288 ff.).
- Crown land records card index, 1786–1868 (film 1544230 ff.). Card index of personal and place names extracted from various types of land records: surveyors' letters, land rolls, land sales, petitions, etc.

The original records are at the Archives of Ontario in Toronto.

Archives of Ontario. *Preliminary Inventory of the Records of Record Group 1.* 2 Vols. (Ottawa: The Archives, 1988). Preliminary inventory of the records of the Office of the Surveyor-General, 1763–1845; Crown Lands Department, 1827–1905.

Heir and Devisee Commission (1st), Upper Canada. Land records, 1784–1857 (film 1305909 ff.). Heir and Devisee Commission records include case files, reports, and minutes, along with the Surveyor-General's notes for Quebec and Ontario. The records after 1804 were created by the second Heir and Devisee Commission. The original records are at the National Archives in Ottawa, Ontario.

Districts
Eastern, 1784–1841
Johnstown, 1782–1840
Midland, 1784–1841
Home, 1787–1837
Western, 1787–1841
London, 1803–41

Niagara, 1802–19
Niagara and Home, 1788–1804, 1820, 1856
Gore, 1816–24
Newcastle, 1798–1835
Bathurst, 1840–1

Townships
Ancaster, 1794–9
Blenheim, 1797–9
Beverly, 1796–9
Burford, 1796–9
Charlotteville, 1797–9
Crowland, 1797

Ernestown, 1812
Etobicoke, 1794–9, 1828
Gainsborough, 1794–9, 1828
Grimsby, 1794–9, 1802
Humberstone, 1794–9, 1828
Lansdowne, 1794–9, 1828
Loughborough, 1794–9, 1828

Markham, 1794–9, 1828	Townsend, 1797–1801
Newark, 1794–9, 1802	Vaughan, 1797–1801
Oxford, 1796–9	Wainfleet, 1789–1803
Pelham, 1795–9	Wolford, 1789–1803
Rainham, 1795–9	York, 1789–1803
Saltfleet, 1797–1801	Loyalist claims, 1777–1816
Southwold, 1797–1801	Claims allowed, 1797–1804, 1805–23
Thorold, 1797–1801	

Executive Council, Provincial Secretary, Upper Canada.
- Petitions for land grants and leases, 1791–1867 (film 1832344 ff.).
- Index to Upper Canada Land Board minutes and records, 1765–1804 (film 1851299 ff.).
- Upper Canada Sundries, Civil and Provincial Secretaries, 1766–1841 (film 1819518 ff.).
- Upper Canada Sundries, land petitions, 1790–1855 (Ottawa: National Archives, 1965, film 0477538).
- Manuscript Division, National Archives of Canada. *Upper Canada Sundries, Finding Aid 881: 1776–1858* (Ottawa: The Archives, 1975, film 1025228 ff.). *Finding Aid 881* provides a description of each item.
- Index to surrendered and impounded deeds and leases for Upper Canada, 1787–1848 (film 1851370 ff.). Includes letters patents for grants or leases, surrendered to or impounded by the Clerk of the Executive Council when discovered to be flawed; and the Surveyor General's description of certain land grants used to supply information necessary for the production of letters patent.

The original card indexes and records of the above are at the National Archives in Ottawa, Ontario.

Johnstown District index to Crown lands, 1780–1958, and land grants (Ottawa: National Archives, 1965, film 0477530 ff.). The original records are at the National Archives in Ottawa, Ontario.

Registrar of Deeds, Niagara District. Land records, 1796–1840 (film 0170145 ff.). Niagara District included the present-day counties of Lincoln, Welland, and Haldimand. The original records are at the Registrar's Office in Saint Catharines.

County Records

The following are some, but not all, of the county land records available on microfilm. General registers include transcripts of wills, administrations, etc., involving land transactions. Land records include memorials and other instruments; some may also include indentures and wills.

Registrar of Deeds, Dundas County.
- General register, 1801–1910 (film 1903032 ff.).

- Land records, 1800–1955 (film 0201604 ff.).
- Provincial Registrar's Department. Return of lands patented in Dundas County, 1793–1847 (film 0201605).

The original records are at the Registrar's Office in Morrisburg.

Registrar of Deeds, Glengarry County.
- Abstract index books, 1800–1959 (film 0201715 ff.).
- General register, 1798–1957 (film 1731128 ff.).
- Land records, 1798–1957 (film 0201709 ff.).

The original records are at the Registrar's Office in Alexandria.

Registrar of Deeds, Grenville County. Abstract index books, 1800–1959 (film 0201641 ff.). The original records are at the Registrar's Office in Prescott.

Registrar of Deeds, Haldimand County.
- Deeds and land records, 1788–1954 (film 1927502 ff.)
- General register, 1800–83 (n.p.: London Microfilming, 1959, film 0171287).
- Abstract index books, 1795–1958 (film 0171261 ff.).

Land records for years prior to 1847 are in the records of the Niagara District. The original records are at the Registrar's Office in Cayuga.

Registrar of Deeds, Halton County.
- Abstract index books, 1798–1958 (film 0178978 ff.).
- Land records, 1803–81 (film 0179001 ff.).

The original records are at the Registrar's Office in Milton.

Registrar of Deeds, Kent County.
- Land records, 1789–1954, index, 1797–1957 (film 0105580 ff.).
- Abstract index books, 1800–1957 (film 0105464 ff.).

The original records are at the Registrar's Office in Chatham.

Registrar of Deeds, Lanark County.
- Abstract index books, 1800–1959 (film 0200671 ff.).
- Land records, 1802–1921 (film 0200666 ff.).

The original records are at the Registrar's Office in Perth.

Registrar of Deeds, Norfolk County.
- Land records, 1797–1953 (film 0160664 ff.).
- Abstract index of surveys, 1798–1958 (film 0160638 ff.).
- Department of the Secretary and Registrar. Return of lands patented in Norfolk County, 1797–1877 (film 0160668).

The original records are at the Registrar's Office in Simcoe.

Registrar of Deeds, Prescott County.
* Abstract index books, 1800–1959 (film 0201590 ff.).
* Land records, 1797–1908 (film 0201553 ff.).
The original records are at the Registrar's Office in L'Orignal.

Registrar of Deeds, Russell County.
* Land records, 1806–1978 (film 0201519 ff.).
* Abstract index books, 1800–1959 (film 0201518 ff.).
The original records are at the Registrar's Office in Russell.

Land Companies and Miscellaneous Records
Peter Robinson supervised Irish immigration to Bathurst and Newcastle districts in 1823 and 1825, particularly townships in Peterborough County and Lanark County, and Huntley Township in Carleton County. The emigration was from County Cork, Ireland.

Peter Robinson Papers Located at the Peterborough Public Library, Ontario (Toronto: Archives of Ontario, 1955, film 0394002). Microfilm of manuscript material in the Peterborough Public Library relating to the 1823 and 1825 settlements in the Bathurst and Newcastle districts, and containing ships' lists of emigrants and various records relating to the emigration in 1823 and 1825 and miscellaneous documents, 1828, 1844.

Bennett, Carol. *Peter Robinson's Settlers* (Renfrew, ON: Juniper Books Ltd., 1987).

Coleman, Thelma and James Anderson. *The Canada Company* (Stratford, ON: County of Perth and Cumming Publishers, 1978). Includes a list of early families in the Huron Tract (1835–9) and early settlers in Guelph and Crown Land Reserves (1827–36).

Trace, Mary Kearns. *The Upper Canada Gazette and American Oracle: Index to Personal Names, 1793–1798* (Calgary, AB: Traces, 1988). The paper was published at Newark (Niagara) at and later at York. A great percentage of the names indexed pertain to deed and land grant lists that were published regularly during this time period. The grant lists were printed for all areas in Ontario.

Spragge, Godfrey L. *A Guide to Ontario Land Registry Records* (Toronto: Ontario Genealogical Society, 1994).

Before an immigrant could receive a Crown grant, it was necessary to take an oath of allegiance. Records before 1828 can be found in land petitions, Township Papers, and other land records. After 1828, a seven-year residency requirement had to be fulfilled before the oath could be taken. Those registers are at the National Archives in Ottawa, Ontario (RG B47):

Provincial Secretary's Office, Upper Canada. Naturalization returns, 1828–50 (Ottawa: National Archives, 1980, film 1631550 ff.). Records give name, occupation, residence, and date of naturalization. Sometimes the date of arrival in the province is given. Returns were made annually by the county registrar. These records have been abstracted in McKenzie, Donald A. *Upper Canada Naturalization Records, 1828–1850* (Toronto: Ontario Genealogical Society, 1991).

Lauber, Wilfred R. *An Index of Land Claim Certificates of Upper Canada Militiamen Who Served in the War of 1812–1814* (Toronto: Ontario Genealogical Society, 1995). The information consists of Land Claim Certificates, Certificate B's, discharge papers from the Incorporated Militia, and other supporting documents, and is not yet microfilmed. The original records are in the "C" Series at the National Archives in Ottawa, Ontario.

Suggested Reading

Bennett, Carol. *Valley Irish* (Renfrew, ON: Juniper Books, 1983). History of the Irish in the Ottawa Valley, with concentration on the townships that once formed the old District of Bathurst.

Cameron, Wendy and Mary McDougall. *The Petworth Emigration Scheme: A Preliminary List of Emigrants from Sussex and Neighbouring Counties in England to Upper Canada, 1832–1837* (n.p.: Wordforce, 1990).

Canniff, William. *History of the Settlement of Upper Canada, Ontario, with Special Reference to the Bay of Quinte* (Toronto: Dudley and Burns, 1869, film 0908363).

Casselman, Alexander Clark. *The Story of the Palatines: An Address by Alexander Clark Casselman to the United Empire Loyalists' Association of Ontario, 1900* (Hamilton, ON: Hamilton Branch, United Empire Loyalists' Association of Canada, 1984). History of Palatine immigration to New York and Ontario.

Craig, Gerald M. *Upper Canada: The Formative Years, 1784–1841* (London, ON: McClelland and Stewart, 1963).

Fleming, Patricia Lockhart. *Upper Canada Imprints, 1801–1841: A Bibliography* (Toronto: University of Toronto Press, 1988).

Graeff, Arthur D. *The Pennsylvania Germans in Ontario, Canada* (n.p.: Pennsylvania German Folklore Society, film 1598296).

Guillaume, Sandra. *Sources for Genealogical Research in Ontario* (Salt Lake City: Genealogical Society of the Church of Jesus Christ of Latter-day Saints, 1969, fiche 6039427).

MacDonell, J.A. *Sketches Illustrating the Early Settlement and History of Glengarry in Canada: Relating Principally to the Revolutionary War of 1775–83, the War of 1812–14 and the Rebellion of 1837–8* (Montreal: William Foster, Brown, and Co., 1893, film 0874418).

MacKenzie, A.E.D. *Baldoon: Lord Selkirk's Settlement in Upper Canada* (London, ON: Phelps Publishing Co., 1978). History of the colonization of Baldoon by Scottish emigrants. Many of its settlers settled nearby Wallaceburg (formerly "The Forks") and surrounding townships in Kent County.

McLean, Marianne L. *The People of Glengarry: Highlanders in Transitions, 1745–1820* (Montreal: McGill-Queen's University Press, 1991). Highland communities in Glengarry County that were established by nine group emigrations which left western Inverness between 1785 and 1802 for Glengarry County.

Middleton, Jesse Edgar and Fred Landon. *The Province of Ontario: A History, 1615–1927.* 5 Vols. (Toronto: Dominion Publishing, 1927–8, fiche 6048255 ff.).

Neville, Gerald J. *The Lanark Society Settlers: Ships' Lists of the Glasgow Emigration Society, 1821* (Ottawa: British Isles Family History Society of Greater Ottawa, 1995). Transcript of the ships' lists of the Glasgow Emigration Society settlers that traveled to Quebec for settlement in Upper Canada. The Lanark Society settlers belonged to approximately forty emigration societies under an emigration scheme in 1820 and 1821.

Pioneer Life on the Bay of Quinte: Including Genealogies of Old Families and Biographical Sketches of Representative Citizens (Toronto: Rolph and Clark, 1904, film 0982201). Families listed are of United Empire Loyalist descent, and settled in Prince Edward County and the nearby counties of Hastings, Lennox and Addington, and Frontenac.

Reaman, G. Elmore. *The Trail of the Huguenots* (n.p.: Book Society of Canada, 1965). This includes the history of the French Huguenots from New York who settled on the Bay of Quinte in 1784.

Russell, Victor L. *Ontario's Heritage: A Guide to Archival Resources* (Cheltenham, ON: Boston Mills Press, 1978).

Weaver, Emily Poynton. *The Story of the Counties of Ontario.* 2 Vols. (Toronto: Bell and Cockburn, 1913, film 0982166).

A BRITISH GRENADIER.

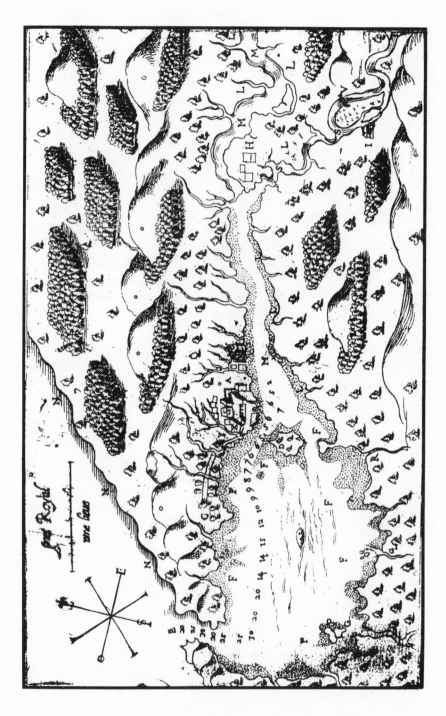

46 Port Royal (National Archives of Canada)

Acadia

Comprised of Île-Royale (Nova Scotia), Île-Sainte-Croix (New Brunswick), and Île-Saint-John (Prince Edward Island), Acadia was one of the earliest French settlements in North America. The Treaty of Utrecht in 1713 ceded most of Acadia to Britain as a permanent possession. In the 1740s, France and Britain were again at war, and troops from New England seized Louisbourg (Cape Breton) in 1745. It was returned to France by treaty in 1748. All of Acadia was under British control by 1763.

Le Grand Dérangement (The Great Uprooting)

From original settlement in 1604, the Acadian population at Port Royal grew from 500 people in 1671 to over 13,000 people in 1755. The Acadian population was left alone for thirty years. In 1755, at the beginning of the Seven Years' War, the claims of Acadian neutrality were no longer accepted by the British, and the deportations began. Over the years, the Acadians were exiled from Nova Scotia, Cape Breton, New Brunswick, Prince Edward Island, and Maine several times: they came to the American colonies, Quebec, and other places in North America. The time line of the diaspora is as follows:

1755: Half of the Acadian population was sent to the American colonies: Massachusetts (2,000), Connecticut (700), New York (250), Pennsylvania (500), Maryland (1,000), Virginia (1,100), North Carolina (500), South Carolina (500), and Georgia (400).

1756: Those Acadians that were sent to Virginia were rerouted to England.

1758: 2,500 Acadians who had escaped to Louisbourg were deported to England and France.

1763: Many of the Acadians who had been transported to the British American colonies emigrated to Quebec, the Maritimes, and the French West Indies (Saint-Domingue, Guadeloupe, and Martinique).

1763–5: Some Acadians who had been deported to the Carolinas, Georgia, and Maryland began to migrate to Louisiana.

1764: Acadians who had been sent from Virginia to England were now sent to France.

1763–83: The remaining refugees on Saint-Pierre-et-Miquelon were deported to France.

1766: 200 Acadians emigrated from Halifax to Louisiana.

1785: 1,500 Acadians emigrated from France to Louisiana.

> **SEE ALSO**
> France
> Great Britain
> Louisiana
> New France
> Quebec

Records of the diaspora that are held by the National Archives in Ottawa, Ontario are:

- List of Acadians deported in 1755.
- Locations of Acadians deported to Connecticut, 1756.[56]
- Petitions of Acadians in Massachusetts, 1755–63, and Acadian families in Boston, Massachusetts requesting to settle in Quebec, 1766 (original records at the Massachusetts State Archives in Boston).
- List of Acadians deported to France, 1758–63.
- List of Acadians residing in Kentucky, Maryland, Pennsylvania, South Carolina, and other colonies, 1763.
- Names of Acadians imprisoned at Saint John and Halifax, 1760–3.
- Shipping list of Acadians to England, 1762–72.

Records at the French National Archives, Section Outre-Mer, Paris (all on film 1077743 ff.), include:

- Emigrants from Acadia, 1760–1804.
- *Rôles des habitants* (Acadian censuses) and lists of refugees for Quebec, Saint-Pierre-et-Miquelon, Île-Royale, and Île-Saint-Jean, 1762–79 (film 1084569), including Saint-Pierre-et-Miquelon, 1764–89; Île-Royale, et Île-Saint-Jean réfugiés en France, 1762-73.
- Lists of refugees and emigrants in various colonies, 1758–1818.
- Refugees at Saint-Pierre-et-Miquelon, 1780–1826.
- Lists of Acadian families in Louisiana, who migrated from Saint-Domingue (Haiti), New York, and Nova Scotia, 1764–9.

Examples of Acadian records at French *Departmental* (state) Archives are:

- Census records for Normandy, 1763–89, at the Departmental Archives in Calvados, Caen.
- Census records of Acadians arriving at Nantes, 1775–6, and for Vienne, 1791, at the Departmental Archives in Vienne, Poitiers.
- Other archives that hold records of the Acadian exiles are: Vannes, Morbihan; Quimper, Finistere; Rouen, Seine-Maritime; Arras, Pais-de-Calais; Cherbourg, Manche; and La Rochelle, Charente-Maritime.

Records at the Louisiana Historical Society in New Orleans include:

- Acadian emigrants to Louisiana, 1784–5 (film 1305383).
- Microfilm copies of records at the National Archives in Ottawa, Ontario.
- Notarial records of Acadians in Louisiana, 1770–1850.

---

[56] This information is also found in *The Public Records of the Colony of Connecticut* 10 (Hartford, CT: Case, Lockwood, and Brainard, 1850–90, film 0908427), 452–3.

Records at the Centre d'Études Acadiennes, Université de Moncton, and the Société Historique Acadienne — both in Moncton, New Brunswick — include microfilm copies of many of the records described above.

The American Canadian Genealogical Society in Manchester, New Hampshire has a large collection of books and microfilm relating to the Maritime Provinces.

Suggested Reading

Arsenault, Bona. *Histoire et Généalogie des Acadiens.* 6 Vols. 2nd ed. (Montreal: Leméac, 1978, film 0873863). The history and genealogy of the Acadians in Nova Scotia, New Brunswick, Prince Edward Island, Quebec, Louisiana, and Saint-Pierre-et-Miquelon.

Brasseaux, Carl A. *The Founding of New Acadia: The Beginning of Acadian Life in Louisiana, 1765–1803* (Baton Rouge: Louisiana State University Press, 1987).

Brasseaux, Carl A. *Quest for the Promised Land: Official Correspondence Relating to the First Acadian Migration to Louisiana, 1764–1769* (Lafayette: University of Southwestern Louisiana, 1989).

Brault, Gerard J. *The French Canadian Heritage in New England* (Hanover, NH: University Press of New England, 1986).

Hebert, Donald J. *Acadians in Exile* (Cecilia, LA: Hebert Publications, 1980, fiche 6010582). This includes records of the Acadians from Acadia, Sinnamary, French Guiana, France, and the West Indies (Guadeloupe, Martinique, Saint-Domingue, and Saint Lucia).

Hebert, Donald J. *Researching Acadian Families* (Ville Platte, LA: Hébert Publications, 1987, film 1697360).

Hébert, Pierre-Maurice. *Les Acadiens du Québec* (Montreal: Editions de l'Echo, 1994). History of the Acadians in Quebec.

Hebert, Timothy. *Acadian-Cajun Genealogy: Step by Step* (Lafayette, LA: Center for Louisiana Studies, 1993).

Jehn, Janet B. *Corrections and Additions to Arsenault's Histoire et Généalogie des Acadiens* (Covington, KY: The Author, 1988, fiche 6088770).

Mahaffie, Charles D. *A Land of Discord Always: Acadia from Its Beginning to the Expulsion of Its People, 1604–1755* (Camden, ME: Down East Books, 1995).

Martin, Ernest. *Les Exilés Acadiens en France au XVIIIe Siècle et leur Établissement en Poitou* (Paris: Librairie Hachette, 1936, film 0924514). The exiled Acadians in France in the eighteenth century and their establishment in Poitou.

Poirier, Pascal. *Des Acadiens Déportés à Boston, en 1755: Un Épisode du Grand Dérangement* (n.p., n.d., film 1597996). The Acadians who were deported to Boston in 1755: an episode of large-scale displacement.

Reed, William B. *The Acadian Exiles, or French Neutrals in Pennsylvania* (Richibouctou, NB: R. Babineau, 1984).

Rieder, Milton P. *The Crew and Passenger Registration Lists of the Seven Acadian Expeditions of 1785: A Listing by Family Groups of the Refugee Acadians Who Migrated from France to Spanish Louisiana in 1785* (Metairie, LA: n.p., 1965).

Rieder, Milton P. and Norma Gaudet Rieder. *The Acadians in France, 1762–1776: Rolls of the Acadians Living in France Distributed by Towns for the Years 1762 to 1776.* 3 Vols. (Metairie, LA: n.p., 1967–73).

Université de Moncton, Centre d'Études Acadiennes. *Inventaire Général des Sources Documentatires sur les Acadiens* (Moncton, NB: The Center, 1975–7).

Wood, Gregory. *A Guide to the Acadians in Maryland in the Eighteenth and Nineteenth Centuries* (Wheaton, MD: The Author, 1995). Traces the history of Acadian migration from Maryland to Louisiana, and those Acadians who remained in Maryland.

Nova Scotia

Originally, Nova Scotia included the provinces of New Brunswick (until 1769) and Prince Edward Island (until 1784). The French established a settlement at Port Royal (Annapolis Royal) in 1605. The British attacked Port Royal in 1709 and captured it in 1710. The British founded Halifax in 1748 with British colonists and German and Swiss Protestants from Friesland, Hamburg, and the Upper Rhine Valley. In 1752 German and Swiss families from Halifax relocated to Lunenburg, Nova Scotia.

Townships were laid out in Nova Scotia in 1759 to attract New Englanders to settle on land vacated by the Acadians. Those who came were primarily from New London, Connecticut and Newport, Rhode Island; others came from Nantucket, Plymouth, and Boston, Massachusetts, and Portsmouth, New Hampshire. In 1772 a group of Highland Scots emigrated to Pictou, and a group of Yorkshire families settled at Chignecto. In 1784, 19,000 Loyalist refugees settled at Nova Scotia. Cape Breton was a French possession until 1763, when it was attached to Nova Scotia. It was separated from Nova Scotia in 1784 and annexed back in 1820.

Church Records and Sources

Anglican parish registers begin in 1752, Catholic in 1702, Congregational in 1762, and Baptist in 1784. Originals or copies of most registers are at the Provincial Archives in Halifax.

Acadian church records: 1705–1955 (film 1319976 ff.). Some of the many records in this series are:

- Saint Mary's (Church Point) and Saint Mandé (Meteghan), catalog of families, 1799–1811.
- Annapolis Royal (Saint-Jean-Baptiste), baptisms, marriages, and burials, 1727–55. There are also records from 1702 that may not have been filmed.
- Father Charles François Bailly for Acadia, baptisms, marriages, and burials, 1768–73.
- Chibouktou, Port Royal, funeral ceremonies, 1705–28.

The original records are at the Acadian Center, Sainte-Anne's College, Church Point.

SEE ALSO
Acadia
France
Louisiana
New Brunswick
New France
Newfoundland
Quebec

Église Catholique, Saint-Charles-Aux-Mines, Grand Pre. Parish registers, 1707–48. The original records are at the Archives of the Diocese of Baton Rouge, Baton Rouge, Louisiana. These records have not been filmed.

Église Catholique, Notre-Dame, Louisbourg, Île Royale. Registres paroissiaux, 1715–58 (film 0959785 ff.). Parish registers of baptisms, marriages, and burials for Louisbourg, Île Royale, now Cape Breton County, Nova Scotia. The original records are at the French National Archives, Section Outre-Mer, Paris.

Église Catholique, Beaubassin. Registres paroissiaux, 1712–48 (Ottawa: National Archives, n.d., film 0476183). Baptisms, marriages, and burials. The original records are at the National Archives in Ottawa, Ontario.

Church of England in Canada, Saint Luke, Annapolis Royal. Parish register transcripts, 1782–1817 (film 0928970). The typescript is at the National Archives in Ottawa, Ontario. The original register is at the Provincial Archives in Halifax, and dates from 1752.

Bailly, Charles François. *Registre de l'Abbé Charles-François Bailly, 1768 à 1773* (Moncton, NB: Centre d'Études Acadiennes, Université de Moncton, 1978). A transcript of the baptism, marriage, and burial register of Father Bailly kept while he lived in Halifax. The records also include New Brunswick.

Campeau, Lucien. *La Première Mission d'Acadie, 1602–1616* (Quebec: Presses de L'Université Laval, 1967). History of the first Jesuit mission to Acadia.

Congregational Church, Chebogue. *The Records of the Church of Jebogue in Yarmouth, Nova Scotia, 1766–1851* (Yarmouth, NS: Stoneycroft Publishers, 1992). Contains a transcript of the original Chebogue Congregational Church records held by the Provincial Archives in Halifax.

De Ville, Winston. *Acadian Church Records.* 5 Vols. (Mobile, AL: The Author, 1964, fiche 6087648 ff.). Compilation of miscellaneous baptismal, marriage, and funeral records from Beaubassin, Rivière Saint-Jean, Mines, missions in New Brunswick, and the parish churches of Sainte, Baie-des-Challeurs, Grande Rivière, Beaubassin, Port Royal, and other places in Acadia and the Gaspé Peninsula and Quebec.

Betts, E. Arthur. *Congregational Churches in Nova Scotia and New Brunswick, 1749–1925* (Sackville, NB: Maritime Conference, United Church of Canada, 1985).

Johnston, Angus Anthony. *A History of the Catholic Church in Eastern Nova Scotia* (Antigonish, NS: Saint Francis Xavier University Press, 1960).

Levy, George E. *The Baptists of the Maritime Provinces, 1753–1946* (Saint John, NB: Barnes-Hopkins, Ltd., 1946, fiche 6110631). This also covers New Brunswick and Prince Edward Island.

Census Records and Sources

Census records of the French dominion begin in 1671, and British censuses begin in 1752. For the original censuses taken by the French, see the section on France.

Trahan, Charles C. *Acadian Census, 1671–1752* (Rayne, LA: Hébert Publications, 1994). This covers Nova Scotia, New Brunswick, and Prince Edward Island.

De Ville, Winston. *The Acadian Families in 1686* (Ville Platte, LA: The Author, 1986).

Census records and poll tax rolls for Nova Scotia, 1770–1838 (film 1376295 ff.). The 1770 census records include areas of New Brunswick that were once part of Nova Scotia. The original records are at the Provincial Archives in Halifax.

La Roque, Joseph de. *Tour of Inspection Made by the Sieur De La Roque: Census, 1752* (Ottawa: S.E. Dawson, 1906, film 1006146). Census of Île-Royale.

Richard, Bernice C. *Nova Scotia 1770 Census* (Chicago: Chicago Genealogical Society, 1972, film 0982213).

Richard, Bernice C. *Nova Scotia: Some Assessment, Tax Grantees, Tenants and Other Lists, 1765–1789: Supplemental to the Nova Scotia 1770 Census* (Chicago: Chicago Genealogical Society, 1985).

Civil Registration and Notarial Records

Records of early civil registration for Acadia (from 1679) are at the Provincial Archives in Halifax. Transcripts of marriage bonds issued at Halifax, Nova Scotia, 1763–1871 (film 1376196 ff.), are at the Provincial Archives in Halifax.

Notarial records contain wills, marriage settlements, land and property transactions, etc. The following are some of the notarial records that have been filmed:

* Notariat, Acadie. Actes de notaire, 1687–1741 (film 0963350).
* Notariat, Acadie. Actes de notaire, 1715–22 (film 0963363).
* Notariat, Acadie. Actes de notaire, 1730–58 (film 0963351 ff.).

- Notariat, Acadie. Actes de notaire, 1730–58 (film 0963353).
- Notariat, Louisbourg, Île Royale. Actes de notaire, 1737–53 (film 0963354).

The original records of the above are at the French National Archives, Section Outre-Mer, Paris.

Loppinot, Jean Chrysostome. *The Loppinot Papers, 1687–1710: Genealogical Abstracts of the Earliest Notarial Records for the Province of Acadia* (Ville Platte, LA: The Author, 1991). Entries concern people from Port Royal (now Annapolis Royal); they also cover New Brunswick and Prince Edward Island.

Court and Land Records and Sources
French Records
The records of the French dominion consist of the *Conseil Superieur de Loiusbourg* (Superior Court of Louisbourg), 1711–58. They contain court proceedings and estate, guardian, and indenture records. The original records are at the French National Archives, Section Outre-Mer, Paris.

Concessions (land records) of Louisbourg, 1720–42, are kept at the French National Archives, Section Outre-Mer, Paris and are filmed for 1735–40 (film 1077743 ff.). Copies of the original records are at the National Archives in Ottawa, Ontario. French land and court records can also be found in notarial records described above.

Marble, Allan E. *Deaths, Burials, and Probate of Nova Scotians, 1749–1799, from Primary Sources.* 2 Vols. (Halifax: Genealogical Association of Nova Scotia, 1990).

British Records
One of the earliest records of English occupation is an allegiance list to the English King, taken in Nova Scotia in 1695. The original list is at the Massachusetts State Archives in Boston. There is a card index to the Archives, 1629–1799 (film 0543878 ff.), which can help identify the contents of this — and possibly other records. There is a filmed copy of the allegiance list at the National Archives in Ottawa, Ontario.

British land and court records begin in 1749 and were recorded on the county level. Some of the records that have been filmed are:

Annapolis County
- Registrar of Deeds. Land records, 1763–1970 (film 0814052 ff.).
- Court of Probate. Estate files, 1763–1925 (film 1838799 ff.).

The original records are at the Annapolis County Courthouse in Annapolis Royal.

Halifax County
- Registrar of Deeds. Deed records, 1749–1903, index, 1749–1967 (film 0530611 ff.)
- Court of Probate. Wills, 1749–1967 (film 0466415 ff.).

The original records are at the Halifax County Courthouse in Halifax.

Pictou County

Registrar of Deeds. Index to deeds, 1771–1967, deeds, 1771–1905 (film 0578943 ff.). The original records are at the Pictou County Courthouse in Pictou.

Gilroy, Marion. *Loyalists and Land Settlement in Nova Scotia* (Halifax: Provincial Archives of Nova Scotia, 1937, fiche 6046551).

Crown land grants begin in 1763 and contain township grants, petitions, survey warrants, survey descriptions, certificates from the Surveyor General, and grants.[57]

Department of Crown Lands, Nova Scotia. Land records, 1763–1914, index, 1784–1877 (film 1378554 ff.). This also covers the county of Sunbury, Nova Scotia, which was re-established as Sunbury County, New Brunswick in 1785. The original records are at the Provincial Archives in Halifax.

Land grants of various counties in Nova Scotia (Ottawa: National Archives, 1965, film 0477530). The original manuscript is at the National Archives in Ottawa, Ontario.

Loyalist land grants date from 1775. Grant applications often included information stating the services claimants had made on behalf of the British Crown during the American Revolution. This information can help in determining the probable areas of origin of refugees in the United States. Most of the services rendered by the refugees had to do with the regional military units to which they belonged.[58]

Smith, Clifford Neal. *Whereabouts of Some American Refugees, 1784–1800: The Nova Scotian Land Grants* (McNeal, AZ: Westland Publications, 1992). Union index to the Provincial Archives (of Nova Scotia) list of land grants, warrants, and escheats in Nova Scotia made to refugees from the American Revolution, published in 1937.

---

[57] For more information on Crown land grants, see Ontario.

[58] For more information on Loyalist claims, see New France.

Peterson, Jean. *The Loyalist Guide: Nova Scotian Loyalists and Their Documents* (Halifax: Provincial Archives of Nova Scotia, 1983, fiche 6010877).

Foreign Protestants who sailed from continental Europe (film 1376197). Contains passenger lists, 1750–3, for the ships *Ann, Speedwell, Gale, Murdoch, Pearl, Betty,* and *Sally,* and also includes victualling lists. The photocopied records are at the Provincial Archives of Nova Scotia in Halifax.

Stayner collection (film 1376187 ff.). The collection includes genealogical material of families in Nova Scotia, historical information, letters, documents, newspaper clippings etc. The original records are at the Provincial Archives in Halifax.

Suggested Reading

Akins, Thomas B. *Acadia and Nova Scotia: Documents Relating to the Acadian French and the First British Colonization of the Province, 1714–1758* (1869. Reprint. Cottonport, LA: Polyanthos, 1972).

Bell, Winthrop Packard. *The Foreign Protestants and the Settlement of Nova Scotia* (1961. Reprint. Camden, ME: Picton Press, 1990).

Campbell, D. *Beyond the Atlantic Roar: A Study of the Nova Scotia Scots* (Toronto: McClelland and Stewart, 1974, fiche 6046662).

Crowell, Fred E. *New Englanders in Nova Scotia* (Cambridge, MA: New England Historic Genealogical Society, 1979, film 1402829).

Elliot, Noel Montgomery. *The Atlantic Canadians, 1600–1900: An Alphabetized Directory of the People, Places and Vital Dates.* 3 Vols. (Toronto: Genealogical Research Library, 1994). Contains an index of over 500,000 names taken from records for the following provinces: Nova Scotia, New Brunswick, Newfoundland and Labrador, and Prince Edward Island, as well as the French islands of Saint-Pierre and Miquelon.

Fergusson, Charles Bruce. *Pre-Revolutionary Settlements in Nova Scotia* (Salt Lake City: Genealogical Society of the Church of Jesus Christ of Latter-day Saints, 1969, fiche 6039428).

Fergusson, Charles Bruce. *State and Provincial Archives, Treasure Houses for Historians and Genealogists: Nova Scotia* (Salt Lake City: Genealogical Society of the Church of Jesus Christ of Latter-day Saints, 1969, fiche 6039401).

Huling, Ray Greene. *The Rhode Island Emigration to Nova Scotia* (1889.

Reprint. Toronto: Canadiana House, 1984, fiche 6049736).

Kirké, Henry. *The First English Conquest of Canada: With Some Account of the Earliest Settlements in Nova Scotia and Newfoundland* (London: Bemrose, 1871, film 1035770).

MacGregor, John. *Historical and Descriptive Sketches of the Maritime Colonies of British America* (1828. Reprint. East Ardsley, England: S.R. Publishers, Ltd., 1968, fiche 6049589).

MacKay, Donald. *Scotland Farewell: The People of the Hector* (Toronto: McGraw-Hill Ryerson, Ltd., 1980, film). Story of the Highland Scots who sailed to Pictou, Nova Scotia in 1773 on the *Hector*.

MacNutt, William S. *The Atlantic Provinces: The Formation of a Colonial Society, 1712–1857* (Toronto: McClelland and Stewart, 1965).

McNeill, John Robert. *Atlantic Empires of France and Spain: Louisbourg and Havana, 1700–1713* (Chapel Hill: University of North Carolina Press, 1985).

Moore, Christopher. *Louisbourg Portraits: Life in an Eighteenth-Century Garrison Town* (Toronto: Macmillan & Co., 1982).

Murray, Hugh. *An Historical and Descriptive Account of British America: Comprehending Canada Upper and Lower, Nova Scotia, New Brunswick, Newfoundland, Prince Edward Island, the Bermudas, and the Fur Countries.* 3 Vols. 2nd ed. (Edinburgh: Oliver and Boyd, 1839, film 0982219).

Norton, Judith A. *New England Planters in the Maritime Provinces of Canada, 1759–1800: Bibliography of Primary Sources* (Toronto: University of Toronto Press in Association with Planters Studies Centre, Acadia University, 1993). This covers Nova Scotia, New Brunswick, and New England.

Punch, Terrence M. *Genealogist's Handbook for Atlantic Canada Research* 2nd ed. (Boston: New England Historic Genealogical Society, 1997). This includes New Brunswick, Prince Edward Island, and Newfoundland.

47 The Maritimes (Library of Congress)

New Brunswick

The first French settlement at New Brunswick was at the mouth of the Sainte Croix River in 1604. Saint John was founded in 1631. The first British settlement was also at Saint John, in 1762. New Brunswick was separated from Nova Scotia in 1784 and settled by 13,000 Loyalist refugees.

Church Records and Sources

Église Catholique, Saint-Pierre-aux-Liens, Caraque. Registres paroissiaux, 1768–1920 (film 0859880). The first part of the register includes entries made by the missionary Charles François Bailly in 1768–73. The registers, 1786–96, were made by the missionaries of South Baies des Challeurs, Restigouche, Miramichi, and Caraquet. The original records are at the Diocesan Archives in Bathurst.

The earliest Anglican parish registers at the National Archives in Ottawa, Ontario begin in the following years: Gagetown (1786), and Dumfries (1791). Other early parish registers are Kingsclear (1791), Northampton (1791), Prince William (1792), Saint Andrews (1787), and Woodstock (1790), which are at the Provincial Archives in Fredericton, some on film.

Civil Records and Sources

Supreme Court in Equity, New Brunswick. Court files, 1784–1912 (film 1508459 ff.). The Supreme Court in Equity was formerly called the Court of Chancery. The original records are at the Provincial Archives in Fredericton.

New Brunswick Crown Land Office.
- Description of land grants, 1763–1868 (film 0862077 ff.). The grants that were recorded before 1784 are at the Provincial Archives of Nova Scotia in Halifax.
- Land petitions, 1763–1860 (film 0843156 ff.).
- Land petitions, 1783–1857 (Fredericton: Provincial Archives, 1979–80, film 1249993 ff.). This is a newer filming of the same records.
- Index to land grants, 1765–1900, New Brunswick (Fredericton: Provincial Archives, 1973, film 1429802).
- Index to land grants, 1785–1852, abstract register of grants, 1785–1828,

SEE ALSO
Acadia
France
New France
Nova Scotia
Quebec

general index of grants, 1785–1830 (film 0851176).
The original records are at the Provincial Archives in Fredericton.

Probate court record indexes for counties in New Brunswick (film 1437508 ff.).
This is a probate court finding aid of the Provincial Archives (of New
Brunswick), containing a brief description of the probate court records for each
county and an alphabetical name index to the probate records. The county
records that began before 1800 are:

Charlotte County (1785)	Sunbury County (1786)
Kings County (1786)	Westmorland County (1787)
Queens County (1785)	York County (1786)
Saint John County (1785)	

Family histories and pedigrees from the Provincial Archives of New Brunswick
  (film 0851133 ff.). Collection of typescripts, manuscripts, and some
  published works at the Provincial Archives in Fredericton.

Suggested Reading

Dionne, Raoul. *La Colonisation Acadienne au Nouveau-Brunswick, 1760–1860:
Données sur les Concessions de Terres* (Moncton, NB: Chaire d'Études
Acadiennes, 1989). The Acadian colonization of New Brunswick, 1760–1860.

Fellows, Robert F. *Researching Your Ancestors in New Brunswick, Canada*
(n.p., n.d., 1979, fiche 6051366).

Hannay, James. *History of New Brunswick.* 2 Vols. (Saint John, NB: J.A.
Bowes, 1909, fiche 6051269).

Monro, Alexander. *New Brunswick, with a Brief Outline of Nova Scotia and
Prince Edward Island* (1855. Reprint. Belleville, ON: Mika Studio, 1972, film
0908697).

Rigby, Ann B. *A Guide to the Manuscript Collections in the Provincial Archives
of New Brunswick* (Fredericton: Provincial Archives, 1977, film 1036745).

Surette, Paul. *Petcoudiac: Colonisation et Destruction, 1731–1755* (Moncton,
NB: Éditions d'Acadie, 1988, fiche 6101565). Contains the history of the
colonization of Acadian villages in the region of the Shepody, Petitcodiac, and
Memramcook rivers, and their destruction during the British military expedition
in 1755.

Taylor, Hugh. *New Brunswick History: A Checklist of Secondary Sources*
(Fredericton: Provincial Archives, 1975).

Prince Edward Island

Originally known as Île-Saint-John, the first settlement was by the French at Port la Joie (Charlottetown) in 1719. British from New England seized the colony in 1745 and held it until 1748. The British took permanent possession of the island in 1758 and renamed it Saint John Island. Saint John Island was annexed to Nova Scotia in 1763 and became a separate colony in 1769. Highland Scots emigrated to the Island of Saint John in 1772. Almost one thousand United Empire Loyalists settled on Saint John in 1784. In the 1790s, Highland Scots from Sutherland settled at Antigonish. The island's name was changed to Prince Edward Island in 1799.

Church Records and Sources

Roman Catholic Church records begin in 1721. Before 1827, Prince Edward Island was part of the Diocese of Quebec. The earliest Anglican registers date from 1777. Many church records have been filmed and are available at the Provincial Archives in Charlottetown and the National Archives in Ottawa, Ontario.

Église Catholique, Paroisse de Île-Saint-Jean. Registres paroissiaux, 1721–58 (film 0959787). Parish registers of baptisms, marriages, and burials for Île-Saint-Jean, including Saint-Pierre-du-Nord, Saint-Pierre, 1721–58, and Saint-Pierre-du-Nord, Notre Dame, 1724–58. The original records are at the French National Archives, Section Outre-Mer, Paris. There are also copies of the parish registers at the Provincial Archives in Charlottetown and the National Archives in Ottawa, Ontario.

Anglican Church of Canada, Saint Paul, Charlottetown. Church records, 1777–1963 (Charlottetown: Provincial Archives, 1977, film 1630129 ff.). The original records are at the Anglican Diocese in Halifax, Nova Scotia.

United Church of Canada, Margate Pastoral Charge, Prince Edward Island. Church records, 1778–1968 (Charlottetown: Provincial Archives, 1980, film 1630118). Records cover localities in the eastern part of Prince County and the northwestern part of Queens County. The original records are at the Provincial Archives in Charlottetown.

Civil Records and Sources

Census records of the French dominion are at the French National Archives, Section Outre-Mer, Paris. See France for more information.

SEE ALSO
Acadia
France
New France
Nova Scotia
Quebec

The following court records are at the Provincial Archives in Charlottetown:

- Court of Probate, Prince Edward Island. Probate records, 1807–1901 (film 0861200 ff.). Will index, some exemplifications,

partitions, sundries, and other documents.
* Court of Chancery, Prince Edward Island. Court records, 1793–1934 (Charlottetown: Provincial Archives, 1979–80, film 1630150 ff.).

Records of Crown land grants from 1767–9 are at the Provincial Archives of Nova Scotia in Halifax. Crown land records after this time are at the Provincial Archives in Charlottetown.

Registrar of Deeds, Prince Edward Island. Land registry records (conveyance ledgers), 1769–1872 (Charlottetown: Provincial Archives, 1979–81, film 1630087 ff.). The original records are at the Provincial Archives in Charlottetown.

Prince Edward Island ship passenger lists (film 1036774). Nine ship passenger lists, 1775–1848. Most of the ships embarked from Scotland.

Suggested Reading

Blanchard, Joseph-Henri. *Histoire des Acadiens de l'Île du Prince-Edouard.* 3rd ed. (Summerside, PE: Williams and Crue, 1976). History of the Acadians of Prince Edward Island, including a census of names for 1728 and 1798.

Bolger, Francis W.P. *Canada's Smallest Province: A History of Prince Edward Island* (Charlottetown: Prince Edward Island Centennial Commission, 1973).

Campbell, Duncan. *History of Prince Edward Island* (Charlottetown: Bremner Brothers, 1875, fiche 6046785). This includes a census of the inhabitants on the Island of Saint John taken in 1798.

Harvey, Daniel Cobb. *The French Régime in Prince Edward Island* (1926. Reprint. New York: Arno Press, 1970).

Illustrated Historical Atlas of Prince Edward Island (1880. Reprint. Belleville, ON: Mika Publishing Co., 1977).

Jones, Orlo and Doris Haslam. *An Island Refuge: Loyalists and Disbanded Troops on the Island of Saint John* (Summerside, PE: Abegweit Branch of the United Empire Loyalist Association of Canada, 1983).

Jones, Orlo. *Family History in Prince Edward Island: A Genealogical Research Guide* (Charlottetown: Prince Edward Island Heritage Foundation, 1981, film 1421868).

Warburton, Alexander Bannerman. *A History of Prince Edward Island from Its Discovery in 1534 Until the Departure of Lieutenant-Governor Ready in A.D. 1831* (Saint John, NB: Barnes, 1923, fiche 6051267).

Webber, David A. *A Thousand Young Men: The Colonial Volunteer Militia of Prince Edward Island, 1775–1874* (Charlottetown: Prince Edward Island Museum and Heritage Foundation, 1990). History of the various volunteer companies that formed the militia during 1775–1874.

Saint-Pierre-et-Miquelon

Saint-Pierre-et-Miquelon is the only remaining French possession in North America. Along with Guadeloupe, Martinique, and Guyane (French Guiana), it holds the status of an Overseas Department of France. The first settlers were French fishermen in 1604. The islands have remained in French control except from 1713 to 1763, and 1793 to 1814, during which time they were occupied by Great Britain. During the Acadian deportations, many refugees escaped to Saint-Pierre-et-Miquelon.

Church Records and Sources

Église Catholique, Notre-Dame-des-Ardilliers, Miquelon. Registres paroissiaux, 1775–1830 (film 1072975). Parish registers of baptisms, marriages, and burials for Miquelon, Saint-Pierre-et-Miquelon.

Église Catholique. Paroisse de Saint-Pierre. Registres paroissiaux, 1763–1822 (film 1072978 ff.) Parish registers of indexes, baptisms, marriages, and burials for Saint-Pierre, Saint-Pierre-et-Miquelon.

The original records are at the French National Archives, Section Outre-Mer, Paris.

There are also parish registers for Saint-Pierre-et-Miquelon at the National Archives of Canada in Ottawa, Ontario. For more information, consult Campeau, Marielle and Patricia Kennedy. *Checklist of Parish Registers* (Ottawa: National Archives, 1975).

Civil Records and Sources

Saint-Pierre-et-Miquelon *recensements* (censuses), 1673–1785, and 1774–1804; and *mémoires généraux* (land records), 1762–1819 (film 1077743 ff.), are at the French National Archives, Section Outre-Mer, Paris. For census and lists of Acadian refugees in Saint-Pierre-et-Miquelon, see Acadia.

Notarial records, 1764–89, can be found at the French National Archives, Section Outre-Mer, Paris, and microfilm copies are available at the National Archives of Canada in Ottawa, Ontario.

Civil registration began in 1816. Ten-year indexes of births, marriages, and deaths for Miquelon, 1816–70 (film 1072978 ff.), and Saint-Pierre, 1823–70 (film 1072971 ff.), are at the French National Archives, Section Outre-Mer, Paris.

SEE ALSO
Acadia
Caribbean
France
French Antilles
New France
Nova Scotia

Suggested Reading

Andrieux, Jean-Pierre. *Saint Pierre and Miquelon: A Fragment of France in North America* (Lincoln, ON: W.F. Rannie, 1983).

Guyot-Jeannin, Olivier. *Guide des Sources de l'Histoire de Saint-Pierre-et-Miquelon: Tome Premier, Archives Publiques de l'Archipel* (Saint-Pierre: The Archives, 1982). Guide to research in the archives of Saint-Pierre-et-Miquelon.

Poirier, Michel. *Les Acadiens aux Îles Saint-Pierre et Miquelon, 1758–1828* (Moncton, NB: Les Editions d'Acadie, 1984). A history of the Acadians on the islands of Saint-Pierre-et-Miquelon, containing vital records, lists of emigrants and deportees, and government censuses.

Coins Struck in France for the Colonies.

Newfoundland and Labrador

Known as Île-de-Terre-Neuve by the French, Newfoundland was England's first North American colony. Portuguese and French fishermen were fishing in the waters off Newfoundland in the 1520s. In the 1540s Basque whalers from France and Spain established whaling stations on Labrador, the Gulf of Saint Lawrence, and most of Nova Scotia. The English entered the enterprise in the 1570s. In 1583 the English officially claimed the island. They established the Newfoundland Company in 1610 and founded Saint John's.

Between 1617 and 1632, several aborted settlements were attempted. The first permanent French colony was established at Plaisance (Placentia) in 1662. By 1670 there were about thirty small English settlements along the coast of Newfoundland, most of the colonists coming from Devon. An English fishery was organized in 1690 that extended from Bonvista to Trepassy. The French destroyed the English settlement at Saint John's in 1692. In turn, the British sacked the French settlement at Port Royal, Acadia in 1710.

The French territory on Newfoundland was ceded to Great Britain in 1713. In 1717 many of the French families in Plaisance began to migrate to Louisbourg, on Cape Breton Island. Irish laborers, mostly from County Waterford, were recruited for settlement on Newfoundland in the 1720s. It was annexed as a province of Great Britain in 1763. In the 1770s British fisheries were opened on Labrador. Newfoundland remained a separate British colony until 1949, when it joined the Dominion of Canada as the Province of Newfoundland and Labrador.

Church Records and Sources

The Anglican Church was established as the official church in Newfoundland in 1583. The earliest parish registers and other ecclesiastical records for Newfoundland and Labrador are:

- Society for the Propagation of the Gospel in Foreign Parts, Anglican Church, 1701–22
- Anglican, Saint Paul's, Trinity, 1752
- Anglican, Bonavista, 1786
- Anglican, Saint John's, Northern Peninsula and Labrador, 1790
- Wesleyan Methodist, Harbour Grace, 1765
- United Methodist, Carbonear, 1792

SEE ALSO
Acadia
France
Great Britain
New France
Nova Scotia

- Moravian, Labrador, 1771
- Congregational, Saint John's, 1775
- Catholic, Port-aux-Basques, 1715–77
- Catholic, Labrador, 1847

The Provincial Archives of Newfoundland and Labrador in Saint John's have original and filmed copies for all of the above except the Catholic records. They also hold copies of most later parish records in Newfoundland and Labrador. The Maritime History Archives of the Memorial University of Newfoundland in Saint John's have copies of the Saint Paul's Anglican Church at Trinity, 1753–1840; they also have copies of Catholic and Anglican parish registers from Ireland, 1750–1850.

Saint Paul's Anglican Church, Trinity, Newfoundland: Index of Names, Baptisms, Marriages and Burials, 1753–1867 (Saint John's: Newfoundland and Labrador Genealogical Society, 1995).

The Catholic Church records mentioned above are at archives in France and Quebec:
- Église Catholique, Paroisse de La Baleine, Île Royale. Registres paroissiaux, 1715–77 (film 0963362). Parish registers for La Baleine, Nova Scotia, including marriages and baptisms for Port-aux-Basques, Newfoundland, 1740. The original records are at the French National Archives, Section Outre-Mer, Paris.
- Église Catholique, Archidiocèse de Québec. Registres paroissiaux, 1662–1848 (film 1311432). Baptisms, marriages, burials, confirmations, and abjurations, including Labrador. The original records are at l'Archidiocèse de Québec in Quebec.

Hugolin, Père. *L'Éstablissement de Récollets de la Province de Saint-Denis à Plaisance en Île-de-Terre-Neuve, 1689* (Quebec: n.p., 1911, film 0856141). The settlement of the Franciscan friars from the Province of Saint-Denis at Plaisance, Newfoundland in 1689.

A History of the Churches in Newfoundland: A Supplement to a History of Newfoundland from the English, Colonial, and Foreign Records (London: Macmillan & Co., 1895, film 1421673).

Civil Records and Sources
The first French *recensements* (censuses) for Terre-Neuve begin in 1671–1711 (film 1098205). The original records are at the French National Archives,

Section Outre-Mer, Paris. English censuses begin in 1675.[59] The original records are in the Colonial Office Papers (CO 194) at the PRO in Kew, Surrey, England. Copies of these records are available at the Provincial Archives in Saint John's, the National Archives in Ottawa, Ontario, and other archives.

Early Census Records of Saint John's Harbour, Newfoundland: 1677, 1794–1795, 1796–1797, 1801–1802 (Saint John's: n.p., 1972, film 1033848).

Other references to British colonists in Newfoundland can be found in the Colonial Office Papers (CO 194), Original Correspondence, 1696–1922, and Register of Correspondence (CO 350).[60] Original Correspondence (CO 194/16) contains papers regarding the Moravian missionaries and their work on Labrador. For a description of what types of records are contained in the Colonial Office Papers, see the section on Great Britain.

The Provincial Archives in Saint John's have the original Surrogate Court records from 1787, Magistrate Court records from 1787, and Supreme Court records from 1795.

Early French land records, *mémoires généraux*, 1762–1819 (film 1077743), are at the French National Archives, Section Outre-Mer, Paris.

Crown Lands Department, Newfoundland. Land records, 1803–1990 (film 1753518 ff.). The original records are at the Department of Forestry Service and Lands, Howley Building, in Saint John's.[61]

The Registrar of Deeds at the Confederation Building in Saint John's has deeds and conveyances dating from 1825. They also hold some wills as early as 1744.

French notarial records are at the French National Archives, Section Outre-Mer, Paris. They cover *actes de notaire*, (notarial records) from 1696–1711 (film 0963360 ff.), 1712–14 (film 0963362), 1714–57 (film 0965951), in Plaisance, Terre-Neuve, now Placentia, Newfoundland.

---

[59] A detailed description of these records can be found in the *Genealogist's Handbook for Atlantic Canada* (Boston: New England Historic Genealogical Society, 1989), 34–6.

[60] Judith Prowse Reid, *Genealogical Research in England's Public Record Office: A Guide for North Americans* (Baltimore: Genealogical Publishing Co., 1996), 36.

[61] For a full description of Crown lands, see Ontario.

Suggested Reading

Barkham, Selma Huxley. *The Basque Coast of Newfoundland* (n.p.: Great Northern Peninsula Development Corporation, 1989). The history and description of the West Coast of Newfoundland, particularly the following islands: Codroy, Flat, Red, Governor's, Benie, Saint John's, and Ferolle.

Budgel, Richard. *A Survey of Labrador Material in Newfoundland and Labrador Archives* (Goose Bay, Labrador: Labrador Institute of Northern Studies, Memorial University of Newfoundland. Includes holdings for the following archives: Centre for Newfoundland Studies, Maritime History Group, Provincial Archives of Newfoundland and Labrador, Them Days Labrador Archive, and United Church Conference Archive.

Cell, Gillian Townsend. *English Enterprise in Newfoundland, 1577–1660* (Toronto: University of Toronto Press, 1969).

Chang, Margaret. *Provincial Archives of Newfoundland and Labrador. A Guide to the Government Records of Newfoundland* (Saint John's: The Archives, 1983).

Elliot, Noel Montgomery. *The Atlantic Canadians, 1600–1900: An Alphabetized Directory of the People, Places and Vital Dates* (Toronto: Genealogical Research Library, 1994). Index of more than 500,000 names taken from a wide range of records for Newfoundland, Labrador, and other locations.

Gosling, William G. *Labrador: Its Discovery, Exploration, and Development* (London: n.p., 1910).

Grenfell, Sir Wilfred Thomason. *Labrador, the Country and the People* (New York: Macmillan & Co., 1909).

Handcock, W. Gordon. *So Longe as There Comes Noe Women: Origins of English Settlement in Newfoundland* (Saint John's: Breakwater Books, 1989). Patterns of migration from the southwest and southern regions of England to Newfoundland from the early seventeenth century, and the process of settlement formation that followed.

Mannion, J.J. *The Peopling of Newfoundland* (Saint John's: Memorial University of Newfoundland, 1977).

Matthews, K. *A Who Was Who of Families Engaged in the Fishery and Settlement of Newfoundland 1660–1840* (Saint John's: The Author, 1971). Index to a collection at the Memorial University of Newfoundland.

Memorial University of Newfoundland, Maritime History Group. *Check List of*

Research Studies Pertaining to the History of Newfoundland in the Archives of the Maritime History Group. 7ᵗʰ ed. (Saint John's: The Group, 1984).

Neary, Peter. *Part of the Main: An Illustrated History of Newfoundland and Labrador* (Saint John's: Breakwater Books, 1983).

O'Dea, Agnes C. *Bibliography of Newfoundland* (Toronto: University of Toronto Press, 1986). Printed works relating to Newfoundland from early voyages to 1975, in national libraries in Canada, the U.S., and Great Britain.

O'Neill, Paul. *The Story of Saint John's, Newfoundland.* 2 Vols. (Erin, ON: Press Porcepic, 1975–6).

Pitt, Robert D.W. *Encyclopedia of Newfoundland and Labrador* (Saint John's: Newfoundland Book Publishers, 1967).

Prowse, Daniel Woodley. *A History of Newfoundland from the English, Colonial, and Foreign Records* (London: Macmillan & Co., 1895, film 1421673).

Punch, Terrence M. *Genealogist's Handbook for Atlantic Canada Research.* 2ⁿᵈ ed. (Boston: New England Historic Genealogical Society, 1997).

Quinn, David B. *Newfoundland from Fishery to Colony* (New York: Arno Press, 1969).

Researching Your Family's History in Newfoundland and Labrador (Saint John's: Newfoundland and Labrador Genealogical Society, 1986).

Roy, Pierre-Georges. *Inventaire de Pèces sur la Côte de Labrador Conservées aux Archives de la Province de Québec.* 2 Vols. (Québec: n.p., 1940–2). Inventory of documents about the coast of Labrador, conserved at the Archives Nationales du Québec.

Seary, E.R. *Family Names of the Island of Newfoundland* (Saint John's: n.p, 1977). The files for this manuscript are at the Memorial University of Newfoundland in the Folklore and Language Archive.

Thomas, Roberta and Heather Wareham. *A Guide to the Holdings of the Maritime History Archive of the Memorial University of Newfoundland* (Saint John's: Maritime History Archive of the Memorial University of Newfoundland, 1991).

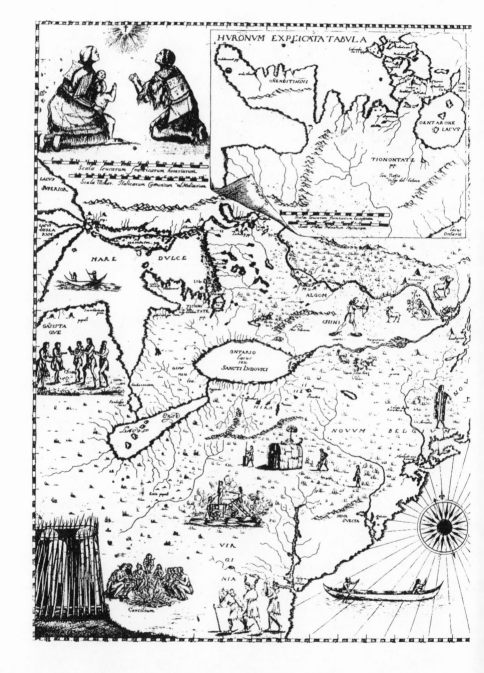

48 Jesuit map of Huronia, 1657 (National Archives of Canada)

Rupert's Land

In 1670 the Hudson's Bay Company was granted a charter by the English Crown for the area known as Rupert's Land, named for Prince Rupert, a cousin of King Charles II. At this time French traders were already operating trading posts in the Upper Mississippi and the Great Lakes area. By 1685 the English had established six forts on the Hudson Bay and James Bay, including York Factory (Manitoba) and Fort Albany. For a brief period the French captured these and other forts, until they closed most of their posts in 1696.

After the Treaty of Utrecht in 1713, control of the area was given to Great Britain, although the area continued to be disputed for many years. British Fort Churchill was built in 1717. The French built Fort Rouge (at a site near Winnipeg, Manitoba) in 1738. French trading posts on the Saskatchewan River were founded in the 1740s. Cumberland House (Saskatchewan) was founded by the Hudson's Bay Company in 1774, and the Company opened posts on Lake Athabasca (Alberta) in 1777.

The Northwest Company was organized in 1779. Spain established a fur trading post at Santa Cruz de Nuca (Nootka) on Vancouver Island from 1789 to 1795. The Hudson's Bay Company extended its posts to the Arctic Ocean, at the mouth of the Mackenzie River, in 1789, and founded Fort Augustus (Edmonton, Alberta) in 1794. A Russian post was opened at Sitka (Alaska) in 1799. By 1805 the Northwest Company had also expanded into Athabasca (Alberta) and the Pacific Coast.

In 1809 the Northwest Company built Fort Gibraltar (Winnipeg, Manitoba). The Red River Colony (Manitoba) was founded in 1812 by Highland Scots and some Swiss, Irish, and a group of mercenaries called the *de Meurons*. By 1815 the Hudson's Bay Company had established forty-two posts and the Northwest Company, fifty-nine, and both companies merged in 1821.

The border between United States and British territory was established at the forty-ninth parallel in 1818. All of the territory held by the Hudson's Bay Company was sold to the Canadian government in 1870. The provinces of Alberta, British Columbia, Manitoba, Saskatchewan, and the Northwest and Yukon territories were partially or completely created from this land.

SEE ALSO
Great Britain
New France
Ontario
Quebec
Wisconsin

Church Records and Sources

Early church records are kept in diocesan archives. A Roman Catholic parish was established at Red River in 1818 and an Anglican one in 1820. The Manitoba Genealogical Society has been extracting the Anglican parish registers for the Diocese of Rupert's Land.

Église Catholique, Mission de Saint-Joseph, Cumberland House, Saskatchewan. Registres paroissiaux, 1846–1915 (film 1033190). Parish registers. The original records are at the l'Église de Saint-Joseph, Cumberland House, Saskatchewan.

Kipling, Clarence. Kipling Collection, MG 25, G 62: Kipling Index (film 1851502). Kipling's index combines his transcripts from the Anglican parish registers of Saint John's, 1820–82, and Saint Andrew's, 1835–84; and the Roman Catholic parish registers of Saint Boniface, 1824–34. The original records are at the National Archives in Ottawa, Ontario.

MacDonald, Wilma. *Guide to the Holdings of the Archives of the Ecclesiastical Province and Dioceses of Rupert's Land* (Winnipeg: Saint John's College Press, 1986). Includes Anglican archives of Ecclesiastical Province of Rupert's Land, and the following dioceses: Athabasca, Brandon, Calgary, Edmonton, Keewatin, Mackenzie River, Qu'Appelle, Rupert's Land, Saskatchewan, and Saskatoon.

Civil Records and Sources

The Hudson's Bay Company Archives were filmed by the PRO in Kew, Surrey, England (see Great Britain). The original records have been transferred to the Provincial Archives of Manitoba in Winnipeg. The archives have been filmed through 1904 and may only be obtained through interlibrary loan from the Provincial Archives in Winnipeg to any public library. Some of the material contained in the manuscripts are:

➤ journals and correspondence, 1703–1894
➤ censuses, 1827–33, 1835, 1838, etc.
➤ contracts, employee records, etc., 1774–1904
➤ wills, 1717–1903
➤ ships' logs, 1751–1904
➤ land grants, 1811–71

A finding aid to the records is *Microfilm Register and Interlibrary Loan Finding Aid* (Winnipeg: Hudson's Bay Company Archives, Provincial Archives of Manitoba, 1988–9, film 1730847 ff.). This provides an inventory of microfilm numbers with brief descriptions of the records in the archives.

There are also records of the Hudson's Bay Company in the Colonial Office Papers, British North America, Original Correspondence, 1816–68 (CO 6) at the PRO in Kew, Surrey, England.

Rich, Edwin Ernest. *Minutes of the Hudson's Bay Company, 1671–1674* (Toronto: Champlain Society, 1942).

Oliver, E.H. *The Canadian North-West, Its Early Development and Legislative Records: Minutes of the Councils of the Red River Colony and the Northern Department of Rupert's Land* (Ottawa: Government Printing Bureau, 1914).

Martin, Archer E.S. *The Hudson's Bay Company's Land Tenures: And the Occupation of Assiniboia by Lord Selkirk's Settlers with a List of Grantees under the Earl and the Company* (1898. Reprint. Washington, DC: Library of Congress, 1979, film 1723747).

Manitoba census records, 1831–70 (Ottawa: National Archives, 1964, film 1375923). Censuses for Red River, 1827–56, were taken by or for the Hudson's Bay Company. The 1870 census was taken under the direction of Canada's Department of Agriculture.
Red River Settlement and province of Manitoba typed card index to the nominal census returns, 1832–70 (film 1420272 ff.). The original records are at the Provincial Archives of Manitoba in Winnipeg.

Martin, Chester Bailey. *Red River Settlement: Papers in the Canadian Archives Relating to the Pioneers* (n.p.: Archives Branch, 1910, film 0982391). Collection of the Selkirk Papers in the National Archives in Ottawa, Ontario.

Duckworth, Harry W. *The English River Book: A North West Company Journal and Account Book of 1786* (Montreal: McGill-Queen's University Press, 1990).

Wallace, W. Stewart. *Documents Relating to the North West Company* (Toronto: Champlain Society, 1934).

Suggested Reading

Briggs, Elizabeth. *Handbook for Reading and Interpreting Old Documents; With Examples from the Hudson's Bay Company Archives* (Winnipeg: Manitoba Genealogical Society, 1992).

MacBeth, R.G. *The Selkirk Settlers in Real Life* (1897. Reprint. Washington, DC: Library of Congress, 1990, film 1723762). History of the Selkirk settlers in the Red River Settlement, with particular emphasis on various aspects of daily life.

Newman, Peter C. *Empire of the Bay: An Illustrated History of the Hudson's Bay Company* (Markham, ON: Penguin Books Canada, Ltd., 1989).

Rich, Edwin Ernest. *The History of the Hudson's Bay Company [1670–1870]*. 2 Vols. (London: Hudson's Bay Record Society, 1958–9).

Willson, Beckles. *The Great Company: Being a History of the Honourable Company of Merchants-Adventurers Trading into Hudson Bay* (1900. Reprint.

Washington, DC: Library of Congress, 1990, film 1723751).

Part Seven

Resources for further research

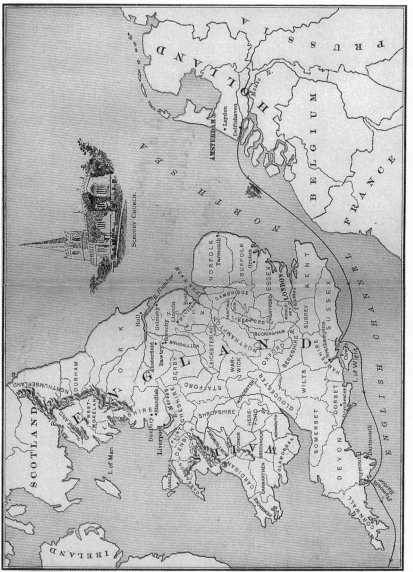

49 Homes of the Pilgrims in England and Holland (D.H. Montgomery, *The Leading Facts of English History*. London: Ginn & Co., 1912)

Religious Groups in the New World

Roman Catholic

The Catholic Church was the official church of all Spanish, Portuguese, and French colonies. From the time Franciscan missionaries accompanied Columbus on his second voyage, the Catholic Church was a continuing presence in the New World. Record keeping became obligatory after the Council of Trent in 1563, although there are parish registers that date from the early 1500s. By 1600 five archdioceses existed in Spanish America.

North America's first Catholic settlements were at Saint Augustine, Florida in 1565 and Santa Fe, New Mexico in 1598. Jesuits attempted a mission in Virginia between 1570 and 1572. Recollets (Franciscans) were active in New France (Canada) from 1611 and Jesuits from 1625. Maryland was settled in 1634 by a grant to the Calvert Family, which was Catholic, and was the only English colony to allow Catholicism, except from 1649 to 1657 when it was banned. Catholicism was the least accepted religion in the English colonies because England's two main enemies, France and Spain, were Catholic nations. In 1740 Parliament forbade the colonies to naturalize Catholics, also known as Papists. They could not vote or hold office in any colony; however, they were allowed to worship and to engage in commerce. This policy remained in effect until 1774, when the Quebec Act officially granted French Canadians freedom of worship. There were about 25,000 Catholics in the original thirteen colonies at the time of the Revolution.

Curran, Francis X. *Catholics in Colonial Law* (Chicago: Loyola University Press, 1965).

Ellis, John T. *Catholics in Colonial America* (Baltimore: Helicon Press, 1963).

Gongora, Mario. *Studies in the Colonial History of Spanish America* (Cambridge: Cambridge University Press, 1975).

Hummling, Virginia. *U.S. Catholic Sources: A Diocesan Research Guide* (Salt Lake City: Ancestry Publishing, Inc., 1995).

Moir, John Sargent. *Church and State in Canada, 1627–1867. Basic Documents* (Toronto: McClelland and Stewart, 1967).

Payne, Stanley G. *Spanish Catholicism: An Historical Overview* (Madison: University of Wisconsin Press, 1984).

Schwaller, John F. *The Church and Clergy in Sixteenth-Century Mexico*

(Albuquerque: University of New Mexico Press, 1987).

Moravians

The Moravian Church was founded in Kunewalde, Moravia in 1457. Originally a militant sect, they were defeated in battle at White Mountain (Prague) in 1620 (during the Thirty Years War). The first Moravians settled in Savannah, Georgia in 1734, but moved to Bethlehem, Northampton County, Pennsylvania in 1741. Another settlement from Germany was established in Bethlehem, Pennsylvania in 1741. Moravian missionaries were sent to Saint Croix, in the Virgin Islands (1732), New York (1752), Wachovia, North Carolina (1753), and Labrador (1771).

Fliegel, Carl J. *Index to the Records of the Moravian Mission Among the Indians of North America* (New Haven: Research Publications, 1970). Contains 135,000 entries classified as Indian, white, geographic name, Indian nation, mission, etc., from the 1700s through about 1820. Localities include New York, Connecticut, Pennsylvania, Ohio, Michigan, Indiana, Georgia, and Ontario. The original records are also available on film (film 1017681 ff.) and at the Archives of the Moravian Church in Bethlehem, Pennsylvania.

Gollin, Gilliam S. *Moravians in Two Worlds: A Study of Changing Communities* (New York: Arno Press, 1967).

Hamilton, John Taylor. *A History of the Movavian Church: Or the Unitas Fratrum, or the Unity of the Brethren, during the Eighteenth and Nineteenth Centuries* (1900. Reprint. New York: AMS Press, 1971).

Murphy, Patricia Shaubah. *The Moravian Mission to the African Slaves of the Dutch West Indies, 1732–1828* (Saint Thomas: Caribbean Research Institute, 1969).

Lutherans

The Lutheran Church was founded in 1517. The first Lutheran services in North America were held at Port Churchill, Hudson Bay, Canada in 1619.[62] The first Swedish Lutherans arrived in 1637 in the group of settlers on the Delaware River and in New Amsterdam in the 1620s. A congregation was organized in New York City in 1648. Palatine Germans founded Germantown, New York in 1709. Most Lutherans settled in Pennsylvania and Georgia. The church was officially organized in America in 1748.

---

[62] Sueflow, August R. *Church Records in the United States: Records of the Lutheran Churches of America* (Salt Lake City: Corporation of the President, 1969, fiche 6039392).

Nelson, E. Clifford. *The Lutherans in North America* (Philadelphia: Fortress Press, 1980).

Qualben, L.P. *Lutheran Church in Colonial America* (New York: Thomas Nelson, 1940).

Roeber, A.G. *Palatines, Liberty, Property: German Lutherans in Colonial British America* (Baltimore: Johns Hopkins University Press, 1993).

Anabaptists and Mennonites

The Anabaptist reform movement originated in Zurich in 1524. It spread into The Netherlands, were they were known as Mennonites. Protestant evangelists also spread the movement into Germany in the 1540s. The Amish Mennonites formed their own more conservative sect in 1693. The first Amish came to America in the 1720s and settled in Lancaster County, Pennsylvania.

Gratz, Delbert L. *Mennonite History: Studies in Anabaptists and Bernese Anabaptists and Their Descendants* (Goshen, IN: Mennonite Historical Society, 1953).

The Mennonite Encyclopedia: A Comprehensive Reference Work on the Anabaptist-Mennonite Movement. 4 Vols. (Hillsboro, KS: Mennonite Brethren Publishing House, 1955–9).

Schelbert, Loe. *Swiss Migration to America: The Swiss Mennonites* (New York: Alfred A. Knopf, 1980).

Huguenots and Walloons

The Huguenot (French Protestant) movement began in 1546 and was organized by synod in 1559. Walloons were native to northern France and southern Belgium, and the earliest congregation dates from 1571. The Massacre of Saint Bartholomew's Day in 1572 created many refugees who fled to Protestant European countries. In 1598 the Edict of Nantes granted religious freedom in France but it was repealed in 1685, abolishing the Protestant Church in France and beginning another major emigration. The refugees settled in exile in England, Germany, The Netherlands, and Switzerland. In the New World they settled at Fort Caroline, Florida in 1562, but the settlement was destroyed by the Spanish. Other settlements began in the French Antilles (from 1625), New Amsterdam (1623), Virginia (1621), Acadia and Quebec (1620s), from the Palatinate to New York (1678), South Carolina (1680), Massachusetts (1685), Rhode Island (1686), and North Carolina (1707).

Baird, Charles W. *History of the Huguenot Emigration to America.* 2 Vols. (1885. Reprint. Baltimore: Genealogical Publishing Co., 1966).

Currer-Briggs, Noel and Royston Gambier. *Huguenot Ancestry* (Chichester, Sussex: Phillimore, 1985).

Lart, Charles E. *Huguenot Pedigrees.* 2 Vols. (London: Saint Catherine Press, 1924–8, film 0441654).

Church of England (Anglican, Protestant Episcopal)

Anglican Church records begin in 1556. It became the official church in Virginia (1619), in four counties of New York (1693), South Carolina and Maryland (1706), North Carolina (1715), and Georgia (1758). The American colonies were placed under the episcopacy of the Bishop of London in 1691. The Society for the Propagation of the Gospel in Foreign Parts was founded in 1701 under the auspices of the Bishop of London to engage in missionary work in the colonies. As of 1701 there were only two clergymen of the Church of England in New England.[63]

Because of the size of the parishes in the south, a minister could not attend all services. One missionary wrote that it took him ten to twelve weeks to cover his parish. By 1775 there were almost 250 Anglican churches from Maine to Georgia. The first bishops were not installed in the American colonies until 1787. As a bishop was the only one who could perform the rite of confirmation, there are no confirmation records for America before 1787. [64]

Manross, William Wilson. *A History of the American Episcopal Church* (New York: Oxford University Press, 1935).

Oliver, David D. "The Society for the Propagation of the Gospel in the Province of North Carolina." *Proceedings, North Carolina Historical Society* V (1910): 1.

Congregational

The Puritan movement was influenced by the Calvinists but began at the inception of the Anglican Church in 1559 (Acts of Supremacy and Unity). Its goal was to purify the Anglican Church from the effects of Catholicism. A separatist congregation of Puritans from Scrooby, Nottinghamshire — fleeing from persecution — settled at Leiden, The Netherlands for a period of twelve years. They were called the Leiden Separatists, or Pilgrims, but referred to themselves as Saints. The Pilgrims contracted sponsors to colonize in the

---

[63] Charles F. Pascoe, *An Historical Account of the Society for the Propagation of the Gospel* (London: The Society, 1901), 41.

[64] John T. Humphrey, *Understanding and Using Baptismal Records* (Washington, DC: Humphrey Publications, 1996), 33.

Americas, eventually settling at New Plymouth, Massachusetts in 1620 — a third-choice location after Virginia and Bermuda.

The Dorchester adventurers who had settled at Cape Ann (Massachusetts) in 1623 went bankrupt, and they combined with Puritans from London and East Anglia to form the New England Company, re-chartered as the Massachusetts Bay Company. The Puritans settled at Naumkeag (Salem) in 1629 and Mishawaum, Shawmut (Boston), Mystic (Medford), and Watertown in 1630. From there other settlements sprang up in Massachusetts, Connecticut, New Hampshire, Maine, and Rhode Island. Another Puritan company, called the Providence Company, settled Providence Island, off the coast of Nicaragua, in 1630.

The fundamental difference between the Puritans who settled the Bay Colony and the Pilgrims who settled the Plymouth Colony was that the Puritans of the Bay Colony were not leaving England only for religious freedom; they meant to be in control of their own government, ruled by righteous "Saints." The local congregation was the highest authority, not a bishop, and the place of worship was called a meetinghouse instead of a church. In Massachusetts the Cambridge Platform was adopted in 1648, outlining a strict orthodox code. The Half-Way Covenant adopted in 1662 allowed some compromise regarding church franchise (membership). After the witchcraft trials of the 1690s the church was reorganized into councils, providing some centralized control.

Puritans considered marriage a civil contract, and there are no marriages recorded in church records before the 1690s.

The so-called Great Awakening (as it was later to be known) began in 1737 in Massachusetts. Its premise was that the emotions as well as the intellect needed to be involved in the spiritual experience; people's hearts needed to be touched so that their lives could be changed. Churches that grew in membership from this movement were Presbyterian, Baptist, and Methodist.

Levy, Babette, M. "Early Puritanism in the Southern and Island Colonies." *Proceedings of the American Antiquarian Society* LXX (1960): 293–8.

Miller, Perry. *The New England Mind: From Colony to Province* (Boston: Beacon Press, 1953).

Morgan, Edmund S. *The Puritan Dilemma: The Story of John Winthrop* (Boston: Little, Brown, 1958).

Wertenbaker, Thomas J. *The Puritan Oligarchy: The Founding of American Civilization* (New York: Charles Scribner's Sons, 1947).

Presbyterians

Presbyterianism began as a reform movement based on the teachings of John Calvin. One of the first Presbyterian churches in America was organized at Jamestown, Virginia in 1611, and another at Rehobeth, Maryland in 1684. Most came in the migration of the Ulster Scots to America and settled in Virginia, Maryland, Pennsylvania, and New Jersey. Some Presbyterians migrated from the Philadelphia area to the southern colonies and established a college in South Carolina in 1735.

Benedetto, Robert and Betty K. Walker. *Guide to Manuscript Collections of the Presbyterian Church in the United States* (Westport, CT: Greenwood Press, 1990).

Gillett, E.H. *History of the Presbyterian Church in the United States of America.* 2 Vols. (Philadelphia: Westminster Press, 1864).

Gregg, William. *History of the Presbyterian Church in the Dominion of Canada* (Toronto: Presbyterian Publishing, 1905).

Revill, Janie. *A Compilation of the Original Lists of Protestant Immigrants to South Carolina* (1939. Reprint. Baltimore: Genealogical Publishing Co., 1968).

Smylie, James H. *American Presbyterians: A Pictorial History* (Philadelphia: Presbyterian Historical Society, 1985).

Reformed Dutch

The Reformed Dutch Church became the state church of The Netherlands in 1588. A large Dutch colony was established at Recife, Brazil in 1629 and remained there until they were expelled by the Portuguese in 1654. A Reformed Dutch congregation formed by a minister from Brazil began to meet in New Amsterdam in 1628, and a church was built in 1642. The church was the official church in the New Netherland Colony until 1664. The Reformed Church separated from the mother church and formed the Synod of the Reformed Churches of New York and New Jersey in 1784.

Fiske, John. *The Dutch and Quaker Colonies in America* (New York: Houghton Mifflin, 1899).

Gasero, Russell L. *Guide to Local Church Records in the Archives of the Reformed Church in America and Genealogical Resources at the Gardiner Sage Library, New Brunswick Theological Seminary* (New Brunswick, NJ: Historical Society of the Reformed Church of America, 1979, fiche 6046480).

Wabeke, B.H. *Dutch Emigration to North America, 1624–1860* (New York: Alfred A. Knopf, 1942).

Baptists

The Baptist Church was founded in England in 1609. A group broke away and formed the Particular Baptists in 1633. The first Baptist Church in the colonies was founded in Providence, Rhode Island in 1639. For most of the seventeenth century they were persecuted because of their opposition to infant baptism and demand for separation of church and state. A small Welsh Baptist church was organized in Swansea, Massachusetts in 1663. Baptists also settled in Pennsylvania in 1688, and the first association of Baptist churches was formed there in 1707. The Free Will Baptists were organized in 1727, and the German Seventh-Day Baptists in 1728. As dissenters, Baptists were frequently required to take oaths, which can be found in town records in Maine, Vermont, and elsewhere.

Colonial Baptists: Massachusetts and Rhode Island (1652. New York: Arno Press, 1980).

Hester, H.I. *Southern Baptists and Their History* (Nashville, TN: Broadman Press, n.d.).

McLaughlin, William G. *New England Dissent, 1630–1833: The Baptists and Separation of Church and State.* 2 Vols. (Cambridge: Harvard University Press, 1971).

Starr, Edward Caryl. *A Baptist Bibliography, Being a Register of Printed Material by and about Baptists.* 25 Vols. (Rochester, NY: American Baptist Historical Society, 1947–76).

Reception of the Quakers

Different colonies had various ways of discouraging the Friends from attempting to put down roots. Some means of persecution were:

New Hampshire, 1651: Quakers were dragged behind a cart from town to town and whipped in each town.

Massachusetts, 1656: Anyone sheltering Quakers could be fined 40 shillings. Quakers banned from the colony and returned were subject to mutilation and execution (the last Quaker execution in Massachusetts was in 1661).

Connecticut, 1658: Those bringing Quakers into the colony were fined £50; Quakers who "communicated with citizens" four times suffered their tongue to be bored through with a hot poker.

Society of Friends (Quakers)

The Religious Society of Friends was founded in England in 1650. Initially they experienced considerable persecution in America: four Quakers were executed in Massachusetts between 1659 and 1661. Despite this, they were able to establish several meetings in Massachusetts by 1680. The first yearly meetings held in Rhode Island were in 1661, although they were made illegal in 1665.

Meetings were organized in Baltimore in 1672, Virginia in 1673, North Carolina in 1676, New Jersey in 1678, Pennsylvania in 1681, New York in 1696, and North Carolina in 1698. In 1674 Quaker proprietors purchased the province of West Jersey; they were the first settlers of Pennsylvania in 1681. Their beliefs stressed equa-lity among all people; they would not take oaths or perform military duties or pay taxes for military support. Quakers began to migrate from Massachusetts to Nova Scotia in 1762. A large group of Loyalist Quakers resettled from the new American states to Nova Scotia and New Brunswick in 1783.

Bowden, James. *The History of the Society of Friends in America*. 2 Vols. (London: W. and F.G. Cash, 1850–4, film 1425524)

Carey, Patrick W. *The Quakers* (Westport, CT: Greenwood Press, 1993).

Durham, Harrier F. *Caribbean Quakers* (Hollywood, FL: Dukane Press, 1972).

Hinshaw, William Wade. *Encyclopedia of American Quaker Genealogy*. 6 Vols. (1936–50. Reprint. Baltimore: Genealogical Publishing Co., 1973, fiche 6051371 ff.). This covers records in North Carolina, Pennsylvania, New York, Ohio, Delaware, Indiana, Maryland, and Virginia.

Dunkards (Church of the Brethren)
Members of the German Baptist Brethren, the Dunkards emigrated from Germany to America and established a church at Germantown, Pennsylvania in 1719. Another large group arrived in 1729. The sect, the Brethren in Christ, was founded in Pennsylvania in 1770, and in Canada in 1788. [65]

Braumbaugh, Martin G. A *History of the German Baptist Brethren in Europe and America* (Mount Morris, IL: Brethren Publishing House, 1899, film 0824393).

Durnbaugh, Donald F. *The Brethren in Colonial America: A Source Book on the Transplantation and Development of the Church of the Brethren in the Eighteenth Century* (Elgin, IL: Brethren Press, 1967).

Methodism
Methodism began in England in 1735 as a reform movement within the Anglican Church. By 1760, congregations were being formed in America. It was officially

---

[65] G. Elmore Reagan, *The Trail of the Black Walnut* (1965. Reprint. Baltimore: Genealogical Publishing Co., 1993), 25.

set apart from the Church of England in 1784 as one of the Dissenters.

Davidson, E.H. *The Establishment of the English Church in Continental American Colonies* (Durham: Duke University Press, 1936).

Kirby, James E., Russell E. Richey, and Kenneth E. Rowe. *The Methodists* (Westport, CT: Greenwood Press, 1997).

Judaism

Exiled from Spain in 1492 and Portugal in 1497 as victims of the Inquisition, the first Jewish settlers came to the New World in 1492. Many also fled to Amsterdam at that time. A sizable Jewish community was established by the Dutch at Recife, Brazil, in 1629. The site of the oldest synagogue in the Americas was built there in 1651. There were also Jewish communities in the Dutch colony of Curaçao and Suriname while it was an English colony. The first Congregation was established in Curaçao in 1652, and a synagogue was built in 1692. When the Portuguese expelled the Dutch from Brazil in 1654, the refugees migrated to Barbados, Curaçao, the Antilles, and New Amsterdam (New York).

At this time Jewish merchants began appearing in southern New England, but the only real settlement was at Newport, Rhode Island in 1658. A Jewish burial ground was purchased there in 1678 by Jews from Barbados. Another group arrived from Curaçao in 1693. Jews in North America were few in number and economically self-sustaining. The first synagogues in North America were built at New York (1730), and Newport (1759). The Congregation Bevis Marks in London helped to finance the Georgia colony. In 1733 a group of Jews settled at Savannah. A congregation was organized in 1735. The settlers, fearing attack from Spanish Florida, migrated elsewhere in 1749 but returned after 1763. A group of Jews migrated from New York to Philadelphia in the 1730s and to Charleston, South Carolina in 1740, establishing congregations in 1747 and 1749, respectively. By the time of the Revolution, there were about 1,500 Jews, in congregations in Newport, New York, Philadelphia, Charleston, and Savannah. In Canada, small communities existed in Trois Rivières and Montréal, Quebec by 1776.

Bennet, Ralph G. "Genealogical Resources in the Caribbean Available for Jewish Researchers." *Caribbean Historical and Genealogical Journal* III (January 1995): 25-9, III (April 1995): 12-13, III (July 1995): 4-7, III (October 1995): 14-17, IV (January 1996): 13-16, IV (April 1996): 16-18.

Cohen, Martin A. and Abrahan J. Peck. *Shepardism in the Americas: Studies in Culture and History* (Tuscaloosa: University of Alabama Press, 1993).

Liebman, Seymour B. *The Inquisitors and the Jews in the New World: Summaries of Procesos, 1500–1810, a Bibliographic Guide* (Coral Gables, FL: n.p., 974).

Marcus, Jacob R. *The Colonial American Jew, 1492–1776.* 3 Vols. (Detroit: Wayne State University Press, 1970).

Olitsky, Kerry M. *The American Synagogue: A Historical Dictionary and Sourcebook* (Westport, CT: Greenwood Press, 1996).

Preisler, Julian H. *Pioneer American Synagogues: A State by State Guide* (Bowie, MD: Heritage Books, 1997).

Schappes, Morris U. *A Documentary History of Jews in the United States, 1654–1875.* 3rd ed. (New York: Citadel Press, 1971).

Suggested Reading

Alleson, William Henry. *Inventory of Unpublished Material for American Religious History in Protestant Church Archives and Other Repositories* (Washington, DC: Carnegie Institute, 1910).

Gaustad, Edwin Scott. *Historical Atlas of Religion in America* (New York: Harper and Row, 1976).

Hill, Samuel S. *Religion in the Southern States, A Historical Case Study* (Macon GA: Mercer University Press, 1983).

Kirkahm, E. Kay. *A Survey of American Church Records.* 4th ed. (Logan, UT: Everton Publishers, 1978).

Mead, Frank and Samuel S. Hill. *Handbook of American Denominations.* 8th ed. (Nashville: Abingdon Press, 1985).

Melton, J. Gordon. *The Encyclopedia of American Religions.* 3rd ed. (Detroit: Gale Research, 1989).

Mode, Peter. *Source Book and Bibliographical Guide for American Church History* (1921. Reprint. Boston: J.S. Canner and Co., 1964).

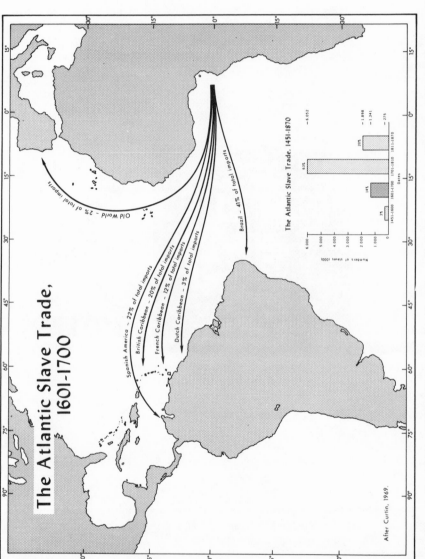

50 Atlantic slave trade, 1701 to 1810 (Cathryn L. Lombardi, et al., *Latin American History: A Teaching Atlas*. Madison: University of Wisconsin Press, 1983)

Africa and the New World

Portugal was the first European power to explore West Africa. A slave market was opened in Lisbon in the fifteenth century, and the first slaves were brought from Africa in 1441. Africans were first transported to the New World when the Spanish colony on Hispaniola required a supply of labor to work in the mines; European diseases gradually annihilated the Amerindian population in the Caribbean, Central Mexico, and the Andes.

Africans were imported to Santo Domingo in 1502 and in 1510, but it was not until 1518 that large numbers of slaves began to arrive as slave labor to work in the sugar plantations. Sugar was first cultivated in Santo Domingo in 1493. It began to be shipped to Europe in 1516. Sugar cultivation rapidly spread to Mexico (1520), Puerto Rico (1524), and Peru (1533).

Brazil was shipping sugar to Lisbon by 1526. By 1550 there were 70 sugar mills in operation. During the sixteenth century most of Europe's sugar came from Brazil. During the seventeenth century it was also heavily cultivated in the West Indies, competing for Brazil's share of the market. Plantations were established on the English, French, and Dutch islands. Cultivation began at Barbados in 1642 and at Guadeloupe in 1647.

The first African slaves in English North America were imported to Virginia in 1619, although they remained a small minority of the population until the eighteenth century. In the North, New Netherland (New York) was the largest importer of slaves, having been founded by the slave traders of the Dutch West India Company. The number of black slaves in New England was negligible: amounting to only two percent of the population by 1760.

After 1538 Spain granted *asientos* (licenses) to shipping firms, under which they contracted to transport a certain number of slaves to Spanish colonies during the period of contract. Portugal held the monopoly on the slave trade during the sixteenth century. Dutch (and French to a lesser extent) shipping transported most of the slaves in the seventeenth century. The eighteenth century was dominated by Great Britain (*asiento* from 1713), and France (*asiento* from 1700–13). Minor enterprises were conducted by the Danes, Germans, and Swedes.

The slave trade in New England in the seventeenth century was centered in Boston, Massachusetts. Puritans went into competition on a small scale with their Dutch neighbors in New Netherland. Most of the slaves were brought in by the Dutch West India Company and the English Royal African Company after being "island-seasoned" for a few years in the West Indies.

During the seventeenth century much of the labor in English and French colonies was supplied by indenture contracts. By 1700 this was no longer cost effective, and the African slave market became the major source of labor. In 1697 the Royal African Company lost its monopoly on the slave trade, paving the way for enterprising independent English businessmen to legally engage in trading.

The so-called Triangle Trade developed in the eighteenth century from the sale of New England rum in Africa. After the end of Queens Anne's War, English-American ships were allowed into the French West Indies, trading African slaves in the West Indies and molasses (from sugar) from the West Indies to New England (to make rum). Barbados, Cuba, Jamaica, and Martinique in particular had successful slave-based sugar plantations.

Almost 1,000 ships left Rhode Island for Africa between 1709 and 1807, importing 106,544 slaves.[66] After receiving the slaves for rum at the British colony of the Gold Coast in Africa, the transit was made to the sugar islands in the Caribbean, primarily Barbados and Jamaica, and in later years South Carolina, Georgia, Virginia, and Cuba. Molasses or sugar was received for slaves (tobacco and rice from the southern colonies) or bills of exchange.

Most of the slaves taken to the West Indies and America during the sixteenth, seventeenth, and eighteenth centuries were from West Africa. West African society was divided into tribes, each tribe being ruled by a chief. Each had its own language. Plural marriage was practiced. Land ownership was communal except in Yorubaland, where it belonged to the family.

When the African people were removed to the New World, they lost touch with their established society. The slave owners were at all not interested in preserving African ways of living. Different tribes were mixed on each plantation to lessen the chances of rebellion, resulting in the fragmentation of the African languages.

The journey known as the Middle Passage was a triangular voyage from Plymouth (England) to Guinea (Africa) to the West Indies (usually Barbados or Martinique). Many Africans died during these voyages. They were packed on shelves between the ships' decks, and brought on deck once daily so their shelves could be washed down. Male slaves were shackled together at the wrist and leg.

---

[66]James A. Rawley, *The Transatlantic Slave Trade: A History* (New York: W.W. Norton, 1981), 359–60.

In the efforts to market the slaves, buyers would be influenced by a perceived set of characteristics indigenous to various African cultures. As buyers' preferences became apparent, the distribution of the slaves was directed to the regional marketplace; however, some colonies were not interested in the African origins. For example, the planters in South Carolina exhibited a definite bias toward tall slaves, preferably from the Senegambia, and disliked slaves from Angola (Ibo people), but planters in Virginia were not as particular. [67] Sometimes the origins on the shipping lists were deliberately altered to increase saleability.

Colonies took advantage of the slave importation to make a little profit for themselves. All of the thirteen original colonies levied duties on imported slaves except Connecticut, Delaware, New Hampshire, and North Carolina.

Total Estimated Slave Imports to the Americas, 1451–1870

> **British North America**   532,000
> **Spanish America**   1,687,100
> **British Caribbean**   2,443,000
> **French Caribbean**   1,655,000
> **Dutch Caribbean**   500,000
> **Danish Caribbean**   50,000
> **Brazil**   4,190,000[68]

The mortality rate of Africans who died at sea is estimated to be 25% or higher in the early years. An average of one sailor in five also died during transit.

The following information was abstracted from the types of records immediately following the table, to give an idea of what information can be found in colonial records. Some records have been abstracted and published; however, most searches still require some original research.

---

[67] Philip Curtin, *The Atlantic Slave Trade, A Census* (Madison: University of Wisconsin Press, 1969), 155–8.

[68] James A. Rawley, *The Transatlantic Slave Trade: A History* (New York: W.W. Norton, 1981), 428.

Location in Africa / Export	Tribe/People/ Region	Destination
Angola	Mbundu, Kwanza River	Barbados, Brazil, Cuba, French Guiana, Guadeloupe, Haiti, Jamaica, Martinique, Mississippi, Nevis
Ardra and Whydah		Barbados, Jamaica, Nevis
Barbados (re-exports)	Angola, Ivory Coast, Senegambia	South Carolina, Virginia
Benin and the Calabros (Nigeria)		Barbados, Jamaica, Nevis
Benin, Bight of (Nigeria)	Foin/Fon, Arada, Juda, Popo, Thiamba, Cotocoli, Nago/Oyo Yoruba	Brazil, British Guiana, Cuba, French Guiana, Haiti, Jamaica, Saint Croix, Saint Thomas
Biafra, Bight of (Nigeria)	Ibo, Calabari, Moco/Moko, Ara/Aro	Cuba, French Guiana, Haiti
Brazil (re-exports)	Senegambia, Sierra Leone, Angola, Bight of Benin, Ivory Coast, Liberia	Argentina, Bahamas, British Honduras, Cuba, Guadeloupe, Mississippi, Puerto Rico, Saint Croix, Saint Thomas, Suriname, Uruguay
Cameroon, Gabon	Balala/Lala	Mexico
Cape Province, South Africa	Zozo/Xhosa	Mexico
Casamance	Cazanga/Kassanga	Peru
Congo		Cuba, French Guiana
Congo River	Manicongo/ Bakongo	Mexico, Peru
Congo-Brazzaville	Enchicho/Tio or Teke	Peru

Location in Africa / Export	Tribe/People/ Region	Destination
Cuba (re-exports)		British Honduras, Puerto Rico
Dahomey (Benin)	Popos, Fo, Gun	Haiti
France (Bordeaux, Nantes, Rouen, La Rochelle) (re-exports)	Senegambia, Angola, Bight of Benin	Cuba, French Guiana, Guadeloupe, Haiti, Martinique, Puerto Rico, Suriname, Trinidad
Gold Coast (Ghana)	Ashanti	Jamaica
Gold Coast (Ghana)	Akan/Mine, Cormanti	Brazil, British Guiana, Cuba, French Guiana, Haiti, Jamaica, Saint Croix, Saint Thomas
Guinea (upper)	Caboverde/Lebu	Mexico
Guinea (east coast)	Tierra Nova	French Guiana, Guadeloupe, Haiti, Martinique, Mexico, Peru
Guinea-Bissau	Bañol/Banyun, Biafara/Biafada, Bran/Bram	Bolivia, British Guiana, Haiti, Jamaica, Mexico, Peru, Virginia
Ivory Coast and Liberia (British Windward Coast, Portuguese Costa da Mina)	Aquia, Bobo, Canga	Barbados, Brazil, British Guiana, Cuba, French Guiana, Haiti, Jamaica, Nevis
Jamaica (re-exports)		South Carolina, Virginia

Location in Africa / Export	Tribe/People/ Region	Destination
Liverpool, London, and Bristol, England (re-exports)		Barbados, Dominica, Georgia, Grenada, Jamaica, Leeward Islands, North Carolina, Saint Lucia, Saint Vincent, South Carolina, Tobago, Trinidad
Luanda	Angola/Ambudu	Bolivia, Chile, Peru
Madagascar	southeast African peoples	Cuba, Nantes, France (for re-export)
Mount Cameroons	Ambo/Northwest Bantu	Peru
Mozambique	southeast African peoples	Cuba, Haiti, Jamaica, Mexico, Peru
Nigeria (south)	Yoruba, Ido	
Nigeria (north)	Hausa, Mandingans, Fulani (Muslim)	West Indies
Safi, Morocco	Zafi/Safi	Mexico
Senegal	Bioho/Bissago	Mexico
Senegal Valley	Tucuxuy/Tukulor	Mexico
Senegambia (Gambia)	Mandinga/Malinke	Mexico, Peru
Senegambia	Cap-Vert/Cape Verde Islands	French Guiana
Senegambia (Senegal)	Jelof/Wolof, Berbesi/Serer	Bolivia, Mexico, Peru

Location in Africa / Export	Tribe/People/ Region	Destination
Senegambia (Senegal and Gambia)	Fula/Fulbe, Bambara, Wolof	Barbados, Brazil, Cuba, French Guiana, Guadeloupe, Haiti, Jamaica, Mississippi, Nevis, Peru, Puerto Rico, South Carolina, Virginia
Sierra Leone	Zape/Landuma, Baga, Temne	Brazil, Cuba, French Guiana, Guadeloupe, Haiti, Jamaica, Martinique, Mexico, Mississippi, Peru, Puerto Rico
South Carolina (re-exports)	Jamaica Senegambia	Georgia, Maryland, North Carolina, Virginia

Where to look for places of origin of African slaves

Space does not permit a comprehensive list of all the possible sources that can be searched to look for African origins. Although the likelihood of tracing an *individual* ancestor across the water is not promising, by carefully examining shipping and other records it is definitely possible to find an area of origin.

Spanish records (see also Spain)
➢ Notarial registers, inventories of estates, colonial and Spanish archives
➢ Records of *asientos* (licenses to trade in slaves), AGI, Seville
➢ Land and property records, colonial archives

British records (see also Great Britain)
Records at the PRO in Kew, Surrey, England contain records on Britain's own enterprise in the slave trade and its efforts to suppress the trade in the nineteenth century.
Treasury Office and Treasury Solicitor's Records:
➢ Company of Merchants Trading to Africa (T 70), including the Royal Company of African Adventurers, 1663–72, the Royal African Company of England, 1672–1750, and the Company of Merchants Trading to Africa, 1750–1821
➢ Compensation paid to slave owners, 1812–46 (T 71)

➤ Shipping and trade returns, colonies, 1680–1867 (T 64)
➤ Captured slave ships, 1801–8 (TS 10)
Foreign Office Papers:
➤ Returns of slave vessels
➤ General correspondence on the slave trade, 1816–92 (FO 84)
➤ Slave Trade Commission, Cape Town, 1843–70 (FO 312)
➤ Slave Trade Commission, Havana, 1819–69 (FO 313)
➤ Slave Trade Commission, Jamaica, 1843–51 (FO 314)
➤ Slave Trade Commission, Sierra Leone, 1819–68 (FO 315)
➤ Spanish claims, 1790–1823 (FO 316)
➤ Embassy and Consular Archives for Brazil, including slave trade registers for Portugal, 1858–71 (FO 131)
Colonial Office Papers:
➤ Negroes shipped and delivered by the Royal African Company, West Indies Papers (CO 318)
➤ Admiralty Court records (CO 155)
Privy Council Records:
➤ Reports of the Lords of the Committee of Council for Trade and Foreign Plantations
Board of Customs and Excise Records:
➤ Ledgers of imports and exports, 1697–1780 (Customs 3), and America, 1768–73 (Customs 16)
Admiralty Court records:
➤ African station correspondence, 1797–1932 (ADM 123)
Slave registers and returns (Treasury Office Papers, Colonial Office Papers), and local archives: i.e. Bermuda slave registry, 1821–34 in the Bermuda Archives, Hamilton (film 1857077), and Antigua Court of Common Pleas, registers of slaves, 1817–33, in the Antigua and Barbuda National Archives, Saint John's (film 1873590 ff.).
Exchequer's Office records:
➤ West Indies slave compensation payments after emancipation, 1835–42 (AO 14), (NDO 4)
➤ King's Remembrancer port books, 1565–1798 (E 190)
Runaway slave advertisements in newspapers (West Indies and North America)
Harleian Manuscripts, British Library, London

Danish Records
➤ *Danske Cancelli* (Danish Chancery) records of testamentary manumissions, 1746–99, Rigsarkivet, Copenhagen
➤ *Generaltoldkammer* (General Customs Office) records, Rigsarkivet, Copenhagen
➤ Enumeration of Free Coloured, Saint Croix, Saint John, and Saint Thomas, 1833; sea pass protocols for vessels, 1782–1868 (RG 55), National Archives, Washington, DC

➤ Moravian missionary records, various archives in Germany and the United States

➤ Newspapers: *Royal Danish American Gazette* (Christiansted, Saint Croix), and the *Saint Thomas Tidende* (Charlotte Amalie, Saint Thomas)

French records (see also France)

➤ *Déclaration de retour* (declarations of shipments), in French archives containing port records; most records at the Archives Départmentales Loire-Atlantique, Nantes; also records at departmental archives in Bordeuax, La Rochelle, Le Havre, Saint-Malo, Lorient, and Marseilles

➤ *Rôles d'armement et désarmement*, 1700–1800 (captain and armateuer's names, destinations, crew information, name of ship), Nantes

➤ *Rapports des capitaines*, 1714–78 (investors), Nantes

➤ *Acts de propriéte*, 1693–1791 (details of expedition, including arrivals and departures, number of slaves traded, number of slaves delivered, and crew deaths), Nantes

➤ Colonial records, French National Archives, Section Outre-Mer, Paris, such as *registres des libertés et affranchisements*, 1776–7 (film 1093928), which are emancipation records for Haiti

German records

➤ Slave trade regulations, 1837, 1842, Lübeck State Archives

➤ Slave trade prohibitions, 1845–6, Kiel State Archives

Portuguese and Brazilian records (see also Portugal and Brazil)

➤ Export records for Portuguese African ports in archives in Lisbon (some have been published)

➤ Import records, Archives of Bahia, Brazil

➤ Notarial and parish registers kept by Luzo-Brazilian priests, 1500–1900

➤ Archives of the Cathedral of Olinda, Brazil, some published in *Cartas Jesúiticas*, 1550–1568 (Rio de Janeiro: The Archives, 1887).

Database project

The W.E.B. DuBois Institute of Afro-American Research at Harvard University has created a searchable database of Atlantic slave trade voyages from the seventeenth century to 1860. There are only about 1,000 voyages entered for the years 1588 to 1660; the bulk of the 27,000 entries fall in the late seventeenth to nineteenth centuries. That database is available on CD-ROM. See Eltis, David, Stephen D. Bahrendt, David Richardson, and Herbert Klein. *The W.E.B. DuBois Transatlantic Slave-Trade Data Base* (Cambridge: Cambridge University Press, 1998).

Life in the New World

Africans accompanied the Spanish from the time of their earliest explorations in the Americas and the Caribbean. As the slave population in English North

America slowly increased, the codes prescribing their behavior and eliminating their rights were written in the fashion of the West Indian colonies, modeled after the Barbados code of 1644. Punishment could be severe: in 1728 some slaves convicted of conspiracy in Antigua were burned alive or drawn and quartered.

African Roots

Cultures in West Africa generally trace lineage through the maternal line and take the mother's name rather than that of the father. An heir of a male would be his mother's brother or his sister's son. Plural marriage was practiced. Land ownership was usually communal.

North American Colony	Date of First Slave Laws	Date Slave Code Written
Canada (New France)	1709 (legalized)	—
Connecticut	1650	—
Delaware	1721	—
Georgia	banned from 1735–49	1750
Maryland	1638	1663
Massachusetts	1641	—
New Hampshire	1714	—
New Jersey	1668 (East Jersey)	1682
New York	1644 (Dutch)	1712
North Carolina	1669	1715
Pennsylvania	1700	—
Rhode Island	1652	—
South Carolina	1669	1691/1712
Virginia	1660	1661

African music found its way into the music of European culture. The following dances all have their origins in African ritual dance:

➤ *Beguine*: Afro-French, originated in Martinique
➤ *Rhumba, conga, mambo*: Afro-Spanish, originated in Cuba

➤ *Habanera*: Afro-Spanish, from Havana, Cuba, precursor of the tango (from the African *tagana)*
➤ *Cumbia*: Afro-Spanish, originated in Colombia
➤ *Samba*: Afro-Brazilian, derived from the Angolan wedding dance known as the *quizomba*[69]

Miscegenation

Interracial marriage was prohibited by law in virtually every North American colony by the early eighteenth century, although many children of mixed racial heritage were born in the southern plantation society from unions between the whites and their black slave mistresses. These children were regarded as slaves. This prohibition was not practiced in Brazil and most Latin American countries. While in North America slaves were treated as chattel property, the enslaved Africans in Latin America retained some of their social and religious rights and were, in some cases, encouraged to work for their emancipation. Today Latin America has one of the most racially intermixed populations in the world.

Terms for racial mixture and degree of blood vary from place to place. Sometimes the same word could have an entirely different meaning in two societies, such as *creole*, meaning a person of mixed race in North America, but in Latin America a *criollo* was a white Spaniard of colonial birth. These terms can provide important clues in tracing ancestry. Some illustrations are:

➤ **Louisiana**: Some names actually indicated the percentage of black blood. *Mulatto* (black and white), *quadroon* (mulatto and white), and *octoroon* (quadroon and white) are a few of the labels used in a rather rigid caste system.
➤ **Brazil**: Slaves were distinguished between African-born and Brazilian-born. African slaves were known as *Nacão, Africana, Cabinda, Mocambique, Benguela*, etc. Brazilian-born slaves were called *pardo, mulato, cabra, crioulo*, etc.
➤ **Latin America**: Terms for race were defined in a *régimen de castas* (caste system). Generally those of mixed race were known as *color quebrado* (broken color), meaning half-breed, a combination of white, black, and Indian blood. Some of the many names used are *albrarazado, barcino*, and *coyote* (Indian, African, and white), *jíbaro, lobo*, and *cambujo* (Indian and African), *mulato, negro fino*, and *ochavado* (African and white).

Children were usually named for relatives of the mother, although many were forced to adopt European names that were favored by their masters in addition to keeping their African names. There are instances of surnames or *titles* being used to reflect either the surname of the first slave owner or the first ancestor

---

[69] Much of this information is from Benjamin Quarles, *The Negro in the Making of America* (New York: Macmillan & Co., 1964), 30–1.

born in Africa.

Where to look in church records for slaves

Between 1664 and 1706, Maryland, New Jersey, New York, North and South Carolina, and Virginia passed laws renouncing baptism as a vehicle for emancipation. The New England colonies, Georgia, and Pennsylvania did not have such laws.

➢ Quaker monthly meeting records after 1754 (manumissions); possibly some membership records from 1657.

➢ Baptist records after 1750 (baptisms). The first African-American congregation in Virginia was founded in Lunenburg in 1758.

➢ Roman Catholic records after 1693, in Florida (also notarial and militia records).

➢ Congregational Church records from earliest baptisms and covenant owners (few records before 1700), marriages from the 1690s..

➢ Anglican records: baptisms after 1727; see parish registers, Society for Propagation of the Gospel (SPG): Lambeth Palace Transcripts. Series A and B, also records at the SPG Library in London. Marriage registers, West Indian colonies, from the earliest settlements. Religious instruction of slaves was required by law in the Bahamas as of 1725.[70]

➢ Moravian records: missionaries were active in the West Indies and in some colonies in British North America after 1732.

➢ Reformed Dutch records: the church required slaves to receive a religious education after 1644.

Other sources of information:

➢ Newspaper advertisements for sales of slaves; also ads for runaways.

➢ Court records of crimes and misdemeanors; South Carolina and Pennsylvania had separate slave courts; after 1715 slaves in North Carolina were tried in a freeholders' court. In Virginia an act of 1692 required all slaves accused of capital offenses to be tried in a county court of oyer and terminer without a jury.

➢ Slave registers found in court records: in Pennsylvania the Court of Quarter Sessions maintained slave returns, i.e. Bucks County (film 1433970), Lancaster County (film 1433968), and Cumberland County (film 1465915).

➢ Tax records, rateables, tithables. In Virginia all slaves and free Negroes over sixteen were deemed tithables in 1723. The law was amended in 1748 to include only slaves and wives of free Negroes, and amended again in 1769 to exempt the free females.[71]

---

[70] Gail Saunders, *Slavery in the Bahamas, 1648–1838* (Nassau: The Nassau Guardian, 1985), 5.

[71] Jane Purcell Guild, *Black Laws of Virginia* (Lovettsville, VA: Willow Bend Books, 1995), 131–4.

➢ Colonial records, titled such as Colonial Records, Records of Governor and Council, Governor and Assembly, Governor and Company, etc.

➢ Records of admiralty courts convened in the colonies.

➢ Southern colonies: inventories of estates; transfers of ownership of land, particularly inheritances; slaves were inherited as personal property in the southern colonies (except from 1705–48 in Virginia, when they were defined by law as realty).

➢ New England: slaves were regarded as personalty (moveables or personal property); likewise with tax lists, poll lists, returns of rateable property, etc. Usually called servants rather than slaves, they also had rights as persons and could inherit both land and personal property from their masters, or purchase it.[72] They could also serve as witnesses, give evidence, make contracts, appeal a ruling, or bring suit in court, practices not allowed in New York or the southern colonies. They also were entitled to trial by jury. African Americans in New England also served in militias, and their names appear on muster lists; they served on vessels, both warships and privateers and merchantmen. For these services they were paid the same wages as whites.

➢ Manumission records, such as those found at the Pennsylvania Abolition Society in Philadelphia for 1780–1840 (film 1731983 ff.), from various eastern states, including New Jersey, Maryland, Pennsylvania, Delaware, Georgia, and Virginia, and British manumissions for slaves from Trinidad, Barbados, and Jamaica.

➢ Southern and Mid-Atlantic colonies: land records include slaves as transfers of property; manumissions may also be recorded in land records. In South Carolina, mortgage records, 1734–1860, index, 1709–1840 (film 0022627 ff.), at the South Carolina State Archives in Columbia contain predominantly "mortgages of negroes."

➢ Plantation records contain diaries, or "daybooks," which kept accounts of slave labor, sometimes including births of children and the name of the mother.

A series of plantation papers has been filmed by the University Publications of America in Frederick, Maryland and edited by Kenneth Stammp. Although generally titled to date from the Revolution through the Civil War, many actually begin in the early eighteenth century. There are reel guides published for each series. The following is a small selected representation of what is available on microfilm. Each series contains many additional records.

Series A, South Caroliniana Library, University of South Carolina (1986, film 1534196 ff.).
• Thomas family diaries and papers, plantation books, 1702–1887
• Read-Lance family papers, plantation journals, slave records, accounts,

---

[72] Slaves were also known as servants in Virginia until the mid-seventeenth century.

1677–1865
- Heyward family papers, slave books, plantation books, account books, diaries, 1708–1866
- Miller-Furman-Dabbs family papers, land records, list of Negro and white church members, genealogical notes, 1771–1827

Series B, South Carolina Historical Society (1985, film 1534237 ff.).
- Thomas Porcher Ravenel papers, diaries, daybooks, slave lists, 1731–1867

Series D, Maryland Historical Society (1985, film 1534260 ff.).
- Hollyday family papers, land records, correspondence, accounts, slave lists, 1677–1811
- Oden family papers, 1755–1832

Series E, University of Virginia Library, Charlottesville (1985, film 1534274 ff.).
- Tayloe family papers, journals, account books, farm journals, 1708–1861
- John Ambler papers, correspondence, accounts, daybooks, 1767–1879
- "Pocket" Plantation papers, accounts, slave sales, estate papers, daybooks, 1748–74, overseer's papers, accounts, receipts, 1794–1851, daybooks, journals, 1784–1826, ledgers, slave birth lists, estate account books, 1788–1826
- Berkeley family papers, correspondence, estate papers, accounts, 1536–1774, Bible records, 1745–1885
- Gilliam family papers, accounts and receipts, correspondence, slave-trade papers, 1828–65
- Barbour family papers, accounts, daybooks, plantation and farm books, 1785–1866
- County Line Church of Christ records, first two volumes
- Bruce family papers, indentures, business papers, deeds of trust, 1746–1860

Series F, Duke University Library, North Carolina (1986, film 1549774 ff.).
The Deep South
- Henry Watson, Jr., papers, indentures, 1765–1869

South Carolina and Georgia
- William Gibbons, Jr., papers, 1728–1803
- George Noble Jones papers, 1786–1872
- John Ball papers, 1773–1833
- William Sims papers, 1770–1837

North Carolina, Maryland, and Virginia
- Henry Toole Clark papers, 1757–1873
- Samuel Smith Downey papers, 1762–1802
- Battaile Muse papers, plantation records, daybooks, 1748–1865
- Henry Fitzhugh papers, 1746–89
- Thomas Yuille, John and George Murdoch papers, 1754–7
- Robert Carter papers, deeds of emancipation, daybooks, 1772–93
- William Bolling letters and papers, 1724–1813
- James McDowell II papers, 1767–1858
- William Henry Hall papers, 1738–1902

Series G, Barker Texas History Center, University of Texas at Austin (1987, film 1549858 ff.).

Texas and Louisiana

- James Franklin Perry and Stephen Perry papers, daybooks, register of Negroes, 1786–1874
- Julien Sidney Devereux papers, daybooks, 1787–1865
- William Massie Collection papers, estate records, register of Negroes, 1766–1865

Series J, Southern Historical Collection, Library of the University of North Carolina (1989–92, film 1672791 ff.).

- Correspondence of Bennehan, Duncan, and Cameron families, daybooks, deeds and indentures, surveys, land plats, 1757–1865
- Pettigrew family papers, 1761–1908
- Hubard family papers, 1741–76
- Hairston and Wilson families, account books, 1772–1822

South Carolina

- Thomas Middleton plantation books, 1734–1813
- Josiah Smith, Jr., letter books, 1771–84
- Grimball family papers, 1683–1905
- Elliott and Gonzales family papers, plantation journals, 1701–1865
- Bacot family papers, 1767–1887
- Boykin family papers, 1748–1860
- Singleton family papers, 1759–1888

Georgia and Florida

- Mackay and Stiles family papers, plantation and slave records, 1790–1865
- Arnold and Screven family papers, 1762–1865
- Alexander and Hillhouse family papers, 1758–1915
- Jackson and Prince family papers, plantation accounts, 1784–1880
- Branch family papers, 1788–1866

Louisiana

- Andrew McCollam papers, 1792–1858
- Brashear and Lawrence family papers, 1802–50
- Avery family papers, 1796–1850
- John G. Devereux papers, 1791–1890
- Phanor Prudhomme papers, plantation records, 1804–56
- William Dunbar account books, 1776–1847
- Guion family papers, 1789–1927
- Minor family papers, 1763–1900
- Norton, Chilton, and Dameron family papers, 1760–1926
- Quitman family papers, 1784–1838
- James Thomas Harrison papers, 1770–1896
- Hughes family papers, 1790–1857
- William Ruffin Smith papers, 1772–1909

Alabama
- William Stump Forwood papers, 1786–1860
- Miscellaneous business letters, 1747–1929
- George Washington Allen papers, 1778–1928
- Lipscomb family papers, 1791–1867

Tennessee and Kentucky
- Calvin Jones papers, 1785–1838
- Polk and Yeatman family papers, plantation records, 1773–1871
- Michael D. Shoffner papers, 1777–1873

Virginia
- Charles W. Dabney papers, account and daybooks, 1744–1865
- Fredericks Hall plantation books, 1727–75
- Burwell family papers, 1750–1828
- Crenshaw and Miller family papers, 1751–1916
- James McDowell papers, writings and notes on slavery, 1728–1896

Tidewater and coastal plains, North Carolina
- Langdon, Young, and Meares family papers, 1771–1877
- Strudwick family papers, 1701–1826
- Gillespie and Wright family papers, 1735–1870
- Thomas David Smith McDowell papers, 1735–86
- Lewis family papers, 1757–1956
- Archibald Hunter Arrington papers, 1744–1865
- Brownrigg family papers, 1736–1863
- Skinner family papers, plantation journals, 1705–1900
- Peter Evans Smith family papers, 1739–1885
- Lewis Thompson papers, 1723–1848
- William Henry Wills papers, diaries, 1712–1865
- Grimes family estate papers, 1713–1859

Piedmont North Carolina
- William Eaton papers, 1725–1893
- William Johnson papers, 1760–1890
- Person family papers, 1739–1907
- Papers of the Hamilton, Coleman, Tarry, and Watkins families, 1757–1882
- Stephen Moore papers, 1767–1869
- Walter Alves papers, 1771–1807
- John Steele papers, 1759–1838
- Macay and McNeely family papers, 1746–1872
- Leonidas Chalmers Glenn papers, 1752–1907
- Rufus Reid papers, 1772–1884

Western North Carolina
- Hamilton Brown papers, 1752–1890
- James Gwyn papers, 1653–1852

Series K, Colonial Williamsburg Foundation Library, Shirley Plantation Collection, 1650–1888 (1993, film 1844996 ff.).
- Correspondence and business papers, 1650–1888, plantation journals, order

book, account books, 1815–59, account books, plantation and naval journals, 1842–72

Series L, Earl Gregg Swem Library, College of William and Mary, Williamsburg, Virginia (1993, film 1844318 ff.).

- Carter family papers, 1667–1862
- Jerdone family papers, 1736–1918
- Skipwith family papers, 1760–1977
- Austin-Twyman papers, 1765–1865

Series M, Virginia Historical Society, Richmond (1994, film 1985945 ff.).

- Tayloe family papers, 1650–1870, account books, land records, 1650–1871
- Carter family papers, letters, accounts, land and legal papers, 1703–58
- Custis family papers, correspondence, accounts, legal papers, 1683–1858
- Fairfax family papers, 1756–87
- Jenings family papers, 1737–1837
- Lee family papers, letters, diaries, legal papers, 1667–1814
- Mercer family papers, accounts, correspondence, legal papers, 1656–1869
- Peckatone plantation papers, accounts, correspondence, 1664–1920
- Bassett family papers, correspondence, accounts, 1728–1852
- Byrd family papers, letters, correspondence, 1757–1867
- William Chamberlayne papers, 1766–1831
- Douthat family papers, correspondence, accounts, 1795–1895
- Hunter family papers, correspondence, 1770–88, correspondence, accounts, lists of slaves, diaries, 1827–73
- Woolfolk family papers, correspondence, accounts, legal papers, slave papers, 1780–1856

Slave rebellions and the Maroons

Slave rebellions in the West Indies were more frequent than in other parts of the New World. The first recorded rebellion was on Hispaniola in 1522. Most rebellions took place on Jamaica: some involving thousands took place in 1730, 1760, 1766, 1776, and into the nineteenth century. In 1795, at the end of the Second Maroon War, almost 600 Maroons were exiled from Jamaica to Nova Scotia and then deported to Africa in 1800.

Maroon comes from the Spanish word *cimarron*, meaning runaway. This term was used for Africans who successfully escaped from slavery. Their goal was to form their own communities and to reestablish West African society and culture. In many cases, this included owning black slaves of their own. The Maroons — also known as Bush Negroes — trace their genealogy through the maternal line, and the birth of a daughter was celebrated because it meant the family line would continue.[73]

The first Maroon bands were formed in Cuba and Puerto Rico in the early sixteenth century. There were also bands of Maroons on Antigua, Barbados, and Saint Kitts. In 1655 a Maroon community began in the Blue Mountains in Jamaica, at Nanny Town.

In the eighteenth century, Maroon settlements were viable only on the larger islands of Cuba, Hispaniola, Guadeloupe, and Jamaica. In 1750 there were about 3,000 Maroons on Hispaniola. Saint Vincent and Dominica, inhabited by the Carib Indians, were also places of refuge for runaways. The Maroon community on Saint Vincent assimilated with the indigenous Caribs. The community on Dominica survived until 1814.

In the sixteenth and seventeenth centuries, slaves from the Guinea coast of West Africa were able to rebuild a full tribal culture in the forests of Suriname. By the end of the seventeenth century, some 6,000 former slaves had established villages in the colony's bush. In North America small Maroon communities existed in Spanish Florida, Georgia, South Carolina, North Carolina, and Virginia. The largest of these was the Great Dismal Swamp settlement on the border of North Carolina and Virginia.

Dates of Abolition of the Slave Trade and Emancipation

Country	Abolition of slave trade	Emancipation
Brazil	1851	1888
Denmark	1792 (as of 1803)	1848
France	1792/1819	1848
Great Britain	1808	1834 (after seven years apprenticeship)
Mexico	1817	ca. 1830
Netherlands	1814	1863
Portugal	1836	1871

---

[73]For a chronological list of slave rebellions in the West Indies, see Jan Rogoziński, *A Brief History of the Caribbean* (New York: Meridian Books, 1992), 158–60.

Country	Abolition of slave trade	Emancipation
Spain	1820	1873 (1879 in Cuba)
Sweden	1824	1846
United States	1787 (as of 1808)	1862 (effective 1863)

Campbell, Mavis C. *The Maroons of Jamaica: A History of Resistance, Collaboration, and Betrayal* (Westport, CT: Greenwood Press, 1988).

James, C.L. *Out of the House of Bondage: Runaways, Resistance, and Marronage in Africa and the New World* (London: Frank Cass, 1986).

Katz, William Loren. *Breaking the Chains: African-American Slave Resistance* (New York: Atheneum Books, 1990).

Price, Richard. *Maroon Societies: Rebel Slave Communities in the Americas* (Baltimore: Johns Hopkins University Press, 1979).

Suggested Reading
General
Blackburn, Robin. *The Making of New World Slavery: From the Baroque to the Modern, 1492–1800* (New York: Verso, 1997).

Burnside, Madeline Smith. *Spirits of the Passage: The Transatlantic Slave Trade in the Seventeenth Century* (New York: Simon and Schuster, 1997).

Curtin, Philip. *The Atlantic Slave Trade: A Census* (Madison: University of Wisconsin Press, 1969).

Davidson, Basil. *The African Slave Trade: Pre-Colonial History, 1450–1850* (Boston: Little, Brown, 1961).

Donnan, Elizabeth. *Documents Illustrative of the Slave Trade to America.* 3 Vols. (Washington, DC: Carnegie Institute, 1930–5). Essential reference to searching slave ship records.

Miller, Joseph C. *Slavery and Slaving in World History: A Bibliography, 1900–1991* (Madison: University of Wisconsin Press, 1991).

Miller, Randall M. *Dictionary of Afro-American Slavery* (Westport, CT: Greenwood Press, 1997).

Mintz, Sidney W. *Sweetness and Power: The Place of Sugar in Modern History* (New York: Viking Penguin, 1985).

Nash, Gary B. *Red, Black and White: The Peoples of Early America* (Englewood Cliffs, NJ: Prentice-Hall, 1974).

Quarles, Benjamin. *The Negro in the Making of America* (New York: Macmillan & Co., 1964).

Rawley, James A. *The Transatlantic Slave Trade: A History* (New York: W.W. Norton, 1981).

Sharp, William F. *Slavery on the Spanish Frontier* (Norman: University of Oklahoma Press, 1976).

Wiecek, William M. "The Statutory Law of Slavery and Race in the Thirteen Mainland Colonies of British America." *William and Mary Quarterly* XXXIV (1977): 258–80.

Williams, Eric. *Capitalism and Slavery* (Chapel Hill: University of North Carolina Press, 1944).

Windley, Latham A. *Runaway Slave Advertisements: A Documentary History from the 1730s to 1790.* 4 Vols. (Westport, CT: Greenwood Press, 1983).

Wright, Donald. *African Americans in the Colonial Era: From African Origins through American Revolution* (Arlington Heights: University of Chicago Press, 1990).

Africa

Koelle, Sigismund W. *Polyglotta Africana* . . . (London, 1854). Republished in Dalby, David. "Provisional Identification of Languages in the *Polyglotta Africana*." *Sierra Leone Language Review* 1 (1964): 83–90.

Mannig, Patrick. *Slavery, Colonialism, and Economic Growth in Dahomey, 1640–1960* (Cambridge: Cambridge University Press, 1982).

Newbury, Colin W. *The Western Slave Coast and its Rulers: European Trade and Administration Among the Yoruba and Adja-Speaking Peoples of South-Western Nigeria, Southern Dahomey, and Togo* (Oxford: Clarendon Press, 1961).

Thornton, John K. *Africa and Africans in the Making of the Atlantic World,*

1400–1600 (Cambridge: Cambridge University Press, 1992).

Thornton, John. "Central African Names and African-American Naming Patterns." *William and Mary Quarterly* L (1993): 727–42.

Bahamas
Saunders, Gail. *Slavery in the Bahamas, 1648–1838* (Nassau: The Nassau Guardian, 1985).

Barbados
Dunn, Richard S. *Sugar and Slaves: The Rise of the Planter Class in the English West Indies, 1624–1713* (Chapel Hill: University of North Carolina Press, 1972).

Brazil
Conrad, Robert E. *World of Sorrow: The African Slave Trade to Brazil* (Baton Rouge: Louisiana State University Press, 1986).

Freyre, Gilberto. *The Masters and the Slaves: A Study in the Development of Brazilian Civilization* (New York: Alfred A. Knopf, 1963). Originally published as *Casa-Grande e Senzala* (Rio de Janeiro: José Olympio, 1946). Contains excellent glossary that includes the Portuguese names for African tribes and peoples, i.e. Daomeianos, people of Dahomey.

Nielsen, Lawrence J. *The Special Problems of Research and Documentation of Slave Families in Brazil* (Salt Lake City: Corporation of the President, 1980, fiche 6085821).
Queirós Mattoso, Katia M. de. *To Be a Slave in Brazil, 1500–1888* (New Brunswick: Rutgers University Press, 1986).

Taylor, Quintard. *African Families, Black and White, Slave Families on the Fazenda and Plantation: A Comparison of Brazil and the United States, 1750–1850* (Salt Lake City: Corporation of the President, 1980, fiche 6085857).

Canada
Hamelin, Jean. *L'Esclavage au Canada Francais: Histoire et Conditions de l'Esclavage* (Quebec: Les Presses Universitaires Laval, 1960).

Trudel, Marcel. *Dictionnaire des Esclaves et de leurs Propriétaires au Canada Français* (Ville LaSalle, PQ: Hurtubise, HMH, 1990). Dictionary of slaves and their landowners in French Canada; includes Quebec, Kingston, Ontario, parts of New York, Crown Point, Indiana, Detroit, Michigan, and Pittsburgh, Pennsylvania.

Winks, Robin W. *The Blacks in Canada: A History* (New Haven: Yale University Press, 1971).

Caribbean (General)

Bush, Barbara. "The Family Tree is Not Cut," In *Slave Women in Caribbean Society, 1650–1838* (Bloomington: University of Indiana Press, 1990).

Goveia, Else M. *Slave Society in the British Leeward Islands at the End of the Eighteenth Century* (New Haven: Yale University Press, 1965).

Klein, Herbert S. *African Slavery in Latin America and the Caribbean* (New York: Oxford University Press, 1986).

Radcliffe, Virginia. *The Caribbean Heritage* (New York: Walker and Co., 1976).

Sheridan, Richard. *Sugar and Slavery: An Economic History of the British West Indies, 1623–1775* (Baltimore: Johns Hopkins University Press, 1974).

Connecticut

Steiner, Bernard. *History of Slavery in Connecticut* (1893). Reprinted in *Slavery in the States* (New York: Negro Universities Press, 1969).

Cuba

Aimes, Hubert F. *A History of Slavery in Cuba, 1511–1868* (New York: n.p., 1907).
Marrero, Levi. *Cuba: Economía y Sociedad.* 2 Vols. (Madrid, 1973).

Ortiz, Fernando. *Hampa Afro-Cuban: Los Negros Esclavos* (Havana: Revista Bimestre Cubana, 1916).

Delaware

Munroe, John. "The Negro in Delaware." *South Atlantic Quarterly* LVI (1957).

Denmark

Higman, B.W. *Slave Society in the Danish West Indies* (Baltimore: Johns Hopkins University Press, 1992).

Highfield, Arnold R. and Vladimir Barac. *History of the Mission of the Evangelical Brethren on the Caribbean Islands of Saint Thomas, Saint Croix, and Saint John* (Ann Arbor, MI: Karoma Publishers, 1987). English translation and edition of Oldendorp, C.G.A. *Geschichte der Mission der Evangelischen Brüder auf den caraibischen Inseln S. Thomas, S. Croix, und S. Jan* (Barbary, Germany, 1777).

Pedersen, Svend E.G. "The Scope and Structure of the Danish Negro Slave Trade." *Scandinavian History Review* 19 (1971): 149–97.

Trade." *Scandinavian History Review* 19 (1971): 149–97.

Dominican Republic
Veras, Ramón Antonio. *Inmigración — Haitianos — Esclavitud* (Dominican Republic: Ediciones de Tallar, 1983).

Florida
Siebert, Wilbur H. "Slavery and White Servitude in East Florida, 1726–1776." *Florida Historical Quarterly* 10 (1931): 3–23.

France
Stein, Robert Louis. *The French Slave Trade in the Eighteenth Century: An Old Regime* (Madison: University of Wisconsin Press, 1979).

Georgia
Slave Bills of Sale Project. 2 Vols. (Atlanta: African-American Family History Association, 1986, fiche 6049830 ff.)

Smith, Julia Floyd. *Slavery and Rice Culture in Low Country Georgia, 1750–1860* (Knoxville: University of Tennessee Press, 1985).

Wood, Betty. *Slavery in Colonial Georgia, 1730–1775* (Athens: University of Georgia Press, 1984).

Great Britain
Craton, Michael. *Sinews of Empire: A Short History of British Slavery* (Garden City, NY: Anchor Books, 1974).

Davies, K.G. The *Royal African Company* (New York: Atheneum Books, 1970).

Walvin, James. *Black Ivory: A History of British Slavery* (Washington, DC: Howard University, 1983).

Guadeloupe
Vanony-Frisch, N. "Les Esclaves de la Guadeloupe à Fin de l'Ancien Régime d'Apres les Sources Notariales [1770–1789]." *Bulletin de las Société d'Histoire de Guadeloupe* 63–4 (1985).

Jamaica
Patterson, Orlando. *The Sociology of Slavery: An Analysis of the Origins, Development, and Structure of Negro Slave Society in Jamaica* (London: Stein and Day, 1967).

Latin America (see also Caribbean)
Mellafe, Rolando. *Negro Slavery in Latin America* (Berkeley: University of California Press, 1975).

Vilar, Enriqueta Vila. *Hispanoamerica y el Comercio de Esclavos* (Seville, 1977).

Louisiana
Allain, Mathé. "Slave Policies in French Louisiana." *Louisiana History* XXI 2 (1980): 127–37.

Taylor, Joe Gray. *Negro Slavery in Louisiana* (Baton Rouge: Louisiana State University Press, 1963).

Maryland
Brackett, Jeffrey R. *The Negro in Maryland: A Study in the Institution of Slavery* (Baltimore: Johns Hopkins University Press, 1889).

Main, Gloria L. *Tobacco Colony: Life in Early Maryland, 1650–1720* (Princeton: Princeton University Press, 1982).

Massachusetts
Twombley, Robert C. and Robert H. Moore. "Black Puritan: The Negro in Seventeenth-Century Massachusetts." *William and Mary Quarterly* XXIV (April 1967): 224–42.

Middle Colonies (General)
Kulikoff, Allan. *Tobacco and Slaves: The Development of Southern Cultures in the Chesapeake, 1680–1800* (Chapel Hill: University of North Carolina Press, 1986).

Mississippi
Sydnor, Charles S. *Slavery in Mississippi* (New York: Negro Universities Press, 1933).

The Netherlands
Emmer, Pieter C. "The History of the Dutch Slave Trade, A Bibliographic Survey." *Journal of Economic History* XXXII (September 1972): 728–47.

Postma, Johannes Menne. *The Dutch in the Atlantic Slave Trade, 1600–1815* (Cambridge: Cambridge University Press, 1990).

New England (General)
Greene, Lorenzo J. *The Negro in Colonial New England, 1620–1776* (1942.

Reprint. New York: Atheneum Books, 1974).

Jordan, Winthrop D. "The Influence of the West Indies on the Origins of New England Slavery." *William and Mary Quarterly* XVIII (1961): 243–50.

New Jersey
Cooley, Henry S. *A Study of Slavery in New Jersey* (Baltimore: Johns Hopkins University Press, 1896).

New Jersey Society for Promoting the Abolition of Slavery. *Cases in the Supreme Court of New Jersey Relative to the Manumission of Negroes and Others Holden in Bondage* (Burlington, NJ: Isaac Neale, 1794, film 1035620).

New York
McManus, Edgar C. *A History of Negro Slavery in New York* (Syracuse, NY: Syracuse University Press, 1966).

North Carolina
Bassett, John S. *Slavery in the State of North Carolina* (1896. Reprint. New York: AMS Press, 1972, film 1036142).

Kay, Marvin L. and Lorin Lee Cary. *Slavery in North Carolina, 1748–1775* (Chapel Hill: University of North Carolina Press, 1989).

Spindel, Donna J. *Crime and Society in North Carolina, 1663–1776* (Baton Rouge: Louisiana State University Press, 1989).

Pennsylvania
Blockson, C.L. *Pennsylvania's Black History* (Philadelphia: Portfolio Associates, 1975).

Smith, Billy G. and Richard Wojtowicz. *Blacks Who Stole Themselves: Advertisements for Runaways in the Pennsylvania Gazette, 1728–1790* (Philadelphia: University of Pennsylvania Press , 1989).

Peru
Bowser, Frederick, P. *The African Slave in Colonial Peru, 1524–1650* (Stanford: Stanford University, 1974).

Portugal
Mauro, Frédéric. *Portugal et l'Atlantique au XVIIe (1570–1670) Etude Economique* (Paris: Ecole Pratique des Hautes Etudes, 1960).

Saunders, A.C. *A Social History of Black Slaves and Freedmen in Portugal, 1441–1555* (Cambridge: Cambridge University Press, 1982).

Puerto Rico

Díaz, Soler L.M. *Historia de la Esclavitud en Puerto Rico, 1493–1890.* 2nd ed. (Rio Piedras: Editorial Universitaria, 1970).

Coll y Toste, Cayetano. *Historia de la Esclavitud en Puerto Rico: Información y Documentos* (San Juan: Sociedad de Autores Puertorriqueños, 1972). History of slavery in Puerto Rico, with copies of original documents relating to slavery.

Rhode Island

Coughtry, Jay. *The Notorious Triangle: Rhode Island and the African Slave Trade, 1700–1807* (Philadelphia: Temple University Press, 1981).

Crane, Elaine Forman. *A Dependent People: Newport, Rhode Island in the Revolutionary Era* (New York: Fordham University Press, 1992).

South Carolina

French, Austa M. *Slavery in South Carolina and the Ex-Slaves, or, the Port Royal Museum* (New York: The Author, 1862, fiche 6049356).

Gutman, Herbert George. *The Black Family in Slavery and Freedom, 1750–1925* (New York: Vintage Books, 1976).

Sirmans, M. Eugene. "The Legal Status of the Slave in South Carolina, 1670–1740." *Journal of Southern History* XXVIII (1962): 426–73.

Wood, Peter H. *Black Majority, Negroes in South Carolina from 1670 Through the Stono Rebellion* (New York: Alfred A. Knopf, 1974).

Southern States (General)

Bancroft, Frederic. *Slave Trading in the Old South* (1931. Reprint. Columbia: University of South Carolina Press, 1996).

Stammp, Kenneth M. *The Peculiar Institution: Slavery in the Ante-Bellum South* (New York: Alfred A. Knopf, 1956).

Virginia

Guild, Jane Purcell. *Black Laws of Virginia* (1936. Reprint. Lovettsville, VA: Willow Bend Press, 1996).

THE AFRICAN'S LAMENT.

Minchinton, Walter E., Celia King, and Peter Waite. *Virginia Slave-Trade Statistics, 1698–1775* (Richmond: Virginia State Library, 1984).

Morgan, Edmund S. *American Slavery, American Freedom: The Ordeal of Colonial Virginia* (New York: W.W. Norton, 1975).

Schwarz, Philip J. *Twice Condemned: Slaves and the Criminal Laws of Virginia, 1705–1865* (Baton Rouge: Louisiana State University Press, 1988).

Westbury, Susan. "Slaves of Colonial Virginia: Where They Came From." *William and Mary Quarterly* XLII (1985): 228–37.

Colonial Sources in Denmark

Kongelige Bibliotek

The Kongelige Bibliotek (Royal Library) of Copenhagen holdings include most of the books that have been published in Denmark, including colonial history.

Landsarkivet for Sjælland

Landsarkivet for Sjælland. *Københavnske Kirkebøger*. 2 Vols. Copenhagen: Landsarkivet for Sjælland, 1974). Inventory of the parish registers of the city of Copenhagen and suburbs housed at the provincial archives in Copenhagen, including some from the Danish West Indies.

Rigsarkivet

The Rigsarkivet (National Archives) in Copenhagen have microfilm copies of parish records for all of Denmark, and sixteenth- through eighteenth-century records of censuses and emigration.

Suggested Reading

Searching for Your Danish Ancestors: A Guide to Danish Genealogical Research in the United States and Denmark (Saint Paul: Danish Genealogical Group of the Minnesota Genealogical Society, 1989).

Westergaard, Waldemar. *The Danish West Indies Under Company Rule, 1671– 1754, with a Supplementary Chapter, 1755–1917* (New York: Macmillan & Co., 1917).

Vore Gamle Tropekolonier (Copenhagen: Fredmad, 1966). The Danish colonies in the West Indies (U.S. Virgin Islands), East Indies (Indonesia), and the Gold Coast (Ghana).

WOMEN OF SABLES D'OLONNE, LA VENDEE, FRANCE.

Colonial Sources in France

France's present-day possessions in the Americas have the status of *Départements d'Outre-Mer* (overseas departments). They are Martinique and Guadeloupe in the West Indies, Guyane in South America, and Saint-Pierre-et-Miquelon in North America. Records in French archives that specifically refer to the Acadian deportations in the eighteenth century can be found in the section on Acadia.

Archives Nationales, Section Outre-Mer, Paris

The national and departmental archives of France use a classification system of *fonds* (holdings), which are organized in series, A–Z. A–H are documents prior to 1790. The French National Archives Overseas Section contains many records relating to colonization in the New World, particularly the West Indies, French Guiana, Nova Scotia, Newfoundland, Prince Edward Island, Quebec, and Saint-Pierre-et-Miquelon. There are also records of the settlements in Michigan, Louisiana, Alabama, Mississippi, and the area known as "the Illinois." Examples of the variety of their holdings are:

- Lists of French citizens living at Fort Louis (Mobile, Alabama), 1721 and 1732
- Notarial records from Saint-Domingue (Santo Domingo), 1701–76
- Original duplicates for colonial parish records through 1776
- Land records for Cape Breton, Nova Scotia, 1720–43

A large collection of census and land records has been filmed: Gouverneur-général, Guadeloupe. Recensements générales, 1665–1802 (Paris: La Société Français du Microfilm, 1967, film 0719957 ff.). Census records for Guadeloupe, including Saint Martin, Marie-Galante, Saint-Barthélemy, and La Désirade; Saint Kitts and Nevis; Haiti; Saint Vincent; Saint Croix; and Grenada.

Recensements des colonies Françaises (film 1077743 ff.). Collection of censuses, land grants, and other documents for the former French colonies, including:

North America: Recensements et dénombrements (censuses)
Acadia (all), 1671–1755
Île-Saint-Jean (Prince Edward Island), 1728–58
Île Royale (Nova Scotia), 1713–90
Louisbourg (Cape Breton, Nova Scotia), 1735–43
Terre-Neuve (Newfoundland), 1673–1785
Saint-Pierre-et-Miquelon, 1673–1785, 1774–1804, 1818

North America: Concessions and *mémoires* (land records)
Terre-Neuve (Newfoundland),
Saint-Pierre-et-Miquelon: mémoires généraux, 1762–1819
Concessions dans l'Île Royale (Nova Scotia), 1720–36 and 1754–68
Concessions à Louisbourg (Cape Breton Island), 1735–43

West Indies: Recensements (censuses)
Guadeloupe, 1664–1800
Saint-Barthélemy, 1681–1767
Saint Martin, 1682–1767
Marie-Galante, 1680–1782
La Désirade, 1767
Martinique, 1664–1788
Saint Christopher, 1665–1701
Saint-Domingue, 1730–85
Les Antilles, 1671–1782
La Grenade, 1669–1755
Saint Croix, 1681–95
Saint Vincent, 1732
Sainte Lucia, 1730–89

West Indies: Concessions and *mémoires* (land records)
Compagnie des Indes, concessions, 1748–89

French Notarial Records

When parish registers are not available, *actes notariés* (notarial records) can substitute for the missing records. Types of notarial records are:

➤ *baux* (leases).

➤ *ventes* (sales).

➤ *quittances* (quit-claim deeds).

➤ déguerpissement (abandonment of land).

➤ *contrats de mariage* (marriage contracts).

➤ *testaments* (wills).

➤ *inventaires après décés* (inventories of estates).

➤ *partages* and *successions* (property division among the heirs of an estate).

➤ *actes de tutelle* (guardianship agreements).

➤ *engagements* (indentures).

For more information see Bernard, Gildas. *Guide des Recherches sur l'Histoire de Familles* (Paris: Archives Nationales, 1981).

Recensements du Québec. 7 Vols. (n.p., n.d., fiche 6046792). Transcripts of censuses at the Section Outre-Mer, including:

• Censuses of 1661 and 1667 of New France
• Trois-Rivières, 1760–2, 1765
• La Ville de Québec, 1744, 1762
• Terreneuve et Plaisance (Newfoundland), 1671–1711
• Montréal, 1731, 1765
• La Pariosse de Québec, 1792, 1795, 1798, 1805
Section Outre-Mer.
• Inventaire des greffes des colonies Françaises, 1718–1810 (film 0789108). Inventory of colonial court records deposited in the French National Archives.

- Inventaire sommaire de l'Etat civil des colonies, les hôpitaux, et les recensements (film 0789107). Inventory of abstracts of civil and census records for the French colonies, seventeenth to nineteenth centuries.
- Inventaires des recensements des colonies Françaises, 1664–1818 (film 1069589). Inventory of censuses of the French colonies in the French National Archives.
- Répertoire numérique des papiers publics des colonies: registres paroissiaux et d'Etat civil (film 1811894). Archival holdings list for the archives of the former French colonies.

Archives Nationales. *Guide des Recherches Sur l'Histoire des Familles* (Paris: Archives Nationales, 1981).

Archives Nationales. *Guide des Sources de l'Histoire de l'Amérique Latine et des Antilles dans les Archives Françaises* (Paris: Les Archives, 1984). Guide to the sources of the history of Latin America and the West Indies in French archives.

Saint-Seine, Xavier. *Etat des Registres Paroissiaux des Colonies Conservés aux Archives Nationales, Section Outre-Mer* (Paris: Centre Généalogique, 1968, film 0789107). List of parish registers of the colonies maintained by the National Archives of France.

Bibliothéque de l'Arsenal, Paris
The library's holdings on the Americas are mostly from the eighteenth century. The archives of the Bastille are here and include the records of over 50,000 prisoners sent to the French colonies. These have been indexed. Material from the *Archives de la Bastille* include:
- Dossiers of prisoners, A–Z (1693), D–Z (1694), A–E (1711), I–L (1717), etc.
- "Affaire du Canada," 1761–72: investigations of fraud in Canada, imprisonments, and punishments.
- Documents regarding transport of prisoners to Louisiana and Caynenne (1719–20).

Catalogue des Manuscrits de la Bibliothèque de l'Arsenal. 8 Vols., Supps. (Paris: 1895–99, 1904–).

Bibliothéque Nationale, Paris
In the Department of Manuscripts, the *Manuscrits Français* are numbered in series and contain many documents relevant to colonial America. Brief examples of the vast holdings follow:
- **6233–56.** Colonization of French Guiana (1763–4).

- **6653.** Confirmation of the establishment of the Congrégation des Filles in Montréal, Canada (1653).
- **6682.** Letters of naturalization granted to Dutch subjects allowing them to engage in commerce and exploration in America (1670).
- **9063.** Swiss regiment, in the service of the King of France: troops embarking for Louisiana, agreement to secure families for Louisiana, etc.
- **2549.** Notes, memoranda, copies of documents, etc., relating to the maritime colonies, 1667–1735, including the establishment of Recollets (1716) and a Conseil Supérieur and three bailiwicks (1717) on Île Royale (Cape Breton).
- **2552.** Colonial documents, 1729–32, including censuses of the parishes, hospitals, religious houses, mills, and sugar refineries on Martinique, 1729.
- **532.** Lists of officers serving in Quebec (1667), marine officers in the colonies (1711), officers serving in Santo Domingo (1718), etc.
- **871.** List of passengers on the *Charente* bound for Louisiana, and from New Orleans to Brest and Rochefort.
- **9035.** Census of Detroit (1750).

Catalogue des Manuscrits Français, Ancien Fonds. 5 Vols. (Paris: n.p, 1868–1902). Catalog of the series, *Manuscrits Francais*, first series.

Departmental Archives

Departmental archives throughout France hold *actes d'engamement* (indenture records), notarial collections, and passenger lists, particularly at port archives. The archives at Nantes have an admiralty collection containing crew and indenture lists from 1690 and passenger lists from the mid-1700s to Guadeloupe, Martinique, Saint-Domingue, and Louisiana.

The archives at La Rochelle also contain passenger and indenture lists which have been abstracted in *Engagés pour le Canada au XVIIe Siècle Vus de La Rochelle,* by Gabriel Debien (Quebec: Laval University, 1952, film 0982154), listing the names of indentured men who came to Canada and the West Indies from western France, 1634–1715. The records are based on notarial records and passenger lists in the departmental archives of La Rochelle. Copies of the original records are also available on microfilm at the National Archives of Canada in Ottawa, Ontario.

The departmental archives at Toulon have a naval collection containing *matricule du bagne* (records of prisoners), 1649–1705, brought to the New World in bondage. Most of the prisoners — including Huguenots — were sent to the West Indies, Canada, and Louisiana. There are also *engagements* (indenture agreements), 1634–1822, at departmental and port archives in Saint-Malo, Dieppe, Rouen, Nantes, and Bordeaux.

Archives de la Marine, France. *Répertoire Numérique des Archives du Arrondissment Maritime, Série O, Bagnes de Toulon, Marseille, Prison Gervais* (Paris: n.p., 1925, film 0962567).

The departmental archives of Bas-Rhin at Strasbourg contain lists pertaining to emigration to the Americas from the seventeenth to nineteenth centuries (fiche 6001483).

Suggested Reading

Allen, Cameron. *Records of Huguenots in the United States, Canada and the West Indies with Some Mention of Dutch and German Sources* (Salt Lake City: Genealogical Society of Utah, fiche 6039362).

Ardouin-Weiss, Idelette. *Les Actes Notarialés Anciens: Lexique* (Tours: Centre Généalogique de Touraine, 1990). Dictionary of terms used in notarial records.

Astorquia, Madeline. *Guide des Sources de L'Histoire des États-Unis dans des Archives Françaises* (Paris: France Expansion, 1976).

Auger, Léon. *Vendéens au Canada aux XVIIe et XVIIIe Siècles: Fleurs de Lys et Léopards* (Quebec: Association Vendée-Québec, 1990). Emigration, immigration, and history of early immigrants from the Vendée region of France into Canada.

Auger, Roland J. *Tracing Ancestors Through the Province of Quebec and Acadia to France* (Salt Lake City: Genealogical Society of Utah, fiche 6039358).

Beauregard, Marthe F. *La Population des Forts Français d'Amerique, XVIIe Siècle: Répetoire des Baptêmes, Marriages, et Sépultures Célébrés dans les Forts et les Établissements Français en Amérique du Nord au XVIIIe Siècle* (Montreal: Editions Bergeron, 1982). Baptisms, marriages, and burials for the French forts in North America in the eighteenth century.

Beers, Henry Putney. *French and Spanish Records of Louisiana: A Bibliographical Guide to Archive and Manuscript Resources* (Baton Rouge: Louisiana State University Press, 1989).

Bottin des Communes: Hameaux, Ecarts, Lieux-Dits, France Métropolitaine et Outre-Mer (Paris: Didot-Bottin, 1988). Gazetteer for France and the overseas departments of Réunion, Guyane, Guadeloupe, Saint-Pierre-et-Miquelon, and Martinique.

Bourrachot, Lucile. *Les Départs de Passagers Commingeois par le Port de Bordeaux au XVIIIe Siècle Suivi d'Une Liste Nominative* (Tarbes, France:

Imprimerie Saint Joseph, 1970, film 0824130). The departures of passengers from Comminges, port of Bordeaux, in the eighteenth century to the West Indies and Canada, including names, ages, etc.

Bourrachot, Lucile. *Les Départs de Passagers Quercynois pour les Antilles et le Canada au XVIIIe Siècle par le Port de Bordeaux* (n.p.: Société des Etudes du Lot, 1967). The departures of passengers from the old French province of Quercy (now Lot and Tarn-et-Garonne) for the French West Indies and Canada in the eighteenth century via the port of Bordeaux.

Crouse, Nellis M. *French Pioneers in the West Indies, 1624–1664* (New York: Columbia University Press, 1940).

Debien, Gabriel. *Liste des Engagés pour le Canada au XVIIe Siècle* (Quebec: Laval University, n.d., film 0962700). List of men indentured for Canada in the seventeenth century.

Debien, Gabriel. *Engagés Pour le Canada au XVIIe Siècle Vus de La Rochelle* (Quebec: Laval University, 1952, 0982154). Indentured men who came to Canada from Western France, 1634–1715.

Extraits des Archives des Ministeres de la Marine et de la Guerre a Paris: Canada, Correspondance Generale . . . 1755–1763 (Quebec: L.J. Demers et Frere, 1890, fiche 6048926). Extracts from the archives of the ministers of the Navy and of War in Paris, 1755–63.

Fournier, Marcel. *Les Bretons en Amérique du Nord: des Origines à 1770* (Quebec: Société de Généaloie de Québec, 1987, fiche 6101309).

Houpert, Jean. *Les Lorrains en Amérique du Nord* (Quebec: A. Naaman, 1985). The Lorrainian emigration to North America, 1640–1914.

Jensen, C. Russell. *The Role of the Notary in European Family Life* (Salt Lake City: Corporation of the President, 1980, fiche 6085791).

Lanctot, Gustave. *Filles de Joie ou Filles du Roi: Etude sur l'Emigration Féminine en Nouvelle-France* (Montreal: Editions du Jour, 1966). Study of early feminine emigration to New France.

Law, Hugh T. *Tracing Ancestors from the United States to France* (Salt Lake City: Genealogical Society of Utah, fiche 6039359).

Leland, Waldo G. *Guide to Materials for American History in the Libraries and Archives of Paris* (Washington, DC: Carnegie Institute, 1932).

Northcutt, Wayne. *The Regions of France: A Reference Guide to History and Culture* (Westport, CT: Greenwood Press, 1997).

Ozanam, Didier. *Les Sources de l'Histoire de l'Amerique Latine: Guide du Chercheur dans les Archives Français* (Paris: Reports of the Institute of Advanced Studies of Latin America, 1963). Sources of Latin American history: guide for research in French archives.

Roy, Joseph-Edmond. *Rapport Sur les Archives de France Relative a l'Histoire du Canada* (1911. Reprint. Washington, DC: Library of Congress, 1990, film 1723759). Report on the archives of France relative to the history of Canada.

Surrey, N.M. *Calendar of Manuscripts in the Paris Archives and Libraries Relating to the History of the Mississippi Valley to 1803* (Washington, DC: Carnegie Institute, 1926).

Trabajos y Conferencias (Madrid: Universidad de Madrid, 1954). Includes articles on French emigration to the Americas in the colonial period and the social conditions of Indians in the eighteenth century.

Weiss, M. Charles. *History of the French Protestant Refugees, from the Revocation of the Edict of Nantes to Our Days: With an American Appendix by a Descendant of the Huguenots.* 2 Vols. (New York: Stringer and Townsend, 1854).

ST. MALO.

Costume about the Middle of the Seventeenth Century.

Colonial Sources in Great Britain

The British Library, London

The British Library holds the following materials on the American colonial period: maps and charts, ships' logs, plans and proposals for settlement, information on shipping, trade, slave transportation, and exploration. The Library also holds one of the largest collections of West Indian newspapers.

Andrews, Charles M. *Guide to the Manuscript Materials for the History of the United States to 1783: In the British Museum, in Minor London Archives, and in the Libraries of Oxford and Cambridge* (Washington, DC: Carnegie Institute, 1908. Reprint. New York: Kraus Reprint Corporation, 1965, film 0873858).

Nickson, M.A.E. *The British Library: Guide to Catalogues and Indexes of the Department of Manuscripts* (London: n.p., 1978).

County and Municipal Record Offices

County and municipal record offices — and burgh and regional offices in Scotland — may contain records with information on emigration, transportation of prisoners, indentures, letters of denization, estates, etc. Types of records useful in tracing immigrant ancestors are:

apprenticeship registers	orphan court registers
burgess registers	quarter sessions records
bishops' transcripts	removal orders
Church of England parish registers	settlement papers
ecclesiastical court books	shipping, crew, and passenger lists
militia lists	title deeds
marriage license bonds and allegations	wills, administrations, inventories
Nonconformist parish registers	wills, register copies

Wills proved in county probate courts are useful because they can name relatives who have emigrated to the colonies. Many of the county offices have been inventoried in the *National Inventory of Documentary Sources* (Cambridge: Chadwyck-Healy, 1985, index on fiche 6341118 ff.), also known as "NIDS." For specific county information, see the Family History Library Catalog under ENGLAND — COUNTY — ARCHIVES — INVENTORIES. Another important finding aid for county records is Moulton, Joy Wade. *Genealogical Resources in English Repositories* (Baltimore: Genealogical Publishing Co., 1994).

Many county record offices contain transportation bonds, which are bonds that bind the master of a ship to transport prisoners to America. Between 1615 and 1776, some 50,000 convicts were transported. One of the best illustrations of the value of municipal record offices is to look at the Bristol Record Office in Avon. In 1654 the Council of the City of Bristol enacted an ordinance requiring that a system of enrollment be set up to record the names of all indentured servants embarking from the port of Bristol. They are transcribed in Coldham, Peter W. *The Bristol Registers of Servants Sent to Foreign Plantations, 1654–1686* (Baltimore: Genealogical Publishing Co., 1988). The destinations were Maryland, Virginia, and the West Indies.

Another example of this type of holding can be found in the Chester City Record Office, Cheshire. In the records of the Court of Quarter Sessions of the Peace are transportation bonds, 1731–75, and transportation contracts, 1764–75 (film 1472457).

The Northumberland County Record Office holds the records for the county Court of Quarter Sessions of the Peace. Orders for transportation, 1768–1808 (film 1068703), include a landing certificate for the "Port of South Potomack in Virginia." The certificate is dated 27 April 1772, and gives the name of the ship, the captain, and the prisoners put ashore.

Parish registers also contain information to make a connection to a place of origin. References to emigration, marriages, births, baptisms, burials, and other events were kept in the registers. For instance, a marriage of "Nathanyall Carey to Elizabeth Walker, of Charlestowne, New Ingland [Charlestown, Massachusetts]," was recorded in the parish register of Saint Mary's, Lancaster, on 9 July 1674. The registers of Saint Mary's Church are kept at the Lancashire Record Office in Preston (PR 3262/1/1–51,57–60). They have also been microfilmed from 1599–1900 (film 1526146 ff.), and contain baptisms, marriages, burials, and marriage banns.

Lambeth Palace Library, London

Lambeth Library contains records concerning the Church of England jurisdiction in the colonies, before the establishment of colonial bishoprics. The records include general correspondence, missionary papers, etc. Related manuscripts are the Fulham Palace Papers of the Bishops of London and the papers of the Archbishop of Canterbury.

- Manross, William W. *The Fulham Palace Papers in the Lambeth Palace Library, America Colonial Section: Calendar and Indices* (Oxford: Clarendon Press, 1965).
- Manross, William W. *S.P.G. Papers in the Lambeth Palace Library: Calendar and Indices* (Oxford: Clarendon House, 1974).

• *The New World: A Catalogue of an Exhibition of Books, Maps, Manuscripts, and Documents Held at Lambeth Palace Library . . .* (Westminster: The Church Information Board, 1957).

Missionary society records contain information regarding missionaries, society minutes, diocesan records, etc. Three such organizations are the Company for the Propagation of the Gospel in New England (founded 1649), the Society for Promoting Christian Knowledge (founded 1698), and the United Society for the Propagation of the Gospel (founded 1701). The papers for these societies are part of the Fulham Palace Papers. Some are also available on microfilm at selected libraries, including the Library of Congress in Washington, DC.

United Society for the Propagation of the Gospel in Foreign Parts, London

Founded in 1701, the archives of the Society hold the reports of the missionaries that were active in the Americas in the eighteenth century. There is also an extensive library available on-site. Manuscripts are organized as follows:

• Letters, 1702–99, relating to New England, New York, New Jersey, Pennsylvania, the Carolinas, Georgia, and Nova Scotia
• Letters, 1721–86, relating to Newfoundland, Nova Scotia, Pennsylvania, British Guiana and British Honduras, and the West Indies
• Letters, 1738–52, relating mostly to New England, but contain materials on all British colonies
• Letters, 1756–86, relating to Connecticut, Massachusetts, New Jersey, Nova Scotia, and Pennsylvania
• Journals of the Proceedings of the Society, containing abstracts of letters

Pascoe, C.F. *Two Hundred Years of the S.P.G., 1701–1901* (London: The Society, 1901).

Perry, William Stevens. *Historical Collections Relating to the American Colonial Church.* 5 Vols. (New York: AMS Press, 1969, fiche 6049573 ff.).

Rhodes House Library, Oxford

The Rhodes House Library holds a large collection of materials relating to the West Indies, in microform, books, and manuscripts. Their collection includes:
• Diaries, journals, and maps
• Correspondence of colonial governors and officials
• Records of the London Anti-Slavery Committee, founded 1823
• Records of the British and Foreign Anti-Slavery Society, founded 1839, with card indexes of writers and place-names from Brazil, British and Dutch Guiana, Costa Rica, Cuba, Haiti, Mexico, Panama, Peru, Puerto Rico, and the West Indies

- Mico Charity apprenticeship records, prior to emancipation, 1835–42, from Antigua, the Bahamas, Barbados, British Guiana, Cayman Islands, Dominica, Jamaica, Montserrat, Saint Lucia, Saint Vincent, Tobago, and Trinidad
- Other apprenticeship records for Anguilla, Argentina, Bolivia, Colombia, Cuba, Grenada, Jamaica, Mexico, Peru, Saint Kitts, and Texas
- The Oxford Colonial Records Project: transcriptions of the North Manuscripts relating to the West Indies, 1670–1879

For more information see Frewer, Louis B. "Rhodes House Library, Its Functions and Resources." *Bodeleian Library Record* 6 (October 1956) and 3 (January 1964).

Windsor Castle, Royal Archives

Among the colonial records at the Archives are the Duke of Cumberland Papers, 1750–60, relating to New York, Nova Scotia, Pennsylvania, and the West Indies.

The Public Record Office, Kew, Surrey

Th Public Record Office (PRO) is a repository for original source documents, many of which relate to the colonial period. Much of the material has been abstracted or transcribed into compiled collections. These works vary in their degree of accuracy and completeness, and only the most reliable are identified here as resources.

The PRO record groups are designated as classes. They are identified by letter codes, thereafter followed by a class number and a piece number. There are numerous published finding aids that help in locating these references. The major classes at the PRO relating to colonial research are:

Admiralty **(ADM)**
Exchequer and Audit Department:
American Loyalist Claims Commission
   (AO) *(See also New France)*
Board of Trade **(BT)**
British Transport Historical Records **(BH)**
Chancery **(C)**
Colonial Office **(CO)**
Court of King's Bench **(KB)**
Exchequer **(E)**

Foreign Office **(FO)**
Gifts and Deposits, **(PRO)**
High Court of Admiralty **(HCA)**
Prerogative Court of Canterbury **(PROB)**
Privy Council **(PR)**
State Papers **(SP)**
Treasury **(T)**
Treasury Solicitor **(TS)**
War Office **(WO)** *(See also New France)*

Admiralty (ADM)

The Office of Marine Causes was established in 1546 (prior records are under Privy Council). Some of the Admiralty Office classes contain records regarding prisoner of war lists **(ADM 103)**, records of the Royal Marines **(ADM 157)**,

Royal Navy officers service records (**ADM 196**), wills of seamen (**ADM 48**), naval courts martial (**ADM 1**), ships' pay books (**ADM 32-5**), and ships' musters (**ADM 36-9**). Some of the records are found in other series, such as the Admiralty reports found in the Treasury Solicitor's Office (**TS 10**), which are entry books of prize, captured slave ships, etc. Admiralty records are generally germane to more administrative naval matters, as opposed to the High Courts of Admiralty, which contain records of crimes committed on the high seas, etc. (See High Court of Admiralty).

Index to bounty papers, 1675-1822 (**ADM 106**, film 0824518).
Index to commission and warrant books, 1695-1742 (film 0824516).

Rodger, R.A.M. *Naval Records for Genealogists* (London: HMSO, 1988).

Board of Trade (BT)
The early records of the Board of Trade include *Registrar of General Shipping and Seamen , Agreements, and Crew Lists, Series 1, 1747-1860* (**BT 98**), which contains muster rolls and crew lists of merchant seamen, arranged by port.

Board of Trade, Naval Office Shipping Lists:
* East Florida, 1764-9 (film 0964006).
* Georgia (film 0964005).
* Maryland, 1689-1754 (film 0964007).
* Massachusetts, 1686-1765 (film 0965841 ff.).
* New Hampshire, 1694-5, 1723-69 (film 0964004).
* New Jersey, 1722-64 (film 0965866).
* New York, 1713-65 (film 0965862 ff.).
* South Carolina, 1716-67 (film 0964002 ff.).
There are also colonial shipping lists in the Colonial Office records.

British Transport Historical Records (BH)
The Hudson's Bay Company Archives, dating from 1667, were originally gathered in London in the 1920s. The original records have been returned to the Provincial Archives of Manitoba and are available on microfilm at the PRO. For more information, see Rupert's Land.

Public Record Office. *The British Transport Historical Records Collection: A Provisional Guide* (London: PRO, 1977).

For other records on Hudson's Bay, see Colonial Office Papers, original correspondence, 1675-1759 (**CO 134**), and entry books, 1670-1789 (**CO 135**).

Chancery (C)

Chancery Court records deal with civil disputes involving land, inheritance, marriage settlements, etc. **(C 103–114)**. Some of the more important classes are:

- Association Oath Rolls: swearing allegiance to the Crown.
- Close Rolls: private deeds that were folded before being sealed.
- Feet of Fines: records of title-holders of land.
- Manor Court Rolls: proceedings of the manor court regarding transactions between the landlord and the tenants, including sales and lists of slaves. Some of the Manor Court Rolls are at other repositories, including private collections.
- Other proceedings of the Chancery Court.

List of Records of the Chancery, Petty Bag Office to 1842. Vol. 25 (London: List and Index Society, 1967).

Gandy, Wallace. *The Association Oath Rolls of the British Plantations, A.D. 1696* (1922. Reprint. Baltimore: Clearfield Co., 1994). The localities include Antigua, Barbados, Bermuda, Montserrat, Nevis, New York, Saint Kitts, and Virginia.

Colonial Office (CO)

Colonial Office papers date from 1574 and refer to the departments that had oversight for colonial administration. The main classes of early records in the Colonial Office are:

- Colonial papers: general records referring to more than one colony, may contain censuses and other population returns, militia returns, etc.
- Original correspondence: may include original parish registers, censuses, petitions, tax lists, lists of inhabitants, pensions, land grants, newspapers, prisoner lists, local court records, etc. Parish registers and non-conformist registers may also contain lists of emigrants.
- Entry books: may include patents for grants of land, petitions, etc.
- Acts: may include local acts and ordinances, including private naturalizations.
- Sessional papers: legislative proceedings.
- Government gazettes: may include notices of vital records, obituaries, tax lists, court notices, applications for licenses, jury and voter lists, militia lists, notice of land sales, wills, naturalization applications, port entries, parish relief registers, etc.

Great Britain, Public Record Office. *Calendar of State Papers — Colonial Series: Preserved in the . . . Public Record Office.* 44 Vols. (London: HMSO, 1860–1969). The following volumes contain material relating to America and the West Indies:

Vol. 1, 1574–1660	Vol. 19, 1701	Vol. 32, 1720–1
Vol. 5, 1661–8	Vol. 20, 1702	Vol. 33, 1722–3
Vol. 7, 1669–74	Vol. 21, 1702–3	Vol. 34, 1724–5
Vol. 9, 1574–1676	Vol. 22, 1704–5	Vol. 35, 1726–7
Vol. 10, 1677–80	Vol. 23, 1706–8	Vol. 36, 1728–9
Vol. 11, 1681–5	Vol. 24, 1708–9	Vol. 37, 1730
Vol. 12, 1685–8	Vol. 25, 1710–11	Vol. 38, 1731
Vol. 13, 1689–92	Vol. 26, 1711–12	Vol. 39, 1732
Vol. 14, 1693–6	Vol. 27, 1712–14	Vol. 40, 1733
Vol. 15, 1696–7	Vol. 28, 1714–15	Vol. 41, 1734–5
Vol. 16, 1697–8	Vol. 29, 1716–17	Vol. 42, 1735–6
Vol. 17, 1621–99	Vol. 30, 1717–18	Vol. 43, 1737
Vol. 18, 1700	Vol. 31, 1719–20	Vol. 44, 1738

A collection of documents selected from the PRO relating to the Palatine immigration from the Colonial Office and Treasury Papers (film 0087881) has been microfilmed, and includes correspondence of:

- Secretary of State (1708–27), New York (**CO 5**)
- Board of Trade (1708–10), Jamaica (**CO 137**)
- Entry books of letters (1706–9), Jamaica (**CO 138**)
- Board of Trade (1706–5), Virginia (**CO 5**)
- Entry book of letters (1709–10), Carolina (**CO 5/289**)
- Secretary of State (1702–29), Carolina (**CO 5**)
- Board of Trade (1708–12), New England (**CO 5**)
- Entry books of letters (1708–15), New England (**CO 5**)
- Secretary of State (1702–10), America and West Indies (**CO 5**)
- Secretary of State (1696–1731), Bahamas (**CO 5**)
- Board of Trade (1726–31), Bahamas (**CO 23**)
- Secretary of State (1704–25), Leeward Islands (**CO 152**)
- Board of Trade, Nova Scotia and Cape Breton, 1726–30 (**CO 217**)
- Entry books of letters (1720–49), Nova Scotia and Cape Breton (**CO 218**)
- Board of Trade (1705–21), New York (**CO 5**)

Another series of selected transcripts of **CO 5** has been filmed (film 1549671 ff.) that duplicates some of the previous records, but also includes different papers:

- New England, original papers, 1710–52
- Colonial governors' correspondence, 1743–61
- Board of Trade plantations, general papers, 1689–1783
- Board of Trade Indian affairs, 1756–75
- Board of Trade correspondence to the Virginia Board of Trade, 1699–1773
- Board of Trade correspondence to the Virginia Secretary of State, 1696–1777
- Board of Trade entry books on proprietary colonies, 1696–1775
- French and Indian War, 1754–63
- Instructional commissions to colonial officials, 1702–84
- The American Revolution, 1772–84

Correspondence from Antigua and the Leeward Islands with the Board of Trade (**CO 152,** film 1818355 ff.), for the years 1727–30, 1734–5, and 1744–7 contains parish records, court records, tax lists, and military records. Parish registers are from Antigua, Falmouth, Nevis, Saint Kitts, and Montserrat. There are also Colonial Office papers for British Honduras (**CO 123, 124**). Some Admiralty Court records have also been included in this series, such at the court records for Saint Kitts (**CO 155**).

Oaths of allegiance taken by foreign Protestants in Jamaica, Maryland, Massachusetts, New York, Pennsylvania, South Carolina, and Virginia between 1740 and 1800 (**CO 5, 324**) have been abstracted in Giuseppi, M.S. *Naturalizations of Foreign Protestants in the American and West Indian Colonies* (1921. Reprint. Baltimore: Genealogical Publishing Co., film 0908978).

Thurston, Anne F. *Sources for Colonial Studies in the Public Record Office, I: Records of the Colonial Office, Dominions Office, Commonwealth Relations Office, and Commonwealth Office* (London: HMSO, 1995).

Court of King's Bench (KB)
The Court of King's Bench records contain swearing and oath rolls (**KB 24**), 1708–12, including foreign Protestants who were required to produce a sacrament certificate (**KB 22**), 1767, and 1728–1828. This was considered a form of naturalization. These records have been indexed in the collections of the Huguenot Society (Vol. XXVII: 78–107).

Exchequer (E)
The office of King's Remembrancer was cognizant for taking notes of debts and other matters of which the Court needed to be informed. It issued *Exchequer Court Licenses to Pass Beyond the Seas*, 1558–1677 (**E 157**), including registers of passengers, which have been abstracted by several authors. The registers date from 1634–9 and 1677.
- Hotten, John Camden. *The Original Lists of Persons of Quality: Emigrants; Religious Exiles; Political Rebels; Serving Men Sold for a Term of Years; Apprentices; Children Stolen; Maidens Pressed; and Others Who Went from Great Britain to the American Plantations, 1600–1700, with Their Ages, the Localities Where They Formerly Lived* (1880. Reprint. Baltimore: Genealogical Publishing Co., 1962, fiche 6051412). This has been superseded by Peter Coldham's *Complete Book of Emigrants* (see page 764).
- Brandow, James C. *Omitted Chapters from Hotten's Original Lists of Persons of Quality*... (Baltimore: Genealogical Publishing Co., 1982). For more information on the missing parishes, see Barbados.
- Sherwood, George F.T. *American Colonists in English Records: A Guide to Direct References in Authentic Records, Passenger Lists Not in "Hotten"*

(1932. Reprint. Baltimore: Genealogical Publishing Co., 1978, film 0874190). The records are abstracted from the Exchequer records, the Privy Council Papers, the Prerogative Court of Canterbury, Chancery proceedings and bills, records of the Drapers' Company (London), the Harleian Manuscripts at the British Library, the Commissariot of Edinburgh, miscellaneous parish registers, etc.

Foreign Office (FO) and State Papers (SP)

State Papers are one source of information about people who were shipped to the colonies or had a death sentence commuted to transportation. These records are also found in other classes: Patent Rolls (**C 66**), Treasury Papers (**T 1**), and Quarter Sessions records in local record offices. Records of the Foreign Office before 1782 are also among the State Papers. The records include wills, naturalizations, passport registers, estates, and sometimes vital records.

Records of the slave trade are also found in the Foreign Office Papers, extending into the nineteenth century. They include Havana, 1819–69 (**FO 313**), Jamaica, 1843–51 (**CO 314**), Cape Town, 1843–70 (**FO 312**), and Sierra Leone, 1819–68 (**FO 315**). The papers on Sierra Leone include emancipations of slaves shipped form Jamaica to Nova Scotia to Africa.

State Papers, Spanish Series, 1485–1603 (London: HMSO, 1879–1916).

Atherton, Louise. *Never Complain, Never Explain: Records of the Foreign Office and State Paper Office, 1500–1960.* PRO Readers Guide No. 7 (London: PRO Publications, 1994).

High Court of Admiralty (HCA)

The High Court of Admiralty's jurisdiction was divided into two courts:

➢ Ordinary or Instance Court: civil cases and Admiralty Droits — suits relating to disputes, wages, collision, salvage and droits; and criminal cases tried in the session of Oyer and Terminer and General Gaol Delivery — murder, warrants for piracy, etc.

➢ Prize Court: prizes taken form an enemy in time of war; registers of letters of Letters of Marque and Reprisal.

Some of the important classes include:

- Oyer and Terminer Indictments, 1604–1797 (**HCA 1**)
- Oyer and Terminer Examination of Pirates, 1601–1768 (**HCA 1**): Bermuda, New England, New York, Pennsylvania, and Virginia
- Prize Acts, 1643–1786 (**HCA 3**): indexes cases before the high court by ship, captain, and plaintiff
- Prize Exemplifications, 1603–1768 (**HCA 14**): copies of judgments or orders, including evidence regarding appeals from colonial courts
- Prize Papers, 1661–1855 (**HCA 32**)

- Prize Sentences, 1643–1854 **(HCA 34)**
- Prize Appeals Acts, 1689–1813 **(HCA 41)**
- Prize Appeals Papers, 1689–1833 **(HCA 42)**
- Libel files, 1603–1739 **(HCA 24)**: includes appeals from Vice-Admiralty Courts in the colonies
- Instance Papers, 1629–1778 **(HCA 15)**, 1772–1806 **(HCA 16)**: arranged by ships' names
- Letters of Marque, declarations, 1689–1814 **(HCA 26)**: records of privateering
- Letters of Marque, bonds, 1549–1815 **(HCA 25)**
- Slave trade reports, 1821–91 **(HCA 35)**, 1837–76 **(HCA 36)**
- Slave Trade Advisor to the Court, 1821–97 **(HCA 37)**: registers of liberated slaves, crew lists, etc.

Coldham, Peter W. *English Adventurers and Emigrants: Abstracts of Examinations in the High Court of Admiralty with Reference to Colonial America* (Baltimore: Genealogical Publishing Co., 1984). The localities include Virginia, the Plymouth Colony, Newfoundland, and Canada.

Vice-Admiralty Courts were established in overseas dominions after 1697 over waters which could not be adequately policed by the High Court of Admiralty in England. Appeals were made to the High Court in England, which declined in importance after 1700. Vice-Admiralty Courts held jurisdiction over:

➢ ordinary marine causes: wages, bottomry, claims, salvage, etc.
➢ prize cases: about one third of the case load, where it was necessary to establish that ships and cargo that had been captured had belonged to an enemy
➢ breaches of acts of trade: infractions and ships engaged in illegal trading, smuggling, etc.
➢ trials for interloping: infringing on licensed trading companies
➢ treaty infringements

Vice-Admiralty Court records can be found listed under individual colonies, in this section as shipping lists under Board of Trade, and in court proceedings, 1636–1875 **(HCA 49)**, including:

- Guadeloupe, 1811–15
- Jamaica, 1662–3, 1747–8
- New York, 1777–83 (transferred from New York to England in 1784, also in **HCA 24, 32**)
- Bahamas, Barbados, Jamaica, Virginia, South Carolina, Rhode Island, Pennsylvania, and New York, 1723–39. Virginia records have been published in George Reese. *Proceedings in the Court of Vice-Admiralty of Virginia, 1698–1775* (Richmond: Virginia State Library, 1983).
- Vice-Admiralty records in Assignation books, 1689–1796 **(HCA 43)**, for courts in Bermuda, East Florida, Halifax (Nova Scotia), Jamaica, New

York, and Saint Kitts
- Captured letters from Bordeaux, France to America (1778), and from Havana to New Orleans, Louisiana (1783)
- Appeals, 1750–1800 **(HCA 45)**
- South Carolina, 1716–89 (film 1549527 ff.). The original records are at the National Archives in Washington, DC (M1180).

Prerogative Court of Canterbury (PROB)
The Prerogative Court of Canterbury **(PCC)** proved all wills involving those who died outside of England and still held property within the country. As the highest probate court in England, it was also the court of first instance when a will involved an overseas claimant.
- Province of Canterbury Prerogative Court. Probate records, 1526–1856 (film 0172524 ff.). The original records are at the PRO.
- Coldham, Peter W. *American Wills and Administrations in the Prerogative Court of Canterbury, 1610–1857* (Baltimore: Genealogical Publishing Co., 1989).
- Coldham, Peter W. *American Wills Proved in London, 1611–1775* (Baltimore: Genealogical Publishing Co, 1992).
- Mathews, John. *Hints for Tracing an Anglo-American Pedigree in the Old Country: With a List of Wills from 1700 to 1725 in the Prerogative Court of Canterbury, England, of Testators Living or Dying in America and the West Indies* (Washington, DC: Library of Congress, 1981, film 1429855).

Privy Council (PC)
The Privy Council advised the King on matters concerning petitions to the Crown, as a court of last resort in cases of appeal, and in administrative decisions involving the affairs of government. In 1615 a Privy Council order authorized the first criminals to be transported to the Americas. The Privy Council registers **(PC 2)** contain petitions of those wishing to emigrate, or already residing in the colonies, including lists of convicts. Plantation Books **(PC 5)** also contain material on emigration and colonial government and land issues.
- *Acts of the Privy Council, Colonial Series, 1613–1783.* 6 Vols. (London: HMSO, 1908–12).
- "British Privy Council Records: Their Usefulness in Caribbean Research." *Caribbean Historical and Genealogical Journal* I 2 (April 1993): 13–14.

The Peter Wilson Coldham Collection

Peter Wilson Coldham is the author of two series considered to be the standard works on Anglo-American colonial immigration (all published by Genealogical Publishing Co., Baltimore, not available on microfilm). He has made accessible many of the classes of the PRO (and other repositories) that contain primary source documents on emigrants to the New World. In addition to the published volumes, the series are also available as a single CD-ROM (Genealogical Publishing Co./Broderbund, 1996), which includes approximately 140,000 names.

Coldham, Peter W. *The Complete Book of Emigrants in Bondage, 1614–1775* (1988–92). An alphabetical listing of English convicts transported to colonial America taken from records of the Assize Courts, Courts of Quarter Sessions, Patent Rolls, Treasury Papers, etc. There is also a supplement.

The Complete Book of Emigrants series covers the following years:
*   *The Complete Book of Emigrants, 1607–1660* (1987). Emigrants from Barbados to Virginia, and records taken from Chancery and Exchequer offices, including missing records from Hotten.
*   *The Complete Book of Emigrants, 1661–1699* (1990). Records from state and parliamentary papers, customs and treasury records, apprenticeship records, port books, criminal transportation orders, estate records, and county and town records.
*   *The Complete Book of Emigrants, 1700–1750* (1992). Records from plantation apprenticeship bindings (Liverpool and London), port books (Bristol, Liverpool, Newcastle, Whitehaven, Southampton, Portsmouth, Poole, Weymouth and Lyme, Exeter, Bideford, Dartmouth, and Plymouth), and convict pardons on condition of transportation (Patent Rolls for 1700–19).
*   *The Complete Book of Emigrants, 1751–1776* (1993). Records include port books, plantation apprenticeship bindings, and Treasury records.

Other publications not on CD-ROM:
*   Coldham, Peter W. *Emigrants from England to the American Colonies, 1773–1776* (1988). Includes every emigrant officially recorded as leaving from an English port between 1773 and 1776.
*   Coldham, Peter W. *Child Apprentices in America from Christ's Hospital, London, 1617–1778* (1990).

Treasury (T) and Treasury Solicitor (TS)
- Loyalist claims, 1777–1812 (**T 79**)
- East Florida Loyalist claims, 1786–1820 (**TS 11**)
- Refugee and militia lists, 1780–1856, "Americans sufferers in East Florida orders," 1789–95, and Loyalist allowances, 1780–1835 (**T 50**)
- Muster rolls of colonial regiments in the French and Indian War from Connecticut, Massachusetts, New Hampshire, and Rhode Island (**T 64**)
- Blathwayt's Journal, 1680–1718 (**T 64**), including transcripts from William and Mary College in Williamsburg, Virginia (see Virginia).
- Claims from the British settlers in East Florida, 1740–89 (**T 77**)
- Lists of criminals transported to America (**T 1, 53**)
- West Jersey (New Jersey) Society records, 1675–1921, including some land in Pennsylvania and New England (**TS 12**)
- Embarkation lists of German Palatines arriving at New York, 1708–10 (**T 1**)
- Records of the slave-trading companies, 1660–1833 (**T 70**), including the Company of Royal Adventurers (incorporated 1663), the Royal African Company of England (incorporated 1672), and the Company of Merchants trading to Africa (incorporated 1750)
- Santo Domingo Claims Committee, 1794–1812 (**T 81**)
- Slave Registration and Compensation, 1812–46 (**T 71**)
- Berbice Commission, British Guiana, 1812–17 (**T 89**)
- Deeds for Crown lands, 1668–1803 (**T 64**)
- Jacobite rebellion papers, 1745–53 (**TS 20**, film 1485247 ff.).

Calendar of Treasury Books and Papers, 1729–1745 . . . 5 Vols. (London: HMSO, 1897–1903).

Treasury Board Papers . . . 1745–1755. Vol. 120 (London: List and Index Society, 1976).

Treasury Solicitor and H.M. Procurator General Class List: Part I. Vol. 147 (London: List and Index Society, 1978).

Cameron, Viola Root. *Emigrants from Scotland to America, 1774–1775: Copied from a Loose Bundle of Treasury Papers in the Public Record Office, London, England* (Baltimore: Southern Book Co., 1959, fiche 6049039).

War Office (WO)
Records of the War Office include muster and pay lists, militia records, administrative records, muster books, Army lists, officers' records, etc. For more information on volunteers and units serving in American colonies (**WO 28, 42, 97**), see New France. Series include:
- Letters from various officers serving in South Carolina and Virginia to Commander-in-Chief, and letters from Commander-in-Chief to officers serving in South Carolina and Virginia, 1757–63 (**WO 34/47-8**) (London:

PRO, n.d., film 1303171). Also includes some monthly and weekly returns, applications for commissions, reports and plans.

- Headquarter records: records relating to Connecticut, 1746-7, and Canada 1775-85 **(WO 28)**
- West Florida letters and papers, 1763-4 **(WO 1/49)**
- American Rebellion entry books, 1773-83 **(WO 36)**
- Amherst Papers, 1712-84, relating to the Thirteen Colonies **(WO 34)**
- Ordnance Office: artillery in America, 1773-7 **(WO 55)**
- Court martial proceedings, home and foreign stations, 1715-90 **(WO 71)**
- Commissariot accounts for New York, 1774-84 **(WO 60)**
- Soldiers' documents, 1760-1872 **(WO 97)**
- Army lists, monthly returns, home and abroad, 1759-1865 **(WO 17)**
- Secretary of War correspondence: America, 1775-1810, West Indies, 1775-1805, deserters, 1744-1833 **(WO 4)**

Gifts and Deposits (PRO)
This series includes the documents donated or deposited with the PRO; it also includes a collection of records transcribed from foreign archives.

- Carleton Papers, 1747-83 **(PRO 30/11, 35, 55, also WO 34)**. See New France.
- Carmichael Smyth Papers, 1805-37, relating to the Bahamas and British Guiana **(PRO 30/35)**
- Manchester Papers, relating to Virginia plantations and Bermuda, 1603-25 **(PRO 30/55)**
- Shaftesbury Papers, containing the original Fundamental Constitutions for Carolina, records of the Ashley River settlement in Carolina; and Jamaica and Barbados **(PRO 30/24)**

Scottish Record Office, Edinburgh (SRO)
Often overlooked by American researchers, the Scottish Record Office in Edinburgh holds classes of records similar in content to those of the PRO. Some of the most important records for tracing immigrant ancestors are:

Admiralty Court **(AC)**
Board of Customs and Excise **(CE)**
Burgh Records **(B)**
Scotland Church Records **(CH)**
Commissary Courts **(CC)**
Court of Session **(CS)**
Exchequer **(E)**
Gifts and Deposits **(GD)**

High Court of Justiciary **(JC)**
Old Parochial Registers **(OPR)**
Privy Council **(PC)**
Register of Deeds **(RD)**
Register of Sasines **(RS)**
Services of Heirs **(SH)**
Sheriff Court **(SC)**

Admiralty Court Records (AC)
Crimes committed on the high seas between 1705 and 1830 are found in the volumes of the Admiralty Court.

Dobson, David. *Scottish-American Court Records, 1733–1783* (Baltimore: Genealogical Publishing, Co., 1991). Identifies those people resident in North America who were engaged in litigation in Scotland, based on the minute books of the Court of Session and those of the High Court of the Admiralty for 1733–83, and also the Court of Session **(CS)**.

Burgh Records (B)

Burgh records contain muniments (title deeds), apprenticeship records, shipping, poor relief, sentences of transportation, etc. Burghs were chartered towns that functioned independently of the county in which they were situated. Many have been extracted in:

Renwick, Robert. *Extracts from the Records of the Burgh of Glasgow, 1697–1717* (Edinburgh: Scottish Burgh Record Society, 1852).

Renwick, Robert. *Extracts from the Records of the Burgh of Stirling, 1677–1711* (Edinburgh: Scottish Burgh Record Society, 1897).

Renwick, Robert. *Extracts from the Records of the Burgh of Peebles, 1652–1714: With Appendix, 1367–1665* (Glasgow: Scottish Burgh Record Society, 1910, fiche 6035500).

Renwick, Robert. *Extracts from the Records of the Royal Burgh of Lanark* (Glasgow: Carson and Nichol, 1893, film 1426091).

Rae, Thomas I. *The Burgh Court Book of Selkirk, 1503–1545* (Edinburgh: J. Skinner, 1960, film 0844784).

Wood, Marguerite. *Extracts from the Records of the Burgh of Edinburgh, 1642–1655* (Edinburgh: Oliver and Boyd, 1937, film 0990416).

Wood, Marguerite. *Register of Edinburgh Apprentices, 1756–1800* (Edinburgh: Scottish Record Society, 1963, film 0844784).

Repertory of Scotland Church Records (CH)

The denominations and records in this series include the Church of Scotland General Assembly Papers **(CH1)**, Kirk Session records, Church of Scotland records **(CH2)**, Quaker Meeting records **(CH10)**, Methodist Church **(CH11)**, the Episcopal Church in Scotland **(CH12)**, United Free Church of Scotland **(CH13)**, Congregational Church **(CH14)**, Unitarian Church **(CH15)**, Roman Catholic Church **(RH21)**, and other related categories are found in this group. Kirk sessions handled the judicial and administrative proceedings of a parish. They contain vital records, church disciplinary matters, residences and parish censuses, admissions, transfers of membership, etc. Testificates are certificates attesting to the moral character of a parishioner who was transferring from one parish to another. Finding aids and inventories for all of the religious groups are on microfiche (fiche 6029985 ff.).

Repertory of Church of Scotland Records (Edinburgh: SRO, 1977–1983, film 0952933 ff.).

Calderwood, D. *History of the Kirk* (London: Woodrow Society, 1848).

Roman Catholic Registers (Edinburgh: SRO, 1971, fiche 6035739). Place index to the Roman Catholic registers in the SRO.

Records of the Church of Scotland: Preserved in the Scottish Record Office and General Register Office, Register House Edinburgh (Glasgow: R.E. Robertson, 1967, film 0844784).

Marshall, James Scott. *Calendar of Irregular Marriages in the South Leith Kirk Session Records, 1697–1818* (Edinburgh: Neill, 1968, film 0844784).

Maxwell, Archibald Strath. *Scottish Society of Friends: "Quakers, " Registers of Births, Proposal of Marriage, Marriages, and Deaths, 1647–1878* (n.p., n.d., film 0832635).

Commissary Court (CC) and Sheriff Court (SC) Records
Between 1650 and 1900, some Scots in North America chose to have their wills registered and confirmed in Scotland rather than in the Prerogative Court of Canterbury. All wills proved before 1801, and some through 1824, were under the jurisdiction of the commissary court. To use these records, it is necessary to know the approximate date of death and where the individual lived in Scotland.

Each commissariot is indexed separately. For a person who died outside of Scotland but left property within Scotland between 1801 and 1875 there may be an executry in the commissary office of the Sheriff Court of Edinburgh (**SC70**). Sheriff Court records are also organized by commissariot.[74]

Dobson, David. *Scottish-American Wills, 1650–1900* (Baltimore: Genealogical Publishing Co., 1991). The original records are at the SRO in Edinburgh.

McCaffray, Charles. *Index to Sheriff Court Districts in Scotland* (Edinburgh: W. Green and Son, 1980).

Court of Session (CS)
Court of Session was the highest civil court in Scotland from 1532. The proceedings include litigation between parties in Scotland and North America, particularly the Chesapeake region, but also the West Indian colonies. Files of cases, *Warrants of the Acts and Decreets*, or *Extracted Processes*, are indexed, 1670–1852, and 1684–1848. See also Scottish Record Office. *Scottish Record Office, Court of Session Productions, 1760–1840* (Kew, Surrey: List and Index Society, 1987).

---

[74]For more information, see Cecil Sinclair, *Tracing Your Scottish Ancestors: A Guide to Ancestry Research in the Scottish Record Office* (Edinburgh: HMSO, 1990), 31–40.

Exchequer (E)
Exchequer records contain many different categories. Forfeited Estate Papers contain records of forfeited Jacobite estates in the eighteenth century. Other records in this series include muster rolls, 1614–1707, before the union of England and Scotland in 1707.

Furgol, Edward M. *A Regimental History of the Covenanting Armies, 1639–1651* (Edinburgh: John Donald Publishers, Ltd., 1990).

Hamilton-Edwards, Gerald. *In Search of Army Ancestry* (London: Phillimore, 1977).

Millar, A.H. *A Selection of Scottish Forfeited Estate Papers, 1715, 1745* (Edinburgh: Scottish History Society, 1909, fiche 6035783).

Gifts and Deposits (GD)
Records that have been loaned to the SRO by individuals, families, organizations, and private concerns are found in this collection, such as the Hay of Houston Papers relating to Barbados. Some of the more important papers are lease and rent rolls, letters, estate papers, indentures, and more.

High Court of Justiciary (JC), Privy Council (PC)
The High Court of Justiciary, from 1672, and the Privy Council of Scotland, 1545–1708, sentenced many people to transportation to the colonies. Prisoners from the Tollbooth of Edinburgh — Covenanters, Jacobites, Highlanders, gypsies, criminals — were transported to New Jersey, New York, Maryland, Virginia, the Carolinas, Bermuda, Barbados, Jamaica, etc.

For Privy Council records see:
Burton, John Hill. *Register of the Privy Council of Scotland, 1545–1625.* 1st Series (Edinburgh: HMSO, 1877–98).
Brown, P.H. *Register of the Privy Council of Scotland, 1625–1660.* 2nd Series (Edinburgh: HMSO, 1899–1908).
Brown, P.H. *Register of the Privy Council of Scotland, 1661–1691.* 3rd Series (Edinburgh: HMSO, 1908–70).

For Justiciary records see:
Cameron, John. *The Justiciary Records of Argyll and the Isles, 1664—1742.* 2 Vols. (Edinburgh: Stair Society, 1949, film 0990279).
Fairely, J.A. *Extracts from the Records of the Old Tollbooth, 1657–1686* (Edinburgh: T. and A. Constable, 1923, film 1559417).
Smith, J. Irvine. *Selected Justiciary Cases, 1624–1650.* 3 Vols. (Edinburgh: Stair Society, 1970–4, film 0990290 ff.).

Old Parochial Registers (OPR)
The Old Parochial Registers are in the New Register House and date from the late 1500s to 1854. They contain births, marriages, and deaths from parishes throughout Scotland. There is an index on microfiche and CD-ROM available at the Family History Library (FHL), and at Family History Centers, that contains about 10.5 million names listed in the Church of Scotland (Presbyterian) parish registers. The registers are the best source of family information before the introduction of civil registration in 1855. Most of the indexed records are available on microfilm through the FHL.

Register of Deeds (RD), Services of Heirs (SH), Register of Sasines (RS)
There are three important types of land records: Sasines, Services of Heirs, and Deeds. The Register of Deeds are in three series: 1554–1657, 1661–1881, and 1812–. They contain not only land records but also marriage contracts, apprenticeships, letters testamentary, and other contracts.
* *Deeds, Minute Books and Index of Deeds and Probate Writs, 1542–1851* (Edinburgh: SRO, 1958, film 0231790 ff.).
* *Index to Register of Deeds, 1661–1696.* 70 Vols. (Edinburgh: HMSO, 1915–, film 0896590 ff.).

Services of Heirs, or Retours, of the Chancery Court, rendered verdicts on the inheritable land claims of the deceased. Some of the heirs had emigrated to the colonies. Sometimes a person who had emigrated left property to family members who were still in Scotland. The Services of Heirs Records are indexed, 1530–1700 (film 0908847), and 1700–1860 (film 0990340), and the original records, 1530–1900 (film 0231260 ff.), are also available.
* *Decennial Index to the Service of Heirs, 1700–1860* (Edinburgh: HMSO, 1870, film 0990340).
* American heirs of deceased Scottish landowners have been extracted in Dobson, David. *Scottish-American Heirs, 1683–1883* (Baltimore: Genealogical Publishing Co., 1990). This includes the document registration date and some Scottish landowner death dates.

Sasines are the instrument of transfer of property from an estate to an heir or another person. The Particular Register of Sasines, 1617–1868, can be used with the Services of Heirs records to find out more information about an estate. The records were recorded in notarial minute books, 1599–1793 (film 0216980 ff.).
* *Index to the General Register of Sasines: 1617–1700* (Edinburgh: SRO, 1958, film 0216970 ff.).
* *Index of Persons, to Abridgments of Sasines: 1781–1868* (Edinburgh: SRO, 1958, film 0217026 ff.).
* Campbell, Herbert. *Abstracts of the Particular Register of Sasines.* 2 Vols. (Edinburgh: W. Brown, 1933–4, film 1426081).

Finding Aids

Bloxham, Ben. *Key to Parochial Registers of Scotland from Earliest Times Through 1854.* 2nd ed. (Provo, UT: Stevenson's Genealogical Center, 1979, fiche 6036348).

British Reference Unit. *Sasines, Services of Heirs and Deeds Register* (Salt Lake City: Church of Jesus Christ of Latter-day Saints, 1981, fiche 6054478). Brief historical background, explanations of, and availability of three types of land records: Sasines, Services of Heirs, and Deeds.

Bumsted, J. M. *The People's Clearance: Highland Emigration to British America, 1770–1815* (Edinburgh: Edinburgh University Press, 1982).

Cory, Kathleen. *Tracing Your Scottish Ancestry* (Baltimore: Genealogical Publishing Co., 1990).

Dobson, David. *Directory of Scots Banished to American Plantations, 1650–1775* (Baltimore: Genealogical Publishing Co., 1984).

Dobson, David. *Directory of Scottish Settlers in North America.* 7 Vols. (Baltimore: Genealogical Publishing Co., 1984–93).

Dobson, David. *Directory of Scots in the Carolinas, 1680–1830* (Baltimore: Genealogical Publishing Co., 1986).

Dobson, David. *The Original Scots Colonists of Early America, 1612–1783* (Baltimore: Genealogical Publishing Co., 1989). Some of the destinations of the colonists and the transportees were Antigua, the Bahamas, Barbados, Bermuda, the Carolinas, Georgia, Jamaica, the Leeward Islands, Martinique, Maryland, Massachusetts, New Brunswick, New Jersey, New York, Nova Scotia, Prince Edward Island, Saint Croix, and Saint Kitts.

Donaldson, G. *The Scots Overseas* (London: Robert Hale, 1966).

Graham, Ian Charles Cargill. *Colonists from Scotland: Emigration to North America, 1707–1783* (1956. Reprint. Baltimore: Clearfield Co., 1994).

Scottish Record Office. *The Emigrants: Historical Background, List of Documents, Extracts and Facsimiles* (Edinburgh: SRO, 1994).

Scottish Record Office. *Finding Aids* (Cambridge: Chadwyck-Healy, 1987–92, fiche 6029985 ff.).

Steel, Donald J. *Court Records as Sources for Family History in Scotland* (Salt Lake City: Corporation of the President, 1980, fiche 6085756).

Suggested Reading

Andrews, Charles M. *Guide to the Materials for American History to 1783, in the Public Record Office of Great Britain.* 2 Vols. (Washington, DC: Carnegie Institute, 1912–14, film 0873858).

Barr, James. *The Scottish Covenanters.* 2nd ed. (Glasgow: J. Smith, 1947, fiche 6026310).

Bell, H.C. and D.W. Parker. *Guide to British West Indian Archive Materials in London and the Islands* (Washington, DC: Carnegie Institute, 1926).

Coldham, Peter W. *Emigrants in Chains: A Social History of Forced Emigration to the Americas of Felons, Destitute Children, Political and Religious Non-Conformists, Vagabonds, Beggars and Other Undesirables, 1607–1776* (Baltimore: Genealogical Publishing Co., 1992).

Crick, B.R. and Miriam Alman. *A Guide to Manuscripts Relating to America in Great Britain and Ireland* (London: Oxford University Press, 1962).

Dobson, David. *American Vital Records from The Gentleman's Magazine, 1731–1868* (Baltimore: Genealogical Publishing Co., 1987). Listings are for Americans in the United States, Great Britain, Jamaica, Antigua, Barbados, and the West Indies.

Filby, P. William. *American & British Genealogy & Heraldry: A Selected List of Books*. 3rd ed. (Boston: New England Historic Genealogical Society, 1983). There is also a supplement, published in 1987.

Ghirelli, Michael. *A List of Emigrants from England to America, 1682–1692 Transcribed from the Original Records at the City of London Record Office* (1968. Reprint. Baltimore: Genealogical Publishing Co., 1989).

Grannum, Guy. *Tracing Your West Indian Ancestors: Sources in the Public Record Office* (London: PRO, 1995).

Herber, Mark D. *Ancestral Trails: The Complete Guide to British Genealogy and Family History* (Baltimore: Genealogical Publishing Co., 1997).

Kaminkow, Jack and Marion Kaminkow. *A List of Emigrants from England to America, 1718–1759, Transcribed from Microfilms of the Original Records at the Guildhall, London* (1964. Reprint. Baltimore: Genealogical Publishing Co., 1989).

Reid, Judith Prowse. *Genealogical Research in England's Public Record Office: A Guide for North Americans* (Baltimore: Genealogical Publishing Co., 1996).

Virginia State Library. *The British Public Record Office: History, Description, Record Groups, Finding Aids, and Materials for American History with Special Reference to Virginia* (Richmond: The Library, 1960).

BRITISH SOLDIERS.

MAYFLOWER.

Plymouth Harbor, England.

Colonial Sources in Germany

Miscellaneous Archives

Records in Germany can be found in the Bundesarchiv (National Archives) in Koblenz, and in *hauptstaatarchiv, landeshauptarchiv* (archives corresponding to a Bundesland), *staatsarchiv, landesarchiv,* (state archives), *kreisarchiv* (county archives), *stadtarchiv* (city archives), and *diözesanarchiv* (diocesan church archives and *kirchenbücher* (local parish registers). Many church records have been filmed by the Family History Library. *Militärakten* (military records) are found in local and state archives. Civil registration did not occur in all of Germany until after 1876. Although some records were destroyed during World War II, many resources have survived.

Types of information that can be found in original parish registers include lists of emigrants to America, such as those found in the registers of Freckenfeld, Bavaria, which have been transcribed in Krebs, Friedrich. "Auswanderer nach den Nordamerikanschen Kolonien im 18 Jahrhundert auf Grund der Einträge Lutherischen Kirchenbuch von Freckenfeld" *Blaetter fuer Pfaelzische Kirchengeschichte und Religiose Volkstunde* 19:3–4 (1952): 99–101 (film 1181767).

The Palatinate

Since 1156 the area on both sides of the Rhine River has been known as the Palatinate. After the Thirty Years' War, Huguenots and Walloons from Alsace-Lorraine, Luxembourg, Hesse, Baden, and Württemberg as well as some Swiss settled in the Palatinate in the towns of Mannheim, Heidelberg, Zweibrucken, and others. It was from this group that the settlers of New Pfalz (on the Hudson River in New York) came in 1678. They also colonized Germantown (Pennsylvania) in 1683, and the area on the eastern banks of the Hudson River in 1709-10.

Records particularly relating to emigration are among the archival holdings in Germany. The following selections have been copied and are available at the Manuscript Division of the Library of Congress in Washington, DC:

➤ Landeshauptarchiv Koblenz, Rhineland-Pfalz: prohibition of emigration, 1764–85, emigration to Pennsylvania, 1717

➤ Generallandesarchiv, Karlsruhe, Baden: emigration to Pennsylvania, 1737, 1745, 1769–71; emigration from the Palatinate to Pennsylvania, 1709

➤ Hessiches Staatsarchiv, Darmstadt, Hessen: regulations regarding emigration, 1630–1779

➤ Bayerisches Hauptstaatarchiv, Munich, Bavaria: emigration from Salzburg to America, 1731; American Jesuit mission letters and records, 1611–1760

➤ Landesarchiv Magdeburg-Landeshauptarchiv, Saxony-Anhalt: Hamburg emigrants to America, investigations, 1802–4

➤ Landesarchiv Speyer, Rhineland-Pfalz: emigration, 1685–1779

➤ Stadtarchiv, Neuwied, Rhineland-Pfalz: land acquisition in America, 1757–66

➤ Stadtarchiv, Frankfurt/Oder, Hessen: emigration, 1733, 1804–5, emigration of citizens from Darmstadt, 1793

➤ Staatsarchiv der Freien und Hansestadt, Hamburg: documents of Lutheran parishes in New York, 1724–60

➤ Mission Library of the Orphanage, Halle (Franck Foundation), Saxony-Anhalt: records of Lutheran parishes in Pennsylvania, 1733–69, Virginia, 1736–8, Georgia, 1733–48, and Nova Scotia, 1776–87

➤ Landesarchiv, Berlin: emigrants with service in the British Army, 1800–5; emigration, 1817–57

➤ Staatsarvhiv, Königsberg, Hessen-Nassau, Prussia (now Kaliningrad, Kaliningrad, Russia, records in archives in Göttingen, Hanover): emigration, 1686–1750 (inventories of archives, 1198–1940, on film 0071083 ff.).

➤ Sächsisches Hauptstaatsarchiv, Dresden, Saxony: documents of the Hoch Teutsche Compagnie, 1706; information regarding Carolina, 1705

➤ Archiv der Brüder-Unität (Moravian Archives), Herrnhut, Saxony: missions in Georgia and Pennsylvania, 1733–50; documents about Pennsylvania and New York, 1735–66; diaries from Pennsylvania, Virginia, New England, Maryland, and New York, 1742–56; papers from Wachau, North Carolina, 1750–4; Georgia and South Carolina colonists, 1762–78; Labrador mission papers, 1750–1869

➤ Staatsarchiv, Breslau, Prussia (possibly now in the Archiwiem Archdiecezjalne we Wrocławiu and the Archiwum Państwowe e Wrocłlawiu, Wrocław, Poland: reports of Catholic missionaries, 1720–39; tariffs in Haiti; emigration to Texas

➤ Stadtarchiv, Hanau, Hessen: Hanau troops in America, 1776–82

➤ Hanover: troops in America, 1775–90

➤ Hesseisches Hauptstaatsarchiv, Wiesbaden, Hessen: emigration of Palatines to Pennsylvania, 1709; the Waldo Colony in Maine

For information on Huguenot and Walloon ancestors, the Deutsche-Hugenotten-Gesellschaft in Bad Karlshofen publishes *Der Deutsche Hugenott* (film 0908257).

Americana in Deutschen Sammlungen: Ein Verzeichnis von Materialien zur Geschichte der Vereinigten Staaten von Amerika in Archiver und Bibliotheken der Bundesrepublik Deutschland und West Berlins (Cologne: Die Gesellschaft, 1967). Americana in German collections: list of materials on American history located in West German archives and libraries.

Learned, Marion Dexter. *Guide to the Manuscript Materials Relating to American History in the German State Archives* (Washington, DC: Carnegie Institute, 1912). Reprinted as *German Americana in Europe: Two Guides to Materials Relating to American History in the German, Austrian, and Swiss Archives* (Bowie, MD: Heritage Books, 1997). There is a two-volume, unpublished supplement at the Library of Congress, written in 1929 and 1932.

Emigrants to and from Germany from the Eighteenth to Twentieth Centuries (n.p., n.d., film 1125001 ff.). These are extracts from the periodical *Deutsches Familienarchiv* (Berlin: Verlag Degner, 1912-). The periodical has also been indexed under Friederichs, Heinz F. *Gesamtregister zum Deutshcen Familienarchiv.* 4 Vols. (Neustadt an der Aisch: Verlag Degner, 1957–89).

Thode, Ernest. *Address Book for Germanic Genealogy* (Baltimore: Genealogical Publishing Co., 1995).

Suggested Reading
Bell, Raymond Martin. *Emigrants from the Wolfersweiler Region of Germany to Pennsylvania, 1730-1750* (n.p., 1982, fiche 6088813).

Bittinger, Lucy Forney. *The Germans in Colonial Times* (1901. Reprint. New York: Russell and Russell, 1968, fiche 6048681).

Bly, Daniel W. *From the Rhine to the Shenandoah: Eighteenth Century Swiss and German Pioneer Families in the Central Shenandoah Valley of Virginia and Their European Origins* (Baltimore: Gateway Press, 1993).

Brandt, Edward R. *Germanic Genealogy: A Guide to Worldwide Sources and Migration Patterns* (Saint Paul, MN: Germanic Genealogy Society, 1995).

Burgert, Annette Kunselman. *Eighteenth-Century Emigrants from the Northern Alsace to America* (Camden, ME: Picton Press, 1992).

Burgert, Annette Kunselman. *Locating Your Pennsylvania German Ancestor in Europe* (Worthington, OH: AKB Publications, 1983).

Burgert, Annette Kunselman and Henry Z Jones. *Westerwald to America: Some Eighteenth-Century German Immigrants* (Camden, ME: Picton Press, 1989).

Diffenderffer, Frank R. *The German Exodus to England in 1709* (1897. Reprint. Washington, DC: Library of Congress, 1954, film 0087880).

Diffenderffer, Frank R. *The German Immigration into Pennsylvania Through the Port of Philadelphia from 1700 to 1775 and The Redemptioners* (Baltimore: Genealogical Publishing Co., 1977, film 1036066).

Eshleman, H. Frank. *Historic Background and Annals of the Swiss and German Pioneer Settlers of Southeastern Pennsylvania, and of Their Remote Ancestors, from the Middle of the Dark Ages, Down to the Time of the Revolutionary War* (1917. Reprint. Baltimore: Genealogical Publishing Co., 1991, film 0844515).

Forsyth, Alice D. and Earlene L. Zeringue. *German "Pest Ships," 1720-1721* (New Orleans: New Orleans Genealogical Research Society, 1969, fiche 6094099).

Hart, Simon. *Lutheran Church in New York and New Jersey, 1722-1760: Lutheran Records in the Ministerial Archives of the Staatsarchiv, Hamburg, Germany* (New York: United Lutheran Synod of New York and New England, 1962).

Hinke, William John. *A List of German Immigrants to the American Colonies from Zweibruecken in the Palatinate, 1728-1749* (n.p.: Pennsylvania German Folklore Society, 1936, fiche 6088522).

Jones, Henry Z. *The Palatine Families of New York: A Study of the German Immigrants Who Arrived in Colonial New York in 1710.* 2 Vols. (Universal City, CA: The Author, 1985).

Knittle, Walter. *Palatine Emigration, Early Eighteenth Century* (1937. Reprint. Baltimore: Genealogical Publishing Co., 1997).

Langguth, Otto. *Pennsylvania German Pioneers from the County of Wertheim* (n.p.: Pennsylvania German Folklore Society, 1948, fiche 6110908).

Learned, Marion D. *Guide to the Manuscript Materials Relating to American History in the German State Archives* (Washington, DC: Carnegie Institute, 1912). Republished in *German-Americana in Europe* . . (Bowie, MD: Heritage Books, 1997).

Lehmann, Heinz. *The German Canadians, 1750-1937: Immigration, Settlement and Culture* (Saint John's, NF: Jesperson Press, 1986).

Roeber, A.G. *Palatines, Liberty and Property: German Lutherans in Colonial British America* (Baltimore: Johns Hopkins University Press, 1993).

Rupp, Israel Daniel. *A Collection of Upwards of Thirty Thousand Names of German, Swiss, Dutch, French and Other Immigrants in Pennsylvania from 1727 to 1776: With a Statement of the Names of Ships, Whence They Sailed, and the Date of Their Arrival at Philadelphia, Chronologically Arranged Together with the Necessary Historical and Other Notes, Also an Appendix Containing Lists of More than One Thousand German and French Names in New York Prior to 1712* (1876. Reprint. Baltimore: Genealogical Publishing Co., 1985, film 1421791). Also includes names of first Palatines in North Carolina and names of Salzburger settlers in Georgia, 1734–41.

Sachse, Julius Friedrich. *Germany and America, 1450–1700* (Bowie, MD: Heritage Books, 1992).

Simmendinger, Ulrich. *True and Authentic Registers of Persons Still Living, by God's Grace: Who in the Year 1709, Under the Wonderful Providence of the Lord Journeyed from Germany to America of the New World and There Seek Their Piece of Bread at Various Places* (1934. Reprint. Baltimore: Genealogical Publishing Co., 1991, film 0874251).

Smith, Clifford. N. and Anna Piszczan-Czaja Smith. *American Genealogical Resources in German Archives: A Handbook* (New York: R.R. Bowker Co., 1977).

Strassburger, Ralph B. *Pennsylvania German Pioneers: A Publication of the Original Lists of Arrivals in the Port of Philadelphia from 1727 to 1808.* 2 Vols. (1934. Baltimore: Genealogical Publishing Co., 1966).

Totten, Christine M. *Roots in the Rhineland: America's German Heritage in Three Hundred Years of Immigration* (New York: German Information Center, 1983)

Verein für Sozailpolitik. *Schriftenreihe de Vereins für Sozailpolitik: Die Ansiedling von Europäern in den Tropen.* Vol. 147 (Munich: Verlag von Duncker and Humbolt, 1913). Publications for the Society of Social Betterment: European settlement of the tropics.

Yoder, Don. *Pennsylvania German Immigrants, 1709–1786. Lists Consolidated from Yearbooks of the Pennsylvania German Folklore Society* (1984. Reprint. Baltimore: Genealogical Publishing Co., 1989).

Yoder, Don. *Rhineland Emigrants: Lists of German Settlers in Colonial America* (Baltimore: Genealogical Publishing Co., 1981).

Colonial Sources in The Netherlands

Gemeente Archief, Amsterdam

This is the repository for the archive of the Dutch Reformed Classis of Amsterdam including the colony of New Netherland, notarial records from 1578 (including deeds). Copies of many of these records are kept at the Gardiner A. Sage Library in New Brunswick, New Jersey.

Amsterdam Gemeente Archief 2. *Fiches Collectie van Dopen, Trouwen en Overlijden: 1553–1811* (film 0441875 ff.). Index to baptisms, marriage intentions, and deaths in church and civil records of Amsterdam.

Diender, G. *Gemeentearchief Amsterdam, Inventaris met Filmnummers* ('s-Gravenhage: The Author, n.d.). Inventory of church records and registers of civil marriages and burials (before 1811) of Amsterdam.

Van den Hoek Ostende, J.H. and P.H.J. van der Laan. *De Archieven in Amsterdam: With English Summary* (Alphen aan den Rijn: Samsom, 1981, film 1393243). The archives of Amsterdam, The Netherlands.

Rijksarchief, Overijssel

Lyst de Noodlijdende Kerken en Personen, die door de Christelyke Synodus van Overissel, 1768 (film 1032847). List of distressed persons and churches in Pennsylvania that received aid from the Christian Synod of Overijssel.

The Spanish Netherlands

From the time of the sixteenth century, The Netherlands were subject to Charles V, German Emperor and King of Spain, a member of the Hapsburg family. His son, Philip II, consolidated control of the region. Protestants of the Dutch Reformed, Lutheran, and Mennonite denominations resisted the persecution from the Inquisition, which began in 1566. The northern provinces of The Netherlands formed a republic in 1579.

Spain continued to occupy the southern provinces (Belgium) and annexed Portugal in 1580. In 1586 England enlisted the support of the Dutch to mount an expedition against Spain and Portugal. It was not until England defeated the Spanish Armada in 1589 that the Dutch began to consider the potential for profit and settlement in the Americas.

Algemeen Rijksarchief, The Hague

The Algemeen Rijksarchief holds Dutch Reformed Church records and emigrant lists for Suriname (Dutch Guiana), the West Indies, and North America.

781

Centraal Bureau voor Genealogie. *Index op Bij het Centraal Bureau voor Genealogie te 's-Gravenhage Aanwezige Microfiches van DTBL Registers van Nederland, Duitsland, Oost-en West Indië en Buitenland.* 3 Vols. ('s-Gravenhage: Centraal Bureau voor Genealogie, 1984). Inventories of the microfiche copies of baptisms, marriages, burials, and membership lists at the Central Bureau for Genealogy in The Hague, including the West Indies.

Centraal Bureau voor Genealogie, Nederland. *Catalogus Microfiches Dopen, Touwen, Begraven, Lidmaten* ('s-Gravenhage: Centraal Bureau voor Genealogie, 1984, fiche 6312615 ff.). Microfiche catalog of baptisms, marriages, burials, and membership records of Dutch in the West Indies and North America.

Bibliothèque Wallonne, Leiden
This library houses a card index to extant Huguenot and Walloon registers, 1500–1828 (film 0199755 ff.), 1644–1858 (film 0199963 ff.), and 1687–1808 (fiche 6312188 ff.). The records include Huguenots and Walloons from The Netherlands, Belgium, England, France, Germany, and the Americas.

Suggested Reading
De Boer, Louis P. *An Inventory of Records of Protestant Churches in The Netherlands Prior to 1664* (n.p., 1941, film 0106780).

Dexter, Henry Martyn. *The England and Holland of the Pilgrims* (1906. Reprint. Baltimore: Genealogical Publishing Co., 1978).

Epperson, Gwen. *New Netherland Roots* (Baltimore: Genealogical Publishing Co., 1994).

Geyl, Pieter. *The Netherlands Divided, 1609–1648* (London: Williams and Norgate, 1936).

Guide to the Sources in The Netherlands for the History of Latin America ('s Gravenhage: The Hague, 1968).

Jaquet, Fritz G.P. *Guide to the Sources in The Netherlands Concerning the History of Asia and Oceania, 1796–1949* (Zug, Switzerland: Inter Documentation Co., 1970-3). Includes information on The Netherland Antilles.

Meilink-Roelofsz, M.A.P. *A Survey of Archives in The Netherlands Pertaining to the History of The Netherlands Antilles* ('s-Gravenhage: n.p., n.d.).

Motley, J.L. *History of the United Netherlands.* 2 Vols. (London: n.p., 1875).

O'Callaghan, E.B. *Documents Relative to the Colonial History of the State of New York: Procured in Holland, England, and France. 15 Vols.* (Albany: Weed, Parsons, and Co., 1853–87, film 0824380 ff.). English translations of documents at the National Archives, The Hague, and the City Archives of Amsterdam, 1603–78.

Parker Geoffrey. *Guide to the Archives of the Spanish Inquisition in or Concerned with The Netherlands [1556–1706]* (Brussels: Drukkerij George Micgiels, 1971). The *Raad van Beroete* (Council of Troubles) records are at the Central Archives of the Kingdom of Brussels, Belgium (original records on films 0720653 ff., 0720991 ff., and 0721576 ff.).

Scheffer, J. de Hoop. *History of the Free Churchmen Called the Brownists, Pilgrim Fathers, and Baptists of the Dutch Republic, 1581–1701* (Ithaca, NY: Andrus and Church, 1921).

Schelhaas, T.N. *Discovering a New World: The Impact of Colonization on the Dutch Family* (Salt Lake City: Corporation of the President, 1980, fiche 6085774).

Sprunger, Keith L. *Dutch Puritanism: A History of English and Scottish Churches of The Netherlands in the Sixteenth and Seventeenth Centuries* (Leiden: E.J. Brill, 1982).

Tammel, Johanna W. *The Pilgrims and Other People from the British Isles in Leiden, 1576–1640* (Peel: Mansk-Svenska Publishing Co., 1989).

Costume about the Middle of the Seventeenth Century.

Colonial Sources in Portugal

Arquivo Nacional da Torre do Tombo

An earthquake in Lisbon in 1755 destroyed many of the existing records. It is also important to note that from 1580 until 1640 Portugal and Spain were united under the Spanish Crown. Most records in Portugal relating to the colonial period are at the Arquivo Nacional da Torre do Tombo in Lisbon.

Bibliotecas e Arquivos de Portugal. 3 Vols. (Lisbon: Ministério da Educação Nacional, 1969–73). Libraries and archives of Portugal, including an inventory of parish registers found in historical archives and the Torre do Tombo in Lisbon; includes a list of archival sources for the study of the history of Brazil.

Inquisição de Lisboa (Lisbon: Laboratórios Fototécnicos, 1975, film 0784501 ff.). Documents of trials of New Christians (Marranos), persons taken prisoner in Brazil, accused of being Jewish, and sent to Portugal to face the Inquisition, 1591–1735. The original records are at the Arquivo Nacional da Torre do Tombo in Lisbon and the archives of Hebrew College, Cincinnati, Ohio.

Ferreira, Carlos Alberto. *Indice Abreviado das Genealogias Manuscritas do Arquivo Nacional da Torre do Tombo* (Lisbon: Imprensa Moderna, 1937, film 1573058). Abbreviated index to manuscript genealogies at the Torre do Tombo in Lisbon.

Miscellaneous Archives

Other institutions in Portugal with Latin American materials are the Histórico Ultramarino (Overseas Historical Archive), the Ministerio de Negocias Extrajeros (Ministry of Foreign Affairs), and the Operto and Evora Libraries, all in Lisbon.

Suggested Reading

Belo, A. Raimundo. *Emigração Açoriana para o Brasil* (Angra do Heroísmo, Portugal: Tipografia Andrade, 1954, fiche 6030520). Azorean immigration to Brazil.

Genealogical Department of the Church of Jesus Christ of Latter-day Saints. *Basic Portuguese Paleography* (Salt Lake City: The Department, 1978, fiche 6001480).

Javierre Mur, Aurea Lucinda. *La Orden de Calatrava en Portugal* (Madrid: Imprenta y Editorial Maestre, 1952, film 0908056). The Order of Calatrava, a military religious order, in Portugal.

Lafuente Machain, Ricardo de. *Los Portugueses en Buenos Aires: Siglo XVII* (Madrid: Tipografía de Archivos, 1931, film 0873683). The Portuguese in Buenos Aires during the seventeenth century.

Leite, Serafim. *A Grande Expedição Missionária dos Mártires do Brasil* (Lisbon: Centro de Estudos Históricos Ultramarinos, 1961). History of the Jesuits in Brazil.

Novinsky, Anita. *Cristãos Novos na Bahia* (Sao Paulo, Brazil: Perspectiva, Universidade de São Paulo, 1972. New Christians (Jews) in Bahia, Brazil, including genealogical tables.

Ryder, Alan Frederick Charles. *Materials for West African History in Portuguese Archives* (London: University of London, Athlone Press, 1965).

Saraiva, António José. *Inquisição e Cristãos-Novos*. 3rd ed. (Porto, Portugal: Editorial Inova, 1969). The Portuguese Inquisition.

Portugal.

View of Lisbon.

Colonial Sources in Spain

Archivo General de Indias (General Archive of the Indies)

The Archivo General de Indias in the Casa Lonja in Seville is the repository for Spanish documents relating to the colonization of the Americas. Records are organized in *legajos* and thereunder by *secciones*. The ship passenger lists from 1509 to 1599 have been published in *Catálogo de Pasajeros a las Indias Durante los Siglos XVI, XVII, y XVIII* (Seville: n.p., 1940–, film 0277577 ff.). Other related works are:

Bermúdez Plata, Cristóbal. *Catálogo de Documentos de la Sección Novena del Archivo General de Indias* (Seville: Escuela de Estudios Hispano-Americanos, 1949). Catalog of section nine of the Archivo General de Indias, including records for Santo Domingo, Cuba, Puerto Rico, Louisiana, Florida, and Mexico.

Chapman, Charles E. *Catalogue of Materials in the Archivo General de Indias for the History of the Pacific Coast and the American Southwest* (Berkeley: University of California Press, 1919).

Peña y Cámara, José Mariá de la. *Archivo General de Indias de Sevilla: Guía de Visitante* (Madrid: Dirección General de Archivos y Bibliotecas, 1958).

Peña y Cámara, José Mariá de la. *Catálogo de Documentos del Archivo General de Indias: Sobre la Epoca Española de Luisiana.* 2 Vols. (Madrid: Dirección General de Archivos y Bibliotecas, 1968; New Orleans: Loyola University, 1968). These include the *Papeles de Cuba*, the provincial archives of the Spanish dominion of West Florida and Louisiana.

Archivo General de Indias. *Regimiento de Infantería de la Luisiana: Relación de los Reclutas Solteros y Casados con Sus Familias Que Se Embarcaron de Santa Cruz de Tenerife con Destino a los Batallones de la Luisiana, 1778–1779* (Seville: The Archive, 1971, film 0908033). List of recruits to the Louisiana Infantry Regiment, who embarked at Tenerife in the Canary Islands for Louisiana on the ships El Santíssimo Sacramento (alias El Tezón), La Victoria, San Ignacio de Loyola, San Juan Nepomuceno, La Santa Faz, and El Sagrado Corazón de Jesús.

Hanke, Lewis. Guía de las Fuentes en el Archivo General de Indias Para el Estudio de la Administración Virreinal Española en México y en el Perú: 1535–1700. 3 Vols. (Madrid: Atlas, 1976). Guide to the sources in the Archivo

General de Indias for studying the administration of the Spanish viceroyalties in Peru and Mexico, 1535–1700.

Archivo General de Indias. *Pasajeros a Indias: Libros de Asientos* (Madrid: Centro Nacional de Microfilm, 1978, film 1223690 ff.). Lists of passengers to the New World, 1509–1701.

Boyd-Bowman, Peter. *Indice Geobiográfico de Cuarenta Mil Pobladones Españoles en America en el Siglo XVI* (Bogotá, Colombia: Instituto Caro y Cuervo, 1964–8). Index of 40,000 Spanish settlers to the Americas in the sixteenth century.

Boyd-Bowman, Peter. *Indice Geobiográfico de Más de 56 Mil Pobladores de la América Hispánica [1493–1519]* (Mexico: Fondo de Cultura Económica, 1985). Geobiographical index of more than 56,000 inhabitants of Hispanic America from the Archivo de Indias and other colonial sources.

Boyd-Bowman, Peter. *Patterns of Spanish Emigration to the New World [1493– 1580]* (Buffalo: University of New York at Buffalo, 1973, film 1410948 ff.).

Catálogo de Pasajeros a Indias Durante los Siglos XVI, XVII y XVIII (Seville: n.p., 1940–, film 0277577 ff.). Lists of passengers from Spain to the New World during the sixteenth, seventeenth, and eighteenth centuries.

Documentación y Archivos de las Colonización Española (Madrid: Ministerio de Cultura, 1980).

Also in the Archivo de Indias are judgments of estates that date from 1753. The records for persons who died in Peru and left debts in Spain have been published by Lohmann Villena in "Indice de los expendientes sobre bienes de difuntos en Perú." *Revista del Instituto Perúano de Investigaciones Genealogicas* 11 (Lima, 1958): 59–133.

Archivo General Militar (General Military Archive)
The Archivo General Militar in Segovia houses most of the records of militia officers, military census records, and *hojas de servicios* (service sheets) of enlisted soldiers during the colonial period. Officers' records are indexed in *Archivo General Militar de Segovia: Indice de Expedientes Personales.* 9 Vols. (Madrid: Instituto Luis de Salazar y Castro, 1959–63, film 1410966).

Archivo Histórico Nacional (Historical Archive of Spain)
Among its holdings the Archivo Histórico Nacional in Madrid has records relating to sixteenth- to nineteenth-century military service records, "Sección Estado," and can be found in *Expedientes de Militares, Siglos XVI al XIX* (Madrid: Hidalguía, 1986), by Emilio de Cárdenas Piera.

Records of military fraternal orders that were created in 1100 are also kept at this archive. Membership was restricted to those of *hildalgo* (noble) status. Documented genealogies of the members are included. For more information on Latin Americans in these orders, see *Los Americanos en Los Ordenes Militares [1529-1900]* (Madrid: Consejo Superior de Investigaciones Científicas, Instituto Gonzalo Fernández de Oviedo, 1957).

The Inquisition in Spain was established in 1480 to prosecute heretics and religious criminals. Courts of the Holy Office were instituted to prosecute suspected infidels and heretics. They were instituted in America in 1569, the first courts being held in Lima in 1570 and Mexico in 1571. Those who acted as officials over the proceedings were required to submit *limpieza de sangre* (proof of purity of blood), containing names, dates, residence, places of origin, family relationships, and pedigree data.

The unfortunate groups who met the criteria for heretic and infidel status were the Spanish Jews, New Christians (converted Jews), and Moors, who were suspected of plotting with foreign enemies. Also on the list for prosecution were the Dutch Protestants in the Spanish Netherlands and the New World. It is interesting to note that — with a few exceptions — the Amerindians did not fall victim to the Inquisition. They were considered too new in the faith and not accountable enough to be judged.

This archive holds the records for Courts of the Holy Office that were created in Cartagena in 1610 (film 1224001 ff. and 1418266 ff.), Lima in 1570 (film 0873987 ff.), and Mexico in 1571 (film 0283553 and 1149544). Some records of the Inquisition can be found in Latin American archives (see individual countries).

Archivo General de Simancas

The Archivo General de Simancas in Valladolid houses military records of Spanish solders who served in the Americas between 1780 and 1810. They are indexed in *Hojas de Servicios de América: Cátalogo XXI del Archivo de Simancas*, by Ricardo Magdaleno (Valladolid: Secretaría de Guerra, 1958). This consists of an alphabetical surname index of men who rendered military service in Spanish colonial America during the eighteenth century. It includes full name, position, name of regiment, years of service, and location of original service records in the Archivo General de Simancas. The records can be found in:

España, Secretaría de Estado y del Despacho de Guerra. Hojas de Servicios Militares de América:
- Chile, 1787–1800 (film 1156330 ff.).
- Colombia and Venezuela, 1814–19 (film 1156358).
- Cuba, 1765–1809 (film 1156324 ff.).
- Florida, Louisiana, and Mississippi, 1787–94 (film 1156353 ff.).

- Guatemala and Nicaragua, 1789–99 (film 1156333).
- Nueva España (Mexico, California, New Mexico, and Texas), 1786–1800 (film 1156334).
- Nueva Granada (Colombia, Ecuador, and Panama, 1787–1800 (film 1156343 ff.).
- San Juan de Puerto Rico, 1793–1800 (film 1156352).
- Santo Domingo, 1786–99 (film 1156352).
- Virreinato de Buenos Aires (including Argentina, Uruguay, and Trinidad and Tobago), 1787–99 (film 1156322).
- Virreinato de Perú, 1793–1800 (film 1156346 ff.).
- Yucatán (including the other Mexican states of Campeche and Quintana Roo), 1784–1800 (film 1156357).

Records of the granting of *titulos nobilarios* (titles of nobility) are found in this archive in the sections for *mercedes* (grants), *privilegios* (privileges), *ventas* (sales), and *confirmaciones* (confirmations). They are described in the heraldic dictionary, *Nobilario Español: Dictionario Heráldico de Apellidoa Españoles y de Títulos Nobilarios,* by Julio de Atienza (Madrid: M. Aguilar, 1948, film 1181816).

A general guide to this archive has been written by Plaza Bares. *Archivo General de Simancas, Guia del Investigador* (Valladolid: The Archive, 1962).

Suggested Reading

Codinach, Guadalupe Jiménez. *The Hispanic World, 1492–1898: A Guide to Photoreproduced Manuscripts from Spain in the Collections of the United States, Guam and Puerto Rico* (Washington, DC: Library of Congress, 1994).

Kern, Robert. W. *The Regions of Spain: A Reference Guide to History and Culture* (Westport, CT: Greenwood Press, 1995).

Konetze, Richard. *La Emigración Española al Río de la Plata Durante el Siglo XVI* (Madrid: Instituto Gonzalo Fernández de Oviedo, Consejo Superior de Investigaciones Científicas, 1952). Spanish emigration to Río de la Plata in the sixteenth century.

Martínez Martínez, María del Carmen. *La Emigración Castellana y Leonesa al Nuevo Mundo, 1517–1700.* 2 Vols. (Valladolid: Junta de Castilla y León, Consejería de Cultura y Turismo, 1993). Emigration from the Spanish Kingdoms of Castile and Leon to the New World from 1517 to 1700.

Medina, José Toribio. *Biblioteca Hispano-Americana, 1493–1810.* 7 Vols. (1898–1907. Reprint. Lexington: University of Kentucky, 1958, film 0164666 ff.).

Queen Isabella of Spain.

CITY OF CADIZ.

STRAIT OF GIBRALTAR.

Colonial Sources in Sweden

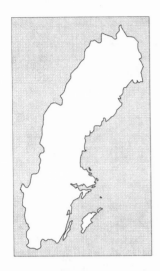

The first Swedish emigration served to establish the New Sweden Colony (Delaware) in 1638. Except for some abortive attempts to build some forts in West Africa, there was no significant emigration until the colonization of Saint Bartholomew (West Indies) in the eighteenth century.

Riksarkivet, Stockholm

There are some emigration records in the provincial archives in Sweden; they also hold church, land, and court records. The Svensk Arkivinformation, SVAR, at Ramsele, Sweden is the research division of the Riksarkivet (National Archives) in Stockholm. They have detailed information about holdings and what has been copied to microfilm.

Some of the original records at the Riksarkivet in Stockholm are:

- Nya Sverige: Handel och sjöfart; kolonier (film 1644295). Diverse transactions and letters concerning the colony of New Sweden in Delaware, 1636–58.
- Handlingar rörande Nya Sverige (film 1364758). Transactions regarding the settlement of New Sweden in Delaware, 1696–1742.
- Svedberg, Jesper. *Svecia Nova: Manuskriptsamlingen* (film 1644295). History of Svecia Nova (New Sweden), in Swedish and Latin by the Lutheran minister Jesper Svedberg, who served as one of the first ministers to the Swedish colony in Delaware.
- Passenger lists of persons who embarked for New Sweden in 1641 and 1649, abstracted in Tepper, Michael. *Emigrants to Pennsylvania, 1641–1819* (Baltimore: Genealogical Publishing Co., 1979).

Jägerskiöld, Olof. *Riksarkivet, 1618–1968* (Stockholm: P.A. Norstedt and Söner, 1968). Guide to the National Archives of Sweden.

Miscellaneous Archives

There are passport journals for Stockholm, 1737–1879, at the Göteborg Provincial Archives in Göteborg, a principal port of Sweden.

A possible source of emigration records are parish registers. An emigrant was given a certificate indicating his membership in good standing and that he had permission to leave Sweden. Many of the surviving records of immigrant churches in the United States are available on microfilm at the Swenson Swedish Immigration Research Center, Augustana College, in Chicago.

The Nord Library in the American-Swedish Historical Museum in Philadelphia, Pennsylvania holds family records dating from the founding of the Delaware Valley settlements.

Suggested Reading

Åberg, Alf. *The People of New Sweden: Our Colony on the Delaware River, 1638–1655* (Stockholm: Natur och Kultur, 1988).

Clay, Jehu Curtis. *Annals of the Swedes on the Delaware.* 3rd ed. (Chicago: Swedish Historical Society of America, 1914, film 1364921).

Det Började vid Delaware: Om Svenska Hembygder i Amerika (Stockholm: Riksförbundet för Hembygdsvärd, 1986). History of the Swedish colony of New Sweden in Delaware from about 1638 to the 1900s.

Evjen, John Oluf. *Scandinavian Immigrants in New York, 1630–1674: With Appendices on Scandinavians in Mexico and South America, 1532–1640; Scandinavians in Canada, 1619–1620; Some Scandinavians in New York in the Eighteenth Century; German Immigrants in New York, 1630–1674* (1916. Reprint. Baltimore: Genealogical Publishing Co., 1972, film 1033525).

Guide to Swedish-American Archival and Manuscript Sources in the United States (Chicago: Swedish-American Historical Society, 1983).

Johnson, Amandus. *The Swedish Settlement on the Delaware: Their History and Relations to the Indians, Dutch, and English, 1638–1664.* 2 Vols. (Philadelphia: University of Pennsylvania Press, 1911).

Keen, G.B. "The Eighth Swedish Expedition to New Sweden." *The Pennsylvania Magazine of History and Biography* 8 No. 1 (1884): 107–8.

Keen, G.B. "The Third Swedish Expedition to New Sweden." *The Pennsylvania Magazine of History and Biography* 3 No. 4 (1879): 462–4.

Lindeström, Rälamb P. *Kort Relation och Beskrivning Över Nya Sverige* (Stockholm: Kungliga Biblioteket, n.d., film 1364759).

Olin, K-G. *Våra Första Amerikafarare: Historien om Finlandssvenskarna i Nya Sverige* (Jakobstad: Ab Olimex, 1988). History and life of Finnish-Swedish emigrants in New Sweden.

Weslager, C.A. *New Swedes on the Delaware, 1638–1655* (Wilmington: Middle Atlantic Press, 1988).

ULRICKSDAL, PALACE OF THE KING.

Colonial Sources in Switzerland

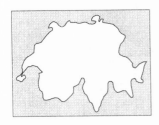

State Archives of Switzerland

The Staatsarchiv (State Archive) in Zurich holds records of *Täufer* (Anabaptist) emigration and land confiscations of emigrants. If the emigrant returned, he was supposed to have his property returned. The archive also has the records of the Reichnungen der Zürcher Vogteien, which recorded tributes paid to the state before emigration. The state archives in Bern and Basel also hold similar records on emigrants.

Faust, Albert Bernhard and Gaius Marcus Brumbaugh. *Lists of Swiss Emigrants in the Eighteenth Century to the American Colonies.* 2 Vols. (1976. Reprint. Baltimore: Genealogical Publishing Co., 1995, fiche 6048998). The records include lists from the state archives in Zurich, 1734–44; the archives in Bern, 1706–95; and the archives in Basel, 1734–94.

Suggested Reading (see also Germany)

Faust, Albert B. *Guide to Manuscript Materials Relating to American History in Swiss and Austrian Archives* (Washington, DC: Carnegie Institute, 1916). Republished as *German Americana in Europe: Two Guides to Materials Relating to American History in the German, Austrian, and Swiss Archives* (Bowie, MD: Heritage Books, 1997).

Haller, Charles R. *Across the Atlantic and Beyond: The Migration of German and Swiss Immigrants to America* (Bowie, MD: Heritage Books, 1993).

Historisch-Biographisches Lexikon der Schwiez. 7 Vols. (Neuenberg: Administration des Historisch-Biographisches Lexikons, 1921–34). Historical and biographical dictionary of the Swiss.

Mennonite Encyclopedia. 4 Vols. (Scottdale, PA: Mennonite Publishing House, 1952–7).

Oehler, Robert. *Familennamenbuch der Schweiz.* 2 Vols. (Zurich: Zürcher Polygraphischer Verlag, 1940, film 0441670). Family name book of Switzerland by geographic area.

Packull, Werner O. *Hutterite Beginnings: Communitarian Experiments During the Reformation* (Baltimore: Johns Hopkins University Press, 1995).

Schelbert, Leo. *Swiss Migration to America: The Swiss Mennonites* (New York: Arno Press, 1980).

Schrader-Muggenthaler, Cornelia. *The Swiss Emigration Book* (Apollo, PA: Closson Press, 1993).

Yoder, Don, ed. *Rhineland Emigrants: Lists of German Settlers in Colonial America* (Baltimore: Genealogical Publishing Co., 1985). Series of articles that include material on the Anabaptists (Mennonites), French Swiss, and other emigrants. Of particular interest is the section, "Swiss Mennonite Family Names," by Leo Schelbert and Sandra Luebking.

ALPINE SCENERY.

Foreign Records at the Library of Congress

The Library of Congress in Washington, DC is a repository for original documents, and it acquires and actively makes copies of records from other archives. The documents regarding Americana in Europe are divided among several reading rooms: the Geography and Map Reading Room, the Rare Book and Special Collections Reading Room, the Microform Reading Room, and the Manuscript Reading Room; there are published materials in other divisions.

For information on the material available in the Microform Reading Room, see Frazier, Patrick. *A Guide to the Microform Collections in the Humanities and Social Sciences Division of the Library of Congress* (Washington, DC: The Division, 1996). This division purchases materials filmed by other institutions, or records from other institutions, including published works, such as:

➢ Papers from the Archivo Franciscano, Instituto Nacional de Antropologia y Historia, Mexico

➢ Papers from the Archivo General de Indias, Seville, Spain

➢ La Collection Mangones (period monographs on the early history of Haiti and the Dominican Republic)

➢ Coleccion de Libros Cubanos (Cuban writings prior to independence with Spain)

➢ Friends House Library, London, digest registers for England and Wales, seventeenth to eighteenth centuries

➢ Methodist Missionary Society Archives, London

➢ Pre-1900 Canadiana (50,000 monographs)

➢ Reformed Protestant sources, 1600s and 1700s, German and Dutch

➢ Translations of Texas censuses and statistics, 1603–1803

The Manuscript Division has systematically been filming records in European and other archives as part of their Foreign Copying Program. There are no up-to-date finding aids that have been published or are available online, but the reading room of the division has finding aids to use on-site. When searching in the finding aids cabinets it is necessary to look under "F" for "Foreign" to locate all of these records. Copies of foreign manuscripts may be requested through interlibrary loan directly from the Division. Manuscripts may be available on microfilm or in copy form. The most important finding aids are:

• Griffin, Grace Gardner. *Guide to Manuscripts Relating to American History in British Depositories Reproduced for the Division of Manuscripts of the Library of Congress* (Washington, DC: Library of Congress, 1946, film 1698100).

- Bickel, Richard. *Manuscripts on Microfilm: A Checklist of the Holdings of the Manuscript Division* (Washington, DC: The Division, 1973).
- The series of guides published by the Carnegie Institute of Washington, which are cited throughout this book. Originally published in the early twentieth century, they provide a checklist of holdings that — as many pre-date both World Wars — may no longer exist in the original archives.
- *The Harkness Collection in the Library of Congress Manuscript Division: Documents from Early Peru. The Pizarros and the Almagros, 1531-1578* (Washington, DC: USGPO, 1946).
- Warren, J. Benedict. *The Harkness Collection in the Library of Congress Manuscript Division: Manuscripts Concerning Mexico, a Guide* (Washington, DC: Library of Congress, 1974).
- Kent, George O. "A Survey of German Manuscripts Pertaining to American History in the Library of Congress." *The Journal of American History* 56 No. 4 (March 1970): 868–81.

The following unpublished finding aids are available at the Division:
- "Guide to French Reproductions in the Library of Congress."
- "Dutch Reproductions: Manuscript Division — Library of Congress" (1958).
- "Louisiana Colonial Records Project, Archives Nationales."
- "Foreign Copying Project: Reproduction from Repositories in Spain and Latin America."
- "Dutch Manuscripts in the Library of Congress Relating to Brazil."
- "German Reproductions, Manuscript Division — Library of Congress."
- "Czechoslovakian Reproductions: Manuscript Division — Library of Congress."
- Cortes Alonso, Vicenta. *Informe sobre la Coleccion de Manuscritos Relativos a la America Latina en la Biblioteca de Congreso* (1960).

Some of the records available in the Division include:
Argentina
➢ Archivo General de la Nacion, Buenos Aires
Brazil
➢ Bibliotecha Nacional, Rio de Janeiro
➢ Original Dutch records relating to Brazil, 1636–49; records of the Nederlandische West-Indische Compagnie (Dutch West India Company), relating to Brazil, 1568–1650
Cuba
➢ Archivo Nacional de Cuba, Havana: Louisiana and West Florida papers, 1771–81

Czech Republic
➢ Veřenjná a Universitní Knohovna, Prague: papers relating to Jesuit mission activity in New France, 1653–9
France

➤ French National Archives, Paris: Louisiana Colonial Records Project, covering Louisiana, the Gulf of Mexico, Acadia, Newfoundland, Florida, Quebec, New England, Mississippi, Saint-Pierre-et-Miquelon, and the French Antilles

Germany

➤ All of the records listed under individual archives in the Germany section of this book

Great Britain

➤ Fulham Palace Papers, Archives of the Bishop of London
➤ British Library, London: all of the material described in Andrews, Charles M. *Guide to the Manuscript Materials for the History of the United States to 1783: In the British Museum, in Minor London Archives, and in the Libraries of Oxford and Cambridge* (Washington, DC: Carnegie Institute, 1908. Reprint. New York: Kraus Reprint Corporation, 1965, film 0873858).
➤ Lambeth Palace Library, Archbishop of Canterbury manuscripts
➤ Roman Catholic Diocese of Westminster, archives
➤ Society for the Propagation of the Gospel in Foreign Parts, London
➤ Public Record Office: the following classes of records (see the Great Britain section of this book for description):
Admiralty (ADM 1, 31, 49, 50, 80, 97, 98)
Audit Office (AO 1, 12, 13)
Chancery (C 66)
Colonial Office (CO 1, 5, 23, 28, 37, 42, 71, 110, 117, 101, 134, 137, 152, 188, 194, 217, 245, 260, 314, 318, 323, 324)[75]
Foreign Office (FO 4, 5, 16, 75, 84, 97, 115, 353)
High Court of Admiralty (1, 24, 30, 32, 49)
Gifts and Deposits (PRO 30/11, 30/14, 30/47)
Privy Council (PC 1)
Treasury (T 50, 64)
Treasury Solicitor (TS 11)
War Office (WO 1, 4, 6, 28, 34)

Mexico

➤ Archivo General de la la Nacion, Mexico City: California Papers; selected *Real Audiencia* records, 1548–1766

The Netherlands

➤ Geneentearchief, Amsterdam: Compagnie de Cerès, 1791–1825
➤ Universiteitsbiblioteck, Amsterdam: all the material listed in Matteson, David B. *List of Manuscripts Concerning American History Preserved in European Libraries* (Washington, DC: Carnegie Institute, 1925), 3–17.
➤ Algemeen Rijksarchief, The Hague: admiralty records, 1777–83; West Indies Company records, 1623–76
➤ Gemeentearchief, Rotterdam: correspondence between Rotterdam,

---

[75] CO 5 volumes for 1700 to 1784 are on film 1549671.

Amsterdam, and Pennsylvania, 1732; records of eighteenth- and nineteenth-century emigration

Spain

➤ Archivo General de Indias, Seville: *audiencia* papers of Charcas, Chile, Guadalajara, Guatemala, Lima, Mexico, and Santo Domingo; notarial records; the *Papeles de Cuba*

➤ Academia de la Historia, Madrid

➤ Archivo Histórico National, Madrid

➤ Biblioteca del Palacio, Madrid

➤ Archvio General de Simancas, Simancas

➤ Biblioteca Publico, Toledo

➤ Original records of the Spanish dominion of East Florida, 1783–1821

The Pillory.

Index